CW00967662

In the
Language
of Kings

Fiction

Ofay

The Boots of the Virgin

Under the Fifth Sun: A Novel of Pancho Villa

In the Yucatán

Non-fiction

The Death of the Great Spirit: An Elegy for the American Indian

The Oppressed Middle: Scenes from Corporate Life

Jews Without Mercy: A Lament

Power Sits at Another Table: Aphorisms

While Someone Else Is Eating (editor)

Latinos: A Biography of the People

*A Nation of Salesmen: The Tyranny of the Market and
the Subversion of Culture*

New American Blues: A Journey Through Poverty to Democracy

Riches for the Poor: The Clemente Course in the Humanities

In the
Language
of Kings

An Anthology of Mesoamerican Literature—
Pre-Columbian to the Present

Miguel León-Portilla and Earl Shorris

with Sylvia S. Shorris, Ascensión H. de León-Portilla, and Jorge Klor de Alva

W. W. Norton & Company New York • London

Since this page cannot legibly accommodate all the copyright notices, pages 719–720
constitute an extension of the copyright page.

The text of this book is composed in Fairfield Medium with the display set in Cochin
Composition by Allentown Digital Services
Manufacturing by The Maple-Vail Book Manufacturing Group.
Book design by Chris Welch
Production manager: Andrew Marasia

Library of Congress Cataloging-in-Publication Data

In the language of kings : An anthology of Mesoamerican literature—Pre-Columbian to the
present / [edited by] Miguel León-Portilla and Earl Shorris with
Ascensión H. de León-Portilla . . . [et al.].
p. cm.
Includes bibliographical references and index.
ISBN 0-393-02010-X
1. Indian literature—Mexico—Translations into English. 2. Indian literature—Central
America—Translations into English. I. León Portilla, Miguel. II. Shorris, Earl, 1936–

PM3097.E1 I5 2001
897—dc21   00-069564

W. W. Norton & Company, Inc., 500 Fifth Avenue, New York, N.Y. 10110
www.wwnorton.com

W. W. Norton & Company Ltd., Castle House, 75/76 Wells Street, London W1T 3QT

1 2 3 4 5 6 7 8 9 0

Para los tocayos,
Miguel Diego León-Portilla Hernández
y
Michael Laurino Shorris

Contents

Book III: Other Mesoamerican Literatures 615

With flowers and songs
I give life to the new sun.
With flowers and songs
I greet the dawn.

Foreword

On the Pleasures of the Amateur

Earl Shorris

Half a century ago, in El Paso, Texas, a boy could travel by trolley on a Saturday afternoon to the unknown world. I found it there, in the old gray stone public library, in the pale light of a December day when snow can cover the high desert. I was drawn by accident, by the way the light slanted in through the small high windows, to a book bound in green leatherette stamped with the title *Incidents of Travels in Central America, Chiapas, and Yucatan.*

I had never imagined anything like the tales and pictures contained in those yellowed pages. Dreaming full, I stood with my back against the shelves, and was transported to Mayab, the home of Kukulcan, the place where the Xiu and Itza contended for their destiny. Since then, John Lloyd Stephens and the great anthropologists who came before and after him have been at my side, whispering dreams and ideas to an amateur, holding him in never-ending thrall.

Over all the years since then I have never ceased dreaming; I have been the consummate amateur, captive not only of the Maya, the Nahuas, and the Mixtecs, but of their translators, those scholars of the library and the ruin, those who brave dengue fever and those who pit themselves against the unpunctuated lines, the vague letters, the bastion of codes and centuries.

These scholars, these adventurers in other minds, are the special gift to the amateur. Their disagreements, the manner in which they proceed, sometimes gracefully, often rancorously, from one dream to the next, are to them a series of wars, victories, and catastrophes; but to the amateur, the wars of the professionals are windows into the dreamworld.

Do I mean to suggest here that the worlds of the ancient Mesoamericans did not exist? that they were dreamed? No one who has climbed a pyramid or attended a class taught in Maya or Nahuatl can doubt the origins of the dream, but no one who has considered Johann Gottfried von Herder's seventeenth-century arguments about our relation to the ancient Greeks can doubt that we must be dreaming. We can never be ancient Greeks or Mexica; reading is dreaming. This is a book of literature, not of science.

We read: "Tezcatlipoca said to Quetzalcoatl . . . ," and immediately we are dreaming. And if we readers are amateurs, our dreams are informed by the translators—we are twice dreaming. Unlike the professional, who exists on the nectar of the myth of anachronism, the amateur concedes that the reader is also a writer; the amateur enjoys the luxury of the literary arts.

Pity the poor professional who argues against the authenticity of the *Popol Vuh* or the *Florentine Codex*. With admirable rigor and foolish expectations, the last in line searches for some antithesis to guarantee a place in the history of dreaming. But what is authenticity? In what might be called a Nahua poetics or a Nahua version of Plato's *Symposium*, a group of poets gathered in a garden in the fifteenth century to discuss art and life. They began by saying that the poet or singer had descended there (into the garden or into the world), but from where? What is the provenance of art? of the artist?

They, too, wondered what is real, authentic. In one poem or song (*cuicatl*) after another, the Nahuas ask if we truly live on earth. Is it only a dream? Do they mean language? thought? life itself? Is the reader dreaming Heidegger? Derrida? Saint Paul?

Only the most recent work is approachable in its original intent, and even then it must endure the betrayals of translation, geography, and culture. If the old texts were uncorrupted, they would be corrupted the moment they were read. For a line to be scientifically authentic, it would have to be read by a Mexica or Maya noble of the fifteenth century.

Or an amateur born 500 years later, a reader in the thrall of literature.

Diego de Landa and Bernardino de Sahagún were amateurs, clerics by profession. Landa wrote as an amateur. He irritates us now, he angers us, for he burned the painted books, the Maya codices. Sahagún became the greatest professional ethnographer of all time, the source. This was no Herodotus swallowing stories about monsters. Sahagún was orderly, skeptical, intent upon learning Nahua culture and religion even though his avowed purpose was to destroy the religion.

Charles Dibble and Arthur J. O. Anderson translated the work of Sahagún's informants into lovely, but curiously antiquated English. Perhaps it was their way of giving a sense of authenticity to the work, of assisting the amateur to dream, but it was not necessary.

The brilliant plain English translations of Sahagún's work by James Lockhart and Thelma Sullivan are no less the stuff to excite the dream of reading. Lockhart and Sullivan avoided the attempt to recreate a moment that can only be reassembled out of the two sources of the past: the past itself and the scholars who search out the past and convey it to us.

In Mexico, Angel Maria Garibay K., another cleric, worked diligently to bring more Nahua literature into the present, but it was not until the work of Miguel León-Portilla, another amateur, trained as a philosopher, that the quality of dreaming for this reader and thousands of others entered the world of thinking. In *La Filosofía Nahuatl,* published in the United States as *Aztec Thought and Culture,* the young scholar who was to become the foremost Mexicanist of our time reconsidered the Nahuas as human beings who had developed a philosophical view of life. He engaged the ethics and ontology of the Nahuas, and in one book changed forever the way people thought of Mesoamerica.

León-Portilla ended any consideration of the state cultures of Mesoamerica as the lives of savages, curiosities, somehow less than us. True, only the Maya had developed a form of writing incorporating symbols for sounds as well as things and acts, but the Nahua and Mixtec codices could be read and understood in much the same way as the pictographic versions *(Bibliae Pauperum)* of the Old and New Testament were used in sixteenth-century Europe.

In a shameful conceit, some of the professionals who doubt the "authenticity" of Mesoamerican literature based on readings of the codices would not deny that the *Bibliae Pauperum* represented quite adequately the literature of their own religion and culture. Today, of course, the illustrated article and advertisement have combined the two forms of "reading" in a manner amusingly like the Nahua and Mixtec codices or the Maya mix of phonetic and glyphic writing. Alberto Manguel, in his *History of Reading,* offers charming insights on the subject.

Whether oral literature, like that of the Nahuas and Homer, is less authentic or of less value in some way because it was not written down with a quill or an Apple Powerbook has no importance for the reader lucky enough to be an amateur. The Fitzgerald translation of the *Iliad* is a marvel, as are the translations by Richmond Lattimore and Robert Fagles, but they are not the same. The authenticity of the work is the beauty of the words on the page. Perhaps the real Homer or Homers, Greeks or Serbs or Albanians, reducing the anachronism to absurdity, had the eyesight of an eagle. It matters not at all to the amateur, who has been blessed by Fagles, Lattimore, Fitzgerald, and all their magnificent predecessors—and by the person or persons who may or may not have been Homer.

There is one *Cantares Mexicanos* in Nahuatl, another in English by John Bierhorst, and very soon there will be a third in Spanish by Miguel León-Portilla, working with two Nahuatl-speaking scholars from Milpa Alta, Librado Silva Galeana and Francisco Morales Baranda. Yet another is the English version that my wife Sylvia (whose first language is Spanish) and I have made of portions of the *Cautares.*

The *Popol Vuh,* which some writers refer to as the Maya Bible, has had three fine translations into English. The amateur may read with pleasure the

work of Adrián Recinos or the version in prose form by Munro Edmonson or
the wonderfully literary version by Dennis Tedlock. The professionals groan
over each of the translations, they grouse at each other, but there is yet another wonder here for the amateur—the curiously Hegelian progression of
scholars. Dennis Tedlock, for example, studied with Munro Edmonson. Does
the pupil excel the master or is the pupil merely different from the master?
Are there two masters?

This war, this Hegelian progression is in itself a drama about drama, a
dream of dreams for the amateur. More. Michael Coe wrote *Breaking the
Maya Code* about such wars among the professional Mayanists.

Working on this book has been all that an amateur could hope for, like
finding John Lloyd Stephens again. Better. To work with Miguel León-Portilla
is to encounter encyclopedic knowledge of the field gathered in a delightfully
witty and welcoming man, and to join in some small way his concern for indigenous people. The other professionals, those who make the gift of dreams
to amateurs, are soft-spoken scholars, worldly men and woman who appear
to live in awe of the thought and language of Mesoamerica. They, like León-
Portilla, look through time, and the ravages of Mesoamerica's encounter
with Europe, to find the truest stuff from which to dream.

I have also enjoyed the chance to work with Jorge Klor de Alva, and I
lament his decision to leave this project and the field to become president of
the University of Phoenix; were it not for his interest at the early stage, this
book, which I had been planning for more than two decades, might never
have come about. It was my good fortune to spend many wonderful days together with him planning this work and gathering material for it.

The Maya section of the book has been enhanced and to some degree
shaped by professionals: Dennis Tedlock, the author of literary translations
from Quiche Maya and one of the more interesting minds I have encountered; Gary Gossen, the proponent of humility and champion of clarity
among professionals; the grand and generous Mayanist Munro Edmonson;
and in Yucatan, Eleuterio Po'ot Yah, who was Edmonson's informant for several of his major works; as well as Alejandra García Quintanilla, Miguel Angel
May May, Sylvia Terán, Roger Arellana, Raúl Murguía Rosete, and the students of our Escuela de Alta Cultura Maya—Hunab Ku. Robert Laughlin—
translator of twentieth-century material from Chiapas—and the relentlessly
accurate linguist William Hanks also offered their thoughts.

The contemporary sections have been greatly aided by Natalio Hernández
Xocoyotzin, the prize-winning poet and former director of the Casa de los Es-
critores en Lenguas Indigenas. The renowned poet and president of the
Casa, Juan Gregorio Regino, also contributed to our work.

Although he began as a graduate student employed as a research assistant,
the brilliant young scholar Peter Sigal became a teacher as well.

Each one has some criticism to offer of the work of the others, although they are respectful of their colleagues, artists rather than adversaries. Will one of them prove some day to have been correct? Unless a Mesoamerican noble of the fifteenth or early sixteenth century appears to judge their work, we shall have to assume that all of them and none of them are correct.

Is it possible that even as we move further from the pre-Hispanic world of Mesoamerica, we will continue to get closer to the exact reproduction of the thoughts of that time? On the face of it that seems unlikely, and yet one can be certain that it will happen.

The limit of future work is set by losses long past. The tragedy of the European invasion of Mesoamerica is best characterized, I believe, in a single line from *Maya Cosmos* by Linda Schele: "*Hom,* the old K'ichean word for 'ballcourt,' is now the word for 'grave.'" She went on to say that when she and David Friedel and their colleagues began their work, they "wrote with such authority," but now "have become uncomfortable with that voice, instead bearing witness."

Scholars have discovered how to read the Maya glyphs. Perhaps. The discovery has come time and again, and there has always been a later discovery to prove that all previous work was less than imagination, error. Now, the efforts of both Dennis Tedlock and Linda Schele have come together in the translation of glyphs from Palenque. Professionals will scour the glyphs and debate the English words for decades to come. To an amateur, however, it is literature, fuel for dreaming, the beginning of the long voyage that leads from here to Mesoamerica and home again to rediscover ourselves in light of what they thought and did.

They were there. Through the intermediary called literature, we engage them, over time, as they were, and as they changed. Amateurs, readers, in dreams we infer the past and the other. As long as there are doubters and readers, it is still a ball court, not a grave.

Acknowledgments

In addition to those mentioned earlier, we are grateful to the J. Paul Getty Trust for the assistance of Peter Sigal and for the clerical help during several weeks of Jorge Klor de Alva's year as scholar in residence, and to the calm, careful, and always good-humored Drake Bennett for shepherding all the parts of a very complex manuscript.

Starling Lawrence, novelist and editor, helped to shape this work, making it more accessible to the general reader. In addition to his title as *h-meen* of Norfolk, we must add *tlamatini* of Fifth Avenue.

During the last days of work on this book at Miguel León-Portilla's home in the state of Morelos, we often spoke with amazement of the ability of Ann Adelman, who copyedited the manuscript of nearly 1,100 pages. "Does she know Nahuatl? Are you sure she doesn't know Nahuatl?" León-Portilla said.

It seemed impossible for someone without knowledge of Mesoamerican languages to have done such thorough and thoughtful work. This book bears her mark, as it bears the mark of Starling Lawrence and the authors/editors. We are grateful to her not only for her contribution, but for her willingness to take on such a large task when she had other pressing business.

In the
Language
of Kings

How to Use This Book

Although this is primarily an anthology of work chosen for its literary value, it also serves as a documentary history of much of Mesoamerica. The Nahua and Maya sections are arranged chronologically as well as by literary form. The Mesoamerican works at the outset of the anthology are the most certainly pre-Hispanic, since we have evidence in stone and painted books (codices) of their origin.

Where it seemed necessary to us and our editor, Starling Lawrence, we have added introductory notes to specific works to make them more accessible to the reader. Instead of the usual footnotes in a book such as this, we have produced an ample Glossary of Names, Terms, and Concepts (p. 647), which may be useful to the reader for other reading as well as for this work.

In place of a bibliography arranged in alphabetical order, Ascensión Hernández de León-Portilla, author of a major two-volume bibliography of Nahuatl works, has written a Bibliographical Essay (p. 674), placing the development of Mesoamerican studies in historical context. Since this anthology includes selections from a majority of the great works of Mesoamerican literature, the provenance of the individual selections serves as a fairly complete bibliography of primary sources.

All guides to orthography and pronunciation for Mesoamerican languages are open to discussion, but the guide included below should enable the reader quickly to get over the discomfort of hearing and saying aloud words and sounds that are very foreign to an English or Spanish speaker's ear. When words in Mesoamerican languages do not come trippingly off the tongue of English-speaking readers, we suggest that they simply let it be. One need not become a Nahua or Maya or Mixtec to enjoy the literature; translation after all must serve some cross-cultural purpose.

However, translation of ancient languages implies great variants: for example, the third edition of the *Maya/Spanish Dictionary* compiled by Alfredo Barrera Vásquez (Mexico City, 1995) runs to more than 1,400 very large

1

pages, but the *Dictionary of Hocabá* compiled by Eleuterio Po'ot Yah and Victoria Bricker (Salt Lake City, 1998) is a useful 400-page supplement. And there are others. In the case of several translations from sixteenth-century Spanish, we have had the benefit of Sylvia Sasson Shorris's knowledge of Ladino (a form of Spanish relatively unchanged since the end of the fifteenth century).

As we know from the history of our own English language, the changes over long periods or even brief periods in a living language are enormous. Almost every work included here can be said to be translated from a living language; thus the variant interpretations of words and concepts are the danger as well as the delight of the scholar's work. In general, we have followed the rule of using Mexican spelling—i.e., accents and tilde—for proper names and eliminated all but the tilde for most other words. In previously published material we have otherwise endeavored to reproduce the work as it was published, except for editing for sense or space and the conversion to block prose of some work that was produced in other forms.

Translation of Mesoamerican names may often lead the reader astray. The English translation of Nezahualcoyotl is "Fasting Coyote," but it means no more about the great Nahua poet's life or work than Armstrong or Shoemaker does for someone living in Boston. We have generally avoided using translations in the text, offering them instead in the glossary. We are particularly indebted to Munro Edmonson for his permission to print the material from the books of the Chilam Balam in block form and updated language.

In several cases, such as the *Rituals of the Bacabs* and the *Popol Vuh,* more than one reading is presented. Readers will have the opportunity to decide which is most pleasing in English.

Clearly, the invasion and conquest of Mexico is a prominent theme in both Nahua and Maya literature, and on occasion the same event was seen from several points of view, as in the Tlaxcaltecan war poem about the capture of Cuauhtemoc and the far more complete historical accounts from the *Florentine Codex.*

As a general rule, when the word "God" appears here, it refers to the Christian God, not to some unnamed Mesoamerican deity. A good clue to how this came about can be found in the four chapters from the Dialogues of 1524 (Book I, section 8) between the Franciscans and the surviving Mexica wise men and priests.

Orthography and Pronunciation

Many Mesoamerican languages began to be written in Roman letters during the first half of the sixteenth century. Such was the case with Nahuatl,

Otomi, Yucatec Maya, Quiche, Cakchiquel, Zapotec, and Mixtec, among others. The adaptation of the Latin alphabet to represent the phonemes of these languages was the work of several friars, assisted by Indian collaborators.

At about the same time they also prepared the first grammars and vocabularies of the native languages, some of which were published in Mexico, where printing was introduced as early as 1539. In the process of using the alphabet, they had to face many problems due mainly to the great differences in the phonemic systems of the Mesoamerican languages compared to those of Latin or Spanish. Because of this, one often finds inconsistencies in the spelling and writing of indigenous words.

In this anthology we have respected such inconsistencies, for they point up the complex processes necessitated in the transfer of literary productions into alphabetic writing from spoken tradition and/or painted books with glyphic characters. Thus, one will find numerous personal names spelled in variant forms, such as Montezuma, Moctezuma, Motecuhzoma, and Moteucsoma; place names like Texcoco, Tezcoco, and Tetzcoco; and common words such as that for "lord" in Nahuatl: *tecuhtli, tecutli, teutli,* and even *tectli;* for "god," *teotl, teutl;* for "flower," *xochitl, xuchitl,* and even *suchitl; The Discourses of the Elders* may be *huehuetlatolli* or *huehuehtlatolli.*

Among the various Mesoamerican languages there are notable differences that must be mentioned here. In the case of Nahuatl (the language of the Aztecs or Mexicas), most writers say that it is generally pronounced in accordance with the phonetic value of most of the graphemes of the Spanish language. Important exceptions are the following: for *a, e, i, o,* although pronounced as in Spanish (*a* as in "father"; *e* as in "pet"; *i* as in "feed"; and *o* as in "pomp"), one has to add the existence, seldom registered in writing, of long and short vowels. The *u* is often interchangeable with *o,* and in writing is also employed in dipthongs such as *hue*—as in *huehuetl,* "drum"—and *hui*—as in *xihuitl,* "year."

Finally, we should note that *x* is pronounced as in the English word "she"

tl is a digraph, as in "Atlantic"

tz is another digraph, as in "tsar"

h or sometimes an apostrophe ('), often called a saltillo (little jump), indicates a glottal stop, as in "coopt"

Nahuatl words are stressed on the next to the last syllable.

Nahuatl Pictographic Techniques*

Direct depiction

The god Huitzilopochtli

Ideograms

| "water" | "stone" | "mountain" | "sun, day" |
| *atl* | *tetl* | *tepetl* | *tonatiuh* |

Phonetic transcription

| Çoquitzinco | Quauhnahuac | Huiztlan |
| ("little mud place") | ("next to the trees") | ("next to the spine") |

Transparent ideograms

temple burning   leader pierced by dart

Sources: Sahagún, 1905–57, Vol. VI, cuaderno 2 ("Primeros Memoriales"); *Codex Mendoza*; Matrícula de Tributos; Historia Tolteca-Chichimeca.

*James Lockhart, *The Nahuas After the Conquest* (Stanford, CA: Stanford University Press, 1992), p. 329.

Maya Writing

From among nearly thirty existing Mayan languages, we have chosen Yucatec to illustrate their most salient phonemic traits:

Vowels, as in Nahuatl, are written and pronounced with a similar value as in Spanish and Latin. They also may be long and short, although this is rarely indicated in writing. Double vowels in Maya are frequent and indicative of different words, as in *kan*, "snake," and *kaan*, "sky"; *hun*, "one," and *huun*, "paper."

As with the consonants, the early grammarians devised special signs or graphemes to represent specific Maya phonemes. The following is to be noted: *dz* for *ts'*.

As in Nahuatl, also in Yucatec Maya and other cognated languages, one has to describe the phonetic value of the following employed letters: *X* as *sh* in "English." Preceded artificially by an *i*, it represents the female gender prefix, as in the name of the goddess *Ix Chel*. A parallel procedure was adopted to represent the male gender prefix, which actually is an *h*, in this case preceding it with an *a*, as in *Ah Kin*, "He of the Sun" (a priest of the Solar cult). In the Mayan languages, there are several explosive consonants. To distinguish them from those non-explosive, two procedures were introduced: either to double the consonant, as *pp*, or by adding an apostrophe after the consonant, as *p'*, *ch'*, *tt*, *t'*, and *th*.

In most lowland Mayan languages, *l* is subtituted for *r*. The prosodic accent depends upon the length of the vowel and the constriction of some syllables that receive greater stress.

Other languages from which compositions translated into English are included here share some of the phonemic traits of Nahuatl and Maya, such as the glottal stops and the characteristic pronunciation of the *x*, *ts*, and *h*. They include the relative height of pitch, in fact, a phoneme of the language that is indicative of a different meaning in a word. For those interested in the pronunciation and writing of such languages as Tarascan, Otomi, Zapotec, and Mixtec, we refer to Norman A. McQuown, ed., *Linguistics, Handbook of Middle American Indians*, Vol. V (Austin, TX: University of Texas Press, 1967), and its Supplements: Munro S. Edmonson, ed., *Supplement of the Handbook of Middle American Indians*, Vol. II (Austin, TX: University of Texas Press, 1984).

The Maya Syllabic Chart

	a	e	i	o	u
	(glyphs)	(glyphs)	(glyph)	(glyphs)	(glyphs)
b	(glyphs)	(glyph)	(glyph)		(glyphs)
ch	(glyphs)	(glyphs)	(glyph)		(glyph)
ch'	(glyph)			(glyphs)	
h	(glyphs)		(glyphs)	(glyphs)	(glyphs)
c	(glyphs)		(glyphs)	(glyph)	(glyph)
k	(glyph)				(glyphs)
l	(glyphs)	(glyph)	(glyphs)	(glyph)	(glyph)
m	(glyphs)		(glyph)	(glyph)	(glyphs)

The Maya writing system is a mix of logograms and syllabic signs; with the latter, they could and often did write words purely phonetically. This chart shows the Maya syllabary as it has been deciphered thus far. It should be kept in mind that, due to homophony, the same sound is usually represented by more than one sign; and that some of these signs may also act as logograms. With the exception of the top left row of boxes, in which each sign stands for a syllable consisting of vowel only, each box contains one or more signs representing a

	a	e	i	o	u
n					
p					
s					
t					
tz					
dz					
u					
x					
y					

consonant-vowel (CV) syllable; the consonants are at the left, and the vowels at the top. Thus all signs in the top right box would be pronounced nu.

As an example of syllabic writing, a Maya scribe would have written the word pitz, "to play ball," with the signs for pi and for tzi , combined thus:

Source: Michael D. Coe, *Breaking the Maya Code* (London and New York: Thames & Hudson, 1992), pp. 280–81.

General Introduction

Miguel León-Portilla

The Mesoamerican World

Mesoamerica—a large part of present-day Mexico and Central America—has a history embracing thousands of years of intellectual and artistic creativity. As a cultural area it began to develop, more than a thousand years B.C., along the coast of the Gulf of Mexico, not far from the land of the Maya. Many peoples living in the central highlands, in Oaxaca and the Maya area, were influenced by the Olmec culture, which is generally characterized as the "mother culture."

The emergence of larger communities in which social stratification and economic specialization began to develop presaged the birth of urbanism. Archeological investigation has unveiled the settlement patterns manifest in the building not only of ceremonial complexes but of truly civic centers in Mesoamerica. Teotihuacan, Tikal, Yaxchilan, Chichen Itza, Palenque, Monte Alban, and later Cholula, Uxmal, Xochicalco, Tula, and the metropolis of Mexico-Tenochtitlan with their temples, palaces, schools, marketplaces, and houses for the common people, in a network of plazas, streets, avenues, and canals, stand out among the many examples of Mesoamerican urbanism.

Magnificent architecture, mural painting, stone sculpture, gold, silver, and gemwork, and polichrome pottery flourished in a great variety of forms. Inscriptions on stelae, written and painted books, positional mathematics—including the concept of zero, an extremely precise calendar, and a highly elaborated worldview—are among the major intellectual accomplishments of the Mesoamericans.

Literary work, in several languages, developed along with these other artistic and intellectual accomplishments. Archeologists and epigraphers have unearthed and deciphered some of the oldest materials that may be described as literature, written not with letters but with glyphs and images. From the centuries of the Mesoamerican pre-Classic horizon, antedating the Christian era, some inscriptions on stone have survived which tell of the deeds of famous rulers. Such is the case of the stelae of Monte Alban, in Oaxaca, dated 600–300 B.C. Other carved stones found in Izapa, Chiapas, introduce us to the sacred universe conceived by the very ancient Maya. On stele 5, the supreme divine pair appears at the center of the world, She and He resting on both sides of a great cosmic tree whose roots penetrate a ground surrounded by the divine waters, and whose upper branches reach the heavens, the whole bracketed by two feathered serpents, a sacred space in which several humans, priests and artists, perform their duties. Teotihuacan, the metropolis known for its great pyramids and other monuments, which flourished in the central plateau some centuries later, during the Mesoamerican Classic period, also offers testimony to the beliefs and deeds of its inhabitants. There one can contemplate mural paintings representing gods, humans, and animals, from whose mouths emanate speech scrolls inscribed with glyphs. Most likely, these represent enunciations of songs, discourses, or narrations, evoking oral tradition, the main vehicle for expressing human thought and feelings.

During the Classic period, most of the traits characteristic of Mesoamerican civilization merged and consolidated, as in the case of the pantheon in which the supreme dual god—Our Father, Our Mother—is accompanied by many other divine local deities, "his children." A worldview, religious celebrations, complex social and political organization and other cultural patterns, as well as the arts, local differences notwithstanding, acquired their unmistakable shape. All this is reflected in what is known of the literature produced during that time.

We can approach this literature through the Maya inscriptions on stone, mural paintings, ceramics, and other objects. And it is not only the inscriptions, now in the process of decipherment, that convey literary expressions; the images themselves also express ideas and words. Most often on stelae, but also in murals and polichrome ceramic vases, the glyphic texts appear accompanied by images. One could say that the images somehow take the place of oral discourse because the mere contemplation of them illuminates and animates what the text expresses.

Maya stelae and paintings, using texts and images, speak about the achievements of rulers and warriors, bringing together both divine and human acts. For example, some polychrome cylindrical vases use paintings and glyphs to convey episodes that were told alphabetically in the *Popol Vuh*, the Maya Quiche Book of the Council. Also in Oaxaca, and to a lesser degree in central Mexico, carved slabs portray images, and complex scenes, sometimes accompanied by glyphs, which tell about a variety of occurrences. After the still only partially explained collapse of Classic Mesoamerica at the beginning of the tenth century, a final period of autonomous existence developed, which was interrupted by the Spanish invasion in the sixteenth century.

This post-Classic period, being the closest to the encounter with Western civilization, is the time from which most of what we know as pre-Hispanic literature derives. While inscriptions on stone became scarce, and most of the pre-Hispanic pictoglyphic books were destroyed by the conquerors, two forms of transmission survived. One was the art of book painting, which made possible the production in the early colonial years of hundreds of manuscripts, similar in various degree to the old codices in their style and contents. These manuscripts, often including glosses in Nahuatl or other languages, are of religious, ceremonial, astrological, historical, tributary, and geopolitical nature. Tradition, surviving in the minds of the elders, no doubt helped in the production of such works.

This and the fact that some of them are probably copies of lost pre-Hispanic manuscripts, make of them, along with the few extant works antedating the Conquest, invaluable testimonies, enabling us to penetrate the worldview and history of Mesoamerica. Some of Oaxacan-Mixtec origin, and others from central Mexico, vividly tell stories of great interest: for instance, the deeds of the Mixtec ruler Tiger's Claw told in the *Selden Codex,* or those of Nezahualcoyotl, the poet and ruler of Tezcoco, a kingdom allied with Mexico-Tenochtitlan, according to the *Codex Xolotl.*

The oral tradition, which in pre-Hispanic times was systematically preserved in the priestly schools, survived in various forms. One was in texts written by means of the alphabet which numerous Mesoamericans learned from the friars only a few years after the Conquest. This rescue occurred in several places in Mesoamerica, mainly in central Mexico, Oaxaca, and the Yucatan peninsula. The *Annals of Tlatelolco,* the *Legend of the Suns,* the *Toltec-Chichimec History,* and other texts in Nahuatl are examples of this. For their part, the books of the Chilam Balam, priests of Yucatan, belong to a sacred historical and astrological literature whose contents have been compared to those of the few extant pre-Hispanic Maya codices.

The oral tradition was also rescued by some friars who wished to know about "indigenous antiquities." That was the case with researches carried out by friars Andrés de Olmos and Bernardino de Sahagún in the central highlands; by Francisco de Burgoa in Oaxaca; Diego de Landa and Bernardo de Lizana in Yucatan; and Francisco de Ximénez in Guatemala. Many compositions—songs, narrative, discourses, and historical accounts—were thus transcribed either in native languages or Spanish translation. The best way to appreciate the authenticity of such materials has been to compare them with other productions unquestionably derived from Mesoamerican civilization: the testimony of stone or the surviving indigenous books.

At least a significant part of the literary legacy of pre-Hispanic Mesoamerica was thus saved from oblivion. The native scribes who could "read" the pictoglyphic books, or listen to those who had preserved the ancient tradition, made alphabetic transcriptions of songs, poems, prayers, narrations, legends, annals, discourses, conundrums, and other compositions. For a long time the manuscripts in which this literature—in Nahuatl, Maya, Quiche, and other languages—was transcribed remained on the dusty shelves of several monastery libraries, in the possession of private individuals, or in some vicere-gal repositories in Mexico. Other texts, sent to Europe for various reasons, formed part of the collections of noblemen or were placed in royal and church libraries, including that of the Vatican.

By the nineteenth and twentieth centuries, some of these manuscripts, sagaciously acquired by antiquarians and others, found a home in public li-braries, museums, and additional repositories in Europe, the United States, and Mexico. Scholars began to study them, first as historical or ethnological testimonies, then more recently as works of literary value.

Modern researchers scrutinize, translate, and comment on whatever can be identified as an expression of Mesoamerican literature. This includes archeological findings from various Mesoamerican periods, inscribed stelae, mural paintings, polichrome vases and other objects bearing images and glyphic texts, books of pre-Hispanic provenance or from the early colonial times, as well as the many works from the oral tradition that were recorded alphabetically.

Voices Never Silenced

Mesoamerican culture and its literary creativity survived the Spanish invasion in many forms. Employing the alphabet adapted to represent the phonemes of many indigenous languages, native scribes—working mainly in Nahuatl and both Yucatecan and Quiche Maya, but in other languages as well—con-tinued to produce a large variety of written texts. While some were of their own invention, others were dictated to them by their composers or by those interested in committing the ancient oral tradition to writing.

Most of the scribes had learned their office at the schools established by Franciscan friars in native towns. By 1540, there were several hundred young people who had mastered the art of alphabetic writing in their languages. Two colleges were also established to give young Mesoamericans a more sophis-ticated education. One was the College of the Holy Cross in Tlatelolco, the twin city of Mexico-Tenochtitlan; the other that of Tirepetio, not far from Val-ladolid in Michoacan.

In both colleges, friars like Bernardino de Sahagún, Juan de Gaona, Alonso de la Vera Cruz, and Agustín Focher, trained in famous Spanish or French universities—Salamanca or the Sorbonne of Paris—became profes-sors, working side by side with some Nahuatl and Tarascan elders knowl-edgeable in branches of their own ancient learning, such as medicine, pharmacology, manuscript painting, the calendar, and historiographic annals. This was probably the best aspect of the encounter of two worlds. Everyone learned from everyone else: the friars learned from the native sages, who learned from the monks, and their students learned from both.

We know the names of some of the Mesoamerican young people who were taught in these colleges and later became professors or distinguished themselves in other activities; among them, Antonio Valeriano, Martín Jacobita, Pedro de San Buenaventura, Juan Badiano, Martín de la Cruz, and Antonio Huitziméngari. Their accomplishments include not only close collaboration with the friars, but their own compilation of valuable testimonies about the ancient culture.

They also produced compositions themselves, mainly poetry and historical accounts. Hernando Alvarado Tezozómoc, Domingo Chimalpain, Cristóbal del Castillo, and Gaspar Antonio Xiu stand out for their literary achievements, examples of the indigenous literature of the colonial years.

A narration which has many of the dramatic aspects of a play has been attributed to Antonio Valeriano. It tells of the appearance of the Virgin of Guadalupe on the hill of Tepeyac. This text, known as *Nican Mopohua* ("Here is recounted"), uses concepts and expressions fron ancient Nahua songs and from the "Discourses of the Elders." Its poetry appears intended to convey the Christian message to the Indians in terms of "flower and song" (the metaphor used in Nahuatl to mean poetry).

Anonymous accounts describing the Spanish invasion from the indigenous perspective are examples of Mesoamerican epics at their best. In them, one can hear the voices of Nahua, Maya, Quiche, Cakchiquel, and Tarascan individuals who witnessed the sudden and dramatic confrontation. This literature, contrary to what many had believed, encompasses a rich gamut of works in Nahuatl, and to a lesser degree in other Mesoamerican languages.

One would not usually include among literary compositions complaints or denunciations addressed to local or viceregal authorities or even to the king, nor would one consider titles to property, or most letters and testaments, in this category. And Christian plays and discourses might appear at first to be outside the realm of Mesoamerican literature. However, it is in such works that we find descriptions of events which deeply affected the everyday lives of the people. In this sense, these works have unintended literary merit, as will be made clear by the compositions selected for this anthology.

There are also compositions in indigenous languages by well-known persons of Spanish descent. Perhaps the most illustrious examples are the poems—*tocotines*—by the celebrated poetess Sor Juana Inés de la Cruz. Translations were also made of Spanish classics into Amerind languages. A mestizo ecclesiastic, Bartolomé de Alva Ixtlilxóchitl, actually put into Nahuatl comedies belonging to the Spanish classic literature, including the work of Lope de Vega and Pedro Calderón de la Barca.

When Mesoamerican Literature Took Refuge in
the Hearts of the People

In contrast to the blossoming of Mesoamerican literature during the colonial period, indigenous voices were almost silent during the first hundred years of independent Mexico.

While the ancient Mesoamerican texts began to awaken the professional interest of scholars in Europe, the United States, and Mexico, the various governments of Mexico, having in mind national unity, fostered the assimilation of the Indians. The government forced the Indians to abandon their languages, minimizing them as useless dialects, and to speak Spanish, which they referred to as the national language. As Mesoamerican languages died, the number of speakers of those languages still alive began to decline. In that context, the mere idea of literary production among the Indians would sound chimerical.

Yet, to quote William Faulkner, "they endured." Often living in extreme poverty, at once despised and exploited, many of them still managed to preserve what they most cherished: ancestral traditions, moral values, and language. In their religious celebrations, they intoned the songs their parents had taught them, as well as some of their own invention. Seated together, perhaps at night around a bonfire, the elders told stories about the origins of all that existed: the supreme Father and Mother, the world, animals, plants, and the people. They passed on ancient wisdom in the form of admonitions delivered on special occasions: to boys or girls who had reached the age of discretion or were about to get married, at the birth of their sons, and, finally, at the funeral of a member of the community.

The best proof that beautiful words can take refuge in the hearts of the people is, of course, the literature itself. At first, it was the harvest of those who patiently entered into dialogue with Mesoamericans who knew about themselves and their traditions. This was mainly the work of ethnographers and linguists. More recently, Mesoamericans of various linguistic groups have become deeply concerned with the preservation of their culture, particularly their language and literature.

This anthology, unlike many earlier small collections of Mesoamerican literature, includes not only ancient material but also literature produced during the most difficult times for maintaining indigenous culture. Some, like the Chamula Origin Story and the Chorti tale of "What the World Used to Be Like," come from the Maya; others from Oaxaca, among them a Zapotec "Historical Legend" and a surprising Mixtec account, which sounds like a Mesoamerican modern reading of a page from a pre-Hispanic codex, "The Man Born of a Tree" (p. 69). Among the Nahuatl compositions with similar provenance are poems like "Little mother mine, when I shall die" ("Madrecita") (p. 383), and the play entitled *The Tepozteco.*

Fortunately, the many people who collaborated in producing this anthology are not alone in abandoning an apparently scholarly, but in fact naive, attitude that considered these compositions mere ethnographic materials obtained from Indian "informants."

Mesoamerican Literature Today

Something unexpected and quite wonderful happened during the last quarter of the twentieth century: A growing number of Mesoamericans took up pen, typewriter, or computer and produced widely varied literary works. At first they were influenced, perhaps overly so, by what they had read of their own ancient literature. They went back again and again in poetry and narrative to describe the sufferings of their people, and to denounce, with good reason I might add, the injustices that had been committed against them. It was a necessary and important beginning. Little by little, they have opened new windows to seeing and expressing their experience. Today, prestigious publishing houses are finding an audience for their work.

Among the authors whose work is included here, the Nahuas Luz Jiménez and Librado Silva Galeana are much praised for their narrative skills; Natalio Hernández Xocoyotzin, Alfredo Ramirez, and José Antonio Xochime for their poetry. The Maya writer Humberto Ak'abal is known for both prose and poetry, Briceida Cuevas Cob for poetry, Miguel May May for both fables and essays. Oaxaca has been fertile soil for writers of prose and poetry, including Andrés Henestrosa and those who work with Victor Hernández Cruz. The Mazatec María Sabina, famous for her esoteric knowledge of the mushroom-eating ceremony, composed chants of great beauty and profound meaning, work that has high literary value. Another Mazatec, Juan Gregorio Regino, has become widely known for his poetry, including a poem about María Sabina. And there are others as well, one of whom, the Tlapaneco Abad Carrasco Zúñiga, has produced a lovely poem about language with which the anthology ends—an eloquent corroboration of the very thoughts expressed here.

Through many ups and downs, Mesoamerican literature has not only survived for more than 2,000 years but now flourishes once again, meriting an anthology such as this, the first to consider the entire production as a single, continuing literature.

It is true of course that the impact of Western civilization affected the living patterns and thinking of the original peoples of the Americas. But it is also true that while the imposition of foreign culture hurt the innermost cultural self of the Mesoamericans, it did not efface it. Different languages and cultures have co-existed, influencing each other, shaping the "face and heart" (a Nahua metaphor meaning character) of what is today Mexico.

It has taken many years, and cost much blood and suffering in an as yet unresolved struggle, for the countries of Mesoamerica, notably Mexico, to recognize their multicultural and plurilinguistic identity. This is not exceptional in the world today. Global cultural trends induced by hegemonic powers—nation-states and transnational corporations—tend to homogenize worldviews, beliefs, and moral values. The method now relies heavily on technology, but the damage to individual cultures bears a strong resemblance to the aims of the colonial empires of earlier centuries.

Then and now, literary output has played and continues to play a crucial role. It gives utterance to ideals and remembrances, images of the self and others in poetry, narrative, and discourse, which exert deep cultural influence. The great literatures of the world testify to this. Mesoamerica, whose influence now reaches all of northern Mexico, most of Central America, and the Southwest of the United States, has never been silent.

The Mesoamerican Ethos

We have considered the long literary history of Mesoamerica. It is now time to ask how, over such a long period, with participants of so many different languages, a sort of Mesoamerican unity can exist. Can we say that there is a Mesoamerican *ethos*, or shared tone of sentiment, attitudes, and worldview; of values and forms of behavior, the sense of belonging to a family, both nuclear and extended; of being part of the community as a whole formed by those who speak the same native language and participate in the same cultural traditions? The answer is that such an ethos exists and cannot be denied; evidence of it is widely apparent.

In accordance with their ethos, it would be unthinkable for the Mesoamericans, even today, to think of themselves as unattached entities, kinless, isolated in any way. They understand that the cycles of feasts and religious ceremonies during the solar year help them immensely to reinforce the vital feeling of belonging to a sacred time and space. This ethos is the realm where humans are born, establish links of close relationship with others, work, marry, have their children, and fearlessly accept their own death as a point of encounter with Her, Our Mother/Him, Our Father. Such beliefs and attitudes are very far from those of modern Western culture. Nevertheless, these beliefs and attitudes, variously nuanced, have given meaning to the lives of millions of Mesoamericans.

This ethos serves also as the inspiration for Mesoamerican literature. Although at first one might expect such literature to reflect an archaic or primitive stage of cultural development, the texts speak to the contrary. Many surprises await those who would delve into the universe—magical, portentous, rich in meanings—that the Mesoamericans have created for themselves.

For us, ambivalent creatures at the beginning of a new millennium, understanding and enjoying the work collected here can be a deeply humanistic experience. However, these works were conceived in a social and cultural milieu totally different from that of Western tradition. In order to make the most rewarding connection to them, the reader should know something of the Mesoamerican spiritual universe.

The Ultimate Reality

When there was still night, in a primeval time, the gods earned, through their own voluntary sacrifice and death, the restoration of the Sun, moon, earth, and human beings. The universe in which Mesoamericans have lived—and many still think in this manner—has been established, destroyed, and reestablished several times: four according to the Maya, five in the Nahua tradition. This conception, which parallels that of the *kalpas* or recurrent cosmic ages in Hindu thought, has provided some Mesoamericans, like the present-day Maya Tzotzil of Chiapas, with a temporal frame of reference wherein they locate the most significant happenings of their own modern history.

There are more than twenty testimonies—archeological representations, codices, and texts in several indigenous languages—which speak of those ages or "Suns" that have existed. In many of them, reference is made to the supreme divine pair, *Tonantzin, Totahtzin,* Our Mother, Our Father, *Ometeotl,* the dual god, to whom the origin and successive restorations of the universe are attributed. He/She, Begetter, Conceiver, resides in the uppermost of the heavens; in the center of the world as depicted in the Mixtec codices *Selden Roll* and *Gómez de Orozco,* and in the one from the central plateau known as *Vatican A* and the Maya *Tro-Cortesiano.*

Tonantzin/Totahtzin, Our Mother/Our Father, the supreme divine pair, continues to be worshipped in Mesoamerica today. Many people in Mexico, Indians and non-Indians (mestizos), when asked whom they revere most— God the Father, the Son, or the Holy Spirit—frequently answer that they have recourse in their needs to Our Mother Guadalupe and Our Father Jesus.

Today, as in the past, the supreme divine pair continues to be thought of as the ultimate source of life for other gods, now in the form of Christian saints, or for human beings, animals, and plants with their respective destinies. All that exists on the celestial levels, on the surface of the earth with its four cosmic quadrants and the center, as well as in the underworld, has its origin and is governed by Him/Her, Our Father/Our Mother.

One very important trait of the Mesoamerican pantheon is that most, if not all, of its members exist and act in pairs, reflecting the ultimate nature of the supreme dual god. Thus, for instance, Tlaloc and Chalchiuhtlicue are, respectively, the god of rain and the goddess of the terrestrial waters;

Mictlantecuhtli and Mictlancihuatl, Lord and Lady of the Region of the Dead; Quetzalcoatl and Cihuacoatl, Feathered Serpent or precious twin, and the Feminine Twin, the word *coatl* meaning both "serpent" and "twin"; Tlaltecuhtli, who is at once Lord and Lady of the Earth; Cinteotl, god and goddess of maize; Xochipilli and Xochiquetzal, the Prince of Flowers and She the-Flower-precious-as-a-quetzal-feather. The Quiche Maya *Popol Vuh,* as one might expect, is a story of twins.

Tezcatlipoca is a god deserving particular attention. He appears in various texts and codices as the Red and Black One, or as Tezcatlipoca, Smoking Mirror, and Tezcatlanextia, the Mirror who makes things visible. And, as is also the case with gods like Tlaloc and Quetzalcoatl, Tezcatlipoca can play the role of a divine quartet, being present in the four cosmic quadrants and in the four previous ages of the world. The Mesoamericans found a Christian parallel in the several saints who appeared by pairs or who acted as divine quartets. Thus, Saints Joachim and Anna are the parents of the Virgin Mary; Saints Peter and Paul are the columns upon which the church rests; the four evangelists, Matthew, Mark, Luke, and John, are part of the key quartet of the Gospels. This was expressed in the social and religious organization of the Christianized Mesoamerican communities: as in the past, they maintained a quadripartite distribution, each ward of their villages and towns presided over by its correspondent god or patron saint.

Tezcatlipoca, Lord of the Smoking Mirror, had a special relationship with the God of Duality. He/She, the ultimate origin of whatever exists, acted, so to speak, through his/her various children, the other gods, but particularly through the portentous Tezcatlipoca. He was held in such esteem and reverence that, in prayers addressed to Him concerning pestilence, famine, or war, those who prayed to Him not only recognized Him as their principal god but also acknowledged that He was "all-powerful, the invisible, the untouchable one." And among other titles they gave Him, the following were often repeated:

Tlacatle, Totecoe, Tloque Nahuaque, Ipalnemoanie, Ioalle, Ehecatle, O Moyocoya, O Monenequi, Totecoe, Titlacaone, Iaotzine, O Teyocoyani.

Master, Our Lord, Lord of the near, of the nigh, You by whom we live, Night, Wind, O you who invent yourself, O you who do as you please, Our Lord, You whose servants we are, Warrior, O inventor of the human beings.

These invocations denote such high attributes that researchers have often thought they pertained to the supreme dual god. But in fact they are primarily associated with Tezcatlipoca, who, on account of his many portentous performances, was taken as "their principal god." A summary approach to several Mesoamerican books of paintings and glyphic characters will bring to light more of the personality of this god, who also appears in close relationship to Quetzalcoatl.

Let us turn to *Codex Fejervary-Mayer*, a pre-Hispanic manuscript from central Mexico. On the first page, a horizontal image of the universe, as conceived by the Mesoamericans, is shown. It depicts the four cosmic quadrants and the region of the center, accompanied by the nine Lords of the night hours, two in each quadrant, and Xiuhtecuhtli, Lord of Time and Fire, in the center. Two arrangements of the *tonalpohualli*, the astrological calendar, accompany the space image to indicate the recurring presence of time.

According to an ancient text, Xiuhtecuhtli, seen in the middle of the picture, is the "Mother, Father of the gods, who dwells in the navel of the earth." Four streams of blood converge on Xiuhtecuhtli from the four quadrants of the universe. The stream from the east originates from a hand of Tezcatlipoca, painted yellow; the stream from the north begins where the stump of a leg of the same god is visible; the stream from the west comes from the vertebrae and ribs of his skeleton. Finally, a head with Tezcatlipoca's painted facial decorations and other attributes indicates the origin in the south of the fourth current of blood. The god of the Smoking Mirror is thus present and acting in the four cosmic quadrants, for he is as one of his names says, *Tloque, Nahuaque,* Lord of the Close, of the Near.

Tezcatlipoca is represented on many other pages of the same codex, and on the very last one he appears surrounded by the 20 day signs, each one combined with 12 dots, the whole completing a *tonalpohualli*, the astrological calendar of 260 days, each of them the bearer of destinies. This image, which also appears in the pre-Hispanic codices *Borgia* and *Vatican B,* points to the god's presence in all the moments of time, and to the meaning of another of his names, *Monenequi,* He-who-does-as-he-pleases in his inescapable relationship with human destinies.

Tezcatlipoca, also known as *Tetzahuitl,* "the Portentous One," is represented in the codices in a great variety of forms. In some instances the Red Tezcatlipoca fights with his double, the Black Tezcatlipoca, in a sort of mysterious divine dialectic. He also appears in the Nahuatl texts rendered alphabetically after the Conquest, often acting with or against Quetzalcoatl, suggesting that if, in the Mesoamerican realm of the divine, duality as a complementary principle played a key role, the idea of confrontation had also a crucial significance. Thus one reads how both Tezcatlipoca and Quetzalcoatl, having fought in previous ages over governing the various Suns, cooperated in the restoration of the earth in the fifth cosmic age. To do so, they brought down from heaven the god/goddess of the earth, a monster full of eyes and mouths. Tezcatlipoca and Quetzalcoatl, transforming themselves into two great serpents, seized the earth monster and exerted such pressure on him/her that they finally divided the monster into two parts, making the heavens from one and the earth from the other.

The legendary cycle of Quetzalcoatl, both as god and as high priest of the Toltecs in the metropolis of Tula, stands in clear contrast to such cooperation. There, in a compelling story included in this anthology (p. 185), Tezcatlipoca appears accompanied by two wizards causing the ruin of the city and the flight of Quetzalcoatl.

In their various periods, Mesoamerican cultures have given birth to epic poems, lyric chants, and diverse forms of narrative whose subject is related to the primordial actions of the gods. Magnificent examples of this are provided by the *Popol Vuh,* Book of the Council of the Maya Quiche, and the *Florentine Codex,* where stories such as the deeds of the Hero Twins and the portentous birth of Huitzilopochtli, the patron god of the Mexica, are told. But Mesoamerican literary works are not only concerned with the world of divine beings. They also have an ethical component; that is, they consider how human beings behaved and should behave. Using legendary and historical accounts, as well as the admonitory speeches or "Discourses of the Elders," they constantly refer to concepts alien to Western culture, concepts which must be elucidated to help the reader understand and enjoy this literature to the full.

A Key Mesoamerican Concept: Men and Women "the Deserving Ones"

Mesoamericans had a specific and important notion about the origin and nature of human beings in the present cosmic age. Various texts in Nahuatl, Yucatec Maya, and Maya Quiche are particularly revealing. One, which occurs in two different manuscripts, tells what happened once the gods had restored the earth, Sun, and moon, as a result of their own immolation in a primeval region known as *Teotihuacan,* "Where-one-becomes-a-god."

Quetzalcoatl, the Feathered Serpent god, symbol of divine wisdom, was asked by the other gods to restore human beings after their destruction at the end of the penultimate cosmic age. Quetzalcoatl went to *Mictlan,* "the Region of the Dead," in search of the precious bones of men who had lived in previous ages. In the Region of the Dead, Quetzalcoatl had to overcome many obstacles; but once he finally gathered the precious bones, he took them to *Tamoanchan,* the place of origin, abode of the supreme dual god. There the Mother Goddess ground them up and put them into a precious vessel.

Quetzalcoatl still had to transmit new life to the ground-up human bones. To do that, He bled his penis, and as the drops of blood fell on the bones, they came to life. Since they had done penance along with the gods, they deserved life, *tlamacehuaya,* for while they were in Teotihuacan the gods had also restored the Sun and present age. They said: "The human beings have been born—the *macehualtin,* the deserving ones."

In fact, the word *macehualtin*, "the deserving ones by the gods' penance," became synonymous with human beings not only in Nahuatl but also, as a loan, in several other Mesoamerican languages. It is true that later a differentiation was introduced between *macehualtin*, "human beings" (understood as the common people), and *pipiltin*, "those of lineage," members of the nobility, the ruling class. But this did not alter the idea that all men and women, whether of noble lineage or commoners, essentially were *macehualtin*, "deserving by the gods' penance."

The concept of *tlamacehua* denotes the essential relationship human beings have with their gods, who by their own penance and sacrifice deserved—brought into existence—the human beings. The gods did this because they were in need of beings to worship them, to provide sustenance to nourish their lives. Man also had to perform *tlamacehualiztli*, "penance, the act of deserving through sacrifice," including the bloody sacrifice of human beings. If the gods "did penance for us"—*topan otlamaceuhqueh*—man ought to follow their example, to deserve his own being on the earth with his blood and life.

Actions often described as "utterly detestable human sacrifice," the consuming of small pieces of flesh from the human victim, the blood-smeared effigies of the gods, were elements that Mesoamericans thought essential to proper behavior in terms of *tlamacehualiztli*. If the gods had sacrificed themselves when it was still night there in Teotihuacan, and if, only in this way, with their blood, had they deserved the restoration of the world, then to repeat that primeval act was indeed to give in return, to repay and also restore. The victims of the sacrifice were thus named *teomicqueh*, "the divine dead." With these *teomicqueh*, man repaid the gods and did his part in maintaining the life on earth, in the heavens, and in the shadows of the underworld. There is a discourse of one *tlahtoani*, "high ruler," in which he advises his sons to take firm hold upon whatever is related to this concept:

> In this way one approaches *Tloque, Nahuaque*, "The One Who Is Near," "The One Who Is Close," where there the secrets are removed from His lap, His bosom, and where He recognizes one, causes one to deserve things [*quimacehualtia*]. Perhaps He causes others to merit, to deserve [*quitemacehualtia*] virility, the rank of eagle warrior, the rank of tiger warrior. There He takes, He recognizes the one who prays well to Him. In his hands He places the eagle vessel, the eagle tube [instruments for the sacrifice].
>
> This one becomes father and mother of the Sun. He provides drink, He makes offerings to those who are above us [*Topan*] and in the Region of the Dead [*Mictlan*]. And the eagle warriors, the tiger warriors revere Him.

With these words to his sons, the high ruler unveiled the meaning of the actions they should take, including that of "providing drink and sustenance" to the gods through human sacrifice. To achieve proximity to *Tloque,*

Nahuaque—in this case most probably referring to Tezcatlipoca—was diffi-cult. But if rulership, government, were to be alive, were to be deserved, *tla-macehualiztli,* the act of deserving it, should be reenacted.

In order to deserve divine benevolence, a good *tonalli* or destiny, many rites were also carried out in the privacy of the home. The word *tonalli* de-rives from the verb *tona,* meaning "to be warm and for the Sun to shine." It denotes the "warmth of the Sun, radiance, shining," and consequently the span of time in which this occurs, i.e., "the day." But as the days (and all other periods of time) provide the stage for the divine action, the *tonalli,* or days, bring with them the destinies for good or ill that will affect both individuals and entire peoples. Mesoamericans today, like many Asians and all those who have faith in horoscopes in the rest of the world, prepare themselves to cope with their destinies. In places like Oaxaca, Chiapas, and Guatemala, one often hears Mesoamericans speaking about their own *tona.*

To influence their destiny or *tonalli,* the Mesoamericans engaged in a great variety of public sacrifices and other acts. These were timed to accord perfectly with the day count of eighteen groups of twenty in the solar calen-dar. The rites' day names are described in several codices, including the *Bor-bonicus* and *Tellerianus,* and in some texts written in Nahuatl using the Roman alphabet.

After the Spanish Conquest, a syncretic religious attitude developed, bringing together both Christian and Mesoamerican concepts: Jesus, the son of Tonantzin, Our Mother, had done penance for humankind; He had ac-tually been put to death in a bloody sacrifice. Once again, men and women had become deserving because of Him, who was already known as *Ipal-nemoani,* Giver of Life. To repay for this and to obtain a good *tonalli,* Mesoamericans performed new kinds of *tlamacehualiztli,* penance or acts of deserving through sacrifice. Processions during Holy Week, pilgrimages to such sanctuaries as the famous site of the appearance of Our Mother Guadalupe in Tepeyac,[1] and of Our Father, the Lord of Chalma, as well as many holidays during the year, provide occasions to do *tlamacehualiztli,* thus bringing about favorable destinies, and above all, salvation. In this way, the ancient Mesoamerican culture reinterpreted the Christian dogma taught by the friars.

The Tonalli: *Human Destinies and the Beyond*

The *tonalli,* destiny, depended upon what Our Mother/Our Father had de-served and conceded to a person when he or she was born. Whatever possi-

[1]Tepeyac is the name of the modern city. The site at which the Virgin appeared is the hill of Tepeyacac.

bility might exist to modify the *tonalli* had to be sought in the *tonalpohualli* book of destinies. There, in the manuscripts called *tonalamatl*, "papers related to the destinies," one could find an indication of the most useful action, on any determined date, that would give something in return in order to foster the best possible life in the divine flow. This of course presupposed the *tlamacehualiztli*, the act of meriting and deserving what is "appropriate and righteous," that Our Mother/Our Father had determined for us when He/She placed our destiny in the womb of our terrestrial mother.

To live attuned to the rhythms of time was thought to be of primary importance. Only on a certain day could a person perform proper *tlamacehualiztli* to bring about a good destiny. Besides consulting the *tonalpohualli*, the 260-day calendar system, and the *xihuitl*, the 365-day solar count, those who knew about destinies concentrated upon other cycles of time, which presupposed more complex forms of correlation based on astronomical observations.

Stargazing (there were no instruments other than the naked eye) became the occupation of some priests and other members of the ruling group. Centuries of observation of the movements of the celestial bodies had actually led to the structuring of the basic calendrical systems. The precisely situated astronomical observatories of the Maya can still be seen in various restored cities. Visitors are regularly astonished by the way in which the Maya sited these and other structures to conform with astronomical phenomena ranging from the position of Venus to the solstices.

This stargazing enabled them to introduce corrections to the calendar, which brought it one ten thousandth closer to the solar year than the Western calendar after the Gregorian correction. As a Nahuatl text expresses it, one had often to consult with "those who guide us and instruct how our gods must be worshipped. Those who see, who dedicate themselves to observing and measuring with their hand the running and the crossing of the stars in the sky." Thanks to those observers and measurers of celestial movements, a number of other cycles of primary importance to the Mesoamericans were charted: the cycle of the Great Star (Venus); the Moon, including its eclipses; the Pleiades, closely related to the fifty-two-year cycle; and several other constellations and celestial phenomena.

Astronomical observation was not only linked to the accuracy of the calendar and to whatever was ruled by it, but also to the cult of the gods; to the basic duties of a person as a member of his family, group, town, chiefdom; and to his activities as farmer, warrior, artist, merchant, and so on. In other words, the very existence of the Mesoamericans presupposed observation of the sky. Without skywatchers, the ethos of this people, its distinguishing spirit, its genius would have developed along very different lines, if it had developed at all.

The Sun was central to all Mesoamericans—priests and skywatchers, rulers, members of the nobility, and commoners. He was the most revered manifestation of the Giver of Life and the one to whom blood sacrifices had to be offered so that the present cosmic age would continue to exist. The Sun, *Tonatiuh*, he "who causes light and warmth to exist," is also the source of the *tonallis* or destinies. He determines them; he is the supreme ordinator of time.

Considering what awaited them in the beyond, Mesoamericans saw the Sun as one of their ultimate possible destinies. Men who perished in the battlefield or as sacrificed captives would accompany the Sun on its daily course from dawn to the zenith.

Women who died in childbirth, as if with a prisoner in the womb, would become companions to the Sun from the zenith to the sunset. A manifestation of this survives still today in several localities bearing the name *Cihuatlan*, "place of women," along the west coast of Mexico.

Other possible destinies existed in the beyond, but they had no relationship to the behavior, good or bad, of people on earth. Mesoamericans considered that immanent consequences affected human beings while they were alive in accordance with their conduct. Destinies in the beyond mostly depended on the various forms of death. Those who were drowned or struck by a thunderbolt, being chosen by Tlaloc, god of rain, were taken by him to Tlalocan, his paradise. Children who died in infancy also found a home there. To them Tlalocan was a kind of Limbo, where they passed four years, until their *tonalli* brought them back to live on earth.

Mictlan, the abode of the dead, was the common house where most humans had to go. A sort of Greek Hades or Hebrew Sheol, it was an obscure place that people reached after having surmounted a series of obstacles. In Mictlan, their fate was to accompany Our Lord and Lady of the Region of the Dead, a manifestation of Our Father/Our Mother, in the most profound level of the universe.

Mesoamericans could contemplate their ultimate destiny in various places, generally using sculptures or paintings as guides to the possibilities. There is, for instance, a mural painting in one palace in Teotihuacan that probably represents Tlalocan. In the archeological zone of El Zapotal in Veracruz, inside a temple, an impressive sitting sculpture of Mictlantecuhtli, Lord of the Region of the Dead, was discovered, and there is another representation of the same god and his feminine counterpart in the main temple of Tenochtitlan. *Codex Vatican A* also includes images of the Mictlan, the Tlalocan, and the Sun's heaven.

Among the Maya, one can see representations of the *Xibalba*, the Region of the Dead described in the *Popol Vuh,* in some of the polychrome cylindrical vases of the late Classic period mentioned earlier. New interpretation of the destiny of the beheaded ballplayer, carved in bas-relief on the wall of the great ball court at Chichen Itza, gives further credence to the Maya view of the beyond.

A large part of the Chilam Balam books of *Chumayel* and *Tizimin* is devoted to the year count of the Maya, and there is little doubt now that among the great wars fought between the Maya city-states were those based on the "seating of the cycle," the ceremonial period of years so vital to Maya life. The Maya prophecies, too, were based on cyclical notions founded in the calendar.

Although it is extremely difficult for the Western mind to grasp, the Maya concept of time, in which certain persons or priests were known as "day-keepers," considers time as both encompassing and made up of discrete parts. Maya documents often speak of Venus and the Sun as twins, with Venus, which appears first in the morning sky, as the older twin. Even today, in the villages of the Yucatan, the diviners or "doers" known as *h-menes,* or *h-meeno'ob* (to use the proper orthography and Maya plural), study the position of the Morning Star in its relation to the Sun to predict the destinies of their clients or patients. Recent incantations used by *h-menes* show the influence of Christianity, as can be seen in the invocation of the rain god, Chac, included here (p. 556).

With This You Shall Live

Books of paintings, indigenous texts, and several Spanish chroniclers tell how children and young people were educated in the *calmecac* or priestly schools, and in the *telpochcalli,* the houses for youth. At home and in the schools, self-control, respect for the others, and knowledge about what a boy or girl should aspire to, were matters of the greatest concern.

Discourses in several native languages, alphabetically transcribed in the sixteenth century, and some modern works based on ancestral wisdom but adapted to new circumstances, offer perhaps the best examples of the moral values most cherished then and now by Mesoamericans.

These ethical discourses are fine examples of the way in which beauty and wisdom come together in Mesoamerican literature. We have included such discourses from Nahua, Maya, Zapotec, and other groups to demonstrate some of the salient principles that shaped the "faces and hearts" (the metaphor meaning character) of those who were enlightened by a big torch that did not smoke (another metaphor).

The idea that the earth, where it is our destiny to live, is a dangerous place, painful and without repose, was inculcated in the Mesoamericans from early childhood. Boys and girls had to prepare themselves to face the shattering winds, sicknesses, famines, wars, all sorts of misfortunes. They had to realize that they came to live with others on the earth. This deeply instilled sense of belonging also meant being accountable for whatever they might be asked to do on behalf of others, including the community as a whole.

Children were taught to humble themselves, to respect others. They were told that, as in a mirror, they should contemplate those who lived in the past—the great-grandfathers, the forefathers, those who gained merit, who were skillful, and above all knew what was good and righteous—and follow that path.

In service of the gods, they were to do acts of penitence, to bathe at dawn, then to sweep and clean the place where they lived. Students in the ordinary schools learned to cultivate the fields, go to war, prepare themselves for marriage, and be ready to take part in whatever work was needed by the community. Listening to the words of admonition addressed to them, readers will appreciate what was said to be the ultimate aim of such education: "Act, cut wood, work the land, plant cactus, and you shall have drink, food, and clothing. Thus, shall you live. For this you should be known, praised. Someday you will tie yourself to a skirt, to a blouse [you will get married]. What will she drink? What will she eat? Is she going to live off the air? You are the support, the remedy; you are the eagle, the tiger."

The education offered in the priestly schools was much more sophisticated. There the students were taught to speak well, mastering the subtleties of their own language, and for the Nahuas the reverential forms. They learned by heart the ancient songs, the old stories, the prayers, and the most celebrated discourses.

Following the contents of their books of paintings and characters—and in the case of the Maya, complex phonetic and glyphic representations—they were introduced to the divine wisdom, astronomy, and the calendar; and to the art of composing poems, narrations, and discourses. And especially in the schools of Nahua nobles, they were taught not to be arrogant and greedy but to behave as true human beings, developing a heart firm as a rock and a face like that of the sages.

Comparing the principles that were norms of conduct in pre-Hispanic Mesoamerica with the realities seen in the everyday lives of those who inhabit the same land today, doing their best to survive, one cannot fail to note that the heritage endures. Despite alien influences and impositions, Mesoamericans have still managed in large measure to remain true to themselves.

These Are Our Flowers, These Are Our Songs

A great part of Mesoamerican literature was, and to a lesser degree still is, recited and performed in the open air. The feasts that were described in great detail in the codices and in alphabetically written texts, and those that take place in contemporary communities, provide time and place for the recitation of a wide variety of compositions. The participants, surrounded by the rest of the community, are often arrayed in multicolored garb. There is usually music and dance. The audience listens to the vibrant sounds of wooden drums, flutes, conch shells, rattle gourds, and other instruments. Songs, prayers, and discourses are spoken or chanted. Dialogues, often in the form of a play or a pageant, such as the *Rabinal Achí*, may also be part of the festival.

In dealing with these Mesoamerican works, some important distinctions have to be kept in mind. It is true that all were produced by peoples who shared basically one worldview, and one and the same culture, developed over more than 3,000 years. Nevertheless, differences existed in the thinking and feeling of these peoples that were mirrored in their voices, paintings, and glyphic characters.

The first distinction has to do with the procedures followed to preserve and transmit what we now term their literature. On the eve of the Spanish invasion, oral tradition and the painted books were the purveyors of literature, particularly in the temples and schools. After the encounter, things radically changed. The friars managed to adapt the Roman alphabet to represent the phonemes of the Mesoamerican languages. As Angel María Garibay put it, "the indigenous word remained in the luminous prison of the alphabet."

All but a very few of the compositions included here have come down to us through this form of transmission. It cannot be denied that in the process of transferring them into alphabetic writing, there were distortions of the ancient oral tradition and the contents of the painted books and glyphic characters. So too, the ancient texts that were chanted at feasts or delivered as "readings of" or commentaries on the codices were exposed to various external influences. In an effort to bring the reader as close as possible to the ancient Mesoamerican forms of transmitting expression, "readings" of some inscriptions on the monuments and of glyphic texts accompanying the paintings in pre-Columbian books have been included here.

Although they are not easy to comprehend, it is possible to experience and enjoy these direct approaches to the contents of a Maya stela and the pages of a codex. Similarly, the reader can listen to the oral "ancient" history provided by two contemporary Mixtecs of Oaxaca. In the modern version of their language, they give an account of the origin of their people which appears to be an accurate rendering of the pages of two ancient Mixtec codices (see Book III, section 1).

In contrast to these direct presentations of Mesoamerican expression, most of the works included here derive from versions committed to the alphabet either by native scholars or by friars anxious to learn about indigenous beliefs in order to more effectively replace them with Christianity. A large part of the Mesoamerican literature that has come down to us has gone through such a process. It could not be otherwise, for most of the ancient books were reduced to ashes. As to the inscriptions on stelae and other monuments, the work mainly of the Maya, only recently have epigraphers begun deciphering them. To compensate for the limited access to those sources, we must turn to the abundant alphabetic renditions done in the sixteenth and seventeenth centuries.

Questions have been raised about the authenticity of texts obtained in this way; but modern translators working in European languages have delved into these critical questions and succeeded in distinguishing interpolations and other kinds of alterations from what is an authentic rendition of indigenous expression. For the texts included in this anthology, their agreement with archeological findings, extant inscriptions, and other independent transcriptions of the same or very similar compositions enables us to discern their authenticity as part of the ancient Mesoamerican culture, while not denying the influences of Western culture. Of course, with documents and writings from the colonial period and later centuries, it is far easier to identify their provenance.

The wish to set down in stone, on deerskin, or amate paper (produced from the fig tree) the history and thought of a people impelled the Mesoamericans to develop various forms of writing—pictographic, glyphic, and phonetic—early in their history. Hieroglyphic writing was common among the Maya at the beginning of the modern era. There were words in use then for book (*huun*), page (*valeh*), and even for a writer (*ah tz'ib*).

A culture and history so carefully preserved before the invasion was not to be obliterated in a few centuries. Nor would it permit the imported and imposed culture to exist unaffected, even in the case of the new religious literature. A careful reading of what were once thought to be entirely Western (Christian) documents, such as the *Nican Mopohua* relating the appearance of the Virgin of Guadalupe, reveals strong Mesoamerican influence both in form and content.

Yet another distinction must be drawn, this one related to the assembling of this literature or literatures. For organizational purposes beyond mere chronology, one must distinguish, however arbitrarily, certain subareas and linguistic contexts. We have chosen three. One is that of the Nahuatl-speaking peoples. A second comprises the several Mayan nations (Yucatec, Quiche, Cakchiquel, Tzotzil, Ch'ol, etc.). The third, multivariate in itself, encompasses many of the other peoples: Otomi, Zapotec, Mixtec, Mazatec, Mixe, who belong to the Otomanguean linguistic stock, and a few more, considered unrelated to any other, such as the Purepecha from Michoacan.

The Spiritual Setting and Creativity of the Nahua

Endowed with a great capacity for expansion, the Nahua built their main settlements in the semi-arid central plateau of Mexico. There, those places which successively became their metropolises—Teotihuacan (at least in part inhabited by Nahua people), Cholula, Xochicalco, Tula-Xicocotitlan, Culhuacan, Tezcoco, and Mexico-Tenochtitlan—exerted political, economic, and religious dominance.

The vast regions to the north, ecologically in many respects similar to the great North American Southwest, exhibit some early stages of an attenuated Mesoamerican penetration. To the Nahua, that area was their place of origin.

Systematic expansion of the Nahua into the humid mountain slopes and the coast plains bordering the Pacific and Atlantic oceans took place in discrete stages. In the years of Aztec or Mexica hegemony, they subdued a large part of the present-day states of Veracruz and Tabasco, as well as of Guerrero, Oaxaca, and Chiapas. This means that their inhabitants, people like the Totonac, Huaxtec, Mixtec, and Zapotec, had to pay tribute and provide personal services to the Nahua.

Dominance was also exerted through commerce. Since time immemorial, the *pochteca* or merchants had established permanent routes that took them to very distant places in Tabasco, Campeche, Chiapas, and Guatemala. Tribute and trade brought both necessities and precious commodities to the Nahua cities. In the days of Mexico-Tenochtitlan, the *pipiltin,* those of lineage—the supreme high ruler or *huey tlahtoani,* the other dignitaries, high priests, chiefs of the army, judges, teachers at the priestly schools, scribes and wise men—profited most from the uninterrupted flow of tributes and personal services provided by the conquered polities. Not only animals but many tons of maize, beans, chile peppers, fruits, cotton, paper, amber, cacao beans, tobacco, and luxury goods—gold, jewels, feather headdresses, fine cloaks, war attire, sandals, shields, arrows and other weapons—were brought into the city. Stocked at the royal warehouses, they were later distributed through a well-established market system, as well as by other methods, according to the people's requirements.

The efficiency of the resulting political, social, and economic system made it possible for some priests, sages, and artists to enjoy the leisure that is indispensable to the creative life. One very important element was their acquaintance or rediscovery of what they described as the *Toltecayotl,* the summing up of the Toltec creations. Whatever was considered good and admirable appertained to the *Toltecayotl,* which in itself was credited to the wisdom and benevolence of the high priest Quetzalcoatl. According to several Nahuatl, Yucatec Maya, and Quiche texts, and some Mixtec codices, he had lived devoted to the cult of the god whose name he had made his own. He was also the ancestor, divine and human, of the nobles or *pipiltin* from among whom all high rulers were chosen.

Images of the Feathered Serpent, carved during successive periods, testify to Quetzalcoatl's divine presence in the various Nahua metropolises. One of them was carved in the Quetzalcoatl pyramid within the "citadel" of Teotihuacan. Representations of another of his revered forms—that of

Tlahuizcalpantecuhtli, Lord of the Dawn and of the Morning Star—were painted in various murals and in tripoid polychrome cylindrical vases.

Monuments in Xochicalco, in the present-day state of Morelos, bear eloquent reminders of Quetzalcoatl in the feathered serpents carved on their walls and on several stelae, many of them accompanied by calendric registers evoking the wisdom attributed to this most revered personage. There, as in Teotihuacan, symbols of songs and prayers appear in the speech scrolls coming out of the mouths of the priests and even of several sacred animals.

In Cholula, Tula-Xicocotitlan, and other centers like Tenayuca, Tezcoco, and Mexico-Tenochtitlan, and in places as far from the central highlands as Chichen Itza in Yucatan, as well as other Maya and Oaxacan areas, effigies of the Feathered Serpent, who is also known as the Morning Star, and Ehecatl, the god of wind, appear. And with them always the reminder of his confrontation with Tezcatlipoca. He and his Aztec manifestation, their patrongod Huitzilopochtli, who fosters war and bloody sacrifice, appear often in contrast to the deeds and the words of wisdom and peace attributed to Quetzalcoatl.

This contrast is tangible in monuments which can be described as the "official" art of the Aztecs, among them the Temple of the Sacred War. This pyramid, with an altar above and a stairway of thirteen steps, evokes the levels of the heavens in the vertical image of the universe. On the altar there is a solar disk with the four-movement glyph. This is the calendric date of the present cosmic age, the one destined to be the glory of the Mexica nation. Tezcatlipoca appears to the left of the Sun, and to his right, Huitzilopochtli; the glyph of water and fire—war—comes out of their mouths and hands. On top of the altar, bas-reliefs of Xiuhcoatl, the Fire Serpent, the invincible weapon of Huitzilopochtli, and 2-Reed, the date of the founding of the Aztec metropolis, are visible. On the back of the monument appears an eagle on the cactus (*nopalli*), with human hearts instead of prickly pears. The eagle is the Sun, who, as indicated by a glyph, summons them to war.

Truly a book in stone, this monument has other glyphs reminiscent of Tezcatlipoca and Huitzilopochtli: 1-Flint and 1-Death, respectively. In addition, 1-Rabbit and 2-Reed, the first days of the fifty-two-year cycle, evoke the date on which the ceremony of the New Fire took place. Other gods are also present: Tlaloc, god of rain; Tlahuizcalpantecuhtli, Lord of the Dawn; Xiuhtecuhtli, Lord of Fire; and Xochipilli, Prince of Flowers, the ones who sacrificed themselves in the primeval Teotihuacan to permit the movement of the Sun when the present cosmic age began.

War, conquest, the taking of captives, bloody sacrifices, the power and glory of the high rulers are the subjects of many of the monuments erected in Mexico-Tenochtitlan. Open books indeed, they speak about the conquests achieved by Motecuhzoma I, and Tizoc; the ascension to the throne of Motecuhzoma II; and the consecration of the new temple. But most important of all was their representation in the main temple of Tenochtitlan of the portentous birth of Huitzilopochtli, with his mother Coatlicue and his adversary sister Coyolxauhqui, who started a divine cosmic war in the belief that she could thus avenge the dishonor of the birth of Huitzilopochtli, the child of an unknown father. At least six sculptures of the decapitated Coyolxauhqui have been unearthed, all of them testimonies to the victory of Huitzilopochtli, the invincible patron god of the Aztecs. A magnificent example of Nahuatl epic poetry, included here in Book I, section 2, vividly tells the story of the birth and the victory at Coatepetl, the Mountain of the Serpent, which was recreated in stone as the main temple in the heart of the Aztec metropolis.

A Literature Rich in Contrasts

War and conquest on the one hand, peace and wisdom on the other, co-existed in the world where Huitzilopochtli-Tezcatlipoca and Quetzalcoatl were worshipped. The literature portrays the contrasting ideas of the Nahuas in many forms. There are the *yaocuicatl,* songs of war; the *cuauhcuicatl* and *ocelocuicatl,* chants of the eagles, chants of the jaguars; descriptions of battles, death by the obsidian blade; flowery wars to take captives and obtain blood to foster the life of the Sun; the conviction that, as long as the world exists, the glory, the renown of Mexico-Tenochtitlan will endure.

The great festivals held in the open air, accompanied by the sound of drums, flutes, conch shells, and rattle gourds; the dancers in magnificent array, shields and darts in their hands, were the occasions—and they were frequent—to sing the sacred hymns, the war songs, exalting the power of the nation and its role in maintaining the movement of the Sun.

This worldview co-existed with the legacy attributed to Quetzalcoatl. The *xopancuicatl,* spring songs, and the *icnocuicatl,* chants of orphanhood and deep reflection, speak different words. They praise friendship and enjoyment of what the Earth, Our Mother, gives to women and men. They concentrate upon the great mysteries of human existence: suffering, death, the beyond, and the possibility of speaking the truth on earth. Metaphors and clusters of metaphors bring to mind a variety of flowers, precious birds, brilliantly colored feathers, books of paintings, life as a dream, the rapture caused by hallucinogenic mushrooms, the gifts of the Giver of Life, springtime and the golden ears of corn, the beat of the kettledrum and the playing of flutes and conch shells. Parallel expressions, recurrent phrases, variant forms of rhythm are among the most commonly employed stylistic devices in these poems.

There are indications in the manuscripts that some of these works may be ascribed to particular authors. The most probable known author, Lord Nezahualcoyotl (1402–1472), ruler of Tezcoco, suffered terrible persecution by political enemies during his childhood and early youth. Although they had murdered his father, he managed to defeat his tormentors by forming an alliance with the Mexica. His reign of more than forty years was a golden age. Some thirty chants are attributed to Nezahualcoyotl, whose reputation as sage and poet was perhaps unparalleled. Themes recurring in his work include the brevity of all earthly existence, the purpose and value of human action, the mysteries surrounding death and the supreme deity, Our Father/Our Mother. Nezahualcoyotl's poetry inevitably leads the contemporary reader as it did the ancient Nahuas to describe him as a *tlamatini*, "one who knows something."

The ancient annals also mention other composers or poets, among them Tlaltecatzin of Cuauhchinanco, who lived in the fourteenth century and left us an imaginary conversation with an *ahuiani*, a woman of pleasure, in which he intermingled his craving for pleasure with his own search for the supreme Giver of Life.

The list of Nahua poets includes a woman, Macuilxochitzin, to whom a chant is attributed in which she shows her tenderness and compassion in her attempt to save the life of a vanquished Otomi warrior who had wounded the Mexica ruler Axayacatl in battle.

One of the most extraordinary of many pieces about the Nahua lords is a dialogue convoked by Tecayehuatzin of Huexotzinco to discuss the possible meanings of *in xochitl, in cuicatl,* "flower and song"—that is, poetry itself, symbolism, and what we would understand today as art. The dialogue probably took place around 1490 in a garden near the palace of Tecayehuatzin. As the host, he offered his friends, the other poets, a chocolate drink and some tobacco. The ensuing conversation (given in Book I, section 1) contains deep philosophical insights. Aquiauhtzin, a noble from Ayapanco, a town close to the volcano Popocatepetl, proposed several questions new to the princes: Are flowers and songs perhaps the best remembrance man can leave on earth? Or are they the best kind of language for attempting to speak with the Giver of Life?

The dialogue included expressions of doubt. If we ignore which sort of truth man can reach here, how can we dare to affirm that poetry has any value? To Xayacamach of Tlaxcala, flower and song (the metaphor meaning poetry), like the hallucinogenic mushrooms, is the only good means of self-intoxication, the way in which one flees sadness and suffering. After listening to other opinions, the host, Lord Tecayehuatzin, dares to say something which, he hopes, all will agree on: flower and song makes friendship on earth possible.

Dialogues in a poetical vein, chants of war, joy, and deep reflection, were invoked alongside the solemn sacred hymns, which were often esoteric expressions, essential to the feasts marked by the solar calendar. Other recitations followed the contents of the books that preserved the history of the Nahuas.

Some of the *xiuhamatl,* or annals, were redacted several decades after the Conquest. They tell the revised Aztec version of their history, as ordered by one of their high rulers, Lord Itzcoatl. Claiming that there were many falsehoods in the old books which spoke of the humble beginnings of the Aztec nation, he decided that a glorious new narrative should be written. The contents of some of these new books were later transcribed as alphabetical texts. The *Annals of Tlatelolco,* those of *Cuauhtitlan,* and the *Legend of the Suns,* are examples of this. In them one frequently finds expressions such as "It is here," "One sees here," indicative of the process of following and "reading" the painted images and glyphic characters.

One has to keep in mind at this point that there are several annals, poems, discourses, and other compositions in Nahuatl that cannot be ascribed to the Aztec (or Mexica). They were produced by people of other polities such as Tezcoco, Tlaxcala, and Huexotzinco, and even in some small towns where Nahuatl was also spoken. While their poetry may often reflect similar concerns, their annals vary both in content and in the interpretation of some occurrences. Such was the case with the historical narratives which indigenous chroniclers like the Tezcocan Fernando de Alva Ixtlilxóchitl or the Chalcan Domingo Francisco Chimalpain incorporated in their works composed after the Spanish invasion.

Another genre found among most, if not all of the Nahua, from ancient times to the present, merits special attention, for it contains their ethics. Known as *huehuehtlahtolli* or "ancient word," they were transmitted as discourses to be delivered on particularly important occasions during the life cycle of either individuals or the community. In praising the spirituality and didactic value of the *huehuehtlahtolli,* friar Bartolomé de las Casas wrote:

> Are there any discourses better conceived, or more voluntary, and more relevant, to the transformation of human life into virtuous action? Could perhaps Plato, Socrates or Pythagoras, or after them Aristotle, think of something more appropriate than these discourses with which these peoples constantly instructed their sons? What else is taught by the Christian law, with the exception of what pertains to the faith?

These discourses were recognized by the Spaniards as such an extraordinary testimony of indigenous wisdom that one collection of them in Nahuatl, with an abridged Spanish version, was published in Mexico City in 1600. Many years later, on the occasion of the Quincentennial of the Encounter of Two Worlds, a Nahuatl scholar and writer, Librado Silva, and I republished these texts with a complete Spanish translation in a printing of 615,000 copies, which sold out in just five years, proof perhaps of the interest they have awakened.

Nahuatl literature is far from dead. We have already mentioned the extant corpus produced in colonial days. The examples included in this anthology and other *Yancuic Tlahtolli* or "The New Word,"—poetry and narrative by contemporary authors working in their own native language—should be taken as a hopeful sign: the language endures. Nahuatl, the vehicle for wisdom, history, and deep feeling for more than 2,000 years, continues to be spoken, and literature in Nahuatl is well disseminated.

The Divine and Human Background of Maya Cultural Achievements

In the long history of the Maya, notwithstanding the many factors they shared with their neighbors—social and political organization, basic religious beliefs and practices, the calendar, a propensity for waging wars of conquest, and the use of long-distance commerce as a source of prosperity—the Maya developed patterns of living which have a unique face and heart (personality).

The realm of the Maya comprised two principal geographic settings:

The lowlands of the north include the Yucatan peninsula and adjacent areas of Guatemala's Peten, Belize, and the great Usumacinta river basin in Chiapas. The northern half of the peninsula, flat country, relatively dry, contrasts with the humid tropical forest to the south.

The Maya highlands, located in southern Guatemala and parts of Chiapas, have as backbone an important mountain range in which pines, grasses, and oaks abound. Both in the high- and lowlands agricultural practices include a slash-and-burn system, which alternates intervals of seeding with fallow periods during which the land is regenerated and the brush that must be burned to produce ash for the thin layer of soil can grow. The most intense cultivation of corn took place in the southern lowlands. In the densely populated highlands, almost all of the available land was used for growing crops, mainly corn and beans, chile peppers and squash.

A geocultural division—northern, central, and southern—has been introduced by modern Mayanists, in which the first two are located within the lowlands. Maya culture flourished there during its classic splendor. Although there were early manifestations of remarkable cultural development, it is mainly at the base of the mountains in such places as Izapa near the Chiapas-Guatemala border and Abaj Takalik, some thirty kilometers from the Pacific Ocean, that stelae of great interest for the origins of the Maya worldview have been discovered. In Izapa, scenes represented in bas-relief somehow anticipate—like that of stela 5 (described on p. 9)—what centuries later was to be depicted in some polychrome cylindrical vases of the late Classic period (around A.D. 600–900), and in the extant pre-Hispanic codices. Concepts and words spring forth from the images carved on the Izapa stelae to tell of both the divine and human universe conceived by the Maya. Here, and in the early dates registered in the neighboring site of Abaj Takalik, we have in stone the first pages of what was to be the rich and subtle Maya literature.

The earliest registered dates in the system known as the Long Count have been discovered along a narrow zone beginning in the northwest, near the border of the present states of Veracruz and Tabasco, and running in a southeasterly direction across Chiapas to the piedmont area of Izapa–Abaj Takalik. The Long Count is one of the greatest Mesoamerican intellectual achievements. As it spread throughout the Maya world, it was to play a crucial role. The Long Count was structured on the basis of three fundamental mathematical principles. One is a positional vigesimal system in which the values of the registered numbers increase by 20s from bottom to top. In such systems, one can represent any figure imaginable employing only three symbols, one of which implied the discovery of another key concept, that of zero, which was unknown to the Europeans until they received it from India through the Arabs in the Middle Ages. A shell denotes the idea of zero. A dot has the value of a unit which, depending on its position in a column from bottom to top, may have the value of 1, 20, 400, 8,000, and so on. The third symbol is a bar denoting the number 5, or more precisely "five times," in accord with its position within the various layers of vigesimal positions. Thus, one bar represents 5 if placed on the lowest layer; 5 times 20 = 100 on the second; 5 times 400 = 2,000 on the third; 5 times 8,000 = 40,000 on the fourth; and so on. To indicate, for instance, the number 40,127, one would write:

    ▬▬▬▬ = 40,000 (5 × 8,000)

    ◁▷ = 0 [0 is expressed as a shell symbol in Maya mathematics]

    •   ▬▬▬ = 120 (6 × 20)

    •• ▬▬▬ = 7 (2 + 5)

The third principle was the establishment of a fixed point of departure when applying such a mathematical system to the reckoning of time in terms of the Long Count. A sequence of glyphic signs was employed to register a given date which would not be repeated for 374,440 years, an extraordinary accomplishment in any chronological system humankind may devise.

On the top of any Long Count's inscription, a large introductory glyph appears, with a central element that varies in accordance with the group of twenty days (*uinal* or month) in which the registered date falls. On the inferior layers, reading from left to right and from top to bottom, the glyphs represent the numbers of *baktuns* (20 × 7,200 = 144,000 days); *katuns* (20 × 360 = 7,200 days); *tuns,* 360 days; *uinals,* 20 days; and *k'ins,* units from 1 to 19. One of the 260 day signs of the *tzolkin,* the count of the days universally used in Mesoamerica since time immemorial, accompanies these glyphs. That sign indicates the terminal date corresponding to the sum total of days elapsed since the starting point of the Long Count chronological system. Those days are the multiple parts of which an age or cosmic day was composed. All the reckonings of the Long Count can be taken as points of encounter in time, where various gods and other divine forces convene, causing events that are particularly significant in the world where humans live.

Other glyphs appear at the bottom of the various Long Count inscriptions, including one denoting for a given date the corresponding deity from among the Nine Gods—the *Bolontiku*—of the lower world. A supplementary series tells the age of the moon, the length of the lunar "month," the number of the lunation, and also provides a correction formula for maintaining the count of 365 days, which in fact was worked out closer to the true length of the tropical year than it is in the European Gregorian calendar.

Both the vigesimal positional system and its application to the calendric Long Count are intellectual accomplishments that made it possible for those who developed them to perceive—but more than that, to recall, contemplate, scrutinize, and anticipate—everything with a mathematical rigor from which they drew many consequences. Since each moment or period of time conveys a divine presence and a destiny, the Maya believed and continue to believe that one's every act should be attuned to it. This means seeing the world as a stage where everything develops following a mathematically rigorous order. To unveil that order, the priests—*ah k'inob,* "those of the Sun and time"—had to search their books of destinies in an effort to penetrate the mysteries which only divine wisdom would reveal.

The sequence of the very early Long Count registers can be traced in the area already delimited from Veracruz-Tabasco and across Chiapas to Abaj Takalik in southwestern Guatemala. In summary form:

Stela C of Tres Zapotes, Veracruz, appears to bear the oldest known Long Count date, corresponding to November 4, 291 B.C., or to September 2, A.D. 31, according to the two existing correlations of the Maya and Gregorian calendars. The inscriptions, accompanied by a jaguar mask on the other side of the stela, could be understood as recording some mythical occurrence. One of them may be a date in what was perhaps the latest period of the Olmec culture.

Stela 2, found at Chiapa de Corzo in what later was properly Mayaland (Mayab), bears a Long Count date equivalent to December 7, 36 B.C. Stela 1 of El Baul in the Abaj Takalik archeological zone is dated March 4, 31 B.C. Accompanying this Long Count date is the figure of a dignitary, probably commemorating his accession to the throne as in other stelae of the Maya Classic period.

There are other Long Count inscriptions:

Stela 1 of La Mojarra, Veracruz, with two dates corresponding to A.D. 143 and A.D. 256, in the context of a now partially deciphered long glyphic inscription

The Tuxtla statuette (Maya date corresponding to A.D. 162) incorporated in a human figure with a buccal duck mask

One in a jade plaque, known as "Leiden," with a date equivalent to A.D. 320. It commemorates the victory of a Maya ruler whose carved image appears with a defeated enemy beneath his feet, a scene found in many other Maya stelae of the Classic period.

On the other hand, it is true that writing and the calendar had developed in Mesoamerica centuries before the appearance of the Long Count inscriptions. In Monte Alban, Oaxaca, numerous stelae of "the dancers" and those found in association with monument J, from 600–300 B.C., bear ample evidence to this. There, as in many other sites, the *tonalpohualli* or *tzolkin*, "count of the days," interrelated with the *xihuitl* or *haab*, "solar year," with its twenty day signs and numerals from 1 to 13, made it possible to register dates indicating the days, the hours of the day and night, the "months" (groups of twenty days), the years, and the cycles of fifty-two years. In the Monte Alban stelae, these calendric glyphs, as well as glyphs of personal and place names, have been identified, which tell us where wars and other important events took place.

The great differences between these inscriptions and those of the Long Count derive not only from the mathematical rigor of the latter but from the worldview that is reflected in them. Long Count dates always refer to cosmic ages in which all units of time, the *dramatis personae*, are gods whose entrances, actions, and exits in the world of human beings carry with them all kinds of meanings, including predictions of fortune good or bad. Thus, the chronological inscriptions which function as part of the structure of the Long Count are themselves the great chapters of a history—human and divine—in a universe whose deepest substratum is time.

K'in, the Sun, day, age, and, simply, Time, is conceived as an atmosphere in which the visages of the gods—which are part of the calendric glyphs— become manifest cycle after cycle. The norm of life was to attune oneself with what has been, what is, and what would be the implications of time. The movements of the celestial bodies thus occupied an important place in the field of attention of those concerned with Long Count calculations. In a unique conjunction of cosmic historiography and mathematical mythology, there were gods and humans whose representations proliferate in the stelae, lintels, and monuments at such sites as Tikal, Uaxactun, Yaxchilan, Piedras Negras, Calakmul, Río Azul, Tonina, Bonampak, Copan, Quirigua, El Naranjo, Pusilha, and many other places in the Maya central area.

While a growing number of archeologists keep unearthing monuments in Maya sites only recently explored, the epigraphers for their part are now enriching their readings of the inscriptions. Thus, one speaks of "forests of Kings," referring to those who built the great Maya centers and who fought wars of conquest like the one carried out by Tikal against Uaxactun; of the dynasties of Palenque and Yaxchilan; indeed, of the full gamut of events that occurred on the eve of the collapse of the Classic Maya period.

The deeds of the rulers, their lineages, blood sacrifices, lives and deaths, everything related to the universe of the gods—always with precise dates and on stages connected to other cosmic events—were told in this rich Maya narrative made up of inscriptions and images. This was a historiography and art told in the open air on the façades of temples and palaces, on stelae and altars in broad plazas. Architecture and ritual space, besides being conceived in imitation of a divine, sacred geography, were the receptacle of these inscriptions and icons, libraries in stone and mural paintings.

Maya literature of the Classic period, now being deciphered, was also preserved and transmitted in codices from the same period, vestiges of which have been discovered. Other objects, mainly polychrome ceramic vases, convey texts and images, telling stories like those of the *Popol Vuh*, rewritten using the Roman alphabet centuries later. From these one can reconstruct the accounts of the cosmic ages, past and present, some of whose episodes the Long Count registered with mathematical rigor.

The collapse of the Classic period did not mean the end of Maya literary creation. While many cities had been abandoned by the tenth century A.D., as had Teotihuacan in central Mexico, others nonetheless continued to exist or began to flourish. Such was the case of Chichen Itza, Uxmal, Mayapan, Coba, Tulum, and Champoton in northern Yucatan; Tayasal in the Guatemalan Peten; and Zaculeu, Nejab, Iximche, Utatlan, and Solola in the southern highlands. The Toltec invasions brought about many changes. No more stelae were erected; the Long Count system fell into oblivion; and Maya literature took a different path. Time, however, continued to be an obsession. A simplified form called *ukahlay katunob,* "the Count of the *Katuns,"* or thirteen periods of twenty years, became universally employed. In it, each *katun* received its calendric designation depending on the name of its last day, which is always an *Ahau,* "Lord," with reference to the Sun, preceded by a numeral from 1 to 13. The *uinals* or groups of twenty days, and the *k'inob,* the days themselves, kept the same names that they had in the Long Count.

The four extant Maya codices—which bear the names of the cities in which they are preserved, Dresden, Paris, and Madrid, in addition to that of a New York City club, Grolier—are examples of a literature that includes astronomical and astrological expression. Some readings of this literature are offered here, esoteric expressions dealing with human destinies that depend on the favorable or ominous "burdens" carried on by various gods in an unending series of time periods whose ends are also beginnings. And in the codices as in the stelae and other monuments, figures of men, animals, and plants accompany the texts, recreating the Maya concept of the universe as an ever-changing stage on which divine presences may coincide with human actors at any given moment.

Transferring Maya Literature to the Alphabet

Although most of the Maya codices were reduced to ashes, the ancient word did not completely vanish. As happened with the Nahua of central Mexico, there were native sages and priests among the Yucatec Maya, Quiche, Cakchiquel, and others, who learned the alphabet from the friars and used it to write down historical and legendary accounts, songs and texts, recording events in which past, present, and future intermingle and fuse, always with rigorous recordings of time in terms of the Count of the *Katuns*.

The *Annals of the Cakchiquels* tell their story from ancient origins up through the Conquest and its aftermath. We also have early colonial literary works which contain vivid descriptions of the violent encounter with Pedro de Alvarado, the ferocious captain in the command of Hernán Cortés, and more laconic recordings of other events up until 1601. The sources of these annals can be found in the oral tradition and probably in the reading of ancient codices.

There are other historical texts of similar origin: the *Title of the Lords of Totonicapan;* the *Codex of Calkini,* written in Yucatec Maya; and, obviously, the historical part of the *Popol Vuh.* In addition to these narratives, some of which include chants, we have the *Songs of Dzitbalche.* Although they were found copied in an eighteenth-century manuscript, their contents and form of expression suggest a more ancient origin. A few of them—"The Watcher," "The Birds," "The Flower Song," and "Orphan Song" included here—have the texture of works from an earlier period. Echoes of the old tradition can also be found in "A Lacandon Song," "A Chorti Curing Ritual," and "Bright Star of Evening," from the Chontal.

The books of the Chilam Balam (written by Yucatec Maya priests and prophets) deserve special consideration. Fourteen of them are known; five others were lost. They represent at once remembrance of the past, consciousness of the present, and prophecies of the future. They speak not only of what will be but also of what has already happened, seen from the perspective of a cyclical conception of time, the uniquely Maya perspective in terms of which everything must be understood.

Each of these books was written by several different people, each of whom lived in a different period and all of whom made additions to the work. Thus, these books have the unusual attribute of being compositions which, like the cycles of time, are renewed again and again, permitting the recording of events that were brought into the world by the gods who determine human destinies.

This explains how these texts, inspired by the codices and oral traditions and then written down in Roman letters in the sixteenth century, contain narrations, chants, and prophecies about events that happened much later, some of them in postcolonial Mexico. The Maya ethnologist Alfonso Villa Rojas was amazed by an event that occurred in Tusik, Quintana Roo, in 1936. He was reading a text from the *Chilam Balam of Chumayel* to a group of Maya elders when one of them asked permission to read out a fragment of a manuscript they were writing. To his surprise, the fragment was very similar to Villa Rojas's text. Several excerpts from the books of the Chilam Balam are included here, among them "The Birth of the Uinal" (p. 457) and "The Ceremonial of the Baktun" (p. 458).

Despite terrible adversity, Maya literary production has not ceased, and it is rich beyond expectation. Aside from the great variety of subject matter, there is in Maya literature a subtle thread interwoven across the centuries of a complex cultural history. That thread has to do with the concern for finding what has been, is, and could be the place of the person and the community in cosmic time and space. This concern, which is of primordial importance, is expressed in the planning and architecture of their urban centers, conceived as a reflection of cosmic sacred space. It is also perceptible in what are now known as the Mayan arts and sciences: sculpture, painting, astronomy, calendric reckoning, astrological computation, pharmacology, and medicine. But above all, these primordial concerns are manifest in Maya literature.

This is the thread running through them since their first appearance on stelae bearing dates in terms of the Long Count, and then in the codices and texts transferred to the alphabet, particularly the *Popol Vuh*, the various annals, and the books of the Chilam Balam. In the codices, the main concerns are the births and deaths of previous cosmic ages, the nature of men and women made of corn in our own age, the origins, existence, and future of the Maya Quiche nation. The various annals, like those of the Cakchiquel and the Xiu, as well as the histories, prayers, chants, and prophecies of the Chilam Balam, are like a mirror in which one anxiously seeks to perceive what is hidden.

Songs and incantations, proverbs, a Chamula (Maya Tzotzil) origin story, the proclamation of Juan de la Cruz, battle songs, stories of slavery, contemporary stories, fables, and poems—all that belongs to colonial and modern literature in several Mayan languages reflects in subtle forms the worldview that has nourished Maya identity for so many centuries. As with other Mesoamerican nations, Maya identity has been in danger, but it too has been reconstructed, fitting together its parts, integrating what the people were, are, and expect to be. In these pages a window opens to permit contemplation of the many meanings linked to the ultimate core of being Maya.

Works of Other Mesoamerican Peoples

We have delved a little into the souls of two of the most talked about Mesoamerican nations. The Nahua (from Teotihuacan to Mexico-Tenochtitlan) and the Maya, those living in the Yucatan peninsula, Chiapas, Guatemala, Belize, Honduras, and adjacent regions. Their linguistic differences aside, they have more than a few elements in common. Many have to do with their quotidian lives. Most of their crops and forms of cultivation are similar: they have a basic diet of corn, squash, beans, and chile. Mesoamericans are so closely attached to corn that they believe their bodies were formed of it, as their narratives and poems make clear. Methods of cultivation include slash and burn in the humid tropical lands; irrigation, and the seasonal methods based on the rainy season, are most common in the high plateaux. Since it is a permanent preoccupation, agriculture appears frequently in Mesoamerican literature: hymns to the gods of rain and corn, prayers in periods of famine, references to communal work, possession of the land, tributes and markets.

Social stratification existed all over Mesoamerica; one finds mention of it everywhere in the monuments, codices, and expressions of oral tradition. The ruling group, for instance, had a prominent presence in the early monuments of the Olmecs, the Zapotec of Oaxaca, the Maya, Teotihuacans, Xochicalca, and other peoples.

Mixtec and Nahua codices contain the genealogies and histories of their lords and ladies, and also speak of the services and tributes provided to them by the common people. Mesoamerican urbanism, with its magnificent temples, palaces, schools, marketplaces, also had distinct classes of living arrangements for the elite and the common people, reflecting their conception of social duality, derived from the divine duality, both existing in a sacred space, according to several depictions in the codices.

The literature of Mesoamerica, like that of every other people on earth, mirrors the life of the people, from the sacred to the quotidian. It gives us details, in historical context. The work reached extremes of mathematical precision and subtle meanings among the Maya, but on the whole all the literature was based on the same cyclical premises. The calendar round of fifty-two years and the count of the days and destinies was followed universally.

Cultural elements similar to those of the Nahua and Maya, including glyphic writing, although not nearly so advanced as in the case of the Maya, existed among other Mesoamericans. Examples of their literary creations have been included here in Book III: Mixtec stories; Otomi, Zapotec, and Mazatec songs; Tarascan narratives.

This is not an anthology of the works of lost cultures, defunct peoples and languages. It celebrates a living tradition, not only ancient works but also those from the colonial period and the ensuing years of independent Mexico when indigenous voices were forced to take refuge in the heart of the community. Now, as Mesoamericans once again raise their voices to tell stories, record history, and create flower and song, some of the best of their writing has won the distinction of an audience in the English language. Their work confirms the truth that a Nahua poet expressed more than five hundred years ago:

My flowers will not come to an end,
my songs will not fall into oblivion,
I, the singer, raise them up;
they are scattered, they are bestowed.

May you enjoy the wisdom and beauty of Mesoamerica.

Four Pre-Columbian
Documents

T he pre-Columbian works now extant include glyphs, some of which were incised in stone and others that survive in ink or paint on deerskin or amate paper (the bark of the fig tree), pictographs carved in stone, and paintings made on deerskin and amate paper. From these works one can see quite clearly that Mesoamerica underwent great changes after the invasion of the Europeans, but the Mesoamerica we know is not merely a "construction" of European and European-influenced artists and writers. Nor was a historical consciousness or complex worldview imposed upon the original inhabitants. In the four works—accompanied by documentary reproductions— that follow, one can sense, if only for a little while, Mesoamerica as it was.

In the first, previously unpublished example, "Temple of the Sun-Eyed Shield" (p. 43), the poet and anthropologist Dennis Tedlock, working with material from the late Linda Schele, provides an entry to the world of Palenque—a world that collapsed centuries before the invasion. Of all the works in this anthology, this may be the most foreign to the contemporary Western mind. The second example (p. 49) also comes from the Maya. The literary version here was based upon a linear translation of the *Dresden Codex,* one of the few surviving Maya painted books. Historians are now able to read a second level of information in the drawings. Alejandra García Quintanilla, for example, has noted what appears to be a drawing of a locust, growing in size and importance, that is connected with the death god, which probably indicates the advent of one of the plagues that have come to the Yucatan peninsula. For the Maya who read the codices and knew of the events written and depicted in them, this was most likely not hermetic, as it is for contemporary readers and undoubtedly was for the invading Spaniards, who burned most of the codices.

The Nahua Myth of the Suns is yet another example of the similarity in structure between pre-Hispanic and pre-Columbian works. As the accompanying reproductions of stone carvings (p. 44) show, the four Suns were at the foundation of Nahua thinking. The idea of various creations occurs again in Maya literature, as one can see in the excerpts from the *Popol Vuh* included in Book II. The structure of myth followed by historical material mentioned by Tedlock in the Palenque glyphs occurs in this work as well.

The fourth example, "The Man Born of a Tree" (p. 69), occurs in several Mixtec codices and has clearly come down to more recent times relatively unscathed by European cultural influences.

Temple of the Sun-Eyed Shield*

This temple, the second highest of three, is on the northwest side of the plaza at Palenque, opposite the Temple of the Tree of Ripe Corn. Originally all three temples were like this one in having an entrance hall with three doors (see photo). Beyond the central door is an inside door that opens into the chapel, and inside the chapel is a further door that opens into the sanctuary. Like the sanctuaries in the other two temples, this one is a miniature house with three carved stone tablets on its back wall.

On the central tablet (see next page), the standing figures are again Sun-Eyed Sky Jaguar at the ages of seven (left) and forty-nine (right), and again the captions (shown in gray) refer to his designation as his father's successor and his actual accession to the Egret lordship. Both figures bear emblems of lordship in their outstretched hands. The boy holds a bundle of folded paper (the "white paper" mentioned in the caption) and, resting on top of it, the Flint Icon (named in the captions of the Temple of the Tree of Ripe Corn). The man holds a figure of the god named Icon of the Smoking Mirror, whose guardian spirit is the planet Mars and who serves as the patron deity of rulers in general.

Between the two figures, supported by crossed spears, is the Sun-Eyed Shield that gives the present temple its name. The face on the shield belongs to a god whose guardian spirit is visible not as the sun, but as the planet Jupiter. The shield rises over a four-cornered royal dais that stands for the four-cornered surface of the earth. And just as the royal persons on each side stand on the backs of captives taken in war, so the platform of the earth rests on the backs of two lords of the underworld who were defeated by the divine predecessors of earthly kings. All four supporting figures rest in turn on a row of symbols that show them to be in a sacred place in the earth, namely a cave. Sky Jaguar (at both ages) stands with his feet in this lower world, but like the Sun-Eyed Shield, he rises above it.

*Translation by Dennis Tedlock, art by Linda Schele, previously unpublished; both by permission of the author.

Sky Jaguar's father, whose own reign began at the age of twelve, "saw five score years" in the sense that the eighty years of his life began within a formal twenty-year segment of the Mayan calendar, spanned three more segments, and ended during a fifth.

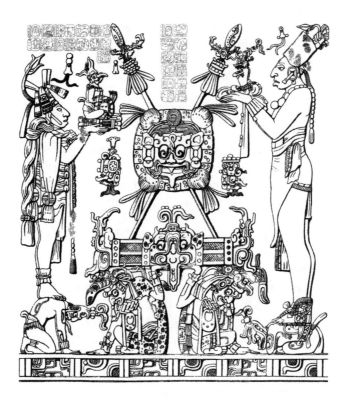

Flanking the picture are tablets filled with a text (shown on the following four pages). As in the other temples, the narrative moves from mythic events into history. Both parts of the story include sacrificial rites in which a spirit is summoned from the underworld. White Egret at the Water, a moon goddess, brings forth her second-born son, Sun-Eyed Shield, and Sun-Eyed Sky Jaguar brings forth the ghost of her human namesake, his own grandmother.

On Nine Night Six Point he was taken up into the temple, he entered the tree, this ballplayer whose guardian spirit is an egret. On Thirteen Lord Eighteen Yellow Sun he came down, this tender sprout, this small creature . . . whose guardian spirit is an egret, this flower of the Holy Lord of the Council of Egrets.

On Eight Foot Three Song, the white paper was handed to him, to Sun-Eyed Sky Jaguar whose guardian spirit is an egret, this flower of the lord who saw five score years, Sun-Eyed Shield, this blessed child whose mother is Lady Medicine, this Lord of the Holy Council of Egrets.

This account of years begins under the dawn sign.

After one times four centuries,

plus eighteen score years,

Since the present world began on August 11, 3114 B.C., 275,466 days had passed and it was now October 23, 2360 B.C.

plus five single years,

plus three score

and six days,

the date was Thirteen Death,

wearing the black hawk as its night, Nineteen Deer,

and twenty-six days ago the moon had emerged

with four months behind her. . . .

The name of the present month (in the right column) has not been deciphered.

is the name of the new month of twenty-nine days.

Eleven and two score days plus one year had passed

since the Icon of Abundance was planted

in its place on One Wind

July 22, 2587 B.C.

Ten Penance, and after that

came the emergence of Sun-Eyed
Torch, the guardian spirit

The planet Jupiter rose in the
east.

who wears the sun on his chest,
 the jaguar who lost his head

in the White . . . House, the
 White Bone House,

Snake Bath,

The right-hand glyph is the
head of a celestial dragon.

Smoke . . . ,

Sun-Eyed Lord of the Shield.

After six and three score days,
 plus five single years,

October 23, 2360 B.C.

plus eighteen score years, plus
 one times four centuries,

and after he had circled the heart
 of Sixth Sky,

Jupiter traveled a retrograde
loop in the sixth
constellation of the Mayan
zodiac, later rising again after
a period of invisibility.

he then emerged from nowhere,

he who is the skewer, the cord

Sun-Eyed Lord of the Shield
appeared because Mother of
Split Place drew sacrificial
blood from her tongue.

of Mother of Split Place,

White Egret by the Water, Lady
 of the Holy Council of Egrets.

Sixteen and five score days,

plus eighteen single years, plus
 twelve score years,

plus nine times four centuries
 after the marking

of the sky with the image

The hearth formed by Alnitak, Saiph, and Rigel in Orion reached the middle of the sky at dawn on August 11, 3114 B.C.

of the First Three Hearthstones on Four Lord

Eight Kiln, it happened

on Two Wax Fourteen Cluster:

July 21, 690

the guardian spirit who rejoined

the divine triplets was Sun-Eyed Lord of the Shield.

There was a conjunction of Jupiter (Sun-Eyed Lord), Mars (Smoking Mirror), and Saturn (Corn Silk) just west of Antares.

With the change to Three Earth

Fifteen Cluster, the one who turned around

in the western Quetzal Jaguar sanctuary

On July 22 the ruler of Palenque who is named below dedicated the Temple of the Sun-Eyed Shield, the westernmost of the three Quetzal Jaguar temples. That night the three planets were joined by the moon.

inside the home of the burners of incense

was the one whose guardian spirit is an egret,

Sun-Eyed Sky Jaguar, Lord of the Holy Council of Egrets.

On the third day he summoned a ghost,

which rose up from the Hollow Tree

sky position. He was down below

Quetzal Tree Mountain. Three and twelve score days,

The name "Sun-Eyed" distinguishes this Sky Jaguar from an earlier one. He performed his seance on July 23, when the moon had moved past the three planets and into the Milky Way (Hollow Tree), which stood straight up on the horizon as midnight approached. His three temples are at the foot of Quetzal Tree Mountain.

plus six single years, plus seven
   score years

November 18, 496

after Twelve Lord Eight Deer,

with the entry into the tree of
   succession

Entry into the tree is a
ceremony in which the heir
to a lordship is designated;
Yellow Pendant Peccary was
the immediate predecessor of
the earlier Sky Jaguar.

of Yellow Pendant Peccary, which
   happened

at Cloudy Center, what occurred

on Nine Night Six Point

On June 15, 641, Mars and
Jupiter were in conjunction
with Spica in Virgo, and five
days later came the summer
solstice.

was another entry, and five days
   after

his entry into the tree of
   succession came the great day

of Sun-Eyed Sky Jaguar, who has
   an egret as his guardian spirit

and Corn Silk as well.

It was eighteen and two score
   days, plus six years

after Two Death Nineteen Bat,

May 21, 635

when he emerged, that he
   entered the tree of succession.
After twelve and eight score
   days plus one year, on Thirteen
   Lord

Sun-Eyed sky Jaguar
completed his succession
rituals when he descended
from the temple on
December 4, 642. It had
been one solar year and six
moons since the opening
ritual, and ten years since
the count of the current
score had begun.

Eighteen Yellow Sun, with the
   count at ten years,

he came down after entering the
   tree.

Dresden Codex (pp. 46–50)*

The god of the Great Star,
star of the morning, appears in the east.
The God that brings the rain
is the victim of his sacrifice.
Misfortune, woe is man!
The sickness that he sends
for the second planting of the corn,
woe is the God of corn!

The God Lahun Chan,
Great Star,
comes out in the east.
Chacbolay, the jaguar,
is his sacrificial victim.
It is the misery of the ripe corn.
God of the merchants and of the north,
woe is the lord!,
great sacrifice,
woe is the god, Hac, turtle, there shall come a drought!

He who is lord of the night, the Great Star,
comes out of the east.
The God of corn is the victim of his sacrifice.
His punishment, his sickness come from the east,
they are sent to his fields of corn.
Misery for man.
Kukulcan, Great Star,
comes out of the east.
The turtle God (the rain) is the victim of his sacrifice.
Misery of the god of the sun face,
Kinich Ahau, the lord of the Sun.
Unhappy destiny, that of the god who brings the rain.
Sickness and ruin
come from the god . . .

*Yuri Knorosov and Sophie D. Coe, Institute for Mesoamerican Studies, State University of New York, Albany, NY. Spanish non-linear translation: Miguel León-Portilla, *Literaturas Indigenas de Mexico*, Fondo de Cultura Economica, Mexico City, 1992; English version, Sylvia and Earl Shorris.

The god of the chill of the dawn,
Great Star, morning star,
comes out of the east.
The divine fish is the victim of his sacrifice.
Misfortune for the lord of the merchants,
he of the north,
the divinity sends sickness and ruin
to the lord of corn.

Dresden Codex, Sächsische Landesbibliothek, Dresden

Sun Stone. From left to right: 4-Ehécatl, 4-Quiáhuitl *(lluvia de fuego),* 4-Atl and 4-Océlotl, *Museo Nacional de Antropologia, Mexico City.*

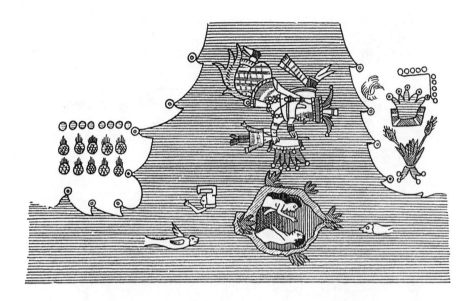

Above: *Sun of Water.* Below: *Sun of Winds.* Vatican Codex A, *fol. 4v y 6r.*

Above: *Sun of the Rain of Fire.* Below: *Sun of the Earth (Sun of the Ocelot).*
Vatican Codex A, *fol. 6v y 7r.*

Myth of the Suns and the Toltec-Chichimec Origins of the Mexica People. Or *Tlamachilliztlatolzazanilli* ("The Wisdom Discourse of Fables")*

The manuscript was bound in the *Codex Chimalpopoca* and is traditionally titled *Leyenda de los Soles, Legend of the Suns,* or *Manuscript of 1558.*

I

Here is the wisdom-discourse of fables, how in ancient times it happened that the earth was established, and each individual thing found its place. This is the manner in which it is known how the sun gave rise to so many things, two thousand five hundred and thirteen years before today, the 22nd of May, 1558.

This sun, Nahui Ocelotl, 4 Jaguar, endured 676 years. Those who lived here first were eaten by jaguars on [the day] 4 Jaguar, of this sun. And they ate chicome malinalli, 7 Grass, which was their sun-sustenance, and so they existed 676 years until they were savagely devoured in 13 years, and so they completely perished and were abolished. And then the sun disappeared. And their year was the year Ce Acatl, 1 Reed. And they were first eaten under this same day-sign 4 Jaguar, so by just this means they were abolished and totally destroyed.

This sun is named Nahui Ecatl, 4 Wind. Those who lived in this second place were swept away by the wind; during the sun 4 Wind it was. And this way they were destroyed: they became monkeys. Their houses and even their trees were all swept away by the wind. This sun itself was carried away by the wind. Their sun-sustenance was matlactlomome cohuatl, 12 Serpent. And so they lived 364 years; thus they were utterly destroyed: in one day they were swept off by wind. Under the single day-sign 4 Wind they were destroyed, and their year was 1 Flint.

This is the sun Nahui Quiyahuitl, 4 Rain. And these are the ones who lived during the sun Nahui Quiyahuitl, which was the third. And thus they were destroyed, in a rain of fire; they were all transformed to birds. And the sun itself also burned; all their houses burned. And so they lived 312 years, and so they were totally destroyed by a rain of fire in only one day. They ate chicome tecpatl, 7 Flint; it was their sun-sustenance. And their year is 1 Flint, and in only one day-sign, 4 Rain, thus they were destroyed: they became the Pipiles, whose speech sounds like turkey-talk. This is why today children are called "little gobblers."

This sun is called Nahui Atl, 4 Water. And the water gathered for 52 years. These are the ones who lived in the fourth age, the sun of 4 Water. And

*Roberta H. and Peter T. Markman, *The Flayed God,* (San Francisco: HarperCollins, 1992), pp. 131–47. Translated from the Spanish by Willard Gingerich.

so they lived 676 years and so they were destroyed, were inundated: they were transformed into fish. In only one day the heavens came down to inundate them, and they were destroyed. And they ate nahui xochitl, 4 Flower, it was their sun-sustenance. And their year was 1 House and on the single day-sign 4 Water they were destroyed; all the mountains were destroyed. And thus the water gathered for 52 years.

And so their years are finished.

II

Then Titlacahuan, "Our Master," [Tezcatlipoca] called forth the one known as "Our Father" and his consort known as "Nene." He said to them, "You will want nothing more. Hollow out a large ahuehuetl log: you will enter it during the vigil of Toçoztli when the heavens will come crashing down." And so they entered it, and then he sealed them in. He said, "You will have a single ear of corn to eat and likewise your woman will have one." When they had finally consumed all the kernels, they heard the water outside declining. Their log no longer moved. Then they opened the log, they saw a fish, they struck a fire from the wood and cooked the fish for themselves. Then the gods Citlallinicue and Citlallatonac gazed down on them and said, "Who has made fire? Who is now smoking up the heavens?" And so then Our Master Tezcatlipoca descended; he scolded them and said to them, "What are you doing, Grandpa? What is this fire?" Then he struck off their heads and reattached them over their buttocks; they became dogs. And here at the sign 2 Reed [you can see] the way in which the heavens were smoked up.

Here are we ourselves, this was already us. Here the fire-starting sticks fell and here the heavens were inundated in the year 1 Rabbit. Here it is [shown] how the fire-starting sticks fell when fire appeared, and here how darkness covered everything for twenty-five years. And here the heavens came to a stop in the year 1 Rabbit. And while the heavens were arrested, then the "dogs" smoked them up, as already mentioned, off there in the distance.

And so finally the fire-starting sticks fell and Tezcatlipoca lit a fire, so that once again the heavens filled with smoke in the year 2 Reed.

III

And then the gods called an assembly; they said, "Who will be seated there, now that the heavens have come to a halt and the Earth Lord has come to a halt? Gods, who will be seated?" Then the gods

Citlallinicue, Citlallatonac;
Apantecutli, Tepanquizqui;
Tlallamanqui, Huictlollinqui;
Quetzalcoatl, Titlacahuan;

were distressed.

And then Quetzalcoatl went off to Mictlan, the Region of the Dead, where he came before the Lord and the Lady of Mictlan. Then he said, indeed he did, "I come to take away the jade bones which you so honorably guard." And so then the Lord of Mictlan said to him, "What is it you will do, O Quetzalcoatl?" And again he said, indeed he did, "The gods are anxious to know who will be settled on the earth."

And so once again the Lord of Mictlan spoke. "Very well; Blow on my conch trumpet and carry it four times around my jade throne." But the conch trumpet had no holes for finger-stops. Then Quetzalcoatl called the worms who filled it with holes, and then bees and hornets quickly rushed inside and filled it with sound so that the Lord of Mictlan heard it.

And then once again the Lord of Mictlan said, "Very well, take them." And then the Lord of Mictlan said to his messengers, the Mictecans, "Tell him, O gods, that he must leave them." And Quetzalcoatl then came forward and said, "I will take them, once and for all." And then he said to his spirit-double, his nahual, "Go tell them that I will leave them." And the nahual came saying loudly, "I will leave them."

Then Quetzalcoatl went up quickly and took the jade bones, those of the man on one side and of the woman on the other. In this way he took them: he wrapped them in a bundle which he carried up with him.

And once again the Lord of Mictlan said to his messengers, "O gods, Quetzalcoatl is in fact carrying off the jade bones! Gods, go dig a pit." Then they went to dig it, so that Quetzalcoatl fell down into it. He was startled by a covey of quail and fell down as though dead, scattering the jade bones across the ground and the quail nibbled and pecked at them.

Soon Quetzalcoatl revived; he began to weep and said to his nahual, "How can this be?" His nahual answered, "As it must. Things have gone wrong but let us go on."

Then Quetzalcoatl gathered up the bones and made a bundle and carried them at once to Tamoanchan. And as soon as he brought them the goddess named Quilaztli, who is also Cihuacoatl, ground them in her jade bowl. And then Quetzalcoatl bled his penis over it.

Then all the aforementioned gods performed penance, Apanteuctli Huictlollinqui, Tepanquizqui, Tlallamanac, Tzontemoc, and the sixth, Quetzalcoatl. And then they said, "The gods have given birth to men, the common people," for certainly they performed penance in our behalf.

IV

So once more they spoke: "What shall they eat, O gods? Already they are searching for nourishment, a sun-sustenance." Then the ant went to take kernels of corn from within the Mountain of Food-Stuffs. Quetzalcoatl encountered the ant and said to it, "Tell me where you went to get it." Persistently he questioned the ant but it did not wish to tell him. Finally it said, "Over there," and led him to the place.

Then Quetzalcoatl transformed himself into a black ant, accompanied the first ant, and they went into the mountain together. That is, Quetzalcoatl followed the red ant to the storage bin, gathered up the corn and carried it quickly to Tamoanchan. There the gods chewed and ate of it and then fed it to us, to nourish and strengthen us.

And then they said, "What shall we do with this Mountain of Food-Stuffs?" Then Quetzalcoatl went and tried to pull it with ropes, but could not lift it. So then Oxomoco performed divination with the kernels and also Cipactonal, his wife, performed divination (Cipactonal is the woman). They said the kernels revealed that only Nanahuatl would be capable of breaking open the Mountain of Food-Stuffs. Then the attendant gods of Tlaloc, the Tlaloque, lords of rain, appeared: the Blue Tlaloque, the White Tlaloque, the Yellow Tlaloque, the Red Tlaloque, and Nanahuatl broke open the corn.

And the food-stuffs were all stolen away by the lords of rain; the white, black, yellow and red corn, beans, chia, amaranth, fish-amaranth—everything was stolen.

V

The name of this sun is 4 Motion. This is now our sun, the one under which we live today. This is its figure, the one here, because this sun fell into the fire at the sacred hearth in Teotihuacan. It is the same sun as that of Topiltzin, "Our Beloved Prince" of Tollan, Quetzalcoatl. Before becoming this sun, its name was Nanahuatl, who was of Tamoanchan. Eagle, Jaguar, Hawk, Wolf, 6 Wind, 6 Flower—all are names of this sun.

This thing is called the "sacred hearth," and it burned for four years. Tonacateuctli and Xiuhteuctli called to Nanahuatl and told him, "Now you shall become guardian of heaven and earth." He was much saddened and said, "What are the gods going about saying? I am only a sickly person." They also summoned there Nahuitecpatl, "4 Flint," who is the moon. Him the Lord of Tlalocan, Tlaloc, called upon, and also upon Napateuctli. Then Nanahuatl fasted in penance. He took up his maguey thorns and his pine branches upon which to offer them. The moon provided his own thorns. Nanahuatl was the first to offer sacrifice, then the moon sacrificed also. The moon used quetzal feathers for branches and jade for thorns, and incense.

When four days had passed, they coated Nanahuatl in chalk and down feathers and he went to throw himself into the fire. Nahuitecpatl made a kind of female song for him. Then Nanahuatl fell into the fire and afterward the moon fell also but only into the ashes. When Nanahuatl fell, the eagle lifted him and carried him off. The jaguar could not carry him, but only leapt into the fire and was spotted. Then the hawk smoked himself and the wolf was scorched. None of these three was able to carry him.

And so when Nanahuatl came to the sky, the high gods Tonacateuctli and Tonacacihuatl bathed him and sat him on a mat of flamingo plumes and wrapped his head with red bands.

And then he spent four days in the heavens; he stood still at the sign 4 Motion. For four days he did not move. The gods asked, "Why doesn't he move?" Then they sent Itztlotli to speak and inquire of the sun. He said to him, "The gods say, 'Ask him why he will not move.'" The sun answered, "Because I require the blood of their legitimacy and their reign."

Then the gods consulted with each other and Tlahuizcalpanteuctli, Lord of the House of Dawn, became angered and said, "Why don't I put an arrow into him? He'll wish he had never been detained!" Then he shot at the sun but missed him. For this the sun shot Tlahuizcalpanteuctli; he shot him with the flaming plumes of the cuetzalin-papagayo and suddenly covered over his face with the nine heavens together. This was Tlahuizcalpanteuctli, the ice-god.

Then the gods Titlacahuan and Huitzilopochtli and the goddesses Xochiquetzal, Yapaliicue, and Nochpaliicue gathered in council, and from then on the gods in Teotihuacan began to die.

And when the sun rose into the sky, then the moon, which had fallen in the ashes, went also. He had no sooner arrived at the edge of the sky than Papaztac came to smash his face with a rabbit-jar. Then the female demons and other demons came out to meet him at the intersections of roads and said, "May you be welcome." Nevertheless they stopped him there and clothed him in rags and came to make offerings. And when the sun came to halt at 4 Motion it was also at sunset.

VI

[At this point in the manuscript the scribe inserts a crude pictographic sketch outlining the mythic precincts of Tula (Tollan) with Topiltzin Ce Acatl Quetzalcoatl, "Our Beloved Prince 1 Reed Quetzalcoatl," standing at its center. Marking the four comers are his "four-part" temples: "Serpent House," "Gold House," "Jade House," and "Turquoise House." (In the *Anales de Cuauhtitlan* these are called "his turquoise-plank house, his coral-inlay house, his whiteshell-inlay house, and his quetzal-feather house.") Under the sign for town, which appears to bear the name "Xicococ," the names of Ce Acatl's parents, Mixcoatl and Chimalman, are joined by what looks like a long umbilical, being cut in the center by a detached arm and hand. Directly below the arm stands Topiltzin. Mixcoatl's age at the time of his son Topiltzin's birth, thirty-nine, is written in the upper-right corner of the pictograph, above the date 1 Flint.]

And so Mixcoatl had lived 39 years. His wife was named Chimalman. And Topiltzin lived 56 years [the drawing indicates fifty-two, the figure given in other accounts]. In the same year 1 Reed in which he moves, here he also leaves his city, Tollan. And here he died on 4 Rabbit in Tlapallan.

In the year 1 Flint the Mixcoa, "Cloud Serpents," were born, they were created. Iztacchalchiuhtlicue, "White Jade Skirt," bore the Four Hundred Cloud Serpents. They entered a cave and when they had entered the cave, again their mother gave birth; then "the Five" were born, also Cloud Serpents: this one is named Quauhtliicohuauh, "Eagle's Twin," this second is named Mixcoatl, "Cloud Serpent," this third, a woman, is named Cuitlachcihuatl, "Wolf Woman," this fourth is named Tlotepe, "Hawk Mountain," and this fifth is named Apanteuctli, "Lord of the River."

And when they were born they entered the water, they threw themselves into the water; then they emerged again and were nursed by Mecitli, she who is Lord [sic] of the Earth, Mecitli. And so it is that today we are "Mexica," not actually "Mexica" but "Mecitin."

And then the sun sent forth the Four Hundred Cloud Serpents. Giving them arrows, darts and shields, he said, "Here is that with which you will satisfy my thirst, with which you will serve my table." [He gave them] arrows, precious-feather arrows, fletched with quetzal plumes, heron plumes, troupial plumes, roseate spoonbill plumes, flamingo plumes, cotinga plumes. "And, furthermore," [he said] "she is your mother, Lord of Earth."

But they did not perform their calling, they only shot at birds, they only enjoyed themselves; so it is that place is called "Bird Arrow." And occasionally they caught a jaguar; they did not offer it to the sun. When they did capture a jaguar, they decorated themselves with plumes and down, they slept with women, drank tzihuac liquor and wandered about completely drunk, wandered about completely intoxicated.

So the sun then called "the Five" who had been born later. He gave them tzihuac arrows and lords' shields and said, "Listen carefully now, my sons; you must destroy the Four Hundred Cloud Serpents who offer nothing to Our Father, Our Mother." So they gathered together in a large mesquite, from which the others saw them and said, "Who are these, so like ourselves?" And the time came to make war: Quauhtliicohuauh hid inside a tree; Mixcoatl hid within the earth; Tlotepetl hid within a hill; Apanteuctli hid in the water; and his older sister, Cuetlachcihuatl, hid in the ball court. And so when the Four Hundred came near, none of the Five were left in the mesquite tree. Then the tree cracked open and fell on them and out came Quauhtliicohuauh, the earth shook and out came Mixcoatl from within the earth, the hill erupted and fell down and out came Tlotepetl, the water boiled and out came Apanteuctli. So then they eliminated and destroyed the Four Hundred, and then served the sun at his table and gave him to drink. Others who had escaped came to supplicate and plead with them, saying, "We have been a great trouble to you. Please, won't your Honors go in to Chicomoztoc, 'Seven Caves'; certainly it is your beloved cave. Won't your Graces please go in, since it is your beloved home? Could it be that you have just now damaged your caves, your home? We will only sit outside the cave."

VII

Then there came down two deer, each with two heads, and also these two cloud serpents named Xiuhnel and Mimich, who hunt in the Sacred Lands.

Xiuhnel and Mimich pursued the two deer, trying to shoot them. A night and a day they pursued them and by sunset they were tired. They consulted each other and said, "You build a hut there and I'll build one here." The malicious ones had not yet arrived.

Then they came, they who were deer but had become women. They came calling, "Xiuhnel, Mimich, where are you? Come, come to drink; come to eat." And when they heard them they said to one another,"—Hey, why don't you answer?"

Then Xiuhnel called to them and said, "You come here, sister." She came and said to him, "Drink, Xiuhnel." Xiuhnel drank the blood and then immediately lay down with her. Suddenly she threw him down and came face down upon him, then devoured him, tore open his breast.

Then Mimich said, "She has actually eaten my elder brother!" The other woman was still standing and calling, "Lover, come and eat." But Mimich did not call her. Instead he took the firesticks and lit a fire, and when it was lit, ran and threw himself into it.

The woman, pursuing him, also entered the fire. She followed him there the entire night, until noon of the following day. And then he descended into a thorny barrel cactus, fell into it, and the woman fell down after him. And when he saw the star-demon had fallen, he shot her repeatedly. Only then could he turn back.

Then he returned, parting and tying his hair, painting his face and weeping for his elder brother who had been eaten. Then the fire gods heard it and they went to bring the woman, Itzpapalotl, "Obsidian Butterfly."

Mimich went in the lead. And when they took her, they burned her and she burst into bloom. First she blossomed into the blue flint; the second time she blossomed into the white flint, and they took the white and wrapped it in a bundle. The third time she blossomed into the yellow flint, but no one took it, they only watched. The fourth time she blossomed into the red flint which no one took. And the fifth time she blossomed into the black flint which no one took.

Mixcoatl, Cloud Serpent, took the white flint for a god and wrapped it and carried it in a bundle, and then went off to make war in a place called Comallan. He went carrying his goddess of flint, Itzpapalotl. And when the Comalteca learned of it, they came out to meet Mixcoatl and placed food before him, and with this put his heart at rest.

And then he went to Tecanma where also his heart was rested. They said to him, "What does the Lord wish? May he be satisfied here. Bring him his beloved tzihuac, that I might here chop it up and serve him." And then he went to Cocyama where at once he came pulling down the high places [village temples]. And he conquered there in Cocyama then went to Huehueto-can and conquered in Huehuetocan, then went to Pochtlan and came there to conquer also.

And then when Mixcoatl went to conquer in Huitznahuac, the woman Chimalman came out to confront him. He spread out his shield and filled it with arrows and atlatl darts. She stood naked, without skirt or shift. When he saw her Mixcoatl shot his arrows: the first went over her and she only turned aside slightly; the second arrow passed by her side and she deflected it; the third she simply caught in her hand; and the fourth she passed be-tween her legs. And being thus that Mixcoatl had shot four times, he trans-formed himself and immediately went away.

The woman fled away at once to hide in a cave among the canyons. And again Mixcoatl came to prepare and supply himself with arrows. And again he went to look for her but saw no one. So then he attacked the women of Huitznahuac, and the women of Huitznahuac said, "Let us go in search of her." They went to take her; they said, "Mixcoatl is searching for you. On your account he is mistreating your younger sisters." Then when they had gone to take her, they came to Huitznahuac. Then again Mixcoatl went and again met her, finding her exposed as before. Again he lay down the shield and the ar-rows and again he shot at her. Again the arrow went over her head, and one went by her side and one she caught in her hand and one passed between her legs.

And then when this had occurred, he took the woman of Huitznahuac, the one who is Chimalman, and lay with her and so she became pregnant.

VIII

And when he [Topiltzin, also called 1 Reed] was born, for four days he caused his mother to suffer. Then 1 Reed was born and as soon as he was born his mother died. And 1 Reed was then raised by [the divine women] Quillaztli and Cihuacoatl. And being already grown, he accompanied his fa-ther on campaigns. In this way he became exercised in arms, in a place called Xihuacan, where he took captives.

The Four Hundred Cloud Serpents are uncles of 1 Reed; they despised and killed his father, and after killing him went to bury him in Xaltitlan. 1 Reed then went in search of his father; he said, "What is this about my fa-ther?" Cozcaquauhtli, "King Vulture," then said, "Well, they killed your fa-ther; he lies over there where they went to bury him." So he went and took him and seated him in his temple, Mixcoatepetl, "Mixcoatl Mountain." And the uncles who had killed his father were Apanecatl, Zolton, and Cuilton.

Then he said, "How will I dedicate the temple?" "If with only a rabbit, with only a snake, we will be angered; better would be a jaguar, an eagle, a wolf," [the uncles] said. 1 Reed spoke when they said this, "Very well, so it will be." Then he called the jaguar, the eagle, the wolf; he said to them, "Won't you come in, uncles? They say with you I must dedicate my temple. Certainly, you will not die. Instead you will eat men and with them indeed will I dedicate my temple." The ropes which tied the man-eaters by their necks were rotten. And so then 1 Reed called the moles and said to them, "O uncles; won't you come here? We will tunnel into our temple." And the moles then promptly scraped down and tunnelled and 1 Reed entered into it and emerged at the summit of his temple.

And the uncles [who had killed his father] said to him, "We will light fire with the fire-starting stick there on the summit." The jaguar, the eagle and the wolf were most delighted to see them and thought them worthy of being wept for. And as they came reviving, returning to their senses, 1 Reed himself lit the fire with the fire-starting stick. Then the uncles became enraged, and they came up, Apanecatl rushing to the front. And then 1 Reed rose up and threw into his face a polished clay vessel so that he came falling down.

And then he quickly seized Zolton and Cuilton and whistled to the man-eaters, who proceeded to kill them. He brought them together and cut their flesh a little. And when they had tormented them then they cut open their chests.

And then 1 Reed conquered once more in a place called Ayotlan. And when he had conquered there, he went on to Chalco and Xicco where he conquered also. And having conquered there he went to Cuixcoc where he also conquered. And then he went to Zacanco where he also conquered; then he went to Tzonmolco where he also conquered; then he went to Macatzonco where he also came to conquer; then he went to Tzapotlan where he also came to conquer; then he went to Acallan where he crossed a river and also there conquered well.

So he came to Tlapallan. And then in that place he became sick and was ill for five days until he died. And when he had died in honor there, they immolated him, he was burned.

And so then in Tollan no one remained. Huemac was installed as Speaker, and the second was this one named Nequametl, the third this one named Tlalchicatzin and the fourth this one named Huitzilpopoca. These four succeeded Topiltzin.

IX

The Speaker of Nonohualco is named Huetzin. . . . [text partially damaged] They were startled and horrified; they saw the tlacanexquimilli, the night-being without head or arms, the "long man." This then is the one who ate people. And then the Toltecs said, "O Toltecs, Who is this man-eater?" Then they guarded him, they seized him; and having seized this huge young man, toothless, lipless and filthy-faced, they killed him. And having killed him, they opened him up to look inside, and found no heart, no guts, no blood. Then he stank, and whoever smelled him died and even he who did not smell him but only passed by. And in this way many died. Then they dragged him but he would not move, and the rope broke. And those who fell died where they fell. And when he did move, everyone died wherever he went, he devoured everyone. And when he did move along, everyone adorned him, the lineage-bearers, the elders, the princes' sons, the matrons. They tied him with eight ropes and dragged him along to Itzocan. And then he stood up. Those who dragged him did not let go of the ropes but were carried along dangling from them. And all who took hold of the ropes were lifted up and dragged along.

X

And so then Huemac played ball; he played ball with the lords of rain, the tlaloque. And the lords of rain said to him, "What shall we wager?" Huemac said, "My jade and my quetzal plumes." And again they said to Huemac, "None other than this shall you also win: our jade and our quetzal plumes."

Then they played and Huemac beat them. So the lords of rain went to transform that which they would give to Huemac, the ripe maize ear and their quetzal plumes, the green maize leaves in which the ear swells. But he would not accept them; he said, "Can this be what I have won! Was it not jade? Was it not quetzal plumes? Take this stuff away!"

So then the lords of rain said to him, "Very well; 'Give him the jade and the plumes and take away our jade and our quetzal plumes.' " And they took them and went away, then said to Huemac, "Very well, for now we are hiding our jade; the Toltecs will continue to work in suffering but only for four years."

And then the hail fell; it fell to the height of the knee, destroying all food-stuffs. The hail fell in the month of Teucilhuitl. And then especially on Tollan the sun shone; the trees, the nopal, the maguey all dried up; even the stones broke, everything disintegrated because of the sun.

And the Toltecs struggled and died of hunger. Then a sacrificial prisoner, who was probably kept guarded in some place by his uncle [his captor], miraculously, somehow bought himself a chicken, made himself tamales from it and ate them. And in a place called Chapoltepeccuitlapilco, on Mt. Chapoltepec, an old woman sat selling paper banners. He went and bought from her a banner and then went to be sacrificed on the stone known as tech-catl.

And when the four years of famine had passed, the lords of rain again appeared there in Chapoltepec where there is water. Then suddenly to the surface of the water rose a green ear of maize that had been chewed upon, and a certain Toltec man happened to see it, took up the chewed ear, and chewed it himself. And then from out of the water came a priest of Tlaloc who said, "Mortal, have you learned something here?" The Toltec responded, "O most certainly, Our God. It has already been a long time that we lost it for ourselves." Then the other spoke: "Mortal, that is very good; sit here while I speak to the lord." And he returned once more into the water but did not tarry long; then once more he emerged bringing with him an armload of fully ripened ears. Then he spoke: "Mortal, deliver this to Huemac. And tell him the gods request the daughter of Tozcuecuex, the Mexitin [Mexica], for truly as they will eat this, little by little in a sacred manner she will be eating the Toltecs. For indeed the Toltecs will be destroyed and the Mexica will come to extend themselves. And over there at Chalchiuhcoliuhyan in Pantitlan they will go to deliver her."

And so then he went to tell everything to Huemac; thus he said just as Tlaloc had commanded it. And then Huemac was filled with contrition and wept; he said, "So it will certainly be; so the Toltecs will indeed depart; so Tollan will indeed be destroyed." Then he sent to Xicococ two messengers, Chiconcohuatl and Cuetlachcohuatl, to request of the Mexica the young woman named Quetzalxochtzin who was not very old, still a little lady.

So then they went there to Xicococ, and they spoke: "Here have we been sent by Huemac; he says, 'The lords of rain have shown themselves in a sacred manner. They request a young Mexica woman.'" And so the Mexica fasted for four days and fasted as for a death. And when the four days were completed, then they carried her to Pantitlan; her father went with her. Then they sacrificed her.

Then again there the lords of rain appeared and spoke to Tozcuecuex: "Tozcuecuex, don't be lost in your grief, for you will be with your young lady. Open your tobacco pouch." There they placed the girl's heart and all the many and varied food-stuffs. They said, "Here indeed is what the Mexica shall eat, for the Toltecs will certainly be destroyed."

And so then suddenly the clouds gathered and it began to rain furiously; for four days and four nights it rained without ceasing and the water was eaten by the earth. Then sprouted all the different green edible plants and all the herbs and grasses. And all the food-stuffs were created and brought to life.

And then the Toltecs planted; twenty and forty days passed and the young maize plants were full; very soon all the food-stuffs were produced. The year-sign under which all these food-stuffs were produced is 2 Reed.

In 1 Flint the Toltecs were destroyed. Then Huemac went into the cave at Cincalco. Some returned and others dispersed themselves in all directions.

XI

And then the Mexica came, traveling in this direction. 1. Tezcacoatl Huemac. 2. Chiconcohuatl. 3. Cohuatlayauhqui. 4. Cuitlachcohuatl. Thirteen years. 1 Reed. [The narrator is reading literally a pictographic text of some sort; then he explains:] And the names of the four protectors who led them in their departure are—name of the first lord, Cohuatlayauhqui; name of the second, Cuitlachcohuatl; name of the third, Chiconcohuatl; name of the fourth, Tezcacohuatl (this one was Huemac). They served as protectors for thirteen years, always wanderers.

And here they are coming from Colhuacan, from Aztlan; here the Mexica are fleeing, 58 years. 1 Flint. Here it shows they lived in Chapoltepec still in the time of Huitzillihuitl; they lived there forty years. 13 Rabbit. Here it shows they lived in Colhuacan, in Tizaapan, twenty-five years.

When the Toltecs departed in 1 Flint, the Mexica were arriving at the same time; they came from there, from Xicococ and it took them thirty-seven years to arrive at Chapoltepec. There they stayed, in Chapoltepec, for forty years. And then the Colhua rented them out as slaves; the Xaltocameca came to rent them. There the Mexica settled for a time, as the saying goes, "I'll only sleep here nearby you, because I'm headed over yonder." So they "slept" there near the Colhua but in such a way that it seemed they went there only to guard them. And then they [the Mexica] suddenly fled from the Colhua; in this way the Mexica violated Colhua law: they said, "We will enter the Colhua houses" [i.e., marry Colhua women?].

And the Xaltocameca and the Quauhtitla were householders [i.e., former Chichimecs who now lived in permanent towns]; the Acolhua, the Tenayo, the Azcapotzalca, the Quahuaca, the Macahuaca, the Xiquipilca, the Matlatzinca, the Ocuilteca, the Cuitlahuaca, and the Xochimilca; and others were there under protection of the Colhua.

These Colhua captured the Mexica chieftain Huitzillihuitl. Then the Mexica were robbed of their woman, the princess. And other Mexica escaped into the tule marshes at Acocolco and went to camp there for six days.

And here it shows the arrival on dry land here at Tenochtitlan, which was still nothing but tule marsh, still nothing but a reedy place; there the Mexica endured their labors for fifty years. No one was their Speaker.

The Mexica kept exclusively and singlemindedly to their own affairs. Year 51. 2 House: Colhuacan, Tenayocan. And here it was that the Mexica made their first conquests: only Colhuacan and Tenayocan.

1. And it was also there that Lord Acamapichtli was installed as The Speaker. He ruled twenty-one years. 20. 1 Flint: Xochmilco, Cuitlahuac, Quauhnahuac, Mizquic. And here are shown the conquests which he made: Xochmilco and Cuitlahuac and Mizquic and Quauhnahuac. In four places he conquered.

2. And here it is indicated that the son of Acamapichtli, named Huitzillihuitl, ruled for twenty-one years; here he ruled—21. 9 House: Xaltocan, Acolman, Otompan, Chalco, Tetzcoco, Tollantzinco, Quauhtitlan, Toltitlan. And here are shown the conquests which he made. Eight cities Huitzillihuitl conquered.

3. And here it is indicated that the son of Huitzillihuitl, named Chi-

malpopocatzin, ruled; for ten years he was The Speaker. Chalco, Tequix-quiac. 10 years. 4 Rabbit. And here are shown the two cities which Chi-malpopocatzin conquered.

4. And here it is indicated that the son of Acamapichtli, named Itzcohu-atzin, was made The Speaker, and so he was Speaker for thirteen years. 13. 1 Flint. And here are all the conquests which Itzcoatzin made: Azcapotzalco, Tlacopan, Atlacuihuayan, Coyohuacan, Mixcohuac, Quauhximalpan, Quahuacan, Teocalhuiyocan, Tecpan, Huitzitzillapan, Quauhnahuac, Tetz-coco, Quauhtitlan, Xochmilco, Cuitlahuac, Mizquic, Tlatelolco, Itztepec, Xiuhtepec, Tzaqualpan, Chalco, Yohuallan, Tepequacuilco, Cuecallan.

5. And here it is shown that the son of Huitzillihuitl, named Ilhuicami-natzin Moteucçomatzin the Elder, was made The Speaker, and so he ruled for twenty-nine years. 29. 1 House. And here are the conquests which Mo-teucçomatzin the Elder made: Coaixtlahuacan, Chalco, Chiconquiyauhco, Tepoztlan, Iyauhtepec, Atlatlauhcan, Totollapan, Huaxtepec, Tecpatepec, Yohualtepec, Xiuhtepec, Quiyauhteopan, Tlalcocauhtitlan, Tlachco, Quauh-nahuac, Tepequacuilco, Cohuatlan, Xillotepec, Itzcuincuitlapilco, Tlapa-coyan, Chapolicxitla, Tlatlauhquitepec, Yacapichtlan, Quauhtochco, Cuetlaxtlan.

6. And here is indicated how the grandson of both Speakers Moteucço-matzin the Elder and Itzcohuatzin, named Axayacatzin, was made The Speaker; he ruled for twelve years. 12. 4 Rabbit. And here are all the places which Axayacatzin conquered: Tlatelolco, Matlatzinco, Xiquipilco, Tzinacan-tepec, Tlacotepec, Tenantzinco, Xochiyacan, Teotenanco, Callimayan, Mete-pec, Ocoyacac, Capolloac, Atlapolco, Qua. . . .

[The manuscript ends here at the bottom of page 10; the rest has been lost.]

The Man Born of a Tree:
A Mixtec Origin Myth*

With my humble pardon, I will give you some words about what happened very long ago, what the ancestors have said.

A man went to the mountains. He had been there for eight days when he saw the sacred madroño tree. He went to it and made a hole in its side, and

---

*"The Man Born of a Tree: A Mixtec Origin Myth," interlinear translation by Thomas J. Ibach. *Tlalocan,* vol. VIII (1930), pp. 246–47, edited by Earl Shorris. Text provided by mono-linqual Mixtec speakers, Serafio Martinez Ramos and Badilio Gómez Cruz.

Codice Vindobonense, National Library of Vienna, p. 37.

he had intercourse with it. After three or four months passed he saw that the tree was swollen. And then he knew that the stomach of the tree was swollen, and he counted the months.

When the months were complete he went there, and he made a hole in the tree's stomach, and saw a little man inside. He took that little man and carried him home. And when he arrived at his house the little man came to life. His name was "fourteen strengths."

When he grew up he was very strong. He worshipped that tree, because he was born from its stomach.

Where the tree stood, it was not upright, but he went and embraced the tree and made it stand upright from its roots.

The tree grew as before; it would never dry up, it would never die.

The man grew slowly and became stronger and stronger. And then he went to the cave in San Lucas so that he could chase the stones from the cave with a whip, because in the old times the stones were like the domesticated animals that belonged to the people.

When he arrived at the "cross of the avocado tree" with the stones, the sun arose and killed him, because until then, when the man called "fourteen strengths" was born, there had not been a sun.

When he died there, the stones also died; they are still there.

Underneath the "cross of the avocado tree" the sacred man died, the one called "the man of fourteen strengths."

This is all of the story of long ago, the story the ancestors told.

The New Geography of
Mesoamerica

The Mesoamerica cradle exists now only in stone and contemplation. The great helmeted heads, the werejaguar babies are virtually all that remains. What the Olmecs said and how they said it, with what sounds, tones, stops, we shall probably never know. We know only that they began and that their influence was not limited to the flatlands between the great rivers at the side of the Caribbean Sea.

There was Olmec influence in the world of Teotihuacan and Tula to the northwest of the cradle and then the Maya to the south. The great city-state of the Mexica in the high plateau came late in the evolution of the culture, but not last, for it spread everywhere, to the four cardinal directions, in works of war and trade. Then the Spaniards came, and there was a moment when the culture that sprang from the Olmec cradle could have entered its grave. But the Mesoamerican ethos survived. It contracted, and then began to spread again.

After the Spanish invasion, Mesoamerican culture moved north into the states that had been Yaqui, Raramuri, Paquime territory. Along the Rio Bravo, to mention just one area, the people the Spaniards had named *Manso,* meaning "Docile," hunter-gatherers of the northern highlands, slowly adopted the culture that flowed north from Tenochtitlan. The northern villages themselves were reconfigured in the style of the central plateau. The zocalo of Tenochtitlan appeared in El Paso del Norte. The diet of the hunter-gatherers grew more sophisticated, the gods of the north came more and more to resemble the gods who were born or discovered by the Olmecs who lived in what is now the state of Tabasco.

Some of these changes came as a result of the northward migration of people from the more densely populated south and some were brought by the Spaniards who had become "Mexicanized." The cake of cornmeal filled with meat, vegetables, fish, or fruit took its Nahuatl name, *Tamal-li,* to villages from Chihuahua to Colorado and California.

With the continuing northward migration of indigenous people and people of mixed Spanish, indigenous, and sometimes African ancestry, Mesoamerican culture began to mix with the Northern European culture that dominated so thoroughly in the early centuries of what is now the United States. Just as the combination of Spanish, African, and indigenous origins had produced the mestizaje, sometimes still described as *la raza cosmica,* the cosmic race, in Mexico, the continuing northward migration produced a new mestizaje in the United States.

When the northern boundary of Mesoamerican culture reached to Canada and beyond, spread by railroad workers, migrants, and people fleeing the Revolution of 1910, Mesoamerican culture bearers underwent a series of name changes: Mexican, Mexican American, Latin American, and Chicano, the last perhaps the most politically aware and active incarnation.

The Chicano concept was defined in his column in the *Los Angeles Times* by Ruben Salazar, a journalist who was born in Chihuahua and murdered by sheriff's deputies in East Los Angeles. In his definition, Salazar spoke of the Chicano as one who was aware of his indigenous heritage and who defended it.

When Salazar wrote his column in 1970, only politically active young people and a few scholars were concerned with the Mesoamerican heritage of Mexicans and people of Mexican descent in the United States. For many people of the older generation, their Spanish heritage was more desirable. They did not want to be considered "Indians," and perhaps with good reason, for no group of human beings in the United States had suffered more at the hands of the government than those who were known as Indians.

The Chicanos were a new generation; one might best describe them as culturally courageous. They were neither ashamed nor fearful of their indigenous ancestors. Instead, they sought strength in their cultural patrimony.

However, separation from Mexico and the effects of Mexico's ambivalent attitude toward its indigenous people (a mixture of homage to pre-Hispanic times and discrimination and impoverishment now) complicated the nature of the northward spread of Mesoamerican culture. Some Chicanos began to speak of the southwestern United States as Aztlan, the place of origin of the people who moved south into Mexico and adopted the Mesoamerican ethos. Others preferred to abandon Mesoamerica in favor of European culture.

Cultural migration, of course, is an individual decision today in the Americas. Toltec troops will not move north into the United States as they once moved south into the lands of the Maya. Nonetheless, the Mesoamerican ethos affects that of the United States, particularly for people of Mexican national origin, just as the Toltec ethos affected the Maya.

The nature of the spread of Mesoamerican culture northward will depend to a large extent upon what is available. If the culture is limited largely to repasts provided by fast-food restaurants spiced with smatterings of the intellectual achievements of Mesoamerica, it will have been an unfortunate journey.

Many Chicanos and others of Mexican descent who do not use that appellation have begun to seek out the deeper values of Mesoamerica in the art and literature that originated in the cradle of the Olmecs. Until now, a single source of Mesoamerican literature from Palenque to the present has not been available in English, and much of the literature has not been available in English in any form.

Although one book cannot be more than a small part of the great Mesoamerican wave that rolls north, it is the editors' hope that this collection may help to enrich that wave, both for English readers of Mexican descent and for those who want to enjoy the experience of communicating with one of the world's great original cultures.

—Earl Shorris

Book I

Nahua
Literature

The Nahua literary tradition antedates the Spanish invasion by several centuries. It continued after the invasion through the colonial period, remained alive in independent Mexico, and at present a sort of Nahua literary renaissance is taking place.

Most of the Nahua compositions come out of central Mexico, Nahuatl having long been a lingua franca in Mesoamerica, but there are also works in Nahuatl from places far from where it was or still is spoken.

Many of the compositions derive ultimately from the ancient codices or books of paintings and glyphic signs, and also from the oral tradition, which was systematically conveyed in the *calmecac,* or priestly schools. There, as an ancient text puts it, the students "were taught proper discourse . . . and especially the songs with which they invoked the gods," songs later inscribed in their books. "And they were also taught the count of the days, the book of dreams and the book of years."

Based on their merits, a number of these students came to occupy important positions as teachers, functionaries in the political administration, or as priests, artists, and scribes/painters of the books in which their philosophy, art, and culture were both preserved and enriched.

Nahua literature of the pre-Hispanic tradition can be found in a few extant codices that survived the systematic destruction carried out by those who believed the work was inspired by the devil. It can also be studied in numerous books painted and inscribed during the early colonial period, and in texts using the Roman alphabet, which were derived both from readings of the codices and from the oral tradition. This literature comprises sacred narratives, hymns, prayers, poetry, *Discourses of the Elders (Huehuehtlahtolli)*, historical accounts, proverbs, and conundrums. During the colonial period, several indigenous literary works were redacted as alphabetical texts, often at the instigation of the friars. Texts like the *Huehuehtlahtolli* were transcribed in this way. In some of these and in numerous songs one can easily detect Christian interpolations. New compositions also appeared, many of them reflecting the harsh conditions suffered by the people.

There is an outstanding Nahua narrative of the Conquest, which Miguel León-Portilla has described in his *Broken Spears* (1992) as the "Vision of the Vanquished." It consists of several dramatic accounts of the struggle that brought about their subjugation to Spanish rule. Soon after the Conquest, a copious Christian literature began to develop. It included proselytizing texts; popular forms of theater; letters of complaint, often carrying descriptions of daily life; litigations; and even a dialogue between surviving indigenous sages and the Franciscan missionaries. To all this must be added the works of native chroniclers such as Alvarado Tezozómoc and Domingo Chimalpain, who did their best to preserve the memory of the grandeur of the Nahuas.

Literature in Nahuatl produced during the years of independent Mexico up to the present includes various genres derived from two different sources: One is from the oral tradition, and has been collected by ethnographers and linguists. It includes poems, songs, legends, and tales. The other, more recent source is the personal creative work of a growing number of Nahua writers, authors of the *Yancuic Tlahtolli* or "New Word." This continuation includes poetry and narrative arising out of the experiences of both the community and the individual author.

Map of the Valley of Mexico*

*From Miquel León-Portilla, *Fifteen Poets of the Aztec World* (Norman, OK: University of Oklahoma Press, 1992), p. xii.

❧ 1 ❧

Songs and Poems

*I*n addition to the codices, sacred hymns, histories, and ethical works
(Huehuetlahtolli), other manuscripts in which the Nahua tradition
is preserved include alphabetic renditions of a large number of compositions in poetic form. A collection known as the Cantares Mexicanos
(Mexican Songs), kept at the National Library in Mexico City, and another whose bizarre title is Romances de los Señores de Nueva España, preserved in the Benson Latin American Library of the University
of Texas at Austin, are the two main works in this genre.[1] The former was
the result of the concern of more than one native who collected the
songs in the sixteenth century for the benefit of a missionary interested
in them. As for the Romances, there is evidence that leads us to conclude
they were assembled in the same century by the Tezcocan chronicler
Juan Bautista Pomar.

Various literary subgenres can be identified in these works. The icnocuicatl, songs of orphanhood, are often described as metaphysical
poems. They contain questions reminiscent of those proposed at other
times and places by what in European culture are called philosophers.
Among recurring questions expressed in poetic form, these works raise
the problem of speaking the truth in this world, the evanescence of existence, the ethical dilemma of distinguishing good actions from bad, a
concern for human destiny in the beyond, and how to approach the
mysteries surrounding ultimate realities. Readers familiar with European philosophy will recognize the same concerns that preoccupied Im-
manuel Kant: "What can I know? What ought I to do? What can I
hope? And what is man?"

[1]There is a facsimile edition, by Miguel León-Portilla, National Autonomous University of
Mexico, 1994, of the *Cantares;* and a Spanish translation, by Angel María Garibay K., National
Autonomous University of Mexico, 1964, of the *Romances.*

In contrast, the Nahuas also composed poems called cuecuech-
cuicatl, or tickling songs, often accompanied by stirring or provocative
music and dance. And there were a few salacious stories. It is true that
in some instances, as in "The Story of the Tohuenyo" (p. 109), which the
modern reader may interpret as an erotic poem, the intention was not to
produce a bawdy narrative but to recall a significant event.

Yaocuicatl, *"songs of war," also known as* cuauhcuicatl, ocelocuicatl
or "eagle songs, tiger songs," abound in this literature. These stories of
great warriors, conquests, and struggles were accompanied by music and
dance. Xochicuicatl *and* xopancuicatl, *"songs of flowers" and "songs of*
springtime," are expressions of joy and happiness. They evoke all that is
considered good on earth: friendship, love, poetry itself. They refer fre-
quently to flowers and their attributes, to birds and butterflies, precious
stones, bracelets and necklaces, as well as to musical instruments—
drums, flutes, conchshells, rattles, bells—painted books, foaming choco-
late, tobacco, and anything else that produces pleasure, or in some
instances visions, considered prophetic, resulting from eating hallu-
cinogenic mushrooms. In this last context, songs tell of the inner expe-
rience of those consuming the mushrooms.

1. Metaphysical Poems

WE COME ONLY TO DREAM

Thus spoke Tochihuitzin,
thus spoke Coyolchiuhqui:

We only rise from sleep,
we come only to dream,
it is not true, it is not true,
that we come on earth to live.
As an herb in springtime,
so is our nature.
Our hearts give birth, make sprout,
the flowers of our flesh.
Some open their corollas,
then they become dry.

Thus spoke Tochihuitzin,
thus spoke Coyolchiuhqui.

Cantares Mexicanos, fol. 14v, from Miguel León-Portilla, *Fifteen Poets of the Aztec World* (Norman, OK: University of Oklahoma Press, 1992), p. 153.

THE GIVER OF LIFE

The Giver of Life is a mocker:
we pursue only a dream,
oh friends of ours,
our hearts trust,
but truly he mocks.

Being moved, let us enjoy ourselves,
in the midst of the greenery and the paintings.
The Giver of Life makes us live,
he knows, he decides,
how we men will die.

Nobody, nobody, nobody,
truly lives on earth.

Cantares Mexicanos (1994), fol. 13v; from Miguel León-Portilla, *The Aztec Image of Self and Society* (Salt Lake City: University of Utah Press, 1992), p. 169.

SONG OF TLALTECATZIN OF QUAUHCHINANCO

I come to guard the mountain,
somewhere is its story,
with flowers is painted
the Giver of Life, the community.

You have been left in your home,
you, Tlaltecatzin,
you suspire there, you speak.

I alone I sing
to Him, who is my God,
in our place where the lords command,

the flowering chocolate drink is foaming,
the one which intoxicates men with its flowers.

I yearn,
my heart has tasted it,
my heart has been inebriated,
my heart knows it.

O red songbird of the supple neck!
Fresh and burning,
you show your garland of flowers.
You, Mother!

Sweet woman,
precious flower of toasted maize,
you only lend yourself,
you will be abandoned,
you will have to go away,
there will be a defleshing.

Here you have come,
before the lords,
you marvelous being,
in an erect pose.
Upon the mat of yellow and blue feathers,
there you stand proudly.
But, precious flower of toasted maize,
You only lend yourself,
soon you must be abandoned,
you will have to go away,
there will be a defleshing.

The flowering chocolate drink is foaming,
the flower of tobacco is passed round,
if my heart would taste them,
my life would become inebriated.
But here
on the earth,
you, O lords, O princes,
if my heart would taste them,
my life would become inebriated.

I only suffer and say:
may I not go
to the place of the fleshless.

Is anyone there who will become the owner of my heart?
Alone I must go,
my heart covered with flowers.
Quetzal feathers,
precious jades,
so perfectly polished,
will be destroyed.
Nowhere on earth is their model,
thus let it be,
but let it be without violence.

The text of this poem has been established on the basis of the two extant Nahuatl transcriptions of it in *Cantares Mexicanos*, fols. 30r and v, and *Romances de los Señores de Nueva España*, fols. 7r–8r. Translation by León-Portilla, *Fifteen Poets of the Aztec World*, pp. 68–69.

In the following long poem, which comes down to us in the form of a dialogue, a group of Nahua nobles meet in the palace of Tecayehuatzin, in Huezotzinco, not far from the modern city of Puebla, to discuss the origins of what we today speak of as art. The conversation expands from questions of art to speak of friendship and love. The Nahua fascination with language (Nahuatl *means "clear speech") may be seen in such lines as "listen to the dream of a word." The character of the poem is revealed in the first few lines, when Tecayehuatzin speaks of the provenance of the singer, which we may take to mean the question of the divine inspiration of art.*

POETICS:
A DIALOGUE OF FLOWER AND SONG

[*TECAYEHUATZIN*][2]

Where do you live, singer?

[2]The speaker's name appears as an aid to the reader in following the dialogue. Speakers were indicated only by context in the original manuscript, *Xochicuicatl*, which is also known by a Spanish title, *Canto Florido*.

He comes now to set up the drum
adorned with quetzal plumes,
woven with golden flowers.

You will delight the princes,
the lords, the eagle knights, the tigers.

In reality he just descended
to the place of the drums.
Now the poet lives;
he unfolds the songs of the Giver of Life,
he strews them about
as if they were quetzal plumes.

The bell bird responds,
trilling;
he offers flowers, he disseminates our flowers.

In the place where I hear his word,
truly his, the word of the Giver of Life,
that is where the bell bird answers,
where he responds,
trilling,
offering flowers, disseminating our flowers.

Your precious words
fall like a gentle rain of quetzal plumes.

Ayocuan, he, Cuetzpal,
who truly knows the Giver of Life,
also said this.
Thus he arrived, the lord whose praise
is like a finely polished, precious bracelet,
who delights the one God.

If there is a place where some truth exists on earth,
perhaps the Giver of Life is aware of it?
If I could borrow
for a moment,
or for all time,

the jades, the bracelets, the princes,
with my song I would gather the nobles
in the place of drums
and surround them with flowers.

For a moment here in Huexotzinco,
I, Lord Tecayehuatzin,
intertwined the jades, the quetzal plumes,
I brought the lords together,
I surrounded the nobles with nothing but flowers.

The beautiful flowers, the beautiful songs
come from the heart of the sky.
Our yearning makes them ugly,
our inventiveness ruins them.

[AYOCUAN]

Ah, in truth, it is the Chichimeca Lord Tecayehuatzin,
rejoice with him!

Friendship is scattered about
like a rain of flowers from the precious tree;
that flower, redolent of the night,
intertwines with the precious ones of the tender corn.
The lords, the princes, wander among the trees,
sipping as they go.

Over there in your circle of flowers,
among the fragrant boughs,
where the birds warble,
your lovely song,
which you so rightly sing,
is a golden bell bird.

Perhaps you, quechol bird,
are from the Giver of Life?
Perhaps you speak for God?
As soon as you see the dawn,
you set yourself to singing.

Although my heart desires only the flowers of the shield,
those who belong to the Giver of Life,
what can my heart do?
Have we arrived, have we sprung up on earth in vain?
Shall I perish like the flowers?
Will my fame eventually fade away,
will my renown be nothing on earth?
At least flowers, at least songs!

What can my heart do?
Have we arrived, have we sprung up on earth in vain?

Let us rejoice! Here, among friends,
let there be embraces.
We live on the flowered earth.
Here, no one will bring to an end the flowers, the songs;
they endure in the house of the Giver of Life.

Only a moment on earth,
is it the same in Quenonamican?
Is there still joy?
Is there friendship?
Or is it only here on earth that we have come to know each other?

I, Lord Ayocuan, listened to a song over there;
hearing him play the flute,
as if it were a strand of flowers.

He has only responded to you,
he has answered from inside the flowered house,
Aquiauahtzin, Lord Ayapancatl.

[*AQUIAUHTZIN*]

Where do you live, oh my God, Giver of Life?
I search for you,
I, the poet,
sometimes am saddened by you.
I give you only joy.
Only *izquixochitl*, fragrant flowers,
precious fragrant flowers,

are arrayed here inside the verdant house,
the house of painting.
I give you only joy.

Those from afar, from Tlaxcala,
are singing
with tiny bells of jade,
in the place of the drums.

The intoxicating flowers, Lord Xicotencatl of Tizatlan,
Camaxochitzin, are gladdened by song;
they await the word of the one God.

Is it this way in your house, Giver of Life?
In that beyond, in the place of the flower mat,
the princes entreat you.

Many kinds of flowering trees stand
in the place of the drums.
Where you stay, entwined with quetzal feathers,
the beautiful flowers are strewn.

The bell bird lives above
the quetzal feather mat,
and sings.
There, the lord answered him,
and the eagle and the tiger please him.

Let us dance, friends,
among the strewn flowers,
in the place of the drums!

Who is awaited?
Our heart is only grieved.
Listen only to Him, to God,
who descended from the center of the sky.
He comes singing,
and with the music of their flutes
the angels respond.

[*CUAUHTENCOZTLI*]

Our drum stands adorned, resplendent;
it only grieves me.
I, Cuauhtencoz,
am adorned with sadness.

Are men perhaps real?
Soon our song will not be real.

What is standing?
What will come about?
Do we live over there,
is that where we are?

You are in need, my friend,
I should take you along,
so that you could stand on your feet there.

[*MOTENEHUATZIN*]

Where am I singing?
Our friends, you, who speak here,
what are you saying?

The prince, Coyolchiuhqui, comes there
where the patio extends;
weeping, he comes to sing
in the heart of the house of spring.
Sad flowers, sad songs;
I hate everything that changes here.

In truth there is much grieving,
we walk in sorrow.
At the gathering of the lords,
those who govern,
I, Motenehuatzin, entwine the nobility
with my songs, with quetzal plumes.
Oh, Lord Telpolohuatl,
we all live inside the house of spring.
Sad flowers, sad songs;
I hate everything that changes here.

I have heard a song,
I contemplate the water of the verdant time;
he goes there at the break of dawn,
calling to the bird *xiuhquechol,* to the *elotototl,*
he is the lord Monencauhtzin.

[*TECAYEHUATZIN*]

You, our friends,
those who are now
within the house of the cacao flowers
of *xiuhquechol,* the bird of God,
O that I could offer the precious planting!
O that I could meditate upon the laughter of the jade flutes.
The princes may be summoned by the drums;
inside the flowery house
the lords shake the turquoise-colored drums,
they make them resonate.

[*MONENCAUHTZIN*]

Listen! He is trilling,
he sings in the branches of the flowered tree;
the shaking of the tiny metal bells is heard,
it is a quechol bird, that precious hummingbird;
the lord Monencauhtzin
fans himself with plumes of the *zacuan* bird,
extending its wings among the flowery drums.

They rise, the flowers rise;
the flowers are budding
in the presence of the Giver of Life.
He has answered you.

You shall ask the bird of God
to alight over there.
As many as there are songs, so great is your wealth.
You please others,
the flowers are excited.

I go everywhere,
I speak everywhere, I, the poet.
Precious fragrant blossoms
are scattered there,
in the flowery patio
within the house of butterflies.

[XAYACAMACH]

They all come from afar,
from where the flowers stand,
those that make gyrations,
those that set the heart to spinning.
They come with arms outstretched,
scattering garlands of flowers, fragrant flowers.
He entered over there,
on the flower mat.

The house of the singing books
is truly your house,
says Xayacamach;
the cacao flower intoxicates your heart.

A beautiful song resounds;
Tlapalteuccitzin intones his song;
his flowers profuse the air with perfume;
the cacao flowers are strewn.

[TLAPALTEUCCITZIN]

You, our friends,
I have been searching for you,
I retrace the fields one by one.
Here you are!
Delight us! Tell your stories,
Only I have arrived,
I, your friend.

Do I come among the beautiful flowers
perhaps to introduce
an irritating one?

Can it be so?
Am I perhaps the naif, the one in need?
Oh you, our friends!

Who am I? I go flying,
I compose something, I sing the flowers,
the butterflies of song;
I should be delighted
if my heart knew.

I come from that which is above us;
I, the quechol, bird of the verdant time,
have descended,
I have arrived on earth,
opening my wings in the place of the drums.
My song is raised,
it comes out of the earth, it springs forth.

So I also cultivate the flowery songs;
I emerge beside you,
with cords of precious metal I bind my bowl,
I, who am your friend, the one in need.

I stand watch where the flowers bud,
I am your friend;
in time of rain I cover my house
with leaves of colored blossoms.

Rejoice!
With this, I am happy in the fields of God.
Be very glad!
He who is adorned with flower necklaces
is truly the Lord.

Perhaps we shall come to life once more?
As the heart knows,
we have come to live but once.

I have arrived
upon the branches of the flowering tree.
I am the hummingbird,
I perceive the fragrance,
it delights me;
my words are sweet, delicious.

God, Giver of Life,
who is invoked with flowers,
we bow, we give you pleasure
in the place of the drums,
Lord Atecpanecatl.

The drums are kept there,
watched over,
in the heart of the house of spring.
Your friends, Yaomanatzin, Micohuatzin,
Ayocuatzin, watch over you,
the sighs of the lords are flowers.

[AYOCUAN]

A city besieged, a city hated,
Huexotzinco,
surrounded by cactus, attacked with arrows,
Huexotzinco.

The drums, the great tortoise shell,
are abandoned in your house,
in Huexotzinco;
in that far place, where Tecayehuatzin stands vigil.
The lord Quecehuatl plays the flute and sings,
all alone in his house,
in Huexotzinco.

Listen! God, our father,
descends;
in his house the tiger drum
resounds,
the song of the drum has remained there,
there.

Like a flower, the precious mantle
is brought inside the house of books.
So the earth and the forest are watched over,
so the One God is watched over.

There are fiery arrows
in your precious house.
My golden house of painted books
is your house, God.

Friends,
listen to the dream of a word:
In the spring the golden budding of the corn
brings us to life,
enabling us to see.
The ear of corn
the color of the *tlauhquechol* bird
turns into our necklace.
Oh, friends, this we know:
it has gone to quiet your heart.

Cantares Mexicanos, fols. 9v–11v; translation into Spanish, Miguel León-Portilla; English version, Sylvia and Earl Shorris.

In this poignant "Song of Loss," we again encounter the participants in the dialogue, but the subject has changed from art and life to death and the ultimate realities.

SONG OF LOSS

Where is He, God, Giver of Life?
Where do You live?
Your poor friends await you.
They are grieved by songs;
with flowers they search everywhere
for what they so greatly desire;
they beseech your heart for
fame and honor.

I merely speak, remember;
nothing equals the misery.
What will bring peace to my heart?
And will the sadness then end for me, the man of Huexotzinco?

Perhaps my mother, perhaps my father
are waiting for me over there?
What will bring peace to my heart?
Will I finally put an end to my orphan's life?

I sent someone, there is happiness,
there is pleasure here, friends;
your cotton mantles, your necklaces are over there,
and I suffer privation.
Will nothing give me happiness?
Will I enjoy nothing here, among the people?

Dominion,
friendship, nobility, are intertwined.
No one will come from over there.
Will nothing give me happiness?
I want it, I long for it on earth.
Will I enjoy nothing here, among the people?

To You, Lord of the Close and Near,
we offer happiness here.
Yet You value us only as a flower;
the reward at your side is as nothing, Giver of Life,
We, your friends, merely wither.

You shatter precious stones,
You erase paintings,
everyone goes over
to the region of the dead,
to the region where we all go to lose ourselves.

How do You think of us, oh One God?
Is this the way we live?
Shall men go this way now
to be lost in the place of our perdition?
Where must we go?

For this alone I weep.
Thus You are wearied, Giver of Life.
The jades are shattered,
the quetzal plumes are broken.

You mock us, we are nobodies,
you have no regard for us,
you finish us off here.

We offer your sacrifice to You,
your temple, your sustenance, Giver of Life.
No one says that he is an orphan at your side.
You are invoked.

You turn the jades green,
You bring forth quetzal plumes.
Are they your heart, Giver of Life?
No one says that he is an orphan at your side.
You are invoked.

Do we live in the good place?
Let us be happy, we are together but briefly;
honor is acquired for all time.
If no one is truly your friend,
they ask for the loan of your beautiful flowers,
only your yellow flowers,
for but a brief time.

The entire nobility
appears before your mat,
before your seat of honor,
in the heart of the plain,
the dominion, the command,
and are caught up in your flowers of war,
your yellow flowers.

We say nothing true here, Giver of Life,
but speak only as from dreams,
from which we shall soon awaken;
we tell the truth to no one here.

If in truth polished jades are given You,
Giver of Life,
with necklaces of flowers You are invoked,
You are implored.
Perhaps there are nobles, eagles, tigers.
We tell the truth to no one here.

The Giver of Life mocks us.
We express only a dream, oh friend;
our heart knows—
in truth, He, God, mocks us.
Needful though we may be,
we could be happy
among the paintings,
in the heart of the house of spring.
The Giver of Life, he makes us live.
This He knows, this He says:
we men die,
no one, no one, no one truly lives here.

I was born in vain,
in vain I came to be born here on earth;
although I have come forth, I have been born,
I am destitute.
I say, What shall I do?
The princes have come to present themselves,
may I not offend them.
How shall I be prudent?
Am I rising to the place I deserve?
I am only a needy one.
Will my heart suffer?
My friend, it is hard to live here on earth.

How does one live here among the people?
Perhaps there is no reason why we live.
I offend people.
This is the only truth:
I show my reverence,
only in peace,
only with bowed head do I go among the people.

Do not be troubled, my heart,
let nothing you imagine.
In reality, we are abandoned on earth;
truly, the pain increases,
close to you, at your side, Giver of Life.

I remember our friends, I miss them,
perhaps they will come again?
Perhaps then they will come to life?

We lose everything,
for we live only once here on earth.
May your heart not be saddened,
near Him, close to the Giver of Life.

For this I am anguished, I weep,
I was also left an orphan among the people of the earth.
What does your heart desire, Giver of Life?
May your displeasure go away;
may the orphanhood not increase at your side,
You, God, God.
Do You desire my death?

Perhaps we have no joy on earth?
Is this the way you, our friends,
come to take your pleasure on earth?
So we suffer,
all the people here.

Only in the heart of the sky do you create
your word, oh God.
How have you wished it?
Perhaps You will be annoyed here?
Did you have to hide your fame,
your glory, here on earth?
How have you wished it?

No one can be a friend of the Giver of Life,
you, oh, you, tigers,
our friends, you saw that.
Where are we really going?
Oh, princes, we suffer here.

May those who hate us,
who cause us to die,
be made to suffer;
we shall dare,
we shall all go over there, to Quenonamican.

May I not offend you.
I only go on suffering
in the presence of the Giver of Life, God;

He removes us, he alienates us from His fame,
His glory, here on earth.
Yet we shall be happy.
I had to abandon you, my friends, to your lords.

In reality, no one can be
in the presence of the Giver of Life, God;
He removes us, He alienates us from His fame,
His glory, here on earth.
Yet we shall be happy.

You have listened to your heart; your troubled heart.
Look at us! Judge us!
We live here in the presence of the Giver of Life.
May you never die,
may you live forever here on earth!

I, I say it,
only a little,
only as an ear of new corn,
have we come to know ourselves on earth;
we have come only to wither, friends.
May the orphanhood end,
may our sadness be gone from here.

What shall we eat, oh friends?
With what must we cheer ourselves?
Where is our song born,
where are our drums born?
I am anguished on earth.
Where does He live?
May friendship be entwined,
may the community be entwined!
Perhaps I have come to appear in the place of the drums?
Perhaps I still have come to raise my voice in song?
For this alone am I here.
Somewhere, perhaps,
in the fog, the shadow,
I must offer myself.
We should trust you, my heart.
Perhaps this is our house here on earth?
I cannot help but suffer,
we live in this place of affliction.

Where shall I go to take sustenance,
where shall I ask for it?
Perhaps I shall sow it again, as if it were a flower,
perhaps that which gives sustenance will be sown again?
Will my mother, my father perhaps give tender fruits,
will they come to give full ears of corn on earth?
I weep for this,
no one cares about the rest,
we were left orphans on earth.
The road to the region of death is straight,
the road to the region of the dead, Tomoyan, Ximoayan.
Is it really possible to live in Quenonamican?
Perhaps we believe it in our hearts?
In the chest, the coffer, you enclose the people,
you hide them, Giver of Life.
Perhaps I shall see them over there,
perhaps I shall contemplate your countenance, my mother, my father?
Perhaps they will come to give me their song,
their word, that I miss.
No one cares about the rest,
we were left orphans on earth.

The flowers arrive. They could be riches,
they could be adornments, oh you, our lords.
They present themselves again,
they come resplendent;
only in springtime,
when the flowers have come to the forest,
do I go near the Cempoalxochitl.

I sing only inside the house of turquoise,
inside the house of the jewels, I speak,
I the singer.

Think of it, we should remember Quenonamican,
your house is over there, where there is no flesh,
where we are truly going.
We are common people,
therefore, in order to live you must stand before Him,
you must know God.

What are you thinking?
What do you remember, friends?
You do not think now of us,
the blooming, the beautiful flowers
which are as the sadness of the Giver of Life.
All we think,
all we remember,
saddens us here.

It happened, oh, princes, there was pain;
with suffering comes the resurgence of life, oh God.
Come, you, my friend,
what are you thinking?
What is it that you endlessly remember on this earth?
Do not be saddened, it is only that way here,
I know that it is the abandonment, the pain.
We live in anguish always here on earth.

Your anguish, your bitterness,
toward the Giver of Life, has come here now;
and lives on.
The eagles, the tigers, should be mourned,
for we must die here,
no one remains.

Think, oh princes of Huexotzinco,
even if you were jades, even if you were precious metal,
you would still go over there to the place of the fleshless,
to Quenonamican;
no one remains.

I weep, I grieve,
I remember the jades, the precious turquoise,
that you have hidden,
that you have concealed, One God.
And how then shall our heart be,
and what then will end our sadness?
I only suffer.
If your flower is true,
if your beautiful songs are true,
perhaps Ayocuatzin will come again?
Perhaps I will see him again?
Must I summon him once more in the place of the drums?

We lift our voices in song,
the songs of the One God,
and with this, strengthen our friendship.
You offer us to the community.
Tochihuitzin said,
Coyolchiuqui said:
We have just awakened from a dream;
we have come only to dream,
it is not true, it is not true,
that we have come to live on earth.

We have come up like the spring grass;
it sprouts, it revives our heart;
our bodies are flowers,
some blossom, then wither,
said Tochihuitzin.
Only your word, your annoyance,
will shine through.
It is a joke, you toy with us here.
No one is capable, no one can speak
the word of the Giver of Life.

Although it may have been Huemac,
the lord Tozozomoc is eulogized,
a hermit,
that is how he was,
Cuetzal Ozomatlin, the lord of Tlachquiehuitl,
they become old, they only go down there,
on earth no one has power, no one has power.

May the forest stand,
may it last forever!
Ayocuan, he, Cuetzpaltzin,
came to say it.

In Tlaxcallan, in Huexotzinco,
the pungent flowers,
the cacao flowers have been given,
so that the earth may endure.

I become intoxicated, I weep, I am saddened;
I know it, I say it, I remember it.
God willing, I will never die,
God willing, I will never perish.

I shall go
to the place where one lives,
where no one dies.
God willing, I will never die,
God willing, I will never perish.

You adorn us with your wealth,
you princes, Cuahtli Iztac, Petlacalcatl,
you do not leave the flowers of the shield idle;
with them you ignite Xayacmachan,
you make it strong.

Orphanhood will increase in Quenonamican.
You, princes, does anyone want to go?
Would you like to look over there
where our older brothers live,
where your sorrow, your pain,
your flowers and your songs exist?
We shall receive you, Patlacalcatl, Cuauhtli Iztac—
when will the One God,
that One by whom we live here,
grant it?

He leads the people with compassion,
it makes the day go on
that the One by whom we live, God,
is the possessor of all that is good.
He befriends the people on his mat—
when will the One God,
that One by whom we live here,
grant it?

The flowering tree stands in Tamoanchan,
in the house of God.
We were created there,
we were warned.
We were enveloped by the word of the Lord,

He, our God,
by whom we live.

I forge our beautiful songs
as if they were precious metal
and polish them as if they were jades
and turquoises.
Thus you swaddle us four times in Tamoanchan, God,
Giver of Life.
Be happy in verdant times,
in the heart of the house of spring.

With your wealth, your grace, it is possible to live,
Giver of Life, Possessor of the earth.
Here, you rock, you move.
My house, my home on earth
is yours.
Thus one lives now on your mat,
where You are feared.
No one close to You says that
You view the people with compassion,
or that you choose it for yourself.

For yourself, You look with pity on the people
in the place where You wait.
In your house, the Giver of Life looks after something for you,
Xiuhtzin, Coyolchiuhqui, Xihuitl Popoca, Moquihtzin.
No one close to You says that
You view the people with compassion.

You lived with songs,
you bloomed with flowers, you, princes,
I, Zacatimaltzin, Tochihuitzin;
the garland of flowers is coming over there now.
The Giver of Life
bestirs His drum, His rattle.
Your songs are written in the books,
you offered them in the place of the drums.
Motenehuatzin shakes his head,
with the war of the flowers, the One God is gladdened.

Cantares Mexicanos, fols. 12r–15r; Spanish translation, Miguel León-Portilla; English version, Sylvia and Earl Shorris.

THE MUSHROOM DRINK

I have taken the mushroom drink,
    my heart weeps,
    I am but a pauper;
    on this earth I grieve.

Cantares Mexicanos, fol. 17r; Miguel León-Portilla.

IN THE HEART OF THE SKY

I alone say to the Giver of Life:
Do not be annoyed, do not be intransigent,
God willing, we might live close to you,
in your house alone, in the heart of the sky.
Do I perhaps tell some truth here, Giver of Life?
We are only dreaming,
we have only come to quickly awaken ourselves from the dream;
what I say on earth,
we cannot say to anyone here.

Cantares Mexicanos, fols. Xr–Xv; Spanish translation, Miguel León-Portilla; English version, Sylvia and Earl Shorris.

2. Bawdy Poems

Here the mood changes to the wit and charm of the women of Chalco, a town close to the great volcanos. This song is an early feminist work, in that the women challenge their Mexica conquerors, saying that the men of Chalco may have been defeated, but not the women.

The Song of the Women of Chalco

You, my little sisters, get up,
let us go, let us go, we will seek flowers,
let us go, let us go, we will cut flowers.

Here they reach up, here they grow tall,
the flowers of water and fire,
the flowers of the shield, that appeal to men,
the flowers of glory;
the flowers of war.

Beautiful flowers,
flowers above,
with them, I adorn myself,
these are my flowers,
I am from Chalco,
I am a woman.

I desire, I long for flowers,
I desire, I long for songs,
I have a yearning, here in the place
we spin,
in the place our life is spent.

I sing his song,
to the lord, little Axayacatl,
I weave my song with flowers,
I put flowers around it.

A lovely song is like a painting,
like the fragrant flowers that give joy,
my heart values this on earth.

What does this mean?
Your word for me is worth this much,
you, with whom I do it, you, little Axayacatl,
I weave flowers into you,
I put flowers around you,
I lift you up to join us together,
I awaken you.
That is how I please
you with whom I do it,
you, little man, Axayacatl.

My friend,
my little friend, you,
Lord Axayacatl,
if you are really a man,

here is where you can fight to prove it.
Don't you have the strength to continue?

Do it in my warm vessel, much
light on fire.
Come, put it in, come, put it in:
It is my joy.
Come to give me that little thing,
you, let it rest.

We will have to laugh, be happy,
there will be pleasure,
I will have glory,
but no, not yet, do not hurl violently.
little friend, you, lord, little man, Axayacatl.

I, I am trapped,
my little hand slides round and round,
now come, now come.
Do you want to touch my breasts,
even my heart.

Will you ruin
what I value most,
will you finish it;
with flowers the color of the bird of fire,
I will make my womb move for you,
here it is: I make an offering to your chin.

As a precious flower of toasted corn,
as the bird with the rubber neck,
as a flower of the raven, your cloak of flowers,
on your flower-covered mat you lie.
You lie down on the precious mat,
in a house that is a cave of precious feathers,
in the mansion of the paintings. No more.

But even in your house I am sad,
you, my mother, I may no longer be able to spin.
I may not be able to weave,
it is all for nothing that I am a girl.
I am a young girl,
and they say I have a man.

There is suffering,
it is a place of despair on the earth.
So I brood sadly,
I desire evil,
I have become desperate.
I say to myself, come, child,
I want to die.

O my mother, I am distressed,
here I have my man,
I can no longer make the bobbin dance,
I cannot throw the shuttle stick:
my little child,
you laugh at me.
What is left for me?
I will do it!

Perchance with a feathered shield one will be sacrificed
in the field of battle?
I will offer myself, I will offer myself,
my child, you laugh at me.

Little fiend, my little child,
you, lord, little man Axayacatl,
let yourself be by my side,
offer yourself,
make the man in you speak.
Don't I know them,
have not I heard
of your enemies, my little child?
But for now, here by my side, forget.
Even though we are women,
you may gain nothing as a man.
Flowers and songs
from the woman who shares your pleasure,
my little child.

O man-child, my lord, you, great lord,
you, little man Axayacatl;
you still have not begun and
already you are displeased,
little friend. I am going home now,
my little child.

Have you bewitched me;
you have spoken lovely words.
Here, now there is drunkenness,
inebriate yourself!
Is there happiness in our house?

Have you bought me,
did you acquire me for yourself, my little child?
Perhaps you will sell me,
my pleasure, my intoxication?
Do you scorn me, are you displeased,
little friend? I am going home now,
my little child.

You, my friend, you the woman who offers herself,
see how the song endures,
in Cohuatepec, in Cuauhtenanpan.
How it reaches over us, and then is gone,
Maybe the woman in me does crazy things,
my small heart grieves. How should I make love,
to the one who is my man.
The skirts, the blouses,
the women, of our men,
of those we brought to life.

Knead me like corn dough,
you, lord, little man Axayacatl,
I will give you all of me,
I am here, my little child, I am here, my child.
Be glad, our worm rises.
Are you not an eagle, a jaguar,
do not you use these names, my little child?
Don't you play dirty tricks
on your enemies at war?
Now, in the same way, give yourself to pleasure.

My skirt and blouse are nothing,
here I am,
just a woman;
he comes to surrender his harmonious song
he comes here to surrender
the flower of his shield.

Are we not somehow the same,
I, the woman from Chalco,
I, [our former ruler] Ayocuan?

I want there to be women like me,
from afar, from Acolhuacan,
I want there to be women like me,
who are Tepaneca.
Are we not somehow the same,
I, the woman from Chalco,
I, Ayocuan?

They are ashamed I have become your mistress.
My little child,
perhaps you would treat me
like poor Cuauhtlatohua?
Slowly take off your skirts,
open your legs, you Tlatelolca,
you who shoot arrows,
look here to Chalco.

Shall I wear feathers,
my little mother,
shall I paint my face,
how should he see me,
my companion in pleasure?
Before your face we will leave openly,
perhaps they will be angry,
there in Huexotzinco, Xayacamachan,
in Tetzmelocan.

I, a woman, have rubbed my hands with,
I approach with my skirt of prickly fruit,
with my blouse of prickly fruit.
I will see them all dead.
I want the Huexotzincas in Xaltepetlapan,
the captive of Cuetlaxtlan.
the crafty Cuetlaxteca,
I will see them all dead.
How do I know this?
The boy calls me, the lord, little man
Axayacatl,
he wants to have his pleasure with me.

Because of me
you will have two to care for,
my little child.

Does your heart desire it so,
thus, little by little, let us tire each other.
Perhaps your heart is unwilling, my little child,
as you enter here, your pleasure,
your home.
Does your heart desire it so,
thus little by little, let us make each other tired.

How will you make love to me,
my companion of pleasure?
Let us do it this way, together,
are you not a man?
What is it that confuses you?
You circle my heart with flowers,
they are your word.
I will show you the place where I weave,
the place where I spin,
I will remember you, little friend.
What is it that troubles you, my heart?

I am an old whore,
I am your mother,
a lusty old woman,
old and without juice,
this is my profession, me, the woman from Chalco.
I have come to please my blooming vulva,
my little mouth.
I desire the lord,
the little man, Axayacatl.
Look on my flowering painting,
look on my flowering painting: my breasts.
Will it fall in vain,
your heart,
little man, Axayacatl?
Here are your small hands,
now take me with your hands.

Let us take pleasure.
On your mat of flowers,
in the place where you live, little friend,
slowly, slowly surrender to sleep,
rest, my little son,
you, lord Axayacatl.

Cantares Mexicanos, fols. 72r–73v; from León-Portilla, *Fifteen Poets of the Aztec World*, pp. 273–80.

The Story of the Tohuenyo

In the form of a portentous occurrence, the poet tells the story of the seduction of the daughter of the tlahtoani *of Tula. It becomes a comic tale of the plot of the* tlahtoani *to get rid of the highly sexed seducer, resulting in a battle, crowds of dwarves, and finally a comic denouement that readers must discover for themselves.*

And I have here another thing
that Titlacahuan[3] did,
something that turned out to be a wonder:
He transformed himself, taking the face and body of a Tohuenyo.
Going about naked, dangling the thing,
he went to sell chile,
setting himself up in the market, in front of the palace.

Well then, on to the daughter of Huemac,
who was very attractive,
desired and sought after
by many of the Toltecs,
who wanted to make her their wife.
But Huemac did not grant this,
he was not giving his daughter to anyone.

Well, this daughter of Huemac
looked toward the market
and she noticed the Tohuenyo: the one with the thing dangling.
The moment she saw it,
she went into the palace.

[3]A manifestation of Tezcatlipoca, noted for his ability to change form.

And for that reason the daughter of Huemac took sick,
she became tense, got a high fever,
as she felt poorly
because of the bird—the male organ—of the Tohuenyo.

And Huemac soon found out
his daughter was sick.
Then he told the women who cared for her:
"What happened, what's going on?
How did my daughter get this fever?"
And the women who cared for her answered:
"It is the Tohuenyo, the one that is selling chile:
he set the fire, he caused the yearning;
it started with that, that is why she fell ill."

And Lord Huemac,
in light of this, gave orders:
"Toltecs, look for the one who sells chile,
you will find the Tohuenyo."
And soon he was sought everywhere.

And as no one turned up,
the herald began to announce
from the Hill of Proclamations:
"Toltecs, perhaps you have seen the chile vendor somewhere,
the Tohuenyo? Bring him here.
The Lord is looking for him."

They made inquiries right away,
they went all around Tula, and although they made a great effort,
they did not see him,
he was nowhere to be found.
Then they came to tell the Lord
that they had not seen the Tohuenyo anywhere.

But soon the Tohuenyo himself appeared,
just to install himself
where he had appeared the first time.
And when the Toltecs saw this,
they ran to tell Huemac,
they said:
"The Tohuenyo showed up."

To which Huemac said:
"Hurry up and come here."
The Toltecs quickly went to bring the Tohuenyo,
they made him come before the Lord.

And when they brought him before the Lord,
Huemac immediately began to question him:
"Where is your house?"
The other responded:
"I am a Tohuenyo,
I go about selling a little chile."
And the Lord Huemac said to him:
"Well, is that any way to live, Tohuenyo?
Put on the breechclout, cover yourself."
To which the Tohuenyo responded:
"Well, that's how we are."

So the Lord said:
"You have aroused a yearning in my daughter;
you will cure it."

The Tohuenyo answered:
"My Lord, who is foreign to me,
this is not to be.
Kill me, have done with me,
death to me!
Is that what are you telling me?
Even though I am only a poor vendor of chile."
Then the Lord said to him:
"Of course not, you will cure her,
do not be afraid."

In short order they cut his hair,
they bathed him, and after that,
they anointed him,
they put on a breechclout, and tied the cloth.
And when they were done dressing him,
the Lord said:
"Look at my daughter
over there were she is cared for."

And when the Tohuenyo went to see her,
he went to bed with her immediately,

and at that moment the woman's health returned.
Then the Tohuenyo became the son-in-law of the Lord.

And for this they
jeered Huemac;
the Toltecs taunted him, joked about him,
saying: "So the Lord has a Tohuenyo for his son-in-law."

Then Huemac gathered the Toltecs,
and told them: "I have heard that they tell jokes about me,
that I am the object of laughter
for having made a Tohuenyo my son-in-law.
Well, take and leave trickery
in Zacatepec, in Coatepec."

Immediately the Toltecs proclaimed the war;
as one they were all set in motion.
Soon they were on the way
to abandon the son-in-law.

And on the way to the battlefield
they already set the Tohuenyo apart
with all the dwarfs and cripples.
And having set them apart,
the Toltecs went
to take captives
from among their Coatepec enemies.

Then the Tohuenyo said
to all the dwarfs and cripples:
"Don't be afraid,
we'll finish them off here,
they will perish here in our hands."

They thought—
from the way they had tricked the Tohuenyo
and left him to die—
that his enemies would have killed him.

Then they came
to inform the Lord Huemac,
they told him:
"We already left the Tohuenyo,

the one who was your son-in-law, over there."
Huemac thought perhaps it was certain, perhaps it was so,
and he was very pleased,
because he was ashamed
of having made the Tohuenyo his son-in-law.

But that Tohuenyo,
whom they had gone and abandoned in the war,
when their enemies, from Coatepec,
from Zacatepec, had already come,
he then commanded
the dwarfs and hunchbacks,
he told them:
"Have great spirit,
do not be afraid,
don't act like cowards, don't lose heart,
don't let them cut you down!
This I know:
all of you could take captives,
however, you should kill them any way you can."

And when their enemies
came to fall on them, to oppress them,
the Tohuenyo and his men soon brought them down,
they killed them, they finished them off,
they destroyed many of them;
so many,
that they could not count
the number of enemies they killed.

And when Lord Huemac heard this
he was very perturbed and dispirited:
he soon convened the Toltecs,
he told them:
"Let's look for our son-in-law."
With this he stirred up the Toltecs,
setting them in motion.
They accompanied the Lord, like a mob,
all around him,
to search for the Tohuenyo.

They carried the Toltec adornments,
a headdress of quetzal plumes,

a shield of turquoise mosaic.
When they got close to the Tohuenyo,
they immediately gave him gifts,
they gave him the quetzal headdress
and his shield of turquoise mosaic,
and all of the adornments they carried with them.

With these insignias they go dancing,
dancing the dance of the captive, writhing,
boasting, changing places.
They go singing.
The song blends,
it reverberates.
They play flutes,
the trumpets resound,
the conch shells loft their sound.

And when they had arrived at the palace
they put feathers on the head of the Tohuenyo
and anointed him with yellow,
and painted his face red.
And all of his friends were adorned in the same way.

And at the end Huemac said
to his son-in-law:
"The heart of the Toltecs is satisfied
that you should be my son-in-law.
You have earned it;
take a seat on the ground,
give your feet a rest."

Miguel León-Portilla, *Estudios de Cultura Nahuatl,* Instituto de Historia de la UNAM, vol. 1 (1959), pp. 101, 103, 105, 107, 109; English version, Sylvia and Earl Shorris.

3. War Songs

Four War Songs

SONG OF MOTEUCZOMATZIN

You were forged in the heart of the sky,
Moteuczomatzin;
and you rule in Mexico, in Tenochtitlan.

Here the countless eagles die.
The house of your precious adornments stands shining;
the house of God, our father, is over there.

You have come to live here,
in the heart of the plain.
You came to be entwined for a moment
in the gathering of eagles, the nobility,
the lords Ixtlilcuechahuac, Matlacuiyatzin.

Thus the nobles gain honor,
thus the nobles are renowned:
the little bells are scattered,
the dust yellows.

Have courage, friends,
let us be bold!
Fame and renown are gained over there,
one acquires nobility,
one earns it only
by a flowery death.

Your name, your reputation lives,
oh, princes.
You, my prince Tlacahuepantzin, Ixtlilcuechahuac,
you earned it,
for you went to your death in war.

At the break of dawn in the sky,
myriad birds sing,

they are the precious quechol birds;
the Xiuhzacuan birds take flight.

The chalk, the feather,
is not the place of orphanhood.
You are enveloped
in the place of your flowers,
Motlatocazoma,[4]
where the precious quechol birds,
the Xiuhzacuan birds take flight.

ANOTHER WAR SONG

Here I begin, I the singer:
Flowers, beautiful songs,
spring forth from my heart,
and I display them before the Giver of Life.

Here I dance, I the singer:
Flowers, beautiful songs,
spring forth from my heart,
and I display them before the Giver of Life.

There is the renewing of the eagles,
the blooming of the tigers,
they are the nobility,
they are dominion in Mexico.
With arrows, with shields,
the Lord Ahuitzotl speaks.

May the flowers not be plucked,
Giver of Life.
The dust is raised like smoke
in the center of the plain,
there you adorn them with magnificent jewels,
you engarland them with shields and flowers,
to Nezahualpilli, to Totoquihuatzin,
in Acolhuacan.
With arrows, with shields,
the Lord Ahuitzotl speaks.

[4]A play on words, referring to Motecuhzoma as "the one who angers with his reign."

I am saddened, I weep.
How happy is He!
The shields, the flowers, are brought high,
sorrowfully displayed.
I shall see them, my heart desires it.

There is nothing the Giver of Life loves
like death in war,
like the flowery death;
I shall see it, from afar, my heart's desire.

I seek the beautiful songs
in the place from which they come;
I the needy one
shall not sing in vain.

I have come to see your flowers,
oh Giver of Life,
I the needy one;
let me not sing in vain.

WAR SONG IN THE HUASTECAN STYLE

The rattlebells resound,
the dust of the scorching is raised,
the Huasteco flower of war is raised there,
in Tlacahuepan.

Inside the varicolored cactus,
there, the flowery liquor is found;
Tlacahuepan drinks it.

Listen!
They come singing war songs,
on the mountain of the Otomis we, Huastecos,
are intoxicated.
Our God is celebrated with shields.
The scorching comes, entwining
our flower of the pine, our Huastecos.
Voices like tiny bells.

Our God is celebrated with shields,
He, God.

Tocotocotiti tocotocotiti tinco tinco tinti

His torso painted with precious water,
my great one, my prince Nezahualpilli,
is intoxicated with the flowery liquor of the shield;
the Huastecos dance there,
in Atlixco.

You make the flute of tiger cane
resound,
you scream like an eagle
above your great circular stone.
The noble Huehuetzin is gone now,
there is rapture
with the intoxicating beverage of the flowered shield,
there is rapture,
over there where the Huastecos dance,
in Atlixco.

Perhaps one lives twice?
I say it,
I have come to intoxicate myself,
I the woman.

He dances, he of the painted torso.
Perhaps one lives twice?
I say it,
I have come to intoxicate myself,
I the woman.
In the flowered and precious water,
I intoxicated him,
Matlacuiyatzin goes intoxicated.
They went to the plain together.

With this the flower of precious water is bedecked,
the flower of the scorching, Matlacuiyatzin.
They went to Quenonamican together.

My facial adornment,
the band with which I tie my hair, are fine,

I Teucxoch, I the woman;
he who will hunt with reeds
dances with the people.
May our flowered magic be strengthened,
may we be intoxicated together,
oh, my nephews.

We have only arrived here now,
we have become intoxicated,
I Teucxoch, I the woman.
They who will hunt with reeds
dance with the people.
May our flowered magic be strengthened,
may we be intoxicated together,
oh, my nephews.

Where there is precious water,
it foams,
we intoxicate ourselves,
Mexicas, Chichimecas,
I remember it, and weep.

I, Nezahualpilli, weep,
I shall go to some place,
where the flower of war blooms;
I remember, and weep.

You go whirling up into the air,
like a precious bird,
my great flower, Tlacahuepantzin,
only you followed your father from Quenonamican.
In the interior of the water he sings,
speaks,
the precious flowery liquor intoxicates him;
the princes, the Huastecos,
those who are quechol birds like him, chatter
in the region of the magueys.

It makes Ixtlilcuechahuac happy,
he acquires glory with this,
he takes it from the quetzal's ruined plumes
as if the Huastecos were intoxicated.
In the center of the navel of the water

it is like a great wave of war,
it foamed.
It is the prince Ixtlilcuechahuac, Otomi parrot,
who seizes his ruined quetzal plumes
as if the Huastecos were intoxicated.

The water, the mountain, the city,
the hill of the hummingbird,
is painted with the color of jades.
You are the feather of the quetzal of precious palm,
You are the kind One God, God, my God, Jesus Christ.[5]

You shall never lose your fame,
you, Axayacatl.
The *tlauhquechol,* the *zacuan* bird,
spreads his wings in Xochintlapallan,
oh princes, you my nephews.

My nephews Huitzilihuitl, Mahuilmalinalli,
work with obsidian death.
They shall go away from the flowered water of the hummingbird,
it is boiling in Mexico, here,
with it comes intoxication.

Perhaps you have come to know
the valiant lord Ahuitzotl in his house.
He delivers his jade necklace,
wide as a quetzal feather,
to the One God.

Cantares Mexicanos, fols. 65r–66v; Spanish translation, Miguel León-Portilla; English version, Sylvia and Earl Shorris.

IN THE STYLE OF TLAXCALA

FIRST DRUM

We have come here to Tenochtitlan
to give you strength,

[5]An example of the frequent Christian interpolations in these songs.

Tlaxcaltecas, Huexotzincas.
How will the Lord Xicotencatl hear Nelpiloni?
ea, have courage, ah.

Our chief, Quauhtencoztli,
comes roaring.
Xacaltencoz tells the Captain (Cortés),
and our mother, Malintzin,
that we have arrived at Acachinanco,
ea, have courage!

We should wait for the Captain's boats,
even though his standard, coming down from Tepepolli mountain,
has nearly reached him
and the Mexica commoners fall before him,
ea, have courage!

Go to the aid of our Lords.
Those who have arms of metal
destroy the city,
they destroy all that is Mexican,
ea, have courage!

You must sound your drum,
and exult with wild laughter;
do it so, Ixtlilxochitl,
dance, at the entrance of the eagle
here in Mexico,
your shield of the plumes of the cuezpal bird
whirls in Temalacatitlan,
ea, have courage!

He who is happy in war,
who longs for arms,
the warrior, oh Ixtlilxochitl,
dances, at the entrance of the eagle,
here in Mexico,
your shield of the plumes of the cuezpal bird,
whirls in Temalacatitlan,
ea, have courage!

Meanwhile, our nephews offer themselves,
the warrior Anahuacatzin,

the Otomi Lord Tehuetzquiti,
ea, have courage!

Still, for one moment,
one day,
the war blooms.
Your word, Quauhtemoc,
your beautiful golden nose ring,
gleams in the light of the dawn,
your cotton flower glistens like a quetzal plume.
On the mountain of the hummingbird
you are astonished!

Our city will remain in you,
for the people;
should you still long for it,
there will be a price,
your gilded finery of skins,
your cotton flower that glistens like a quetzal plume.
On the mountain of the hummingbird
you are astonished!

SECOND DRUM

Give your attention
to those who dance with shields,
those who have the aspect of the Otomi,
Tehuetzquiti, Tecoatzin.
Perhaps you will be there?
Let there be dancing!
Sing, my young brothers!
God willing, you will be strong on every road,
you, Cohualihuitl, you Itzpotonqui.
Perhaps you will be there?
Let there be dancing!
Sing, my young brothers!

In truth, we have left it;
listen to it, it is my song,
our city, Tenochtitlan, Mexico,
here.
In truth, I say it, I lift my voice.

We have arrived at Tlatelolco
from the four directions.
May it not happen in vain, Tlaxcaltecas!
Sing, my young brothers!

I only saw him,
I admired him there, the Lord Nanahuacatl.
With shields, with swords,
the Tlaxcaltecas came following
the men from Castile.
They left them beside the water.
We went there.
May it not have been in vain, Tlaxcaltecas!
Sing! my young brothers!

THIRD DRUM

You have sounded your golden drum
of blazing fires,
which was left by the Lords,
who rule.
While Lord Toquiztli dances,
you sing;
with him you make various people happy
so that they are with us, the Tlaxcaltecas.
Among the magueys, the Huexotzincos!

But Cuitlachihihuitl, the ruler
and Lord Tepixohuatzin,
has already appeared
here, in Mexico,
thus, the people who are with us,
the Tlaxcaltecas,
joined together among the shields
(gained fame in war).
Among the magueys, the Huexotzincos!

Lord Apopoca came here to Mexico
to perform the dance of the shield.
Thus, those who wear the folded adornments
are engarlanded here with white flowers of the shield.

With the Lord before you, Tlaxcaltecas,
among the magueys, the Huexotzincos!

Perhaps in truth he has already arrived,
he took the metal staff of the Spaniards.
Thus, those who wear the folded adornments
are engarlanded here with white flowers of the shield.
With the Lord before you, Tlaxcaltecas,
among the magueys, the Huexotzincos!

Motelchiuhtzin comes to show the shield;
it is the festival of the lords;
they are coming.
The conquistadors turn the cannon.
They say to Atoch,
let the dance begin, Tlaxcaltecas,
among the magueys, the Huexotzincos!

The wall of the eagles is destroyed,
the wall of the tigers;
it is the festival of the lords;
they are coming.
The conquistadors took the cannon.
Atoch says,
let the dance begin, Tlaxcaltecas,
among the magueys, the Huexotzincos!

FOURTH DRUM

Have courage, fight,
Tlacatecatl, Temilotzin.
The men of Castile are getting out of their boats.
The chinampancecas,
the Tenochas,
The Tlatelolcas, are besieged.

The Tlacochcalcatl Coyohuehuetzin
went to bar the way.
The Acolhua are coming out
on the great road from Tepeyacac;
the Tenocha are besieged,
the Tlatelolca are besieged.

Oh, God, your sons perish,
how great is the valor of Tenochtitlan!
The Captain of Jade is here in Mexico;
the Tenocha are besieged,
the Tlatelolca are besieged.

The thunder sounds, the cloud spreads,
the fire blackens.
They captured Cuauhtemoctzin,
the Mexican princes are scattered over the water;
The Tenocha are besieged,
the Tlatelolca are besieged.

FIFTH DRUM

Remember Tlaxcaltecas, our nephews,
how we did it in Coyonacazco.
The faces of the Mexican women were left covered in mud,
they were chosen by those who shall rule.

The heart of Aiximachoctzin,
Chimalpaquinitzin,
is never satisfied.
We did it in Coyonacazco;
the faces of the Mexican women were left covered in mud,
they were chosen by those who shall rule.

Tehuexolotzin was captured in Acachinanco;
Tlalmenetzin, Xicotencatl, and Castañeda hurry him;
so it is, so it is.

Run quickly, young brothers!
Tlalmenetzin, Xicotencatl, and Castañeda
are hurrying you, Nelpilonitzin;
so it is, so it is.

In nine days, Cuauhtemoc,
Coanacoch, Tetlepanquetzaltzin,
who were already captured,
were forced to arrive at Coyohuacan,
oh, lords.

They are apprehended,
bound with chains of precious metal,
oh, princes.
Tlacotzin encourages them,
he tells them,
become our nephews.

Lord Cuahtemoctzin says,
my nephew,
where were you captured, imprisoned?
Where do you place yourself, beside the General, Captain?
Ah, it is really doña Isabel.[6]
My nephew,
the lords are captured.

In truth the abandonment increases,
precious jewels and quetzal plumes are intermixed
in Coyohuacan,
my nephew.
Where were you captured, imprisoned?
Where do you place yourself, beside the General, Captain?
Ah, it is really doña Isabel.
My nephew,
the lords are captured.

Cantares Mexicanos, fols. 54r–55v; Spanish translation, Miguel León-Portilla; English version, Sylvia and Earl Shorris.

Song of the Elders

The "Song of the Elders" commemorates the one major defeat of the great Mexica armies, which came at the hands of the people of Michoacan.

Listen: What do the brave do?
Are they not prepared to die?
Do they not wish to offer sacrifices?

[6]Yxapeltzin (Eeshapel + tzin, the honorific), daughter of Motecuhzoma and wife of Cuauhtemoc.

When they saw that their warriors
fled before them,
the gold sparkling
and the banners of quetzal plumes shining green,
O, do not be taken prisoners!
Let it not be you, make haste!

Not those young warriors,
they want to sacrifice them,
if it should happen thus, we will cry like eagles,
we will roar like tigers,
we the old eagle warriors.
O do not be taken prisoners!
You, make haste!

Bold in war,
Axayacatl,
perhaps in my old age
will these words be said of my eagle princes?
Let it not be thus, my grandchildren,
I will have to leave you.
There will be an offering of flowers,
with these will be spared the Warrior of the South.

I am overthrown, I am scorned,
I am ashamed, I, your grandfather Axayacatl.
Do not rest, you strong,
may it not be, if you flee, you are destroyed,
with that falls the power
of your grandfather Axayacatl.

Again and again afflicted,
the Mexica exert themselves.
My grandchildren, those of the painted faces,
from the four sides they sound their drums,
the flower of the shields remains in your hands.
True Mexica, my grandchildren,
they remain in line, they hold firm,
sound their drums,
the flower of the shields remains in your hands.

On the mat of the eagles,
on the mat of the tigers,
your grandfather is exalted, Axayacatl.
Itlecatzin sounds conch shells in the combat,
while the quetzal plumage is obscured.
He does not rest with his shield,
there he begins with darts,
with them Itlecatzin wounds,
while the quetzal plumage is obscured.

We, your grandparents, still live,
our darts, our weapons are still powerful,
with them we brought glory to our people.
Indeed now there is weariness,
certainly there is fatigue.
For this I lament, I, your grandfather Axayacatl,
I remember my old friends,
Cuepanahuaz, Tecale, Xochitlahua, Yehuaticac.
Would that they come here,
each one of those lords
who made themselves known there in Chalco.
The brave ones might come to take up the bells,
the brave ones might encircle the princes.

For this I can laugh,
I, your grandfather,
at your women's weapons,
at your women's shields.
Conquerors of ancient times,
live once again!

Cantares Mexicanos, fols. 73v–74v; from León-Portilla, *Fifteen Poets of the Aztec World*, pp. 172–74.

Tezozomoctli Ascends to the Throne

They come now, only from there, all of them,
from the place of the thorny cactus,
the mesquites, from Chicomoztoc.
You reign here.

Oh, our lords!
The nobility of Colhuacan came to mingle here,
the Chichimeca from Colhuacan is entwined.

Ask for the loan of even a little more time,
you princes, from Tlacateuhtzin,
Huitzilihuitl,
the Cihuacoatl Cuauhxilotl,
and in Totomihuacan, the Tlalnahuacatl.
Ixtlilxochitl is xiuhtototl, only a bird.
When it wearies Him,
He, God,
will come to scatter your water, your mountain, your people.
Because of this Tezozomoctli weeps.

Once the mesquite,
once the thorny cactus,
were abandoned in Hueytlalpan.
This alone is His, God's word.

Where do the flowers go?
Where do they go, those who are called eagle, tiger?
The water, the mountain, the people
are scattered, divided in Hueytlalpan.
This alone is the word of the Giver of Life.

There was happiness, there was satisfaction
for the princes of the world;
where the word of the Giver of Life
is known, it rules.
It is good that they, the jades, the bracelets,
the beautiful ones, come to see,
to know His, God's, heart;
in the place where the feathers, the chalk are plentiful—
only flowers came to know war.

Now the rabbit, the lord of the house of the dead,
the lord of Ahcolmiztlan;
here alone in the night lies our honorable Grandmother,
she Cuetzpaltzin;
the white coyote in Totomihuacan, Tlaxcala,
the Lord Coatzin, Tlalotzin—
only flowers came to know war.

What are you planning,
Lords of Huexotzinco?
Think of Acolihuacan
whose leader was attacked
over there in Huexotlan, Ytztapallocan.
Darkness falls
over the water, the mountain, the city.

Over there the ceiba, the cypress;
over there the mesquite rises,
the cave blazes.
The Giver of Life knows of this.

Tlacateotl, our Chichimeca prince,
why does Tezozomoctliu seem to hate us,
to wish us dead?
Perhaps he wants a war, a confrontation;
did he know Acolihuacan?

Although he suffers, it pleases you, Giver of Life
to the Culhuacan, to the Mexica, to the Tlacateotl.
Perhaps you desire the war, the confrontation,
which you spread to Acolhuacan?

There is only joy on earth.
The shields, the flowers are not sent twice;
the Giver of Life is not satisfied twice;
so it gladdens,
it gladdens the Tlailotlaqui, Xayacamach.

Which of you desires the flowers,
the flowers of night,
the flowers of war?
With this you are adorned,
you princes, Quetzalmamatzin, Huitznahuacatl.

Those who fight
live there, upon the wall of shields.
The dove has come; it sings
to those who live there,
the noble Xiuhtzin and Xayacamach.
You give happiness to the Giver of Life.

Let there be dancing,
make offerings close to the battlefield;
take satisfaction in the place where
the prince became a man.

Adorned with quetzal plumes,
they go now to give happiness to the Giver of Life,
there in Ixtlahuaca, in Tepalcayocan.

Now it falls upon our house;
the Huexotzinco shouts;
the white coyote is in Totomihuacan.

You rise up without joy;
you, Tlaxcalteca, fall upon us here.
You shoot arrows at the city of Huexotzinco.

It will be abandoned,
the land of Totomihuacan will be destroyed.
It will appease your heart,
you princes of Huexotzinco.

In the mesquite,
among the thorned cactus,
where the cypress stands;
be compassionate, Giver of Life,
where all is courage, in Huexotzinco,
only there where the land stretches out.

There is only destruction everywhere,
scattering,
your subject cannot find rest anywhere;
he has come to listen to your song, One God;
invent it, you princes.

It only undermines His word,
you shame the Giver of Life, my princes,
in Tepeyacac.
Where are you really going?
Say it, you Tlaxcaltecans!
Tacomihuatzin has gone
to God's war.

You lined up the Chichimecas
like a necklace of quetzal plumes,
to the Totomihuaques, to the Itzaccoyotl.

The Lord Quiauhtzin is in Huexotzinco.
The Mexicans abhor us, the Acolhuas abhor us.
How, in truth, are we going,
will we go to Quenonamican?

You imagined it, you told it to your fathers,
you lords, Ayocuatzin, Tlepetztic,
and perhaps also Tzihuacpopoca.

He alone was in Chalco,
the one from Acolihuacan, the one from Totomihuacan;
in Amilpan, in Quauhquechollan,
he destroys the mat, the seat of God.

On the earth, the mountain, he is the destroyer;
the world is in torment.
In truth, what will they do?
The water smokes, the staff of the Lord on earth is transformed.
Lord Cacamatl knows the region of the dead already;
in truth what will they do?

Cantares Mexicanos, fols. 7v–9r; Spanish translation, Miguel León-Portilla; English version, Sylvia and Earl Shorris.

In the beginning of the poem below, tone and rhythm are indicated by the first three non-lexical words. One might compare it to such markings as allegro assai *on a Western musical score.*

Song to the Sound of the Drum

Titoco, titoco, titocoti

The earth trembles.
The Mexican begins to sing;
he makes the eagles, the tigers dance.

Come, see the Huexotzincan;
on his eagle mat the Mexican gives voice,
as you say.

You are going to Chiquiuhtepetl;
the clay flowers are set before the Cuauhtepetl,
a cloud of shields begins to spread.

Where the tiny bells resound
the Mexican, Chichimeca, causes the others to die,
a cloud of shields begins to spread.

The tiny bells are raised. Eagles, tigers,
watch from behind their cypress shields.
Flags of quetzal plumes are unfurled
above him, the Mexican who fights.

Look in my direction, at me, the Mexican!
I stand tall in the house of the shields, here I am!
Not one of those close to us
will be my friend.
Where do you live?
What is your Word?
In the divine water, in the scorching, I was born,
alone, I the Mexican.

In Acolihuacan, Nezahualcoyotl,
your divine water foams,
your scorching whirls,
making smoke at the edge of the water.
Titoco, titoco, titocoti.

I, bird of the precious flowered water,
offering the abundance of the fiesta,
am a song.
My heart lives in the sky, in Anahuac;
on the lips of men,
I scatter my flowers.
The princes are intoxicated with them,
they are bedecked with flowers.

I am saddened,
my heart only suffers, I am a singer.

At the edge of the nine waters,
on the flowered earth, you, my friends,
should prepare the shroud.

I the singer make a necklace of beads of jade,
it is my reward.
The jades gleam.
I lift my voice in song,
it intoxicates my heart.
On earth one wears a shroud of flowers.

I sing only with sadness on earth, I the singer,
my sadness emerges from within.
The song intoxicates my heart.
On the flowered earth it is enshrouded.

The Toltec way shall remain in painted books;
I the singer,
my song shall live on earth;
I shall be remembered with songs,
you will remain strangers to me,
I shall go, I shall lose myself,
I shall lie down on the mat of precious feathers.
My mothers will weep,
the tears will fall—
I carry the flowers of the heart of an Otomi
on the shore of the yellow sea.

I suffer,
I am taken to Tlapallan,
where the smoke is rising. I shall go there,
I shall go, I shall go to lose myself,
I shall lie down on the mat of precious feathers.

Cantares Mexicanos, fols. Xr–Xv; Spanish translation, Miguel León-Portilla; English version, Sylvia and Earl Shorris.

4. Otomi Songs in Nahuatl

These were old songs from the Otomi (Ñahñu) that were translated into Nahuatl. The Otomi lived in close proximity to the Mexica, who dominated them. Otomi also indicated a rank among Mexica warriors, suggesting that the Otomi were well respected in war by the Mexica.

Spring Song

A song of exhortation for those who do not earn respect in war.

I, the skillful singer,
    sound my drum,
    thus I awaken, I arouse my friends:
    "Your heart knows nothing,
    there is no light in your heart."
    They sleep through war.
    The darkness of night comes over them.
    I do not speak in vain—they suffer privation,
    they must come to hear the songs of the flowery dawn[7]
    that are scattered but once in the region of the drums.

The flowers of the dawn come forth
    in the place of your flowery war,
    of the Lord of the Close and the Near.
    There are resplendent showers, bringing joy.
    Look upon them with pleasure.
    Is nothing said of them?
    Do they come forth in vain?
    No one, not one desires them?
    Oh, friends, let the flowers not be in vain,
    the flowers of the red liquor of life.[8]

Intoxicate with all your force that which gives us life,
    only in the far place does it endure, only over there does it burst
        forth,
    on the mountain where eagles perch,

---

[7]The reference is to the flowery wars, which they used to get captives.

[8]In all of this verse, speaking of flowers alludes to enemy warriors, the vessels of blood, the red liquor of life.

on the distant rim, in the center of the plain,
on the battlefield—the water, the scorching.[9]
In that other place where the clouds, the divine eagle form,
where the tiger roars,
where the varied stones of precious bracelets are scattered,
where all the good fortune of fine plumes is torn,
is destroyed;
in that place the lords are broken into smithereens.

The princes greatly desire the flowers of dawn.
It is instilled in the people,
he makes them yearn for it,
the one who is in the sky,
whom we know as 1-Movement,[10]
the prince who takes his ease among the gods,
the eagle, the tiger.
He teaches the budding of the flowers,
he intoxicates them with a gentle rain of the heart's flowers.

So you feel, my friend,
in vain you desire flowers on earth.
How are you going to take them?
How will you do it?
You are poor;
consider the lords.
With flowers, with songs, come to see.
Is there no way to launch the arrows?
All of them who are princes,
the *zacuan* birds, the *teoquecholtin,*
the *tzinitzcan,* the *tlatlauhquecholtin,*[11]
those that go adorning themselves,
those that know the center of the plain.

With the flowers of the shield,
with flowers that are the scatterings of eagles,
with manly calm, the princes hold their ground,

---

[9]The *difrasismo teoatl-tlachinolli* is ordinarily translated as "divine water-fire," an expression denoting war. We prefer to translate *tlachinolli* as "scorching."

[10]1-Movement (*Ce-Olitzin*) was one of the date names of Tezcatlipoca. Here it relates to Huitzilopochtli, who is also the Sun that shines in the sky.

[11]We have kept the names of these birds in Nahuatl.

with garlands of torch pine flowers they are adorned.[12]
Ennobled by the beautiful songs, the beautiful flowers;
they are the price of the blood of your bosom;
receive the war, the divine water, the scorchings.
Oh friends, in Tliliuquitepec,
we make the war, in Hueyotlipan.[13]
Proffer your shield,
stand tall, eagle, tiger!

Cantares Mexicanos, fols. 6r–6v; Spanish translation, Miguel León-Portilla; English version, Sylvia and Earl Shorris.

A Sad Otomi Song

In sadness I call upon You,
Lord of the Close and the Near,
my very breath I offer before You.
I suffer on this earth.
Neither joy nor wealth have I ever known.
Perhaps I have come in vain to do something on earth,
because this is not a place where anything can be done.
Surely, nothing flowers, nothing springs forth here,
but affliction.
Because in truth one can only be in peace,
close to You, at your side.
God willing, it will be Him,
God willing, You should wish it so:
That at your side, my soul shall be in peace.
My tears shall dry up beside You, close to You,
Giver of Life.

So those who thirst for something,
who came to receive honor on this earth,
who value no one,
who live without understanding,
who do not heed You, Giver of Life;
in truth, they deceive only themselves.
Thus, they think they shall live on earth forever.

[12]In this group of metaphors, those warriors who go in pursuit of the flowers of war have themselves been taken captive.

[13]The allusion here is to the war begun by the Mexicas in Tliliuquitepec and in Hueyohtlipan, two towns located in the present state of Puebla.

They irritate me,
they drank narcotic herbs;
there they are, I see them:
really, mixitl, tlapatl.[14]
That is why I strive, I suffer.
Surely, they will be seen
in the place of the fleshless.
It matters not who we are,
our hearts will be content.

Let no one upset your heart here on earth,
for we are already suffering, weeping here,
because in truth it will soon be over.
In truth, we only exercise power
as the princes command.
Let this be an example to you, my friend,
you who do not enjoy life,
who are not happy on earth,
who adorn yourself that way.
The flowers of sadness,
the flowers of weeping,
are ruined.
The beautiful sighs
will be offered in sacrifice
to the Lord of the Close and the Near.

I have already adorned myself with the necklace
of the flowers of sadness,
the flowers of the shield of sighs;
it is in my hands
I lift my voice in sad song.
I offer the beautiful song as if it were a jade necklace;
I enclose my jade drum in a sprinkling of flowers,
in the nearness of the sky I sustain my song.
I the singer take it from them, the residents of the sky,
the zacuan tototl, the quetzal bird, the tzinitzcan,
the teoquechol, the trilling quechol,
those who bring joy to the Lord of the Close and the Near.

Cantares Mexicanos, fols. 4v–5r; Spanish translation, Miguel León-Portilla; English version,
Sylvia and Earl Shorris

[14]See Glossary.

Another Sad Song of the Otomi

With tears of melancholy flowers,
I, the singer, prepare my song.
I recall the princes,
the shattered princes,
who were lords,
who exercised their power on earth,
the princes, crushed like quetzal plumes,
broken like pieces of jade,
forced now to labor
in the beyond, where no flesh remains.
Let us hope that it was before their eyes,
let us hope that they were able to have seen,
as it is seen on earth,
the knowledge of the Lord of the Close and the Near.

I sing my sadness,
remembering the lords;
if only they could return, if I could take them,
if I could deliver them from there, from the place of the fleshless.
If only one could live twice on earth,
then they would admire the princes
whom we admired.
Perhaps they would be astonished by love
of the Giver of Life?
Is it possible that this will be our reward?
If only we were able to know it, we the ungrateful.
For this my heart weeps,
I put my memories in order, I the singer.
With tears, with anguish, I remember it.

If only they had heard me,
if I had sung some beautiful song to them,
there in the region of the fleshless;
if only I were still able to give them happiness,
if only I could still give them courage,
in their torment, in their affliction.

Perhaps it should be known?
How must I try?
Shall I never follow them over there?
Shall I never speak to them as I did on earth?

Cantares Mexicanos, fol. 4v; Spanish translation, Miguel León-Portilla; English version, Sylvia and Earl Shorris.

5. Attributed Songs

Although most Nahua compositions are anonymous, some extant manuscripts contain indications that they may be attributed to specific authors. It is fortunate that we can link some ancient Nahua poems with the faces and hearts of their authors, thus proving that in pre-Hispanic Mesoamerica, not everything has to be considered anonymous. Indeed, among the Maya as well, the paintings and glyphic texts of a good number of vases of the late Classic period frequently include an inscription that gives the author's name.

Brief biographies of some Nahua nobles who may have been the true composers of works attributed to them are included here to give background to the works and the circumstances under which they may well have been composed.

Nezahualcoyotl

If any figure of the brief and brilliant florescence of those people we know as the Aztecs merits a major biography, it must be the poet ruler of Tezcoco, Nezahualcoyotl. Born in 1402 into the mixture of Chichimeca (northern) and Toltec (craftsman) culture, he enjoyed the early life of a prince, raised with the attentions of tutors and nobles. At the age of sixteen he saw his father murdered shortly before the conquest of Tezcoco by the Tecpanecs of Azcapotzalco.

Young Nezahualcoyotl survived the defeat, but went into exile, where he lived among the Huexotzincans and Tlaxcalans, studying with the tla-matini (those who know something—wise men) while he established alliances with powerful rulers of those city-states and with the Mexica, who were relatives on his mother's side. In 1430, he and his allies defeated the Tecpanecs at Tezcoco, and soon thereafter took Azcapotzalco. Neza-

hualcoyotl, the warrior tutored by wise men, consolidated his power in Tezcoco.

Once installed again on the throne, where he was to remain until his death nearly forty years later, he embarked upon a dualistic career as philosopher/poet and ruthless warrior/king. This career could be seen as the result of the admixture of Chichimeca warrior and Toltec sage, or perhaps as a replaying of the conflict between the wizard Tezcatlipoca and Quetzalcoatl, the monk of Tula, that lies at the core of the divided soul of the Aztec.

In arranging the death of his loyal follower, Cuacuauhtzin, the ruler of Tezcoco displayed a character trait that compares with the Aztecs' slaughtering and devouring of the daughter of their hosts in the Valley of Mexico. He sent Cuacuauhtzin to certain death in battle so that he could marry his loyal friend's wife. A tragic aspect of the plot came about when Cuacuauhtzin learned of Nezahualcoyotl's treachery, yet ever loyal to his ruler, friend, and fellow poet, Cuacuauhtzin still went into battle, and was killed. His widow was to become the queen of Tezcoco and the mother of Nezahualpilli, the poet and Nezahualcoyotl's successor.

Given his treachery, the terrible experiences of his youth, and his participation in the many wars of the Mexica, one might expect a reign like that of Shakespeare's villainous Richard III. But Nezahualcoyotl presided over decades of great art, architecture, poetry, and philosophy in what may have been a kind of golden age in the Valley of Mexico. Under Nezahualcoyotl, a great temple was built, but unlike any other in the Valley, it was said by Fernando de Alva Ixtlilxóchitl (c. 1578–1650) to have contained no images of gods.

All of this is reflected in Nezahualcoyotl's poetry. He does not deny war and glories, but neither does he accept the state religion. The Toltec aspect of his character, which led him to build a gathering place for artists and intellectuals and to design such projects as an aqueduct to bring fresh water to Tenochtitlan, predominates in his poetry. Neza- hualcoyotl concentrates on a non-anthropomorphic deity, speaking of the Close and the Near, the One Who Created Himself, an unseen yet om- nipresent deity. Is this a step toward monotheism? The reader will have to make that judgment based on the work.

There can be little doubt, however, that Nezahualcoyotl had begun to ask the same questions that dominated the thinking of the pre- Socratics. Perhaps it was because he built botanical and zoological gar- dens and spent time with the astronomers who played such an important role in Mesoamerican culture that he looked upon the natural world with the sense of wonder that is said to be the beginning of philosophy. In his poems, he asks the great questions that have occupied philosophers in every culture. Where does one come from? Where does one go after death? Is there a life after death? And how should a person act while here on earth?

Nezahualcoyotl looked beyond war and pleasure to seek some ultimate meaning for existence. Was it to be found, he asked, in a deity, nature, or in the potential of man and his ability to create beauty here on earth? Readers of twentieth-century philosophy will find in the work of Nezahualcoyotl and other Nahua poets many of the issues that preoccupied the existentialists. But such comparisons are perhaps not useful except as a means for the modern reader in attempting to approach the works, for Nezahualcoyotl, like all the Nahuas, was himself deeply conflicted.

Axayacatl

Unlike Nezahualcoyotl, who was most probably the author of works attributed to him, Axayacatl may not have been the sole author of the works connected to his name. In the poem given below (p. 152), as in the earlier "Song of the Elders," the young man who ruled Tenochtitlan as huey tlahtoani concerns himself with the vagaries of history and war.

The youngest of three sons of Tezozomoctzin, a noble who never took the throne in Tenochtitlan, Axayacatl was apparently the favorite of the great gray eminence of the Tenochas, Tlacaelel, who chose him for what he believed would be the young prince's courage and daring in war. Born in the middle of the fifteenth century, Axayacatl was dead, despairing after a great defeat, by 1480. He was probably no more than twenty years old when he ascended to the throne.

Axayactl fought several great wars and was responsible among other things for the carving of the great Sun Stone, often called the Aztec Calendar Stone. One of the wars, against Tlatelolco, had an almost comic origin. Axayacatl's sister was married to the huey tlahtoani of Tlatelolco, but it was said she had such bad breath that no one, including her husband, could bear to go near her. Her husband preferred the company of concubines, which was understood as an insult to the Tenochas and led to further insulting behavior in return. This eventually culminated in the war in which Axayacatl defeated Tlatelolco and united the two neighboring city-states.

Another war fought by Axayacatl pitted the Tenochas against the Purepecha of Michoacan. Spurred on by his mentor, Tlacaelel, who was interested in taking captives for sacrifice and extending the hegemony of the Mexica, the young ruler led an army of 24,000 into Michoacan, only to be met, defeated, and nearly obliterated by a Purepecha army of

40,000. The "Song of the Elders" (p. 126), which was composed with the help of an older poet, describes this one great defeat of the People of the Sun prior to the Spanish invasion.

Nezahualpilli

The son of Nezahualcoyotl had a passion for the draconian form of justice in sexual matters practiced by the Nahuas. Having found out that a beautiful young woman who had seduced him was married, he sentenced her to death for her infidelity. When her husband complained, Nezahualpilli sent him to prison. Whether the case of the "Lady of Tula" resulted from his puritanical streak or jealousy is open to debate. The facts in the case, if the stories can be described as such, are these:

It began as a passion for wit and a love of poetry. Nezahualpilli fell in love with the brilliant daughter of a merchant and took her as his concubine. She composed poetry, and spoke of philosophical issues with the tlahtoani and his advisers, very much as Pericles of Athens enjoyed the love and talents of his mistress. Nezahualpilli's eldest son, Huexotzincatzin, who was also a poet, wrote a satire, which he addressed to the Lady of Tula. As the tlahtoani's son and concubine spent more and more time together, there were rumors that the relationship was more than a friendship of poets. Nezahualpilli deemed it an act of treason, and applied the law. Although he is said to have wept over his decision, he ordered his own son to be hanged.

Nezahualpilli's life also came to an unhappy end, for the Tezcocan noble, who had supported Motecuhzoma Xocoyotzin and made a famous speech after his election as huey tlahtoani of Tenochtitlan, was the victim of palace intrigues at the end of the Aztec ascendancy. He died at fifty-one years old, having reigned since he was a child. Within a few years of his death the Spaniards would arrive in the Valley of Mexico.

As a poet, Nezahualpilli leaves behind one major work said to have been his own. "Song of Nezahualpilli" (p. 153) could well be described as an anti-war poem, a rare sentiment among the Nahuas. The flowery liquor, the blood of the conquered, which excites the Mexica, does not satisfy him; although he is a warrior, he mourns and bemoans the losses in war. Nezahualpilli suffered the same curious mix of attitudes that preoccupied his father. He, too, appears to have believed in something very like a non-anthropomorphic deity, and yet, like his father, he gave outward obeisance to the grand pantheon. He had some concerns about the less fortunate among his people, and may actually have spoken about the need to care for widows and orphans. From the time he was born *until long after his death, it was rumored that Nezahualpilli was an extraordinary creature with special powers, able to change into an eagle or a jaguar and to live on after his death in some distant cave.*

Cacamatzin

The poem on p. 158, probably by Cacamatzin, the last tlahtoani *of Tezcoco—who was tortured and possibly stabbed to death or hanged by Pedro de Alvarado, at the age of twenty-six—may be thought of as a kind of keening over the end of the pre-Columbian world. However one interprets the work, it is surely elegiac, for it goes back through the famed ancestors of Cacamatzin, and then contemplates the possibilities of life after death. But its great sadness only has full meaning in light of the brief and terrible life of the grandson of Nezahualcoyotl, illegitimate son of Nezahualpilli, brother of Ixtlilxochitl, and most importantly nephew of Motecuhzoma Xocoyotzin.*

Cacamatzin was born in 1494 and took the throne in 1515. But his ascendance was not without complication. His brother, Prince Ixtlilxochitl, revolted against the choice, assembling sufficient support to divide Tezcoco into two warring camps, and sending the city-state into economic and military decline. Shortly after the split between the brothers, news arrived from the Gulf Coast of the landing of strange men in ships as large as mountains. As the strange men marched inland, mounted on beasts larger than deer and bringing with them tubes that made the sound of thunder and spit fire, the question of what do to with them was debated in Tenochtitlan: war or welcome?

Following news of the Spanish alliance with Tlaxcala, Motecuhzoma sent his nephew, Cacamatzin, to meet with the Spaniards and dissuade them from coming into the Valley of Mexico. The Spaniards noted the grandeur of Cacamatzin and his retinue, and moved on Tenochtitlan. By 1520, all three leaders of the Triple Alliance of Tenochtitlan, Tlacopan, and Tezcoco were prisoners of Cortés; but when the captain left the city to put down his Spanish rivals, he put Pedro de Alvarado in charge, and the character of the occupation changed. In his mad quest for treasure, Alvarado turned to the use of torture. One of his victims was Cacamatzin, who was bound hand and foot and seared with burning charcoal, then lowered into a bath of boiling pine resin. Cacamatzin, near death, gave up everything—all the gold, all the treasure.

He survived the torture only to witness the treachery of the Spaniards during the feast of Toxcatl (see Book I, section 4). While the unarmed Mexica sang and danced, the Spaniards entered the main temple and slaughtered them. Motecuhzoma was murdered a few days later. The exact time and manner of Cacamatzin's death cannot be known for certain. The Spaniards wrote that he died in battle during the Spanish flight from Tenochtitlan, but the Nahua historians said he was hanged or stabbed forty-seven times before the Spaniards escaped.

If the song below was indeed left behind by Cacamatzin, it must have been committed to memory by the friends to whom it is addressed during the last days or hours of his life. No matter who spoke the words or how the poem comes down to us, it survives as testament to the philosophical turn of mind with which Mexica nobles faced death and the end of empire.

Cuacuauhtzin

Cuacuauhtzin, who knew of Nezahualcoyotl's plot to kill him, wrote a poem about his impending death. In his "Sad Song" (p. 160), he addresses Nezahualcoyotl directly, speaking of him by his nickname, Yoyontzin, which translates as "Panting One," referring perhaps to the tlahtoani's many affairs.

Macuilxochitzin

Tlacaelel, eminence grise of Tenochtitlan, fathered thirteen children, each by a different woman. His seventh child, Macuilxochitzin, probably born on the day 5-Flower, from which she may have gotten her name, was one of the few Nahua women poets whose names we know, the "Lady of Tula" being another. From stories told about Macuilxochitin by the chroniclers and the details of the last great war planned by Tlacaelel that appear in the poem generally attributed to her, she may have been her father's favorite.

In 1476, the Mexica, under the leadership of Axayacatl, went to war against the Matlatzinca and the Otomi in the Valley of Toluca. Tlacaelel saw the war as one of the final conquests in his plan to establish Mexica hegemony throughout Mesoamerica. He had already seen Mexica troops conquer Cuitlahuac, Mizquic, Xochimilco, Culhuacan, Chalco, and other chiefdoms, extending as far east as the Gulf Coast, where the Huastecas and Totonacs sent tribute to the Valley of Mexico. Tlacaelel's parting words to Axayacatl were to destroy the enemy, making them vassals of the Mexica. He advised against leniency.

During the battle, Axayacatl ran ahead of his troops and was wounded in the thigh by the Otomi captain, Cuetzpal (or Tlilatl). He would have died then and there had not the Mexica forces arrived in time to save him. Cuetzpal was captured, and would have been sacrificed or hanged, but the passionate pleadings of the Otomi women convinced the Mexica to spare him. The "Song of Macuilxochitl" (p. 156) tells the whole story in a poem clearly intended to be performed with accompanying music and dance. "Let the dance begin!" She tells her audience: "Ohuaya! Ohuaya!"

Aquiauhtzin

His "Song of the Women of Chalco" (p. 102), included in the "Bawdy Poems" section, is indeed an erotic poem, a deliberate sexual provocation. The kingdom of Chalco, home of Aquiauhtzin, had been defeated by the Mexica ruler, Axayacatl, and Aquiauhtzin composed the poem to be delivered as a challenge in the presence of the victorious king. Axayacatl had defeated the Chalcans in the field, but the warrior women dare him to conquer them by making love.

Songs of Nezahualcoyotl

THOUGH IT BE JADE

I, Nezahualcoyotl, ask this:
   Do we truly live on earth?
   Not forever here,
   only a little while.
   Even jade breaks,
   golden things fall apart,
   precious feathers fade;
   not forever on earth,
   only a moment here.

Cantares Mexicanos, fol. 17r; Spanish translation, Miguel León-Portilla; English version, Sylvia and Earl Shorris.

WE ARE MORTAL

I comprehend the secret, the hidden:
O my lords!
Thus we are,
we are mortal,
humans through and through,
we all will have to go away,
we all will have to die on earth . . .
Like a painting
we will be erased.
Like a flower,
we will dry up
here on earth.
Like plumed vestments of the precious bird,
that precious bird with the agile neck,
we will come to an end . . .
think on this, o lords,
eagles and tigers,
though you be of jade,
though you be of gold,
you also will go there,
to the place of the fleshless.
We will have to disappear,
no one can remain.

Romances de los Señores de Nueva España, fols. 35r–36r; from León-Portilla, *Fifteen Poets of the Aztec World*, p. 80.

I SHALL NEVER DISAPPEAR

I Shall Never Disappear.
I am intoxicated,
I weep, I grieve,
I think, I speak,
within myself I discover this:
I shall never die,
never disappear.

Let me go to the place
where there is no death,
where death is overcome:
I shall never disappear.

Cantares Mexicanos, fol. 70r; Spanish translation, Miguel León-Portilla; English version, Sylvia and Earl Shorris.

IN YOUR BOOK OF PAINTINGS

O Giver of Life,
who paints with flowers,
who bestows color with songs,
who gives form to all those
who dwell on earth;
in time you will destroy
the eagles, the tigers:
We live here only
in your book of paintings.

You will blot out,
with black ink,
all that was friendship,
brotherhood, nobility.

You give form to all those
who live on earth.
We live here only
in your book of paintings.

Romances de los Señores de Nueva España, fol. 35r; from León-Portilla, *Fifteen Poets of the Aztec World,* p. 83.

SONG OF THE FLIGHT

Live peacefully,
pass life calmly!
I am bent over,
I live with my head bowed
beside the people.
For this I am weeping,

I am wretched!
I have remained alone
beside the people on earth.
How has Your heart decided,
Giver of Life?
Dismiss Your displeasure!
Extend Your compassion,
I am at Your side, You are God.
Perhaps You would bring death to me?

Is it true that we are happy,
that we live on the earth?
It is not certain that we live
and have come on earth to be happy.
We are all sorely lacking.
Is there anyone who does not suffer
here, beside the people?

Would that my heart be not afflicted.
Do not relfect any more,
truly, I scarcely
pity myself here on earth.

Miguel León-Portilla, *Fifteen Poets of the Aztec World*, pp. 90–91.

MY FRIENDS, STAND UP!

My friends, stand up!
The princes have become destitute,
I am Nezahualcoyotl,
I am a singer,
head of macaw.
Grasp your flowers and your fan.
With them go out to dance!
You are my child,
you are Yoyontzin.
Take your chocolate,
flower of the cacao tree,
may you drink all of it!
Do the dance,
do the song!

Not here is our house,
we do not live here,
you also will have to go away.

Romances de los Señores de la Nueva España, fols. 3v–4r; from Miguel León-Portilla, *Fifteen Poets of the Aztec World,* p. 92.

I AM SAD

I am sad, I grieve
I, lord Nezahualcoyotl.
With flowers and with songs
I remember the princes,
those who went away,
Tezozomoctzin, and that one Cuacuauhtzin.
Truly they live,
there Where-in-Someway-One-Exists?
O, that I might follow the princes,
take them, our flowers!
If I could but make mine
the beautiful songs of Tezozomoctzin!
Never will your name perish,
O my lord, you, Tezozomoctzin!
Thus longing for your songs,
I am grieving,
alone I have come to remain saddened,
I withdraw from myself.

I have become saddened,
I grieve.
No longer you are here, no longer,
but in the region Where-in-Some-Way-One-Exists.
You have left us without sustenance on the earth,
for this I withdraw from myself.

Cantares Mexicanos, fols. 25r and v; from León-Portilla, *Fifteen Poets of the Aztec World,* pp. 93–94.

SONG OF SPRINGTIME

In the house of paintings
the singing begins,

song is practiced,
flowers are spread,
the song rejoices.

The song resounds,
little bells are heard,
to these answer
our flowery timbrels.
Flowers are spread,
the song rejoices.

Above the flowers is singing
the radiant pheasant;
his song unfolds
into the midst of the waters.
To him reply
all manner of red birds,
the dazzling red bird
beautifully sings.

Romances de los Señores de la Nueva España, fols. 38v–39r; from Miguel León-Portilla, *Fifteen Poets of the Aztec World*, p. 95.

I AM WEALTHY[15]

I am wealthy,
I, prince Nezahualcoyotl.
I join together the necklace,
the large quetzal plumage;
from experience I recognize the jade,
they are the princes, O friends!
I look into their faces,
eagles and tigers on all sides;
from experience I recognize the jade
the precious bracelets . . .

Cantares Mexicanos, fol. 16v; from León-Portilla, *Fifteen Poets of the Aztec World*, p. 96.

[15]In Nahuatl, *nonnocuiltonohua,* meaning "I have something in abundance," referring here to friends.

HE ALONE

He alone,
the Giver of Life.
Empty wisdom had I.
Perhaps no one?
Perhaps no one?
I was not content at the side of the people.

Precious things you have poured down,
from you comes joy,
Giver of Life!
Sweet-smelling flowers, precious flowers,
with eagerness have I longed for them,
empty wisdom had I.

Romances de los Señores de la Nueva España, fols. 38v–39r; from Miguel León-Portilla, *Fifteen Poets of the Aztec World,* p. 97.

Song of Axayacatl

You are celebrated,
you expressed divine words,
but you died.
He who has compassion for men makes wry faces.
You have made it this way.
Perhaps no man has spoken thus?
He who perseveres becomes weary.
The Giver of Life will not invent anyone once more.
Day of weeping, day of tears!
Your heart is sad.
Will the lords have to come a second time?
Alone I remember Itzcoatl,
for him sadness enters my heart.
Was He weary then,
perhaps fatigue overcame the Master of the House,
the Giver of Life?
He makes no one durable on the earth.
Where will we have to go?
For this, sadness enters my heart.

Cantares Mexicanos, fols. 29v–30r; from León-Portilla, *Fifteen Poets of the Aztec World,* pp. 168–69.

Song of Nezahualpilli During the War with Huexotzinco

I am intoxicated,
intoxicated is my heart:
Day is dawning,
already the zacuan bird is singing
above the inclosure of shields,
above the inclosure of darts.

Be merry, you, Tlacahuepan,
you, our neighbor, of shaven head,
like a Cuexteca with shaven head.
Drunk with the liquor of flowery waters,
there at the edge of the water of the birds,
shaven head.

The jade and plumes of quetzal
with stones have been torn down,
my great lords, those intoxicated with death,
there on the ground planted in water,
at the edge of the water,
the Mexica in the land of the cactus.

The eagle screams,
the jaguar howls,
and you, o my prince, Macuilmalinalli,
here, in the region of smoke,
in the land of red color.
Bravely the Mexica are fighting.

I am intoxicated, I, Cuexteca,
I of the flowery shaven hair,
again and again I drink the flowering liquor.
Let them pass the precious flowery nectar.
O my son,
you, young man and strong,
I grow pale.

Where the divine waters spread out,
there they are inflamed with passion,
the Mexica intoxicated
with the flowery liquor of the gods.

I remember now the Chichimec,
only for this am I saddened,
For this I moan, I Nezahualpilli,
now I remember him.
Alone he is there,
where the flowers of war open their corollas,
I remember him and for this now I weep.

Above the bells, Chailtzin
within the waters rejoices.
with this Ixtlilcuechahuac achieves renown,
takes possession of the quetzal plumage,
the Cuexteca takes the turquoises.
Before the face of the water, within the battle,
under the spell of water and fire,
Ixtlilotoncochotzin rises up in fury,
with this he achieves renown,
he takes possession of the quetzal plumage,
he takes the turquoises.
The bird of the fine plumage is flying,
Tlacahuepatzin, my possessor of flowers;
like rabbits he pursues them, the strong youth,
the Cuexteca in the land of the cactus.

Within the waters they sing,
the divine flowers call out.
They are intoxicated, they shout,
the princes who look like precious birds,
the Cuextecas in the land of the cactus.
Our fathers are intoxicated,
the intoxication of strength.
Begin the dance!
To his house have gone those with the spoiled flowers,
those who had the plumed shields,
those who guarded the heights,
those who took prisoners alive,
now they dance.
Vomiting blood they go
the owners of the spoiled flowers,
those of the flowery shields.

Stained with blood my prince goes,
our yellow lord of the Cuexteca,

the one of the dark-zapote skirt,
Tlacahuepan is exalted
Where-One-Somehow-Exists.

With the flower of the liquor of war
my prince has become intoxicated,
our yellow lord of the Cuexteca.
Matlaccuiatzin is bathed with the liquor of war,
together they go to Where-One-Somehow-Exists.

With divine water, the one of painted torso,
my great, my prince, who as Nezahualpilli behaves,
there the Cuexteca are intoxicated
with the shield's flowery liquor,
a dance is performed in Atlixco.

Make resound
your trumpet of the tigers,
the eagle screams,
upon the circular stone
where the gladiatorial fight takes place.
The old men are leaving,
there the Cuexteca are intoxicated
with the shield's flowery liquor,
a dance is performed in Atlixco.

Make resound your turquoise drum,
inebriated cactus, with flowery water.
Your necklace of flowers,
your pendant of heron feathers,
you of the painted body.
Now they hear it,
the birds with flowery heads
accompany the strong youth,
the owner of the shield of the tiger, who came back.

My heart is sad,
I am young Nezahualpilli.
I look for my captains,
the lord has gone,
the flowering quetzal,
the young and strong warrior has gone,
the blue of the sky is his house.

Perhaps Tlatohuetzin and Acapipiyol will come
to drink the flowery liquor,
here where I weep?

Cantares Mexicanos, fols. 55v–56r, from Miguel León-Portilla, *Fifteen Poets of the Aztec World*, pp. 127–30.

In the poem below, which has been attributed to the daughter of Tla-caelel, the gray eminence behind the Aztec throne, one can see the character of these poems as performance. They were generally accompanied by music played on drums, flutes, conch shells, and rattles, which provided the rhythm for the dance.

Song of Macuilxochitl

I raise my songs,
I, Macuilxochitl,
with these I gladden the Giver of Life,
let the dance begin!

Are these songs carried
to His house,
there Where-in-Someway-One-Exists?
Or are your flowers
only here?
Let the dance begin!

. . .

On every side Axayacatl
made conquests,
in Matlatzinco, in Malinalco,
In Ocuillan, in Tequaloya, in Xohcotitlan.
From here he went forth.
There was Axayacatl
wounded in the leg by an Otomi,
his name was Tlilatl.

That one went in search of his women,
he said to them:
"Prepare a breechcloth and a cape,

give these to your man."
And Axayacatl called out:
"Bring the Otomi
who wounded me in the leg."
The Otomi was afraid,
he said:
"Now truly they will kill me!"
Then he brought a large piece of wood
and a deerskin,
with these he bowed before Axayacatl.
He was full of fear, the Otomi,
but then his women made supplication for him to Axayacatl.

Cantares Mexicanos, fol. 53v; Spanish translation, Miguel León-Portilla; English version, Sylvia and Earl Shorris.

Poets of Various Nations (Altepeme)

1. Texcoco

SONG BY CACAMATZIN

MY FRIENDS

My friends,
listen to this:
let no one live deluded with a pretention of royalty.
The fury, the clashes,
let them be forgotten,
disappear in due time from the earth.

Also, to me alone,
a short time ago they said,
those who were at the ball court,
they said, they murmured:
Is it possible to work mercifully?
Is it possible to act prudently?

I know only myself.
Everyone says this,
but no one speaks truly on earth.

. . .

I only say,
I Cacamatzin,
now alone I remember
Lord Nezahualpilli.
Perhaps they speak there,
he and Nezahualcoyotl,
in the place of the drums?
I remember them now.

Truly, who will not have to go there?
If he is jade, if he is gold,
perhaps he will not have to go there?

Am I perchance a shield of turquoise,
will I as a mosaic be embedded once more in existence?
Will I come again to the earth?
Will I be shrouded in fine mantles?
Still on earth, near the place of the drums,
I remember them.

Romances de los Señores de Nueva España, fols. 5v–6r; from León-Portilla, *Fifteen Poets of the Aztec World,* pp. 143–45.

SONG OF CUACUAUHTZIN

Here they are: my jade drum,
my conch of quechol green
on which I blow;
here I am and here I stand,
I, Cuacuauhtzin;
I, the singer.

Enjoy it now:
may he stand here,
the one whose heart

I have offended.
Here I am and here I stand,
I lift my voice;
I, the singer.

Open your heart,
that I may go there,
you who abhor me and wish my death;
when I am dead and gone,
then perhaps nevermore
shall you weep for me,
be sad for me.
I am going now, my friend,
I am going now.

My heart says
that I shall come no more,
but that I am going now,
I am going now;
I will not return
to be born
upon the much cherished earth.

My heart desires flowers;
I am saddened by songs,
I merely try out songs on earth,
I, Cuacuauhtzin.
I crave flowers;
may they come into my arms.
I am discontent.

Where then shall we go,
so that we shall never die?
Even if I were of jade
or of gold,
I would be pierced and melted;
(would it consume my heart?)
I grieve,
I, Cuacuauhtzin.

Do nothing without enjoyment,
enjoy every single thing, my friends;

will you be joyless,
will you be discontent, my friends?
From where shall I take
beautiful flowers,
beautiful songs?

Does it never bloom twice here?
I grieve,
I, Cuacuauhtzin.
Will you be joyless,
will you be discontent, my friends?
From whence shall I take
beautiful flowers,
beautiful songs?

Cantares Mexicanos, fols. 26r–27v; Spanish translation, Miguel León-Portilla; English version, Sylvia and Earl Shorris.

SAD SONG OF CUACUAUHTZIN

My heart craves the flowers,
that they be in my hands.
With songs I am saddened,
I only try to compose songs on the earth.
I Cuacuauhtzin,
anxiously I desire the flowers,
that they be in my hands,
for I am dispossessed.

Where would we go
that we never have to die?
Though I be precious stone,
though I be gold,
I will be dissolved,
melted down there in the crucible,
I have only my life,
I Cuacuauhtzin, I am dispossessed.

You make resound
your kettle drum of jade,
your red and blue conch shell,
you, Yoyontzin, Panting One,

Now he has come,
now the singer has risen.
For a short time be happy,
come and be present,
those with the sad heart.
Now he has come,
now the singer has risen.

Open the corolla of your heart,
let it tread the lofty heights.
You have hated me,
you have marked me for death.
Now I go to His house,
I will perish.
Perhaps because of me you will weep,
because of me you will be sad,
you, my friend,
but now I will go,
now I am going to His house.
Only this my heart tells,
I will not return,
never will come back to the earth,
now I will go, I am going to His house.

Only useless effort,
enjoy, enjoy, my friends.
Should we not be happy,
should we not have pleasure, my friends?
I will take with me the beautiful flowers,
the beautiful songs.

Never I do it in springtime,
I alone am in need,
alone am I, Cuacuauhtzin.
Should we not enjoy, my friends?
I will take with me the beautiful flowers,
the beautiful songs.

Romances de los Señores de Nueva España, fols. 26r–27v; from León-Portilla, *Fifteen Poets of the Aztec World,* pp. 109–11.

2. Chalco—Plain Song

The Nahua poet or poets who wrote this three-part plain song express various aspects of the philosophy of Mesoamerica. It begins in war and destruction as the fires burn and the arrows fall on Chalco; goes on to speak of the arts that give life its glorious moments; and ends with the notion of orphanhood or abandonment as it raises questions similar to those heard from modern existentialist thinkers.

The term "plain song" was probably added to the poem by a Nahua scholar, using a learned Spanish term, canto llano, *because these works were reminiscent of the tone of Gregorian chant.*

WAR SONG

The drum was raised,
the song spread in Chalco,
here on the plain, in Cocotitlan—
only a singer am I.

The lords dance on the eagle patio;
Motecuhzoma, Nezahualcoyotl,
Chimalpopoca, you gave us joy on the plain,
in Cocotitlan.

The flower of the One God,
lord chichimeca,
revives—
it scatters, it spreads.

This is the way they live, they are born to it,
your friends, the princes.
Ayocuantzin, White Coyote, came but for a brief moment
to bring You joy.

Is it only a provocation to the One by whom we live?
Perhaps He does not want to enjoy himself?

Giver of Life,
Your flowers are pieces of precious metal,
enhanced by the color of jade.

The turtledoves are over there, in front of Him.
There is no other place where your flowers are like this,
flowers of the shield.

Toncohuili, toncohuili, in the palaces
the flowers turn yellow,
the shields are scattered,
the butterflies spread out, sipping honey
from your eagle flowers.
Resplendent,
they divide and divide again the flowers of your shield,
and for this the lord Cuauhteotl weeps.

You stir up the flowered water, the scorching,
you are there, you, princes,
the chichimeca Amecatzin, White Coyote.
Ask the Giver of Life for the loan of His dart and His shield.
He puts the flower of the scorching, the flower of war
in your hand.
Which of you wants it?
Which of you longs for it, you princes?

Yet in peace you give joy to the Giver of Life,
in peace you give happiness to the One God.
The drum stands tall;
although the flowers are open,
you ask for the loan of the chichimeca Toteociteuhtli.

The eagle flags,
the golden shields
bring joy to Cuauhtlehuanitl.

Solemnly, he wishes to offer
your city, Chalco,
to the Giver of Life
here in Amaquemecan, his house.

Have no doubt, you Chichimeca princes,
says God on earth here, in his house,
that there is not already one down and one up.

The Giver of Life troubles us,
you princes,
He speaks over there perhaps;
perhaps Chalco is the place where they are dressed in fine cottons,
the place of the dart throwers.

Your name, your renown will never be lost
in the place of the rattles,
the place of the flower of battle,
the flower of the shield, the clay.
The feathers are strewn in Amaztlalla.
The yolloxochitl is blooming,
here, in Chalco.

Only in orphanhood
is Itztompatepec abandoned.
It never was and never will be like this.
Your heart will be troubled, it will be shamed.
Giver of Life, in your mockery,
You cause the princes to suffer.
Your servant raises a cry.

May the war not fill us with fear;
you are the flowers of the shield, you princes.
In this way alone it depicts, it names the grandmother, the grandfather.
The earth shall be offered.
Your heart will be troubled, it will be shamed.
Giver of Life, in your mockery,
You cause the princes to suffer.
Your servant raises a cry.

Weep! Meditate on it,
you, princes,
you chalcas, amaquemecas,
it is raining darts
and your shield is over my house.

How does He say it, the Giver of Life,
the One God?
The water, the mountain, Chalco, is at war.
Your subjects are scattered,
may this be the final word
of the Giver of Life,
may the One God cause no more suffering!

In the place of the rattles,
in the battle,
where the canes are broken,
here, in Chalco,
the dust yellows,
the houses smolder,
your servant weeps,
here, in Chalco.

The acts of the One God
shall never be lost, never be forgotten;
there is scattering, destruction, in Ytztonpactepec,
the dust yellows,
the houses grow damp,
your servant weeps,
here, in Chalco.

You speak in Tula,
Motecuhzoma, Nezahualcoyotl.
You destroy the earth,
you devastate Chalco, here.
May it pain your heart!

Only you can bring the day to an end on earth,
you destroy it,
you devastate Chalco, here.
May it pain your heart!

Only you can bring the day to an end,
Motecuhzoma; you color the earth
in Acolihuacan.
The Giver of Life grows weary there,
you have been taken to Chalco,
to the interior of the wooden house,
he gives you orders there,
Cuauhteotl has brought your adornments.

But you shall never lose your fame this way,
in the way you have fashioned yourself.
The precious flower, the flower that sustains us,
is scattered, spread about here.

I weep, I am saddened,
I remember the princes,
Nequametl, Totomihuatzi, Ceacatzi,
who have in truth gone to region of the dead.
They gave luster
to the city of Chalco;
its fame will never end.

You are needy, you hate me,
you send me to the region of the dead,
chichimeca, you, Ayocuan, White Coyote.
You sow pain, anguish;
may your heart understand it so, Huexotzinco!

The Giver of Life will tell him over there,
there, in Tlapitzahuacan,
in the interior of the house.
On the flowered patio
the fog lifts,
he weeps, he came to govern Chalchiuhtlatonac.

Listen to his word,
which was said by lord Chichicuepantli,
who fell in the war.
Perhaps in the region of the dead,
the breath, the word of the princes
will still resound?

They go shaking the jades,
shaking the precious feathers;
they have become fleshless in Quenonamican.

Only over there are the princes happy,
the noble Tlaltecatl, Xocuahuatzin,
Tozmaquetzin, Necuamatzin.
The Giver of Life paints but briefly.
Because you are deserving, you are there,
lord Cuateotl, Chalchiuhtlatonac.

Weep, meditate,
remember lord Toteoci.
May he not enter the mysterious waters.

The precious willow tree turns green again,
the word of Tezozomoctli is not finished.

Look in the place of the darts,
Tehconehuatl has left,
Cuappolocatl, Cuauhtecotl have left;
the lords are fleshless;
Cacamatl and Tzincacahuaca left hastily;
this will not turn you into a chichimeca,
our lord Toteoci.

Do not weep, lords of Chalco.
You are pleased, Giver of Life.
You bring the day to a close in Atlixco,
lord Toteoci, lord Cohuatl,
but you are perturbed by the Giver of Life.

You scatter the bracelets, the jades,
you disarrange the wide, precious feathers;
There is weeping, the fall of tears.
For the priest in Huitzilac, the lord Tozan,
there was an edict.

Do you believe it now, priest, Cuateotl?
Does it perturb your heart?
Will the eagle's water be abandoned?
The sky that confronts the earth trembles,
it shakes,
the chichimeca Tlacamazatl is abandoned over there.

The Chalcas are in disarray,
the Huexotzincos are upset.
The Tlailotlaqui [the-one-who-came-back], by yourself,
lord Quiyeuhtzin,
how do you enter Amaquemecan?
You build your ramparts at Chalco,
lord Toteoci.

How do you say it?
The arrows belong to no one, the shields belong to no one.
You send, you order Miccalcalcatl.

The Tlailotlaqui by yourself, lord Quiyeuhtzin,
how do you enter Amaquemecan?
You build your ramparts at Chalco,
lord Toteoci.

Now lord Toteoci and lord Cohuatzin weep,
they are anguished.
Where did Totzin go?
The Chalcas are separated,
some eagles, some tigers
are in disarray over there in Almoloya;
the Chalcas are transformed into Acolhuas, Tepanecas,
Mexicans.

CANTO FLORIDO (*XOCHICUICATL*)

It is but an illusion
that with our songs
we gladden our friends.
You play the precious drum well.
You scatter the flowers, you spread them about—
the flowers wilt.

The song we sing here
is new.
Our flowers, which are also new,
will come to life in our hands.
May there be joy with them,
friends,
with them, may our bitterness,
our sadness, be dissipated.

May no one be sad,
may no one on earth remember.
I have our flowers,
our beautiful songs here.
There is joy with them,
our bitterness, our sadness,
fades away.

We have come here, friends,
to plead for a brief time on earth.

We shall have to leave the beautiful songs,
we shall have to leave the beautiful flowers.

It pains me, Giver of Life,
that we shall have to leave your songs behind.

The flowers sprout again,
they spring forth, green again, interwoven, they bloom.
The flower of song springs from within you,
and you the singer scatter it,
you send it out among the people.

Be joyful, friends,
go and dance in the place where I sing,
in the house of flowers.

I make the jade drum,
your golden drum,
resound here,
God, Giver of Life,
Lord, One God.

Only here are we joyful,
where the bitterness of the princes dissipates.
Cuauhatlapaltzin, Tacxocuauhtzin,
Tepanquizcatzin, Cohuatzin.

You are there in the proximity of precious stones,
you nobles,
Ayocuatzin, Tacxocuauhtzin;
we are a bit happier here.

You mingle with eagles,
you are as harmonious as tigers, oh princes.
With this the flowers are sipped,
and we are a little happier here.

Never, never will your drum be destroyed,
for it is the song of the Giver of Life.
Be joyful, my prince.
Not forever here on earth!

To whom shall we bequeath tomorrow
or the past?
Give happiness to the eagles, to the tigers,
we have no adornment but flowers.

All men are believers
here on earth.
But only for a moment the good ones,
the fragrant flowers, pass before us.

Giver of Life, which are your flowers,
your wealth, your bouquet?
May we beg the loan of the quetzalizquixochitl
here on earth?
Perhaps we shall have to bring them to your house
or must we leave them
in the place of the fleshless?

You, Lord Cacamatl,
have changed into a precious willow,
a ceiba, a juniper.
Now, lord, you renew your water, your mountain,
your city blooms again.

In Amaquemecan, in Totolimpan,
your heart suffers, oh, Giver of Life.
Perhaps they came to break out,
to be green again,
the princes, the lord chichimeca, you Ayocuan,
the priest of Cuauhtliztac?

The house of precious paintings
is like the plumage of a parrot,
and you are there, taking pleasure
in seeking the word of the Giver of Life,
of Him, God.

Before whom,
in whose time was I born,
my God, Giver of Life, God?

The flowers are ringed
in the heart of the house of books,

in the heart of the house of butterflies,
the earth is colored;
your song is spread,
your word is spread,
the voices are heard.
Our Father, One God,
Giver of Life.

There are many quechol birds,
many butterflies,
in your house,
presaging war.
I alone choose your songs,
interweave your jades,
intertwine your ruby and gold
gleaming bracelets.
You are bedecked with these, Father,
your riches are but flowers.

Myriad beautiful birds fly above you,
tzinitzcan birds, red tlauhquechol,
with these you give color to your drum on earth,
your riches are but flowers.

I ask you, priests,
from whence come the intoxicating flowers,
the intoxicating songs,
the beautiful songs?
They come only from over there, from your house,
from the heart of the sky;
the myriad flowers come
only from your house.

The One God, by whom we live,
asks them to come down,
the xiloxochitl flowers are scattered,
above them, the eloquechol bird sings,
He is content, He teaches the people.

In Tollan, in Chalco,
in the house of God,
the precious starling,

the red starling trills,
and above the temple of precious stones
the quetzal bird also trills.

In the jade-colored house,
where the water extends,
the precious hallucinatory flower
achieves perfection.
The tzinitzcan birds are
intermingling,
mixing with the flowers;
among them, the quetzal bird sings,
trilling.

I the singer begin.
My song is entwined with the xiloxochitl,
among the fragrant, flowering trees.

The precious hallucinogenic flowers
dance in the place of the drums;
they live, they are joyous, and they depart.

Beside the repository of jades,
where precious plumes abound,
stands Our Father, God;
like turquoises mounted in bracelets,
the flowers are scattered in the house of paintings.

Then sing, princes,
then gladden the Giver of Life;
the flowered is painted with precious feathers.

The flowers arrive,
the flowers of spring shine with the sun.
Your heart, your body,
is a myriad of flowers, God.

Which of us desires your flowers,
God, Giver of Life?
They are in the hands of Miccacalcatl;
the flowers sprout, bloom, become yellow,
shine with the sun.

I come only from your house,
I, the precious vision flower.
I lift my voice in song,
I give out my flowers.

May the precious tobacco flowers
be tasted;
they are scattered, God apportions your flowers;
take them into your house.

SONG OF ORPHANHOOD

It begins:
The flowers are lifted up,
they stand tall in the place of the drums,
and I am happy.
I have come to hurl myself—
the flowers are engaged.

I alone give happiness to our friends,
in the house of jades,
on the mat of flowers,
where the laughing singer speaks.

If for naught you shall give us happiness,
if for naught you shall sing to us,
perhaps our flowers, our songs should not be glad now,
perhaps our flowers, our songs should not be grateful now.
Perhaps the Eagle prince, Cacamatl
will come again?
Perhaps Ayocuan will come again?
Will Ilhuicamina still make us happy?
I do not know if it is twice
or only once that we depart.

I come only to weep,
I come only to be sad.
The chief, Lord Ayocuan, reprimands us.

You are only glorified,
esteemed here,
close and near to the people;

it is not your time, yet—
my mother, my father do not know it,
for which I weep,
because they are also in the place of the fleshless.

I weep, I am saddened,
I remember only that we have left
the beautiful flowers,
the beautiful songs;
still we enjoy ourselves,
still we sing, ·
we go completely,
we perish.

What is it then that our friends know?
Suffer your unhappy heart.
We are not born twice,
one is not a child on this earth twice;
we only depart this earth.

Still, we are but briefly here,
together, close to the people.
It shall never come about, I shall never be joyous,
I shall never be happy.

Where does my heart live?
Where can I make my home?
Where will my house remain?
Because I am needy here on earth.

Suffer, my heart.
Do not be saddened here on earth.
Perhaps this shall be my destiny.
He knows.
Perhaps I have deserved no more
than to have been born this way?
It would be good if it were so.
One does not live anywhere,
so speaks my heart.

What does God say?
Do we really live?
Have we come to last forever on this earth?

Will I have to leave the beautiful flowers?
Shall I make them go down to Quenonamican?
Only hastily,
only for a brief time,
do we ask for the loan of the beautiful songs.

I begin my song,
I take, I sense your flowers,
Giver of Life,
we play our flowered drums well.
It is our earthly adornment.

Have the flowers been transported?
Are our songs not transported to Quenonamican?
We leave everything behind,
no one shall remain on earth.

Let there be one more day here, friend.
We shall go on to leave
our flowers, our songs.
We shall go on to leave
the earth everlasting.

Be happy, friends, all of you,
be happy!

What do you imagine,
what do you remember, my friend?
Do you not enjoy a song?
Do you not long for the flowers of the Giver of Life?
Be happy in the place of the drums,
set yourself apart,
if that is what your heart desires.

The beautiful butterfly above the crowd is happy,
for it sips of our flowers;
the flowers in our hands,
our fans, our stalks of tobacco mingle
and give off fragrances in the place of the drums,
be happy!

Where will I go? Where will I go?
Straight is His dual road, His road, God's.

Perhaps people are awaited in the place of the fleshless,
or in the heart of the sky?
Or is the place of the fleshless only here on earth?

We depart from the world,
we go from the world to your house, over there.
No one pays attention to those left on earth;
Who asks who are your friends on earth?
Take your pleasure!

May the precious quecholxochitl flowers,
the beautiful red flowers be intertwined:
they are your heart, your word,
my prince, Lord Chichimeca,
you, Ayocuan.
Only for a brief time
do we ask for the loan of them here on earth.

For this I weep,
our death destroys,
ruins our works,
the beautiful songs.
Only for a brief time
do we ask for the loan of them here on earth.

Cantares Mexicanos, fols. 31v–36r; Spanish translation, Miguel León-Portilla; English version, Sylvia and Earl Shorris.

3. *Huexotzinco*

IN THE MANNER OF HUEXOTZINCO[16]

Only flowers of sadness,
sorrowful songs, unfold here in Tlatelolco, in Mexico,
but it is over there that the people make themselves known.

---

[16]Despite the title, this song refers to the abandonment of Tlatelolco and Tenochtitlan after the defeat of the Mexicans by the Spaniards. The end describes the torture of Cuauhtemoc and others. Huexotzinco itself is best represented poetically by the work of Tecayehuatzin in the "Dialogue of Flower and Song," or "Poetics" (p. 81). A brief history of Huexotzinco appears in the Glossary.

Giver of Life, Paper-Covered Countenance,
You alone have done well by us;
there is a place where we the common people shall lose ourselves.

We are needy, woeful are we,
we common people;
we have meditated upon suffering—
it is known.

You disperse,
You endanger your subjects.
In Tlatelolco, the hardship spreads,
the people know suffering.
You weary of this,
it annoys you, Giver of Life.

The weeping spreads,
the tears rain down in Tlatelolco.
The Mexica have gone by water;
already mingling with women they go;
we are going over there, my friends.

So it happened,
the water, the mountain, the city is abandoned.
Smoke rises in Mexico,
the mist spreads,
it is your work, Giver of Life.

Remember, you Mexica,
that He causes his force, his honor to fall only upon us,
He is the One, God, in Coyonacazco.

He greets them with weeping over there, only over there,
the Huitznahuatl Motelchiuh.
They are all going there, the Tlaylotlaqui, Tlacotzin,
the Lord Oquihtzin; they are abandoning Tenochtitlan.

You are in pain, my friends, weep;
we have lost the Mexican nation.
Bitter water,
bitter food.
The Giver of Life has done this in Tlatelolco.

But, ah, Motelchiuhtzin, Tlacotzin
have been taken peacefully;
they fortified themselves with songs in Achinanco
when they were taken to the fire in Coyohuacan.

Cantares Mexicanos, fols. 31v–33v; Spanish translation, Miguel León-Portilla; English version, Sylvia and Earl Shorris.

4. Mexico

THE FALL OF TENOCHTITLAN

Our cries of grief rise up
and our tears rain down,
for Tlatelolco is lost.
The Aztecs are fleeing across the lake;
they are running away like women.

How can we save our homes, my people?
The Aztecs are deserting the city:
the city is in flames, and all
is darkness and destruction.

Motelchiuhtzin the Huiznahuacatl,
Tlacotzin the Tlailotlacatl,
Oquitzin the Tlacatecuhtli
are greeted with tears.

Weep, my people:
know that with these disasters
we have lost the Mexican nation.
The water has turned bitter,
our food is bitter!
These are the acts of the Giver of Life. . . .

THE IMPRISONMENT OF CUAUHTEMOC

The Mexica are besieged in the city;
the Tlatelolcas are besieged in the city!

The walls are black,
the air is black with smoke,
the guns flash in the darkness.
They have captured Cuauhtemoc;
they have captured the princes of Mexico.

The Mexica are besieged in the city;
the Tlatelolcas are besieged in the city!

After nine days, they were taken to Coyoacan:
Cuauhtemoc, Coanacoch, Tetlepanquetzaltzin.
The kings are prisoners now.

Tlacotzin consoled them:
"Oh my nephews, take heart!
The kings are prisoners now;
they are bound with chains."

The king Cuauhtemoc replied.
"Oh my nephew, you are a prisoner;
they have bound you in irons.

"But who is that at the side of the Captain-General?
Ah, it is Doña Isabel, my little niece!
Ah, it is true: the kings are prisoners now!

"You will be a slave and belong to another:
the collar will be fashioned in Coyoacan,
where the quetzal feathers will be woven.

"Who is that at the side of the Captain-General?
Ah, it is Doña Isabel, my little niece!
Ah, it is true: the kings are prisoners now!

Miguel León-Portilla, *Broken Spears* (Boston: Beacon Press, 1992), pp. 146, 148–49.

FLOWERS AND SONGS OF SORROW

Nothing but flowers and songs of sorrow
are left in Mexico and Tlatelolco,
where once we saw warriors and wise men.

We know it is true
that we must perish,
for we are mortal men.
You, the Giver of Life,
you have ordained it.

We wander here and there
in our desolate poverty.
We are mortal men.
We have seen bloodshed and pain
where once we saw beauty and valor.

We are crushed to the ground;
we lie in ruins.
There is nothing but grief and suffering
in Mexico and Tlatelolco,
where once we saw beauty and valor.

Have you grown weary of your servants?
Are you angry with your servants,
O Giver of life. . . .

THE GLORY OF TENOCHTITLAN

On the eagle mat,
The jaguar mat,
Saint Mary is invoked.[17]

He, Giver of Life,
Shield that descends,
Brought the night down on Mexico.
The chalk, the fine feathers,[18]
Are coming, spreading across the earth,
        drawing near.

Your command, your wealth,
You, lords,

[17]León-Portilla explains this astonishing use of Saint Mary in the *Cantares* as an aberration, proving fray Diego Durán's argument in *Historia de las Indias de Nueva España* that such bowdlerizations were used "to conceal the ancient significance of these compositions."

[18]A *difrasismo*, meaning war.

Cuauhtlecoatl, Cahualtzin,
You have been borrowing the glory
    of the Giver of Life,
Shield that descended here in Mexico.

Famously, the city of Tenochtitlan endures,
Bringing glory on itself;
Oh, you princes,
As He, the one God, commands you, his sons,
Let no one fear the beautiful death.

Whose efforts will truly gain
The mat of the shield, the honored place
    of the arrows of God?
Think of this, remember it, you, princes,
Who can disturb the city of Tenochtitlan?
Who can shake the foundations of heaven?

Long live Tenochtitlan!

Cantares Mexicanos, fols. 19v–20r; Spanish translation, Miguel León-Portilla; English version, Sylvia and Earl Shorris.

ꙩ 2 ꙩ

Sacred Narrative

*Compositions in this genre recall primeval events, deeds of the cul-
ture heroes, stories of the early migrations and the settling and
founding of towns, what could be termed the foundations of the culture.
Myth and history intermingle in these accounts of ancient tradition,
often described as* teotlahtolli, *"divine words."*

*An account of the five ages and cosmogonic Suns was included in the
General Introduction. There are several variants of this account which
closely correspond to what is pictorially represented in an indigenous
book and in some stone monuments. The text transcribed here is actually a "reading" done in 1558 of the contents of a codex.*

Frequent referential statements such as "here is" (izcatqui); *"this appears here"* (inezca in nican ca); *"this appears here"* (inin in nican);
"then, next, following on" (niman ic; niman ye ic) *reveal that the account was recited and commited to alphabetic writing, following the pictoglyphic sequences. There is a compound word in Nahuatl meaning the
process of following the contents of a codex or indigenous book:* amox-
oh-toca, *literally, "to follow the way of the book," that is, the sequence
of its paintings and glyphic signs.*

This narrative, today known as the Legend of the Suns, *after recalling the successive foundations and destructions of the Sun, earth,
and man, tells of other happenings. Among them are the finding of
maize, the sacrifice of the gods in a primeval Teotihuacan, and the deeds
of Quetzalcoatl, who is both the divine culture hero and a high priest of
the Toltecs.*

*The mythic cycle of Quetzalcoatl, the Feathered Serpent, god and
priest, is also told in other compositions whose rhythm and beauty reveal
Nahua poetry at its best. In this section we have included the* Hero Journey *from the* Anales de Cuauhtitlan *redacted in 1570. As a god, he symbolizes the wisdom of the supreme divine duality. As a priest and culture*

hero, he was the religious leader of the Toltecs during the second half of the tenth century A.D. *He lived in palaces of various colors which he had built in Tula, his metropolis. There, Quetzalcoatl dwelt in complete chastity, often fasting, devoting his life to meditation and to enriching the culture of his people. But one day three wizards appeared in Tula. Apparently, they wanted to introduce the practice of human sacrifice. The wizards "confused Quetzalcoatl's heart" and brought about his ruin. He abandoned his city and went in search of a Land of Wisdom (the colors red and black). When he arrived at the edge of the ocean, he cast himself into a great fire from which his heart emerged as the Morning Star.*

According to another version, he embarked on a raft of serpents and sailed toward the East, where he disappeared. This story of the great culture hero, also told in Yucatec under the name Kukulkan and in Quiche Maya (as Gucumatz), is perhaps the richest in symbolism and most beautiful of all Mesoamerican narratives.

Contrasting with the peaceful figure of Quetzalcoatl is that of the war god, Huitzilopochtli, the tutelary deity of the Aztecs or Mexicas. A sacred narrative, completely different from those of Toltec origin, provides the story of Huitzilopochtli's birth and immediate triumph over his envious sister and many other siblings.

The Birth of Huitzilopochtli, *as told in the* Florentine Codex *(see Bibliographical Essay), with its great force of expression, has furnished archeologists with a key to understanding the meaning of the main temple of the Mexicas, recently unearthed in downtown Mexico City. There, a carved bas-relief on a large stone was found of a decapitated and dismembered goddess, identified as Coyolxauhqui. She was that malevolent sister of Huitzilopochtli who had urged her brethren to kill him at the very moment his mother Coatlicue was giving birth to him at Coatepetl, "the Mountain of the Serpent." A vivid description of the battle that followed and of how the portentous Huitzilopochtli defeated Coyolxauhqui and her brethren, completes the story.*

The main temple represented the Mountain of the Serpent where Huitzilopochtli was born. That is why, while his effigy and that of his mother Coatlicue were assigned to the top of the temple, the carved figure of the decapitated and dismembered Coyolxauhqui was placed at the bottom.

Another of the sacred narratives concerns the founding of Tenochtitlan. The terrifying story of the marriage of the daughter of Achitometl appears here. It is also one of the versions of the death of the wizard Copil, whose heart was torn from his chest and buried in the earth. A prickly pear cactus (tenochtli in Nahuatl) sprang from the buried heart of the wizard, giving its name to the city-state—Tenochtitlan. In this story, Huitzilopochtli is the name of a priest, suggesting another iteration

*of the connection between gods and humans in Nahua literature.
Huitzilopochtli was, as noted earlier, the tutelary deity of the Mexica.*

A Note on Quetzalcoatl

*Few figures in Mesoamerican culture have generated so much com-
mentary as Quetzalcoatl. He is recognized as the "culture bearer," a role
that leads to comparison with the Greek Prometheus, who was punished by the gods for stealing fire and bringing it to mortals. Quetzalcoatl
is a more complex figure, for he appears in both human and divine
form, representing the duality of the supreme deity. His role as culture
bearer is undisputed by gods or humans; rather, it is his character that
is tested. In one version, Quetzalcoatl, the pure one, is tempted by the
trickster Tezcatlipoca, succumbs, and for his act (there is no concept of
sin as we know it among the Nahuas) he throws himself into a fire from
which his heart emerges, rising into the sky to become the Morning Star,
thus transcending death and governing the cycles of time.*

*The difference between Quetzalcoatl and Prometheus (Forethinker)
is that the Greek culture hero, also known as the supreme trickster, is
punished by the gods, while the Nahua culture hero recognizes the flaw
in human behavior and himself repents. How one interprets this aspect
of Quetzalcoatl's life is key to the view one holds of Nahua culture in general and Nahua morality in particular.*

*It leads among other things to the question of the character of the
Nahua poets, who consider the origins of art, the meaning of human existence, the value of friendship, and at the same time agree to wars of
conquest and the sacrifice of human beings, as merited by the gods. The
tension between those who were opposed to human sacrifice and those
who understood it as the ultimately reverential act exists in Quetzalcoatl.
But the story may also be read as the fall from innocence.*

*If one were to think of the Mesoamerican gods as aspects of the
supreme god, Ometeol, the Dual God, Our Mother/Our Father, the por-
trayal of the deities could be understood as the aspects of human nature
magnified and made comprehensible. In considering the meaning of
the gods and their existence, one must never forget the materialist origin of their invention: Corn goes underground as seed and then reappears as the corn plant. Compare this to Quetzalcoatl finding the bones
of humans, grinding them up, and bleeding his male member to give
them sustenance. How should that be interpreted? As the need to sacrifice humans to the gods or as the need to pray for rain to bring the corn*

back to life? Readers who want to understand the work to its fullest may find the Quetzalcoatl figure the key to entering the thinking of the ancient Nahua world.

His name, like that of Prometheus, connects him to the arts, for quetzal *in its adjectival form means "beauty" in Nahuatl. The Nahuas divided the character of Prometheus into two distinct persons, opposed to each other—Tezcatlipoca the trickster and Quetzalcoatl the pure and beautiful—following the Mesoamerican principle of duality.*

QUETZALCOATL'S HERO JOURNEY

I

1 Reed: It is recounted, it is said, in this year was born Quetzalcoatl, the one called Our Honored Prince High Priest One Reed Quetzalcoatl; and it is said his mother's name was Chimalman. And also in this fashion was Quetzalcoatl placed within his mother's womb: she swallowed a precious green stone, it is told.

[Years] 2 Flint, 3 House, 4 Rabbit, 5 Reed, 6 Flint, 7 House, 8 Rabbit, 9 Reed.

In this year 9 Reed Quetzalcoatl searched for his father, when he had come to a little knowledge, being now nine years old. He said, "What is my dear father like? May I see him? May I look on his face?"

And then he was told, "He has died with honor, he is buried there. Go look upon him."

Then Quetzalcoatl went there at once and dug up his bones and buried them again in the temple of the one called Quilaztli.

[Years] 10 Flint, 11 House, 12 Rabbit, 13 Reed, 1 Flint, 2 House, 3 Rabbit, 4 Reed, 5 Flint, 6 House, 7 Rabbit, 8 Reed, 9 Flint, 10 House.

In this year died in honor the Lord Speaker of Cuauhtitlan, Huactli, who had ruled for sixty-two years. He was the Lord Speaker who knew not the sowing of maize, the edible foodstuffs. His people knew not the making of tilmal capes. They wore only skin clothing; their food was only rabbits, snakes, birds, and deer. Nowhere did they keep houses, but only wandered from place to place.

11 Rabbit: The lady Xiuhtlacuiloxochitzin was installed as Speaker. Her grass dwelling stood at the side of the market plaza where Tepextitenco is today. And the city, Cuauhtitlan, passed to her since she was the wife of Huactli, it is said, and because she spoke often to the devil Itzpapalotl.

12 Reed, 13 Flint, 1 House, 2 Rabbit: This year Quetzalcoatl arrived there in Tollantzinco, where during four years he built his House of Fasting, his House of Turquoise-inlaid boards. From there he passed to Cuext-

lan, from which place he laid a bridge across the water which, it is said, still survives.

3 Reed, 4 Flint, 5 House: In this year the Toltecs took Quetzalcoatl and installed him on the throne there in Tollan and he was their priest; in another part his story has been written.

6 Rabbit, 7 Reed: Lady Xiuhtlacuiloxochitzin died; she had ruled twelve years in Cuauhtitlan.

8 Flint: In this year Ayauhcoyotzin was installed as Lord Speaker of Cuauhtitlan at the place known as Tecpanquauhtla.

9 House, 10 Rabbit, 11 Reed, 12 Flint, 13 House, 1 Rabbit, 2 Reed: (It is the word of Tetzcoco that in this year died Quetzalcoatl, Our Lord of Tollan Colhuacan.) In this year 2 Reed he built his House of Fasting, his place of penance and of prayer. He, Our Lord One Reed Quetzalcoatl, carefully laid out his four houses: his turquoise-plank house, his coral-inlay house, his whiteshell-inlay house, and his quetzal-feather house where he prayed frequently, performed penance and observed his fasts.

And at the exact hour of midnight he went down to the place called Atecpan Amochco, by the water, and there he humbly inserted his penitential spines, which he did as well on the heights of Xicocotl and Huitzco and Tzincoc and Nonohualcatepec. And his penitential spines were made of precious greenstone and he offered them up on a bed of quetzal feathers. And for incense he burned turquoise, greenstone, coral; and his blood offerings were of serpents, birds, butterflies which he sacrificed.

And it is recounted, it is said he prayed often, he sought godhead in the depths of heaven and invoked it by the names

Citlalinicue, Citlallatonac
Tonacacihuatl, Tonacateuctli
Tecolliquenqui, Eztlaquenqui
Tlallamanac, Tlallichcatl.

And the place to which he cried out was known as Omeyocan Chiucnepaniuhcan, "Duality Above Nine Heavens."

And so in this manner he knew those who there kept their dwellings, calling upon and petitioning them insistently in most honorable humility and contrition.

And finally it was he who revealed the grandeur of wealth: jadestone, turquoise, gold—yellow and white, coral, mother-of-pearl, plumage of the quetzal, the cotinga, the roseate spoonbill, the troupial, the trogon and the heron. And he revealed the multicolored cacao as well as multicolored cotton. He was a great Toltec, a grand artisan, in all his earthenware, painted blue green, white, yellow, red and a multitude of colors.

And in the time that he lived he began, he founded his temple and set its serpent columns, but he did not finish and he did not give up hope.

And in the time that he lived he did not show his face before the people; deep within his house he lived where he was protected.

And his heralds kept him, in many places they enclosed him well.

And in every place he stayed, in each and every place were his heralds, and there were the Jadestone Mat, the Quetzal Mat, the Gold Mat of his authority.

And it was recounted, it has been said, his House of Fasting was built in four parts.

And it is recounted, it is said, how many times in vain the Human Owl sorcerers sought to humiliate Quetzalcoatl so that he would make his offerings of humans, that he would sacrifice men.

But he never desired it nor consented. For greatly did he love his common people, his Toltecs, and his offerings, the sacrifices he made continually, were but serpents, birds and butterflies.

And it is recounted, it is said that the owl sorcerers became greatly angered and began tormenting, mocking and humiliating him, saying they wanted in this way to make him miserable. And thus would they drive him out, and truly it was done.

[Years] 3 Flint, 4 House, 5 Rabbit, 6 Reed, 7 Flint, 8 House, 9 Rabbit, 10 Reed, 11 Flint, 12 House, 13 Rabbit, 1 Reed: In this year Quetzalcoatl died. And it is said he went to Tlillan Tlapallan, to die there.

Then was Matlacxochitl installed as Speaker in Tollan.

II

Now, it is recounted how Quetzalcoatl conducted himself when he disregarded the desire of the owl sorcerers that he should make human offerings, that he should sacrifice men.

The owl sorcerers counseled together, those whose names were Tezcatlipoca, Ihuimecatl and Toltecatl. They said, "Certainly it is necessary that he abandon the city, which we will occupy." They said, "Let us brew the pulque which we will give him to drink; so he will be corrupted and so he will no longer perform his sacramental penances."

And then Tezcatlipoca said, "I say we must give him his own body, that he should see it." And so it would be done, that in this way they might punish him with great severity. Then Tezcatlipoca went ahead, carrying a small, double-sided mirror, enwrapped.

And when he had arrived where Quetzalcoatl was, he said to the heralds who protected him, "Please do the honor of saying to the High Priest: 'Truly, Telpochtli, the Young Man, has come to you and wishes most humbly to deliver to you, to humbly show before you your body.'"

And the heralds went in to him and delivered the message. Quetzalcoatl said to them, "What is this thing, grandfather-heralds, what is this body of mine that he has brought here? Examine it; then he will enter."

But he did not wish them to see it. He said, "Truly, I myself must show it to him; tell him this." They went to tell him, "He will not consent. He very much wishes to show you himself." Quetzalcoatl said, "Let him come in, grandfathers."

They went to summon Tezcatlipoca who came in and greeted him saying, "My beloved Prince and High Priest One Reed Quetzalcoatl. I salute your grace, and I arrive to set before you your beloved body." Quetzalcoatl said, "You have wearied yourself in this work, grandfather. From where did you come? What is this thing you call my 'body'? Show it to me."

He said, "My Beloved Prince and High Priest, certainly I am your humble subject. I come from the lower slopes of Mt. Nonohualca. Won't you please look upon your beloved body?"

Then he brought him the mirror and said, "May it please you to know, to look upon yourself, my Beloved Prince, for you will appear there in the mirror."

So then Quetzalcoatl looked upon himself, and he was overcome with horror. He said, "If my subjects see me, perhaps they will flee." For his eyelids were swollen, his eyes sunken deep in their sockets, his face all heavily pockmarked and furrowed; he was a monstrous sight. When he had seen himself in the mirror, he said, "My subjects shall never see me; I will stay here."

Then Tezcatlipoca turned away and withdrew; he called urgently for Ihuimecatl so that they might fully abuse him. Ihuimecatl said, "Let Coyotlinahual 'Shape-shifting Coyote,' the feather-artist, go in to him now." The shape-shifter listened to their suggestion, that he would be the one sent. Coyotlinahual the feather-artist said, "It is good. Let me be the one to go, the one to see Quetzalcoatl."

Then he went, and said to Quetzalcoatl, "My Beloved Prince, I come to say to your grace in all reverence, come out, show yourself before your subjects. Permit me to array and prepare you so that they might look upon you." Quetzalcoatl said to him, "Prepare them, grandfather, I will see what they are."

And so then Coyotlinahual the feather-artist fashioned them; first he made Quetzalcoatl's plumed headdress, then his turquoise inlay mask. He took red with which to paint his mouth; he took yellow with which to stripe his face. Next he prepared his serpent teeth, then his beard of cotinga and roseate spoonbill feathers across his lower face.

And so he arrayed him in his attire and he was Quetzalcoatl. Then he handed him the mirror, and when he looked on himself he was very pleased with what he saw. Then Quetzalcoatl abandoned forthwith the place where he was guarded.

And so then Coyotlinahual the feather-artist went to Ihuimecatl and said, "Certainly I have caused Quetzalcoatl to emerge. Now it's your turn." He replied, "That's fine."

Then he befriended one named Toltecatl and they went off together, and they arrived at a place called Xonacapacoyan where they met with a farmer named Maxtlaton who guarded Toltec Mountain.

And then they also grew herbal greens, tomatoes, chili, green corn and beans, and in only a few days it was done. And there also were magueys in that place which they requested of Maxtlaton. For only four days they fermented the pulque. Next, they collected it; they found wild honeycombs and with these they collected and mixed the pulque.

Then they went to the home of Quetzalcoatl there in Tollan. They took all their herbs, their chili, etc., and the pulque. They arrived and requested entrance, but those who guarded Quetzalcoatl refused them. Twice and three times they returned but were not received. The last time they were asked where was their home? They responded and said, "Why, there on Priest's Mountain, Toltec Mountain." And hearing this, Quetzalcoatl said, "Let them come in." They entered and greeted him and then finally gave him the green herbs, etc.

And when he had eaten, they entreated him once more: they gave him the pulque. But he said, "No, I will not drink it; I am fasting. Does it not intoxicate? Is it not fatal?" They answered him, "Do taste it with your honorable finger. It is certainly strong and fresh."

Quetzalcoatl tasted it with his finger and found it good. He said, "Allow me to drink, grandfathers; three drinks." "You must drink four," the owl sorcerers said to him, and they gave him the fifth, saying, "This is your ritual libation."

And when he had drunk it, they served it to everyone, to all the heralds they gave five drinks. They made them completely drunk.

Then again the owl sorcerers spoke to Quetzalcoatl and said, "My Beloved Prince, may it please your grace to sing. This is the blessed song it shall honor you to lift up." Then Ihuimecatl raised the song:

"My house of quetzal, quetzal
my house of troupial
my house of redshell—
I must already lose them
for my carelessness, An ya!"

And Quetzalcoatl was now full of joy; he said, "Bring my sister, Quetzalpetlatl. Let us be drunken together!" So his heralds went to Mt. Nonohualca where she practiced her meritorious penances. They said to her, "My Beloved Princess, noble lady of fasts, Quetzalpetlatl: We have come for you;

the High Priest Quetzalcoatl awaits you. Will it not please you to go into his presence?" She answered, "It is good, herald grandfather; let us be off."

And upon arrival she sat herself beside Quetzalcoatl and they served her the pulque, four drinks and then the fifth, her ritual libation. The seducers Ihuimecatl and Toltecatl then also raised another song before the sister of Quetzalcoatl:

> "My sister, Where now will you live?
> O Quetzalpetlatl, let's make ourselves drunk!
> Ay, ya, yya, yn, ye, an."

When they were fully drunken, they no longer said, "If it were not for the merit we earn . . . ," nor did they go down to the water's edge, nor any more plant spines in their bodies. At dawn they performed no sacraments and when the sun appeared they were stricken with anguish, their hearts were orphaned in remorse.

Then Quetzalcoatl spoke and said, "O how unfortunate I am!" And then he composed the lament of his exile; he sang there:

> "No longer is even a single day-sign counted in my house;
> Let it be here, aya, where he was guarded, let it be here.
> Let it already be, let it happen,"

he chanted,

> "He who owns the body of earth can be but miserable and afflicted.
> All that is precious is no more;
> Certainly I return to sober virtue."

The second time he chanted his song:

> "Aya, she had formed and shaped me,
> she who is my mother, an ya,
> Coacueye, the goddess;
> ah, her son, yyaa,
> I weep, yya, ye an."

And when Quetzalcoatl had sung, all his heralds were overcome with sadness and wept also. Then they also sang and raised the chant in that place:

> "Aya, He gave us a life of abundant riches;
> He who is my Lord, he, Quetzalcoatl.
> Lost, your jadestone headdress;

the tree, broken and bleeding.
Let us look already upon him,
Let us weep also."

And when the heralds finished singing, then Quetzalcoatl said to them there, "Grandfather heralds, let it be finished. Let me abandon the city, let me go. Send word that a stone sarcophagus be made." Then they quickly prepared the sarcophagus and when it was prepared and finished, they laid Quetzalcoatl within it.

And he had lain in the sarcophagus only four days when he became ill. Then he said to his heralds, "Let it be finished, grandfather heralds. Let us depart. Conceal and hide all around the felicity and the rich prosperity we have revealed, and all the property of our inheritance."

And the heralds did as he said. They hid them well in the place where Quetzalcoatl's bath was, a place called Atecpan Amochco.

So then Quetzalcoatl left. He rose up, summoned his heralds, and wept deeply for them.

Then they departed in search of Tlillan, Tlapallan, Tlatlayan "The Black, the Red Land, Place of the Burning."

And he looked upon every place and traveled everywhere, but no place was satisfactory to him. And when he found at last the place he sought, then once more he wept in sad contrition.

And it was again on the day 1 Reed, it is recounted, it is said, when he arrived at Teoapan Ilhuicaatenco, "Along the divine water, At the shore of heavenly water." Then he halted and stood; he wept, took up his vestments and adorned himself in his insignia, his turquoise mask, etc.

And when he was fully adorned then with his own hand he set himself on fire, he offered himself up in flame.

So the place where Quetzalcoatl went to immolate himself came to be called Tlatlayan, "Place of the Burning."

And it is said that even as he burned, his ashes emerged and arose: and there appeared, before the sight of everyone, all the birds of great value which emerged and rose into the sky. They saw the roseate spoonbill, the cotinga, the trogon, the heron, the yellow parrot, the scarlet macaw, the white-bellied parrot, and every other bird of precious plumage.

And when the ashes were extinguished, then arose his heart, the quetzal bird itself; they saw it. And so they knew he had entered the sky within the sky.

The old ones used to say he was transformed to the dawn star; thus it is said that when Quetzalcoatl died this star appeared, and so he is named Tlahuizcalpanteuctli, "Lord of the Dawn House."

They used to say that when he died he did not appear for four days; he went to live in Mictlan, the Nether World, they said.

And also in another four days he made for himself arrows. So in eight days appeared the great star which was named Quetzalcoatl, and this, they said, is when he was enthroned as Lord.

And so they knew when he came to appear, each individual tonal or day-sign under which he falls upon men, he fires his arrows, he is provoked. If on 1 Crocodile, he shoots arrows at old men and women all alike; if on 1 Jaguar, if 1 Deer, if 1 Flower, he shoots well-born children; and if on 1 Reed, he strikes all the ruling speakers, as also on 1 Death. And if on 1 Rain, he shoots the rain; rain will cease. And if on 1 Motion, he shoots the young men and women; and if on 1 Water, then drought comes.

Each of these day-signs, therefore, was held in veneration by the elders, both men and women.

So it is recounted how for Quetzalcoatl all was in vain. He was born under a day-sign 1 Reed and he also died under 1 Reed. Thus it is completely read, thus it is exhausted, fifty-two years or one full calendar round. So it all came to an end in this year 1 Reed.

It was said that Matlacxochitl took his place as Speaker there in Tollan.

Roberta H. and Peter T. Markman, *The Flayed God* (San Francisco: HarperCollins, 1992), pp. 369–77, translated by Willard Gingerich.

2. The Founding of Tenochtitlan

Here it is told, it is recounted,
how the ancients who were called, who were named,
Teochichimeca, Azteca, Mexitin, Chicomoztoca, came, arrived,
when they came to seek,
when they came to take again possession of their land here,
in the great city of Mexico Tenochtitlan. . . .
In the middle of the water where the cactus stands,
where the eagle raises itself up,
where the eagle screeches,
where the eagle spreads his wings,
where the eagle feeds,
where the serpent is torn apart,
where the fish fly,
where the blue waters and yellow waters join,
where the water blazes up,
where feathers came to be known,
among the rushes, among the reeds where the battle is joined, where
    the peoples
from the four directions are awaited,
there they arrived, there they settled. . . .

They called themselves Teochichimeca, Azteca, Mexitin.
They brought along the image of their god,
the idol that they worshipped.
The Aztecs heard him speak and they answered him;
they did not see how it was he spoke to them. . . .
And after the Azteca, Mexitin sailed here from Aztlan,
they arrived in Culhuacan. . . .
They went everywhere in Culhuacan,
in far-off Culhuacan, in Tona ichuacan or Tonallan.
All of them journeyed far—
the people of Michoacan, kin of the Mexicans,
and the people of Malinalco—
for all of them came.

And when they (the Aztecs) abandoned the people of Michoacan,
the men and women were amusing themselves
in the water at a place called Patzcuaro.[1]

They made off with the men's capes and breechcloths
and they took the women's skirts and huipiles.

The men no longer had breechcloths;
they went about with their bottoms bare,
rather, they go about with their bottoms bare, uncovered.
The women gave up their blouses and the men became wearers of
    huilpiles.
In this manner they abandoned the people of Michoacan.

And the reason Huitzilopochtli went off and abandoned his sister,
    named Malinalxoch, along the way,
that all his fathers abandoned her while she was sleeping,
was because she was cruel,
she was very evil.
She was an eater of people's hearts,
an eater of people's limbs—it was her work—
a bewitcher of people,
an enchanter of people.
She put people to sleep,
she made people eat snakes,

---

[1]Material in parentheses has been inserted by the author, Ms. Sullivan, for clarity.

she made people eat scorpions,
she spoke to all the centipedes and spiders
and transformed herself into a sorceress.
She was a very evil woman;
this was why Huitzilopochtli did not like her,
this was why he did not bring his sister, Malinalxoch, with him,
that they abandoned (her and) all her fathers while they were sleeping.

Then the priest, Huitzilopochtli spoke,
he addressed his fathers, called the "idol-bearers" . . . he said to them,
"O my fathers, the work that Malinalxoch does is not my work.
When I came forth, when I was sent here,
I was given arrows and a shield,
for battle is my work.
And with my belly, with my head,
I shall confront the cities everywhere.
I shall await the peoples from the four directions,
I shall join battle with them,
I shall provide people with drink,
I shall provide people with food!
Here I shall bring together the diverse peoples,
and not in vain, for I shall conquer them,
that I may see the house of jade, the house of gold, the house of quetzal
    feathers;
the house of emeralds, the house of coral, the house of amethysts;
the sundry feathers—the lovely cotinga feathers, the roseate spoonbill
    feathers,
the trogon feathers—
all the precious feathers;
and the cacao of variegated colors,
and the cotton of variegated colors!
I shall see all this,
for in truth, it is my work,
it was for this that I was sent here.
And now, O my fathers, ready the provisions. Let us go!
Off there we are going to find it . . . !"
And when the sister of Huitzilopochtli, called Malinalxoch,
whom they had abandoned while sleeping,
whom they had gone off and abandoned,
when Malinalxoch awakened, she wept.
She said to her fathers, "O my fathers, where shall we go?
My brother, Huitzilopochtli, has abandoned us by trickery.

Where has the evil one gone?
Let us seek the land where we are to dwell. . . ."
Then they saw the mountain called Texcaltepetl;
they established themselves upon it. . . .

Along the way Malinalxoch became big with child,
and the child of Malinalxoch, a son named Copil, was born.
His father's name was Chimalquauhtli;
he was king of Malinalco. . . .
The others settled at Coatepec. . . .
The Mexicans erected their temple, the house of Huitzilopochtli
and they laid down Huitzilopochtli's ball court
and constructed his skull-rack.
Then they blocked the ravine, the gorge,
and the water collected, it filled up.
This was done at the word of Huitzilopochtli.
Then he said to his fathers, the Mexicans,
"O my fathers, the water has collected.
Plant, sow, willows, bald cypresses, reeds, rushes and water-lilies!"
And the fish, frogs, ajolotes, crayfish, dragonfly larvae, ahuihuitlame,
    ephydrids,
and the salamanders multiplied,
and also the izcahuitli,
and the birds, ducks, American coots, and the "red-shouldered" and
    "yellow-throated" grackles.
And Huitzilopochtli said,
"The izcahuitli are my flesh, my blood, my substance."
Then he sang his song,
They all sang and danced; the song was called Tlaxotecayotl and also
Tecuilhuicuicatl;
he composed it there.
Then his fathers, the Centzonhuitznahua, spoke, they said to
    Huitzilopochtli,
"O priest, the work for which you came shall be done here.
You shall await the people,
you shall meet in battle the people from the four directions,
you shall arouse the cities.
With your belly, with your head,
and your heart, your blood, your substance,
you shall capture them,
that you may see what you promised us—
the many jades, the precious stones, the gold, the quetzal feathers and
    sundry precious feathers,

the cacao of variegated colors,
the cotton of variegated colors,
the diverse flowers, the diverse fruits, the diverse riches.
For, in truth, you have founded,
you have become the ruler of your city, here in Coatepec.
Let your fathers, your vassals, the Aztecs, the Mexicans, gather here!"
   the Centzonhuitznahua beseeched him.
Huitzilopochtli became enraged,
"What are you saying?" he said.
"Do you know?
Is it your work?
Are you greater than I?
I know what I must do!"
Then, atop the temple, his house, Huitzilopochtli began to array himself.
When he had arrayed himself,
when he had arrayed himself for battle,
he painted his face the color of a child's excrement,
he made circles around his eyes,
and he took up his shield. . . .
Then he went off;
he went to destroy, he went to slay his uncles, the Centzonhuitznahua.
On the sacred ball court he devoured his uncles;
and his mother, she whom he took as his mother, called
   Coyolxauhcihuatl. . . .
he cut off her head there and devoured her heart,
Huitzilopochtli devoured it. . . .

The Mexicans were frightened.
The Centzonhuitznahua had thought that the city was to be there in
   Coatepec,
that Mexico was to be there,
but Huitzilopochtli did not want it so.
He made a hole in the dam where the water had been,
and the water broke the dam.
All the bald cypresses, willows, reeds, rushes and water lilies withered.
All the fish, frogs, ajolotes, ephydrids and insects,
and the crayfish and dragonfly larvae that lived in the water died. . . .
and all the birds perished.

Then Huitzilopochtli set out,
he went off with his fathers, his vassals, the Mexicans.

They came, they settled behind Chapultepec in a place called
   Techcatitlan. . . .
Then Huitzilopochtli gave orders to the Mexicans. . . .
he said to the idol-bearers,
"O my fathers, wait, for you shall see,
wait, for I know what is to happen.
Gird yourselves, be courageous.
Gird yourselves, prepare yourselves.
We shall not dwell here,
we shall find it (the place) off there,
there is where we shall possess it.
Let us await those who shall come to destroy us . . . !

. . .

The son of Malinalxoch, sister of Huitzilopochtli, whose name was
   Copil, spoke,
he said to her,
"O my mother, well I know that your brother is off there."
"Yes, your uncle, named Huitzilopochtli, is yonder," she said. "He
   abandoned me,
he abandoned me while I was sleeping,
he abandoned me by trickery along the way.
Then we settled here in Texcaltepeticpac."
"Very well, O my mother," said Copil.
"I know that I must look for him in the place he has found
   contentment,
in the place he has settled.
I shall destroy him,
I shall devour him,
and I shall destroy, I shall vanquish his fathers and the vassals that he
   took with him.
Well I know all the gifts that are marked for him who is to see, who is
   to behold the manifold riches.
And it shall be I.
Mine shall be the knowledge of all the sundry jades and gold,
of the quetzal feathers and the other feathers,
of the cacao of variegated colors,
of the cotton of variegated colors,
of the diverse flowers and diverse fruits.
O my mother, be not sad.
I go now to seek out the evil one, my uncle. . . ."

Then he came.
He arrayed himself, he adorned himself, he who was called Copil.
He was very evil,
he was a greater sorcerer than his mother, Malinalxoch;
Copil was a very evil man.

He came in the year 1-House, 1285
and in the place called Zoquitzinco he transformed himself.
Once more he came, and in the place called Atlapalco he transformed
    himself.
He came once again and in the place called Itztapaltemoc he
    transformed himself,
and because Copil transformed himself,
because he turned himself into a flagstone,
it is now called,
it is known as Itztapaltetitlan.

After Copil was transformed,
after Copil had transformed himself into a flagstone,
he returned again to his home,
to Texcaltepeticpac.
Soon afterward Huitzilopochtli sees and knows
that Copil, his nephew, has grown,
and tells his priests:
"Oh, my parents, be ready,
for my nephew, the crook, is coming,
and I am going to destroy him."
Before long, he met him there in Tepetzinco,
and when he saw him, he said:
"Who are you?
Where are you coming from?"
And Copil answered,
"I am he whom my sister brought into the world."
And Huitzilopochtli said again:
"Where is your home?"
And Copil said:
"There in Texcaltepeticpac."
Then Huitzilopochtli said,
"Well, are you not
he whom my sister, Malinalxoch, brought into the world?"
"Yes, I am he," Copil said,
"and I shall capture you, I shall destroy you!
Why did you abandon my mother while she was sleeping?

Why did you abandon her by trickery?
I shall slay you!"

"Very well," Huitzilopochtli said, "Come ahead."
They pursued each other with cunning,
and they captured Copil in Tepetzinco.
When he was dead he (Huitzilopochtli) cut off his head and slashed
   open his chest,
and when he had slashed open his chest, he tore out his heart.
Then he placed his head on top of Tepetzintli, which is now called
   Acopilco,
and there the head of Copil died.

And after Huitzilopochtli slew him,
he ran off with Copil's heart.
And the idol-bearer, called Quauhtlequetzqui, came upon
   Huitzilopochtli.
When he encountered him, he said,
"You have wearied yourself, O priest."
"Come, O Quauhtlequetzqui," he said.
"Here is the heart of the evil one, Copil.
I have slain him.
Run with it into the rushes, into the reeds.
There you shall see the mat of stone
on which Quetzalcoatl rested when he went away,
and his seats, one red and one black.
There you shall halt and you shall cast away the heart of Copil."

Then Quauhtlequetzqui went off to cast away the heart.
When he came to the place he had described to him,
he saw the Mat of stone,
and he halted there and cast away the heart;
it fell in among the rushes, in among the reeds. . . .
The place where Quauhcoatl stopped and cast away the heart,
we now call Tlalcocomoco. . . .

Then the Mexicans went to Acuezcomac,
they passed through Huehuetlan, Atlixocan, Teoculhuacan, Tepetocan,
   Huitzilac,
Culhuacan, Huixachtla, Cahualtepec, Tetlacuixomac.
They settled in Tlapitzahuayan in the year 2-Rabbit, 1286. . . .

In the year 11-Reed, 1295 . . . the Mexicans passed through
    Zacatla. . . .
The people of Chalco drove them out,
they stoned them.
Once again they went to Chapultepec. . . .
Behind Chapultepec all the Tepanecas, Azcapotzalcas and Culhuacans,
the Xochimilcas, Cuitlahuacas and Chalcas besieged the Mexicans. . . .
The Mexicans were besieged in Chapultepec in 2-Reed, 1299.

Then the Mexicans moved to Acuezcomac.
Then they came, they settled in Mazatlan,
and all the Mexicans gathered in Tepetocan.
The from there they went to Culhuacan.

Coxcoxtli was the king of Culhuacan. . . .
Then Huitzilopochtli said to the Mexicans,
"My fathers, say to Coxcoxtli, 'Where shall we live?' "
They addressed Coxcoxtli, they said to him,
"O lord, O king, we are beseeching you.
Where shall we go?
We have known this to be your city.
Have mercy on us with a small piece of your land on which we may
    live!"
Coxcoxtli replied, he said, "Very well."
He summoned his Culhuacan chiefs, he said to them,
"Where shall they live?"
"O lord, O king, let them go there," his chiefs said.
"Let the Mexicans live beside the mountain, here in Tizaapan."
Then they took them, they established them in Tizaapan.
They advised Coxcoxtli, the king, they said, "O lord, O king, we have
    taken the Mexicans to Tizaapan."
"Good," Coxcoxtli said, "They are monstrous, they are evil. Perhaps
    they will meet their end there,
perhaps they will be devoured by the snakes,
for it is the dwelling place of many snakes."

But the Mexicans were overjoyed when they saw the snakes.
They cooked them,
they roasted them over the fire, and they ate them. . . .

In the year 13-Reed 1323,

the Mexicans had passed, had spent twenty-five years in Tizaapan
   Culhuacan.
Then Huitzilopochtli spoke to his fathers, he said to them,
"O my fathers, another person shall appear whose name is Yaocihuatl.
She is my grandmother and we shall have her.
And hear this, O my chiefs, we are not to remain here.
We shall find (the place) off there.
There is where we shall possess it. . . .
And now gird yourselves,
make yourselves ready,
for you have heard that Yaocihuatl, my grandmother, will manifest
   herself there.
I command that you go,
that you ask Achitometl for his child, his daughter.
You are to ask him for his precious child,
for I know I shall give her to you."
And then the Mexicans went off,
they went to ask Achitometl for his daughter.
The Mexicans spoke to him, they said,
"O my prince, O lord, O king, we your grandfathers, we your vassals,
   and all the Mexicans,
pray that you grant, that you give us, your jewel, your quetzal feather,
your daughter, our granddaughter, the princess.
There, beside the mountain in Tizaapan she will keep guard."
Achitometl said, "Very well, O Mexicans, you may take her with you."
He gave her to the Mexicans.
They went off with the daughter of Achitometl,
they brought her,
they settled her in Tizaapan.
Then Huitzilopochtli spoke . . . he said to them,
"O my fathers, I order you to slay the daughter of Achitometl and to
   flay her.
When you have flayed her, you are to dress a priest in her skin."
Then they slew the princess and they flayed her,
and after they flayed her, they dressed a priest in her skin.
Huitzilopochtli then said,
"O my chiefs, go and summon Achitometl."
The Mexicans went off, they went to summon him.
They said, "O our lord, O my grandson, O lord, O king . . .
your grandfathers, the Mexicans beseech you, they say,
'May he come to see, may he come to greet the goddess.

We invite him.' "

Achitometl said, "Very well. Let us go."

He said to his lords, "Let us go to Tizaapan,

the Mexicans have invited us. . . ."

They took along rubber, copal, papers, flowers, and tobacco,

and also what is called the "lord's food" to set down in offering before
    the goddess. . . .

And when Achitometl arrived in Tizaapan, the Mexicans said, as they
    received him,

"You have wearied yourself, O my grandson, O lord, O king.

We, your grandfathers, we, your vassals, shall cause you to become ill.

May you see, may you greet your goddess."

"Very good, O my grandfathers," he said.

He took the rubber, the copal, the flowers, the tobacco, and the food
    offering,

and he offered them to her,

he set them down before the false goddess whom they had flayed.

Then Achitometl tore off the heads of quail before his goddess;

he still did not see the person before whom he was decapitating the
    quail.

Then he made an offering of incense and the incense-burner blazed up,

and Achitometl saw a man in his daughter's skin.

He was horror-struck.

He cried out, he shouted to his lords and to his vassals.

He said, "Who are they, eh, O Culhuacans?

Have you not seen?

They have flayed my daughter!

They shall not remain here, the fiends!

We shall slay them, we shall massacre them! The evil ones shall be
    annihilated here!"

They began to fight. . . .

The Culhuacans pursued them, they pursued the Mexicans,

they drove them into the water. . . .

The Culhuacans thought that they had perished in the water,

but they crossed the water on their shields,

they crossed on their arrows and shields.

They bound together the arrows, called tlacochtli,

and those called tlatzontectli,

and, sitting upon them, they crossed the water. . . .

and sitting upon the shields they crossed the water

when the Culhuacans pursued them.

And they came into the rushes, into the reeds at Mexicatzinco. . . .

There they dried their battle gear which had become wet,

their insignias, their shields—all their gear.

And their women and children began to weep.

They said, "Where shall we go? Let us remain here in the reeds. . . ."

And then the old Mexicans, Quauhtlequetzqui, or Quauhcoatl, and also
the one called Axolohua went off,

they went into the rushes, into the reeds

at the place that is now called Toltzalan Acatzalan;

the two of them went to look for the place they were to settle.

And when they came upon it,

they saw the many wondrous things there in the reeds.

This was the reason Huitzilopochtli had given his orders to the idol-
bearers, his fathers,

Quauhtlequetzqui, or Quauhcoatl, and Axolohua, the priest.

For he had sent them off,

he had told them all that there was in the rushes, in the reeds,

and that there he, Huitzilopochtli, was to stand,

that there he was to keep guard.

He told them with his own lips,

thus he sent off the Mexicans.

And then they saw the white bald cypresses, the white willows,

and the white reeds and the white rushes;

and also the white frogs, the white fish, and the white snakes that lived
there in the water.

And they saw the springs that joined;

the first spring faced east and was called Tleatl and Atlatlayan,

the second spring faced north and was called Matlalatl and also
Tozpalatl.

And when they saw this, the old men wept.

They said, "Perhaps it is to be here.

We have seen what the priest, Huitzilopochtli, described to us when he
sent us off.

He said, 'In the rushes, in the reeds, you shall see many things.' And
now we have seen them, we have beheld them!

It has come true, his words when he sent us off have come true!"

Then they said, "O Mexicans, let us go, for we have beheld them.

Let us await the word of the priest;

he knows how it shall be done."

Then they came, they sojourned in Temazcaltitlan.

And during the night he saw him, Huitzilopochtli appeared to the idol-
bearer, called Quauhtlequetzqui, or Quauhcoatl.

He said to him, "O Quauhcoatl, you have seen all there is in among the
    reeds, in among the rushes,
you have beheld it.
But hear this:
There is something you still have not seen.
Go, go and look at the cactus,
and on it, standing on it, you shall see an eagle.
It is eating, it is warming itself in the sun,
and your hearts will rejoice,
for it is the heart of Copil that you cast away where you halted in
    Tlalcocomoco.
There it fell, where you looked, at the edge of the spring,
among the rushes, among the reeds.
And from Copil's heart sprouted what is now called tenochtli. There we
    shall be,
we shall keep guard,
we shall await, we shall meet the diverse peoples in battle.
With our bellies, with our heads,
with our arrows, with our shields,
we shall confront all who surround us
and we shall vanquish them all,
we shall make them captives,
and thus our city shall be established.
Mexico Tenochtitlan:
where the eagle screeches,
where he spreads his wings,
where the eagle feeds,
where the fish fly,
and where the serpent is torn apart.
Mexico Tenochtitlan!
And many things shall come to pass."

Then Quauhcoatl said to him. "Very well, oh priest. Your heart has
    granted it.
Let all the old men, your fathers, hear."
Then Quauhcoatl gathered the Mexicans together,
he had them hear the words of Huitzilopochtli;
the Mexicans listened.
And then, once more, they went in among the rushes, in among the
    reeds, to the edge of the spring.
And when they came out into the reeds,
there, at the edge of the spring, was the tenochtli,

and they saw an eagle on the tenochtli, perched on it, standing on it.
It was eating something, it was feeding,
it was pecking at what it was eating.
And when the eagle saw the Mexicans, he bowed his head low.
(They had only seen the eagle from afar.)
Its nest, its pallet, was of every kind of precious feather—
lovely cotinga feathers, roseate
spoonbill feathers, quetzal feathers.
And they also saw strewn about the heads of sundry birds,
the heads of precious birds strung together,
and some bird's feet and bones.
And the god called out to them, he said to them,
"O Mexicans, it shall be there!"
(But the Mexicans did not see who spoke.)
It is for this reason they call it Tenochtitlan.
And then the Mexicans wept, they said,
"O happy, O blessed are we!
We have beheld the city that shall be ours!
Let us go, now, let us rest. . . ."

This was in the year 2-House, 1325.

From Fernando Alvarado Tezozomoc, *Crónica Mexicayotl*, translated by Thelma D. Sullivan, *Tlalocan*, VI (UNAM, 1971), pp. 313–35.

3. The Birth of Huitzilopochtli

The Aztecs greatly revered Huitzilopochtli; they knew his origin, his beginning, was in this manner:

In Coatepec, on the way to Tula, there lived, there dwelt a woman named Coatlicue. She was the mother of the four hundred gods of the south and their sister, Coyolxauhqui. And this Coatlicue did penance there: she swept, which was her task; thus she did penance in Coatepec, the Mountain of the Serpent.

One day, when Coatlicue was sweeping, a ball of fine feathers fell on her. Coatlicue picked them up and put them in her bosom. When she finished sweeping, she looked for the feathers she had put in her bosom, but found nothing there. At that moment Coatlicue was with child.

The four hundred gods of the south, seeing their mother was with child, were very annoyed. They said, "Who has done this to you? Who has made you with child? This insults us, dishonors us."

And their sister Coyolxauhqui said to them: "My brothers, she has dishonored us. We must kill our mother, the wicked woman who is now with child. Who gave her what she carries in her womb?"

When Coatlicue learned of this, she was very frightened. She was very sad. But her son Huitzilopochtli spoke to her from the womb, he comforted her: "Do not be afraid, I know what I must do." Having heard the words of her son, Coatlicue was consoled, her heart was quiet, she felt at peace.

But meanwhile the four hundred gods of the south came together to make a decision, and together they decided to kill their mother, because she had disgraced them. They were very angry, they were very agitated, as if the heart had gone out of them. Coyolxauhqui incited them, she inflamed the anger of her brothers, so that they would kill her mother. And the four hundred gods made ready, they attired themselves as for war.

The four hundred gods of the south were like captains; they twisted and bound up their hair as warriors arrange their long hair. But one of them, named Cuahuitlicac, broke his word. He went immediately to tell, to reveal to Huitzilopochtli, what the four hundred had said. And Huitzilopochtli replied to him: "Take care, be watchful, my uncle, for I know well what I must do."

The four hundred gods were determined to kill, to do away with their mother, and they began to prepare, with Coyolxauhqui directing them. They were very robust, well equipped, adorned as for war. They distributed among themselves their paper garb, the anecuyotl [girdle], the nettles, the streamers of colored paper; they tied little bells on the calves of their legs. Their arrows had barbed points.

Then they began to move, they went in order, in line, in orderly squadrons. Coyolxauhqui led them. But Cuahuitlicac went immediately up onto the mountain to speak to Huitzilopochtli from there: "They are coming now."

Huitzilopochtli replied, "Look carefully. Which way are they coming?"

Then Cuahuitlicac said, "They are coming through Tzompantitlan."

And again Huitzilopochtli said, "Where are them coming from now?"

Cuahuitlicac replied, "Now they are coming through Coaxalpan."

And once more Huitzilopochtli asked Cuahuitlicac: "Look carefully. Which way are they coming?"

"Now they are coming up the side of the mountain."

And yet again Huitzilopochtli said, "Look carefully. Which way are they coming?"

Then Cuahuitlicac said, "They are at the top now, they are here, Coyolxauhqui leads them."

At that moment Huitzilopochtli was born. He put on his gear, his shield of eagle feathers, his darts, his blue dart-thrower, the turquoise dart-thrower. He painted his face with diagonal stripes, in the color called "child's paint." He arranged fine plumage on his head, he put on his earplugs. And on his left foot, which was withered, he wore a sandal covered with feathers. And his legs and arms were painted blue.

And the so-called Tochancalqui set fire to the serpent of candlewood, the one called Xiuhcoatl, which obeyed Huitzilopochtli. With the fire serpent he struck Coyolxauhqui, he cut off her head, and left it lying there on the slope of Coatepetl. The body of Coyolxauhqui went rolling down the hill, it fell to pieces, her hands, her legs, her body fell in different places.

Then Huitzilopochtli was proud; he pursued the four hundred gods of the south, he chased them, drove them off the top of Coatepetl. And when he followed them down to the foot of the mountain, he pursued them, he chased them all around the mountain, as if they were rabbits. He made them run around it four times. In vain they turned to attack him, rattling their bells and clashing their shields. They could do nothing, gain nothing, they could not defend themselves. Huitzilopochtli chased them, he drove them away, he humbled them, he destroyed, he annihilated them.

Even then he did not leave them, but continued to pursue them. They begged him repeatedly, saying, "It is enough!"

But Huitzilopochtli was not satisfied, he pushed on forcefully, he pursued them. Only a few were able to escape him, to avoid his reach. They went toward the south, and because they went toward the south, they are called gods of the south.

When Huitzilopochtli had killed them, when he had given vent to his wrath, he stripped off their gear, their ornaments, their anecuyotl; he put these on, he took possession of them, he introduced them into his destiny, he made them his own insignia.

And this Huitzilopochtli, as they say, was a prodigy, because he was conceived only from fine plumage which fell into the womb of his mother, Coatlicue; he never had any father. The Aztecs venerated him, they made sacrifices to him, honored him, and served him. And Huitzilopochtli rewarded those who did so. And his cult, as it was practiced from the most ancient times, came from there, from Coatepec, the Mountain of the Serpent.

Florentine Codex, Book III, chapter 1; from Miguel León-Portilla, ed., *Pre-Columbian Literatures of Mexico* (Norman, OK: University of Oklahoma Press, 1969), pp. 43–48.

⚛ 3 ⚛

Sacred Hymns, Prayers, and Ceremonies

*S*everal codices, among them the Borbonicus, Magliabecchi, *and* Vatican A, *as well as several chronicles, contain pictures and texts related to the sacred feasts, according to the solar calendar. Following the agricultural cycle, gods and goddesses are invoked and worshipped in various forms, including the offering of human sacrifices. The ceremonies were accompanied by music, dances, and chants. In this context the twenty sacred hymns, transcribed from the oral tradition of the elders by fray Bernardino de Sahagún, were intoned.*

A selection of these hymns includes those in honor of Xipe Totec, Our Lord the Flayed One, a fertility god; Cihuacoatl, the Female Twin or Female Serpent, a title of the Mother Goddess; Tlaloc, god of rain; and of Tezcatlipoca, Smoking Mirror, one of the manifestations of the supreme God of Duality, Ometeotl. Although the language of these hymns is esoteric, one can glimpse some of the subtleties inherent in this sacred literature.

Besides evoking the main attributes of these gods, the sacred hymns refer to other themes, including war and the primordial Mesoamerican staple, maize. Here, the reader should keep in mind the interdependent relationship between humans and maize: neither can survive without the other.

From among the many Nahua prayers that have survived, one of the several addressed to Tezcatlipoca, the god of the Smoking Mirror, is offered here. Pronounced with anguish whenever a cocoliztli *or pestilence afflicted the people, two points are emphasized. One is the nature of the calamity itself; the other, Tezcatlipoca's need for human service. If the pestilence continued, the moment could arrive when there would be nobody left alive to provide him with the sacrifices he required.*

A text about the act of purifying the heart (p. 222), a rite of confessing sexual transgressions, with the ceremonial expressions of the priest

*dedicated to the service of the goddess Tlazolteotl, She-of-Filth, vividly
recalls a practice that has been compared to the sacramental confession
of the Roman Catholic Church.*

*The description of the feast of Toxcatl in honor of Tezcatlipoca
(p. 217) exemplifies Nahua liturgical literature. In addition to the many
ceremonies carried out at the main temple and elsewhere, it was at feasts
like this that the hymns to the gods were intoned.*

*Taken together, these extracts offer an insight into the religious and
ethical life of the ancient Nahuas.*

1. Hymn to Xipe Totec

SONG OF OUR FLAYED LORD
THE NIGHT DRINKER[1]
(XIPE TOTEC)

Drinker by night, why are you difficult?
 Go in what covers you;
 Apparel yourself in garments of gold.
 This means, you, Night Drinker, our Flayed Lord, why are you
    difficult? Are you angry? do you hide? That is, why does it not rain?
 Teocuitlaquemitl xicmoquenti means, may it rain, may the water
    come.
 My god carries waters of jade on his back.
 The waterway's midpoint is not its way down.
 The quetzal-plume cypress, the quetzal-plume fire snake have left me
    bereft.
 This means, you are my god; your water has descended, your water
    has come.
 Ay Quetzalavevetl: That is, now it becomes the color of the quetzal
    feather, now it is greening, now it is spring.
 Ay quetzalxiuhcoatl nechiaiquinocauhquet: That is, now famine has
    left us.
 Let me go, let me perish.
 I am the green stalk of maize;
 My heart is a precious green stone.
 I shall look at the gold:

[1]*Yohuallana*, "Night Drinker," was a title applied to the priest who presided over the gladiatorial sacrifice, *tlahuahuanaliztli*, the highlight of the *veintena* (20-day cycle) of Tlaxcax-
ipehualiztli, Xipe's particular ceremony. [Sullivan's note]

My heart will repose.

The leader is hardened.

The war lord's been born.

This means, let me go, let me perish, I who am Yoatzin, that is, the green maize stalk; my heart is like a jade.

Ateocuitlatl nocoyaitaz means, whatever is first to form, I shall be tranquil.

My lord the maize, face up!

He fears in vain.

He is the tender maize.

Your god observes you from your hills.

My heart will be at rest.

The leader is hardened, The war lord's been born.

This means, he is my god. Some of his sustenance is growing where there is labor, and what comes up first where there is labor, everyone gives to you first; and when everything has now come up, once again everyone gives you your sustenance.

Thelma D. Sullivan, *Primeros Memoriales* (Norman, OK: University of Oklahoma Press, 1997), pp. 146–48.

2. Song of Cihuacoatl

The eagle, the eagle Quilaztli,

Her face has been painted with the blood of a snake.

In eagle plumes dressed she comes sweeping the road.

Bald cypress of Chalma, now Colhuacanian.

This means, Eagle-woman. Her face has been painted with serpent blood, and of eagle feathers is what is called her eagle headdress, which is on her (head). She has been brought there to Colhuacan.

Fir branches of our sustenance,

Maize ear in the godly field,

With rattle sticks she is supported.

This means, when the maize was planted,

it was done in the divine field. With rattle sticks they dug; thus they planted.

The thorn, the thorn lies in my hand.

The thorn, the thorn lies in my hand.

With rattle sticks in the godly field

She is supported.

Vitztla means, in my hand lie my rattle sticks with which I sow, with which I dig.

The broom lies in my hand.
With rattle sticks in the godly field
She is supported.
Malinalla, victli means, with the digging stick she sweeps; that is, with it she works in the divine field and with her rattle stick she has dug, she has planted.
Thirteen Eagle is our mother, Chalman lady.
He fills me with the glory of his cactus dart,
He who is my lord Mixcoatl.
This means, Thirteen Eagle is my sign. I am your mother and you people of Chalma are my children. Take the cactus dart; fill me with it.
Our mother, warrior-woman,
Our mother, warrior-woman,
Deer of Colhuacan who is covered with feathers.
This means, I am your mother, the warrior-woman. My home is there in Colhuacan, and I give someone an eagle feather with which she becomes an eagle.
The sun has shone, war goes on.
The sun has shone, war goes on.
Let men be dragged up; they will come to an end.
The deer of Colhuacan is covered with plumes.
This means, the sun has shone, the day has dawned. Let there be war, let captives be taken, let the land be decimated. I give people eagle feathers.
Eagle feathers are your facial paint,
Of the fighter is your facial paint.
This means, captives have been taken. His face is painted with eagle feathers.

Thelma D. Sullivan, *Primeros Memoriales*, pp. 143–44.

3. Hymn to Tlaloc

O, Tlaloc!

O Lord, Our Lord, O Provider, O Lord of Verdure
Lord of Tlalocan, Lord of the Sweet-Scented Marigold, Lord of Copal!
The gods, Our Lords, the Providers
the Lords of Rubber, the Lords of the Sweet-Scented
Marigold, the Lords of Copal,

have sealed themselves in a coffer, they have locked themselves in a
    box.
They have hidden the jade and turquoise and precious jewels of life,
they have carried off their sister, Chicomecoatl, the fruits of the earth,
and the Crimson Goddess, the chile.

Oh, the fruits of the earth lie panting;
the sister of the gods, the sustenances of life,
feebly drags herself along,
she is covered with dust, she is covered with cobwebs,
she is utterly worn and weary.

And behold the people, the subjects are perishing!
Their eyelids are puffy, their mouths as dry as straw,
their bones are desiccated, and they are twisted and gaunt,
their lips are thin, their necks pale and scrawny.

And the children, the little ones—
those who barely walk, those who crawl
those still on the ground making little piles of earth and broken bits of
    pottery
and the infants lashed to their boards and slats,
all of them are hollow-eyed.

Everyone knows anguish and affliction,
everyone is gazing upon torment;
no one has been overlooked.

All living things are suffering.
The troupial and roseate spoonbill drag themselves along,
they topple over and lie prostrate on their backs,
weakly opening and closing their beaks.
And the animals: the dogs of the Lord of All and the Everywhere are
    reeling;
they take refuge among us, vainly they lick the earth.
Man and beast alike are crazed for the want of water,
they die for the want of water,
they are perishing, they are wasting away, they are vanishing!

The breast of our mother and father, Lord of the Earth, is dry;
no longer can she nourish, no longer can she feed,
no longer can she suckle what sprouts, what comes forth,
what is the very life of the people, their food and their sustenance.

Oh, the sustenances of life are no more, they have vanished;
the gods, the providers, have carried them off,
they have hidden them away in Tlalocan;
they have sealed in a coffer, they have locked in a box,
their verdure and freshness—
the cuphea and fleabane, the purslane and fig-marigold—
all that grows and puts forth,
all that bears and yields,
all that sprouts and bursts into bloom
all vegetation that issues from you
and is your flesh, your generation and renewal.

It is the jade, the armlet, the turquoise—
the most precious, the only precious thing there is;
it is the sustenance, the substance, the life of the world,
whereby those who are alive, live
and talk and rejoice and laugh.
Oh, the fruits of the earth, the green and growing things have gone,
they have hidden themselves away!

O Lord, Our Lord, Lord of Tlalocan, O Provider!
What does your heart will?
By chance have you let this fall from your hand?
Is it to be thus? Is this all? Is this the end?
Are the people, the multitude, to die out, to vanish from the earth?
Is the city to be left empty and desolate?
Is this all? Is it to be thus?
Was it so ordained Above and in the Region of the Dead?
Was it so decreed for us? Was it so determined?

But all the little ones suffer—
Those who barely walk, those who crawl, those on the ground still,
the infants lashed to their boards and slats,
who are sensible of nothing—
give them, at least something to eat,
at least provide them with something,
for as yet they do not reason.

If we have vexed the Above and the Region of the Dead
If our foulness and corruption rose up,
If it wafted up to the Above, to the heavens,
then, perhaps this is all; perhaps, this is the end.
Perhaps, at this very moment darkness shall come

and all shall perish, all shall disappear from the earth.
What can we say? What is the use? To whom can we appeal?
It has been ordained.

At least let the common people have fullness and abundance;
let them not know total dissolution.
Their hearts and bodies are in torment,
day and night their hearts burn, their hearts are on fire!
A monstrous serpent is within them
slavering and panting and shrieking;
It is terrifying how it burns, how it shrieks, how it howls!

Perhaps now is coming true, now is coming to pass,
what men and women of old knew, what they handed down:
that the heavens over us shall sunder,
that the demons of the air shall descend
and shall come to destroy the earth and devour the people,
that darkness shall prevail, that nothing be left on the earth.
Our grandmothers and our grandfathers knew it,
they handed it down, it was their tradition
that it would come to pass, that it would come to be.

And now to the ends of the earth, to the outmost bounds of the earth,
the land is devastated.
It is all over now, it is the end;
the earth's seeds have withered,
like old men and women they have shriveled,
and nothing has food, no one shall give food and drink to another.

O, Our Lord, let it not go on like this,
Let there be fullness and abundance for all!

Or, let pestilence seize the people in its grip,
Let the Lord of the Region of the Dead do his work, take up his duties.
Then, perhaps, Chicomecoatl and Centeotl shall sustain them, shall
    succor them a little;
perhaps, into their mouths she shall put a drop of corn gruel, a scrap of
    food,
as provisions for their journey.

Or let the Sun, the Eagle Ascendant, the Precious Child, the Valiant
   One,
the Brave Warrior, the Everlasting Resplendent One, do his work.

Then the people, and the Eagle and Jaguar Knights shall rejoice,
for in the middle, in the center of the battlefield they shall be charred,
and their hair shall scatter, their bones whiten, their skulls split open.
And they shall know the House of the Sun,
where the sun is amused, where his praises are sung,
where the nectar of sundry sweet and fragrant flowers is sipped,
where the Eagle and Jaguar Knights,
the brave and valiant who die in battle, are glorified.

And the little child, the tot,
still a chick, still a mite, not sensible to anything,
as jade, as turquoise, he shall go to heaven, the House of the Sun;
a perfect jade, a perfect turquoise, a smooth and lustrous turquoise,
is the heart he shall offer the sun.

And your sister, Chicomecoatl, shall sustain him,
the sister of the gods, the Providers, shall enter his belly,
and thus he shall be provided for his journey;
she shall lift him to that far-off place.
For she alone is our flesh and bones,
she alone is our staff and support,
she alone is our strength and fortitude;
she is man's entire recompense.

O Lord, Our Lord,
the people, the subjects—the led, the guided, the governed—
now behold, now feel, now are filled to bursting
with searing pain of affliction.
Their flesh and bones are stricken by want and privation,
they are worn, spent and in torment;
indeed, the pain reaches to the heart of them.
Not only once, or merely twice
do they behold, do they suffer death!
And the animals, also.

O Lord, O King,
Lord of Verdure, Lord of Rubber, Lord of the Sweet-Scented Marigold!
May it be your will,
may you, at least, cast a sidelong glance at the people.
They are going, they are perishing, they are vanishing, they are breaking
   and crumbling,
they are disappearing from the earth,
the suckling infants are wizened and dying,
the little ones that crawl are wasting away!

May it be your will, O, Our Lord,
may you grant that the gods, the Providers,
the Lords of the Sweet-Scented Marigold and the Lords of Copal do
   their work,
that they see their tasks on earth.
May bounty and good fortune be unleashed,
may the sweet-scented marigold rattles shake,
may the rattleboards of the mist clatter,
may the gods don their rubber sandals!
Oh with a sprinkle, with a few drops of dew,
may you succor, may you aid, Tlaltecutli, Lord of the Earth, who feeds
   and nourishes man!
And may you comfort the anguished fruits of the earth,
beloved child, sister of the gods,
who feebly drags herself through the rows,
who is wilting and withering in the rows!

Let the people be blessed with fullness and abundance,
let them behold, let them enjoy, the jade and the turquoise—
the precious vegetation,
the flesh of Our Lords, the Providers, the Gods of Rain,
who bring, who shower down, the riches that are theirs alone.
And let the plants and animals be blessed with fullness and abundance,
let the troupial and roseate spoonbill sing,
let them flutter their wings, let them sip the sweet nectar.

Oh, let not the Gods of Rain loose their wrath and indignation,
for the people are enfeebled
and they shall frighten them, they shall strike terror into them.
Let them not lash themselves into a fury,
but let them only take, let them only strike the one who is theirs, who
   was born,
who came into the world, marked for Tlalocan,

who is their property, their possession.
Let them not deceive the people
that inhabit the forests and open plains,
that dwell in the wild, untilled fields.
Neither let them do this:
let them not blight the trees, the magueys, the prickly pears, and all
    that grows,
for they are the root of the life of the people,
the sustenance of the poor and hapless,
those living in misery and want, the destitute,
who have nothing to eat in the morning, nothing in the evening,
who go about empty, their stomachs rumbling.

O Lord, Beloved Lord, O Provider!
May it be in your heart to grant, to give, to bring comfort to the earth
and all that lives on it and all that grows on it.
And you who inhabit the four corners of the universe,
you Lords of Verdure, you the Providers,
you the Lords of the Mountain Heights, you the Lords of the
Cavernous Depths

I call out, I cry out to you:
come, bring yourselves here,
comfort the people, slake the thirst of the earth;
the earth and the animals, the leaves and the stalks
are watching and waiting and crying out.
O Gods, Our Lord, make haste!

Thelma D. Sullivan and T. J. Knab, *A Scattering of Jades* (New York: Simon & Schuster, 1994), pp. 152–59.

4. Invocation of Tezcatlipoca

O master, O our lord,
O lord of the near, of the nigh,
O night, O wind,
now in truth I come to appear before you,
to reach you.
Before you I come jumping over ridges,
I come sidling up,
I who am a commoner, unrighteous, evil.
Let me not meet your annoyance, your wrath.

And do you dispose as you will. . . .
In truth now you incline your heart,
you dispose.
And it was ordained above us,
it was arranged in the land of the dead,
in the heavens,
that we have been forsaken.
In truth now your annoyance, your anger,
descends, it gathers;
you who are the lord of the near, of the nigh.
Castigation, pestilence grow; they increase.
For the plague is reaching the earth.

O master, O our lord,
truly now already the common folk go;
they already perish.
Already there is havoc,
already the common folk, the vassals, are destroyed.
Already the babies, the children are [as if] crushed, shattered. They are
    those who know nothing,
those who pile up earth [and] potsherds;
those on the ground, who lie on the board,
stretched out on the board.
For already the infants are destroyed,
the eagle-warriors, the ocelot-warriors,
the old men, the old women,
the middle-aged women, the middle-aged men,
the mature unmarried men.
For already your city is destroyed.

O master, O our lord,
O lord of the near, of the nigh,
indeed your wrath, your anger, already take glory,
enjoy, take pleasure, delight in the castigation.
It is absolutely true . . . there remain placed, implanted, pestilence
    upon [your people]
even as you sprinkle, scatter,
the dew of the reed upon them.
And so you castigate them with icy water,
with nettles, with curved fangs.

And here, in truth, now,
O master, O our lord,

O night, O wind,
O Moyocoyatzin, O Titlacauan,
how can your heart wish it?
How can you wish it?
Have you already abandoned your vassals?
Is this perchance all?
Is it perchance this way?
Will perchance the common folk go, perish?
Will the governed come to an end?
Will emptiness, darkness prevail in the city?
Will it not be?
Will your miserable city choke with trees, fill with stones?
And your places for holding vigil,
where your mounds, your pyramids are located,
will they fall to pieces, will they break up?

Is this perchance to be no more?
Is this to be all?
It is perchance this way?
Will the castigation abate no more,
will your annoyance, your anger be reversed?
Will your wrath, your annoyance, no more be placated?
Have we perchance just been forsaken?
Has it perchance been ordained above us;
has it perchance been declared in the land of the dead?
Perchance no longer is there castigation with icy water?
perchance no longer is there castigation with nettles?
Perchance in truth now there will be darkness forever?
Will you no longer look back upon the common folk?

For—ah!—thus are they destroyed,
those who are restless in sickness,
who toss from side to side,
who nowhere can do anything;
whose teeth, whose mouths [are filled with] dirt.
For darkness is fallen; all are as if drunk;
they just fall somewhere.
And this [people] is as if destroyed,
for nevermore is there knowledge of one,
for deep darkness prevails,
for no longer does one concern himself for another,
for the trainable ones, the teachable ones, the children,
the suckling babies, those who are unlearned, already starve.

It is nothing but truth:
mothers, fathers have abandoned them;
the filth of the aged ones envelops them.

Alas, O master, O our lord,
O lord of the near, of the nigh,
O compassionate one: truly, now may your rage have passed.
May the vassals, the common folk,
have enjoyed, have benefited from castigation.
And your city has taken you by the ear,
you have tugged at the flank;
it has been punished with icy water, with nettles;
for truly now the reprehension of one, the confronting of one,
the curved fang,
have brought one benefit,
even as the dew of the reeds
has sprinkled, showered, scattered upon one.

O master, O our lord,
the city is as a baby, a child.
Perhaps it has heard, perhaps it has exhorted itself,
perhaps of its own accord it has tugged at its flank, at its ear. Perhaps it
    has reflected upon as much.
Perhaps of its own accord it has punished itself, castigated itself,
perhaps it has chided itself, exhorted itself,
so that in your hands they animate one another,
they encourage one another, they chatter.

May this yet be all, O master, O our lord,
O precious nobleman, O precious person;
may it [have reached] its end.
Conclude it, stem it.
May your annoyance, your anger, abate, be reversed;
may your wrath, your fury, be placated;
may your annoyance pass. Does not death prevail?
Where indeed is there to go, in vain?
For our tribute is death;
[it is] awarded us in common as merited.
And on earth there prevails the coming to pay the tribute of death.
For there will be the following after, the approaching
to your progenitor Mictlan tecutli, Cueçalli, Tzontemoc,
who remains unsatiated, who remains coveting.
He remains thirsting there for us,
hungering there for us, panting there for us.

O master, O our lord,
consider yet those who lie on the board, those who are on the ground,
those who know nothing,
the poor, the miserable, the useless,
those who rejoice not, the discontented,
those who never have the necessities of life,
those never comfortable of bone, of flesh,
those who all together live suffering great pain, great affliction of
   hearing.
Perchance somewhere you will require the eagle warrior, the ocelot
   warrior;
perchance he will go there to the house of the sun.
Perchance he will follow Quauhtleuanitl,
the blotched one, the brave warrior.
Perhaps he will provide drink, will provide food above us,
in the land of the dead, the heavens.

May this be all;
cease amusing yourself,
O master, O our lord,
O lord of the near, of the nigh,
O lord of the earth,
O Moyocoyatzin, O Titlacauan!
May the smoke, the cloud [of your ire] cease;
may the fire, the blaze [of your rage] be extinguished!
May the earth be at rest!
May the roseate spoonbill, the troupial sing;
may they preen themselves.
May [your people] call to you, supplicate you, know you!

This is all.
Thus I fall before you, I throw myself before you;
I cast myself into the place whence none rise, whence none leave,
the place of terror, of fear.
May I not have aroused your annoyance;
may I not have walked upon your fury.
O master, O precious nobleman, O our lord,
perform your office, do your work!

Arthur J. O. Anderson and Charles E. Dibble, *Florentine Codex of Fray Bernardino de Sa-hagún*, 12 vols. (Santa Fe, NM: School of American Research and the University of Utah Press, 1950–82), Book VI, chapter 7.

The goddess Tlazolteotl (goddess of filth) was able to wash away acts of sexual transgression.

5. Prayer to Tlazolteotl

O master, our lord,
O lord of the near, of the nigh,
you have taken, you have heard the commoner thus troubled,
who has reported before you, who has placed before you
his stench, his rottenness.
But perhaps he has come ridiculing you,
or he has come going amiss, going astray in your presence.
Perhaps he himself has come to plunge himself
into the torrent, from the crag,
or has come to cast himself there.
And perhaps he has come to place himself in the thongs, the snare.
Perhaps he has come to take the paralysis,
the blindness, the rottenness,
the tatters, the rags.

Perhaps certainly now, O master, O our lord,
O lord of the near, of the nigh,
perhaps he has come really to bind himself.
Perhaps he has retracted, swallowed,
suppressed a word or two;
for of his own will he acts,
he mocks himself;
for you are near, O master, O our lord,
O night, O wind.
He has just come,
just come to stand,
to speak, to pass;
for there rest the blue water, the yellow water
with which you bathe, with which you wash the common folk.

And perhaps he has come to take his destruction, his exaltation.
And perhaps he has come to do himself good:
perhaps he has come to unclothe, to strip himself [of his faults];
    perhaps he has come to show himself to you in all parts.
What is done is done;
what is performed is performed,
as if he had slipped, he had tripped;

as if in your presence he had gone astray, gone amiss;
and as if truly he had dirtied himself,
had hurled himself into the bottomless pit,
into the water, into a cave.
Truly, he is a common person;
. . . he goes carrying with him that which troubles him, perverts him,
and that which afflicts his bones,
his body,
his mind,
his heart;
and it eats, it drinks,
it disturbs his heart, his body.
And it becomes his stick, his stone;
his sighing, his fright;
his wonderment.
It becomes his resolution to improve his way of life.

And you are here.
It is not the work of man.
Although he has done it, although he has performed it,
it has been ordained.

And now, O master, O our lord,
O lord of the near, of the nigh,
as the commoner has troubled you, as he has offended you,
will perhaps your fury, your anger,
be placated, be turned?
May [the pardon] of the common person be complete, be achieved?
Because he takes fright,
he sighs when he turns to himself,
when he reflects upon, when he remembers
what he has done, what he has performed.
He weeps, he sorrows,
he eats out his heart when he acknowledges how he has offended you,
how he has wronged you.
He takes fright, he is terrified.

May your fury, your anger yet be placated;
may it yet be averted,
O master, O our lord.
Now, here, bathe him, wash him.
May he descend;
put him in the blue water, in the yellow water,

in the sea, in the deep waters
where you wash one, where you bathe one.

And may he go.
May he weep. May he be sad.
May he do penance.
May your words come forth.
Command of him that which your heart will require,
that which he will do, that which he will perform on earth,
how he will live.
And advise him how he will live.

The soothsayer, the confessor, addressed the one who confessed; he said
to him:

Here you hide,
you have come to place yourself,
. . . to pass the uninhabitable place, the place of fright,
where stand the torrent, the crag.
The cliff, the gorge, the crag stand sheer,
stand ashen, stand reddened:
the place where there can be no standing, no place of exit.
And there are placed one above another, joined one to another,
the cord, the snare,
the trap.

And you have descended,
you have cast yourself into the water, into the cave,
from the crag.
You have put yourself in the cords, into the snare,
which let one not escape.
[Your faults] are deadly . . . destroying . . . savage.
Perhaps you have retracted
or you have suppressed, you have swallowed
your stench, your rottenness,
your blackness, your filth;
ugly,
stinking,
rotten,
it is diffused, it is known,
it goes into the land of the dead, into the heavens.
Your stench, your rottenness are reaching the entire world.

And now, here,
you have given yourself, you have consulted with the master, our lord,
the lord of the near, of the nigh,
who can especially be offended,
who is especially wrathful, who is angered;
who tomorrow, the next day will hide you, will place you underfoot,
will send you to our common home,
the land of the dead.
There your mother, your father, Mictlan tecutli,
remains panting . . . coveting,
. . . thirsting for you . . . hungering for you.

And to you he will give, on you he will place
your desert, your merit,
which you have brought down, which you have required of our lord:
blindness, paralysis,
tatters, rags,
the miserable cape.

And you shall suffer, you shall endure misery;
you shall be poor on earth.
Your heart, your body will suffer torment, pain.
Torment, pain, fatigue will reach to your nose.
And as to this: you are here, you have been good to yourself,
for you have consulted the one who knows,
who sees things [within] wood, within stones.
And he knows, he sees things within you;
he hears what you say within yourself.

And as to this: what have you done, what have you performed?
For of your own volition
you have put yourself in the cords, into the snare;
for you have cast yourself into the water, into the cave,
from the crag.

You were good, you were fine when you were sent here,
when your mother, your father, Quetzalcoatl,
made you, created you.
You were cast, you were perforated [as] a precious green stone, a bracelet,
a precious turquoise.
You have sprouted, blossomed,
come to life, been born
[as] a precious green stone, a precious turquoise.

But just of your own volition
you defile yourself, dishonor yourself,
dirty yourself;
you live,
you cast yourself into excrement, into filth,
into that which you do, into that which you perform.
That in which you roll, in which you play
—the bad, the evil, the filth—
has dishonored one, dirtied one.
Of your own volition you have wallowed in filth, in refuse.
Even as if you were a baby, a child,
who plays with the dung, the excrement,
so have you bathed yourself, rolled yourself [in filth].

And as to this:
now you have given it, you have manifested it
to the lord of the near, of the nigh.
You have consulted, you have revealed it
to the bather of people, the washer of people.
Perhaps it is not in jest,
perhaps this is no little thing,
for you have descended where the blue waters,
the yellow waters,
the deep green waters
rest,
where the lord of the near, of the nigh,
washes one, bathes one.

You have just come;
you have just come to emerge, you have come to appear;
for you have descended into, you have beheld
the land of the dead, the heavens.
Now our lord has caused the sun to shine,
has caused the dawn to break.
Now you cause the sun to appear, to come forth.
Now once again you are rejuvenated, you emerge as a child.
Once again you become as a baby.
You become, you are hatched a young parrot,
a precious green stone, a precious turquoise.
Once again, newly, you sprout, you are hatched,
you are born on earth.

And go in peace and quiet;
go softly.
Yet try your feet out.
For a few days you will vex our lord of the near, of the nigh,
the night, the wind.
Behave yet humbly, sadly, modestly.
Live in this way; live so doing.
And give yourself exclusively to your weeping, your sorrowing;
go calling to our lord in sadness.

Do not presume.
Our lord of the near, of the nigh,
hears you,
knows of things within you,
hears within you when you have offended him.
What is happening to you?
What are your beginnings? What are your roots?
[Our lord] will wish for you that which his heart will determine.

Will he, perchance, here in the world, show you
the invisible, the frightening,
the painful,
the torment,
the affliction?
And perhaps he will hide you, put you underfoot,
send you to our common home,
the land of the dead.
Where you await the word of the lord of the near, of the nigh, the night,
    the wind,
himself,
the earth will crumble, the place will be made excrement.
And he will determine in the manner he will desire;
he will ruin,
burn,
break up,
scatter the earthen structure, the reed enclosure,
the mound of earth
which in vain you have put together.

And as to this:
be yet careful;
stand forth;
pay attention.

Be not as you are.
May your heart be otherwise.
May your manner of life be otherwise.
Take utmost care.
May you not falter again in something.
Be ever cautious.
And can you, perhaps, as a human being,
behold the lord of the near, of the nigh,
the youth, Moyocoya, Titlacauan,
Tezcatlipoca?
For he is the night; he is the wind.

Sweep;
clean;
arrange, order things.
[Otherwise] you wilt reject, offend
the master, the youth,
who goes appearing among us;
who lives everywhere,
who finds his amusement,
and works,
and goes seeking his friend.

And as to this:
do you go, especially to the sweeping.
Take care of the cleaning.
And now you are to clean things;
you are to clean yourself, you are to bathe slaves;
you are to dance, you are to sing.
And behold, you are to castigate yourself;
you are to fast,
you are to fast for a year.
And you are to draw blood.

And because you have found pleasure in filth, in vice,
you are twice [daily] to pass twigs,
once through your ear[lobe],
once through your tongue,
especially because of adultery,
and because at some time you have hurt, you have harmed,
your neighbor with your words.

And because at some time you have depreciated the things of our lord,
have failed to provide food,
you will provide, will offer as your duty,
the paper, the incense.

And see to him who thirsts, who hungers;
who goes moistening his lips, chewing his fingernails;
who goes skin and bone, who goes like a skeleton.
Take from your mouth the morsel;
share it;
offer it.

And clothe him who goes naked, who acquires not
that which to hang from his neck, from his loins.
For your body is also as his,
especially the sick one,
for he is the image of the lord of the near, of the nigh.

Be careful; be yet careful.
Pay close attention.
May the lord of the near, of the nigh,
recreate you.
This is all; take yourself hence.

Arthur J. O. Anderson and Charles E. Dibble, *Florentine Codex of Fray Bernardino de Sahagún,* Book VI, chapter 7.

☙ 4 ☙

Huehuetlahtolli
("Discourses of the
Elders")

*T*he beauty of the language is the salient of this literary genre. The Huehuetlahtolli, *"Ancient Word"* or *"Discourses of the Elders,"* conveyed the ancient wisdom in the most elegant Nahuatl prose. As fray Bernardino de Sahagún, who transcribed many huehuetlahtolli, wrote, they have to do with the "rhetoric, moral philosophy, and theology of the Mexican people, including curious things touching upon the subtleties of their language and very delicate things touching upon moral virtues."

The Huehuetlahtolli *amount to hundreds of pages. Choosing from among them is difficult. Some of the work included here provides an insight into the conjunction of religious and moral life: greetings to the pregnant woman, the words pronounced at the bathing of the baby boy and girl. Works relating more to daily life include the salutation to an elderly noblewoman and other dialogues spoken by well-educated boys and girls.*

The reader will also find proverbs and conundrums, the latter important lest one think the Nahuas lived a humorless life. Nothing could be farther from the truth. Although it was a highly formalized society, especially among the upper classes, and punishment for infractions of transgressions such as adultery, theft, and so on was draconian, the Nahuas, like all Mesoamericans, had a lively wit. Metaphor played a powerful role in religious, poetic, and even daily speech. The difrasismo *or kenning, the use of two concrete terms to convey an abstraction, is one kind of metaphor. Others selected here will give the reader a different insight into the complex and often arcane language of the songs and poems.*

It is remarkable that today in many Nahua communities the huehuehtlahtolli, as well as many of the ancient proverbs and conundrums, are still alive. Examples of contemporary expressions will appear later when we look at modern Nahua literature.

Florentine Codex, *Book VI*

1. GREETING THE PREGNANT WOMAN

Here are told the words of greeting with which they greeted or with which they exhorted the pregnant one; with which the youth's parents admonished her. And they told her to thank the gods for their blessings; and to guard herself that nothing abort the conceived baby. They made her see all the ills by which abortion might result. And when they had admonished her, they exhorted her mother, her father. And they also replied. And the pregnant one likewise exhorted her father-in-law, her mother-in-law.

"O my beloved granddaughter, O precious person, O precious bracelet, O precious green stone, O precious turquoise, O hair, O fingernail: truly now the god, the ruler, the lord of the near, of the nigh, has remembered you. Within you he wishes to place a life; he wishes to provide you with a precious necklace; he wishes to provide you with a precious feather. [Is it because] perhaps you have sighed? Perhaps you have wept? Perhaps you have reached out your arms to him? Perhaps you have supplicated our lord, the night, the wind, [at] the division of the night, [at] midnight? And perhaps you have held vigil? Perhaps you have been industrious in sweeping, and in offering incense? Perhaps at this time our lord has instructed you, has shown you mercy? Perhaps for this reason it was determined above us, in the land of the dead, in the beginning, that our lord wishes to place life within you? Perhaps it is true that, perchance, the lord, our prince, Quetzalcoatl, the creator, the author, has permitted it? And perhaps Ome tecutli, Ome ciuatl stated it? Perhaps the instruction was that a child be born.

"And do not speak to yourself; do not say: 'Already I am carrying something; already I am this way; already I am pregnant.' And do not become proud, do not become arrogant! Our lord will know of that within you; he knows of things, he sees within the rock, the tree. Soon something will befall you; our lord will bring about for us the death of our child. Soon something will therefore cause the baby, the tender thing, to be stillborn. And also the lord of the near, of the nigh, will bring sickness, pestilence down upon you. For truly our desire for a child is fulfilled by our lord. And indeed you have blasphemed, you have taken it jokingly.

"Perhaps, as your merit, perhaps there emerge the thorn, the maguey of your great-grandfathers, of your forefathers, which they go bequeathing to you. Perhaps [our lord] desires that the spine, the maguey which the old men planted deep in the soil, should sprout, should flower. Perhaps our lord wishes to make images, likenesses of those whom he has destroyed, whom he has hidden. Perhaps he wishes to lift the heads of those who will go increasing in dignity.

"And now, O my beloved daughter, O youngest one, be especially welcomed! Be especially careful; let there be your tears, your sighs. Be diligent in the sweeping, the cleaning, the arranging of things, the cutting [of wood], the fanning [of the fire], and the offering of incense. Hold vigil. Do not practice the sweetness, the agreeableness of sleep. Especially sigh with all your might; [say]: 'How will it be in a few days? How will this be with us?'

"And behold still another thing: be a guardian of the treasure of our lord. Let there be no mockery by you. And do nothing to cause sickness to the blessing of our lord with which you are adorned. Guard yourself never to seize, to raise up anything very heavy. Do not take excessively, do not give yourself excessively to the sweat bath. Do not kill it; do not overdo the heat [of the sweat bath].

"And behold also: may the eagle, the ocelot hear it, that is to say, her husband, our son, the eagle, the ocelot, N., who is seated [here]. Here is a word with which we command you, because we are knowledgeable, we who are the old men. Do not make too much sport with the one who is with you. Especially are you not to be excessive in the carnal act, for you will harm that with which our lord has adorned you. It will cause it to be feeble; it will come forth with lamed fingers [and] toes. If perhaps something is our merit, if the creation of our lord is born, it will be covered with filth. And truly it is said: 'You will die in childbirth. For this will cause the baby to be stuck, when no longer at the proper time the semen goes forth; for it exceeds glue in adhesiveness. It is so adhesive, so viscous, that you will thereby perish.'

"And do not view that which is evil, that which frightens one. The old men, the old women departed saying how you were to act. O my beloved daughter, O youngest one, O little dove, O little one, this is all. By this your mothers, your fathers, your forefathers, the old men, the old women who are here encourage you, animate you. And all things they make clear to you; everywhere they cause you to conduct yourself, everywhere they instruct you that you are their precious necklace, that you are their precious feather. They hide nothing, they cover nothing, because they are wise. And of this may you take much heed; may you be especially welcomed. May you not be endangered by something, may nothing cause you to take sick, may you not be harmed by something. May we all yet have faith in our lord, as to how it will grow light, how it will dawn, what he by whom we live will dispose. O youngest one, be heedful."

Then [one of his kinsmen] admonished the mothers, the fathers, or the mothers-in-law, the fathers-in-law. He supplicated them; he said to them:

"You who are present, you who possess precious necklaces, you who possess precious feathers, here truly now are those who were cut from your bosoms, from your laps, N. [and N.], who are here; they are your hair, they are your fingernails. Truly, now, we have acquired veritable wealth by virtue of our lord, for we have beheld in the coffer, in the reed chest, that which we should not discern, that which we should not behold, that which we should not understand. Perhaps our lord has mistaken us for others, for they have gone, our lord has removed those who go becoming the real mothers, the real fathers, the old ones. And in their absence we perform foolishness, babyishness, childishness. Where, truly, can we get them? Have they perchance departed to a place whence they will not return? Will they perchance in a short time come passing by? Will they come appearing? Will they perchance perform the duty of mothers, the duty of fathers? For they have departed forever; for our lord has placed them in a coffer; he has placed them in a reed chest. For we know that it has been forever; they are gone forever, completely finished. For here we obtain the reward in their behalf; in their absence we listen for them.

"And behold, truly now, what does our lord desire? Perhaps we shall obtain something as merit; something as desert. Perhaps we shall merit that of which we here dream, that which we here see in dreams. We speak in the land of the dead. In what manner is your precious necklace, your precious feather, our granddaughter, arrayed? Yet in our time, in our presence, may we marvel at the coming of light, the dawning, which our lord will bring about. May we look into his countenance [to know] in what manner our lord will reward us.

"For you are already here; motherhood, fatherhood are exercised here. Consummate your motherhood, your fatherhood; still admonish, still cry out to them although they are already like those not babies, not children; no more wishing to perform in negligence, no more wishing to perform reluctantly on earth, [and yet] they are rude, peevish. We beseech you that your spirit, your words, may yet be consummated. May they yet weep, may they yet sorrow, may they yet sigh. Perhaps it will come to pass in that which we desire as merit. Certainly we only dream, we only see in dreams; likewise the lord of the near, of the nigh, may be wrathful, may change the manner in which he will dispose. May you be here that your words [not] be in vain."

The mother, the father [of the maiden] replied to those who had made the entreaty. They said: "You have inclined your hearts, your bodies; you have suffered aches and pains in your heads, in your stomachs; may we not here have exposed you to maladies, to sickness and pestilence. You have taken to yourselves, you have grasped the word or two of your duty as mother, as father, which yet our lord accords you. In the meantime, you become protectors: you become the silk cotton tree, the cypress. Still you take from them the bundle, the carrying frame; you help carry the bundle for those who already reside beyond, those whom our lord has destroyed, has hidden: our forefathers, those who bequeathed, who as they departed placed on your backs, on your shoulders the bundle, the carrying frame, the burden, that which is to be carried, that which is to be borne, the duty of motherhood, the duty of fatherhood.

"And now the coffer, the reed chest are open; there issues the word or two of your motherhood, your fatherhood, which the old men, the old women, our ancestors, brought forth for you as they departed, and which you have taken from them, which you have learned from them: that which lies inert, which lies folded in your laps, in your breasts; which you have preserved, guarded, for your beloved children, the teachable ones, the trainable ones, the babies, the children who are here. Though like these, perhaps they already think themselves discreet; they do not yet imagine that to no avail they live on earth. They know not if perhaps the earth is a very good place where perhaps there is rejoicing. Perhaps they will contrive to find pleasure in sleep. Perhaps they will not engage in sweeping, in the offering of incense. And perhaps they will not say: 'What, if anything, is the lord of the near, of the nigh, determining for us in perhaps five days, in ten days?' Perhaps we shall obtain, perhaps we shall merit, perhaps we shall realize that of which we dream, that which we see in dreams, his possession, his creation, the life which our lord wishes to present. You have finished your words; everywhere you have made them known to them; everywhere you have caused them to reflect; nothing more have you left out. And also like them, we who are the old men, we who are the old women have once again taken, grasped [the counsel] such that you are our mothers, you are our fathers, such that once again we become your sons. You have shown mercy; you have inclined your hearts. We take, we clutch in our fists that which has come forth, that which flew out as a spark, your motherhood, your fatherhood. Truly, you have taken, you have grasped a word or two, wherefore we assemble here by the grace of our lord. We are gathered, we come together in behalf of, in regard to the baby, the girl, the maiden, your precious necklace, your precious feather, your hair, your fingernail, and the spine, the thorn of those who have gone, those whom our lord has destroyed, whom he has hidden, those who have gone on to remain beyond, your ancestors. And behold, truly, our lord wishes to show mercy in giving a precious necklace, a precious feather. He wishes to give it to your humble one. Our lord wishes to place a life within the maiden. For this he by whom we live has assembled you here. And this you have received, you have heeded. And behold this is that which we shall say, for certainly we still dream, we see in dreams that perhaps something will be the desert, the merit of the children who are here. Perhaps [our lord] will cause his creation to emerge on earth, for we exist, we live, we speak in darkness. Let us yet have faith in our lord as to how he will determine, for he still reigns, for truly he still disposes for us. Pay good heed, O our lords, O my sons. Find repose. May our lord rest you in peace."

The one with child, the one already pregnant, responded to the words which the old men had spoken. She said:

"My progenitors, my lords, precious persons, I have caused you to fall, to falter on the road; I have caused you torment. And you know so much of our lord, you know his secrets. No little thing have I caused you to forget, for already here I have rejoiced exceedingly, have enjoyed pleasure, for I have taken your motherhood, your fatherhood, the incomparable in your breasts, the wonderful, the precious. Perhaps somewhere I shall reject them; perhaps somewhere there we shall reject them. For here, hearing them, is your humble one, N. Our lord hath bound us together; he has made us one. Who will so remember it? Verily, you have grasped [the news], you have received it; for in truth you have heard that our lord inclines his heart to grant such as is a precious necklace, a precious feather. Ah, truly, our lord wishes to concede [the child]. Ah, it is said I have ruined my pregnancy. And behold, in what manner is our lord determining for me? Perhaps something is my desert, my merit; perhaps the child will come to be born on earth; perhaps our lord will cause that with which I am adorned to see the light of day.

"And here is your humble one. Our hands are together; we go holding hands. Perhaps he will see, perhaps he will know, perhaps he will behold the face of that which is his blood, his color, recognizable as his. Perhaps it will be his image. But on the other hand, the lord of the near, of the nigh, may laugh at us. Perhaps our lord will completely destroy the tender thing. Perhaps something will cause the baby, the tender thing to sicken. Perhaps something will cause it to be stillborn; our lord will leave us [still] desiring a child. Certainly we are weepers, we are sorrowers. Let us have faith in our lord; perhaps something is our desert, perhaps something is our merit. My progenitors, precious persons, my lords, find repose."

Arthur J. O. Anderson and Charles E. Dibble, *Florentine Codex of Fray Bernardino de Sahagún*, Book VI, chapter 25.

2. BATHING THE BABY

The midwife stood facing the west. Then the midwife bathed the baby. . . . She said to him:

"Eagle warrior,
ocelot warrior,
valiant warrior,
youth, my youngest son,
you have come to arrive on earth.
Your mother, your father,
Ome tecutli, Ome ciuatl
have sent you.

You were cast, you were bored in your home,[1]
the place of duality, [over] the place of the nine heavens.
The lord of the near, of the nigh,
Topiltzin Quetzalcoatl,
has given you.
And now arrive with your mother, Chalchiuhtliicue,
    Chalchiuhtlatonac."

Then she made him taste the water. She said to him:

"Take it, receive it.
Here is wherewith you will endure,
wherewith you will live on earth,
wherewith you will grow, wherewith you will develop.
Behold, we have completely merited our sustenance on earth.
Take it!"

Then she placed water on his breast; she said to him:

"Here is the blue water,
the yellow water,
which cleanses our hearts,
so that they be purified;
which washes away our filthiness.
Take it!
May it cleanse,
may it purify your heart;
may it cleanse it."

Then she poured water on the crown of his head. She said to him:

"My youngest son, my youth,
take, receive the water of the lord of the earth,
our sustenance, our refreshment,
which is that which cleanses one, that which bathes one.
May the heavenly water,
the blue water,
the deep green,
go into your body;
may it remain in your body.
May it remove, may it destroy

[1]A *difrasismo*, meaning "you have been formed as if you were made of precious metal."

the manner of things you were given
with which you were arrayed in the beginning—
the bad, the evil;
for we are still left in its hands; we merit it;
for even before, our mother, Chalchiuhtli icue, knows of it."

Thereupon she bathed him all over; she massaged him. She proceeded speaking to him:

"Wherever you are,
as you are a baby cast down to earth:
go, move!
Now the baby lives again; he is born again;
now he becomes clean, he becomes pure again.
Our mother Chalchiuhtli icue casts, perforates him again."

Thereupon she raised him as an offering to the heavens. She said:

"Here is your little creature.
You have sent him, you have given him to the earth,
a place of pain,
a place of torment,
a place of penitence.
Array him, inspire him!
You are the master,
you are Ome tecutli, you are Ome ciuatl."

A second time she raised him up; she raised him as an offering to the heavens. She said:

"I address you, I cry out to you,
you who are mother of the gods,
you who are Citlallatonac,
you who are Citlalicue.
Whatsoever is your spirit, give it to him.
Give your spirit to the commoner."

A third time she raised him as an offering to the heavens. She said:

"Now, you who are dwellers in the heavens,
you who are heavenly noblemen,
you who are assembled in the heavens:
here is the commoner.

Whatsoever is your spirit, give it to him.
Give your spirit to him that he may dwell on earth."

A fourth time she raised him as an offering to the heavens. She addressed, she cried out to the sun. She said:

"Our mother, our father,
Tonatiuh, Tlaltecutli:
here is the commoner,
your troupial, your roseate spoonbill,
the eagle, the ocelot.
Unto you I declare him,
unto you I commend him,
unto you I raise him as an offering—
to you, the resplendent one, the turquoise prince,
the eagle,
the ocelot which is ashen, which is well blotched,
the brave warrior, the valiant warrior.
He is your possession, your property;
he is dedicated to you.
For this was he created,
to provide you drink,
to provide you food,
to provide you offerings.
He belongs to the battlefield there,
in the center, in the middle of the plains."

Then she took up the shield, the bow, the spear. She said:

"Here are the instruments of war,
the little shield, the shield,
the spear, the long one, the curved one,
which are for your gladness, for your praise.
Provide that which you provide [for warriors],
whatsoever his desert, his merit, his lot.
Perhaps he will be able to arrive by you.
Perhaps he will be able to go there;
perhaps he will go to know your home,
the place of contentment, the place of happiness,
there where the eagle warriors, the ocelot warriors,
the valiant warriors, those who died in war, rejoice,
are glad, are happy,
remain gladdening you, remain giving cries to you.

Perhaps the poor commoner will be able to arrive by them.
Show him mercy, master, ruler."

If [his name were] Yaotl, the midwife spoke man's talk. She said to him:

"O Yaotl, O Yaotl,
take your shield, take the spear,
the little shield which is for the gladness of the sun.
O Yaotl, O Yaotl,
know the interior of the plains, the middle of the plains,
the battlefield.
O Yaotl, O Yaotl,
you will gladden the sun, Tlaltecutli.
You will provide him drink, you will provide him offerings.
You belong with the eagle warriors,
with the ocelot warriors,
with the valiant warriors, those who died in war,
who gladden, who cry out to the sun.
O valiant warriors,
come, eat the umbilical cord offering of Yaotl."

Arthur J. O. Anderson and Charles E. Dibble, *Florentine Codex of Fray Beruardino de Sahagún,* Book VI, chapter 32.

3. CUTTING THE UMBILICAL CORD

Then the midwife cuts the child's umbilical cord, she removes the umbilical cord. And she takes what is called the afterbirth, which had covered the baby, which had enveloped him. She buries this in a corner [of the house]. The child's umbilical cord is kept. It is set out to dry. Later (the warriors) take it with them to battle.

(The midwife addresses the infant boy.)
My beloved child, my precious one,
here are the precepts, the principles
your father, your mother, Yohualtecutli, Yohualticitl, have
laid down.
From your body, the middle of your body, I remove, I cut the umbilical
    cord.
Know this, understand this: home is not here.
You are the Eagle, you are the Jaguar,
you are the precious scarlet bird,

you are the precious golden bird of Tloque Nahuaque;

you are his serpent, you are his bird.

Only your nest is here.

Here you only break out of your shell,

here you only arrive, you only alight,

here you only come into the world.

Here like a plant, you sprout, you burst into bloom, you blossom.

Here like a fragment struck from a stone, chipped from a stone, you are
born.

Here you only have your cradle, your blanket, your pillow where you lay
your head.

This is only the place of arrival.

Where you belong is elsewhere:

You are pledged, you are promised, you are sent to the field of battle.

War is your destiny, your calling.

You shall provide drink,

you shall provide food,

you shall provide nourishment for the Sun, for the Lord of the Earth.

Your true home, your domain, your patrimony is the House of the
Sun in heaven,

where you shall shout the praises of, where you shall amuse, the
Everlastingly Resplendent One.

Perhaps you shall merit, perhaps you shall earn,

death by the obsidian knife in battle.

This cord is removed from your body,

that comes from the middle of your body,

That I take from you,

is the property, the possession of the Lord of the Earth, of the Sun.

And when war stirs, when war breaks out,

it shall be put into the hands of the Eagles, the Jaguars, the valiant
warriors.

They shall give it to your mother, your father, the Sun, the Lord of the
Earth.

They shall bury it in the middle, in the center, of the battlefield,

and with it you shall be pledged, you shall be promised to the Sun, to
the Lord of the Earth.

With this you shall make yourself an offering,

with this your name shall be inscribed,

your name shall be set down, in the middle, in the center of the
battlefield,

so that you are not forgotten,

so that your name, your glory are not.
This precious object taken from your body
shall be counted as your offering of maguey thorns,
tobacco, reeds, pine branches.
It shall be your act of penance, it shall stand as your vow.

And now let us be hopeful.
Perhaps you shall merit,
perhaps you shall be worthy of some reward.
Work, my precious child!
May Tloque Nahuaque mold you, provide for you;
may he adorn you.

If the child is a girl, when the midwife cuts the umbilical cord, she says
 to her:
My beloved daughter, my little girl, you have wearied yourself, you have
 fatigued yourself.
Our lord, Tloque Nahuaque, has sent you here.
You have come to a place of hardship, a place of affliction,
a place of tribulation.
A place that is cold, a place that is windy.

Listen now:
From your body, from the middle of your body, I remove,
I cut the umbilical cord.
Your father, your mother, Yohualtecutli, Yohualticitl, have
ordered, have ordained:
that you shall be the heart of the house.
You shall go nowhere,
you shall not be a wanderer.
You shall be the covering of ashes that banks the fire,
you shall be the three stones on which the cooking pot rests.

Here our lord buries you, inters you,
and you shall become worn, you shall become weary.
You are to prepare drink, you are to grind corn,
you are to toil, you are to sweat, beside the ashes, beside the hearth.

Florentine Codex Book VI, translated by Thelma D. Sullivan and T. J. Knab, *A Scattering of Jades,* pp. 136–41.

4. THE MIDWIFE ADDRESSES THE NEWLY DELIVERED WOMAN

O my daughter, O valiant woman, you worked, you toiled.
You soared like an eagle, you sprang like a jaguar,
you put all your strength behind the shield, behind the buckler; you
    endured.
You went forth into battle, you emulated our mother, Cihuacoatl
    Quilaztli,
and now our lord has seated you on the Eagle Mat, the Jaguar Mat.
You have spent yourself, O my daughter,
now be tranquil.
What does our lord, Tloque Nahuaque will?
Shall he bestow his favors upon each of you separately, in separate
    places?
Perhaps you shall go off, and leave the child that has arrived.
Perhaps, as small as he is, the creator will summon him, will call out to
    him,
or perhaps, he shall come to take you.
Do not be boastful [of the child].
Do not consider yourself worthy of it.
Call out humbly to our lord, Tloque Nahuaque.

Florentine Codex Book VI, translated by Thelma D. Sullivan and T. J. Knab, *A Scattering of Jades,* pp. 141–42.

5. INVOCATION OF THE WARRIOR WOMAN

The woman who dies with a child in her womb, who is called Mocihuaquetz-qui, at the moment she died was deified, they say. When she was still lying there, when her body was still reposing there, the midwife invoked her, prayed to her, supplicated her, entreated her. She said to her:

O Chamotzin my little child,
O, Quauhcihuatl, O little one, little dove, O my daughter!
You have labored, you have toiled,
your labors have come to rest;
you have worked with your mother, the goddess
Quauhcihuatl, Quilaztli.
You took up, you raised aloft, you wielded the shield, the buckler,
that your mother, the goddess Cihuacoatl, Quilaztli, placed in your
    hand.

Awake! Arise! Stand up!
It is now day, it is now dawn.
The scarlet glow of daybreak has risen, the dawn has come up;
the flame-tinged curassow and the flame-tinged swallow are singing
    now,
so sing the sundry flame-tinged roseate spoonbills.
Arise! Stand up! Array yourself!

Be off, betake yourself to the good place, the fine place,
the House of your mother and father the Sun!
Let his sisters, the divine celestial women, take you to him,
they who always and forever know joy and happiness,
gladness and delight,
next to, beside, our mother and father the Sun,
amusing him, shouting his praises!

O my little one, my daughter, beloved mistress,
you have wearied yourself, manfully you have fought.
By your labors you have won Our Lord's noble death, glorious death;
truly, now, you have toiled for it, well you have merited it;
the good, the fine, the loving death was your recompense, your reward.
By chance have you died in vain?
Perhaps you have died, it has been your penance.
Who is granted what you have merited?
Eternally you shall live and know joy and gladness
next to, beside, our mistress, the divine woman.

Farewell my daughter, my little one!
Go to them, join them
let them take you, let them receive you.
Be with them, amusing, shouting the praises of our mother and father,
    the Sun,
accompany them wherever they go in their rejoicing.

O my little one, my daughter, my mistress,
you have gone off leaving us behind,
you have gone off kicking us away, we the old men and women,
you have departed flinging aside your mother and father.
But was it you who willed it?
You were summoned, you were called!
And what now!
In your absence, with your back turned, we shall perish!
What now?

A pauperous old age filled with misery,
and we shall end our days beside others' walls, in the corners of others'
    houses!

O our mistress, may you think of us,
may you remember us in our deprivation!
It is as if we were beholding it,
as if we were imprisoned in it here on the earth.
Verily, we are twisted by the heat, and by cold, icy winds,
wizened, trembling, streaked with dirt and mud,
our entrails are filled only with misery; are helpless!
May you think of us, my precious daughter, Quauhcihuatl, divine
    woman.
For you have gone on to be happy;
in the good place, the fine place where you now dwell,
and beside, next to Our Lord, you now live.
You behold him now with human eyes,
you invoke him now with human voice.
May you pray to him for us, may you invoke him for us!
With all this we commend ourselves to you.
It is finished.

Florentine Codex, Book VI, translated by Thelma D. Sullivan and T. J. Knab, *A Scattering
of Jades*, pp. 145–47.

The Bancroft Dialogues[2]

An Elderly Noblewoman congratulates a mother on her two sons having
turned out well.

Ah my lady, how fortunate are you to whom the Giver of life, our Engenderer and Creator, has given these precious jewels and emeralds. The creatures of our Lord are growing very big, turning out very big.
    Consider our home Mexihco Tenochtitlan, the place of the dike, or the
palaces in all the other places; hardly anyone who is born grows up, they just

---

[2]*The Bancroft Dialogues* comprise several brief works in classical Nahuatl which are valued
both for their content and for the diacritical marks used by the anonymous person who redacted
the *Huehuetlahtolli*. It is the only known text containing these indications of glottal stops and
vowel forms. The work is housed at the Bancroft Library of the University of California, hence
the name.

die off. It is the same in Tlacopan, Azcapotzalco, and Itztapalapan, wherever there have still been nobles. Here in our home of Tetzcohco, your birthplace, things are also coming to an end.

There were innumerable rulers and nobles who were relatives of the former lord Acolmiztli Nezahualcoyotl, and also the son Acamapichtli Nezahualpilli and the Chichimeca nobles. Back when I was growing up there was an infinite number of them. And how many noble houses there were, the palaces of the former nobles and rulers! It was like one big palace. There were countless (minor) nobles and lesser relatives, and one could not count the commoners who were dependents, or the slaves; they were like ants.[3] But now everywhere our Lord is destroying and reducing the land, we are coming to an end and disappearing.

Why? For what reason? Perhaps we have incurred His wrath and offended Him with our sins and wrongdoing. But what are we to do? Since we are His creatures and entirely in His hands and He is our Engenderer and Creator, let us await His command as to what His will will be for us in the future. Let us do all we can to raise up children; let parenthood flourish. Let our children, our offspring, be made to look after the proper and good so that they will truly fear and serve our Lord the All-pervasive, and so that they can live peacefully among other people; especially today they greatly need to be well looked after, because evil and bad behavior are greatly growing, increasing, and hardening in them; hardly are they born when they begin not to care about anything, not to obey, to have no shame.

Back when I was brought up, the boys who were children of rulers were taught and raised at the Tlacatecco (a temple); the lord Tecuepohtzin, the Cihuacoatl, and the senior priest, the great priest, themselves saw to them, and also the Quetzalcoatl (a priest). They (the adults in charge) got them up right at midnight; they (the children) sprinkled and swept everywhere. Next they left for the edge of the woods and carried fir and ferns with which they adorned (the temples).

Now was that already the house of our Lord?

They were still just demons' temples, of Tezcatlipoca, Hulitzilopochtli, or Tlaloc, and of other demons who were false gods.

Next they washed and bathed themselves, even though it was very cold. And by the time it had cleared and become full day, they had prepared the adornment everywhere. Then they (the adults in charge) threw down on the ground to them (the children) an old tortilla each, or perhaps (two each) if they were a little larger; they treated them like little dogs. And when they had breakfasted, they (the adults in charge) began teaching them how to live, how to obey, and how to honor people, to give themselves to the good and to relinquish and shun evil, bad behavior, and excess.

---

[3]The authors have used words and phrases in parentheses to clarify the text.

How much wisdom and prudence they absorbed there! And as to how they were punished, if they did the least thing wrong, it was very frightening; they hanged them up, they set them in the smoke of burning chiles, they hit them with nettles and beat them with switches on their calves and elbows, they stuck maguey spines in their ears, they put their heads close to the fire and scorched them.

And likewise at midday, when the sun was very hot, they sent them to the edge of the woods; they (the children) carried wood, bark, and kindling. They ran vigorously, no one idled or went along shoving people down; all ran prudently and went with fear and respect, and in a very short while they returned. And when they (the children) had arrived again, they (the adults in charge) fed them the same way, they just threw down on the ground to them one or two old tortillas each, with which they had their midday meal.

And when they had eaten, right away they (the adults) began teaching them again: again (i.e., resuming from the morning a list of things taught), to some how to do battle, or how to hunt, how to shoot a blowgun or how to hurl stones; they were taught all about the shield and the handsword, and how to hurl spears and darts with a spear thrower; also about netting and snaring. Others were taught the different crafts: featherwork, how (small) feathers and plumes were arranged; also mosaic work, goldsmithery, jewel cutting, and metal polishing; and also (codex?) painting, woodworking, and the various other crafts.

Others were taught song composition and oratory and the science known as "the drum and the rattle" (i.e., music), and also the science of the heavens, how the sun and moon and stars, called the Ninefold, move; and then what are called divine codices which talked about the All-pervasive, the Creator of humanity, though they also were about the former false gods with whom people used to delude themselves, for it was still the time of darkness, and the light of our Lord, the faith, had not yet reached them. And indeed, some they took to the fields or the flower gardens to teach them how to sow seeds, to plant trees and flowers, and to cultivate and work the land. They taught them all it was needful for them to know by way of service, knowledge, wisdom, and prudent living.

Likewise within the houses, where the ladies were in their quarters, the girls were taught all the different things women do: sweeping, sprinkling, preparing food, making beverages, grinding (maize), preparing tortillas, making tamales, all the different things customarily done among women; also (the art of) the spindle and the weaver's reed and various kinds of embroidery; also dyeing, how rabbit down or rabbit fur was dyed different colors. And in the same way (as with the boys) those who did something wrong or did not take care were severely punished. And they were all well cared for: no men, no matter who, entered there; taking care of them was the exclusive domain of the elderly noblewomen.

And every eighty days they went to the Tlacatecco and heard the eighty-day speech of the lord ruler Acolmiztli Nezahualcoyotl, and there the lord Tecuepohtzin admonished them and cautioned them. And the commoners were raised in the same way; the youths were raised in the school at the youths' house, and the girls at the women's temple, where the female penitents were enclosed and fasted.

Oh, this is how the ancients who left us behind lived and ordered things; they took very great care. But how we raise our children today is a very different thing; bad behavior is no longer feared, for they no longer fear adultery, theft, drunkenness, and other kinds of bad behavior, because it is no longer punished as it used to be punished long ago, when they forthwith hanged (strangled?) and destroyed people.

For I still saw it myself and it happened before my eyes, when the daughter of the lord Axayacatl, ruler of Mexihco Tenochtitlan, committed adultery with Maxtla of the house of Tezonyohcan (Tezayuca) and with Hultzilihhuitl, that it was done on a grand scale and countless people were punished, who were hanged (strangled?) and crushed with stones along with the lady: some stewards, some artisans, and some merchants, and also the ladies-in-waiting and dependents of the lady.

All the world assembled, people came from the towns all around to behold; the ladies brought along their daughters, even though they might still be in the cradle, to have them see. Even the Tlaxcalans, and the people of Huexotzinco and Atlixco, although they were our enemies, all came to see; the whole roof of the house of the Cholulans (merchants' or foreigners' quarters?) was brimful. And as to how the lord ruler Nezahualpilli fed people, there were all the containers with hollow bases, the reed baskets, and the sauce bowls, by which the Mexihcah were very much put to shame.

And likewise I saw how they hanged (strangled?) the lord Huexotzincatzin, who was the eldest son of the lord ruler Nezahualpilli; he was punished just for composing songs to the lady of Tollan (Tula), his stepmother, one of the wives of the lord.

And he (Nezahualpilli) came back and shut himself up in his palace; the lord Nezahualpilli named the palace "the place of tears," because he wept greatly over the death of his beloved son.

Likewise I saw how Cuauhtliztactzin, younger brother of Huexotzincatzin, was punished just because he built himself a residence of his own, not by order of the lord. And I saw other noblemen and ladies whose wrongdoings were forthwith punished, as well as the rulers of cities (subject to Tetzcohco). Tzotzomahtzin of Cuauhtitlan was punished for drunkenness. If I mentioned all of them here, it would be a very long time before I finished telling it.

And so, my lady, let our grandchildren be very well taken care of, for the world is a difficult place; they will fall into misdeeds and descend to the abyss, or they may make friends with some delinquent boys and they will be accused of something and punished. Make every effort, oh my mistress and lady, oh precious personage.

Frances Karttunen and James Lockhart, *The Art of Nahuatl Speech: The Bancroft Dialogues* (Stanford, CA: UCLA Latin American Center Publications, 1987), pp. 170–83.

Greeting of a woman who passes by the house of her relatives on the way to the market.

Do stay seated, my lady, I (don't wish to) disturb you, for I'm just passing by your place here to ask about you, whether you are enjoying a bit of the health of our Lord, for it's been a while since I've seen your faces. What I have come about is to look into things at the market, for so it is with us who are afflicted (us ordinary mortals).

Reply.
Greetings, my child, my dear daughter. You have entered your home; will you stay a while? And thank you, yes, our Lord is keeping us somewhat healthy, and somehow we are scraping along on His earth. And is the Giver of life also keeping you and my brother-in-law and the children whom you have for a time a bit healthy likewise? Or has he sent some illness down upon them? Although it is here (in the general vicinity), it is quite a distance (from your house to ours). How are we to know how our Lord is causing you to fare?

(Response of the woman on her way to the market.)
Thank you, my lady, we too enjoy a bit of the health of the All-pervasive; your brother-in-law is in good health, and your humble servants the little children are healthy. You said that though it is here (in the vicinity), it is quite a distance (from your house to ours). That's why we neglect you and don't come to ask about you; forgive us before our Lord.

The woman going to the market takes her leave.
Stay at rest (don't get up), I'm leaving you now. After I've been at the market, it could be I'll come by your place again; may our Lord keep you.

Reply.
Take it easy now; thank you for having come entering here on our account; don't let us detain you. May our Lord guide you.

Congratulations to a married couple.
Oh my youngest ones, you owe thanks to our Lord and to our Mother the holy church which governs us for tying you together and uniting you. Go con-

ducting and leading yourselves calmly and prudently; let the words of the Giver of life, His sacrament that He has made your property and inheritance, come to fruition. Exert all your effort (do your best to follow all the admonitions), my children; serve your God and ruler. Do not let yourselves go, do not follow wild ways; do not fall into the abyss of sin. You, the groom, since you are the head and trunk of the maiden here whom our Lord has vouchsafed to you, are to busy yourself and work at what people need, water and food, the grain (sustenance) that gives us bones and flesh. You are not to lie in sleep and pleasure; you are to be wakeful and take care of things in your domicile. You are to be finding out and leaping from your bed to see what people in your house and home daily need, for it is not just any burden that has been put upon you. And you, my daughter, you are to be the same way in guarding the household of our Lord. You are no longer to give yourself to childishness, for you are to be wakeful and take care of how you conduct and manage things in your house. When it is still dark you are to rise and sweep and sprinkle the entryway and patio of our Lord, and then also (you are to see to) the food and drink that people need; and then also (you are to use) the spindle and the weaver's reed, so that you will please your husband whom our Lord has vouchsafed to you, for as a woman you are to take care of things, watch over things, and not let things go to ruin in your house and home; and keep yourself so that you do not live in vice and badly, for this is why you will be loved and honored. Oh my youngest ones, my children, exert all your effort. Perhaps our Lord will give you a long life, or perhaps His punishment will come, for we do not know how we will live in the future on His earth. Only with these few words do I address you and kiss your hands and feet; I (do not wish to) make you ill (with long talking), I (do not wish to) disturb your spirits, my youngest ones, my children. May our Lord God the Giver of life grant you health.

(The same speaker to the parents.)

And you the parents who are here, the creatures of our Lord, your jewels and plumes (your children) owe thanks to you; perhaps you will be so fortunate that the Giver of life will cause things to go well with them; perhaps through them you will be relieved and cured, perhaps your weeping, sorrow and sighing will come to fruition, and perhaps the Master of heaven and earth will inspire those whom you have brought up and raised to be good; perhaps through them you will have peace of mind, and creatures of our Lord will split and break off from them, will bloom and flower, so that you will see and recognize yourselves in them. Have confidence in the All-pervasive, be awaiting His future pleasure. That is all with which I awkwardly pass before you, I bow down to and address you. I (do not wish) to distract you (with further talk), my nobles, I (do not wish) to make you ill.

(The same speaker to the governor of the town and after that to the members of its council.)

Oh lord, o ruler, oh my youth, oh my noble, I (do not wish to) make you ill, to distract your lordship and rulership. Your mothers and fathers (those present) here are enjoying your lordship and rulership. Are they so fortunate that you come entering here on their account and they detain you? They owe you thanks. Let them enjoy your lordship, rulership, and dignity. And as to the humble man (the groom) here who today has taken and enjoyed the sacrament of our Lord by which our Mother the holy church unites and joins (the couple), perhaps they will appreciate and honor the way you have come here on account of them, that you have come to honor them and manifest your lordship and rulership. Oh lord and ruler, your vassals, your fathers, mothers, and progenitors (aides) owe you thanks. Are you indeed lending yourself to them for a time, since they are your vassals and you are the great tree in whose protective shadow and under whose governance they are, oh lord, oh my nobleman? And here are you, our lords, who care for the governance of the city (the city council members), who have led here the lord our youth, our grandchild (the governor); he owes you thanks, and so do the parents (of the bride and groom) present here whose weeping and sorrow our Lord has heard, so that today those whom they have brought up and raised, the young woman and child (i.e., the woman so recently a child herself) and the humble man, today enjoy His sacrament, by which our Mother the holy church has united them. Let them enjoy your beneficence and your parenthood. This is all with which I address you, with which I kiss your hands and feet, my youths, my nobles.

The governor replies to the latter speaker.

Oh Pablo, all owe you thanks, the parents present here owe you thanks, and the humble youth here and our daughter who have enjoyed today the sacrament of our Lord, by which our Mother the holy church has united them in matrimony. What will the All-pervasive, the Giver of life desire for them? Let us be awaiting of Him whether He will give them health, whether He will give them a good portion of His time, whether He will guide them well in His service, which is especially to be desired, since He united them so that they have enjoyed holy matrimony. You have spoken generously, my progenitor; do take a seat and rest.

Another nobleman replies to the same.

Oh my youngest, the lord our grandson (the governor) owes you thanks, and so do the parents present here, the raisers and educators of children, and the relatives, whose weeping and sighing have been realized and heard by our Lord. And our son and daughter here, who today have experienced the sacrament of our Lord the Master of heaven and earth and of our Mother the holy church, which governs us, so that it tied them and united them in matrimony (likewise owe you thanks). And we your elder brothers owe you thanks, for here we jointly honor the sacrament of our Lord, and we are enjoying the charity of the parents present here. All owe you thanks, my youth; do take a seat and give your body rest.

The mother of the groom to the same.

My male child, my offspring, the lord ruler, our head who governs us, who has come entering here on our account, owes you thanks. Are we his vassals so fortunate as to enjoy his lordship and rulership? Is he indeed lending himself to us for a while? We are his subjects and in his charge, for he governs us. And our lords who guide the city owe you thanks, as do the humble young man and woman here on whose account we now face (the assembled) city, because they have enjoyed the sacrament of our Lord the Giver of life, because our Mother the holy church has united them in matrimony. Perhaps it (the marriage?) will become our good fortune. And also here we the parents profit from what you have said, and it has been the good fortune of us the relatives (to hear it). Let us rejoice that our Lord has brought us together here. My male child, precious personage, proper man, do rest, put your body to rest.

(Greeting to a group of nobles.)

Do remain seated, my nobles. I (do not wish to) distract you; it's already late. How do you feel? Has our Lord given you the good fortune of a bit of His good health? That is all with which I bow down before your dignity and kiss your hands and feet.

Reply.

Greetings, oh Pablo. Thank you (for the inquiry); yes, we are enjoying a bit of the health of the Giver of life, who has united us here. How then? Only so late (not until now) you come by, our friend? Etc.

What the bride-negotiators say to the parents of the bride requested by the king of Tetzcohco (Texcoco).

Oh lord, oh ruler, oh my nobleman, oh lady, we bow down to your lordship and rulership, we kiss your hands and feet, for the lord ruler (name), who governs the city, your home, of Acolhuahcan Tetzcohco, has sent us here before you, and he says: "Let the lord ruler within the waters, who is in charge at our home of Mexihco Tenochtitlan and in our place of origin Atzacualco (place of the dike), the lord (name) and the lady (name), listen, since that which forms the tuft and tassel of the tree of rulership has taken my fancy, I want and desire that I might enjoy their precious emerald, their fine turquoise, their bracelet that was forged and perforated at the throat and in the womb of the lady (i.e., their daughter), the relic and bloom of the rulers who have come to guard the city, (to occupy) the seat of authority in our home Mexihco Tenochtitlan. May they place her next to me, may they adorn her for me and show her to me, since the time has come, and I am not merely lending myself to her; she is my jewel and plume. And if we are so fortunate, and the city is so fortunate, that the All-pervasive, the Master of heaven and earth, the Creator and Engenderer of people, should hear our weeping and sorrow, we will be so fortunate that one or two of His creatures will split and break off from us, who will have their time in governing the city. When we have come to rest and to an end, there will be light through them, since that is why we exist, since that is why we have come to obey our Lord, the Master of heaven, earth, and the underworld. Let me quickly hear word from them how a party will come to bring the lady our elder sister to come to govern her city and occupy (her? its?) throne, where it will come to fruition that she will console me, and her (little) brothers-in-law and sisters (sisters-in-law) and her vassals will be looking up to her." Oh our lords, oh rulers, these are the words of the lord ruler your nephew that you hear. May we hear a few words from you with which we can go to console the lord ruler, since he is waiting, since it is here that he has taken a fancy, oh our lords, oh rulers, oh lady, oh my lords.

Reply of the parents of the girl.

Greetings, oh rulers who have come entering here on our account, we (do not wish to) detain you or bring illness upon you. Are we so fortunate that you have fatigued yourselves crossing hills and plains coming here on our account? Although our home of Tetzcohco Acolhuahcan (is in the vicinity), it is a good stretch away. The lord ruler our nephew has spoken generously; we owe him thanks, and his vassal, older sister, and (unworthy) girl, whom we have for a while, owes him thanks. Is he indeed lending himself to her? She is of his line, let her go and serve him, let her be as she should be as a woman, as a person of high descent, born of important people. Where else should she go? This is why the Master of heaven and earth engendered her and caused her to be born, that she might take the fancy of the lord ruler our nephew. What will be the will of the All-pervasive? Perhaps she will serve Him (him?) for a lifetime and be in charge of His (his?) household, where she will do His (his?) bidding, and perhaps we will be so fortunate as to see one or two of His (his?) creatures, our grandchildren, through whom there will be light (on the city) when our Lord gives him rest, and one of them will relieve him of his burden and one day come to rule. Well, oh lords and rulers, what should we say then? Let it be so done, let what the lord ruler our nephew desires be realized; here are all the Mexihca Tenochca lords and rulers, who jointly concur. We await word from him that his humble servant the maiden is to go. Take to your feet, oh rulers, thus inform and consult with the lord ruler our nephew. We (do not wish to) detain you, to disturb your spirits. Take it easy then, oh our lords, oh rulers.

The king, now married, greets his recently arrived bride.

Greetings, oh lady, you have arrived at your home, where you will do the bidding of our Lord the Master of heaven and earth. What will be His will? Perhaps I will enjoy you for a whole lifetime. And greetings to you, oh rulers, oh ladies; I (do not wish to) inconvenience or detain you; do enter your home.

A nobleman of the court of the king greets the recently married queen.

Oh our mistress, oh noblewoman, oh lady, oh precious one, oh precious personage, oh precious jewel, oh emerald, oh bracelet, oh fine turquoise, many greetings; you have arrived in your city, where it will come to fruition that you will serve the lord ruler, and your brothers and sisters-in-law and your vassals will be looking up to you. What will be the wish of our Lord the Master of heaven, earth, and the underworld? Perhaps we will be so fortunate as to have you for a lifetime, and I wonder if we will also be so fortunate that a jewel and plume of ours will split and break off from you, will bloom and blossom out from your womb and throat, the sprout and blossom of the lord ruler, the Tlacateuctli; perhaps our Engenderer, the Master of the created, the Creator, the Giver of life, our divine Lord, will grant, engender, create, bring to life, and quicken one or two (children) who will be the illumination and splendor of the city, through whom there will be light, and who will relieve the lord ruler of his burden when the Giver of life, the All-pervasive, should summon and call to him. Well, oh our mistress, oh our lady, I (do not wish to) bring you illness (through long talk). Exert every effort, always have confidence in our Lord and pray to Him; call for His mercy, to benefit you and make you deserving, and that you gently and prudently watch over His household, and that the city and the commoners be so fortunate as to enter into your protective shade. This is all with which I appear before you and bow down to your ladyship and womanly rulership, with which I kiss your hands and feet, with which I bow down to you and with which your city bows down to you and addresses you, for I speak for the city here before you, oh lady, oh my noble person.

The same speaks to the married king.

Oh our lord, oh personage, oh ruler, oh youngest one, oh precious one, oh bracelet, fine turquoise, emerald, plume, oh ruler of the city, we have been so fortunate that you have tied on the precious bracelet, have placed at your throat the precious necklace with radiating pendants, and on your head you have raised the wide plumes; you have brought together the nobility and dignity to which your city looks up and of which it is enamored, and which your vassals will be expecting and awaiting. Rejoice greatly in the beneficence of our Lord the Giver of life. What will be His will in the future? Let us be hoping that perhaps we will be so fortunate that one or two of the creatures of our Lord the Giver of life will bloom and flower, perhaps there will be forged and perforated the precious emerald and fine turquoise which (who) will take up your burden and through whom there will be light when the Master of heaven and earth summons and takes you. Let us enjoy what our city today is seeing and beholding, oh lord, oh ruler. This is every last thing with which I bow down to you and kiss your hands and feet, oh lord our lord.

Salutation to the queen after giving birth.

Oh our mistress, oh lady, oh emerald, oh jewel, oh turquoise, oh bracelet, be of good cheer, for now it has been the will of our Lord the Master of heaven and earth that He has seen and heard the weeping and sorrow of your city, and the precious bracelet, the precious emerald has been forged and perforated, and we have been so fortunate that a boy has been born. Perhaps if he grows up he will become the fortune of the city, of the commoners. As the All-pervasive, the Master of heaven and the underworld dispatched him, do not neglect his breastfeeding, see to it that your attendants care for him. Exert every effort (taking care of the boy), oh our mistress, oh lady. I (do not wish) you to take ill or for your spirit to be disturbed. May you profit from your diet, oh personage, oh lady, oh my noblewoman.

Congratulations to the king on the birth of the child.

Oh personage, oh lord, oh our ruler, oh precious one, oh precious personage, your city and the commoners have been fortunate; we have been so fortunate that today you have seen the precious emerald, the fine turquoise, that has split and broken off from you, that our Lord the Master of heaven and earth, the Engenderer and Creator of people has given you. May your city behold, enjoy, and rejoice in the precious emerald, the fine turquoise, the bracelet that He has given and sent you and that you now take as your necklace and bracelet. We have been fortunate, oh personage, oh our lord, oh ruler.

Salute to the dead king.

Oh personage, oh ruler, you have already worked and served, and the governance of your city, while it was in your charge, was as it should be, for it was not quietly and gently (but with much effort) that you governed your city. The suffering and pain from tiring and fatiguing yourself have come fully to an end and a conclusion; you have left your city in peace, (as in peace you came to occupy the mat and seat of authority, peacefully you arranged and settled things for the Giver of life. Truly indeed you spent all your breath, truly indeed you exerted yourself on behalf of the city. You stretched yourself out (were active) before our Lord, you did not idly hide your hands and feet under your cape. And now there is silence and darkness in your city. Your vassals are wrapped in weeping and sorrow, as are the nobles whom you have left orphaned; our Lord has made (the city) a desolate place. Have you not gone to, reached your forebears and progenitors? You have gone to and reached our Parent. From the place where people go, not just somewhere, will you come back again? Will you return? Are your city and your offspring to expect you in the future (to be awaiting you for a time)? No, never again. For that is all, that is enough; you have gone once and for all, the torch and light have gone out and been snuffed, the city of the All-pervasive lies silent and dark. Let the commoners weep and sorrow, and let the tears of the well born, the nobles, sprinkle and scatter down. Let them cry in sorrow to the Giver of life, the All-pervasive; let them say, "Alas, woe to us who have been left orphans." Let there be weeping, sorrowing, and sighing; let the tears sprinkle and scatter down. Do rest, rejoice next to your grandfathers and forebears whom you have gone to and reached in the fleshless place, our eternal home. This is all with which I greet you and bow down to you, with which I appear before the public, oh lord ruler.

The same gives condolence to the noblemen on the death of the king.

Oh our lords, oh rulers, oh nobles, oh citizens, thus today the lord (name), whom our Lord the Master of heaven, earth, and the underworld has effaced and sequestered, has gone to rest. He has put aside and left the bundle and carrying frame, the means of bearing the heavy, unliftable, unbearable load of government. Does he not still haunt his city, which lies in silence and darkness, which the All-pervasive has made a place of desolation? Does he not still haunt what now is an entirely deserted place, the governorship that the lord ruler, the Tlacateuctli, abandoned and orphaned, he who presides (presided?) here, he over whose body we weep, whom for a short time the city borrowed, dreamed, and saw in its sleep, for our Lord has summoned and called to him. Let the city provide safekeeping for his body. The All-pervasive has already put (his soul) in the refuge of the dead. Has he not gone to and reached his forebears and progenitors? He has gone to and reached our Parent, he has gone to our eternal home, the place without a chimney, for he has already extinguished (the flame), he has gone to the place without fleas, the place where people go that is not just somewhere. Will he come back again? Will he still return? It is over, it is enough, it ended once and for all, it was forever, the city knows it is entirely finished, and he will not emerge and rise in the future. He has gone, he has disappeared, the torch and light have been snuffed out, the city of the All-pervasive and Giver of life lies silent and dark. So that here at this time he has relinquished and put up the bundle and carrying frame, the means of government; in peace he has abandoned the city, as in peace he occupied the mat and seat of authority, and peacefully he arranged and settled things for the Giver of life. Truly indeed he expended all his breath, truly indeed he exerted himself on behalf of the city. He stretched himself out (was active) before our Lord, he did not idly hide his hands and feet under his cape; he exerted all his effort, his spirit suffered, not quietly and gently did he sit on the throne of the All-pervasive. He knew no sleep, no food, he suffered on account of the city, he kept vigil and went without sleep, he sighed and wept, he disquieted himself over the commoners when he was on the throne of our Lord and governed the city. Oh our lords, oh rulers, oh nobles, oh citizens, make every effort; let the weeping, sorrow, tears and sighs increase and flourish. This is all with which I appear before you, bow down to you, and encourage your spirits. Be of good cheer. I (do not wish to) cause you to take ill (with my long talking), oh our lords, oh rulers, oh noblemen.

Frances Karttunen and James Lockhart, *The Art of Nahuatl Speech*, pp. 107–37.

Ceremonies of Sacrifice—Florentine Codex

In the Mesoamerican worldview, sacrifice was considered necessary to the main-tenance of the Sun, meaning light and life. As the gods sacrificed themselves to give life to man, so man sacrificed to maintain the lives of the gods, especially the Sun. According to the Nahua texts: "Because the gods sacrificed themselves for us (topan otlamaceuhque), *we humans are* macehualtin *(those who exist by the sacrifice of the gods).*

Human sacrifices took place during the feasts as they occurred during the solar year. The following texts, collected by fray Bernardino de Sahagún, de-scribe two feasts and the celebration of a victory, when the captives were brought into the city.

1. TLALOC—THE RAISING OF THE TREE

Quauitl eua: This day came, and when it was this [month], a feast was then celebrated for the Tlalocs.

Everywhere on mountain tops, blood sacrifices were made and sacrificial banners were hung. Blood sacrifices were made at Tepetzinco, or there in the very gulf of the lake at a place called Pantitlan.

At this place they left consecrated papers and set up long poles called cuenmatli by means of which would come to pass greenness, sprouting, and growth.

And there they took children, known as "human banners"—those who had two cowlicks of hair and whose day signs were favorable. They were sought everywhere, and bought. It was said, "These are precious blood-offerings. [The rain gods] receive them with rejoicing; they wish for them; they are thus satisfied and given contentment." With them the rains were sought; rain was asked.

And everywhere, in the houses, in each home, in each of the quarters where the young warriors were trained, and in each tribal temple, everywhere they erected the slender green poles; on them they placed white paper flags dotted with large and small drops of liquid rubber.

And they took [the children] to many [different] places. [First was] Quauhtepec. And the one who died here bore the same name Quauhtepetl. His paper vestments were brown.

The second place where one died was the top of Mount Yoaltecatl. The human banner [the child to be sacrificed] had the same name—Yoaltecatl. His paper vestment was black striped with red.

The third place was Tepetzinco, where died a girl called Quetzalxoch, a name which they took from Tepetzintli, [also] named Quetzalxoch. Her array was blue.

The fourth place was Poyauhtlan just at the foot and in front of Mount Tepetzinco. The name of him who died was Poyauhtecatl. Thus he went adorned: he was arrayed in rubber, stripes of liquid rubber.

The fifth place, there in the midst of the lake, was a place named Pantitlan. He who died there had the name Epcoatl. The vestments in which he went, having put them on, were set with mussel shells.

The sixth place to which they carried [a victim] was the top of [the hill of] Cocotl, and also he went bearing the name Cocotl. His array was varicolored—part red, part brown.

The seventh place was on the summit of Yiauhqueme, and also the human banner bore the name Yiauhqueme. The clothing which he bore was completely brown.

These were the places where [the children] died, as blood offerings, as human banners.

And all went with head-bands with sprays and sprigs of quetzal feathers; they had green stone necklaces, and they went provided with green stone bracelets; they provided them with bracelets of green stone. Their faces were painted with liquid rubber, and spotted with a paste of amaranth seeds. And they had sandals of liquid rubber. All went in glorious array; they were adorned and ornamented; all had valuable things on them. They gave them paper wings; wings of paper they had. They were carried in litters covered with quetzal feathers, and in these [the children] were kept. And they went sounding flutes for them.

All mourned much; men wept for them; men loosed their tears for them; they mourned them and they groaned.

And when they reached the place of vigil, in the Mist House, here was spent the night in vigil. Vigil was kept for them by the priests and the quaquacuitli who were the old priests. [And if] any of the priests separated themselves from them, they were called mocauhque (they who are abandoned); no longer did [such an one] join others in intoning chants; no longer was he needed; no more was he counted [among them].

And if the children went crying, their tears coursing down and bathing their faces, it was said and understood that indeed it would rain. [For] their tears signified rain. Therefore [men] were joyful; thus were their hearts at rest. Hence they said: "Truly, soon rain will set in; yea, now soon we shall have rain." And if one who was dropsical was [met] somewhere, they said "It will not rain for us."

And when the rains were about to end, when they were soon to finish, to close, then the cuitlacochin bird cried—a forecast that continual, soft rain was about to set in. Then came the gulls. And also came the falcons, flying with much clamor. And they forecast when would come the ice, and that it would freeze.

And at the time called Quauitl eua, there on the round sacrificial stone appeared and came into view all those who were to be sacrificial victims. And of those who were thus to die, it was said, "They raise poles for the striped ones." They were brought to Yopico, [Xipe] Totec's temple. There they made them fight in mock battle, in the same manner as they would later die, [when] they would tear their hearts out of them. They counterfeited this with them. [Using] tortillas of ground corn which had not been softened in lime [as mock hearts], they thus cut their hearts out.

And four times they appeared before the people. They were looked at; they were made to be seen by the people; they were made known. They gave them and provided them their paper vestments.

The first time they were given, and ornamented with, red; they were [dressed] in red; their paper garments were red.

The second time their paper ornamentation was white.

The third time they again bore their red vestments.

The fourth time, white.

This last time, they ornamented them and gave them presents; for this last time, they wore [this array]—so that in it their fate would come, they would be slain, they would breathe their last, they would be the [sacrificial] striped ones. For this last time, they took their red array.

No more did they change [their garments]. And they ornamented them as the striped ones with liquid rubber.

And those who had captured prisoners, who had captives whom they had taken, also anointed themselves with red; they covered themselves with feather down; their hands and feet were covered with white turkey feathers.

And also they were given costly insignia; [but] not given [to keep] always only that they should smoke with them; that they should dance the captives' dance with them.

Only thus they appeared and were seen; only thus men marveled at them; only thus [garbed] they celebrated the feast; only thus did one make known to men that his captive was to be offered as a sacrifice.

And he bore his shield, which went resting on his arm, and he carried his rattle stick, which he went rattling, and he proceeded planting his rattle stick on the ground, and it rattled and jingled.

And all those who had captives, those who had taken prisoners, were thus garbed—they whose captives would be offered as sacrifices when the Feast-day Tlacaxipeualiztli came.

2. OLD WOLF

. . . Then were rewarded the seasoned warriors who had brought word of the great veracity of the four-hundred count.

And in this wise the messengers entered; if the flesh of men had been taken captive, it was thus soon made known—all came tying and binding their hair, for the flesh of men had been taken and they thus made it evident. And much did the common folk rejoice when they saw them [and noted] that they came binding [their hair]. They said "And so the flesh of men has been taken captive; for all the messengers go with bound [hair]!" And if some came separate [from the others], and came no more with their hair tied and bound, but went with it quite loose, thus they made it known that [our men] had been made captive and that there had been losses in the war. And when the common folk saw them, then a cry of grief arose. Then they said, "And so there have been losses!"

And the noblemen, when they had taken some captives, did not anoint themselves with yellow but rather stained themselves with red ochre, which they put on all over; and they were pasted with eagle down. And Moctezuma rewarded them all with princely capes and breech clouts of great value and high honor, and with preciously wrought quetzal feather devices [ornamented] with gold, and with shields with, perhaps, quetzal feather garlands—very rich shields.

And if one's captives came alive, then he had stewards guard them, and they took great care of them lest they take sick; perhaps it might be twenty or forty that they would guard.

And at the time when the captive was to die, then, Moctezuma presented the captor a device [with] quetzal feather cups so that possessing it he might slay him as a sacrifice. It did not belong to him; but having it he slew the victim, and he danced with it. He had his rattle stick with him, or the obsidian butterfly or quetzal feather cup [device] set with gold, which he carried upon his back. Possessing it, he slew him as an offering.

And the captive he then took there where he was to die, upon the round sacrificial stone; he proceeded to take the captive by the head, and lead him up there where they would slay him in the gladiatorial sacrifice. The one known as Old Wolf led him by the hand—he in whose care lay the captives, as if they had become his sons. And then he gave [the victim] his four pine cudgels, which he would hurl at his adversaries. And he gave him his shield, and his war club—not edged with obsidian blades but only pasted with feathers.

And those who contended against him in gladiatorial sacrifice were the fire priests and the [other] priests. And the captor remained standing below; he stood regarding his captive. He who died was indeed before [his captor].

And after this, when the Old Wolf had arrayed the captive, thereupon he went, and gave him to drink wine which was called the gods' wine. He took it to him [in] a vessel [painted like] reeds and edged with feathers. When [the victim] had drunk, then he raised [the wine] in dedication [toward] where the sun came forth. So [Old Wolf] did with all the shields and war clubs; he raised all of them as offerings which he gave the captive. When Old Wolf had offered the captive [wine] and made him drink it, thereupon the slayer of the sacrificial victim went forth in order to sacrifice him. [He had] his shield and his war club edged with obsidian blades and covered with feathers.

And when he had drunk, then he struck at the captive, who likewise struck back. And if the captive were of stout heart, if he were verily a chieftain, really manly, perhaps three or four men fought him. Then, when he fell, they indeed slew him as a sacrifice. And if he were not manly, not a chieftain, then he cast himself there on the round sacrificial stone, and did not fight. Forthwith was he stretched out upon his back, and then they gashed open his breast, seized his heart, and raised it in dedication there [toward] where the sun came forth.

And after the sacrifice was offered, thereupon those who had made the sacrifice, who had slain [the victim], the priests, each one danced with the heads [of the captives], carrying them with them. And Old Wolf wept at this; he wept for his sons who had died.

And the [captives] they then flayed; when it was dawn they were already flayed. [They] stood wearing [their] skins. Of each captive who died, their skins were all worn. Then they assembled at Yopico, in the courtyard of the devil. They had their shields, their war clubs, and their rattle sticks. And also came together the great chieftains, the battle-drunk, all important personages. With them were their staves; the pine staves lay in their hands, and they went carrying them.

And when deep night was overspread, they did not take upon their wrists their shields, but took only their staves, as they awaited the time that the sun would burst forth. And when he came forth, thereupon the tototecti placed themselves in order—verily, all of them. And the chieftains, upon this, also placed themselves in order and contended against the tototecti. Perhaps they faced each other in the four directions. And then the chieftains started forth and fell upon the tototecti; they tickled their navels. Very swiftly they tickled them, and then they took after them and went skirmishing with them there in the place where they were, a place called Totectzontecontitlan. There the chieftains turned back; their only task had been to leave them there.

And when this had taken place, thereupon the tototecti visited house after house. Nowhere did they omit a house or one's home. Indeed everywhere they entered; and the common folk, seasoned to this, awaited them in order to offer them the things with which they expected them—bunches of ears of maize, tortillas made of uncooked maize, and tamales of maize, amaranth seed, and honey mixed together. For the whole day they went from house to house, [thus treated with] esteem.

And the next day, or [during the next] twenty days, wherever [one of them] went, perhaps in the market place, he begged, and that which he begged he gave to the owner of [the dead] captive. He gave him his share, perchance, of chili, salt, or staves, or pine wood, or grains of maize—all which lay in the marketplace. Each day [he did] the same.

Arthur J. O. Anderson and Charles E. Dibble, *Florentine Codex of Fray Bernardino de Sahagún,* Book II, chapter 20, Book VIII, chapter 20, and Appendix B.

3. THE FEAST OF TOXCATL

The feast and blood sacrifices made during all the days of the fifth month, which was called Toxcatl [meaning "dryness," a twenty-day period within the spring dry season in central Mexico].

In the month of Toxcatl, the great feast of Tezcatlipoca was held. At that time he was formed and set up. Wherefore his impersonator, who had lived for one year as Tezcatlipoca, died.

And at that time the new impersonator, who would again live for one year, was offered to the people.

For many impersonators lived so, whom guardians kept and maintained. Perhaps there were ten. There were elect captives, chosen when captives were taken. Then one was chosen if he was good to look upon and fair of body. Then such were taken, and the guardians cared for them. But one whom they destined to be a slave, the captor slew.

For he who was chosen was of fair countenance, of good understanding and quick, of clean body—slender like a reed; long and thin like a stout cane; well-built; not of overfed body, not corpulent, and neither very small nor exceedingly tall.

For anyone who was formed thus defective, who was too tall, the women said to him: "Tall one; headnodder, handful of stars!" He who was chosen impersonator was without defects.

He was like something smoothed, like a tomato, or like a pebble, as if hewn of wood. He did not have curly hair, but straight, long hair; he had no scabs, pustules, or boils on the forehead, nor skin growths on the forehead, nor was he large-headed, nor with the back of the head prominent; nor of a head shaped like a carrying-net, nor with the structures of the crown yet soft; not broad-headed, nor with a square head; not bald, nor with a bulbous forehead; not of swollen eyelids, nor enlarged ones; not with swollen cheeks; not of disfigured eyes or cheek, nor with swollen face; not with cleft chin; not with a gross face, nor a downcast one; not flat-nosed nor with wide nostrils, nor with an arched, Roman nose nor a bulbous nose, nor bent nor twisted nor crooked—but his nose should be well-placed, straight; not thick-lipped nor gross- nor big-lipped, nor with bowl-like ones, nor enlarged; neither one who stammered, nor one who talked as if his tongue were pierced for a ring; nor one with welts on his tongue; nor one who spoke a barbarous language, or spoke thickly, or lisped, or was dumb; nor buck-toothed, nor large-toothed or fang-toothed, nor of yellowed teeth, nor darkened, nor decayed—but his teeth were like seashells, well arrayed in order; his teeth were not shaped like bowls. Neither had he scarred eyes, nor poor vision, nor squinting eyes, nor scarified; not blinded, nor of small seedlike eyes, nor angry-eyed, nor sunken, nor hollow, nor cuplike, nor stupid-looking, nor gouged, pierced, or wounded; nor had he a scarred neck, like one who had been choked, nor one with lacerations, nor with double chin, nor with pocks on the neck. Not with protruding or long ears, nor with torpid neck, nor hunch-backed, nor stiff-necked, nor with neck elongated, much elongated, nor twisted, nor kinked; neither with unduly long hands, nor lacking one hand, nor wanting both hands, nor fat-fingered; not emaciated, nor fat, nor big-bellied, nor of prominent, hatchet-shaped navel, nor of wrinkled stomach; nor cringing; not of hatchet-shaped buttocks; nor of flabby buttocks or thighs.

He who was thus without flaw, who had no bodily defects, who had no blemishes, no moles, who had no lacerations or wrinkles on his body, they then looked well that he be taught to blow the flute; that he might pipe and play his flute well; and that with it he hold his flowers and his smoking tube and blow and suck upon it, and smell the flowers.

Thus he went bearing his flute, his flowers, and his smoking tube together as he walked through the streets.

And while he yet lived and was cared for in the house of the guardian, before he appeared before the people, care was taken that he might be prudent in his discourse, that he might talk graciously, converse well, and greet people agreeably on the road, if he met anyone.

For he was much honored when he appeared as the impersonator; because he was the likeness of Titlacaucan; he was acknowledged as our lord, treated like a lord; one begged favors, with sighs; before him the common people bowed in reverence and kissed the earth.

. . .

And for one year he lived thus; at the feast of Toxcatl, he appeared before the people. And when the man died who had been impersonator for one year, he who had led the way, he who had cast the spear for one year, who had given commands for one year, forthwith was chosen to be set in his place, from all whom the temple guardians had saved and cared for at the time that the captive appeared before them.

Thereupon he began his office; he went about playing his flute. By day and by night he followed whatever way he wished.

His eight young men went following him. Four of them had fasted for a year; their hair was shorn like the hair of slaves, cut and clipped, not smooth like a gourd, nor cut too short, not made like growing whiskers on the head.

And four warriors, who instructed youths in the art of war, were similarly shorn. Their hairdress lay upright on their foreheads.

Then Moctezuma adorned the impersonator well and arrayed him in varied garb; he provided him his appropriate indumentary [array]. He ornamented him, he adorned him in great pomp with all costly articles, which he caused to be placed upon him; for verily he took him to be his beloved god. His face was anointed with black; it was said: "He fasts with blackened face." A thick layer of black was smeared on his cheeks. White feathers were placed upon his head—the soft down of eagles. They placed it on his hair, which fell to his loins.

And when he was attired, he went about with sweet-smelling flowers upon his head, a crown of flowers. And these same were hung over both shoulders, as far down as his armpits. This was called "the flowery garment."

And from both ears hung curved, gold, shell pendants. And they fit his ears with ear plugs made of a mosaic of turquoise. And he wore a shell necklace. Moreover, his breast ornament was of white sea shells.

And then his lip plug was a slender snail shell lip plug. And hanging from his shoulders was what was like a cord bag called icpatoxin.

Then they placed golden bracelets on both upper arms, and on both wrists they put carved bracelets with precious stones, covering almost all the forearm. And he put on his net cape like a fish-net of wide mesh with a fringe of brown cotton thread. And his costly breechclout reached to the calves of his legs.

And then they placed his bells on both legs, all golden bells, called oioalli.

These, as he ran, went jingling and ringing. Thus they resounded. And he had princely sandals with ocelot skin ears. Thus was he arrayed who died after one year.

When the feast of Toxcatl was drawing near, when it was approaching him, when it was coming to him, first they married him to four women whom they sought out for him. He was in the month of Uey Toçoztli.

And he left off, scattered in various places, and abandoned the ornaments he had had, in which he had walked about fasting, painted black. His hair was shorn; he was given a tuft of hair tied upon his forehead, like that of a war captain. Thus they bound his hair, knotting it with brown cotton thread called tochiacatl; and they tied to his long hair his forked heron feather ornament with single quetzal feathers attached.

Only twenty days he lived, lying with and married to the women. Four women he lived with, who also were cared for, for one year, in the guardian's house.

The first one was named Xochiquetzal; the second Xilonen; the third, Atlatonan; the fourth, Uixtociuatl.

And still on the eve of Toxcatl, still five days from it, on the fifth day before it, when in five days the feast day of Toxcatl would come, then they began to sing and dance.

. . .

When he arrived where he was to die, where a small temple stood, called Tlacochcalco, he ascended by himself, of his free will, to the place where he was to die. When he climbed the first step, as he passed one step, he shattered his flute, his whistle, etc. there.

And when he had mounted all the steps, when he had reached the summit, then the priests fell upon him; they threw him on his back upon the sacrificial stone. Then one cut open his breast, seized his heart, and raised it as an offering to the sun.

For in this manner were all these captives offered up. But they did not roll his body down; rather, they lowered it. Four men carried it.

And they strung his severed head on the skull-rack. Thus he ended in the adornment in which he died . . . when he went to die there at Tlapitzauaian.

And this betokens our life on earth. For he who rejoices, who possesses riches, who seeks and covets our lord's sweetness, his gentleness—riches and prosperity—thus ends in great misery. For it is said: "None come to an end here upon earth with happiness, riches, and wealth."

And here in Mexico, when it was the month of Toxcatl, they set up and formed a figure of Uitzilopochtli, here at the Temple of Uitznauac, in the tribal district. They placed it on the serpent bench. . . .

They covered Uitzilopochtli's mequite wood framework with fish amaranth dough; for his figure was always hewn of mesquite wood, which they covered.

Then they placed upon him his raiment; they put on him his sleeveless jacket, on which human bones were painted.

And over it they laid a mantle, his cape of maguey fibre, like a network cape.

And they fitted on his paper crown, adorned with feathers, called anecuiotl. On his feather headdress stood a flint knife, also made of feathers, half of it being blood-colored.

Then they arrayed him in a godly, costly cape, made, embellished, and designed all in precious colored feathers, with the red eye border, all thus edged with the feathers of the red spoonbills. And in the center lay a great golden disc.

And his bones were made of fish amaranth dough, shaped like cylinders. . . . They piled them before the figure, until they were hip high.

And the cape which covered them . . . was designed with skulls, palms of hands, hip bones, ribs, legs, the lower arm bones, and the outlines of feet. . . .

And yet one more thing was spread before him: they cast down what was named the sacred roll. In this form it was named his breechclout.

And this was a paper, white paper and not yellow paper, a finger thick, a fathom wide, and twenty fathoms long.

With ceremonial arrows, arrows hardened in fire, they supported it; they were made only that they might carry the paper; that his breechclout might be carried.

They were plumed with white turkey feathers in three places: first on the point, second on the shaft, and third on the end.

When they had ornamented the figure . . . they brought it to the foot of the Temple. . . . And when they had come to the top, they placed the paper roll upon the serpent bench . . . then all came down.

. . .

They caused the women to begin the dance; they danced leaping, dancing in the fashion of women. And the women were in the middle, holding their sacrificial banners in both hands. They danced and leapt about. And the priests also danced. It was called "the leap in the month of Toxcatl."

There were paper rosettes fastened upon the priests' foreheads; they decked their heads with white feathers. And they smeared honey on their lips; their lips were gleaming. They had paper breechclouts. And their black feathered staves had jackdaw feathers in the form of a cup, and a round ball at the base also of black feathers. The black feathered staves also were called black rain-bird staves.

And where they went grasping the staves were papers painted with black scroll designs. And these priests, as they danced, made circles with and struck their black feathered staves on the ground.

And only in the tribal temples were those who beat the drums for them, seated upon the ground. They beat the upright drums; they sat beating rattles; they sat rattling gourd rattles and beating turtle shells.

And all the masters of the youths, the young seasoned warriors, and the youths were spread out, dancing elsewhere a dance called the serpent dance. . . .

And also a number of young women danced, having so vowed, a popcorn dance. As thick tassels of maize were their popcorn garlands. And these they placed upon the girls' heads. And they were painted; down to the thighs they were bedecked with feathers. And these reached up to their upper arms. And they went mingling with and among those who danced.

Of these, it was said that they . . . embraced Uitzilopochtli. And these girls were very well guarded, that none might covet them, nor ravish them.

And all who danced the serpent dance were well watched, that none might fall into covetousness.

And if anyone were seen seducing one of the girls, then the masters of the youths threw him to the ground. They dragged him; they stepped upon him as he lay stretched out; they trampled upon him. For he had committed a crime in the temple; for he had done a wrong. They said to him: "Truly, penitence is done here; a feast is held here."

And as night fell during the dance, so closed the day of feasting. And the next morning . . . there was dancing again. All danced the serpent dance.

And Ixteucale, he who had lived together with Titlacauan, died on this day. And they also named him Tlacauepan and Teicautzin.

And his paper raiment was painted with black discs. On his paper crown were eagle feathers. His headdress hung in disorder. Upon the crown of his head rested a flint knife made of red feathers.

And also he had his network cape; over it hung a small net bag; and his ornament, like a priest's maniple, hung from his arm. It was of the skin of a wild beast. He fastened shells to his legs. He danced with the others; he danced the serpent dance. He went first in line guiding the others.

And purely of his free will, when he wished, he would die. When he wished, then he delivered himself to the place where he would die.

Priests called tlatlacanaualti seized him, stretched him out on the sacrificial stone, held him, and cut open his breast. They lifted up his heart as an offering to the sun.

And they also strung his head on the skull rack. So he came to his end, even as Titlacauan, whose head was strung on the skull rack.

And at this time, the priests cut the skin: with a stone knife they cut the skin of youths, young boys, and even small children yet lying in their cradles. Thus they cut the skin of their stomachs, their breasts, both upper arms, and both forearms.

This was done only at the time of the feast of Toxcatl, when it ended, each year.

Arthur J. O. Anderson and Charles E. Dibble, *Florentine Codex of Fray Bernardino de Sahagún*, Book II, chapter 24.

⑥ 5 ⑥

Proverbs, Conundrums, and Metaphors

*T*he first set of metaphors is from the Florentine Codex *of fray Bernardino de Sahagún, Book VI: Rhetoric, Moral Philosophy, and Theology. The second set is from the prelude to the* Huehuetlatolli *by fray Andrés de Olmos. In the work of Sahagún, the metaphor precedes the explanation. Olmos, as will be apparent, gave the explanation followed by the metaphors.*

A Scattering of Jades *contains 120 examples of "metaphor," but in fact more than a few seem too direct to merit that description, while many of the proverbs could be described as metaphors.*

Lest the reader conclude that the Nahuas spoke a clumsy and forbiddingly sesquipedalian language, it should be noted that an English phrase may often be contained in a single word in Nahuatl. For example, Mixtitlan, Ayauhtitlan, *two words used to stand for the Spaniards who invaded Mexico, translates as "From out of the clouds, from out of the mists." Sahagún explained, "This was said about people very illustrious and very great, who cannot be looked at, who had never been known, who had never been beheld anywhere."*

Excerpts from fray Bernardino de Sahagún, the *Florentine Codex*, Book VI: Rhetoric, Moral Philosophy, and Theology

Proverbs

A page is sent.

This is said about someone who is sent with a message and fails to return with an answer, or else does not go where he was sent. It is said for this reason. They say that when Quetzalcoatl was the king of Tollan, two women were bathing in his pool. When he saw them he sent some messengers to see who they were. And the messengers just stayed there watching the women bathing and did not take him the information. Then Quetzalcoatl sent another of his pages to see who the bathers were and the same thing happened; he did not return with an answer either. From that time on they began, they started saying: *A page is sent.*

Here, there, and everywhere.

This is said about a person who enters where he should not enter, sticks his hand where he should not stick his hand, and quickly takes part in whatever others are doing.

Polished eye.

This is said of a person who is very astute in the manner of finding, of discovering, what is necessary, or who quickly sees what is difficult in an enigma.

One can dig a little in this world.

This is said when one time we are able to put away a little something, and another time we are in need. Sometimes one can, sometimes one cannot.

No one on earth is an umbilical cord.[1]

We should not sneer at anyone; meaning, we should not disdain anyone even though he appears to warrant disdain, as he might be a wise man, or learned, or able.

A word is his meal.

This is said about the person who is wounded by any little thing and immediately starts quarreling with people. When lightly reprimanded he replies angrily and he squabbles with the other, or whenever anything is said he starts arguing and shouting.

Brazen-faced, truly a face of wood.

This is said about the person who is not bashful or timid with others. He rushes ahead of illustrious people.

He eats his excrement over again.

This is said if someone gives something to another, such as food or a cape. Then he asks for it back, he takes it away from him.

---

[1]I.e., something that is thrown away. There is a play on words here: *xictli,* "umbilical cord," and *xictia,* "to look down upon someone."

He marched straight into poverty.

This is said when I manage to accumulate something after a long time and someone comes along and steals it, or else I throw it away on the road and it falls into someone else's hands.

Ash-faced.

This is said about someone who has done or committed something, an iniquity or thievery. He thinks no one knows about it, but his disgrace is already widely known, it has been bruited about. Therefore they say about this person: *Ash-faced.*

The world[2] spills out.

This is said when we are very poor, when hardly anything comes out. One way, such as mantles or food, by which it is evident that someone is poor and in great want. One's rags are very old and torn, barely covering one. They are worn thin, falling apart, and one's body is spilling out. As a result, it began to be said: *Now the world spills out;* or *Now the world is spilling out.*

Can a hummingbird see that much?

This is said when we share a tortilla or some food divided into tiny pieces. If someone says, "*Can a hummingbird see that much?*" for a hummingbird has a very thin beak, and when he sips nectar even from a very tiny flower he sips very little of it.

Swallow's beak.

This is said about a person who talks a great deal, who is full of words.

Because of him my face becomes wide.

This is said when someone's child—a boy or a girl—or else someone's pupil, was well taught, well brought up, and is commended for his good upbringing. Consequently, the child's parent or teacher is also being commended. Therefore, they say with regard to the child: *Because of him my face becomes wide.* Or, *I make someone's face wide, you make someone's face wide.*

Possibly a mouse drank it.

This is said when we are fighting for something and give up, such as, when players, competing in a game of throwing wooden balls, simply give up and lose the game. This is when they say: *Possibly a mouse drank it.*

He has not yet set his head.

This is said about someone who does not devote himself to one thing ex-

---

[2]*Tlalticpac*, which means "the earth, the world," but also "the penis."

clusively, who does not stick to anything. Perhaps he studies singing; he does not master it. Then he wants to learn Latin and he does not master it either. Then he studies Spanish and he does not learn this either. About a person who does this, they say: *He has not yet set his head.*

With someone's help I became a vulture.

This is said when I have nothing to eat and through the offices of a friend I eat a little of his food. Should someone ask me if I have eaten, I reply: *With someone's help I was vulturing.*

The sun is not hot when it has just risen: after it has been traveling its course awhile, then it becomes hot.

This is said about a person who has just married, as he is still very poor when he starts out in life. However after a little time has gone by he is consoled, as he may now have laid by something.

Where have we come from?

This is said when someone hurts us deeply or wants to do us harm and he is not our enemy but our friend. Hence one retorts: *Where have we come from?*[3]

A glorious face.

This is said about a person who, outwardly, makes a good appearance but does nothing well, executes nothing well. He can do absolutely nothing. This is especially said of women who appear to embroider and spin well but in reality can do nothing well; they just deceive people. For this reason they say: *A glorious face.*

His nose has lost its power.

This is said when certain tidings are untrue, when they are imparted wildly and cannot be proven anywhere. For instance if someone says, "They say the emperor is dead," this is not true. So one says: *His nose has lost its power.* But if it were true, then one would say: *His nose certainly is powerful.*

Moderation is proper.

We should not dress in rags, nor should we overdress. In the matter of clothing we should dress with moderation.

When I am a coyote I shall see it.

This is said when someone claims to have done something. For example, he says: "I went to Castile," or "I went to Guatemala." Or, he says: "I was mayor." But this is not true, he is just lying. For this reason, they say: *When*

---

[3]That is, "Weren't we friends?"

I am a coyote, I shall see that he went to Castile, or Guatemala, or that at some time he was a mayor!

Every one of my nits has heard it!
    This is said when a person tells another something and he repeats it many times, he says the same things over and over again.

He makes a stew of all the chameleons he catches.
    This is said when someone is given a task to do that is not difficult, but he regards it as difficult; or he receives an insignificant order that he considers dangerous and is upset.

He hung himself with a piece of rug.
    This is said when I make an accusation against someone because of some trifling thing and he retaliates with something serious that puts me in difficulties; or when something, such as a cape or a cup, is slightly ripped or cracked, and when I want to repair it, it rips or cracks more. Then one says: *He hung himself with a piece of rug.*

This is all that was born.
    This is said when we say something that is brief, not long and drawn out, and it is quickly concluded. When it is over we say: *This is all that was born.*

Someone who arranges his intestines artistically.
    This is said of an artisan, such as a feather artist, who does his work beautifully and designs it well, so that it goes, so that it is sold quickly.[4]

Once again it shall be, once again it shall exist, sometime, somewhere.
    What happened long ago and no longer happens, will happen another time. What existed long ago, will exist again. Those who are living now, will live anew, will exist once more.

Conundrums

What is a little blue-green jar filled with popcorn? Someone is sure to guess our riddle; it is the sky.

What is it that is seized in a black stone forest and dies on a white stone slab? Someone is sure to guess our riddle; it is a louse that we take from our head, put on our nail and then kill.

---

[4]This means to arrange one's feelings, or to feel something deeply.

What is a little darky who writes with a piece of lead? A snail.

What is a little mirror in the middle of fir trees? Our eyes.

What is a mountainside that has a spring of water in it? Our nose.[5]

What are they that go pushing along wrinkled faces? The knees.

What is an "I go this way, you go that, and over there we shall meet"? A breechcloth.

What is a little white stone holding up quetzal feathers? An onion.

What is it that we enter in three places and leave by only one? Our shirt.

What is it that you quickly take from its hole and cast on the ground stiff? It is the mucus from the nose.

What is a cardinal going first and a crow following behind? Something burning.[6]

What is it that in one day becomes big with child? A spindle.

What is it always standing by the hearth curving upward? A dog's tail.

What is a red stone that goes jumping along? A flea.

Thelma D. Sullivan and T. J. Knab, *A Scattering of Jades*, excerpted from pp. 185–204.

Metaphors

My heron feather headdress, my jacket of ropes.[7]
This means: When the city gives me a responsibility I become a slave. If I hurt the city in some way, if I endanger it, I shall be put in jail.

On the side, on the sly.
This was said when someone was admonished many times over but turned

[5]The Dibble and Anderson translation of this conundrum is known to every student of the Nahuas. "What is that which is a hill whence there is a flow? Our nose."

[6]Dibble and Anderson: "What is the scarlet macaw leading, the raven following? The conflagration."

[7]When a slave was purchased, he was given a headpiece of white heron feather to indicate that he was sold. Both words are synonymous with slave and servitude.

a deaf ear and regarded it with disdain. When he was tied up and taken away, these words were said to annoy him: *Do not glance at me obliquely and askance, for I have done my duty.*

Smoke and mist: fame and glory.

This was said about a king not long dead whose *smoke and mist,* meaning his *fame and glory,* had not yet vanished; or, about someone who had gone far away but whose fame and glory had not faded.

The jaguar mat, the eagle mat.

This means where the strong and valiant are, whom no one can vanquish. For this reason they say: "*The eagle mat and the jaguar mat* are laid out there." And they also said: "There stand *the jaguar wall and the eagle wall,* which protect the city," which means *water and mountain.*[8]

The tail and the wing.

This means the common people. For this reason the subjects are called *tails and wings,* and the king, lord of the *tails and wings.*

You are stepping on your face, you are stepping on your teeth.

This was said about a king or noble who said something that was not proper and mortified someone, something that he ought not to have said. He was told: "Be still! Be prudent! You are *stepping on your face.*" This means: "You have disgraced yourself." And he was also told: "You dirty yourself, you dishonor yourself, you mar your life and your words."

There was a sowing, there was a scattering.

This was said of a royal orator who counsels the people well. After he spoke, after the sermon had been preached, they understood its truth and they told him: "The people have been enriched, they have become wealthy. *There has been a sowing, there has been a scattering* of precious jades, etc."

Obsidian blades, hardened arrows.

These words were said about one person who hated another and was constantly plotting to do something monstrous to him. He went about saying: "How can I do something to that scoundrel?" He was always looking for a way to do something sinister, to do something evil to another.

---

[8]*Altepetl,* made up of *atl,* which means "water," and *tepetl,* "mountain." In *The Nahuas After the Conquest,* James Lockhart defined the *altepetl* as "the ethnic state." He went on to explain that "it refers to territory, but what is meant is primarily an organization of people holding sway over a given territory." Lockhart suggests a comparison to "early Mediterranean city-states."

Saliva, spittle.

These words mean falsehood and untruth. It was said to the king or noble who believed all the lies he heard.

"Do not tell lies and falsehoods in the presence of the king," the liar was told. "Investigate it thoroughly, look at it closely."

Your wall, your enclosure.

This was said of those who served in some capacity, such as tribute collectors or captains. Or it was said of a king or a noble who governed the people, as he was like their *wall and enclosure,* encircling and surrounding them. For whatever would befall the people would first befall the king or noble.

The jug holder; the tortilla folder.[9]

This is said to a king or noble who is beset by sorrow. They told him: "Do not grieve so, do not turn away from the *straw base of the jug and the folded tortilla.* Take a little something. Do not neglect yourself, as your grief may turn into sickness."

Heart and blood.

These words were said of chocolate because in the past it was precious and rare. The common people and the poor did not drink it. For this reason it was said: *Heart and blood,* worthy of veneration. They also said it was deranging and it was like the mushroom, for it intoxicated people, it made them drunk. If a commoner drank it, it was considered scandalous. In the past the rulers or great warriors, or the commander of the army or the commander of the arsenal, and perhaps two or three people who were rich drank it; it was considered something grand. They drank chocolate in small amounts, it was not drunk immoderately.

Chaff and straw.

This means lies, which are something bad, something wrong. it was said to someone who was rotten, who was a disturber of the peace, and deceitful. "Lies, which are evil and wrong, have stuck to you like *chaff and straw."* To someone who dedicated and devoted himself to lying, they said: *"Chaff and straw* are what you feed on, you liar, you agitator!"

The black and the red of the ancients.

This was said of the traditions of the ancients, the way of life they established. One lived by it, or perhaps did not live by it. Therefore it was said: "Do not let *the red and the black of the ancients perish!"* This means the traditions.

---

[9]Synonyms for food and drink.

Or: "Why do you destroy the way of life, the *black and the red of our grand-fathers, the ancients?"*

EXCERPTS FROM FRAY ANDRÉS DE OLMOS

Rootstock, or first father, or originator of a family line, ruler or governor.

Hair of the head, rope, entrails, nourishment, root, someone's hair, someone's grandfather.

Arrogant, one who holds no one in esteem, who debases others and who is disdained.

He walks on people's faces, people's heads, he treads on people, he tramples people underfoot. He rises up against people, he sits on people, he places another on the mat and seat, he is aggressive. He insists on being honored, insists on being respected. He respects no one, he goes about without respect for anything, but walks on the face, on the head of his name, his honor. He is arrogant, he kicks people's mat and seat, hence respects nothing.

The slave.

He who is an axe, a tumpline, the earth, the mud, the stones, the wood, who has heron feathers and a jacket of ropes, whose place of being, whose dwelling place is the urinal, the dung heap.

Thelma D. Sullivan and T. J. Knab, *A Scattering of Jades,* excerpted from pp. 204–32.

❦ 6 ❦

Historical Narratives

*T*he Xiuhamatl, *"Books of the Years"—including the* Historia Tolteca-Chichimeca, *which covers the period from the ruin of Tula through the Conquest—recorded important events in the lives of both rulers and people. Several ancient codices preserved this material year by year, using glyphic characters and paintings. The codices* Boturini, Az-catitlan, Mexicanus, *and others describe the long march of the Mexica as they searched for the place that their tutelary god Huitzilopochtli had chosen for them. Several manuscripts in Nahuatl, employing the alphabet introduced by the Spanish friars, also record the genealogies, wars, and most important events of the Mexica and other Nahua peoples, such as the Tezcocans, Tlaxcallans, and many more.*

In this work, the Conquest narrative occupies a place of distinction both for its importance and dramatic character. Through material taken from various sources, one can come to understand the "Vision of the Vanquished," that is, the testimony of the Other, who speaks about the confrontation in which he took part, until finally he contemplated the total ruin of the Mexica nation.

The Annals of Tlatelolco—*the twin city of Mexico-Tenochtitlan—include genealogical and historical literature about the principal polities of central Mexico, and also a brief but intensely human account of the Spanish Conquest. Beginning with the news of the sighting of the Spaniards off the Mexican Gulf Coast, it describes the massacre in the main temple of Tenochtitlan. This is followed by the so-called Night of Sorrows, when Hernán Cortés and his men had to slip out of the Mexican metropolis at night only to be furiously attacked by the Mexica; their return several months later; the eighty-day siege of the city, its fall, and the subsequent events: the flight of the people, the exaction of gold, and the torture of the young ruler Cuauhtemoc. All are part of this vivid eyewitness testimony, a masterpiece of Nahuatl epic literature.*

The Conquest narrative included in the Florentine Codex *of fray Bernardino de Sahagún, pioneer of modern ethnographic research, was dictated by Nahua elders who took part in the fight against the Spaniards. It opens with the omens taken as foretelling the arrival of the Spaniards. The account goes on to describe the first encounters with them, Motecuhzoma's intense terror, Cortés's first entrance into the city, the treacherous massacre at the main temple, the Spanish flight, and the terrible plague of smallpox that spread through the city. Then comes the return of Cortés, the launching of his brigantines to lay siege by water while the army attacked by land, the Spanish assaults, and the suffering of the people, culminating in the surrender of the Mexica, and its meaning for those who survived.*

Contrary to what one might expect, the Nahua, as well as the Maya and other Mesoamerican peoples, did not remain silent about the Spanish invasion and their resistance to it. Beside these firsthand accounts, others were redacted alphabetically in several indigenous languages as well as in codices employing paintings and glyphic characters. These testimonies offer eloquent proof that history can preserve the viewpoint of the vanquished.

Extract from *Historia Tolteca-Chichimeca*

The "Books of the Years"[1]

Thirteen Rabbit year. At this time the Spaniards were sighted at the seashore, when they came.

One Reed year. At this time the Spaniards arrived, and the one called the Marqués came. And when they arrived, the Tlaxcalans met them in Tlaxcala; the rulers greeted them and addressed them politely <or gave them gifts>.

And at this time they wrought destruction at Cholula, also in One Reed year.

And at that point the Tepeyacac people relinquished the rulership they had held; they had held it for fifty-three years.

And at that point the ruler Tequanitzin died, and don Alonso de Castañeda assumed the rulership.

Two Flint Knife year. At this time we of Quauhtinchan, Tepeyacac, Tecalco, Tecamachalco, and Quecholac were defeated. We all, we people of

---

[1]The author here uses square brackets to indicate explanatory material and arrow brackets < > to indicate variant text.

Quauhtinchan, Tecalco, and Tepeyacac, took refuge at the river [or the river Atoyac].

Three House year. At that point we began to serve people at the orders of the Marqués, and the person we served was named Francisco de Orduña. What we gave him was ten light cloaks, also ten loincloths, also ten women's blouses, also ten skirts, and ten pieces of gold, ten hen turkeys, and four hundred measures of shelled maize, just measured with a small woven palm basket.

Four Rabbit year. At that point twelve friars came.

Five Reed year.

Six Flint Knife year.

Seven House year. At that point we began to give labor service to people; it had been three years that we had been given to two Spaniards and were serving them.

Eight Rabbit year. At that point we relinquished our fields in Xicotenco Teteltitlan; the people of Xicotenco are on them.

Nine Reed year.

Ten Flint Knife year. [We gave the type of tribute cloak called] *patolquachtli*.

Eleven House year.

Twelve Rabbit year. At that point our father, named fray Juan de Rivas, established himself in Tepeyacac. At that point was founded the faith, Christianity, and at that point people were baptized and married.

Thirteen Reed year.

Also in this year we were given a tribute quota, so that we <gave various things>, and four thousand [measures] of maize, and sixteen measures of wheat that we were to plant, and eighty measures of beans, and eighty [measures] of chiles, and sixteen measures of chia, and sixteen [pieces of] salt, and twenty turkey hens, and thirty commoners [to work]. At that time the *patolquachtlis* that we had been giving to both Alonso de Valencia and Juan Pérez de Artiaga were stopped. We gave twenty-four thousand of them during four years. And don Tomás, the Tecpanecatl [lord], was hanged at that point. And at that point our father named fray Juan de Rivas established himself at Tepeyacac.

One Flint Knife year.

In this year the Spaniards settled at Cuetlaxcohuapan [Puebla]. The person who first established himself there and governed was named [Saiavillez]. And at that point we began in fact [to pay the tribute in the kind of cloak called an] *itzcallotl*; at that point we relinquished <paying various kinds of tribute>.

Two House year. At this time came the judge named Sandoval; the president [of the Audiencia of New Spain] sent him here about the boundaries, concerning how the Totomihuaque formed their boundary. It took place in the presence of our father fray Cristobal de Zarnora, who acted as witness.

Three Rabbit year. At this time the church of San Juan Bautista was inaugurated. And we cleared ground for cultivation at Otlamaxalco.

Four Reed year. At this time the church of San Francisco in Tepeyacac was inaugurated, and their market was moved <from Tlaitec>.

Five Flint Knife year.

Six House year.

Seven Rabbit year. Don Agustin <came as judge>.

Eight Reed year.

Nine Flint Knife year.

Ten House year. For the second time don Agustin de Osorio came as judge concerning the lands here in Quauhtinchan. Don Antonio de Mendoza, the viceroy, sent him, and our fathers fray Juan de Rivas and fray Diego de Olarte served as witnesses.

Eleven Rabbit year.

In this year the emperor his majesty's rulership was assumed [i.e., Spanish-style municipal government was introduced]. For the first time alcaldes were placed in office, Toribio Martinez and Baltasar Huitznahuatzintli, and also regidores, constables, a majordomo, and a notary.

Twelve Reed year. At that point we began just raising money to give to our ruler, one peso, and to Juan Pérez one peso and four tomines. At that point we gave up [paying in] long tribute cloaks; the money was substituted instead. And at that point the [duty of delivering] dried grass [for hay] was given to the Chichimeca at Atzomiatla.

Thirteen Flint Knife year. At that time don Felipe de Mendoza assumed office as governor for the first time, along with the alcaldes Juan Bautista and don Diego de Galicia.

At that point attention was given to the boundaries that the Mexica—the Xiloxochcatl, the Quahuitencatl, the Tocuiltecatl, the Tlauhpanecatl, the Atepanecatl—had set up seventy-eight years before by order of the ruler Axayacatzin when the Mexica came to divide the altepetl of Quauhtinchan into five parts.

And at that point the Quauhtinchan rulers, don Alonso de Castañeda, don Diego de Rojas, don Pedro de Luna, don Felipe de Mendoza, don Baltasar de Torres, don Diego de Galicia, and don Baltasar de Lup[. . .], pointed out the boundaries that the Mexica had set up at Axaxalpan, Chichicalotla, Chimalcolco, Ocotochatlauhtli, Tlatzcayo, Acatlan, Atlecuillo, Tzotollo, Tecopilli, and Atzontli, where meanwhile the Tepeyacac people had been sustaining themselves from the lands of the Quauhtinchan people. They put it before the lord viceroy, don Antonio de Mendoza, how the people of Tepeyacac had been sustaining themselves from the lands of the Quauhtinchan people, and the lord heard it favorably.

James Lockhart, *We People Here* (Stanford, CA: University of California Press, 1993), pp. 283–87.

The Fall of Tenochtitlan, 1528

Annals of Tlatelolco

And during all this time, while we were being attacked, the Tenochca appeared nowhere on all the roads here in Yacacolco, Atizaapan, Coatlan, Nonoalco, Xoxohuiltitlan, and Tepeyacac. They became the responsibility of the Tlatelolca alone, and likewise the canals all became our exclusive responsibility.

And the Tenochca who were war captains cut off their hair [to avoid recognition], and all the subordinate leaders cut their hair, and the scraped-heads and the Otomis wrapped up their heads. Nowhere did they show their faces during the time when we were being attacked; only all the Tlatelolca surrounded their leader.

And all their women also shamed and scolded the Tenochca, saying to them, "You are just lying inactive, you have no shame. A woman will never decorate herself to be next to you." Their women went about weeping and imploring the Tlatelolca; and seeing this, the citizens sent word, but nowhere did the Tenochca appear.

But the Tlatelolca scraped-heads and Otomis, the war leaders, were dying from the guns and iron bolts.

The ruler of Acolhuacan, Tencocoltzin, sent word. Those with whom they came to talk were the Ticocyahuacatl of Tlatelolco, Topantemoctzin; the Tezcacoacatl Poyecatzin; the Tlacateccatl Temilotzin; the Tlacochcalcatl Coyohuehuetzin; and the Cihuatecpanecatl Matlalacatzin.

The messengers of Tencocoltzin of Acolhuacan came to say to them, "The lord <Coacatl> Tencocoltzin sends us here and says, 'May the Mexica Tlateloca hear; their hearts burn and smart, their bodies are afflicted. And my heart too has burned and smarted. Whatever little thing I buy for myself [and put] in my bundle or in the folds of my cloak, they look everywhere and take it from me. The citizens are already lost. I say, let the Tenochca be left alone, let them perish by themselves. I will do nothing yet; I will await word of what [the Tlatelolca] say and how many days <they are deferring it>. This is all of my statement that they are to hear.' "

Then the Tlatelolca rulers responded to the speech, telling them, "Thank you, our younger brothers; the Chichimecatl of Acolhuacan is our protector. Here is what he is to hear. Twenty days ago <they> wanted what he says to be done, but now, where have we seen [the Tenochca]? They have entirely hidden their faces. No one proclaims himself a Tenochca any more, for some pretend to be from Quauhtitlan, and some claim to be from Tenanyocan, Azcapotzalco, or Coyoacan. Where do we still see any of them? And those

<whom we do> proclaim themselves Tlatelolca. What are we to do? [Tenco-coltzin] has been kind. Those who toddle and crawl owe him thanks. We await word from our lords."

After we had been being attacked for sixty days, and the Spaniards were coming [fighting] in person, one named Castañeda came shouting at the place called Iyauhtenco. He brought the Tlaxcalans. He shouted in this direction to those who stood watch at the rampart at Tlaxoxiuhco, who were one named Chapoltzin, leader of the Itzpan people, along with the Tlapalte-catl Cuexacaltzin.

He said to them, "Come here, whoever is there."

They said to each other, "What will they say? Let's just go listen to him."

Then they got in a boat and, stationing themselves at a distance, said to them, "What do you want to say?"

The Tlaxcalans responded, "Where is your home?"

They said to them, "Very well, you are being sought. Come; the god, the Captain is summoning you."

Then they left; then they took them to Nonoalco, at Ayauhcalco, where the Captain, Marina, Tonatiuh [Alvarado], Sandoval, and all the rulers of the various altepetl were gathered.

When they spoke, they said to the Captain, "The Tlatelolca have come; we went to get them."

Marina told them in reply, "Do come here; the Captain says, 'What do the Mexica think? Is Quauhtemoc still such a small child? He has no pity on the children and women; the old men have already perished. Here are the rulers of Tlaxcala, Huejotzingo, Cholula, Chalco, Acolhuacan, Cuernavaca, Xochimilco, Mizquic, Cuitlahuac, and Culhuacan.' "

[The Tlatelolca] said, "The Tenochca have taken great advantage of people; the hearts of the rulers in the [various] altepetl have been pained. Well then, let them leave the Tenochca by themselves, let them perish alone. Perhaps the Tlatelolca will not be pained by it, the way they perished because they took advantage of them."

Then [Cortés] replied to the rulers, "Perhaps it is not as you rulers say."

They said, "Yes, indeed it is; may our lord the god so hear it. Let them leave the Tenochca by themselves, let them perish alone. That is the word that you are to carry to your subordinates."

The god said, "Let them go tell Quauhtemoc. Let them consult, let them leave the Tenochca by themselves. Meanwhile, I am moving to Teocalhuey-acan; word from you about what you have decided will reach me there. And the boats are moving to Coyoacan for a while."

When they heard this, they just replied, "Where are we to get hold of the people they are looking for? We have had a difficult time of it; let us make an effort."

Thus were the Tenochca discussed and agreement reached about them. But [when the Tlatelolca were] in the boat, they shouted, "It is no longer possible to leave the Tenochca by themselves! At this point, after all, they have <relied on us> in the fighting!"

Then [the Spaniards] reached Cuepopan, and at Yacacolco, in Cozcaquauhco, Coyohuehuetzin fought, shooting crossbow bolts, and <hit> four.

And the boats stationed themselves at Texopan. The fighting lasted three days, and they drove us from there. Then they reached the temple courtyard; the fighting lasted four days.

And when they reached Yacacolco here, Spaniards were captured on the Tlilhuacan road, as well as all the people from the various altepetl. Two thousand died there, and the Tlatelolca were exclusively responsible for it.

At this time we Tlatelolca set up skull racks; skull racks were in three places. One was in the temple courtyard at Tlillan, where the heads of our lords [the Spaniards] were strung; the second place was in Yacacolco, where the heads of our lords were strung, along with the heads of two horses; the third place was in Cacatla, facing the Cihuateocalli [Woman-Temple]. It was the exclusive accomplishment of the Tlatelolca.

After this they drove us from there and reached the marketplace. That was when the great Tlatelolca warriors were entirely vanquished. With that the fighting stopped once and for all.

That was when the Tlatelolca women all let loose, fighting, striking people, taking captives. They put on warriors' devices, all raising their skirts so that they could give pursuit.

At this point they made a canopy for the Captain on a sacrificial platform in the marketplace. This was also when they set up the catapult there on the platform. The fighting in the marketplace lasted ten days.

And all this is what happened to us and what we saw and beheld. What we suffered is cause for tears and sorrow. The water we drank was salt. Adobe bricks <dipped in> a well were an exclusive possession, guarded under a shield. If someone tried to toast something, [it had to be guarded] with a shield. We ate colorin wood, grass from the salt flats, adobe, lizards, mice, things full of dust. We fought over eating worms; when they put them on the fire and their flesh began to cook, they picked them out of the fire and ate them.

And we had a price. There was a price for a youth, a priest, a maiden, or a little child. The price for any ordinary person was just two handfuls of shelled maize. Ten cakes of water flies or twenty of grass from the salt flats was our price. Gold, greenstones, tribute cloth, plumes, and all precious things were considered as nothing and just spilled on the ground.

When they had set up the catapult in the marketplace, then they came to deliver Xochitl, the Acolnahuacatl. He died in the war [but was still alive at this time]; Tenochtitlan was his home. For twenty days they had <had him

with them>; they came to the marketplace to deliver him. He attributed himself to Tlatelolco; he did not call himself a Tenochca. When they brought
him, they came taking him on both sides, and a crossbowman and a har-
quebusier came guarding him.

When they left him at Copalnamacoyan, they shouted out, "Here will
come a nobleman." Then the Tlatelolca went to get him; the leader was Tohueyo, a leader from Huitznahuac.

When they had taken Xochitl, the Huitznahauc leader came to report [to
Quauhtemoc] and told him, "Xochitl is carrying a message." Quauhtemoc
told Topantemoc, "You will come to talk to the Captain."

When they came to deliver [Xochitl], the war stopped. There was no more
fighting, no one was taken prisoner. Then they took [Xochitl] and put him in
the Cihuateocalli at Axocotzinco.

When they had put him there, they went to tell Topantemoctzin, Coy-
ohuehuetzin, and Temilotzin, and thereupon also the ruler of the Tenochca.
They said to them, "O my lords, they have come and delivered your agent the
Acolnahuacatl Xochitl. It is said he has some message to give you."

Then they consulted and said to one another, "What do you say?"

Then they all cried out, "Let him not be brought here, for our sacrifices
when we read in the paper and the incense were such that the one who went
to get him should receive the message."

So the same Huitznahuac leader, Tohueyo, went to receive the message.
He caused [Xochitl] to speak and interrogated him about the message he
brought.

The Acolnahuacatl Xochitl said, "The god, the Captain, and Marina say,
'Let Quauhtemoc, Coyohuehue, and Topantemoc hear.[2] They have no pity on
the people, the little children, the old men and women. <It is over here. Is
there to be another rout?> And then let everything be brought: beautiful
women, shelled white maize, turkey hens, eggs, white bread. But perhaps one
should wait to see what the reply is. Let the Tenochca be left by themselves,
let them perish alone.' "

When the Huitznahuac leader Tohueyo had received the message, he
went to give it to the Tlatelolca rulers; sitting among them was the ruler of
the Tenochca, Quauhtemoc. When they had heard the whole message that
the Acolnahuacatl Xochitl brought, the Tlatelolca rulers said to one another,
"What do you say? What is your advice?"

Then the Tlacochcalcatl Coyohuehuetzin said, "Let them summon the
Teohua [custodian of the god]." [When he arrived,] he said to him, "Come;
what is your [pl.] view? How do you see what is in your custody [the ritual
calendar]?"

---

[2]The Captain is Hernán Cortés. Marina is his native interpreter, LaMalinche, whose name
has become synonymous with betrayal of one's own people.

The Teohua, learned with papers, cutter of papers, said, "My lords, listen to what we will say. In only four days, eighty will have passed [since the fighting began]. Perhaps it is the order of Huitzilopochtli that [nothing should be done when that term] is not yet fulfilled. Perhaps you will see [what should be done] secretly <have it revealed to you>. Let us wait out the eighty days, for there are only four more."

But when the time came, it was not approved <by the god>. The war began again. It was the same Tohueyo, Huitznahuac leader, who faced <the enemy> and began the war, with which finally they moved everyone to Amaxac, and the fighting reached there.

Then people were trampled; one ran just on top of people. The water filled up with people. It was through people that <one saved oneself? one died?>.

Thus were defeated the Mexica Tlatelolca, who relinquished their altepetl. There at Amaxac, as to all we had with us, we no longer had shields or war clubs, we no longer had anything to eat. It rained on us all night.

When it was done, when it was over, Coyohuehuetzin, Topantemoctzin, and Temilotzin went and delivered Quauhtemoctzin to the place where the Captain, don Pedro de Alvarado, and Marina were.

When they had been taken into custody, the people began to leave, heading for where there was a way out. Some still had some rags to wrap around their bottoms.

The Christians searched all over the women; they pulled down their skirts and went all over their bodies, in their mouths, on their abdomens, in their hair.

Thus the people left, scattering among the altepetl all around, going into the corners or against the sides of other people's houses.

When we dispersed and the altepetl was lost, it was Three House year. We dispersed in [the month of] Nexochimaco, on a day One Serpent.

When we had dispersed, the Tlatelolca rulers Topantemoctzin, the Tlacochcalcatl Coyohuehuetzin, and Temilotzin went to settle in Quauhtitlan. Great warriors had to find a way to live somewhere or other, wearing nothing but rags. Likewise the women put on just skirts with a skull pattern and painted blouses.

For this reason the rulers were discontent and consulted about it, [saying], "We are perishing for a second time. Some of the people who left are being murdered among the Otomis of Acolhuacan."

Then they consulted, favoring the people, and said, "Let us go implore our lord ruler the Captain."

Then there was a search for gold. People were searched and interrogated to see whether someone perhaps had taken and kept a little gold on his shield or device, or his lip plug or lip pendant, or if someone perhaps had taken something of gold from his gods, perhaps their half-moon nose ornament or their pendant. It was all then collected.

When whatever was found had been collected, they selected as their representatives the Tlapaltecatl Cuexacaltzin, the Tecpanecatl Huitziltzin, the Huitznahuac leader Tohueyo, and the Cuitlachcoacatl Pocontzin; these are the ones who went to deliver the gold to Coyoacan.

When they arrived, they said to the Captain, "O our lord, o ruler, your subordinates the Tlatelolca rulers come to implore you; may the lord take heed. His vassals are afflicted, they are suffering in the various altepetl in the corners and against the sides of other people's houses. The Acolhuaque and Otomis are taking advantage of them, murdering them. Well then, that is what they come to ask about. Here are the lip- and earplugs of your servants, and what was on our gods and on our shields." They laid it before him in baskets.

But when the Captain and Marina saw it they became angry and said, "Is that what is being looked for? What is being sought is what you caused to be lost at the Tolteca canal. Where is it? Let it be produced."

Then the messengers said, "Quauhtemoc took it, and the Cihuacoatl and the Huitznahuatl. They know where it is. Let them be interrogated."

When [Cortés] heard this, he had them tied up tightly, putting them in irons.

Marina replied to them, "The Captain says, 'Let them go and consult their rulers. I thank them. Perhaps the people are truly afflicted and advantage is being taken of them. Let them come back to settle in their home, Tlatelolco; let the Tlatelolca settle on all their land. And tell the Tlatelolca rulers that no one is to settle in Tenochtitlan yet, for it is the conquered area of the gods and is already their home. May they go.' "

When this had happened and the messengers of the Tlatelolca rulers had left, they turned to the Tenochtitlan rulers and interrogated them. At this time they burned Quauhtemoctzin on the feet.

And at dawn they brought them, tied to poles, and they came and tied them to poles at the home [palace] of Ahuitzotzin in Acatliyacapan. The swords and guns belonging to our lords, that they made them drop, came to light there.

And they went to Cuitlahuactonco, to the home of Itzpotonqui, to extricate the gold. When our lords had retrieved it, they took them again, bound, to Coyoacan.

At that point died the Teohua, who was in charge of Huitzilopochtli, and they were interrogating him about where the appurtenances of the demon were located, along with the incense-offering priest of Totec.

At that time they confessed, so that they led people to Xaltocan, to Quachichilco, where his appurtenances, which they had transported there, were being guarded. When the things had been found, they hanged them both in the middle of the road at Maçatlan.

James Lockhart, *We People Here,* pp. 263–71.

The Conquest of Tenochtitlan

Florentine Codex *of fray Bernardino de Sahagún*

1. OMENS

Here it is said that before the Spaniards came here to this land, and before the people who live here were known, there appeared and were seen signs and omens.

Ten years before the arrival of the Spaniards an omen first appeared in the sky, like a flame or tongue of fire, like the light of dawn. It appeared to be throwing off [sparks] and seemed to pierce the sky. It was wide at the bottom and narrow at the top. It looked as though it reached the very middle of the sky, its very heart and center. It showed itself off to the east. When it came out at midnight it appeared like the dawn. When dawn came, then the sun on coming out effaced it. For a full year it showed itself (it was in [the year] Twelve House that it began). And when it appeared there would be an outcry, and people would hit their hands against their mouths as they yelled. People were taken aback, they lamented.

The second omen that happened here in Mexico was that of its own accord the house of the devil Huitzilopochtli, what they call his mountain, named Tlacateccan, burned and flared up; no one set fire to it, it just took fire itself. When the fire was seen, the wooden pillars were already burning. Tongues and tassels of flame were coming from inside; very quickly they consumed all the building's beams. Then there was an outcry. They said, "O Mexica, let everyone come running, it must be put out, [bring] your water jars!" But when they threw water on it, trying to extinguish it, it blew up all the more. It could not be put out; it burned entirely.

The third omen was that a temple was struck by lightning, hit by a thunderbolt. It was just a building of straw at the temple complex of Xiuhteuctli, called Tzonmolco. The reason it was taken for an omen was that it was not raining hard, just drizzling. It was said that it was struck when the sun was shining, nor was thunder heard.

The fourth omen was that while the sun was still out a comet fell, in three parts. It began off to the west and headed in the direction of the east, looking as if it were sprinkling glowing coals. It had a long tail, which reached a great distance. When it was seen, there was a great outcry, like the sound of rattles.

The fifth omen was that the water [of the lake] boiled up; it was not the wind that caused it. It bubbled and made exploding sounds, rising high in the air. It reached the foundations of the houses; it flooded them, and they collapsed. This is the great lake that extends around us here in Mexico.

The sixth omen was that many times a woman would be heard going along weeping and shouting. She cried out loudly at night, saying, "O my children, we are about to go forever." Sometimes she said, "O my children, where am I to take you?"

The seventh omen was that once the water folk were hunting or snaring and caught an ash-colored bird, like a crane. Then they went to the Tlillan calmecac to show it to Moteucçoma; the sun was inclining, it was still full day. On top of its head was something like a mirror, round, circular, seeming to be perforated, where the sky, the stars, and the Fire Drill [constellation] could be seen. And Moteucçoma took it for a very bad omen when he saw the stars and the Fire Drill. The second time he looked at the bird's head he saw something like a multitude of people coming along, coming bunched, outfitted for war, carried on the backs of deer. Then he called the soothsayers, the sages, and said to them, "Do you not know what I've seen, something like a multitude of people coming along?" But when they were going to answer him, what they saw disappeared, and they said nothing more.

The eighth omen was that many times people appeared, thistle-people with two heads but one body; they took them to the Tlillan calmecac and showed them to Moteucçoma. When he had seen them, they disappeared.

2. FIRST ENCOUNTERS

Here it is said what orders Moteucçoma gave when he found out that the Spaniards had returned. The second time they came it was [with] don Hernando Cortés.

He said to them, "Come, o men of unique valor, do come. It is said that our lord has appeared at last. Do go to meet him; listen well, make good use of your ears, bring back in your ears a good record of what he says. Here is what you will take to our lord."

[First] were the appurtenances of Quetzalcoatl: a serpent mask, made of turquoise; a quetzal-feather head fan; a plaited neckband of green-stone beads, with a golden disk in the middle of it; and a shield with gold [strips] crossing each other, or with gold and seashells crossing, with quetzal feathers spread about the edge and with a quetzal-feather banner; and a mirror with quetzal feathers to be tied on his back; and this mirror for the back seemed to have a turquoise shield, with turquoise glued on it, and there were green-stone neck bands with golden shells on them; then there was the turquoise spear thrower, entirely of turquoise, with a kind of serpent head; and there were obsidian sandals.

The second set of things they went to give him were the appurtenances of Tezcatlipoca: a feather headpiece, covered with golden stars, and his golden bell earplugs; and a seashell necklace; the chest ornament, decorated with many small seashells, with its fringe made of them; and a sleeveless jacket, painted all over, with eyes on its border and teased feathers at the fringe; and a cloak with blue-green knots, called a *tzitzilli*, tied on the back by taking its corners, also with a mirror for the back over it; and another item, golden bells tied to the calves of the legs; and another item, white sandals.

Third was the outfit of the lord of Tlalocan: the heron-feather headdress full of quetzal feathers, entirely of quetzal feathers, like a blue-green sheet, and over it [a strip of] shells crossed with [a strip of] gold; and his green-stone serpent earplugs; his sleeveless jacket sprinkled with greenstone; his necklace was a plaited greenstone neckband, also with a gold disk, also with a mirror for the back, as was said before, also with a *tzitzilli*; the cape to tie on, with red rings at the border; and golden bells for the feet; and his serpent staff made of turquoise.

Fourth were likewise appurtenances of Quetzalcoatl, but of a different kind: a miter of jaguar skin, covered with pheasant feathers; a very large green-stone at the top of it, glued on the tip; and round turquoise earplugs, from which hung curved golden seashells; and a plaited green-stone neckband, likewise with a golden disk in the middle of it; and a cloak to tie on, with a border dyed red; likewise, golden bells used on his feet; and a shield with gold inserted in it, with quetzal feathers spread along its edge, also with a quetzal-feather banner; and the curved staff of the wind [god], bent at the top, sprinkled with white green-stone stars; and his foam sandals.

These then were the things, called gods' appurtenances, that the messengers carried with them, and they took many other things by way of greeting: a shell-shaped gold headpiece with yellow parrot feathers hanging from it, a golden miter, etc.

Then baskets were filled and carrying frames were adjusted. And then Moteucçoma gave orders to the aforementioned five [emissaries], saying to them, "Now go, don't tarry anywhere, and address yourselves to our lord the god. Tell him, 'Your agent Moteucçoma has sent us; here is what he is giving you. You have arrived in Mexico, your home.' "

And when they reached the coast, they were taken across [a river or inlet] by boat at Xicalanco. There again they left by boat, taken by the water folk. Everything went into the boats; the goods were placed in boats. And when the boats were full, they left. They cast off and reached [the Spaniards'] boat[s], bringing their own boat close.

Then [the Spaniards] said to them, "Who are you? Where have you come from?"

Then [the emissaries] answered them, "Why, we have come from Mexico."

Again [the Spaniards] replied to them, "Perhaps not. Perhaps you are just claiming to be from there, perhaps you are making it up, perhaps you are deceiving us."

But when they were convinced and satisfied, they hooked the prow of the boat with an iron staff and hauled them in; then they also put down a ladder.

3. ON THE BOAT

Here it is said what happened when Moteucçoma's messengers went into don Hernando Cortés's boat.

Then they climbed up, carrying in their arms the goods. When they had gotten up into the boat, each of them made the earth-eating gesture before the Captain. Then they addressed him, saying, "May the god attend: his agent Moteucçoma who is in charge in Mexico for him addresses him and says, 'The god is doubly welcome.'"

Then they dressed up the Captain. They put on him the turquoise serpent mask attached to the quetzal-feather head fan, to which were fixed, from which hung the green-stone serpent earplugs. And they put the sleeveless jacket on him, and around his neck they put the plaited green-stone neckband with the golden disk in the middle. On his lower back they tied the back mirror, and also they tied behind him the cloak called a *tzitzilli*. And on his legs they placed the green-stone bands with the golden bells. And they gave him, placing it on his arm, the shield with gold and shells crossing, on whose edge were spread quetzal feathers, with a quetzal banner. And they laid the obsidian sandals before him.

And the other three outfits, the gods' appurtenances, they only arranged in rows before him.

When this had been done, the Captain said to them, "Is this everything you have by way of greeting and rapprochement?"

They answered, "That is all with which we have come, o our lord."

Then the Captain ordered that they be tied up; they put irons on their feet and necks. When this had been done they shot off the cannon. And at this point the messengers truly fainted and swooned; one after another they swayed and fell, losing consciousness. And the Spaniards lifted them into a sitting position and gave them wine to drink. Then they gave them food, fed them, with which they regained strength and got their breath back.

When this had been done the Captain said to them, "Do listen, I have found out and heard that by what they say these Mexica are very strong, great warriors, able to throw others down. Where there is one of them he can chase, push aside, overcome, and turn back his enemies, even though there should be ten or twenty. Now I wish to be satisfied, I want to see you, I want to try out how strong and manly you are." Then he gave them leather shields, iron swords, and iron lances. [He said,]

"Well now, very early in the morning, as dawn is about to come, we will struggle against each other, we will challenge each other, we will find out by comparison who will fall down first."

They answered the Captain, saying, "May the lord pay heed, this is not at all what his agent Moteucçoma ordered us. All we came to do was to greet and salute you. We were not charged with what the lord wishes. If we should do that, won't Moteucçoma be very angry with us because of it, won't he destroy us for it?"

Then the Captain said, "No indeed; it is simply to be done. I want to see and behold it, for word has gone to Spain that you are very strong, great warriors. Eat while it is still before dawn, and I will eat then too. Outfit yourselves well."

4. WITCHES, WIZARDS, AND SORCERERS

Here it is said how Moteucçoma sent witches, wizards, and sorcerers to do something to the Spaniards.

Then at that time Moteucçoma sent out emissaries. Those whom he sent were all bad people, soothsayers and witches. He also sent elders, strong warriors, to see to all [the Spaniards] needed as to food: turkey hens, eggs, white tortillas, and whatever they might request, and to look after them well so that they would be satisfied in every way. He sent captives in case [the Spaniards] should drink their blood. And the emissaries did as indicated.

But when [the Spaniards] saw it, they were made sick to their stomachs, spitting, rubbing their eyelids, blinking, shaking their heads. And [the emissaries] sprinkled blood in the food, they bloodied it, which made their stomachs turn and disgusted them, because of the great stench of the blood.

Moteucçoma did this because he took them for gods, considered them gods, worshiped them as gods. They were called and given the name of gods who have come from heaven, and the blacks were called soiled gods.

After that they ate white tortillas, grains of maize, turkey eggs, turkeys, and all the fruits: custard apple, mammee, yellow sapote, black sapote, sweet potato, manioc, white sweet potato, yellow sweet potato, colored sweet potato, jicama, plum, jobo, guava, *cuajilote,* avocado, acacia [bean], *tejocote,* American cherry, tuna cactus fruit, mulberry, white cactus fruit, yellow cactus fruit, whitish-red cactus fruit, pitahaya, water pitahaya. And the food for the deer was *pipillo* and *tlachicaztli.*

They say that Moteucçoma sent the witches, the rainmakers, to see what [the Spaniards] were like and perhaps be able to enchant them, cast spells on them, to use conjury or the evil eye on them or hurl something else at them, perhaps addressing some words of wizardry to them so that they would take sick, die, or turn back. But when they performed the assignment they had been given concerning the Spaniards, they could do nothing; they had no power at all. Then they quickly returned to tell Moteucçoma what they were like, how strong they were, [saying,] "We are not their match; we are as nothing."

Then Moteucçoma gave strict orders; he scolded and charged the stewards and all the lords and elders, under pain of death, that they see to and take care of everything [the Spaniards] might need. And when [the Spaniards] came onto dry land and finally started moving in this direction and coming along the road toward here, they were well cared for and made much of. They were always in the hands of someone as they came progressing; they were very well attended to.

5. AND MOTEUCÇOMA WEPT

Here it is said how Moteucçoma wept, and the Mexica wept, when they found out that the Spaniards were very strong.

And Moteucçoma lamented his troubles at length; he was afraid and shocked. He told the troubles of the altepetl. And everyone was very afraid. Fear reigned, and shock, laments, and expressions of distress. People talked, assembled, gathered, wept for themselves and for others. Heads hung, there were tearful greetings, words of encouragement, and stroking of hair. Little children's heads were stroked. Fathers would say, "Alas, my children, how is it with you, that what is about to happen has happened to you?" And mothers said, "O my children, how is it with you who are to behold what is about to happen to us?"

And it was told, presented, made known, announced, and reported to Moteucçoma, and brought to his attention, that a woman, one of us people here, came accompanying them as interpreter. Her name was Marina and her homeland was Tepeticpac, on the coast, where they first took her.

And then at this time the messengers who saw in each place to everything [the Spaniards] needed began hardly to pause [on arrival in Mexico,] but to run right back [from whence they came].

At this same time [the Spaniards] came asking about Moteucçoma: "What is he like? Is he a youth, a mature man, already old, advanced in age, or an old man but able? Is he aged, is he white-haired?" And they replied to the gods, the Spaniards, "He is a mature man, not corpulent, but slim and slender, on the thin side."

When Moteucçoma heard this, that many and persistent inquiries were being made about him, that the gods wanted to see his face, he was greatly anguished. He repeatedly wished to flee, to hide, to take refuge from the gods. He thought of, imagined, invented, weighed, and turned over in his mind that he would go into a cave somewhere. He made it known to some people with whom he consoled himself, with whom he was comfortable, with whom he frequently conversed, and they said, "The way is known to Mictlan, Tonatiuh ichan [his house], Tlalocan, and Cincalco for remedy, whichever suits you."

The one he preferred was Cincalco. It became well known, word spread among the public. But he was not able to do it, not able to hide and take refuge. He took no steps; it came to nothing. What the rainmakers had said when they influenced and instigated him, confusing him and turning things around on him, when they claimed they knew the way to the above-mentioned places, was not carried out, could not occur. [Moteucçoma] just awaited [the Spaniards]; he strengthened his resolve, mastered his emotions, and resigned himself entirely to whatever he was to see and behold.

6. TLAXCALAN CONSPIRATORS

Here it is said how the Spaniards reached Tlaxcala, [also] called Texcallan.

[The Tlaxcalans] guided, accompanied, and led them until they brought them to their palace<s> and placed them there. They showed them great honors, they gave them what they needed and attended to them, and then they gave them their daughters.

Then [the Spaniards] asked them, "Where is Mexico? What kind of a place is it? Is it still far?"

They answered them, "It's not far now. Perhaps one can get there in three days. It is a very favored place, and [the Mexica] are very strong, great warriors, conquerors, who go about conquering everywhere."

Now before this there had been friction between the Tlaxcalans and the Cholulans. They viewed each other with anger, fury, hate, and disgust; they could come together on nothing. Because of this they put [the Spaniards] up to killing them treacherously.

They said to them, "The Cholulans are very evil; they are our enemies. They are as strong as the Mexica, and they are the Mexica's friends."

When the Spaniards heard this, they went to Cholula. The Tlaxcalans and Cempoalans went with them, outfitted for war. When they arrived, there was a general summons and cry that all the noblemen, rulers, subordinate leaders, warriors, and commoners should come, and everyone assembled in the temple courtyard. When they had all come together, [the Spaniards and their friends] blocked the entrances, all of the places where one entered. Thereupon people were stabbed, struck, and killed. No such thing was in the minds of the Cholulans; they did not meet the Spaniards with weapons of war. It just seemed that they were stealthily and treacherously killed, because the Tlaxcalans persuaded [the Spaniards] to do it.

And a report of everything that was happening was given and relayed to Moteucçoma. Some of his messengers would be arriving as others were leaving; they just turned around and ran back. There was no time when they weren't listening, when reports weren't being given. And all the common people went about in a state of excitement; there were frequent disturbances, as if the earth moved and <quaked>, as if everything were spinning before one's eyes. People took fright.

And after the dying in Cholula, [the Spaniards] set off on their way to Mexico, coming gathered and bunched, raising dust. Their iron lances and halberds seemed to sparkle, and their iron swords were curved like a stream of water. Their cuirasses and iron helmets seemed to make a clattering sound. Some of them came wearing iron all over, turned into iron beings, gleaming, so that they aroused great fear and were generally seen with fear and dread. Their dogs came in front, coming ahead of them, keeping to the front, panting, with their spittle hanging down.

7. MARCH OF THE SPANIARDS TOWARD THE CITY

Here it is said how the Spaniards came from Itztapalapan when they reached Mexico.

Then they set out in this direction, about to enter Mexico here. Then they all dressed and equipped themselves for war. They girded themselves, tying their battle gear tightly on themselves and then on their horses. Then they arranged themselves in rows, files, ranks.

Four horse[men] came ahead, going first, staying ahead, leading. They kept turning about as they went, facing people, looking this way and that, looking sideways, gazing everywhere between the houses, examining things, looking up at the roofs.

Also the dogs, their dogs, came ahead, sniffing at things and constantly panting.

By himself came marching ahead, all alone, the one who bore the standard on his shoulder. He came waving it about, making it spin, tossing it here and there. It came stiffening, rising up like a warrior, twisting and turning.

Following him came those with iron swords. Their iron swords came bare and gleaming. On their shoulders they bore their shields, of wood or leather.

The second contingent and file were horses carrying people, each with his cotton cuirass, his leather shield, his iron lance, and his iron sword hanging down from the horse's neck. They came with bells on, jingling or rattling. The horses, the deer, neighed, there was much neighing, and they would sweat a great deal; water seemed to fall from them. And their flecks of foam splatted on the ground, like soapsuds splatting. As they went they made a beating, throbbing, and hoof-pounding like throwing stones. Their hooves made holes, they dug holes in the ground wherever they placed them. Separate holes formed wherever they went placing their hindlegs and forelegs.

The third file were those with iron crossbows, the crossbowmen. As they came, the iron crossbows lay in their arms. They came along testing them out, brandishing them, <aiming them>. But some carried them on their shoulders, came shouldering the crossbows. Their quivers went hanging at their sides, passed under their armpits, well filled, packed with arrows, with iron bolts. Their cotton upper armor reached to their knees, very thick, firmly sewn, and dense, like stone. And their heads were wrapped in the same cotton armor, and on their heads plumes stood up, parting and spreading.

The fourth file were likewise horse[men]; their outfits were the same as has been said.

The fifth group were those with harquebuses, the harquebusiers, shouldering their harquebuses; some held them [level]. And when they went into the great palace, the residence of the ruler, they repeatedly shot off their harquebuses. They exploded, sputtered, discharged, thundered, <disgorged>. Smoke spread, it grew dark with smoke, every place filled with smoke. The fetid smell made people dizzy and faint.

And last, bringing up the rear, went the war leader, thought to be the ruler and director in battle, like [among us] a *tlacateccatl*. Gathered and massed about him, going at his side, accompanying him, enclosing him were his warriors, those with devices, his [aides], like [among us] those with scraped heads [*quaquachictin*] and the Otomi warriors, the strong and valiant ones of the altepetl, its buttress and support, its heart and foundation.

Then all those from the various altepetl on the other side of the mountains, the Tlaxcalans, the people of Tliliuhquitepec, of Huexotzinco, came following behind. They came outfitted for war with their cotton upper armor, shields, and bows, their quivers full and packed with feathered arrows, some barbed, some blunted, some with obsidian points. They went crouching, hitting their mouths with their hands and yelling, singing in Tocuillan style, whistling, shaking their heads.

Some bore burdens and provisions on their backs; some used [tump lines for] their foreheads, some [bands around] their chests, some carrying frames, some board cages, some deep baskets. Some made bundles, perhaps putting the bundles on their backs. Some dragged the large cannons, which went resting on wooden wheels, making a clamor as they came.

8. ENTERING MEXICO

Here it is said how Moteucçoma went in peace and quiet to meet the Spaniards at Xoloco, where the house of Alvarado is now, or at the place they call Huitzillan.

And when they [the Spaniards] had come as far as Xoloco, when they had stopped there, Moteucçoma dressed and prepared himself for a meeting, along with other great rulers and high nobles, his rulers and nobles. Then they went to the meeting. On gourd bases they set out different precious flowers; in the midst of the shield flowers and heart flowers stood popcorn flowers, yellow tobacco flowers, cacao flowers, [made into] wreaths for the head, wreaths to be girded around. And they carried golden necklaces, necklaces with pendants, wide necklaces.

And when Moteucçoma went out to meet them at Huitzillan, thereupon he gave various things to the war leader, the commander of the warriors; he gave him flowers, he put necklaces on him, he put flower necklaces on him, he girded him with flowers, he put flower wreaths on his head. Then he laid before him the golden necklaces, all the different things for greeting people. He ended by putting some of the necklaces on him.

Then [Cortés] said in reply to Moteucçoma, "Is it not you? Is it not you then? Moteucçoma?"

Moteucçoma said, "Yes, it is me." Thereupon he stood up straight, he stood up with their faces meeting. He bowed down deeply to him. He stretched as far as he could, standing stiffly. Addressing him, he said to him,

"O our lord, be doubly welcomed on your arrival in this land; you have come to satisfy your curiosity about your altepetl of Mexico, you have come to sit on your seat of authority, which I have kept a while for you, where I have been in charge for you, for your agents the rulers—Itzcoatzin, the elder Moteucçoma, Axayacatl, Tiçocic, and Ahuitzotl—have gone, who for a very short time came to be in charge for you, to govern the altepetl of Mexico. It is after them that your poor vassal [myself] came. Will they come back to the place of their absence? If only one of them could see and behold what has now happened in my time, what I now see after our lords are gone! For I am not just dreaming, not just sleepwalking, not just seeing it in my sleep. I am not just dreaming that I have seen you, have looked upon your face. For a time I have been concerned, looking toward the mysterious place from which you have come, among clouds and mist. It is so that the rulers on departing said that you would come in order to acquaint yourself with your altepetl and sit upon your seat of authority. And now it has come true, you have come. Be doubly welcomed, enter the land, go to enjoy your palace; rest your body. May our lords be arrived in the land."

And when the speech that Moteucçoma directed to the Marqués had concluded, Marina reported it to him, interpreting it for him. And when the Marqués had heard what Moteucçoma had said, he spoke to Marina in return, babbling back to them, replying in his babbling tongue,

"Let Moteucçoma be at ease, let him not be afraid, for we greatly esteem him. Now we are truly satisfied to see him in person and hear him, for until now we have greatly desired to see him and look upon his face. Well, now we have seen him, we have come to his homeland of Mexico. Bit by bit he will hear what we have to say."

Thereupon [the Spaniards] took [Moteucçoma] by the hand. They came along with him, stroking his hair to show their good feeling. And the Spaniards looked at him, each of them giving him a close look. They would start along walking, then mount, then dismount again in order to see him.

And as to each of the rulers who went with him, they were: first, Cacamatzin, ruler of Tetzcoco; second, Tetlepanquetzatzin, ruler of Tlacopan; third, the Tlacochcalcatl Itzquauhtzin, ruler of Tlatelolco; fourth, Topantemoctzin, Moteucçoma's storekeeper in Tlatelolco. These were the ones who went. And the other Tenochca noblemen were Atlixcatzin, the Tlacateccatl; Tepehuatzin, the Tlacochcalcatl; Quetzalaztatzin, the Ticocyahuacatl; Totomotzin; Ecatenpatiltzin; and Quappiaztzin. When Moteucçoma was made prisoner, they not only hid themselves and took refuge, they abandoned him in anger.

9. FACE TO FACE

When things were already going on, when the festivity was being observed and there was dancing and singing, with voices raised in song, the singing was like the noise of waves breaking against the rocks. When it was time, when the moment had come for the Spaniards to do the killing, they came out equipped for battle. They came and closed off each of the places where people went in and out: Quauhquiahuac, Tecpantzinco, Acatliyacapan, and Tezcacoac. And when they had closed these exits, they stationed themselves in each, and no one could come out any more.

When this had been done, they went into the temple courtyard to kill people. Those whose assignment it was to do the killing just went on foot, each with his metal sword and his leather shield, some of them iron-studded.

Then they surrounded those who were dancing, going among the cylindrical drums. They struck a drummer's arms; both of his hands were severed. Then they struck his neck; his head landed far away. Then they stabbed everyone with iron lances and stuck them with iron swords. They stuck some in the belly, and then their entrails came spilling out. They split open the heads of some, they really cut their skulls to pieces, their skulls were cut up into little bits. And some they hit on the shoulders; their bodies broke open and ripped. Some they hacked on the calves, some on the thighs, some on their bellies, and then all their entrails would spill out. And if someone still tried to run it was useless; he just dragged his intestines along. There was a stench as if of sulfur. Those who tried to escape could go nowhere. When anyone tried to go out, at the entryways they struck and stabbed him.

But some climbed up the wall and were able to escape. Some went into the various calpulli temples and took refuge there. Some took refuge among, entered among those who had really died, feigning death, and they were able to escape. But if someone took a breath and they saw him, they stabbed him. The blood of the warriors ran like water; the ground was almost slippery with blood, and the stench of it rose, and the entrails were lying dragged out. And the Spaniards went everywhere searching in the calpulli temples, stabbing in the places where they searched in case someone was taking shelter there. They went everywhere, scratching about in all the calpulli temples in searching.

And when it became known [what was happening], everyone cried out, "Mexica warriors, come running, get outfitted with devices, shields, and arrows, hurry, come running, the warriors are dying; they have died, perished, been annihilated, o Mexica warriors!" Thereupon there were war cries, shouting, and beating of hands against lips. The warriors quickly came outfitted, bunched together, carrying arrows and shields. Then the fighting began; they shot at them with barbed darts, spears, and tridents, and they hurled darts with broad obsidian points at them. A cloud of yellow reeds spread over the Spaniards.

10. IN THE PALACE

Here it is said how the war first began, when the Mexica battled with the Spaniards here in Mexico.

And then the Spaniards fortified themselves. From there the Spaniards shot at the Mexica with iron bolts and fired guns at them. And then they placed Moteucçoma in irons. And then all the warriors who had died were retrieved, taken to places, and identified. And wailing arose from the mothers and fathers, crying and weeping over them. First they took them to their various homes, and afterward they brought them to the temple courtyard and assembled them there. They burned them in a particular place called Quauhxicalco. But some were burned only at the various youths' houses.

And when the sun was setting, while there was still a little sunlight, then Itzquauhtzin cried out; from a roof terrace he cried out, saying, "O Mexica, o people of Tenochtitlan and Tlatelolco, your ruler the Tlacateuctli Moteucçoma addresses you, saying, 'Let the Mexica hear: we are not their match, may they be dissuaded [from further fighting].' May the arrows and shields of war be laid down. The poor old men and women, the common people, the infants who toddle and crawl, who lie in the cradle or on the cradle board and know nothing yet, are all suffering. This is why your ruler says, 'we are not their match; let everyone be dissuaded.' They have placed him in irons, they have put irons on his feet."

And when he had finished saying this, the Mexica railed against him, reproaching him. They grew angry and began to fall into a ranting rage. One of them, boiling over and ranting, said to him, "What does Moteucçoma say, you rogue? Aren't you one of his men?" Then there was a clamor, an increasing clamor, and then arrows fell on the roof But the Spaniards held their shields over Moteucçoma and Itzquauhtzin lest the Mexicas' arrows should hit them.

The reason the Mexica were very angry was that [the Spaniards] had entirely annihilated the warriors and killed them treacherously, without warning. They did not neglect to surround the palace; they kept watch at various places where someone might enter by stealth, where someone might secretly deliver bread. Everything that had been being given to them was completely blocked off, absolutely no one delivered anything any more. It was as though they were drying out their innards. And as to those who would try to give them news and inform them, or gain their favor by giving them a bit of food, if they were seen and detected, then they killed them there, they disposed of them, by striking them on the nape of the neck or stoning them.

Once some Mexica were seen delivering arrows fitted with birds' feathers; they let it out that some [others] were secretly getting in. Therefore strict orders were given that good watch should be kept, that each road and canal should be well guarded. Great care was taken to keep a good lookout. And those who had taken in the arrows were doing their duty, sent by the stewards of Ayotzintepec and Chinantlan. Then and there they took their last breaths, their task came to a conclusion. At the canal they struck them on the napes of their necks with heavy pointed sticks.

There was internal strife among the Tenochca, and it was without reason that they seized those who were performing duties, saying, "This is the one," and then killing him. And if they saw a crystal lip plug on someone, they hastened to seize him and killed him, saying, "He too is one of those who go inside and give provisions to Moteucçoma." And if they saw someone who had tied about him a thin tribute-worker's cloak, they hurried to seize him too, saying, "This is another wretched fellow who goes about carrying scandalous and harmful tales, who takes them in to Moteucçoma when he goes to see him." And he who would try to save himself would implore them, saying, "O Mexica, what are you doing? I am not one of them." They told him, "You are one of them, you rogue, you are not doing [your] duty." Then and there they killed him. They were just keeping watch on everyone, going about being careful about everyone; they kept their eyes peeled, the Mexica just watched everyone. They punished many for invented things, who were treacherously killed; they punished them for wrongdoings not their own. And others doing duty work hid themselves, went to shelter, no longer showed themselves to anyone or let themselves be seen, no longer came out among people. They were greatly afraid, limp with fear; they went about taking refuge so that they would not fall into someone's hands.

And when they had the Spaniards closed in their buildings, they fought them for only seven days. They were shut in for twenty-three days, and during each of these days the canals were excavated, widened, deepened, and the sides made steeper. Everywhere the canals were made more difficult to pass. And on the roads, various walls were built, walls were laid here and there. Walls were set up and the passageways between houses made difficult.

And when this was done. . . .

11. SMALLPOX

Here it is said how, at the time the Spaniards left Mexico, there came an illness of pustules of which many local people died; it was called "the great rash" [smallpox].

Before the Spaniards appeared to us, first an epidemic broke out, a sickness of pustules. It began in Tepeilhuitl. Large bumps spread on people; some were entirely covered. They spread everywhere, on the face, the head, the chest, etc. [The disease] brought great desolation; a great many died of it. They could no longer walk about, but lay in their dwellings and sleeping places, no longer able to move or stir. They were unable to change position, to stretch out on their sides or face down, or raise their heads. And when they made a motion, they called out loudly. The pustules that covered people caused great desolation; very many people died of them, and many just starved to death; starvation reigned, and no one took care of others any longer.

On some people, the pustules appeared only far apart, and they did not suffer greatly, nor did many of them die of it. But many people's faces were spoiled by it, their faces and noses were made rough. Some lost an eye or were blinded.

This disease of pustules lasted a full sixty days; after sixty days it abated and ended. When people were convalescing and reviving, the pustules disease began to move in the direction of Chalco. And many were disabled or paralyzed by it, but they were not disabled forever. It broke out in Teotl eco, and it abated in Panquetzaliztli. The Mexica warriors were greatly weakened by it.

And when things were in this state, the Spaniards came, moving toward us from Tetzcoco. They appeared from the direction of Quauhtitlan and made a halt at Tlacopan. There they gave one another assignments and divided themselves. Pedro de Alvarado was made responsible for the road coming to Tlatelolco. The Marqués went and established himself in Coyoacan, which became his responsibility, along with the road coming from Acachinanco to Tenochtitlan, for the Marqués considered the Tenochca great and valiant warriors.

And it was right in Nextlatilco, or in Ilyacac, that war first began. Then [the Spaniards] quickly reached Nonoalco, and the warriors came pursuing them. None of the Mexica died; then the Spaniards retreated. The warriors fought in boats; the war-boat people shot at the Spaniards, and their arrows sprinkled down on them. Then [the main force of the Mexica] entered [Nonoalco]. Thereupon the Marqués sent [his men] toward the Tenochca, following the Acachinanco road. Many times they skirmished, and the Mexica went out to face them.

12. TZILACATZIN OF THE RANK OF OTOMI

Here it is said how the Mexica left their altepetl in fear and came here when they dreaded the Spaniards.

And at this time the Tenochca came entering into Tlatelolco here, weeping and shouting. Many were the tears of the women; the men came accompanying their women, and some of them carried their children on their shoulders. In just one day they abandoned their altepetl. But the Tlatelolca still went to Tenochtitlan to fight.

And at this point Pedro de Alvarado hurled his forces at Ilyacac, toward Nonoalco, but they could do nothing; it was as though they had hit against a stone, because the Tlatelolca made great efforts. There was fighting on both sides of the road and in the water with war boats. When Alvarado tired, he returned and established himself in Tlacopan. But just two days later they sent out all the boats; at first only two came, then afterward all of them, and formed beside the houses in Nonoalco. Then they came onto dry land, and then they began to follow the narrow road between the houses; they came toward the center of them.

When the Spaniards landed it fell silent; not one of the people came out. But then Tzilacatzin, who was a great warrior and very valorous, hurled three stones he was carrying, huge round stones, wall stones or white stones; he had one in his hand and two on his shield. Then he went pursuing the Spaniards, scattering them, forcing them into the water. They went right into the water; those who went down in the water got thoroughly wetted.

(This Tzilacatzin had the warrior [rank] of Otomi, for which reason he wore the Otomi hairstyle, so he looked down on his enemies, even though they be Spaniards, thinking nothing of them. He inspired general fear. When our enemies saw Tzilacatzin, they would hunch down. They strove greatly to kill him, whether shooting him with iron bolts or with guns. But Tzilacatzin disguised himself in order not to be recognized. Sometimes he would put on [his own] device, with his lip pendant and his golden earplugs, and he would put on his shell necklace. He would go with his head uncovered, showing that he was an Otomi. But sometimes he put on only cotton upper armor and covered his forehead with a little narrow cloth. Sometimes to disguise himself he put on a feather hairpiece or wig, with eagle feathers tied at the back of the neck. This was the way in which those who threw people in the fire were attired; he went about looking like one of them, imitating them. He had golden arm bands on both sides, on both arms, shimmering, and he also had shining golden bands on the calves of his legs.)

Then the next day they came again and grounded their boats at Nonoalco, at Ayauhcaltitlan. Also those who go on foot and all the Tlaxcalans and Otomis came, a great abundance of them. The Spaniards came herding them ahead of them. And when they got to Nonoalco, there was fighting and skirmishing; the scene filled with combat and battle. There were deaths on both sides; equal numbers of the Mexica and their enemies were hit. Thus on both sides there were wounded, and the fighting went on day and night.

There were only two great warriors who did not hide their faces, who thought nothing of their enemies, who did not place value on their bodies. The first was named Tzoyectzin and the second Temoctzin. A third was the already mentioned Tzilacatzin.

When the Spaniards tired, when they were unable to do anything with the Mexica, unable to penetrate them, they went away. They entered [their quarters] in very low spirits, their auxiliaries following after them.

13. THE SACRIFICE OF THE SPANIARDS

Here it is told how the Mexica took captives again—according to the count of the Spaniards they captured, there were fifty-three, as well as many Tlaxcalans and people of Tetzcoco, Chalco, and Xochimilco—and how they killed all of them before their former gods.

And at this point they let loose with all the warriors who had been crouching there; they came out and chased [the Spaniards] in the passageways, and when the Spaniards saw it they [the Mexica] seemed to be intoxicated. Then captives were taken. Many Tlaxcalans, and people of Acolhuacan, Chalco, Xochimilco, etc., were captured. A great abundance were captured and killed. They made the Spaniards and all the others go right into the water. And the road became very slippery; one could no longer walk on it, but would slip and slide.

And the captives were dragged off. This was where the banner was captured; that is where it was taken. It was the Tlatelolca who captured it, at the place now called San Martin. They thought nothing of it, they did not take care of it. The other [Spaniards] escaped; [the Mexica] harried them as far as Colhuacatonco, at the edge of the canal, where they re-formed.

Then they took the captives to Yacacolco, hurrying them along, going along herding their captives together. Some went weeping, some singing, some went shouting while hitting their hands against their mouths. When they got them to Yacacolco, they lined them all up. Each one went to the altar platform, where the sacrifice was performed. The Spaniards went first, going in the lead; the people of all the different altepetl just followed, coming last. And when the sacrifice was over, they strung the Spaniards' heads on poles [on the skull rack]; they also strung up the horses' heads. They placed them below, and the Spaniards' heads were above them, strung up facing east. But they did not string up the heads of all the various [other] people from far away. There were fifty-three of the Spaniards they captured, along with four horses.

Nevertheless, watch was kept everywhere, and there was fighting. They did not stop keeping watch because of [what had happened]. The people of Xochimilco went about in boats surrounding us on all sides; there were deaths and captives taken on both sides.

And all the common people suffered greatly. There was famine; many died of hunger. They no longer drank good, pure water, but the water they drank was salty. Many people died of it, and because of it many got dysentery and died. Everything was eaten: lizards, swallows, maize straw, grass that grows on salt flats. And they chewed at colorin wood, glue flowers, plaster, leather, and deerskin, which they roasted, baked, and toasted so that they could eat them, and they ground up medicinal herbs and adobe bricks. There had never been the like of such suffering. The siege was frightening, and great numbers died of hunger. And bit by bit they came pressing us back against the wall, herding us together.

14. THE SPANISH CATAPULT

Here it is said how the Spaniards installed a catapult with which they were going to kill the Tlatelolca by stealth.

And then those Spaniards installed a catapult on top of an altar platform with which to hurl stones at the people. And when they had it ready and were about to shoot it off, they gathered all around it, vigorously pointing their fingers, pointing at the people, pointing to where all the people were assembled at Amaxac, showing them to each other. The Spaniards spread out their arms, [showing] how they would shoot and hurl it at them, as if they were using a sling on them. Then they wound it up, then the arm of the catapult rose up. But the stone did not land on the people, but fell behind the marketplace at Xomolco.

Because of that the Spaniards there argued among themselves. They looked as if they were jabbing their fingers in one another's faces, chattering a great deal. And the catapult kept returning back and forth, going one way and then the other; bit by bit it righted itself. Then it could be seen clearly that there was a stone sling at its point, attached with very thick rope. Then because of that they named it a "wooden sling."

And again they sent out the Spaniards and all the Tlaxcalans. Then they formed up at Yacacolco, Tecpancaltitlan, and Copalnamacoyan. Then at Atecocolecan [the Spaniards] led all those who surrounded us; very slowly they proceeded. And the [Mexica] warriors came in formation, working up their spirits, taking a manly posture; no one was faint of heart, no one was like a woman. They said, "Come running, o warriors! Who are these little barbarians, these little backlanders?" And the warriors went this way and that, sideways; no one stood straight, raised up straight.

(And often the Spaniards changed their appearance, not showing themselves. They got themselves up as the local people do, putting on devices, tying cloaks on to disguise themselves, hiding behind the others. The only way they could be recognized was when they shot someone. Then everyone crouched down and hit the ground; everyone looked and searched closely to see where the iron bolt came from, which way it was aimed. The Tlatelolca warriors were very alert, kept very good watch.)

Very slowly they went along throwing us back, pushing us against the wall. And at Copalnamacoyan, on the Amaxac road, the weapons clashed against one another, there was a head-on encounter.

And in Amaxac a person whose name was Chalchiuhtepehua took shelter behind a wall. He was one of the Mexica from Tlatelolco. He looked closely at a horse in order to spear it, and when he speared it, the Spaniard was unhorsed. Then his companions quickly seized him. Then all the warriors and noblemen went after them, keeping close to them and following behind them. They forced them back again to Copalnamacoyan, where the wall stood. Then the fighting paused; everyone went away and entered his quarters.

15. THE BOATS

Once it happened that all those who were surrounding us, not including the Spaniards, went and assembled at Teteuhtitlan; it was still dark when they took position. Then they began filling in the waters, filling in a small lake called Tlaixcuipan. They seemed to go jostling one another, some carrying stone, some wood, pillars, door lintels, adobes, corner stones, etc. They went about chattering, raising the dust. The reason they did it was that it occurred to them and they imagined that they would plunder the common people who lived beside the road going to Tepeyacac.

And when the [Mexica] warriors saw what they were doing and what their intention was, they considered what they could do. And when they considered well, a boat was brought; they came poling it very slowly, stationing it at the side of the road. No warrior's device could be seen; everything was just covered over. Then another was brought; they came poling it slowly in the same way, and again two more boats were brought, making four. Then two eagle [warriors] and two jaguar [warriors] rose up. The first eagle was Topantemoctzin and the second Tlacotzin. The first jaguar was Temilotzin, and the second Coyohuehuetzin. Then they got started. They vigorously poled one jaguar and one eagle. The boats seemed to fly, heading for Teteuhtitlan to cut them off, to head them off. And when they had gone, again they dispatched two, also one eagle and one jaguar, to throw themselves into their midst. And when they went, wind instruments were played. Then people were plundered, but the warriors cut off some [of the enemy] on the other side.

16. A REVERSAL

When our enemies saw this, they tried to flee. Many died in the water, sinking and submerging, just pulling at one another, as though they had lost their senses and were fainting. They seemed to fall splattering; when they tried to flee they just fell between the logs. When they were dragged out they were completely covered with mud, slimy with mud, entirely drowned. A great many perished, there was a great abundance of deaths. This was the only time that the different [local] people who were our enemies died in great numbers there. And the day after our enemies had died, everything lay silent.

And at this time the Spaniards came to Amaxac; they reached the very place in which the common people lay in extremity. They fully surrounded us, and there was fierce battle, right in Amaxac and on the road going to Tepeyacac. Then [the Spaniards] went into the youths' house called Hueican, because all the youths were gathered there, and then they climbed up to the roof. And then all the common people scattered behind the youths' house;

then everyone scattered into the water. And one great warrior, a scraped-head named Huitzilhuatzin, stood up on the roof above the youths' house. He was like a bulwark, and the people followed him for a little while. But then the Spaniards fell upon them, and they struck him, breaking him apart, cutting him to pieces. Then [the Mexica] let loose with the warriors again and made them let go of the warrior [Huitzilhuatzin]. Then they took him; he was not quite dead. Then they went away, and there was silence.

17. THE QUETZAL-OWL

Then [the Spaniards] set fire to and burned the images of devils there. The warriors still tried to keep in formation. But [the Spaniards] did not shoot the women, only those who came standing up as men. When the fighting stopped, there was only a little sun.

And on the fourth day our enemies moved together in the same way. The Spaniards headed for where the common people were, going very slowly. And a warrior, the Tlacateccatl Temilotzin, tried to spy on them, taking shelter behind a wall. He was dressed as an eagle, and he had an iron sword with which he was going to cut them up. But when he saw that he could do nothing anywhere, he threw himself into the water, ripped into the water. There was a great clamor. Then there was fierce fighting again; it went no farther <than Amaxac>. The battle lasted a full day.

And when it dawned on the fifth day, our enemies the Spaniards and all who surrounded us again attacked all together; they surrounded us entirely, herded us together. There was no place to go; people shoved, pressed, and trampled one another; many died in the press. But one woman came to very close quarters with our enemies, throwing water at them, throwing water in their faces, making it stream down their faces.

And then the ruler Quauhtemoctzin and the warriors Coyohuehuetzin, Temilotzin, Topantemoctzin, the Mixcoatlailotlac Ahuelitoctzin, Tlacotzin, and Petlauhtzin took a great warrior named Tlapaltecatl opochtzin, whose home was in Coatlan, and outfitted him, dressing him in a quetzal-owl costume. That had been the device of Ahuitzotl. Quauhtemoctzin said, "This was the device of my progenitor, my father Ahuitzotl. Let him wear it, let him die in it. Let him dazzle people with it, let him show them something; let our enemies see and admire it." When they put it on him he looked very frightening and splendid. And they ordered four [others] to come helping him, to accompany him. They gave him the darts of the devil, darts of wooden rods with flint tips. And the reason they did this was that it was as though the fate of the rulers of the Mexica were being determined.

The Cihuacoatl Tlacotzin said, "O Mexica, o Tlatelolca, is there nothing left of the way it was in Mexico, of the way the Mexican state was, which was said to be the envoy of Huitzilopochtli that he sends against people, as he used to send the fire serpent, the fire drill at our enemies? O Mexica, you are taking his envoy the dart; you are to aim it only at our enemies. You are not just to cast it on the ground, but hurl it very close to them. And if one or two of them are hit, or if one or two of our enemies are captured, then it is truly our fate that for a little while longer we will <find favor>, while our lord so wishes." Then the quetzal-owl went, with the quetzal feathers waving.

When our enemies saw him, it was as though a mountain had fallen. Every one of the Spaniards was frightened; he intimidated them, they seemed to respect him a great deal. Then the quetzal-owl climbed up on the roof. But when some of our enemies had taken a good look at him they rose and turned him back, pursuing him. Then the quetzal-owl turned them again and pursued them. Then he snatched up the precious feathers and gold and dropped down off the roof. He did not die, and our enemies did not carry him off. Also three of our enemies were captured. At that the war stopped for good. There was silence, nothing more happened. Then our enemies went away. It was silent and nothing more happened until it got dark.

And the next day nothing more happened at all, no one made a sound. The common people just lay collapsed. The Spaniards did nothing more either, but lay still, looking at the people. Nothing was going on, they just lay still.

Here are mentioned all the warriors, the men of great valor, in whose countenances was war, who directed the battle and presided over it: the Tlacochcalcatl Coyohuehuetzin and the lord of Tzilacan, Temilotzin—these are Tlatilolca. And these are Tenochca: the Cihuacoatl Tlacotzin and the Huitznahuatl Motelchiuhtzin. These were the great warriors of Tlatelolco and Tenochtitlan.

18. SURRENDER

Here it is said how the Tlatelolca and Tenochca and their ruler submitted to the Spaniards, and what happened when they were among them.

And when they had gotten him [there and put] him [Quauhtemoctzin] on land, all the Spaniards were waiting. They came to take him; the Spaniards grasped him by the hand, took him up to the roof, and stood him before the Captain, the war leader. When they stood him before him, he looked at Quauhtemoctzin, took a good look at him, stroked his hair; then they seated him next to him. And they fired off the guns; they hit no one, but they aimed over the people, the [shots] just went over their heads. Then they took a [cannon], put it in a boat, and took it to the home of Coyohuehuetzin. When they got there, they took it up on the roof. Then again they killed people; many died there. But [the Mexica] just fled, and the war came to an end.

Then everyone shouted, saying, "It's over! Let everyone leave! Go eat greens!" When they heard this, the people departed; they just went into the water. But when they went out on the highway, again they killed some people, which angered the Spaniards; a few of them were carrying their shields and war clubs. Those who lived in houses went straight to Amaxac, where the road forks. There the people divided, some going toward Tepeyacac, some toward Xoxohuiltitlan, some toward Nonoalco. But no one went toward Xoloco and Macatzintamalco.

And all who lived in boats and on platforms [in the water] and those at Tolmayeccan just went into the water. The water came to the stomachs of some, to the chests of others, to the necks of others, and some sank entirely into the deep water. The little children were carried on people's backs. There was a general wail; but some went rejoicing and amusing themselves as they went along the road. Most of the owners of boats left at night, though some left by day. They seemed to knock against one another as they went.

And along every stretch [of road] the Spaniards took things from people by force. They were looking for gold; they cared nothing for green-stone, precious feathers, or turquoise. They looked everywhere with the women, on their abdomens, under their skirts. And they looked everywhere with the men, under their loincloths and in their mouths. And [the Spaniards] took, picked out the beautiful women, with yellow bodies. And how some women got loose was that they covered their faces with mud and put on ragged blouses and skirts, clothing themselves all in rags. And some men were picked out, those who were strong and in the prime of life, and those who were barely youths, to run errands for them and be their errand boys, called their *tlamacazque* [priests, acolytes]. Then they burned some of them on the mouth [branded them]; some they branded on the cheeks, some on the mouth.

And when the weapons were laid down and we collapsed, the year count was Three House, and the day count was One Serpent

And when Quauhtemoctzin went to give himself up, they took him to Acachinanco; it was already dark. And the next day, when there was a little sun, the Spaniards came again, a great many of them; they too had reached the end. They came equipped for battle, with iron cuirasses and iron helmets, but not with their iron swords and their shields. They all came pressing narrow white-cloths to their noses because the dead made them sick, for they were smelling bad and stinking. They all came on foot, holding Quauhtemoctzin, Coanacochtzin, and Tetlepanquetzatzin by their capes; only the three of them came <in line>. And the Cihuacoatl Tlacotzin, the Tlillancalqui Petlauhtzin, the Huitznahuatl Motelchiuhtzin mexicatl, the Achcauhtli Teuctlamacazqui [senior lordly priest] Coatzin, and the treasurer Tlacolyaotl guarded all of the gold.

Then they went straight to Atactzinco, where the home of the warrior the

Tlacochcalcatl Coyohuehuetzin was. The Spaniards were in a line stretching for two *mecatl*, reaching far off to its end. And when they reached the home of Coyohuehuetzin, they went up on the roof to a platform. Then they sat down. They placed a canopy of varicolored cloth over the Marqués; then he sat down, and Marina sat beside him.

And Quauhtemoctzin was next to the Captain. He had tied on a shining maguey-fiber cloak, each half different, covered with hummingbird feathers, Ocuillan style. It was very dirty; it was all he had. Then Coanacochtzin, the ruler of Tetzcoco, was next. He had tied on only a plain maguey-fiber cloak with a flowered border, with a spreading design of flowers; it too was very dirty. Next was Tetlepanquetzatzin, the ruler of Tlacopan, who likewise had tied on a maguey cloak; it too was dirtied, very dirty. Next was the Mixcoat-lailotlac Ahuelitoctzin. Last was Yopicatl Popocatzin, a nobleman. To the side were the Tenochca Tlacotzin, Petlauhtzin, Motelchiuhtzin mexicatl, the Achcauhtli Teuctlamacazqui Coatzin, and the treasurer Tlacolyaotl.

19. GOLD

Here is told the speech that don Hernando Cortés gave to the rulers in the altepetl of Mexico here, Tetzcoco, and Tlacopan, when the weapons were laid down, questioning them about the gold they had left scattered at the Tolteca canal when they came out and fled from Mexico.

Then the Marqués, the Captain, spoke to the rulers, saying to them, "Where is the gold that was kept in Mexico?" Then they took out of the boats all the gold: the golden banners, the golden miters, the golden arm bands, the golden leg bands, the golden helmets, the golden disks. They laid it all before the Captain, but the Spaniards came to remove it all.

Then the Captain said, "Is this all the gold that was kept in Mexico? You are to produce it all, for our lords are seeking it urgently."

Then Tlacotzin spoke up: "If our lord the god will pay heed, did our lords not take with them all that was brought to our palace when he was there, all of which was turned into bars?"

Then Marina replied, "The Captain says, 'Yes, we took everything that was assembled, and it was stamped. But they made us let it go at the Tolteca canal, they made us drop it there. They are to produce all of it.' "

Then the Cihuacoatl Tlacotzin replied, "Let the god, the Captain, pay heed. The Tenochca <do not appear> in boats, it is not their affair; rather the Tlatelolca took it upon themselves alone to fight in boats and intercept our lords. Was it not perhaps the Tlatelolca who took it all?"

Then Quauhtemoctzin spoke in turn, replying to the Cihuacoatl, "What are you saying, Cihuacoatl? Although the Tlatelolca took it, were not those who took things apprehended? Did they not produce everything? Was it not collected at Texopan? And is this not what our lords took?" Quauhtemoctzin pointed to the gold with his finger.

Then Marina replied to him, "The Captain says, 'Is this all?' "

Then the Cihuacoatl said, "Perhaps some of the common folk removed it, but it will be investigated, our lord the Captain will see it."

Then again Marina replied, "The Captain says that you are to produce two hundred pieces of gold of this size." She measured it with her hands, making a circle with her hands.

Again the Cihuacoatl replied, saying, "Perhaps some woman put it in her skirt. It will be sought; he will see it."

Then the Mixcoatlailotlac Ahuelitoctzin spoke up, saying, "May the lord our lord, the Captain, pay heed. When Moteucçoma was still alive, when there was a conquest somewhere, the Mexica, the Tlatelolca, the Tepaneca, and the Acolhuaque all went together. All of us, some Tepaneca, some Acolhuaque, and some people of the chinampas, moved together when we went to conquer, but when the altepetl fell, then everyone came back, each one heading for his own altepetl. And afterward came the people of that altepetl, the ones conquered, bringing their tribute; what they carried was greenstone, gold, precious feathers, and other precious stones, turquoise, cotinga and spoonbill feathers, and they came and gave it to Moteucçoma. It arrived all together, all the tribute and gold arrived together in Tenochtitlan."

James Lockhart, *We People Here*, pp. 50–57, 63–74, 83–85, 92–96, 108–12, 114–18, 132–142, 181–84, 198–202, 215–18, 230–34, 247–54.

❦ 7 ❦

Nahua Historians of the Colonial Period

*I*n *the midst of tribulation, impelled by the desire to preserve the memory of their own past, some Nahuas set out to search for the testimony they could obtain from the oral tradition and the contexts of the remaining painted books. Their goal was to commit all they could find of interest to alphabetic writing. Chief among these historians were Hernando Alvarado Tezozómoc (1530–1610) and Domingo Francisco Chimalpain Cuauhtlehuanitzin (1579–1660).*

Alvarado Tezozómoc was born to a family of noble lineage. His father, Diego Huanitzin, was a son of Axayacatl, ruler of Tenochtitlan, and of Francisca Moctezuma, daughter of the emperor. While still a young man, he had access to ancient manuscripts that had escaped the destruction that followed the Spanish Conquest. Based on these and oral tradition, he wrote two major works. One, the Crónica Mexicayotl, *preserved in Nahuatl, contains the genealogies of the Mexica nobility from the founding of Tenochtitlan up to the end of the sixteenth century. The other,* Crónica Mexicana, *known only in Spanish, provides a vivid account of the history of the Mexica during the same period.*

Chimalpain Cuauhtlehuanitzin was born in Amecameca, province of Chalco, near the volcanoes Popocatepetl and Iztaccihuatl. He spent most of his life in the colonial city of Mexico, working as an auxiliary in the religious service of the San Antonio Abad church, located in the outskirts of the metropolis. Although he himself was versed in classical Nahua and European history, he consulted with the Chalcan elders about their own history.

A prolific author, Chimalpain wrote eight historical works in Nahuatl about Chalco and, more generally, central Mexico; a book on the history of Culhuacan; an account of the Spanish Conquest; and he also kept a journal. Most of his work has been translated into Spanish, English, French, and German.

We have included an eloquent text by Alvarado Tezozómoc, from the
Crónica Mexicayotl, *in which a message is addressed to the Mexicas or*
Aztecs asking them to preserve for future generations the legacy of their
history, language, and culture.

From the work of Chimalpain we chose a narrative that deals with
the stay of the Mexicas in Chapultepec and the prophetic words of their
priest Cuauhtlequetzqui, proclaiming that the city of Tenochtitlan they
were to found was destined to survive as long as the world existed.

Crónica Mexicayotl

Thus they have to tell it,
thus they have come to record it in their narration,
and for us they have painted it in their codices,
the ancient men, the ancient women.
They were our grandfathers, our grandmothers,
our great-grandfathers, great-grandmothers,
our great-great-grandfathers, our ancestors.
Their account was repeated,
they left it to us;
they bequeathed it forever
to us who live now,
to us who come down from them.

Never will it be lost, never will it be forgotten,
that which they came to do,
that which they came to record in their paintings:
their renown, their history, their memory.
Thus in the future
never will it perish, never will it be forgotten,
always we will treasure it,
we, their children, their grandchildren,
brothers, great-grandchildren,
great-great-grandchildren, descendants,
we who carry their blood and their color,
we will tell it, we will pass it on
to those who do not yet live, who are to be born,
the children of the Mexicans, the children of the Tenochans. . . .

Miguel León-Portilla, ed., *Pre-Columbian Literatures of Mexico*, p. 117.

The Prophecy of the High Priest Tenochtli
by Chimalpain

The year 10 Calli (House)—A.D.—1281

At this time, after the Mexicas had stayed a year in Chapultepec, they were abhorred by many of the Tepanecs. They made war there, in the center of the plain; but when the war was over they had not been able to harm the Mexicas. And because of this, those of Texcaltepec, Malinalco, and Tolocan soon said:

"We should be killing the Mexicas by night, because they are very fierce."

And when the priest, Tenochtli, found out what had happened, he said to the one who was also Cuauhtlequetzqui:

"Oh, Cuauhtlequetzqui! They say that we Mexicas are going to die now. They say that this was told by Copil the wizard, the one who stays in Texcaltepec, the malinacatl; and it is also said that they will come from Tolocan."

And in turn Cuauhtlequetzqui responded: "I am a much greater wizard. I shall wait for them here, for here I guard my hill, Chapultepetl."

And in truth the wizard Copil came to sally forth in the night; he arrived in the company of his young daughter, named Xicomoyahual.

And when they met in combat, they pursued them stealthily by Tepetzinco. There, Copil fell into the hands of Cuauhcholohua, or Cuauhtlequetzqui. After catching him, Cuauhtlequetzqui killed the aforementioned Copil. Cuauhtlequetzqui cut the dead man's chest with a flint knife; split the chest open, tore out the heart, and then called to the priest Tenochtli:

"Come, Tenochtli! I have here the heart of the wizard Copil. I killed him. Bury it there among the reeds, among the cane."

With this, Tenochtli took the heart, then went quickly to bury it there among the reeds, among the cane; as it is said, here stands the *iglesia mayor*. And where Copil, the Tepetzinco, was killed, it is called to this day, Acopilco.

And the young daughter named Xicomoyahualtzin, who accompanied Copil, was later taken by Cuauhtlequetzqui as his wife, and eventually became the mother of Cohuatzontli.

And after Tenochtli went to bury the heart of Copil, he made an offering of fire before Huitzilopochtli.

And Cuauhtlequetzqui spoke again, he said to Tenochtli:

"Even though we have been here (in Chapultepec) for a long time, now you shall go to look there, among the reeds, among the canebrakes, where you went to plant the heart of the wizard Copil, because an offering has to be made, following the orders of our god Huitzilopochtli. The heart of Copil will germinate over there. And you, you shall go, you. Tenochtli, you shall go over there to see how the prickly pear cactus, the *tenochtli*, has sprung forth from the heart of Copil. There on top of it, the eagle stands, destroying, tearing the serpent apart—devouring it. And the cactus, the *tenochtli*, shall be you, you, Tenochtli. And the standing eagle that you shall see will be me.

"This shall be our fame: as long as the world lasts, so long shall last the renown, the glory, of Mexico-Tenochtitlan. . . ."

Chimalpain Cuauhtlehuanitzin translated by Miguel León-Portilla; English version by Sylvia and Earl Shorris.

⚭ 8 ⚭

Christian Proselytizing
Literature

*W*ith the newly imposed rule, things changed radically. The
Nahuas had not only to obey an unknown, distant king but also
*a previously unknown faith. Much of the Nahuatl literature produced
during the colonial period portrays the situation. A dialogue between
some surviving indigenous sages and the twelve Franciscans who arrived
in 1524 exemplifies the early confrontations over religion and meta-
physics in general. Although this dialogue appears to be a prototypical
reconstruction done by fray Sahagún and his indigenous students, it
nonetheless reveals the sort of arguments that were employed by the missionaries and the responses by native elders and wise men.*

*In this dialogue, as in many other texts produced by the missionaries
and their native assistants, one can detect the ideological and linguistic
problems their authors had to confront. Two in particular stand out:
How should they express in the indigenous language subtle concepts derived from the Jewish and Christian religious traditions? And should
they look for equivalents in native religious thought and in the Nahua
language itself?*

*Let us consider some examples. One is provided by the Christian
concept of God, which although derived from Judaism, had became
transformed into that of the divine Trinity: Father, Son, and Holy Spirit.
The friars, as can be seen in the texts they prepared—Christian doctrines,
confessionals, sermons, dialogues, and narratives—hesitated as to how
they should present this. Some who had become acquainted with key
Nahua religious concepts knew, for instance, that there were words in
Nahuatl such as teotl which generically meant god; Ipalnemohuani,
"Giver of Life"; Tloque Nahuaque, "The One Who is Close and Near,"
i.e., omnipresent; and Ometeotl, who was at once Totahtzin, Tonantzin,
"Our Revered Father, Our Revered Mother."*

Other concepts difficult to translate included those related to the devil, the afterlife, Heaven and Hell; sin and the sacraments; and so on. The friars knew that certain concepts in the Nahua religion at least in appearance could be taken as parallel, although they realized it would be very risky to employ their designation in Nahuatl indiscriminately. In reality, it was misleading to designate, for instance, the concept of the Christian Hell by using the word Mictlan, "Region of the Dead," with its radically different connotations as an obscure space situated in the innermost part of the underworld where most of the dead had to go. In the case of the Christian God and that of the Virgin Mary, it could lead into heresy to refer to them as Ipalnemohuani, "Giver of Life" and Tonantzin, "Our Revered Mother." The first term was actually most often employed to designate the god Tezcatlipoca, "Smoking Mirror," one of the sons or manifestations of Ometeotl, the supreme dual god.

To refer to the Virgin Mary as Tonantzin, "Our Revered Mother," was considered dangerous because in Nahuatl that word was applied to the feminine aspect of the same dual god. One can recall here the reaction of friar Sahagún, who for this very reason fiercely opposed the cult of Tonantzin, the Virgin of Guadalupe.

These examples demonstrate the difficulty of the problems the missionaries had to face in their endeavor to present the Christian religion to native Mexicans. From our modern perspective, we can see that they have left us a rich ensemble of texts—some of great beauty, such as the dialogues with the Nahua sages—from which one can begin to comprehend the extent of the spiritual confrontation that took place in the encounter between two worlds.

The friars also prepared vocabularies and grammars for the study of Nahuatl, some of which are still recognized as valuable contributions. For their part, the doctrines, confessionals, sermons, psalms, and translations of parts of the Bible are not only valuable as literature, but provide insight into the syncretic religion created in Mexico during the colonial period. Among the most important are a selection of missionary theater pieces, and the famous Nican Mopohua, which describes the appearance of the Virgin of Guadalupe to the converted Indian, Juan Diego, at Tepeyacac, the place where the ancient goddess Tonantzin, "Our Revered Mother," had been worshipped.

The Dialogues of 1524

(following the text of fray Bernardino de Sahagún and his Indian collaborators)

DIALOGUES AND CHRISTIAN DOCTRINE IN
THE MEXICAN AND SPANISH LANGUAGE BY
WHICH THE TWELVE FRIARS OF SAINT
FRANCIS SENT BY POPE ADRIAN VI AND
THE EMPEROR CHARLES V CONVERTED
THE INDIANS OF NEW SPAIN

Where it tells how the twelve Fathers of Saint Francis spoke the first time they came among us in the heart of the great city Tenochtitlan. They assembled all the lords, all the rulers who were living there.

Our beloved Mexicas, Tenochcas, lords, rulers, you who have come here to inform us, who have come out together here, please listen well, treat with respect what we are going to set forth, take the Word to heart.

So that we make no error, do not look upon us as if we were superior, for we are merely your peers, *macehuales*, common people; moreover, we are men, we are surely not gods. Like you, we are also inhabitants of the earth: We also drink, we eat, we die of the cold, suffer from the heat; we are also mortal, destructible. We are only messengers, sent here, to your homeland, to your water, your mountain, bearing the honorable breath, the honorable word of the Holy Father Pope, who is the great ruler over divine things in the world, everywhere on earth.

Because he toils on your behalf, prepare yourself:

Listen to this, understand it, let it calm the hearts of my children of the new land, the people of New Spain: the Mexicas, Tenochcas, Aculhuaques, Tepanecs, Tlaxcaltecs, Michhuaques, Huaxtecs, and those from cities all around, all the diverse peoples who dwell in the new lands named West Indies, because it was not long ago but only recently that I heard, I learned of their renown, their history. Our dear son the Emperor, Charles the Fifth, King of Spain, made it known to me. He told me:

Oh, our dear Father, in a distant land, which they saw recently for the first time, one group of men on earth discovered the people who are called Indians, and my Spanish subjects, by their determination alone, conquered them. Now, they are also my subjects; they belong to me.

I implore you to order those whom you dedicate to teaching to teach the word of God, so that they can show them the Christian life, because now these gentiles follow objects which they call god, they live making divinities of devils.

You have heard what pertains to you.

. . .

And now, our beloved, here we are, you see us, you know of us. We are the messengers, the envoys, the chosen ones, we twelve. He sent us here, the one who is the great ruler over divine things, who resides in the heart of the great city, the place called Rome. And he gave us his power, which we have brought here, along with the divine book.

There it lies, there it is kept, the honorable breath, the honorable word of the one, the only true God, Lord of Heaven and Earth, Giver of Life, He whom you never knew.

It is not for anything else that we came, that we were sent here; only because of spiritual compassion for you, only for your salvation. The great ruler over divine things desires nothing of this earth, neither jade, nor gold, nor quetzal plumes, nor any other valuable things; your salvation alone is his desire.

Where it tells Who He is, the True God, the Ruler, Giver of Life, Lord of the Close and the Near.

The Holy Father on earth, the great ruler over spiritual things, sent us, we twelve, he commanded us by the divine word to make known to you, the One, the only God, the True God, Ruler, Lord of the Close and the Near, Lord of Heaven, of the surface of the earth, He who created them, who made heaven, earth, and the region of the dead.

And now perhaps you say: It was mere vanity. Your mission has no value, you have come in vain, because [you say] we also have our god there, our lords are here too; we also know him, we respect him, honor him, obey him, serve him; we also call our god Giver of Life. And before him we kiss the earth, we humble ourselves, we make confession, we offer copal, we burn paper, and we fast; we sacrifice people and offer him the entrails, our heart, and many other things. Every twenty days we celebrate the holy days this way.

What else have you come to teach us? Perhaps something not given as law by the lords, the rulers who are gone now, our forefathers who came to live on the land.

Listen, please, our beloved. In truth, we know, we have seen and heard that you have, not only one, but many gods whom you honor, you serve. You have carved countless numbers of these in stone, in wood, and you keep them as your gods. You call them Tezcatlipoca, Huitzilopochtli, Quetzalcoatl, Mixcoatl, Tlaloc, Xiutecuhtli, Mictlantecuhtli, Cihuacoatl, Piltzintecuhtli, Cinteotl, the Four Hundred of the South, the Four Hundred Rabbits, and others beyond counting. But if they were true gods, if they were truly the Giver of Life, why do they ridicule people? Why do they make mockeries? Why don't they have compassion for their own creations? Why do they also cause you countless diseases and afflictions?

You know this very well. But when you are greatly distressed, when you do not know, when you do not find out; then, in your ire, in your anger, you abandon your god. You tell him: Oh you! whose subjects we are, oh, you great sodomite, you wrinkled old woman, you are the enemy on both sides, the one who works with cunning! You have been mocking us, you have been working your whims.

And every day they demand blood, hearts. On account of this they intimidate the people, they make the people faint. Their images, their representations, are very black, very dirty, very revolting. This is the way they are, those which you consider gods, which you follow as gods, those to whom you make offerings. They tormented the people, they drove them to suicide.

But the One who is the true God, who rules, the true Creator of Men, true Giver of Life, the true Lord of the Close and the Near, the One we came to show you, He is not like them. He does not mock people for any reason, nothing deceitful comes from Him, nothing envious, nothing hateful; He desires nothing black, nothing dirty. He despises all that is not good, not upright [everything which was said], because He is unable to see that which He has prohibited, because He is entirely good, entirely upright. In Him, united in One, is all that is good, upright, pure. He is very loving toward people, very compassionate, very merciful, and surpassing all things in his love for people, His mercy for people. For our sake he made Himself human here on earth, a man; He came to make Himself like us, common people; similarly He came to make Himself, to appropriate for Himself, the flesh of common people. He came to die for us, to shed His precious blood for us; He came to save us from the hands of the great evildoers, the perverse and evil-hearted ones, those who hate the people; those who are our enemies, the devils; [those you falsely formed as gods], those you call gods, those before whom you bleed yourselves, you kill each other; those who provoke you to every kind of evil act: to hate each other, to fight each other, to eat human flesh, and other breaches, even worse.

The one God, Ruler, does not mock anyone, He is the great helper of people; He is merciful toward all men on earth. Also, you people here, you who are called Indians, thanks to Him, you live. He is merciful toward you, He loves you, although you do not know Him, you are not aware of Him, you do not regard Him as God, you do not regard Him as the Ruler, you do not regard Him as Lord, He is the One who gives you all earthly things, food and drink, and also the dominion and the power, nobility and dignity. And now He desires to favor you with something greater, still higher, even more precious, if you accept Him with all your heart, if you truly regard Him as your God, as the One who rules over you.

And our beloved, perhaps you say, What is the name of your God, the One you came to make known to us? Let us know Him, let us hear Him.

He is marvelous and consoling, His precious name is Redeemer. His honorable name is Jesus Christ, true God, and true man, Giver of Life, Lord of the Close and the Near, and Savior of Men everywhere in the world. He, as God, never began, had no origin; He exists eternally, always, He who made the heavens, the earth, and the region of the dead. He also made us, we men, we common people. And He made the devils, those whom you hold as gods today.

As God, He is everywhere, He sees everything, He knows everything; there is nothing like Him, so marvelous is He. As a man, He is there in the interior of heaven, in the honored mansion of the Lord. And here on earth is His precious reign, which has not lasted for only some periods of four hundred years.

And now His precious dominion has drawn near to you; you were fortunate to receive the gift, to have been deemed worthy!

Everything you have heard is painted in the divine book.

Where it is told how these lords, these rulers answered.

After the speech of one of the twelve fathers was concluded, one of the lords, the rulers, stood up, greeted the priests, and little by little—one lip, two lips [translating]—he answered their breath, their word. He said:

Our lords, you have striven mightily since you came to this land, for you came to dominate our water, our mountain. From where? What is it like, that place you came from? Did you come out of the clouds, from the mists? Here in front of you, where you are, we study and study, we marvel at the people of the city. Here we grasp, we take hold of the new word, as if it were something celestial you had said.

Here the secret of the Lord, Our Lord, Lord of the Close and the Near, the coffer, the trunk, is revealed, is opened for us. From where His breath, His word is made known, from the place of our lords, the Holy Father and the Emperor, the great ruler sends you here. And you set before us here the turquoises; here we marvel at them, as if before a round jade that reflects flawlessly, without shadow, precious, like the deep green broad plumage of the quetzal.

They are gone: The Lord, Our Lord, destroyed them, He disappeared them—Motecuhzomatzin, Ahuitzotzin, Axayacatzin, Tizocicatzin, and Izcoatzin, the elder Motecuhzoma, and Nezahualcoyotzin, Nezahualpilli, Totoquihuaztli, and also the elder Tezozomoctli—the rulers who came to abide, to live on earth, to watch over, to protect, your seat, your mat, for a brief day, a moment, here in Mexico, in Tenochtitlan, and in Aculhuacan, Tetzcoco, Tlacopan.

If this had happened during their lifetimes, they would have responded to your breath, your word. They would also have entreated you, based on your love for people, which we admire here. But what can we say now? Although we act like lords, we are the mothers and the fathers of the people; can it be that here, in your presence, we must destroy the ancient law, which our grandfathers, our grandmothers deeply believed, and which the lords, the rulers, studied diligently and beheld in wonder?

The priests, those who make burnt offerings and those who merit the high title quetzalcoa, bear us on their shoulders. They direct us in the worship of our gods, from whom the tail, the wing [the people of the town], draw their worth. Wise men, they attend to their work eagerly, day and night, making offerings of copal, burnt offerings, pine boughs, piercing with thorns, letting blood.

The observers, those who concern themselves with the course and the systematic movements of the heavens, according to the periods of the night; those who look [read], who tell [what they read], who spread out [the leaves of] the books, the black ink, the red ink, who are in charge of the paintings, they bear us, they guide us, they show the way. They determine how the year falls, how the reckoning of the destinies and the days, and each one of the complete counts follow their path. They occupy themselves with this, for it is their task, their commission, their duty: the divine word.

We also speak of what is called the divine water, the fire, which is our sole task. We concern ourselves with tribute from the tail, the wing. This is the way one takes his heron feather banner, his vest of thin cords, his baton, his tumpline, the one he puts on his forehead; this is the way he obtains slaves.

Let us assemble the priests, the quetzalcoa, so that we may give them the breath, the word of the Lord, Our Lord. Perhaps they will respond. What we have taken in, what we have acquired from your breast, your head, we must raise on high, our lords. But calm your hearts, your flesh, remain here on your mat, your seat.

This having been said, all the rulers left immediately. They called upon the priests, the ones who make burnt offerings, and the quetzalcoa, brought them out, and assembled them. Then they spoke with each other carefully for a long time. They conferred, not once, not twice, but three times; they listened to the words of those who make burnt offerings as the priests said them. And those who heard this were deeply disturbed, saddened, as if frightened, terrified by a fall. And when the word had come to light, when the discourse had come to agreement, they resolved that the next day all the men would assemble and go together to face the twelve priests.

At dawn, the men gathered and straight away went to the place where the Fathers were. Then they greeted the priests and rulers, and said to them:

Our lords, those whom we hold in high esteem [the priests] have come because they have taken in, they have received your breath, your word. So that they may respond, and so that your hearts may remain calm, let them hear from the beginning what we have heard. Your head, your chest, we shall hold on high.

After the twelve Fathers heard this, they told it all again, every word, from the beginning, for the priests of the burnt offerings. The one who spoke Nahuatl made it come out [in this language], in the same way that the rulers heard it the previous day. And when he came to the end of the discourse, one person, one of the quetzalcoa, drew himself up, greeted the priests, and responded with a discourse that was rather long.

Where it tells how the priests responded.

Our lords, rulers, esteemed gentlemen, you endured great hardships as you drew near this land. Here, in your presence, in front of you, we common people study you, because Our Lord allowed you to arrive. In fact, you have come to govern your water, your mountain. But from where? How have you been directed toward this place from the place of our lords, the house of the gods? You seem to have come out of the middle of the clouds, from the mists, over the immense waters. The Lord of the Close and the Near looks with your eyes, hears with your ears, speaks with your voice. Here, in a certain way, we see Him in human form, we speak to the Giver of Life, to that which is night and wind as to a human, for you are His image, His representative. Because of this, we took in, we grasped the word, the breath of Our Lord, Lord of the Close and the Near, the One you brought with you, this one who rules the world, who sent you here on our behalf. We here are astonished by what you brought: His book, His painting, the heavenly word, the divine word.

Now, what? What can we say, in what manner, what will it be that we tell, that we bring to your ears?

Are we, perhaps, something? Ah, we are mere common people, earthy, muddy, shameless, poor, afflicted, tormented. Indeed, the Lord, Our Lord only lent us the tip of his mat, his seat, and placed us there.

With one lip, two lips, we respond, we return the word, the breath of the Lord of the Close and the Near. With this we come out of his forehead, his hair; by this we cast ourselves into the river, into the ravine. We provoke him, and we gain his irritation, his wrath. Perhaps we are only [going] to our perdition, our destruction. Or have we, perhaps, been slothful?

Where are we really going? Ah, we are only common people, destructible, mortal. Oh! that we might not die. Oh! that we might not perish, even though our gods have died!

But quiet your hearts, your flesh, oh our lords, because we are going to break, to open slightly the coffer, the hamper of Our Lord.

You say that we do not know Him, the Lord of the Close and the Near, maker of heaven and earth. You say that ours are not truly gods. This word you speak is new, and we are bewildered by this, we are very frightened, because our forefathers, those who came to exist, to live on earth did not speak this way. They gave us their laws, which they believed were true; they served the gods, they honored them. They taught us how to serve them, to honor them. We kiss the earth in their presence, we bleed ourselves; we pay our debts in this way, by burning copal and offering sacrifices. Our forefathers said that the gods gave us life, that they gave us worth.

How? Where? While it was still night.

And our forefathers said that the gods provide our sustenance, our food, all that is drunk or eaten: our meat, corn, beans, wild amaranth, and lime-leaved sage. We ask them for the rain, the water that produces all the things on earth.

They are themselves rich, happy; they have goods, they own things; they have the good fortune always to have something sprouting, growing in their house. Where? How? In Tlalocan, where there is never hunger, nor disease, nor poverty.

They also give the people courage, prowess, the taking of captives in war, adornment for their lips, bindings, loincloths, capes, flowers, tobacco, jade, fine feathers, and gold.

When and where were they invoked, implored, revered as gods? It was a very long time ago, it was in Tula, in Huapacalco, in Xuchatlapan, in Tlam-ohuanchan. It was already there in Yohualichan. It was in Teotihuacan. Everywhere in the world they gave them the foundation for their seat, their mat. They gave them majesty, dominion, fame and glory.

Shall we now destroy the ancient natural harmony of life, the law of the Chichimecs, the Toltecs, the Colhuaque, the Tepanecs? For this is the way [we understand] in our hearts to whom we are indebted for life, for birth, for growth, and for development. For this we invoke [the gods], we implore them.

Our lords, do not do anything to your tail, your wing that will disgrace them, that will cause them to perish. This was the way of the men and women of long ago; it was their education, their upbringing.

May the gods not be angry with us, may we not bring their fury, their anger down upon us! And let it not be that, in our presence, the tail, the wing (the people) rise up; let it not be that we cause a riot, that we create confusion, if we should say in this way: We no longer have to invoke the gods, we no longer have to implore them.

Calmly, peacefully, our lords, consider what is necessary. We cannot be calm, and certainly we do not agree, we do not believe it to be true, even though we offend you.

Here they are, the lords, the rulers who are responsible for the city, who bear the world on their shoulders. It is already enough that we have left the mat, the seat, that we have been restrained, removed. If we remain in this place, we will provoke [the lords] to put us in prison. Do with us what you will. This is all that we answer, that we respond, to your honorable breath, your honorable word, oh our lords.

Miguel León-Portilla, *Coloquios y Doctrina, Los Dialogos de 1524* (Mexico: Universidad Nacional, 1986), pp. 101–07, 121–29, 147–67; English version, Sylvia and Earl Shorris.

Fray Bernardino de Sahagún, in conjunction with his Nahua students, composed psalms in Nahuatl. His inspirations were both the Bible and the Cantares Mexicanos.

Christian Psalms

BODILY BLISS, KNOWN AS THE BLESSINGS OF PARADISE: FIFTH PSALM

The precious jades that I also shape with my lips, that I also have scattered, that I have uttered, are a fitting song. Not only are all these a gift for you, beloved son, you who are a son of the holy Church; even more [gifts] are your due, your lot, which God, your King, will give you, will bestow upon you in the Empyrean Heaven, if you follow Christianity well as a way of life.

There in the Empyrean Heaven, there will be seven gifts for you, called Blessings of Paradise. The first is called Vision, by which you will surely look into the face of our Lord God. The second is called Retention, by which you will always possess spirituality.

The third is called Fruition, by which you will always rejoice in spirituality. All of these are spiritual benefactions for your soul. But there are four more heavenly benefactions that pertain to your body.

The first is called Nimbleness; that is, you will not be heavy; nowhere will be distant from you, even though you may furiously hurry somewhere. The second is called Impassibility; that is, the well-being of your body. It will absolutely always be immutable; [the body] will feel absolutely nothing.

The third is called Clarity, resplendence; that is, your body will shimmer, shine, glisten brightly; it will outshine the sun. The fourth is called Subtlety; that is, nothing will obstruct, nothing will knock against your body; it will quickly enter everywhere, even wood, [even] stone; it will penetrate anything. For it passes within it; nothing obstructs it.

All these that have been mentioned will be gifts for you in heaven, you who are a Christian; you will attain them not just for countable years; you will enjoy them absolutely forever.

Arthur J. O. Anderson, *Psalmodia Christiana*, (Salt Lake City: University of Utah Press, 1993), p. 33.

Christian Theater—Holy Week Drama

HOLY WEDNESDAY

Christ:
You who are the supreme noblewoman,
who are my precious mother,
you who are the daughter of the one who lives forever, God the father,
May you know that today,
oh my precious mother,
you who are a very humble one,
it is now the hour, it is now the moment,
it is now that the time has arrived
for the people to be rescued.
And this:
I wish to set off for Jerusalem.
And well do you understand,
oh my precious mother,
that I am a divinity, I am God, I am sovereign,
along with my precious father and the Holy Spirit.
However, it was in your pure womb
that I came to become a man, I came to assume flesh.
Hence, now I am your precious child,
in the sense that I am a man.
And in the sense that I am a man,
I will be made to suffer great fatigue,
because of the misdeeds of the people of the world.
Thus, because of them I now beseech you
may you give me your command, your send-off,
that I may go to Jerusalem,
oh my precious mother.

Mary:
Oh, you who are my consolation and precious child,
you who emerged from my womb,
in the sense that you are a man,
what is this that you are saying?
You are making me very anxious.
Do sit down.
I want to say a few words to you here,
in front of Magdalene, who is standing here.

Christ:
Oh my precious mother,
what is it that you want to say?
May it be that I hear it!

Mary:
My precious child,
my sweet goodness and consolation,
my lord, God, sovereign,
my repose and love,
what is this that you are saying?
From what I see of you,
you must be greatly afflicted,
because your face of utter goodness
has become quite pale, has become quite white,
with anxiety, with sadness.
May you know,
my precious child,
how I see your students:
all the time, because of you
they go about sad, they go about distressed,
the children of Zebedee.
And this
it is true.
Something very frightful will happen to you,
torment, death.
My precious child, my sovereign, my lord,
may you oblige me, may your heart be compassionate!
For I beseech you
that the great pascua [Easter] may occur while you are right here.
Fervently I beseech you.
May it be just because you love me very much,
Since I am your mother in the fleshly sense.

My precious child,
be compassionate!
May you have pity on me,
that you will not go to Jerusalem,
and so that my spirit will not hurt, will not ache because of you!
Quite truly do I say to you,
for it is true,
that as soon as you go you will fall into the hands of others,
thus you will die,
in the great city of Jerusalem.

Christ:
Oh my precious mother, oh noblewoman,
may you know,
that the people of the world are to be greatly favored.
They are to be rescued.
Thus, it is essential that I go to Jerusalem.
My precious father, God, desires it to be so.
It is he who set it down in this way,
so that I would die
because of the misdeeds in the world.
It is true,
oh my precious mother,
that it is very necessary for the people of the world
that I go, that I go up to Jerusalem.
And this:
you will not be able to hinder me,
you will not forestall me,
with your sadness, your weeping.

Fervently I beseech you,
oh my mother,
for it is true, for I will go!

Mary:
Oh, you who are my life, you who are my consolation,
may your soul not reflect upon such a thing,
that you will go away!
Because I know very well
that it is true that you are God, your power is total,
and that you are a human being, you are a man.
May you desire not that you will go away,
my precious consolation and joy!

And although it may seem
as though I hold you in low esteem,
you who are my precious child,
the way I keep responding to your word,
may it be that you pardon me,
by means of your total power.
For I do not wish
that I myself should give you my send-off,
so that the great festival should befall you there in Jerusalem.
And this:
may I be right here near you, next to you
on the pascua.
May you know
that some children, who are living on the run,
or who live elsewhere,
when it is the pascua,
they all come back.
They are consoled beside their mother,
thus together they console one another on the pascua.
This, my precious child,
it is good, what they do,
and it is necessary that they act in this way.
So I just beseech you,
my precious child,
do tell me,
you who are Jesus the Nazarene,
why are you abandoning me
on the very great pascua?
That which is about to happen,
it will not happen to you here.

Christ:
Oh noblewoman, oh my precious mother,
may you know
that everything the prophet of old left, foretold,
it is really the truth,
it is not false word.
And all that happened a long time ago,
that still is only signs,
it will all come true now.
And this:
I will go, I will go cause to come true
all the prophecies

that lie written in the sacred book.
Oh my precious mother, know
that the sky
and all the stars
and the earth,
their strength is nothing whatsoever,
they are not strong.
They will crumble, they will be scattered.
But the sacred word that lies written in the sacred book,
which is quite strong with sacred words,
they are really the truth.
And this:
oh my precious mother,
I will cause them to come true.

Mary:
Oh, how my heart is torn open to its very bottom!
It [is] as if you plunged a knife into it
by answering me in this way,
you who are truly God and sovereign.

My precious child,
why do you afflict me so with sadness?
Do tell me.
Why do you afflict my spirit, my soul,
I who am your mother in the fleshly sense?

Christ:
Oh, you who are filled with goodness, with propriety,
you who are my precious mother,
I speak truthfully to you!
As to how I came down here upon the earth,
it was for this reason:
that I should be made to suffer fatigue, I should be made to hurt,
that upon the cross I should be stretched by my hand.
In the sense that I am a man, I will die there.
And this:
oh my precious mother,
may you exert all your effort!
May you be strong,
may your heart not be very sad!
Well do you know,
oh my precious mother,

I am God, I am sovereign,
none soever is as great as I, as awe-inspiring as I!
However, this is the reason for my being a man,
this is the reason why I came:
I came to heal, I came to rescue the human being,
whom the great demon, Lucifer, had made his slave.
Oh, oh my precious mother,
by this may you be consoled.
And this:
it is already here, it is already beside me,
the time when I will die
so that I may cause to come true, I may confirm the prediction
that the prophet left uttered in regard to me.
So now I beseech you,
may your heart, your soul be not distraught!
For it is true, I tell you with certainty
that it is great, that it is extreme,
the way your precious soul will ache, will hurt,
when you see me with my hands tied.
And this:
oh my precious mother,
soon I will die,
although now you still see me standing alive.

Mary:
Oh, it is very lamentable, it is very saddening,
the way you answer me,
It is true that it is extreme,
the way my heart is afflicted, the way it hurts.
There is no bitter medicine so hurtful to the heart
as the way you answer me.
Oh, you who are the utterly truthful divinity,
you who are the sovereign,
you who are the precious child of eternally living God the father,
I beseech you,
do tell me,
for what reason do you so greatly sadden your mother with
anxiety of the heart,
by wanting to go to Jerusalem?
Why is your heart not compassionate, not pitying,
my precious child?
For what reason?
Do tell me.

Perhaps you do not remember how I gave birth to you
there in the eating-place of the deer?
Perhaps you do not remember my milk,
with which I nurtured you?
Oh, you who live forever, you who are God,
why, for what reason,
will you die, in the sense that you are a man?
And I, who am your mother,
you are going to leave me!
And with whom will I console myself,
how will my heart be joyful,
when I do not look to you for my measure?
Perhaps you do not remember
all the exhaustion, heat, wind, ravines, and hills
we passed through as we went to hide you there in Egypt
when Herod wanted to kill you?
You do remember what I endured,
how I went just carrying you in my arm,
just in my hand you traveled,
when we went to Egypt.
And there were not just a few times when, by stumbling, I might
have let go of you.
And there were not just a few other things I endured for your sake.
And I remember
how I used to worry about you night and day.
Perhaps you do not remember
how I was afflicted,
the anxiety, the affliction,
when I lost you there in Jerusalem,
where you want to go now?
Why do you just forget,
my precious child?
May you thus have pity on me, favor me.
Fervently I beseech you
that you not wish that you will die,
you who are my utterly precious child!
May you obey me!

Christ:
Oh how greatly you sadden me,
you noblewoman,
you who are my precious mother.
With word of affliction you have declared

how I will retreat,
how I will turn things around for myself,
so that I will not die.
Although you have declared many sad words to me,
not so will it be ruined,
that which my precious father has decreed,
that I will die.
May you know,
oh noblewoman, oh my mother,
God, the divinity, the sovereign, who lives forever,
he is a divinity of utterly surpassing goodness.
And he made Adam and Eve, and he placed them
there in terrestrial paradise.
He gave them orders
so that they would stay there,
in the very good place, in the very fine place.
And he gave them orders
that they would not approach, they would not eat
the fruit of the tree of life.
But later on, the Devil, the demon deceived them,
that they stretched out their hand to it, they ate it,
the fruit, the produce, of the tree of life,
which he had prohibited to them.
Thus they fell into the anger of God.
Thus here in the place of weeping, hither he exiled them.
He placed eternal death upon them.
But my precious father, God, has decided
that I will rescue them.
For this reason I will die
As it was with a tree that Adam and Eve erred,
likewise it must be with a tree that I die.
There will come forth eternal rescue,
and there my precious father will thereby be appeased.
And this:
oh my precious mother,
it is essential that I die,
for none soever will be able to enter heaven.
I alone must make things peaceful for them.

Mary:
My precious child,
may you know
that I know this well, I consider it to be true.

Even if you did not actually die,
you would be able to rescue the people of the world
with your very great, total power.
You who are my precious child,
since you are God, you are sovereign,
therefore everything is in your hands.
And may you want it to be this way,
may you do it this way,
such that it be entirely with your word you will say,
"May it be done."
It is true
that immediately the people of the world would be rescued.
And if you do not desire that it be this way,
that you do it this way,
so that the people of the world will be rescued,
then with these things may you make compensation
before your precious father.
The way that they cut your precious flesh a little bit,
such that a great deal of your precious blood issued forth there,
it along with all your wondrous deeds
and your fasting, your good deeds,
with these things may you make things peaceful for the people of
the world before your precious father,
so that he will be appeased.
And this:
may you speak no more of your death!

Christ:
You who are a blessed and perfect maiden,
you who are a noblewoman and sovereign,
you who are my precious mother,
what you have said is very true and correct.
It is true that I have total power.
everything can be done,
whatever I may wish,
since I am the divinity, I am the sovereign.
But first may you know
that in no way will I turn things around.
It is true that I will cause to come true
that which the prophet left foretold.
Regarding me they left it said
that I would rescue people here on earth.
It will certainly come true,

that I will endure everything
that they left declared, which lies written in the sacred book.
Nothing whatsoever will be lost,
even if it is a little spatter of ink.
It will all come true.
And it was he, my precious father, God,
he decreed it,
that is how the words were set down in this way.
And they will not be the least bit broken.
I will cause everything to come true.
Oh my precious mother,
may you not be very sad,
may you not be very distressed on my behalf.
The rescue of the people has already been left in my hands,
the sentence has already been set down.
I will endure everything that is hurtful to people.
And this:
already it has come to arrive,
the day of sadness,
the day of sadness and weeping.
It is necessary that I destroy
the garment of sad fasting for the dead, the winding-sheet of
the dead,
that the people on earth go about wearing.
It is the old error, original sin.
Their souls are dressed in it,
the demon, Lucifer, enslaved them with it.
And this:
oh my precious mother,
if I am not stretched by my hand upon the cross
there on Mount Calvary,
then how will people be rescued?
I speak truthfully to you,
oh my precious mother,
and indeed you know this well.
If I do not cause to come true,
the command of my precious father, God,
then, if I do not carry out,
the command of my precious father, God,
there can be no rescue.
Therefore may you know
that absolutely never will God lie,
he will never break his word,

because he is a truthful divinity.
This:
oh my precious mother,
it is essential that I die,
it is essential for the people of the world.

Mary:
My precious child,
may it be that you desire
that which I say.
May it be that I die first,
so that I will not see
how your precious blood will be spilled
and how your precious flesh will be broken
as you open, as you raise up the road to the refuge of heaven.
May I not see all that will befall you!

Christ:
Oh my precious mother,
Oh, how very piercing, how profound is the affliction
that will befall me
in that time, at that moment!
Nothing is equal to it.
That which you say,
oh my precious mother,
you say it as if you wish
that you might die first.
It must not be.
It will occur in your presence,
how I will be made to suffer.
On the day of sadness,
oh my precious mother,
just with you alone will be in its entirety, will be kept in its entirety,
the sacred belief, the holy Catholic faith.
And also know,
oh my mother,
that at that time it will be most extremely piteous,
for no one will be my friend any longer,
for no one will follow me about any longer,
for all of my students will hide, they will all flee.
And just you alone will be left beside me.
There you will know, there you will see me being hurt.
You will be very faint of heart,

oh my mother.

Mary:
My precious child,
how very piercing, how profound is the affliction
that will befall you!
Nothing whatsoever matches it, is equal to it,
the aching, the hurting
that your heart will know.
How very strong is the sovereign command that was set down,
the sentence of divinity!
How will I be even a little bit happy?
For I will see you then,
when they tie you to the stone column by your hands.
Not just four hundred times will they flog you.
Oh, my heart,
it is as if it is about to issue forth,
it is so distressed, I am suffering so much,
with sadness, with aching.
My precious child,
may you not become very short of breath,
as you are made to suffer fatigue,
but truly with all your heart, according to your wishes,
in this way the torments will befall you.

Louise M. Burkhart, *Holy Wednesday* (Philadelphia: University of Pennsylvania Press, 1996), excerpted from pp. 111–35.

In 1531, according to Antonio Valeriano, a disciple of fray Sahagún, a dark-skinned Virgin appeared to the Christianized Nahua, Juan Diego, on the hill of Tepeyacac on the outskirts of Mexico City. This is the well-known story, first published in 1645, of the apparition of the Virgin of Guadalupe, patron saint of Mexico. In the original Nahuatl version, one can find many elements of the ancient Nahuatl texts. The work has been translated into many languages since its original publication. It is generally reproduced in prose, although in some Nahuatl-speaking towns, recitations are often given either partially or entirely in poetic form.

Christian Epic Literature

NICAN MOPOHUA

HERE IS RECOUNTED
(Nican Mopohua)
AND TOLD
IN
AN orderly fashion how by a great miracle
THE consummate virgin saint Mary,
MOTHER of God, our queen,
FIRST appeared at
TEPEYACAC, called
GUADALUPE.

First she revealed herself to a humble commoner named Juan Diego, and afterwards her precious image appeared in the presence of the first bishop, don fray Juan de Zumarraga. And [here are related] all the miracles she has worked.

IT HAD been ten years since the altepetl of Mexico had been conquered and the weapons of war had been laid down, and peace reigned in the altepetl all around; likewise the faith, the recognition of the giver of life, the true deity, God, had begun to flower and bloom. Right in the year of 1531, just a few days into the month of December, there was a humble commoner, a poor ordinary person, whose name was Juan Diego. They say his home was in Cuauhtitlan, but in spiritual matters everything still belonged to Tlatelolco. It was Saturday, still very early in the morning, and he was on his way to attend to divine things and to his errands. When he came close to the hill at the place called Tepeyacac, it was getting light. He heard singing on top of the hill, like the songs of various precious birds. Their voices were [swelling and fading?], and it was as if the hill kept on answering them. Their song was very agreeable and pleasing indeed, entirely surpassing how the bell bird, the trogon, and the other precious birds sing. Juan Diego stopped to look, saying to himself, "Am I so fortunate or deserving as to hear this? Am I just dreaming it? Am I imagining it in sleepwalking? Where am I? Where do I find myself? Is it in the land of the flowers, the land of plentiful crops, the place of which our ancient forefathers used to speak? Is this the land of heaven?"

He stood looking toward the top of the hill to the east, from where the heavenly, precious song was coming. When the song had subsided and silence fell, he heard himself being called from the top of the hill. A woman said to him, "Dear Juan, dear Juan Diego." Thereupon he stepped forward to go where he was summoned. His heart was not troubled, nor was he startled by anything; rather he was very happy and felt fine as he went climbing the hill, heading toward where he was summoned.

When he reached the top of the hill, he saw a lady standing there; she called to him to go over next to her. When he came before her, he greatly marveled at how she completely surpassed everything in her total splendor. Her clothes were like the sun in the way they gleamed and shone. Her resplendence struck the stones and boulders by which she stood so that they seemed like precious emeralds and jeweled bracelets. The ground sparkled like a rainbow, and the mesquite, the prickly pear cactus, and other various kinds of weeds that grow there seemed like green obsidian, and their foliage like fine turquoise. Their stalks, their thorns and spines gleamed like gold.

He prostrated himself before her and heard her very pleasing and courtly message, as if inviting and flattering him, saying to him, "Do listen, my youngest child, dear Juan, where is it that you are going?" He answered her, "My patron, noble lady, my daughter, I am going to your home of Mexico-Tlatelolco. I am pursuing the divine matters that the representatives of the lord our Lord, our friars, give and teach us."

Thereupon she conversed with him, revealing to him her precious wish. She said to him,

Know, rest assured, my youngest child, that I am the eternally consummate virgin Saint Mary, mother of the very true deity, God, the giver of life, the creator of people, the ever present, the lord of heaven and earth. I greatly wish and desire that they build my temple for me here, where I will manifest, make known, and give to people all my love, compassion, aid, and protection. For I am the compassionate mother of you and of all you people here in this land, and of the other various peoples who love me, who cry out to me, who seek me, who trust in me. There I will listen to their weeping and their sorrows in order to remedy and heal all their various afflictions, miseries, and torments. And in order that this my act of compassion which I am contemplating may come to pass, go to the bishop's palace in Mexico and tell him how I am sending you to put before him how I very much wish that he build me a house, that he erect a temple for me on the level ground here. You are to relate every single thing that you have seen and beheld, and what you have heard. And rest assured that I will be very grateful for it, and I will reward it, for I will enrich you and make you content for it. You will attain many things as my repayment for your efforts and labors with which you go to put in motion what I send you for. And so, my youngest child, you have heard my message. Get on your way, make every effort.

Thereupon he prostrated himself before her, saying to her, "My patron, O Lady, now I am going to carry out your message. Let me, your humble subject, take leave of you for a while." Thereupon he came back down in order to go carry out his errand, coming to take the causeway that comes directly to Mexico.

WHEN HE got inside the altepetl, he went straight to the palace of the bishop, whose name was don fray Juan de Zumarraga, a friar of Saint Francis and the very first priestly ruler to come. As soon as he arrived, he attempted to see him; he implored his servants and dependents to go tell him. After a rather long time they came to tell him that the lord bishop had given orders for him to enter. When he came in, he knelt and bowed low before him. Then he put before him and told him the heavenly Lady's message, his errand. He also told him everything that he had beheld, what he had seen and heard. But when he [the bishop] had heard his whole statement and message, he did not seem to be completely convinced. He answered him, telling him, "My child, do come again, and I will hear you at length. First I will thoroughly look into and consider what you have come about, your wish and desire." He came back out grieving, because his errand was not then carried out.

HE CAME BACK right away, on the very same day. He came straight to the top of the hill and found the heavenly Lady in the same place where he first saw her, waiting for him. When he saw her, he bowed low before her and threw himself to the ground, saying to her:

My patron, O personage, Lady, my youngest child, my daughter, I went to where you sent me, I went to carry out your instructions. Although it was difficult for me to enter the quarters of the priestly ruler, I did see him, and I put before him your message as you ordered me to. He received me kindly and heard it out, but when he answered me, he did not seem to be satisfied or convinced. He told me, "You are to come again, and I will hear you at leisure. First I will thoroughly look into what you have come about, your wish and desire." I could easily see from how he answered me that he thought that perhaps I was just making it up that you want them to build your temple there for you and that perhaps it is not by your order. I greatly implore you, my patron, noble Lady, my daughter, entrust one of the high nobles, who are recognized, respected, and honored, to carry and take your message, so that he will be believed. For I am a poor ordinary man, I carry burdens with the tumpline and carrying frame, I am one of the common people, one who is governed. Where you are sending me is not my usual place, my daughter, my youngest child, O personage, O Lady. Pardon me if I cause you concern, if I incur or bring upon myself your frown or your wrath, O personage, O my Lady.

The revered consummate Virgin answered him,

Do listen, my youngest child. Be assured that my servants and messengers to whom I entrust it to carry my message and realize my wishes are not high ranking people. Rather it is highly necessary that you yourself be involved and take care of it. It is very much by your hand that my will and wish are to be carried out and accomplished. I strongly implore you, my youngest child, and I give you strict orders that tomorrow you be sure to go see the bishop once again. Instruct him on my behalf, make him fully understand my will and wish, so that he will carry out the building of my temple that I am asking him for. And be sure to tell him again how it is really myself, the ever Virgin Saint Mary, the mother of God the deity, who is sending you there.

Juan Diego answered her, saying to her,

My patron, O Lady, my daughter, let me not cause you concern, for with all my heart I will go there and carry out your message. I will not abandon it under any circumstances; although I find the road painful, I will go to do your will. The only thing is that I may not be heard out, or when I have been heard I may not be believed. However, tomorrow, late in the afternoon, when the sun is going down, I will come returning whatever answer the priestly ruler should give me to your message. Now, my youngest child, my daughter, O personage, O Lady, I am taking leave of you; meanwhile, take your rest.

Thereupon he went home to rest.

ON THE FOLLOWING day, Sunday, while it was still very early in the morning and dark everywhere, he left his home and came directly to Tlatelolco to learn divine things and to be counted and also to see the priestly ruler. It was perhaps ten o'clock when they were finished with hearing mass and taking the count, and all the commoners dispersed again. Thereupon Juan Diego went to the palace of the lord bishop; when he got there, he made every effort to see him, but it was with great difficulty that he saw him again. He knelt down at his feet, and he wept and grieved as he told and put before him the message of the heavenly Lady, because he wondered if perhaps the consummate Virgin's message and will that they were to build and erect a temple for her where she designated and wanted it would not be believed. The lord bishop asked and interrogated him about very many things in order to be satisfied about where he saw her and what she was like, and he told it absolutely all to the lord bishop. Although he told him the exact truth about how she was and all that he had seen and beheld, and that she really seemed to be the consummate Virgin, the precious, revered mother of our redeemer, our lord

Jesus Christ, still he was not immediately convinced. He said that it was not by his [Juan Diego's] word and request alone that what he asked for would be done and carried out. Some additional sign was still very much needed so that it could be believed that it was really the heavenly Lady herself who sent him. When Juan Diego heard that, he said to the bishop, "O personage, O ruler, consider what kind of sign it is to be that you request of her, and then I will go ask it of the heavenly Lady who sent me here." And when the bishop saw that he was entirely convinced, that he had absolutely no second thoughts or doubts, he thereupon sent him off.

And when he was on his way, thereupon he [the bishop] ordered some of the people of his household in whom he had full confidence to follow after him and keep close watch where he went, whom he saw, and whom he talked to. But it so happened that thereupon Juan Diego came straight along the causeway, and those who came following him lost sight of him at the place where the ravine comes out near Tepeyacac, next to the wooden bridge. Thought they kept searching everywhere, nowhere did they see him; they returned empty-handed. Not only did they go away vexed because of the loss of time, but it frustrated them and made them angry. They went to tell the lord bishop about it, preparing him not to believe him; they told him that he was only lying to him, only making up what he came to tell him, or that perhaps he only dreamed or saw in sleep walking what he told him and asked of him. They insisted that if he should come again, should return, they would seize him on the spot and punish him severely, so that he would never lie and disturb people again.

ON THE FOLLOWING day, Monday, Juan Diego did not return when he was supposed to take some sign in order to be believed, because when he reached the home of an uncle of his, whose name was Juan Bernardino, a sickness had come upon him [the uncle] and he lay gravely ill. First he went to summon a physician for him, who looked after him for a while, but it was too late; he was already mortally ill. When night had come his uncle asked him that while it was still very early in the morning and dark everywhere, he should come to Tlatelolco to summon one of the friars to go hear his confession and prepare him, because he was fully convinced that it was now time for him to die and that he would not rise again or recover.

IT WAS TUESDAY, still very dark everywhere, when Juan Diego left his home to summon a friar in Tlatelolco. When he came by the hill of Tepeyacac, at the foot of which the road that he took previously passes to the west, he said, "If I just go straight along the road, I am afraid that the Lady may see me, for before you know it she will detain me in order that I should carry the sign to the priestly ruler as she instructed me. May our affliction leave us first; let me first hurry to summon the friar. My uncle is in need and he can't just lie waiting for him." Thereupon he went around the hill, climbing through an opening and coming out on the other side to the east, so that he would quickly reach Mexico and the heavenly Lady would not detain him. He believed that if he went around there, she who sees absolutely everywhere would not be able to see him. He saw her coming down from the hill where she was watching, where he had seen her before. She came to meet and intercept him on the hillside, saying to him, "Well, my youngest child, where are you going? Where are you headed?" And wasn't he a bit bothered by it? Or ashamed? Or startled and frightened by it? He prostrated himself before her, greeted her, and said to her,

My daughter, my youngest child, Lady, may you be content. How did you feel on awakening? Is your precious body in good health, my patron, my very noble lady? I am going to cause you concern. You must know, my daughter, that a poor subject of yours, my uncle, lies very gravely ill. A great illness has come upon him, of which he will soon die. And first I am hurrying to your home of Mexico to summon one of those beloved of our Lord, our friars, to go hear his confession and prepare him, for what we were born for is to come to await our duty of death. When I have carried this out, then I will return here again so that I may go to carry your message, O personage, my daughter. Please forgive me and meanwhile have patience with me. I am not doing it on purpose, my youngest child, my very noble Lady. I will come by quickly tomorrow.

When she had heard Juan Diego's words, the compassionate, consummate Virgin answered him,

Understand, rest very much assured, my youngest child, that nothing whatever should frighten you or worry you. Do not be concerned, do not fear the illness, or any other illness or calamity. Am I, your mother, not here? Are you not under my protective shade, my shadow? Am I not your happiness? Are you not in the security of my lapfold, in my carrying gear? Do you need something more? Do not let anything worry you or upset you further. Do not let your uncle's illness worry you, for he will not die of what he now has. Rest assured, for he has already recovered.

(And at that very moment his uncle recovered, as was learned afterwards.)

When Juan Diego heard the heavenly lady's message, he was greatly consoled and reassured by it. He implored her to send him to go see the lord bishop, taking him some sign or proof, so that he would believe him. Thereupon the heavenly Lady directed him to go up to the top of the hill where he had seen her before. She said to him, "Go up, my youngest child, to the top of the hill, and where you saw me and I spoke to you, you will see various kinds of flowers growing. Pick them, gather them, collect them, and then bring them back down here, bring them to me."

Then Juan Diego climbed the hill. When he reached the top, he was greatly astonished at all the different kinds of precious Spanish flowers that were growing there, blossoming and blooming, although their blooming time had not yet come, for it was right then that the frost was strong. They were very fragrant, and the night dew on them was like precious pearls. He thereupon began to pick them; he gathered every one and put them in his lapfold. But the top of the hill was absolutely no place for any flowers to grow, for it was a place of crags, thorns, brambles, cactus, and mesquite, and if some little grassy weeds should grow there at that time, in the month of December, the frost would devour and destroy them all. Then he came back down, bringing to the heavenly Lady the various kinds of flowers that he had gone to pick.

When she saw him, she took them in her arms; then she put them back in the folds of his cloak, saying to him,

My youngest child, these various kinds of flowers are the proof and the sign that you are to take to the bishop. You are to tell him on my behalf that thereby he should see my will and carry out my wish and my will, and that you, my messenger, are very trustworthy. I give you very strict orders to unfold your cloak only before the bishop and show him what you are carrying. You are to recount absolutely everything to him and tell him how I instructed you to climb to the top of the hill to pick the flowers, and everything that you saw and beheld, so that you may really inspire the priestly ruler to see to it immediately that my temple which I requested of him is built and raised.

When the heavenly Lady had given him the various instructions, he came following the causeway that leads directly here to Mexico. Now he came content, confident that it would turn out well, that he would carry it off. As he came he exercised great care with what he had in his lapfold, lest he drop anything, and he enjoyed the fragrance of the various kinds of precious flowers.

WHEN HE CAME to the bishop's palace, the majordomo and other dependents of the priestly ruler went out to meet him, and he asked them to tell him that he wished to see him. But none of them wanted to; they pretended not to hear him, perhaps because it was still very early in the morning or perhaps because they now recognized him, that he would just annoy them with his hanging around in front of them; their friends who lost him when they were following after him had already cautioned them.

He was waiting for a reply for a very long time. When they saw that he had stood there for a very long time with his head down, that he was doing nothing in case he was called, and it seemed as if he came carrying something that he was keeping in his lapfold, they approached him to see what he came carrying, to satisfy their curiosity. And when Juan Diego saw that he could by no means hide from them what he came carrying and that because of it they would pester him, shove him, or maybe beat him, he showed them by a little glimpse that it was flowers. When they saw that there were all different kinds of Spanish flowers and that they were not in season at that time, they marveled greatly at it and at how very fresh they were, like just opened flowers, pleasant to smell, splendid. They wanted to seize a few of them and take them from him. But all three times when they tried to step forward to take them, they were entirely unsuccessful, because when they were about to grasp them, it was no longer real flowers that they saw but something seemingly painted, embroidered, or sewn on the cloak.

Thereupon they went to tell the lord bishop what they had seen and how the humble commoner who had come several times was wanting to see him and that now he had been waiting there for a very long time for word about his wanting to see him. When the lord bishop heard this, it came to him that it was the proof that would convince him to carry out what the humble person was after. Then he gave orders that he should enter immediately and that he would see him.

And when he entered, he prostrated himself before him, as he had done before, and again he told him all that he had seen and beheld and his mission. He said to him:

My lord ruler, now I have done and carried out what you ordered me. Indeed I went to tell the lady my patron, the heavenly Lady, Saint Mary, the precious mother of God the deity, that you asked for a sign so that you can believe me and build her temple for her in the place where she asks you to erect it. I assured her that I gave you my word that I would bring back to you some sign and verification of her wish, since you left it in my hands. She approved your message, and she gladly accepted your request for some sign, some verification of it, so that her will may be performed and carried out. Well then, today, while it was still very early in the morning, she instructed me to come to see you again. I asked her for some sign of it so that I would be believed, as she said that she would give me [one], and right then she carried it out.

She sent me to the top of the hill where I had seen her before to go cut various kinds of Spanish flowers. When I had cut them, I brought them back to her down there below. She took them in her arms, then put them back in the folds of my cloak in order that I might bring them back to you and give them to you in person. Although I fully realized that the top of the hill is not a place where flowers grow, that it is only a place of crags, thorns, brambles, cactus, and mesquite, I did not for that reason have any doubts.

When I reached the top of the hill and looked about, it was a flower garden, full of all different kinds of fine flowers in the Spanish style, glistening with dew, so that I immediately went to pick them. And she told me that I was to give them to you on her behalf. Thus I am carrying it out, so that in them you may see what you request as a sign to carry out her wish, and it will be seen that my message and my errand are true. Here they are, please accept them.

Thereupon he spread out his white cloak, in the folds of which he was carrying the flowers, and as all the different kinds of Spanish flowers scattered to the ground, the precious image of the consummate Virgin Saint Mary, mother of God the deity, was imprinted and appeared on the cloak, just as it is today where it is kept in her precious home, her temple of Tepeyacac, called Guadalupe.

When the lord bishop and all who were there saw it, they knelt down, they marveled greatly at it, they looked at it transfixed, they grieved, their hearts were afflicted; it was as if their spirits and their minds were transported upward. The lord bishop, with tears and sorrow, implored and asked her forgiveness for not having immediately carried out her wish, her message.

When he arose, he loosened the garment which was tied around Juan Diego's neck, his cloak, on which the heavenly Lady had appeared, on which she had imprinted herself. Thereupon he took it to place it in his oratory.

Juan Diego stayed one more day in the bishop's palace, he detained him for a while. The following day he said to him, "Let us go so that you may show people the place where it is the heavenly Lady's wish that they build a temple for her." Thereupon orders were given for it to be built and erected.

After Juan Diego had shown where the heavenly Lady instructed that her temple be erected, he took his leave, because he wanted to go home to see his uncle, Juan Bernardino, who lay gravely ill when he left him behind to summon one of the friars in Tlatelolco to hear his confession and prepare him, and who the heavenly Lady told him had already recovered.

But they did not let him go alone. They accompanied him to his home, and when he arrived they saw that his uncle was now entirely healthy, that nothing whatever ailed him. And he was greatly astonished at how his nephew came accompanied and was rendered great honor, and he asked his nephew how it happened that he was thus greatly honored. He told him how when he left to call the friar to hear his confession and prepare him, the heavenly Lady appeared to him at Tepeyacac and sent him to Mexico to go see the lord bishop so that he would build her a house in Tepeyacac and how she told him not to worry, since he was already well, by which he had been greatly consoled.

His uncle told him that it was the truth, that she cured him at that very moment, and that he really saw her in exactly the same way as she appeared to his nephew, and that she told him that meanwhile she was sending him [Juan Diego] to Mexico to see the bishop. He [the uncle] was then to go see him too, he was to put absolutely everything before him, he was to inform him of what he had seen and how she had healed him miraculously, and that he was to give her precious image the very name of the consummate Virgin, Saint Mary of Guadalupe, that it was to bear that very name.

Thereupon they brought Juan Bernardino before the lord bishop to inform him and verify it in his presence. The bishop lodged the two of them, him and his nephew Juan Diego, in his palace for quite a few days until such time as the temple of the Queen was erected at Tepeyacac where she appeared to Juan Diego. The lord bishop moved the precious image of the heavenly precious Lady to the cathedral; he removed it from his palace, where it had been in his oratory, so that everyone would see and marvel at her precious image.

There was a movement in all the altepetls everywhere of people coming to see and marvel at her precious image. They came to show their devotion and pray to her; they marveled greatly at how it was by a divine miracle that she had appeared, that absolutely no earthly person had painted her precious image.

Lisa Sousa, C. M. Stafford Poole, and James Lockhart, *Luis Laso de la Vega's The Story of Guadalupe* (Stanford, CA: UCLA Latin American Center Publications, 1998), English text only, pp. 61–89.

Christian Pageant

Every year, on September 8, in the town of Tepoztlan near Cuernavaca, the Nahuas who live in the area celebrate a feast during which they present the following pageant/play, as they have done since ancient times. The dialogue was recorded and translated by Karttunen and Céspedes.

The Tepozteco[1]

Challengers: Mountain-dweller! *(calling, four times)*

Cuauhnahuac: Mountain-dweller! Cuauhnahuac seeks you. Now I come to turn you into earth and dust, and to reduce you to earth and dust I come. What not. . . . Stout is my heart.

Yaotepec: Mountain-dweller! Yaotepec seeks you. Do you fear when you hear of my fame and my words? Now I have come. I come to turn you into earth and dust, and to reduce you to earth and dust I come. And stout is my heart.

Huaxtepec: Mountain-dweller! Now I have come, I come to destroy you, and to turn you to earth and dust I have come. Here am I . . . Huaxtepec. Hear of my fame and my words. Now I have come to destroy you, and to turn you to earth and dust. And to that end I make stout my heart.

Tlayacapan: Mountain-dweller! Tlayacapan seeks you. Now I have come, I come to reduce you to earth and dust, and to earth and dust I will turn you. And stout is my heart.

Tepozteco: Who are you who have come here? Don't you know how to speak properly? Like little dogs you have gone about from house to house. Why is it that right now when I am enjoying myself and rejoicing, enjoying myself and resting, commemorating the birth of our Mother the eternal Virgin, the Mother of God and our precious Mother? Come Cuauhnahuac, come here and tell me why you are seeking me and why you go about looking for me?

Cuauhnahuac: Mountain-dweller! Cuauhnahuac seeks you. And why indeed am I seeking you, and why indeed a . . . am I looking for you? Now I have come. Why here are you not afraid? I will turn you to earth and dust, and to earth and dust I will reduce you.

Where did you abandon our revered gods? You changed your beliefs thanks to those bad priests, you have sinned. Now I will destroy you. And stout is my heart.

Tepozteco: How is it that right at this time, why is it that right now, you have come here when I am enjoying myself, resting, rejoicing, and commemorating the birth of our Mother, the eternal Virgin, the Mother of God and your precious Mother? Come, Yaotepec, come here and tell me: What disturbs you and why you are seeking me?

Yaotepec: Mountain-dweller! Yaotepec seeks you. Do you fear when you hear of my fame and my words? Now I have come, I come to turn you to earth and dust, and to earth and dust I come to reduce you. Where have you abandoned our revered gods? You have given yourself over to foreigners, to those

[1]A dance/pageant as presented in Nahuatl in the plaza of Tepoztlan, Morelos, in 1977.

bad priests. Now listen. I come to turn you to earth and dust, and to earth and dust I come to reduce you. And I make stout my heart.

Tepozteco: Haven't you seen, and don't you know, and haven't you perceived that here I am encompassed by four strong mountains, seven buttes, my seven ravines, and seven springs? Truly they are there. Very stout of heart am I, and red-blooded am I, and my fame is everywhere heard and praised. You come, Huaxtepec, come here and say what brought you here, and why you are seeking me.

Huaxtepec: Mountain-dweller! Huaxtepec seeks you. Why indeed am I calling you? And why am I seeking you? Now I have come. I come to reduce you to earth and dust, and to earth and dust I will turn you. And to that end I make stout my heart.

Tepozteco: How is it that right at this time, why is it that right now you have come here when I am enjoying myself, rejoicing, resting, commemorating the birth of our Mother, the eternal Virgin? Oh, in truth you live as the blind! You do not recognize that light that comes shining from heaven and instructs the good believers. And now draw near, Tlayacapan, come here and tell me why you disturb me and why you seek me.

Tlayacapan: Mountain-dweller! Tlayacapan seeks you. Now I have come, I come to reduce you to earth and dust, and to earth and dust will I turn you. What do you now fear when you hear of my fame and my words? Where have you abandoned our revered gods? You have given yourself over to foreigners, those bad priests. Know what it is that Tlayacapan desires. He had never lost his vision. You will be destroyed and you will perish. And stout is my heart.

Tepozteco: How is it that right at this time, why is it that right now you have come, when I am enjoying myself, resting, rejoicing, commemorating the eternal Virgin, the Mother of God, and our precious Mother? Do you no longer remember when in the town of Cuauhnahuac [Cuernavaca] you were enjoying yourself and rejoicing when at that time you didn't see me, you ignored me, you disdained me like a black ant, you disdained me like a shadow person, and then I through my strength and my power took from you the marvelous teponaztli and ayacachtli? And now, my reverend elders, come and let us beat the drum to relish and rejoice in the memory of their shameful flight. Let us beat the drum for their shameful flight.

(*music*)

Tepozteco: Now come and fear not. For in all truth you are stout of heart and bold. Come listen to that which with my fame and my words I will declare to you.

Truly exalted is our precious Mother the lady Virgin as says the divine author in the book of the wise. There it is said in the holy songs that twelve stars circle her head and that with the luminous moon her feet are supported, thus over all earth and heaven it spreads forth. Here to earth she came to become the Mother of the Son of God who with the Holy Spirit became the only one true God, through God the Father, God the Son, and God the Holy Spirit; these three reverend personages have become the only one true God. And that child of God came here to earth. He came to deliver us from evil. He came to deliver us from our false beliefs, and those benighted children didn't recognize him, but instead they just mocked him. They despised him, and they took him and put the crown of thorns on his forehead at the time when they went about interrogating him. And they arrived there, there at the place of death on the cross. They pierced his hands and feet and like that he died, and then at the end the earth quaked and it grew dark, the sun was covered and all the world lay down in sleep. And now let us keep well in our hearts the bold words. And like that we will follow the good path there to heaven where there was rejoicing, where there was singing, and where we all will greatly praise our precious Mother forever and ever.

Cuauhnahuac: Now we have comprehended what you have declared; we have been baptized. Truly we have walked in darkness. Truly, truly we have lived in darkness. Now he looks upon us with favor for we live in the right and we will go to dwell within this good faith.

Tepozteco: Oh happy day! May it never, never be forgotten, and let us never more harass one another as good brethren, as good true believers, and let us dance with much rejoicing. And let the hostilities draw to a close.

(*music*)

Frances Karttunen and Gilka Wara Céspedes, *Tlalocan,* vol. IX (1982), pp. 119–27.

The Dance of the Great Conquest

This pageant/play, in which the young prince Cuauhtemoc remonstrates with Motecuhzoma for surrendering to the Spaniards, was presented until the early part of the twentieth century in Xicotepec, a town now known as Villa Juarez, in the state of Puebla.

Entrance of Don Fernando Cortes, Marquis of the Valley, Spanish conqueror.

Great Ruler, King Moctezuma, now is the time. Stand up. The light has come to your kingdom.

Music. A cadence to mark time.

Get out of the darkness. Come now into the light. With it forget [your] doubts.

Same music.

And kneel no longer to your gods. Close now your ears to falsehood. Seek now the truth from the messenger of God, the Father. In the sacraments you will reach His light. Acknowledge at once, Emperor, the renown of the chiefs, the fame of the lords who have arrived in your kingdom.

Know, King Moctezuma, that your fame will grow, that your rule will be praised all over the world.

Draw near, Monarch, Emperor, to the divine Lord, God. Know that He is already calling you.

Become acquainted with His table and with the wafer thereon. . . .

Not only the wafer, but in the wafer you see the precious and honored body of the most holy Jesus Christ.

Music. The wafer on the table.

Be a believer, King Moctezuma. You must not be deceived by the sense of sight in your earthly body. It is not the wafer alone, it is only to signify the fullness and the power of the loaf that first becomes the Precious and honored body of Jesus Christ.

In the wine there is but the Precious and honored blood of Jesus Christ, and believe that the ever-living Christ is in the Host. He alone is in the wine, in this one place, but He is in the Host and the wine.

But there are not two or three Christs. There is only one, always alone.

You must not fall into error. You must not doubt, King Moctezurna. Fortify your knowledge. The holy gospel that comes from Heaven does not lie. And the wafer that shall become your food, know truly that it comes from Heaven.

What is in the blessed wafer you shall not approach with levity. Whoever lightly eats of the wafer, it will be his perdition. Whoever eats thereof in grace, it will become his splendor in the place of everlasting happiness, Heaven.

Now the tune "Santiago" will be beaten, to which the Monarch will dance. Afterwards music will be sung. In the middle he will stand up. Still singing slowly he will proceed until he reaches the place of the throne. He will come slowly.

May your Majesty be seated on your throne. Wait for the Spaniard Don Fernando, who brings the belief, the Holy Catholic Faith.

Now Don Fernando will come. They will stand up on both sides, facing each other. A standard-bearer will bring a blue standard. The little tune "Upwards, Boys" will be beaten. With three silver bugles they will walk around and come to the place. A popular piece will be played to sing and dance to.

Captain Don Fernando Cortes, valiant warrior, you bring the light of the Holy Catholic Faith.

Come into this new land, draw near to this kingdom, the great City called Mexico. There the great Lord, Emperor, King Moctezuma established his throne, his seat of government. Moctezuma went and held sway everywhere in this kingdom of the Indies, for great is his power.

Know you also that he has trampled under foot much property, gold and silver, emeralds; his clothing is like the stars of heaven, the light of Emperor Moctezuma shines like the sun.

Here end the verses of this Conquest and Don Fernando Cortes begins to speak to Emperor Moctezuma.

The owner of this is Don Jose Bernardino, the present prosecutor of the village of Jicotepec, a.d. 1840. *Written in the handwriting of Caledonio Eleuterio.*

A walloon will be played, to which Emperor Motecuzoma, the great Lord and Monarch of this new land named America, will dance and recite.

Don Fernando Cortes will speak: O valiant warrior, Emperor Moctezuma, great Lord and Monarch of this new land named America, let me hear your precious word. With this love, not in war, do I come before your lord viceroys. With this I come before all, for I desire to deserve your loving answer.

Now Moctezuma will speak: Noble Captain, Don Fernando Cortes, Marquis of the Valley, valiant warrior, you who are Lord in Spain, with all love, I rejoice at your precious and honored coming, because you bring light, purity, divine belief, Holy Catholic Faith. O valiant warrior, come into this new land. My holdings, my government I give you. I greet you with my kingdom on account of your good government. Come, draw near to my kingdom here, the great City named Mexico.

Now the First King will speak: With leave of my great ruler, Emperor, I beg permission, I understand Your Majesty, noble Lord, valiant warrior, Don Fernando Cortes, Marquis of the Valley, your fame, your gifts. You shall enter there where the great Lord, Emperor Moctezuma, established his throne, his seat of government.

The Second King will speak: With the permission of my great Lord I am allowed to say that we do not bring war. Very good peace prevails throughout his kingdom of the Indies that Moctezuma has made his own and rules, for great is his power and his valor.

The Third King will speak: And indeed great is his power and great is the strength of my Lord, and in no wise do they equal his dominion. If you were to bring war, were to move your shield, here before us were to remain valiant warriors, for only thus with dust and the Emperor leads them, the Emperor would cry out, whereby would be lost, his subjects, altogether you await this government.

The Fourth King will speak: Dominion, majesty he obtained, he made his own, for our great Lord fears nothing. His fame, his gifts will always exist, for which he will be praised for his austerity. For your fame, your gifts we shall appreciate you. Also know you that the property is great. It is not smooth under foot. Gold and silver, emeralds, the clothing of my Emperor shines like the stars.

Now Moctezuma will speak: Don Fernando Cortes Marquis of the Valley, here you have heard the words of my kings and therefore we answer you what I should have answered you. All my kings have now said it, I have now declared it, for with fair words they have made clear the truth, and I also say clearly that I wish to love you, for you say that it is not dominion, not property and not war. Let me hear it that I may rejoice and that the people I lead may be consoled.

Here Don Fernando Cortes will speak: Great Lord, Monarch, listen to my words. You give me permission, and I am the envoy and the subject of the great Lord, Emperor Charles the Fifth, may God keep him, etc.

My king, a Catholic ruler, there in his kingdom is called the King of Castile and leads cities, subjugated great kingdoms: first, the City of León, secondly the City of Cecilia, and of Jerusalem, of Navarra, of Granada, of Toledo, of Valencia, of Alicia, of Malarkey, of Seville, of Jerdena, of Córdova, of Horcefa, of Murcia, of Jaen, of the Algarbis, and of Algeciras, and all the outlying lands called the Eastern and Western Islands, good and majestic lands, mainlands, besides the Boiling Sea, called Islands of the Great Sea, "en" Duchesses and Archdukes of Austria, of Bargainee, of Bramante, of Millas, of Barcelona, of Biscaya, and Molino, all his kingdoms there in Spain and Germany, and which are held by great rulers, Romans and Italians, tall, active before their king Charles the Fifth. I do not enumerate all his holdings, for it is not possible to name all the great kings who have allied themselves to his crown for great is his power, and now know you also truly that not in war do I come to speak with you for here I come to search, for all alone is what I truly tell you whereby he wishes to make you proud. He does not wish to take any of your kingdom away from you, nor your scepter, nor your crown. No. It is possible you may want to leave him and curse him, for only thus it is necessary that he wants to give it to you, for good is what was not good, what is equal to it.

Moctezuma will speak again: Tell me, Don Fernando Cortes, Marquis of the Valley, what I ask you. Your Catholic King, Charles the Fifth, valiant warrior as you come praising him, and what does he want to take away from me? Set me straight on this.

Now Don Fernando will speak: Hear, Emperor, what he wishes to give you, what will become yours. Nothing else does he ask, neither silver nor gold nor your dominion, No, sit; only that you leave off the worship of stone as God, idolatry; that you believe in the one true God, who is seated and lives in the place of heavenly bliss, three persons, who were rightly made into one essence of divinity, called the Holy Trinity, God the Father, and God the Son, and God the Holy Ghost, who, although they are thus three persons, possess only one divine power and are joined together as one Almighty God. Believe thus also that there are many great miracles, and that they have many praiseworthy mysteries, and that is the divine belief, the Holy Catholic Faith and what is believed in Heaven, and that your gods only deceive you, are only idle creatures, malignant spirits whom God cast out of Heaven, threw into the bottomless pit called Hell, where they suffer forever.

Music called cadence will be sung.

Arise. They bring salvation! Listen to the Holy Gospel.

Moctezuma will speak: Don Fernando, and it is quite true what this miraculous coming out of pity says, and you say that your heart well desires your words on account of the faith in your God, your Lord. With all my heart I receive the divine pouring of water on the head, Holy Baptism. To all whom I lead I thus give my command and my desire.

First King now speaks: For great is the miracle of the order of faith.

The Second King speaks: Quite true. I acknowledge this divine novelty.

The Third King speaks: May what Don Fernando says be done quickly, the belief of the one true God who lives in Heaven.

The Fourth King speaks: Of the purity of the faith in Christianity I knew in my soul.

Music called cadence will be sung.
Line up your children, O chiefs. Tell them the answer of faith.

Moctezuma now speaks: Don Fernando, let instruction begin at once here in my Mexican kingdom. May they tell them and may all whom I lead remember it, for all the great states, provinces, may they teach the great chiefs and thus this miraculous joy, the faith, the apparition of the one true God who lives there in Heaven, thus I gave my great order, decree, may they thus cry out for the belief,the Holy Catholic Faith.
All will say: We all confess and we all believe in the belief, in the Holy Catholic Faith.
Music.
King Moctezuma was converted. He instituted the divine faith.
Now Moctezuma speaks. He talks to Don Fernando, who sits down beside

his royal throne. With dignity he says to him: Sit down, Don Fernando. Be seated. I feel with my heart this marvelous pleasure, this joy of the faith.

Don Fernando replies: I obey your royal command.

Music.

It was commanded that the teaching of the Holy Gospel begin in the empire.

Drum and bugle are played. Now a march is played. Straightway Prince Cuauhtemoc stops in surprise. They line up on both sides, a promenade takes place. He brings a red standard, he comes dancing, Don Fernando and the Monarch advance slowly. They sit down, one on each side. Cuauhtemoc passes to the middle, and music will be chanted.

Music.

One of King Moctezuma's officers, of the name of Cuauhtemoc, opposes the faith.

He persuaded all the chiefs and all the common people here in Mexico: Gentlemen, it will be a bad thing to lose faith in all their gods. It will be better for us to go against the Spaniards who have come here. Let them go home to their country.

Now Prince Cuauhtemoc speaks. Slowly all the instruments become silent, and he waxes very wroth in speaking to Moctezuma.

Cuauhtemoc: Emperor Moctezuma, great Lord Monarch, as you are named here in the land called America. And improperly are you so named, for you no longer ought to wear the crown, for you have lost courage, or you are afraid, for thus you do it. Tell me if you dare to speak to this majestic City! Can you give it to those who are down and out in the country they came from? They come to mock you. All those who come here are second-rate or lost-out Spaniards, who come telling you where in their country there are great cities, talking of another king at the head of the empire of Castile, of the name of Charles the Fifth, of Catholic religion, are only stories, lies. I do not believe in any other books. I feel that their words are only like dreams. You have no courage, but I do, and I'll make war and see his strength that it says, I shall see it and many fearful arts will be practised. Here are flints, arrows, new stones, flints that they will take, those who go out to war, fearful warriors, also Chichimecas, like wild beasts, their anger they are keeping, they are making straight my gods, all of them give me all great knowledge, science. I shall lead them, I shall encourage them, all who are got together, and they will show all the forms of war, armies. You will likewise lose your kingdom, your crown and your scepter you will lose, all the fame that I was maintaining for you, because you gave yourself up. I will search for you in your crown and in your kingdom, and you shall suffer the lost ones here present, the bandits, Spaniards, who have come over here. They come to fool you, for you no longer deserve your dominion. I do deserve it, it belongs to me, because I am strong of heart, valiant. I do not want the honor of our gods to come to naught. You shall see, you shall experience who is the one who calls himself, is named Prince Cuauhtemoc. I have in my hands flame, noise, lightning, embers, smoke, sand, dust, winds, whirlwinds, with which I shall drive them back. If they do not want to die, let them go right back to their country. If they don't, here they shall perish, no matter what you do to prevent it.

Moctezuma replies: It is not like that, the words that you speak and what you say, my dear son, Cuauhtemoc, that I bear. Always I love you, and not war does he bring, only the love of humanity does Don Fernando come specially looking for.

Now Cuauhtemoc draws his sword and all take a turn around. When this is finished, he will come forward, run before Don Fernando and punch him in the face, saying these words to him, Cuauhtemoc will say: Stop. Shut your mouth. My heart is on fire, I am thinking of fighting, war. To arms! to arms! My soldiers. Draw your swords. To arms! to arms!

Moctezuma answers: Don't talk like that, my young son, Prince Cuauhtemoc.

Cuauhtemoc: Hush up. I won't listen. To arms! Let the fight begin!

Now they do it. Cuauhtemoc draws his sword, runs around, attacks Don Fernando.

Cuauhtemoc: Draw your sword, you coward. What are you waiting for?

Don Fernando answers: For the honor of my Emperor I pardon it.

Cuauhtemoc: No longer. Why? Escape from me. Do not speak with fear. Let the fight begin. To arms! to arms!

Don Fernando speaks: Saint James, my soldiers, now is the time for you to show your courage in this fight.

All will say: Let them die, let them die, let them perish.

Now the battle will resound. Now there will be fighting and music, and these verses. . . .

Music.

O Ye angels, heavenly seraphs, all ye virgins, come down to this battle! Come to help them. They signify the divine belief. Come, hurry up!

They and God's captain began to make this battle resound. Like the dust and sand the combatants appeared. They made their swords resound. Out came flames of fire. Their swords struck against one another.

. . . . the stones come out of the slings. O you seraphim! catch them. The believer shall not die.

O angels, dominations, virtues, O you saints, help lead them.

In this battle it does not happen as did Saint Michael there in Heaven when they threw out Lucifer with battle, and all the evil spirits. May thus one speech of yours, "he who believes in God shall be saved," said Saint Michael. Amen.

Saints, seraphim, you inhabitants of Heaven, give them strength.

This will be played by drum and bugles, that they may be emboldened, may they take courage.

Help Don Fernando in this battle. May he be strengthened in the faith. May the bugles sound, may they answer one another, may the cries of the brave believers ring out.

Music will be chanted when the battle is over.

Now you have seen what happened, Emperor. The power of my God is very strong. No one can equal it in divine, beloved and honored strength, for He alone made himself the owner and is the keeper of his creatures, and God our Lord, who is seated as a ruler in the place of joy, the place of bliss, that is called the Kingdom of Heaven, He alone created them.

Moctezuma speaks: Don Fernando, here have I now seen, truly I confess the power of your God who is also my God, and I so confess and believe it.

Music.

There died poor Cuauhtemoc. He went to Hell. His perdition took place because of his blindness.

Moctezuma speaks: And all my children whom I lead may they take his [word] forever! Let them rejoice, let them be happy for this sacred belief, in the remembrance of God. In my heart was formed the love of and the belief in God, in which I shall die and go to Heaven.

Music.

Don Fernando Cortes won, conquered and ruled this kingdom, the City of Mexico.

Moctezuma alone speaks: I am glad, I rejoice in this miraculous passion which Don Fernando receives. Let them say these words with me.

Everybody says: He that has joined us here, may he also join us in the place of bliss, Heaven. Long live Don Fernando!

End of all this conquest.

Byron McAfee, "Dance of the Great Conquest," *Tlalocan*, vol. III, no. 1 (1949), pp. 246–73.

Colonial Literature of
Daily Life

*A*rchives in Mexico, the United States, and Europe contain an un-
expectedly large number of texts written in Nahuatl during the
colonial period in Mexico. In those texts, the memory of quotidian events
in many Nahua communities has been preserved. Although the chief
concern in their composition was not literary, some of them provide a
good look at indigenous life under colonial rule. Among other things, we
find public and personal petitions made to the civil and religious authorities, complaints, suits, land documents, texts of agreements, a great
variety of letters, and wills.

A few items of special interest have been included here: the translation of a letter of petition in Nahuatl to King Philip II from the people
of Huexotzinco, who explain why they feel entitled to their request; an
aggrieved husband's vivid denunciation of a local priest who had sexu-
ally harassed the petitioner's wife during confession; and a curious land
document which provides testimony about the agreement reached by
members of a family after prolonged argument. In this last, the dialogues of the participants are recreated, and finally the happy ending
when "Ana Wept for Joy" as her family was reconciled.

Letters and Proclamations

1. Letter of the Cabildo of Huejotzingo to the King, 1560

Catholic Royal Majesty:
    Our lord sovereign, you the king don Felipe our lord, we bow low in great
reverence to your high dignity, we prostrate and humble ourselves before

you, very high and feared king through omnipotent God, giver of life. We have not deserved to kiss your feet, only from afar we bow down to you, you who are most high and Christian and very pleasing to God our lord, for you are his true representative here on earth, you who govern us and lead us in things of Christianity. All of us creatures and subjects of the life-giving God, we poor vassals and servants of your majesty, we people here, we who dwell here in New Spain, all together we look to you, our spirits go out toward you; we have complete confidence in you in the eyes of our lord God, for he put us in your hands to guard us, and he assigned us to you for us to be your servants and your helpers. By our lord God and by your very honored and very high majesty, remember us, have compassion with us, for very great is the poverty and concern visited on us who dwell here in New Spain.

Our lord sovereign, King don Felipe our lord, through our words we appear and rise before you, we of Huejotzingo who guard for you your city—we citizens, I the governor and we the alcaldes and regidores and we the lords and nobles, your men and your servants. Very humbly we address ourselves to you: Oh unfortunate are we, very great and heavy sadness and concern lie upon us, nowhere do your pity and compassion come to us and reach us, we do not deserve, we do not attain your rulership. And ever since your subjects the Spaniards arrived among us, we have been looking toward you, we have been confidently expecting that sometime your pity would reach us, as we also had confidence in and were awaiting the mercy of your very revered dear father the ruler of the world, don Carlos the late emperor. . . .

Oh unfortunate are we, what is to become of us, we your poor vassals, we of Huejotzingo, we who live in your city? If you were not so far away, many times we would appear before you. Though we greatly wish and desire to reach you and appear before you, we are unable, because we are very poor and do not have what is needed for the journey, things to eat on the boat nor the means to pay people for things in order to be able to reach you. Therefore now we appear before you only through our words; we set before you our poor commoners' words. May you only in your very great Christianity and very revered high majesty attend well to this our prayer.

Our lord sovereign, before anyone told us of or made us acquainted with your fame and your story, most high and feared universal king who rules all, and before we were told or taught the glory and name of our lord God, before the faith reached us, and before we were Christians, when your servants the Spaniards reached us and your captain-general don Hernando Cortés arrived, although we were not yet acquainted with the omnipotent, very compassionate holy Trinity, our lord God the master of heaven and earth caused us to deserve that in his mercy he inspired us so that we took you as our king to belong to you and become your people and your subjects; not a single altepetl surpassed us here in New Spain in that first and earliest we threw ourselves toward you, we gave ourselves to you, and furthermore no one intimidated us, no one forced us into it, but truly God caused us to deserve that voluntarily we adhered to you so that we gladly received the newly arrived Spaniards who reached us here in New Spain, for we left our homes behind to go a great distance to meet them; we went twenty leagues to greet captain-general don Hernando Cortés and the others whom he led. We received them very gladly, we embraced them, we saluted them with many tears. . . .

And when they began their conquest and war making, then also we prepared ourselves well to aid them, for out came all of our arms and insignia, our provisions and all our equipment, and we not merely named someone, we went in person, we who rule, and we took all our nobles and all of our vassals to aid the Spaniards. We helped them not only in warfare, but also we gave them everything they needed; we fed and clothed them, we would go carrying in our arms and on our backs those whom they wounded in war or who were simply very ill, and we did all the tasks in preparing for war. And it was we who worked so that they could conquer the Mexica with boats; we gave them the wood and pitch with which the Spaniards made the boats. And when they conquered the Mexica and all belonging to them, we never abandoned them or left them behind in it. . . .

Our lord sovereign, we also declare and manifest before you that your fathers the twelve children of Saint Francis came to us, whom the very high priestly ruler the Holy Father sent and whom you sent, both granting us the favor that they came to teach us the gospel, to teach us the holy Catholic faith, the belief, to make us acquainted with the single deity God our Lord, and likewise God favored and inspired us, us of Huejotzingo, who dwell in your city, so that we gladly received them. When they entered the altepetl of Huejotzingo, of our own free will we honored them and showed them esteem. When they embraced us so that we would abandon the wicked belief in many gods, we forthwith voluntarily relinquished it; likewise they did us the good deed [of telling us] to despise, destroy, and burn the stones and wood that we worshiped as gods, and we did it; very willingly we destroyed, demolished, and burned the temples.

Also when they gave us the holy gospel, the holy Catholic faith, with very good will and desire we received and grasped it; no one intimidated us into it, no one forced us, but very willingly we seized it, and we quietly and peacefully arranged and ordered among ourselves all the sacraments they gave us. Not once was anyone, whether nobleman or commoner, ever tortured or burned over this, as was done on every hand here in New Spain. People of many altepetl were forced and tortured, were hanged or burned because they did not want to relinquish idolatry, and unwillingly they received the gospel and faith. Especially those Tlaxcalans pushed out and rejected the fathers, and would not receive the faith, for many of the high nobles were burned, and some hanged, for combating the advocacy and service of our lord God. But we of Huejotzingo, we your poor vassals, we never did anything in your harm, always we served you in every command you sent and what at your command we were ordered. . . .

Here is what is happening to us: now your stewards the royal officials and the prosecuting attorney Dr. Maldonado are assessing us a very great tribute to belong to you. The tribute we are to give is 14,800 pesos in money, and an equal number of fanegas of maize.

Our lord sovereign, never has such happened to us in the whole time since your servants and vassals the Spaniards came to us, for your servant don Hernando Cortés, former captain-general, the Marqués del Valle, as long as he lived here among us always greatly cherished us and kept us happy; he never disturbed or agitated us. Although we gave him tribute, he assigned it to us only with moderation; even though we gave him gold, it was only very little; no matter how much, no matter in what way, or if not very pure, he just received it gladly. He never reprimanded us or gave us concern, because it was evident to him and he understood well how very greatly we served and aided him. Also he told us many times that he would speak in our favor before you, that he would help us and inform you of all the ways in which we have aided and served you. And when he went before you, then you confirmed him and were merciful to him, you honored and rewarded him for the way he had served you here in New Spain. But perhaps before you he forgot us. What are we to say? We did not reach you, we were not given audience before you. Who then will speak for us? Unfortunate are we.

Therefore now we place ourselves entirely before you, our sovereign lord. And when you sent your representatives, the Presidente and Bishop don Sebastian Ramirez, and the Audiencia judges, Licentiate Salmerón, Licentiates Ceinos, Quiroga, and Maldonado, they themselves realized and confirmed the orders you gave for us people here, us who live in New Spain. In many things they aided us and lightened the very great tributes we had, and with many things that were our tasks they delivered us from and pardoned us all of it. And we your poor vassals, we of Huejotzingo who dwell in your city, when Licentiate Salmerón came to us and entered the altepetl of Huejotzingo, he saw how troubled the altepetl was with our tribute in gold, sixty pieces that we gave each year. The reason it troubled us is that gold is not gathered here and is not to be found here in our altepetl, though we searched for it everywhere. Then at once Licentiate Salmerón abolished it on your behalf and substituted and exchanged money for it; he set our tribute in money at 2,050 pesos. And ever since he assigned it to us, we have kept doing it; we hasten to give it to you, for we are your subjects and belong to you. We have never neglected it, we have never done it badly, we have given the full amount.

But now we are greatly taken aback and very afraid and we ask, have we done something wrong, have we behaved badly and ill toward you, our lord sovereign, or have we committed some sin against almighty God? Perhaps you have heard something of our wickedness and for that reason now this very great tribute has fallen upon us, seven times exceeding all we had gone along paying before, the 2,000 pesos. And we declare to you that it will not be long before your city of Huejotzingo completely disappears and crumbles, because our fathers, grandfathers, and great-grandfathers knew no tribute and gave tribute to no one, but were independent. We nobles who have charge of your subjects are now truly very poor. Nobility is seen among us no longer. Now we resemble the commoners; as they eat and dress, so do we. We have been very greatly afflicted, and our poverty has reached its culmination. Of the way in which our fathers and grandfathers and great-grandfathers were rich and honored, there is no longer the slightest trace among us.

James Lockhart, *We People Here*, pp. 289–95 (English text only).

2. Olinala—Seduction in the Confessional

This letter of complaint was written in 1595 in Olinala, in the present-day state of of Guerrero.

Most Respected Sir:

I Miguel Hernández, a resident of Chiyauhtzinco, respectfully present myself before you, seeking to bring my petition to you, most respected and reverend sir, Judge don Alonso Roiz, ecclesiastical inspector, who is here in the village of Quamochtitla.

And now I bow before you, I kneel, I go to encounter your lordly hand, because when our priest, Bartolomé López, was hearing my wife's confession, he was not confessing her, he was provoking her to sin.

He told her: "My child, you must leave your husband alone for the night."

My wife then told him: "Father, how shall I leave him? He is a fierce man!"

But he then told her: "My child, do not be afraid that he will do something to you, because of what he could find out about you. Really, if you chance to come with me, I will give you a few coins and your blouse and your skirts. And if he, your husband, mistreats you, bothers you, I will immediately put you in the care of my family in Cuetlachcoapan (the city of Puebla). In truth, you will be happy there with them."

But then my wife told him: "Father, he will look for me there, because my husband is a fierce man."

[He answered:] "My child, don't upset yourself, because then I would have to beat your husband, so don't upset yourself."

But, you, sir, you, our revered priest, if you do not watch over us here, with him so close, how will I hold on to [my wife]? If you do not make him leave the village, how will I hold on to her, with him so nearby?

It is six years since he (Father Bartolomé Lopéz) began to incite her to sin with him. It is two years since he whipped my woman, because she did not consent.

But my reverend sir priest, you, the one who does not wish to be praised, the one who said, when he was hearing the confession of the people there beside the altar, "Son, my cane may be raised for punishment, but do not be afraid . . . I am truly a friend to the decent people of the village.

"Am I perhaps being arrogant, because I do not have curly hair?[1] I am simply your friend."

Thus, I say just to you: I beg you, noble sir, governor, that you apply your justice, because he [Bartolomé López] has caused great distress to us, the men of the village. Take pity on us, for this is why you have come, you have come to help us. And so before you I plead for justice.

(signed) Miguel Hernández

Tlalocan, vol. VII (1977), pp. 23–30; Spanish translation, Miguel León-Portilla; English version, Sylvia and Earl Shorris.

3. A *Nahuatl Journal* by a Zapotec Princess, 1525

I, the Noblewoman of the Zapotec, went to ask the Great Ruler of the Children of the Sun named Cortés about the people who make war on me and my children, and want to steal my land. It is true that I went before our Great Ruler of the Children of the Sun named Cortés, and asked him to assist me by sending his people against the Mixtec people.

When our Great Ruler of the Children of the Sun named Cortés heard our request, he sent seven of his children, who perished. The second time he sent four more, who helped me. It is true that the Mexican people know of my story. It is true that I gave them and their children a place to settle, so that no one would make war on their children. Thus I advised the Mexican people to write on paper exactly how it was given to them, because they won it. The Mixtec people who waged war on me surrendered because the Mexican people defeated them. It is true that they surrendered, for the Mexican

[1] Probably referring to people of African descent.

people will tell you in stories how they were given a place for their children to settle.

It is true that when these people helped us, we asked if they would settle next to us. It is true that we left them with that, and now they have their property. They won it and have settled on the land called Acatepetl. As to how they won it, the Children of the Sun know how they came bearing log drums, shields, obsidian-blade clubs, and arrows. It was done joyously through war. They were recognized as the truly famous Mexicans.

It is true that the Mixtecs killed my children and ate them. Likewise, my children who encountered these Mixtec cannibals were beheaded. I went to the Children of the Sun and asked them to help me. Thus, the Mexican people know it and will tell others in stories what happened to us.

First, the leaders requested it. I, Tlacahuepantzin, along with my brother, Tonalyeyecatzin, and my two cousins, Chimalpopoca and Axayacatzin, conferred as to how we would go to ask our Great Ruler of the Children of the Sun, and how the Noblewoman of the Zapotec came to request that he send his children to help her. He sent seven, of which three were eaten and four others perished. Therefore, we went before the Ruler of the Children of the Sun Cortés and all four of us requested that he send us, for we dared to wage war on the Mixtec people.

The Ruler of the Children of the Sun responded: How will it be possible to wage war with just four when seven have perished? We answered him that we four would win it through war. The Ruler of the Children of the Sun asked us to demonstrate how we would be able to do it. We joyously consented to stage a mock battle in the presence of the Ruler of the Children of the Sun.

He ordered us: Enter the fortress and wage war. We entered with log drums, wielding shields, obsidian-blade clubs and arrows and wearing stone sandals. We went in and sought the approval of our Great Ruler of the Children of the Sun. He responded that perhaps what we assembled was good enough, perhaps it would be enough to engage them in battle. We responded: Good. Then he said to us: If you do it joyfully, perhaps you will truly win land for your children. Then we staged the mock battle and advised the Ruler of the Children of the Sun not to be frightened by our actions.

He said: I will not be frightened. And then we started to play with shields, obsidian-blade clubs and arrows. The Ruler of the Children of the Sun said: That's enough, it is true that they will win the land. He truly believed it, so he sent us.

First, the four of us left and arrived in the Mixteca, where we won a little land for our children. Then we four emerged and went to war. We and the Noblewoman of the Zapotec enriched ourselves. We reached Totoltepetl, where our log drums sounded. The Mixtec people heard it. They asked: What's that sound? They were told that the Mexican people had arrived.

The Mixtecs asked: What are they looking for? Let's go see. So they came to ask us the Mexican people why we came and what we sought. We responded that we came to see our land next to the Zapotec, and to see who is fighting with them and wants to steal our land.

Then they replied: We are the Mixtec. What do you want, war?

We responded: War it will be. Then they instructed us where and which day to meet them, so that we could play.

We flew to the hill near the place called Mexicatepelyan, where we beat the log drums. They heard the war song and assembled. Then, on both sides, the war leaders summoned the women and children. When they came to where we were, we started the battle. The wind blew and the earth moved, and they were killed.

We withdrew only when the Mixtec people said: Let it be, for you are truly the famous Mexican people. We will give you a place where your children can settle. Then they gave us our land, up to where it now ends. They gave it to us. We responded how we and the Zapotec people would settle once and for all.

Then the Mixtec people said: It will not be possible. Let the Zapotec stay next to us and we will give you another place to settle. Then they replied to us: It will be all right after all. We left and consulted with the Ruler of the Mixtec people in order to live as brothers, so that we would not kill each other. Then we said: Let it be done. Let them also give us a place to wait for our children to settle. We will not turn back; we will await our children. Never again will there be war. Then they gave us a place to settle called Acatepetl, where the four of us went and waited for our children to come.

It is true that we went to rest near the hill called Huaxacatzin. Also, the Spaniards sat down and rested. It was there that they first sought to fight us. We climbed up Acatepec where we met those who had won the land.

Cortés rebuked us: Who would kill us and who wants to make us slaves? At that very moment we raised the water through a reed from below the ground. Cortés saw how nobody dared to kill us. Then he said: Let there be no more war. Let us live as brothers. We shall settle beside the Mexicans, as brothers.

But the Spaniards were angry that we raised the water over the hill. They began to fight us with great strength until we, the Mexican people, defeated the Children of the Sun. Then they said: That is enough, let it be. You are truly the famous Mexican people, Cortés declared.

We believe in the true ruler God. Like the Spaniards, we died in battle and we sought war.

We captured two blacks.
Like the Spaniards, we won it with war and gunpowder.

We three rulers decreed it: first, the Ruler of the Marquesado, don Fabian de Cervantes; the Ruler of San Martín Mexicapan, don Francisco de los Angeles Vásquez; and the Ruler of Xochimilco, don Marcos de los Angeles. It is true that once and for all we decreed as God ordered, along with the King, as to how an alguacil mayor and an alguacil would be responsible for three places: Xochimilco, San Martin and the Marquesado. It is his duty to patrol, and to punish and jail those who are bad each Thursday. It will be his duty to respect us and serve us food and provide us with drink on every single Thursday. In this manner we established our cabildo. It is true that this way that it is done must never stop. It will always be the alguacil mayor alone who will keep a record of all borders that stop at places with crosses, and with his account he will shed light on the painting. Then he will serve food and provide people with drink, and the people of San Pedro and San Jacinto will notify him of what he should bring. They will bring a little honey that is necessary. Thus it will be done as obliged.

These are all of our orders that we three have set forth for our children and grandchildren to keep forever. This "original conquest" will be in their hands. We three provide our signatures in this altepetl cabecera. We three witnessed our written document. I am the tlatoani of this altepetl of San Martin [in] the year of 1525.

[signed]
don Fabian de Cervantes y Velásquez
don Francisco de los Angeles Vásquez
don Marcos de los Angeles

Lisa Sousa and Kevin Terracino, *UCLA Historical Journal*, vol. 12, no. 43 (1992).

4. Proclamation by don Carlos María Bustamante, 1820— The Malinche of the Constitution[2]

Indians of this world, whose native language is Mexican, and who do not understand nor even know of Spanish except for those words commonly used

[2]This work was almost certainly written first in Spanish, since Bustamante did not know Nahuatl, then translated by a Nahua from the *altiplano* who may have been in prison with Bustamante. The Nahuatl text was translated into Spanish by Horcasitas.

in our wretched commerce, do you know what the Constitution means? You do not know, nor will you ever know if we do not explain it to you in your language.

Listen, then, to something worth knowing, while these things are being established, and you will learn from the experience. Know that you are free of the hardship of the bosses of the haciendas, who make you work from the time the sun came up until it went in, at the end of a whip, not giving you the freedom of straightening up your bodies to take nourishment, without having the whip over you; since they valued more a bunch of wheat that they left uncut in that moment than a hope of his fellow man. What a horror! When these despots treat you this way time and again, run to your judges and shout: Constitution! Constitution! You are no longer servants or any man's slave, you have your country, and you are not subjects of those bosses who make you work on their lands, or fish in their lakes, as it happened on the Hacienda Atengo; in the name of your loved ones, stand up for yourselves to these bosses, for the unhappy fisherman will spend the night on the lake fishing for what the bosses enjoy and not for his loved ones.

Your happiness is in yourselves: in the election of mayors, councilmen, and the others who today have to govern you, look carefully in your villages at those that are more honest men, who have no vices; those who are able to read, and are less ignorant, who will enlighten you, and comply with what is ordered by constitutional law, explaining Article 18 so that you do not permit yourselves to be denigrated by such names as wild indians, darkies, and others invented by despotism.

We are all Spaniards, and you have every right to public employment, like the whites; but see to it that this is viewed as being virtuous and just, and likewise detest the drunkenness that degrades you; be ashamed of having been derided by the others because of this vice, by the disrespect they have shown you, even to thinking of you as brutes. I know well that you are not: that you have an inborn philosophy like other men: and that you know all of the phenomena and meteors of nature by their proper names, and that you are not unaware of their causes: but your constant labor never allows you the opportunity to think that you are rational beings. To separate yourselves more from this labor, go to the schools; teach yourselves your religion and your rights; send your children, so that they do not experience the same fate: that they learn to read, so they will know the great benefit of knowing the Constitution, and they can demand observance of it whenever necessary. If in one of your villages you do not have a school, demand of your priests and municipal administrations that they put one there, because the Constitution mandates it. Do not let them offend your persons, agreeing that they cut your sidelocks, horns, or what they call boats: this is despicable, and is based in the arbitrary and degrading way they have treated you. Take pleasure in what nature has given you, and do not let them shear you like sheep. You should not be dragged to pillories or prisons for small or trifling infractions. The old refrain of twenty-five lashes or a fine of twenty-five pesos because they found you staggering from drink is finished. Do not let the subdelegates drag a hundred pesos out of you for a license to bring your dances to the sanctuaries of Chalma or Guadalupe, because they are horrified by your primitive jumps with which you please your God; it cost you a lot to go from house to house in your villages, collecting from the poor residents, whom they deprive of the necessary sustenance, to deliver the amount to satisfy the thirst of your oppressors.

Come on, my unhappy fellow citizens! open your eyes: take the advice that is given in your own language by those who have seen your miseries with their own eyes: examine, question, and do not rest until you know everything that favors you in the new code; because knowing it, you will be able to protest the abuses that you suffer to your municipalities and provincial councils, for they cannot remedy what they are not aware of.

Lighten your hearts and give thanks to the Eternal: ask for the success of the National Congress, and the good King Ferdinand, who has dispensed with the preoccupations of his forbears to bring happiness to all his children.

Fernando Horcasitas, *Estudios de Cultura Nahuatl,* vol. VIII (1969), pp. 271–78; English translation, Sylvia and Earl Shorris.

Official Texts

1. *"And Ana Wept"—A Land Document*

Ana spoke and said to her older brother Juan Miguel, "My dear older brother, let us be under your roof for a few days—only a few days. I don't have many children, only my little Juan, the only child. There are only three of us with your brother-in-law Juan."

Then her older brother said, "Very well, my younger sister. Move what you have, let all your things be brought up."

Then the woman answered and said, "Thank you very much, my dear older brother, I appreciate your generosity. Even if I should get intoxicated, I declare that I will never act badly in your house, but behave respectfully, and as to my husband Juan here, if he should ever lose respect, well, you are all there, I leave it in your hands as long as you hold the king's staff (are members of the town government)."

Then Juan Miguel spoke and said to his younger sister Ana, "My younger sister, am I going to pick arguments with my brother-in-law, if he goes along behaving himself?"

Now it is far into October, the 20th of the month, and they have spent a whole month here now.

Then Ana said, "Don't let us give you so much trouble; let us take a bit of the precious land of our precious father the saint San Miguel, and there we will build a little house. When the water has gone down and things have dried out, we'll move down."

Then her older brother said, "Let me tell Juan Francisco, and Juan Miguel of Pelaxtitlan, and also Francisco Baltasar, and also Antón Miguel of Teopanquiahuac. Don't worry, younger sister, they will not want . . . Let me go get them right away, and you be making a tortilla or two. There's nothing for you to worry about; there's pulque for them to drink when they come."

Then he went to get them. Then he said to his younger sister, "We're already back, younger sister; come greet us."

Then the four men said, "May God keep you, and how have you been today? Here we are."

Then Ana said, "Do come in."

Then they all came in and sat down.

Then Ana spoke and said to her older brother, "Give them some tortillas, let them enjoy them."

Then the elders answered, "Let us enjoy your hospitality. And is there something that concerns you, lady?"

Then Ana said, "In a moment you will hear what it is that concerns us."

And when they had eaten, Ana came in and addressed herself to them, saying to them, "I have summoned you for a negligible matter. Here is what we beg, that we might apply for a bit of the land of our precious father the saint San Miguel, for we want to put up a hut there. I don't have many children; the only one I have is little Juan alone. May we?"

Then Juan Francisco said, "Let it be given them. What do you say? Let's give it to them! Juan Miguel, take your cattle prod . . . to measure it with. Let's go, lady, and see where you wish it to be."

Then they went. "Where do you wish it to be? Here, or maybe over there? Say where you wish it to be."

Then the woman said, "Let it be here."

Then the lords said, "Then let it be there."

Then Juan Francisco said, "Who is going to measure it out?"

Then the lords said, "Who indeed? Other times, wasn't it good old Juan? He'll measure it out."

Then they said to him, "Come, good Juan, take the cattle prod in your hands and measure it out. Measure out six lengths on all four sides."

And when he had measured it, then they said, "That's how much land we're giving you."

Then Ana said, "Thank you very much; we appreciate your generosity."

Then the rulers said, "Let it begin right away; don't let the stone concern you, but let it quickly be prepared to begin the foundation."

Then Ana said, "Let's go back and you must enjoy a bit more pulque."

Then the rulers said, "What more do we wish? We've already had (enough)."

And Ana wept, and her husband wept, when they were given the land.

Then Ana said, "Candles will be burnt, and I will go along providing incense for my precious father the saint San Miguel, because it is on his land that I am building my house."

Then Juan Miguel said, "We thank you on behalf of your precious father; let it always be so, not. . . ."

When all five lords had spoken, everyone embraced.

Today, Friday, the (20th?) day of the month of October of the year 1583. I did the writing and it was done before me, don Juan Bautista, notary. The rulers convened here in Amaxocotitlan.

Don Juan Miguel, regidor. Don Baltasar Francisco. Don Juan Francisco. Don Juan Miguel of Pelaxtitlan. Don Antonio Miguel of Teopanquiahuac.

James Lockhart, *Nahuas and Spaniards* (Stanford, CA: UCLA Latin American Center Publications, 1991), pp. 70–74.

2. Sula Title—A Land Document and Mythohistoric Tale

Here will be seen and declared how the Mexica, before they settled the site of Mexico City, came to Sula, and they did not permit these Tenochca or Mexica, who are called Tenochtitlan people, to settle. They were walking along and came to Sula, and [the Sula people] came out to meet them, and they could not halt there. The Mexica came along the highway with trumpet and banner, and the people of Sula came there to meet them so that they would not take away their rule; those of Sula came to the defense of their town.

Then one called Aza Persia came shouting, saying, "My lords, you here of Sula, let us make a halt here, for we are very tired and have come walking a very long way."

And then Martin Molcatzin, the Çolteuctli, answered and said, and they said to Martin Huitzcol [sic], "I and all those who are here are the dwellers of this town, and so you can go ahead, for you cannot halt here."

These two Martins who are named here are two brothers, one called Martin Molcatzin and the other Martin Huitzcol, and they said, "Lady Ana Garcia, we are from here and we are sons of the ancients; we were born in this valley and our grandfathers and grandmothers are from here; they came from nowhere else, and they are those of the ancient time (for their ancestors were pagans). And you, where do you come from? Perhaps you have been exiled from somewhere. Go on with you, we have our questionnaires. Just go ahead and take the highway which begins at our border. . . . [here a short recital of borders and measurements] And know and understand that it is not far to where you are to go; you come from a lake, and now you are very close to another lake there ahead. It could be that there would be a place for you there and you would find what you desire. You are already close to the place and they might admit you there. And so have a good trip, you are very close to a town where they might admit you and give you some place."

And when they heard what they told them, they all went away, and Ana María [sic] and her daughter called Juana Garcia began to shout, saying "Señor, señor, you have these lands; señor Çolteuctli, we have heard what you said."

Well, my very beloved sons, I will now tell you and declare that God our lord saw fit to create him whom they call Çolteuctli, who is Martin Molcatzin, who turned himself into a serpent in the manner of a quail. The Mexica, whom they call the people of inside the water, were leaving, and got to the borders of Sula, and just where the border of the people of Sula is, they found a very large and frightful serpent in the fashion of a quail, as to its feathers, and for this reason they called it Çolcoatl [Quail-serpent], and it was all spread out there and frightful. And the Mexica were greatly taken aback, for never had they seen a serpent like that, so they were very frightened, and they went away and the people of Sula were left very content. Because if the Mexica had stayed, they would have ruled the land which the people of Sula possessed, which their ancestors and grandparents left them and which they are still possessing now.

My beloved sons, what we say here occurred this way, and understand it very well. This Martin Huitzcol wanted to feed them, and they were going to give them what they call in their language maçatl ynenepiltzin [deer tongue], which are a kind of small nopal cactus, and they were going to give them what they call tlanquaxoloch [wrinkled knee], which are beans, and as a third food they were going to give them what they call cuentla ococolmic [what has died off in the field], which are squash, and also what they call cempolihuini centlamini [what entirely disappears and ends], which is amaranth seed, and what is to be sprinkled on top of the food, what they say is pointing toward the ground, which is green chile; and they were going to give them quahuitl yxpillotl [what looks down from the tree], which are avocados—this is what they were going to give them last of all. But the older brother, who is Martin Molcatzin, did not want it to be; if they had fed them there, they would have stayed there and not gone away. God our lord orders everything, and so all the food was left behind.

James Lockhart, *Nahuas and Spaniards,* pp. 49–51.

❂ 10 ❂

Modern Nahua Literature

*D*uring the nineteenth century and the early years of the twentieth
century, Nahua literature was reduced to local recitations of songs
and narrations by members of scattered communities in central Mexico
and other regions where the Nahua presence had managed to survive. It
fell to ethnographers, linguists, and folklorists to identify the spontaneous preservers of these works. Thanks to the transcriptions they made,
we know some of these voices.

It was not until the 1970s that a Nahua Yancuic Tlahtolli, "New
Nahua Word," began to be heard. Here and there in Nahua villages and
a few urban centers, some men and women who had kept alive the language of Nezahualcoyotl and fought for the preservation of indigenous
cultural identity felt that they could and should become writers.

Mariano Jacobo Rojas (1842–1936), a native of Tepoztlan in the
state of Morelos, was among the forerunners of the New Nahua Word.
He devoted his life to the preservation of Nahuatl and to fostering literary work in that language. In addition to publishing a grammar, he
wrote a play, Jewel, in Nahuatl.

Pedro Barra Valenzuela (1894–1978) from Chicontepec, Vera Cruz,
wrote Nahuaxochimilli, "A Nahua Garden," in which, with great sensi-
tivity, the poet serenades the exuberant flora and fauna of his homeland.

Luz Jiménez (c. 1895–1965) was born in the delegacion (a political entity within the Federal District of Mexico) of Milpa Alta, where
many Nahuas live. She lived through the Zapatista rebellion of the Revolution of 1910, and later dictated an oral history of her experiences to
the anthropologist Fernando Horcasitas. The best known portions of her
oral history, Life and Death in Milpa Alta: A Náhuatl Chronicle of
Díaz and Zapata (edited by Horcasitas in 1972), and the Cuentos de
Doña Luz Jiménez are included here.

Natalio Hernández Xocoyotzin, a Nahua teacher born in Naranja Dulce, Veracruz, has fought ardently for the survival of Nahuatl and other indigenous languages of Mexico. Among other things, he founded the Association of Writers in Indian Languages, and more recently, the House of Indigenous Writers, supported by the Mexican secretary of education and UNESCO. A brilliant poet himself, he has published several collections.

A comprehensive list of contemporary Nahua writers would include many other names. Suffice it to recall here those of the poets Delfino Hernández, brother of Natalio; Alfredo Ramírez of Xalitla, Guerrero; Jose Antonio Xochime of Santa Ana Tlacotenco in the Federal District; and Joel Hernández of Veracruz.

In addition to the work of Luz Jiménez, modern prose works here come from Miguel Barrios (1905–1960), prolific author and publisher of a journal in Nahuatl, Mexihcatl Itonalama (The Mexican Paper). Born in Hueyapan, Morelos, Barrios determined as a youth to dedicate himself to writing in his mother tongue and helping others to do the same. He assisted the American anthropologist Robert H. Barlow in preparing Spanish translations of several ancient Nahuatl texts, and published his own stories in the journal he edited.

Carlos López Avila (1928–1994), also working with anthropologists and linguists, did his best to maintain the Nahuatl language of Santa Ana Tlacotenco, where he was born, compiling both traditional songs and stories.

Two more teachers of the New Nahua Word deserve special mention here. Librado Silva Galeana and Francisco Morales Baranda were both born in the 1940s in Santa Ana Tlacotenco. After completing their professional studies as primary and secondary schoolteachers in the public schools, they were deeply attracted to their traditional culture and the cultivation of their own language. As participants in the Seminar on Nahuatl Culture at the National University of Mexico, they have made significant achievements. Silva Galeana, who is notable for his mastery of Nahuatl, both classical and contemporary, is the author of stories in which he recreates the daily lives of his people. He has also translated a sixteenth-century collection of huehuehtlahtolli. Francisco Morales Baranda has produced beautiful original work in Nahuatl—both prose and poetry—as well as translations of Nahuatl poetry into Spanish.

These and other contemporary Nahua authors, working today in many literary forms in many parts of Mexico, also organize literary congresses and competitions. They are indeed the hope of the language, the mothers and fathers of its limitless future.

1. The Poet

When the poet was born, his father said, "You have a big mouth, you will be a real crybaby."

The mother answered, "It is not certain. My son will have happy days, he will have a pleasant mission."

He was still very small when he began to get around. He loved everything in the world. He was never in a hurry. His mind, his heart and his feet were on solid ground. He asked often where strength and power came from. When rain and storms came, he stayed in the front of his house to see how the trees were torn loose by the wind, because they did not have firm roots. In the evenings he liked to watch the sky, from which the moon sent her light to mother earth, because at night father sun was absent.

Every day when the poet woke up, he greeted the sun with words straight from the heart. He spoke this way: "Father, my heart greets you on this new morning. Thank you for chasing away the darkness; you know well that darkness is the hiding place of those who have twisted hearts and do bad deeds. Now I can see the path where I will go today without stumbling. Thank you, Father, for yesterday the little flowers were in bloom, and now, with your warmth and protection they can discover your face, because the cold has gone to dwell in other places. My father, I do not want to distract you on your journey, I know that in other directions other children are also waiting for you, I want only to ask that you do not abandon me: be with me wherever you are, guard my spirit and my energy. Send me strength so that my life and my works can flourish."

Time passed quickly. Gray hair covered the head of the poet.

One day two beautiful hummingbirds came to his house and spoke to him this way: "Our father, the sun has sent us, we come to put your heart in harmony, because the shield of your time has stopped turning, your light has been put out, all roads arrive at this place, your life is coming close to its end. You must prepare for the outcome. Don't be sad, this is the way of all the things of the earth: they are passengers; it is like sleeping and waking, only a little while here and nothing more."

Having said this, the hummingbirds conversed with his heart, with respect, they applauded the poet and they wanted to cry, but the poet consoled them, telling them:

"Do not weep, brother hummingbirds, to be sure, we are passengers. But our words bloom forever in the hearts of the men who come after us."

A little while later, three hummingbirds flew by and were lost in the mirroring blue of the sky.

Delfino Hernández Hernández, *In Yancuic Nahuatl Zazanilli* (*New Nahuatl Tales*) (Mexico City: UNAM Instituto de Investigaciones Históricos, 1985); English translation, Sylvia and Earl Shorris.

2. Life and Death in Milpa Alta

THE MEN OF THE SOUTH

The heavens did not thunder to warn us that the tempest was coming. We knew nothing about the storms nor about the owlish wickedness of men.

One day gunfire was heard between the hills of Teuhtli and Cuauhtzin. We were told that it was the Federals fighting against the men of Morelos. There was a lot of shooting. It was the first time we had heard such a thing, and all of Milpa Alta trembled.

The men of Morelos kept passing through the village, and it was said they were on their way to Xochimilco. I do not know why they were against Porfirio Díaz.

These men from Cuernavaca and Tepoztlan spoke our language. They were only peasants, and we did not know why the Federals were afraid of them.

This was the first thing we heard of the Revolution. One day a great man by the name of Zapata arrived from Morelos. He wore good clothes—a fine broad hat and spats. He was the first great man to speak to us in Nahuatl. All his men were dressed in white—white shirts, white pants, and they all wore sandals. All these men spoke Nahuatl more or less as we spoke it. Señor Zapata also spoke Nahuatl. When all these men entered Milpa Alta, we understood what they said. Each of the Zapatistas carried pinned to his hat a picture of his favorite saint, so that the saint would protect him. Each bore a saint in his hat.

Zapata stood at the head of his men and addressed the people of Milpa Alta in the following way: "Come join me! I have risen in arms, and I have brought my countrymen with me. We don't want Our Father Díaz to watch over us any more. We want a better president to care for us. Join the Revolution with us since we are tired of the few cents the rich pay us. There isn't enough to eat or to buy clothes. I want every man to have his own plot of land. He will sow it and reap corn, beans, and other grains. What do you people say? Will you join us?"

Nobody answered. The days passed. The barracks of Zapata and Everardo González were set up in the village. González was told to stay in Milpa Alta to watch over the village.

General Zapata was received in the following way. Everyone in the village went out to receive him. Crowds of men and women came with flowers in their hands. A band played and fireworks burst; and when he had entered, the band played the *diana*.

Several months went by, and Our Father Porfirio Díaz and the Secretary Justo Sierra were not worried about the Revolution. Their great passion was the Mexican people. Wherever there were four children, they were given clothing. Girls were given a blouse and a skirt, and boys were given a shirt and trousers.

Perhaps Señores Díaz and Sierra believe this: "Fathers and mothers will thus learn how to give an education their children. They will send them to school."

The hopes of these great men were fulfilled, and everybody in the village obeyed them.

ZAPATA'S LIEUTENANT

Don Everardo was the general Zapata left in charge of the village. Everyone was to give him—free—tortillas, water, and fodder for the horses and mules. Each district of Milpa Alta had to carry these things to the soldiers' quarters, and all obeyed. Morning and afternoon people took food to the men of Zapata and to their animals. It was about that time that the Zapatistas kidnapped Don Abrán Monterola, and it was never discovered whether they murdered him or not. Another man, Juan Bastida, also disappeared. We never found out what became of them.

This man Everardo summoned the rich to him saying, "You are going to give us money. If you don't we will kill you."

I had an uncle who told me about the way Don Everardo talked to him. "You'll give us money, or we'll chop off your head."

"I have no money," my uncle answered, "and my wife and children have gone up to Tepoztlan."

"I am not going to kill you," Don Everardo said, "because you have spoken the truth."

My mother also went to beg Don Everardo not to kill him because he was a man with many children. So Don Everardo did not kill my uncle Regino. At that time, a general had been killed. His men went to tell Don Evarardo that the general was lying on the ground. Don Everardo ordered my uncle to keep vigil over the corpse of the general, who still wore his gold watch. "If anyone steals that watch," my uncle was told, "you will die!" And so it was that my uncle had to stay up all night with the body of the general.

One day the Zapatistas came down and burned the town hall, the courthouse, and several homes. One of these houses belonged to a rich man by the name of Luis Sevilla.

His house was burned to the ground. It was enough to break your heart to hear the bursting of the grains of corn and the beans. All his domestic animals died in the burning of that house. The next day, the Zapatistas came down again to the village and forced our men to take fodder and water to their horses. All of these things were caused by the Zapatistas.

When the men of Zapata entered the town, they came to kill. They killed the rich because they asked for large amounts of money which the rich were not willing to give up. Then they would take the rich men to the woods and murder them there. They also carried off girls. People said that they took them to the woods and raped them there. These maidens were abandoned forever in the woods, never to return to their homes. No one knew whether they were devoured by wild animals or whether the Zapatistas murdered and buried them there.

THE TEMPEST

It was around then that people speaking Otomí and Zapotec began to enter Milpa Alta. Women accompanied their husbands. These men came with the Zapatistas. They spoke what is called Otomí, and some of the women spoke Zapotec. They called the *tlaxcalli* (tortilla) "chúzcuta." New languages were heard, but I did not understand any of them. Different tongues were spoken in the village when the men of Zapata were there. We could hear them talking. They talked among themselves, but only God Our Lord knows what they were talking about.

These Otomí women and their husbands had come with the forces of Zapata. They lived a life of their own in the village. Men and women would load their pots and children on their backs and take off for the woods to pick ocote pine roots. It can be said that they were the ones who taught us the proper use of the root of the ocote pine. The men carried their shotguns since they came with the troops of Zapata. They shot rabbits and their women went to sell them in the city of Mexico. The Otomí were very good at that sort of thing.

They also carried fruit, green chile, and onions to sell in the city of Mexico. In those times, the people of Milpa Alta were not [good] as traders. The people of the village were shy.

These Otomí women used to put on their blouses, their wrap-around skirts, and their *quechquemitls* and used to go off to buy and sell in the market place. They twisted their rebozos into rings and placed them around their heads. These rings gave them shade.

It was at this time that the men of Zapata came in, through the village of Amilco. Bombs and machine guns burst, and our two schools were destroyed. When these two buildings collapsed, many federal soldiers were buried in their ruins. One of the schools was called Concepción Arenal, and I do not remember the name of the boys' school. The federal soldiers were crushed to death, together with their camp followers, in my school—in the same classroom where I had learned so many things.

My home was also burned down by Zapata because I lived next to the barracks of the federals. The Zapatistas were killing federals until their corpses were like pebbles scattered on the ground.

If we wished to walk in the street, we had to walk over corpses. Many of the villagers were killed since the firing was done with little aim. A girl, standing on the roof of her house, was hit by a bullet and died a little while later. Many other people were slain in the same way.

Not a single federal soldier was left in the streets of Milpa Alta. By this time, Zapata's men had taken hold of the hill of the Teuhtli. The federals had fled towards San Gregorio and Xochimilco, not stopping until they reached Churubusco.

At that time, no one dreamed of the coming of [Venustiano] Carranza's troops.

I was fourteen years old and was frightened—as were all the people of the village—by the gunfire. The Zapatistas were scattered about the hills of Teuhtli, Tijeras, Ocpayoca. The federals were living in the village of Milpa Alta. These men were called federals at the time that Porfirio Díaz ruled.

So it was that from these three mountains the men of Zapata surrounded the federals. They chased them into the woods. Some fled towards San Pablo Oztotepec. They reached the mountain called Cuauhtzin. But there many Zapatistas had gathered. They were hidden among the hills. When they saw the federal soldiers going by, Zapata's men began to shoot. This was the end of the federals—and they were many. Three or four federal soldiers managed to get away. They reached Milpa Alta. And by that time a reinforcement had arrived from the Capital.

It was rumored in the village that Zapata's men were gathering again to provoke the federals. There was a lot of gunfire, and bullets were answered by bullets. Thus passed three of four months. They were only scaring us!

THE MEN OF THE NORTH

If you only knew, professor, all the things that happened to us when Zapata abandoned us! The people of the village will never forgive him for leaving us in the hands of the enemy. Strangers began to arrive, men wearing earrings. One wore a large golden ring in his nose. They spoke Spanish, I think, but we could hardly understand a word they said. They spoke with thick, brutish accents. They were the men of Carranza!

When the Carrancistas invaded our lands, the shooting began again, this time between the men of Carranza and Zapata. Zapata's men were forced to flee into the woods, all the way up the path towards Santa Ana and San Lorenzo. Their flight was like a forest fire, but there were no dead on either side.

The only dead were the people of the village, those who had gotten up early to work in the fields. Those were the ones who died. A man who had gone to get aguamiel from his maguey plants, another who had gone to the woods to gather herbs, a wood-cutter—those were the ones whom death caught on the road!

At the beginning, these Carrancistas seemed to be nice men. They talked to the people of the village and knocked at the doors of the houses. When we came out, they would say, "That's the way we like it! Don't run away from the village. Stay in your houses. If you stay here, you will be safe." And no one ran away from the village.

But later we found out that the Carrancistas were owls. They were devils. They were capable of doing all sorts of evil things. They went into the houses. They stole our chickens, pigs, and food. If they caught us eating, they carried away all the food, together with the tortillas and dishes, leaving us without anything to eat. They would even grab a broken pot and stick it into their pockets. If a man or woman happened to be wearing good clothes, they were stripped on the spot.

It was then that the men of Zapata fled again to the mountains, leaving our lands in the hands of the Carrancistas. But at nine o'clock one night, the Zapatistas came down again and chased the Carrancistas out. The Carrancistas fled as far as San Gregorio Atlapulco and Xochimilco. They stayed there for some time. Carranza's men would attack the village, and those of Zapata fought back with many bullets.

Carranza and the troops of Amaro kept their headquarters in Milpa Alta. One of the streets got to be nicknamed "The Backbone of the Devil." This street lay in the direction of the Teuhtli, where the men of Carranza and Zapata fought. The soldiers of Carranza became weary of running. They were sometimes caught along this road. They were frightened to death because they could see the Zapatistas catching up with them. "We cannot run up here!" they cried. "It looks like the spine of the devil himself! Here they will catch us and kill us on this devilish road."

The men of Carranza stole vestments from the churches of the village and dressed up in them. Once they had put on the holy robes, they suffered accidents and fell off the altars. Others pulled the images of the saints down from the altars to play around with them. But the next morning, the Carrancistas were found dead.

The saint who watched over my quarter was called San Mateo and an angry saint he was! When the Carrancistas entered the village, they boasted that they would strip him of his robes.

One day a man from our district of San Mateo of Milpa Alta was standing in the church with other men of the village, waiting to see what the Carrancistas would do.

"This dirty Carrancista!" the man from our district said. "He has climbed up to the altar where San Mateo stands. He wants to put on the saint's mantle! And the robes of San Marcos, too, the robes of the son of Mateo!"

When they heard these words, the men of the village spoke up. "Do not worry. No one can take anything away from San Mateo. He who dares to touch him will be killed."

"How can he slay us?" one of the men of Carranza asked. "How can he beat us up or shoot us with bullets?"

"You are going to get sick with a sickness called fever," the men of the village said. "And you won't be able to get rid of it, even if you tried walking on your head! For our San Mateo is a terrible saint!"

But the Carrancista took the mantle of San Mateo and brought it down with him from the altar. He tore the cape to bits, and then he began to shake with the fever.

The other soldier who had been standing below cried, "Oh, Mateo, I am not doing you any harm! Nor am I tearing your clothes! I beg you not to send me the fever. Only now do I realize that you are an angry saint, a saint who hits hard. I did not want to believe this. But now I have seen how you struck my fellow Carrancista with fever!"

The sick man lived about two weeks. He shook all over, and no medicine helped him. Because those were times of war, our witch doctors would not attend him. So it was that this soldier of Carranza died.

The day came when a certain Carrancista decided to bring down from her altar the image of Our Mother, Our Lady of the Assumption, the patroness of our village. He called the other soldiers to help him bring Our Mother down. She cares for our village and stands on high. When there is a fiesta, twenty men take her image down and always bind her with strong woven bands to a wooden platform. That is the way she is taken out in a procession.

But the men of Carranza said, "We will bring this woman down. We will strip her of her crown, her earrings and her robes!" They did not know that Our Mother was so heavy.

One of Carranza's men climbed up above the altar and then he realized that she was heavy. He called others to help him. Four men climbed up the altar, so that now there were five. They were going to undress Our Mother! But they tripped on the altar and came rolling down. One hurt his foot, another broke his arms, and the one who had climbed up first bashed his head in.

Those who saw these happenings told others the reason why the soldiers of Carranza got sick and why they broke their bones. From this time on, they stopped doing evil things within the church. And from this time on, they would kneel down to pray.

Other Carrancistas wanted to turn the church into a stable and to keep their horses in the church. But because of the things that had happened, others told them, "Don't keep them in the church! Terrible things may happen to you!" And so, the horses were left in the church yard. This they turned into a stable.

Fernando Horcasitas, English translation of the Nahuatl recollections of Doña Luz Jiménez, *Life and Death in Milpa Alta: A Náhuatl Chronicle of Díaz and Zapata* (Norman, OK: University of Oklahoma Press, 1972), pp. 15–22.

3. Manifestos of Emiliano Zapata

To you, chiefs, officers, and soldiers of the Arenas Division.

What we all suspected has already occurred. That which had to happen today or tomorrow: your separation from those engendered by Venustiano Carranza [president and head of the federal army]. They never favored, nor loved you. They merely deceived you, envied you. They wanted to hurt you, dishonor you, get rid of you. They never behaved as humans toward you.

To turn the face against those who so badly abuse power, honors you, erases the memory of your past deception [when their chief Arenas sided with the federal government].

We hope you will take part in the ideals for which we are fighting. In this manner we will be one, pressed closely against one flag. Thus our unified hearts will excel. Those who make fun of us, the ones engendered by Carranza, will not be able to destroy us.

Join us, our flag belongs to the people. We will fight together. . . . This is our great work which we will achieve in some way, before our revered mother, [the one] called Patria [i.e., homeland or ancestral land].

Let us fight the perverse, wicked Carranza, who is a tormentor of us all. If we work for our unity, we will fulfill the great command: land, liberty, justice. Let us perform our work of revolutionaries and know our duties toward our revered mother the [ancestral] land. This army's command invites you.

That is why I express this word. All those who will follow it, who will fight at our side, will enjoy a righteous and good life. In it we place our word of honor, of sincere men and good revolutionaries.

Tlaltizapan, Morelos, April 27, 1918
The Commander-in-Chief of the Liberation Army,
Emiliano Zapata

SECOND MANIFESTO OF THE SAME DATE
Our great war will not come to an end, will not conclude until that obscure tyrant, envious, who mocks the people, makes their faces turn around, is defeated. He is Venustiano Carranza who dishonors and makes ashamed our revered mother the [ancestral] land, Mexico is the people who keep strong and confront the great possessors of lands—Christians [i.e., hacienda owners and caciques], those who have made fun of us, who hate us. . . . We will receive the valiant ones, our hearts will rejoice being together with them.

Let us keep fighting. We will not rest until we come to possess our lands, those that belonged to our grandfathers, and which the greedy-handed thieves took from us. . . .

It is now more than ever necessary that we all, with our heart and courage, achieve this great work, following those who began the uprising, who preserve in their souls the true aims and have faith in a pure life.

The Commander-in-Chief of the Liberation Army,
Emiliano Zapata

Miguel León-Portilla, *Broken Spears*, pp. 166–68.

4. Doña Luz Jiménez Stories

THE STORY OF THE WHITE WOMAN I

This story originated in the village of Milpa Alta. Our grandparents were telling stories about a hill above Milpa Alta; the dear grandparents were speaking of Teuhtli. They say that the lord called Moctezuma sleeps there, and it is said that he does not sleep alone, since he is guarded by the great nahuaques [sages or witches]. There are other little nahuaques inside the mountains; the people go to petition them for rain. At times the great nahuaques are angry and they refuse to make a gift of water for the milpas. Then all the people get together with the tlamaques and they set an amount to buy turkeys and lambs [because they do not raise them]. Then they agreed to go to the caves with the food.

And Teuhtli said, "Do not depend solely on my wish. I am going to tell what you have to do. Go and see the Tepozteco."

The sages were astonished. "How is it possible that you could have said that we should bring food? We have just come with what you asked us for, and you send us to the Tepozteco! Where should we go? We are very far away."

The Teuhtli says, "Do not be astonished. Go bearing all that you can carry. Tell the Tepozteco to accept what you carry so that he tells you if he will give you water. If not, the milpas will be dry."

They went to the Tepozteco and they told him, "We bring this food so that you will make a gift of water to us. Our milpas are starting to dry up because it does not rain."

"That's good; bring the food. And tell the grandfather [the Teuhtli] that the rain will fall very soon."

And then he said, "Take all that you want from this wooden table. [It held every kind of vegetable: beans, squashes, etc.]. You will offer this; and I expect that right away you will tell me if the milpas are alright. Tell the grandfather [the Teuhtli]. Now the only thing missing is to greet his daughter [the

White Woman]. Tell him how you came up here. In this way you will go to visit his daughter, over there where she is sleeping. You will carry delicious food and you will see that they have priests over there who guard the maiden. While she sleeps, the others watch over her. (Some of) the people who go to greet her are left [bewitched] inside the hailstorm; (they remain) squashed together and do not get out. And this little woman sleeps and the others eat while she sleeps."

Then, having returned, they passed by the Tepozteco and he asked them, "What did you see? Tell me so that I can be sure that you went."

And they brought some hailstones and some stones to hand to the Tepozteco. This indicated that we would no longer lack water and that the milpas would produce well.

THE STORY OF THE WHITE WOMAN II

There was a young maiden called the White Woman. They tell the story that this girl was the daughter of the lord Moctezuma; it is said that he had this daughter. But since she was the only one, her father loved her very much.

She was a maiden, and a youth called Chimalpopoca wanted to marry with Mariquita. It angered the father. He did not want to let the girl go. It angered the father, and he told him, "Chimal, can't you hear what I say? You make me angry and I am going to send you to eternal sleep with my daughter, who will be known as The Hill of the Woman, and you will be called Popocatépetl. So you shall remain in the hills; you are going to stand guard. I do not want the people of the capitol to come, the white belly people. I do not want anyone to make the Indians cry."

THE THREE MEN AND THE WATER

During those years [when the Iztaccíhuatl was formed], three men from distant places arrived [in the village]. They were also Indians. They said that their village was Huizquilucan. They were important people. Perhaps they had been tlamatques [sages] of the kind that are called wizards. They arrived over there at the village of Milpa Alta.

They asked for a little water to drink. But since there was no water, they answered, "We have no water; we are also thirsty." Those from Huizquilucan commenced to laugh, and they lifted up a stone, and water spouted. They said, "Drink all the water you want (but) if you want to have water here, you will have to give us two boys and two girls. Bring these orphans to us and we will bury them together here where the water spouts. In other words, they will stay enchanted. In this way, you will never lack water."

But there was no one who wanted to make a gift of his children. That is why there is never any water.

The end.

THE GENTLEMEN OF CUERNAVACA,
TEPOZTLAN, AND THE POPOCATÉPETL

Over there in Cuernavaca there is another sage (but) I do not remember his name.

On the other side, in the lands of Tepoztlan, there is also a very good man, the Tepozteco. This gentleman is also a great sage.

Later, there was another, the Popocatépetl, so say all those that were called Chimalpopoca. He slept there with the White Woman, the great lady. She is known as the interpreter of Cortés.

Here it all ends.

Fernando Horcasitas and Sarah O. de Ford, *Cuentos en Náhuatl of Doña Luz Jiménez* (Mexico City: National Autonomous University, 1979), pp. 15–22; English version, Sylvia and Earl Shorris.

5. Madrecita

Little mother mine,
when I shall die,
bury me beside the kitchen stove,
and when you go to make tortillas,
weep for me there.

And if anyone should ask:
Señora, why do you weep?
Say that the wood is green,
and the smoke brings out the tears.

M. León-Portilla, *Estudios de Cultura Nahuatl*, vol. XIX (1989), p. 389; English version, Sylvia and Earl Shorris.

6. Coyotes of Today

Some Coyotes are saying
that we Nahuas will disappear,
will vanish,
our language will be heard no more,
will be used no more.

The Coyotes rejoice in this,
as this is what they are looking for.
Why is it that they want us to disappear?
We do not have to contemplate this too long,
because four hundred years have shown us
the aim of the Coyotes.
They are envious of our lands,
our forests and rivers,
our work, our sweat.
The Coyotes want us living
in the slums of their cities,
naked and hungry,
subject to their falsehoods and frauds.
The Coyotes want us to work for them,
they want us to abandon
our communal lands, our labor,
our endeavors and language,
our ways of dressing and living,
our forms of thinking.
The Coyotes desire
to make Coyotes out of us,
and then they will deprive us
of all that is ours,
the fruits of our labor
which has caused us fatigue.
We must strengthen our hearts
with one, two words,
which will illuminate our eyes,
so we can become fully conscious of it.
We have many tasks to perform.
I will add only a few words.
Where and how many
are the Nahuas in Mexico?
We, the Nahuas,
are not just in one place,
we are scattered in sixteen states
and eight hundred and eight municipalities.
One has to understand
that it is not only in our farm[s],
not only in our village[s],
that we Nahuas exist.
Sometimes we hear
that we Nahuas are vanishing,

but the census figures
speak very differently. . . .
Truly we can assert that,
although some want us to disappear,
we Nahuas continue to live,
we Nahuas continue to grow. . . .

Miguel León-Portilla, *Broken Spears,* pp. 169–71.

7. A New Dialogue of Flowers and Songs

by Xochime

Ladies and Gentlemen:

I am a peasant, my village is Momoxco, a community with its roots in the Nahuatl culture.

My elders instilled their language in my soul and taught me to love the harmony of my home in the natural world.

I learned to break open the earth to drop the corn in the lap of the furrow, according to the faith of my ancestors.

I know the state of mind that comes over a peasant when the miracle of germination appears.

I know the ways of the clouds and the wind in the sky above my village Momoxco.

I know the hope of the tasseling of the cornfield and of the young corn in flower.

I also know the sadness that comes over the countryside when the sky does not bless the earth.

I was raised listening to the words of the old ones before the hearthstones of my hut.

And I know what the work of the community is.

My universe is Nahuatl and my ideals are bound to my ancestral culture.

These origins, with their distinct way of life, do they have any value for present-day society?

Are they not, perhaps, withered old values, insignificant trifles?

What use is it to have a sense of identity?

What has this ideal—if that is what it is—got to do with our time?

Does it serve by chance as a model and invite us to look back over our history?

Is it utopian to believe that it is so, because history is an infinite evolution made of the unique events of every people?

Our culture, after many centuries, is shaped by the example of our ancestors in which there abound bloody deeds and injustices. We suffered a merciless intrusion, with the destruction of our cultural values, and during this period of slavery, they imposed rules on us that were alien to our way of life and they compelled us by force to profess beliefs and acts of faith.

We have also endured revolutions and political dealings, and always, without exception, the native has been the everlasting victim.

What administration since our independence has been preoccupied by the rescue and institutionalization of our native languages? Officially, it is a stigma to speak a native language, and the speaker is an "Indian." Therefore our children do not want to know anything of our values.

For the same reason, our cultural heritage is deteriorating by giant steps, and modern colonialism finds us a fruitful field to gobble up.

That is why it is necessary to revive pride in our essence, inquiring of our yesterdays. And that our native tongues are brought out of the oral tradition and transcribed on paper to be included in the educational program of our youth as foreign tongues are included in the academic curriculum.

The issue is the neglect suffered at present by our grandparents' legacy to us.

It is true that we cannot avoid modern life with its amazing technology, but we should also remember that we are not a spontaneous generation; we have a glorious past of many centuries, and we are the vanguard, the link to our living history, with the obligation of keeping our destiny alive, and we would be disgraced if by our neglect the pride of our ancestors were to perish in our hands.

We demand the right and the respect to be recognized as a primary source of our nationalism. Our origins have to stay alive in our souls and in the daily activities of our villages, because they are the principal instrument of our cohesion and identity. Our origins are in our languages. We are not one Mexico without roots, because no people lacks a history.

POEM

One day the Giver of Life
made all that we see,
and also all that we do not see
but which exists.
He made the Spring
with every kind of plant,
and to every one he give its task,
therefore some give fruit,
others give fragrances and flowers
like those that lavish their shade on us
in this garden
of the College of Jalisco.
He also made all the birds,
and to every species he gave its task.
He made some for the delight
of our eyes,
others for nourishment,
and yet others to spread
their trills over the face
of the earth.
One day, the Spirit
of the College of Jalisco
made a Springtime.
He called all the men
of Good Will
from all the horizons,
to come and give forth
jades and emeralds

from their hearts.
It was like a miracle
to hear the sonorous outpouring
of precious stones.

Xochime, *La Antigua y Nueva Palabra* (Jalisco: El Colegio de Jalisco, 1993), pp. 131–40;
English version, Sylvia and Earl Shorris.

8. On a Diet

I lay down without dinner
and that night I dreamed
I ate your heart;
it was due to hunger, I suppose.

While I devoured the fruit,
which was at once sweet and bitter,
you kissed me with cold lips,
colder and paler than ever before;
it was due to death, I suppose.

Amalia Bautista. Spanish translation by Francisco Morales Baranda; English version, Sylvia
and Earl Shorris.

9. Three Works by
Natalio Hernández Xocoyotzin

SPANISH IS ALSO OURS

[Address to the closing session of the 11th Congress of the Twenty-two Acad-
emies of the Spanish Language in Puebla, Mexico, 1998]

May I take a few words to express my pleasure at the spread of the Spanish language, which is used today by many of the world's peoples.

Many years went by, spanning several centuries. Little by little, with great
effort, with many sacrifices, Spanish was brought into the lands of Anahuac,
the Mexican lands, to establish it there. Although our people accepted it, they
did not abandon their own language, their wisdom, or their culture.

At first, our Mexican languages were repressed by Spanish: their development was not permitted, their flowering was obstructed.

Today, we have entered a period of change: Little by little our peoples have begun to reconcile with Spanish, to accept it as their own language, to use it as if it were ours.

Today we know that we are rich because we have many Mexican languages and the Spanish language which is also ours; in this way we are united.

In our country we must look at the Spanish language as an Ahuehuete tree which gives us shade, and whose branches reach out to communicate with us. It is a marvelous tree, nourished and strengthened by the Mexican languages of Anahuac, Ñahñu, Maya, Zapoteco, Rararamuri, Tojolabal, Nahuatl, Purepecha, in all more than fifty languages that remain alive.

All of these languages give roots, a face of its own, a distinct identity to the Spanish that we speak in Mexico.

Surely we must rejoice because Spanish has spread to different peoples of the world. Going forward from here, however, we must work so that the languages of our peoples, the Mexican languages, are developed: so that they spread their flowers and songs.

It pleases me to express these brief words in the beautiful city of Puebla. Precisely here, in the year 1450, the *cuicapihqui,* creators of songs—we say poets now—invited by Lord Tecayehuatzin, gathered to reflect upon the destiny of the word.

All of them agreed that the only permanence on earth is flower and song: poetry, the word.

So I have come to this Congress to share my words in Spanish and in the Náhuatl language, the Mexican language, because they flow at the same time, in a dignified and harmonious way, like flower and song: *in xochitl in cuicatl.*

I ASK MYSELF

I ask myself,
I ask the stars,
the sun,
the wind
and our mother earth:

What gives us life?
What causes us to walk?
What gives us strength and energy?

No one answers me.
I walk alone,
people look at me,
they perceive me,
they recognize me,
they watch me.

Moments later, my own heart answers:
"You know why you
have been put on earth;
answer yourself.

You have the answer!"

WE WALK ALONE

Sometimes I feel that we indians
await the coming of a man
who knows all,
who can do all,
who can help to resolve
all our problems.

But this man who knows all
and can do all
will never come:
because he lives within us,
he is found within us
he walks with us;
he awakens: yet he sleeps.

Spanish translation by the author; English version, Sylvia and Earl Shorris.

10. Lord of Night

by Librado Silva Galeana

It had grown dark.
After a little while
the last rays of light

were over the horizon.
A faint black veil
had covered all that exists.
The silence, lord of the night,
imposed his rule;
only now and then
the flapping of a bird,
the bark of a dog
broke the tranquility of the night.
All is respectful silence
at the hour in which someone leaves this world,
in which he abandons us.

Spanish translation by the author; English version, Sylvia and Earl Shorris.

Book II

Maya
Literature

Inscriptions on stone, many telling of the deeds of both male and female high rulers, and painted books with characters and texts written in Roman letters on a variety of subjects—prophecies, prayers, and songs—form part of what is known as the literature of the Mayas. In contrast with that of the Nahuas, which is expressed in just one language, Nahuatl, the literature of the Mayas has been transmitted in several cognate languages.

This results from two main factors: time and geography. There are more than 2,000 years of Maya history, a period during which a common proto-language differentiated into almost thirty distinct languages across a large area. Thus, the Yucatec Maya—and among their predecessors, the Itza, Xiu, and others—have lived on a flat, scrub-covered peninsula, never too far from the sea, the Gulf of Mexico, and the Caribbean. Other Maya people—among them the Tzotzil, Tzeltal, Ch'ol, Chonatl, Quiche, Cakchiquel, Mame, Tojolabal, Lacandon, Zutuhil, Chuh, Ixil, Jacaltec, Pokoman, Pokonchi, and Chorti—developed their culture and languages in the wooded highlands of Chiapas and Guatemala, or in the tropical jungles of Central America, including the vicinity of the Usumacinta, Motagua, and Hondo rivers.

In this magnificent variety of natural settings, the Mayas built their urban and religious centers, constellations of monuments, temples, and palaces set beside large plazas; an open-air architecture that included schools, ball courts, and, on the outskirts, the dwellings of the commoners. Thousands of stelae, with figures in bas-relief and inscribed texts, are the pages of a literature consecrated to exalting cosmic order and political rule. Even today, visitors to the Maya archeological sites cannot conceal their amazement at the mere sight of what remains. One thinks of places like Tikal in the Peten forest; Yaxchilan, close to the Usumacinta River; Palenque in the Chiapas jungle; and Tulum at the edge of the transparent blue waters of the Caribbean Sea.

Rich indeed is the literature produced by the creators of such splendid centers and their descendants. To encompass their extant compositions, from the Classic period (third to ninth centuries A.D.), to the post-Classic (which lasted until the Spanish Conquest), the colonial years, and those of the independent existence of their respective countries would require a number of volumes. First, it would necessitate reading, transcribing, and translating innumerable inscriptions, not only on stone monuments, but also on murals, vases, pieces of wood, bones, and the amate paper of the few extant painted books or codices. The magnitude of such literature cannot even be reckoned, for no catalogue exists describing the whole corpus of inscribed texts. Besides, a large part of them remain undeciphered. It is only thanks to the recent work of several epigraphists that we have gained entry into a Maya history that for centuries remained sealed.

As to the texts derived from oral tradition or from the glyphic contents of now-lost codices, a vast literature exists, from which we have chosen the major masterpieces here.

The *Popol Vuh*, Book of Council of the Quiche Maya, often considered the Bible of the New World, occupies a place of distinction. Next to it, texts from three of the several books of the Chilam Balam priests testify to the ancestral wisdom of the Yucatec Maya. These works of history and prophecy express a unique conception of time.

Historical literature in a different mood is provided by the *Annals of the Cakchiquels* and the Chontal story of the death in Tabascan territory of the Mexica young ruler Cuauhtemoc.

Songs and incantations found in colonial manuscripts from the Yucatec Maya, as well as from the Chorti, Chontal, and Lacandon, are also part of this anthology. Nor can modern literature from the nineteenth and twentieth centuries in several Maya languages be ignored. Thus, for instance, from the Yucatec Mayas and Chiapas' Tzotzils we have included narratives dealing with the Caste War in the peninsula and the Chamula nativistic movement. Oral literature—including fables, songs, and poems—and finally contemporary works by a growing number of Maya writers in several languages are also represented, proving that many of the languages of the Mayas survive, as does the culture, continuing to evolve in a process that now encompasses more than 2,000 years of civilization.

As we have seen, monuments, stelae, and a variety of objects with inscribed glyphic texts have been unearthed at Maya archeological sites. But for many years, at least since the period following the Spanish invasion, such inscriptions, as well as those in the few extant books or codices, remained closed to modern readers. Repeated attempts to decipher them were all unsuccessful.

Only recently, beginning with Knorosov's work in the late 1950s, was a method of reading these works—inscribed on stone, ceramics, bones, metals, and other materials— discovered. Contrary to what several earlier archeologists had thought, it has been shown that Maya writing is not merely ideographic. As in all systems of writing, it certainly includes ideograms, but also to a much greater degree phonograms (representations of sounds or phonemes). Furthermore, Maya writing developed other graphemes of morphological significance. These indicated the role that a word played in a sentence.

Maya writing is described today as a logo-syllabic system. By "logo," epigraphers mean the employment of glyphs to represent a complete word (*logus*); "syllabic" refers to the presence of other glyphs which, when combined, result in words. These glyphs are often formed by the stylized figure of an object or living being whose name begins with the syllable represented. In addition, there are other "abstract" glyphs denoting morphological markers or other syllables.

The decisive steps leading to the final deciphering of this writing are attributed to an international cast: one Russian American, one Russian, one German Mexican, and two

Americans. Their names are Tatiana Proskouriakoff, Yuri Knorosov, Enrique Berlin, Floyd Lounsbury, and David Kelley. Later on, a good number of researchers added substantially to the contributions of these pioneers of Maya epigraphy; among them, the late Linda Schele deserves special mention.

Mesoamerican literature in this anthology opened with readings from inscriptions from the magnificent metropolis of Palenque, in the state of Chiapas, Mexico. Palenque boasts many monuments with inscriptions—among them the Temple of the Sun-Eyed Shield, the Temples of the Cross, the Foliated Cross, and the Temple of the Inscriptions, with its great funerary crypt. The tablets in the first three temples, as presently deciphered, register the accession to the "mat and the chair," i.e., the enthroning of Lord Chan Bahlum, "Snake Jaguar," in A.D. 683. Inscriptions related to the funerary crypt speak about the Chan Bahlum's famous father, Sun Lord Pacal, "Hand-Shield." An interpretation of a text from the Temple of the Sun-Eyed Shield (see p. 43) was one of the first texts chosen for this anthology, since it is among the oldest Mesoamerican works of literary value to have been deciphered so far.

⑥ 1 ⑥

Sacred Narrative

The *Popol Vuh*

*U*nless some other work of similar magnitude is discovered, the Popol Vuh is likely to remain the "mat" or council place to which everyone must turn to understand the foundations of Maya civilization. The Popol Vuh was written in Santa Cruz Quiche Maya, using Latin script, in the sixteenth century.[1] The work was almost certainly based on material drawn from several sources: a hieroglyphic codex or a combination of several codices, as well as traditional oral recitations. Like any "bible," it contains myths, legends, history, and ethics; and like any bible, it is a living document open to changing interpretations over time.

To read the Popol Vuh as a relic of a dead past would be to misunderstand a classical work of literature, one that is useful in understanding the ancient Maya, but also in thinking about the world in our time. Ontological and ethical questions exist in all human societies; but the Popol Vuh, written by a people who had to struggle to sustain densely populated city-states in a difficult environment, also raises questions of human ecology.

An example of this was given recently by a group of Maya students in a small village in Yucatan near the Campeche border. They had been discussing the third "creation," in which manikins made of wood populated the earth. These men of wood were unable to think, meaning they were without the human attribute of language,[2] but they were able to make all of the things used by humans. Since they could not think, "They

---

[1]Munro S. Edmonson sets the date at 1550–55.

[2]Speech is the defining human attribute in the Mesoamerican view. One is reminded of the words of a later observer, Claude Lévi-Strauss, who wrote: "Whoever says man says language, whoever says language says society."

were not competent," according to the Popol Vuh, so they were destroyed: Their things—grinding stones and pots and jars and griddles—rose up against them and "tore their faces." Then came the flood. The students, all of whom had been to the metropolis of Merida, understood this as a warning against the thoughtless advance of technology. The next day, when a backhoe was brought to the village to dig a trench for a waterpipe, the students pointed to the operators of the roaring, clanging machine, and said, "Look! The men of wood!"

Along with such insights about the contemporary world, the Popol Vuh gives the reader the great metaphor of Xibalba, which plays an important role in Maya religious and agricultural thinking. The underworld (Hell is not a proper translation for Xibalba) is the place where the Sun goes as it sets in the West and from which it arises in the East. The seeds of corn go into the underworld of the earth and are reborn as new corn after the rains of spring. The Hero Twins of the adventures that make up much of the Popol Vuh descend into Xibalba, where they struggle to defeat tigers, bats, and the Lords of Xibalba. They are brilliant tricksters, excellent players of the Maya ball game, irrepressibly human, more than survivors, conquerors of night, darkness, and death.

The title of the work, Popol Vuh or Pop Wuj (there are several orthographies), was not given by the Quiche, but is drawn from the body of the work, and means "Council Book" or "The Book of Counsel." The title could as easily be "This Is Quiche," "The Sacred Book," or "The Book of the Community." The manuscript in Quiche is terse and sometimes ambiguous. It may have been intended as a guide to the glyphs on which it is based.

Beginning with the original redaction, which required interpretation of glyphic material, translation of the work has been exceedingly difficult, of necessity a highly creative literary endeavor. Since then, there have been many efforts to bring the work into other languages, other cultures. It was translated into Spanish by fray Francisco Ximénez at the beginning of the eighteenth century, then into French by Etienne Brasseur de Bourbourg in 1861. The translation by Adrián Recinos was first published in Spanish in 1947 and then in English by Delia Goetz and Sylvanus G. Morley in 1950. A translation in poetic form by Munro S. Edmonson appeared in 1971; and in 1985, Dennis Tedlock published a new and highly interpretive version, with the assistance of Andrés Xiloj, a "daykeeper" or diviner from Momostenango, Guatemala.[3]

---

[3]Most translators from the Maya have worked with a Maya-speaking "informant." For example, Yucatecan Maya materials translated by Munro S. Edmonson and Victoria Bricker have generally been done with the assistance of Eleuterio Po'ot Yah of the Academy of Maya Language in Merida.

Since a "definitive" translation is unlikely or even impossible, selections from the three English translations, all representing different approaches, are included here. The Ximénez manuscript, now in the
Newberry Library in Chicago, offers little guidance to the translator in
the way of punctuation or paragraphing, let alone the arrangement of
lines in poetic form. Nevertheless, some scholars hold that formal Maya
is written and even spoken in couplets, which requires poetic form in
English. Of the translations used here, only the Edmonson work (Prologue) and a small part of the Tedlock translation are in poetic form.

There are also three distinct views of the nature of translation itself
represented here. Edmonson said that his work was intended to hew
most closely to the original language; one might call it "scientific." The
prose version by Recinos (Part I, chapters 2–3, 7–9; Part II, chapters
1–4, 12–14; Part III, chapters 1–8, 10) is more interpretative, but still
intends a scientific reproduction of the Ximénez manuscript. Dennis
Tedlock (all the remaining excerpts), who was one of Edmonson's students at Tulane, has incorporated the scholarship of the scientific tradition into a uniquely imaginative literary work. The reader should be
aware, however, that the Quiche version was a "reading" or retelling of
a work or works, no longer extant, written in glyphic text. Apparently,
some new, post-invasion notions were added to the glyphs not only at the
beginning, but within the body of the work.

Translation from glyphic writing to full speech is exceedingly difficult, as the Tedlock rendering of the work from Palenque in the General
Introduction to this anthology makes clear. Then, the interpretation by
the translator from Quiche to a European language poses such great
opportunities for variance that one has difficulty following the corre-
spondence of the Tedlock and Recinos texts to each other. Readers will
note, among other things, that Tedlock has chosen to translate rather
than merely transliterate names from Quiche to English. This practice
has been widely debated, with no resolution. Many speakers of American
languages now oppose the translation of people's names. Tacuk Ulroan,
a Cup'ik (Eskimo) teacher and scholar, says, "The Indians in the 'lower
forty-eight' made a mistake by translating their names. Kass'aqs [Euro-
peans] don't do that." We do not consider Mr. Virtue virtuous or expect
Ms. Green to be the color of a leaf in summer, but Tashunka Witco will
forever be Crazy Horse. Thus, we have not translated the proper names
in the Recinos version into English, nor translated the proper names in
the Tedlock version back into Quiche. English equivalents of the important Quiche words appear in the Glossary.

In making the selection here, Edmonson's Prologue was thought to
give an indication of the rhythms of the language in the Quiche original. For the story of the twins in their journey to Xibalba, the good,

straightforward prose of Recinos is excellent. For the rest—the beginning of the world, the creation of humans out of corn, the Maya view of the artistic life, etc.—Tedlock offers not only beauty of language but his marvelous ability to infuse work in contemporary English with the spirituality of the Maya.

The translator from Maya to another language must always face the question of connotation as well as denotation, according to the Yucatecan Maya writer, Miguel May May. He chooses the word "horizon" as an example. The Maya, siyan ka'an, is translated in the third edition of the Alfredo Barrera Vásquez Maya dictionary as "horizonte," but ka'an (sky) is preceded by siyan, which means "birth" or "birthplace." May says that the Maya, "birthplace of the sky," is profound rather than merely descriptive. Considering the concept of Xibalba, the birth of corn, the emergence of the Sun at dawn, and so on, there is reason to accept his view that, in this case certainly, the connotations are richer than those of the English or Spanish noun, which is derived from the Greek word for boundary or limit. The theory applies as well to Quiche Maya, the language of the Popol Vuh.

The problem of translation cannot be overlooked; the Popol Vuh read in the original Quiche is a different book, and of course it was yet another book when originally written, for time is as much a betrayal as translation. Fortunately, however, much of its genius shines through all translations, bringing the modern reader into communication with one of the world's great civilizations.

Some elements will seem like Judeo-Christian interpretations of natural phenomena, others will bear a distinct resemblance to the methods of the Greek philosophers, but it will quickly become clear that the Maya are neither Greeks nor Christians; they are Maya. The calendrical elements which almost certainly accompanied the codices that were the basis for the Popol Vuh have been lost, and with them the sense, in this work, of the Maya preoccupation with time and its inextricable relation to space. The ancient Maya were great astronomers and mathematicians, but also indefatigable astrologers and diviners. In contemporary Maya life, divinations and cures include astrology, mathematics, psychology, and an astonishing knowledge of medicinal herbs.

There are five directions in the Maya conception of space, the four quadrants and the center of the world, hence the Maya description of the interrelation of time and space: "Time is a road in five directions."

How the notion of the center of the world connects to Xibalba is not entirely clear; however, the ball court as the entrance to Xibalba has played a role in recent reinterpretations of such acts as the sacrifice of players in the game. It is generally thought now that the beheaded ballplayer in the bas-relief on the wall of the great ball court at Chichen

Itza is not the loser of the game, but the winner. This new interpretation comes from a close reading of the Popol Vuh.

The Popol Vuh *is the best connection we have to a Mesoamerican civilization that has lasted for more than a thousand years, and continues still; it is a compilation of a way of being in the world, a book of gods and humans, a work for the ages.*

PROLOGUE*

This is the root of the former word.
    Here is Quiche by name.
Here we shall write then,
    We shall start out then, the former words,
The beginnings
    And the taproots
Of everything done in the Quiche town,
    The tribe of the Quiche people.
So this is what we shall collect then,
    The decipherment,
The clarification,
    And the explanation
Of the mysteries
    And the illumination
By Former,
    And Shaper;
Bearer
    And Engenderer are their names,
Hunter Possum
    And Hunter Coyote,
Great White Pig
    And Coati,
Majesty
    And Quetzal Serpent,
The Heart of the Lake
    And the Heart of the Sea,
Green Plate Spirit
    And Blue Bowl Spirit, as it is said,
Who are likewise called,

---

*From Munro S. Edmonson, *The Book of Counsel: The Popol Vuh of the Quiche Maya of Guatemala* (New Orleans: Middle American Research Institute, Tulane University, 1971), pp. 3–8.

Who are likewise spoken of
As the Woman with Grandchildren
    And the Man with Grandchildren,
Xipiacoc
    And Xmucane by name,
Shelterer
    And Protector,
Great-Grandmother
    And Great-Grandfather,
As it is said
    In Quiche words.
Then they said everything
    And did it furthermore,
In the bright existence
    And bright words.
This we shall write already within the word of God,
    Already in Christianity.
We shall save it
    Because there is no longer
A sight of the Book of Counsel,
    A sight of the bright things come from beside the sea,
The description of our shadows,
    A sight of the bright life, as it is called.
There was once the manuscript of it,
    And it was written long ago,
Only hiding his face is the reader of it,
    The mediator of it.
Great was its account
    And its description
Of when there was finished
    The birth
Of all of heaven
    And earth:
The four creations,
    The four humiliations,
The knowledge
    Of the four punishments,
The rope of tying together,
    The line of tying together,
The womb of heaven,
    The womb of earth.
Four creations,
    Four humiliations, it was told,

By the Former
  And Shaper,
The Mother
  And Father
Of Life
  And Mankind,
The Inspirer
  And Heartener,
Bearer
  And Heartener of
Light
  And the Race,
Children of the Mother of Light,
  Sons of the Father of Light,
The Mediator,
  The Thinker
Of Everything,
  Whatever exists:
Heaven,
  Earth,
Lake,
  And Sea.

DAWN*

THIS IS THE account, here it is:

Now it still ripples, now it still murmurs, ripples, it still sighs, still hums, and it is empty under the sky.

Here follow the first words, the first eloquence:

There is not yet one person, one animal, bird, fish, crab, tree, rock, hollow, canyon, meadow, forest. Only the sky alone is there; the face of the earth is not clear. Only the sea alone is pooled under all the sky; there is nothing whatever gathered together. It is at rest; not a single thing stirs. It is held back, kept at rest under the sky.

Whatever there is that might be is simply not there: only the pooled water, only the calm sea, only it alone is pooled.

Whatever might be is simply not there: only murmurs, ripples, in the dark, in the night. Only the Maker, Modeler alone, Sovereign Plumed Serpent, the Bearers, Begetters are in the water, a glittering light. They are there, they are enclosed in quetzal feathers, in blue-green.

*From Dennis Tedlock, *Popul Vuh* (New York: Simon & Schuster, 1985), pp. 72–75.

Thus the name, "Plumed Serpent." They are great knowers, great thinkers in their very being.

And of course there is the sky, and there is also the Heart of Sky. This is the name of the god, as it is spoken.

And then came his word, he came here to the Sovereign Plumed Serpent, here in the blackness, in the early dawn. He spoke with the Sovereign Plumed Serpent, and they talked, then they thought, then they worried. They agreed with each other, they joined their words, their thoughts. Then it was clear, then they reached accord in the light, and then humanity was clear, when they conceived the growth, the generation of trees, of bushes, and the growth of life, of humankind, in the blackness, in the early dawn, all because of the Heart of Sky, named Hurricane. Thunderbolt Hurricane comes first, the second is Newborn Thunderbolt, and the third is Raw Thunderbolt.

So there were three of them, as Heart of Sky, who came to the Sovereign Plumed Serpent, when the dawn of life was conceived:

"How should it be sown, how should it dawn? Who is to be the provider, nurturer?"

"Let it be this way, think about it: this water should be removed, emptied out for the formation of the earth's own plate and platform, then comes the sowing, the dawning of the sky-earth. But there will be no high days and no bright praise for our work, our design, until the rise of the human work, the human design," they said.

And then the earth arose because of them, it was simply their word that brought it forth. For the forming of the earth they said "Earth." It arose suddenly, just like a cloud, like a mist, now forming, unfolding. Then the mountains were separated from the water, all at once the great mountains came forth. By their genius alone, by their cutting edge alone they carried out the conception of the mountain-plain, whose face grew instant groves of cypress and pine.

And the Plumed Serpent was pleased with this:

"It was good that you came, Heart of Sky, Hurricane, and Newborn Thunderbolt, Raw Thunderbolt. Our work, our design will turn out well," they said.

And the earth was formed first, the mountain-plain. The channels of water were separated; their branches wound their ways among the mountains. The waters were divided when the great mountains appeared.

Such was the formation of the earth when it was brought forth by the Heart of Sky, Heart of Earth, as they are called, since they were the first to think of it. The sky was set apart, and the earth was set apart in the midst of the waters. Such was their plan when they thought, when they worried about the completion of their work.

FIRST CREATURES*

Then they made the small wild animals, the guardians of the woods, the spirits of the mountains, the deer, the birds, pumas, jaguars, serpents, snakes, vipers, guardians of the thickets.

And the Forefathers asked: "Shall there be only silence and calm under the trees, under the vines? It is well that hereafter there be someone to guard them." So they said when they meditated and talked. Promptly the deer and the birds were created. Immediately they gave homes to the deer and the birds. "You, deer, shall sleep in the fields by the river bank and in the ravines. Here you shall be amongst the thicket, amongst the pasture; in the woods you shall multiply, you shall walk on four feet and they will support you. Thus be it done!" So it was they spoke.

Then they also assigned homes to the birds big and small. "You shall live in the trees and in the vines. There you shall make your nests; there you shall multiply; there you shall increase in the branches of the trees and in the vines." Thus the deer and the birds were told; they did their duty at once, and all sought their homes and their nests.

And the creation of all the four-footed animals and the birds being finished, they were told by the Creator and the Maker and the Forefathers: "Speak, cry, warble, call, speak each one according to your variety, each, according to your kind." So was it said to the deer, the birds, pumas, jaguars, and serpents. "Speak, then, our names, praise us, your mother, your father. Invoke then, Huracan, Chipi-Caculha, Raxa-Caculha, the Heart of Heaven, the Heart of Earth, the Creator, the Maker, the Forefathers; speak, invoke us, adore us," they were told. But they could not make them speak like men; they only hissed and screamed and cackled; they were unable to make words, and each screamed in a different way. When the Creator and the Maker saw that it was impossible for them to talk to each other, they said: "It is impossible for them to say our names, the names of us, their Creators and Makers. This is not well," said the Forefathers to each other. Then they said to them: "Because it has not been possible for you to talk, you shall be changed. We have changed our minds:

"Your food, your pasture, your homes, and your nests you shall have; they shall be the ravines and the woods, because it has not been possible for you to adore us or invoke us. There shall be those who adore us, we shall make other [beings] who shall be obedient. Accept your destiny: your flesh shall be torn to pieces. So shall it be. This shall be your lot." So they said, when they

---

*From Adrián Recinos, English translation by Delia Goetz and Sylvanus G. Morley, *Popol Vuh: The Sacred Book of the Ancient Quiché Maya* (Norman, OK: University of Oklahoma Press, 1950), pp. 84–89.

made known their will to the large and small animals which are on the face of the earth.

They wished to give them another trial; they wished to make another attempt; they wished to make [all living things] adore them. But they could not understand each other's speech; they could succeed in nothing, and could do nothing. For this reason they were sacrificed, and the animals which were on earth were condemned to be killed and eaten.

For this reason another attempt had to be made to create and make men by the Creator, the Maker, and the Forefathers. "Let us try again! Already dawn draws near: Let us make him who shall nourish and sustain us! What shall we do to be invoked, in order to be remembered on earth? We have already tried with our first creations, our first creatures; but we could not make them praise and venerate us. So, then, let us try to make obedient, respectful beings who will nourish and sustain us." Thus they spoke.

Then was the creation and the formation. Of earth, of mud, they made [man's] flesh. But they saw that it was not good. It melted away, it was soft, did not move, had no strength, it fell down, it was limp, it could not move its head, its face fell to one side, its sight was blurred, it could not look behind. At first it spoke, but had no mind. Quickly it soaked in the water and could not stand. And the Creator and the Maker said: "Let us try again because our creatures will not be able to walk nor multiply. Let us consider this," they said. Then they broke up and destroyed their work and their creation. And they said: "What shall we do to perfect it, in order that our worshipers, our invokers, will be successful?"

MANIKINS*

THEN COMES THE NAMING OF THOSE WHO ARE THE MIDMOST SEERS: the "Grandmother of Day, Grandmother of Light," as the Maker, Modeler called them. These are names of Xpiyacoc and Xmucane.

When Hurricane had spoken with the Sovereign Plumed Serpent, they invoked the daykeepers, diviners, the midmost seers:

"There is yet to find, yet to discover how we are to model a person, construct a person again, a provider, nurturer, so that we are called upon and we are recognized: our recompense is in words.

Midwife, matchmaker,
our grandmother, our grandfather,
Xpiyacoc, Xmucane,
let there be planting, let there be the dawning

*From Tedlock, op. cit., pp. 80–94.

of our invocation, our sustenance, our recognition
by the human work, the human design,
the human figure, the human mass.

So be it, fulfill your names:

Hunahpu Possum, Hunahpu Coyote,
Bearer twice over, Begetter twice over,
Great Peccary, Great Tapir,
lapidary, jeweler,
sawyer, carpenter,
Maker of the Blue-Green Plate,
Maker of the Blue-Green Bowl,
incense maker, master craftsman,
Grandmother of Day, Grandmother of Light.

You have been called upon because of our work, our design. Run your hands
over the kernels of corn, over the seeds of the coral tree, just get it done, just
let it come out whether we should carve and gouge a mouth, a face in wood,"
they told the daykeepers.

And then comes the borrowing, the counting of days; the hand is moved
over the corn kernels, over the coral seeds, the days, the lots.

Then they spoke to them, one of them a grandmother, the other a grandfather.

This is the grandfather, this is the master of the coral seeds: Xpiyacoc is
his name.

And this is the grandmother, the daykeeper, diviner who stands behind
others: Xmucane is her name.

And they said, as they set out the days:

"Just let it be found, just let it be discovered,
say it, our ear is listening,
may you talk, may you speak,
just find the wood for the carving and sculpting
by the builder, sculptor.
Is this to be the provider, the nurturer
when it comes to the planting, the dawning?
You corn kernels, you coral seeds,
you days, you lots:
may you succeed, may you be accurate,"

they said to the corn kernels, coral seeds, days, lots. "Have shame, you up there, Heart of Sky: attempt no deception before the mouth and face of Sovereign Plumed Serpent," they said. Then they spoke straight to the point:

"It is well that there be your manikins, woodcarvings, talking, speaking, there on the face of the earth."

"So be it," they replied. The moment they spoke it was done: the manikins, woodcarvings, human in looks and human in speech.

This was the peopling of the face of the earth:

They came into being, they multiplied, they had daughters, they had sons, these manikins, woodcarvings. But there was nothing in their hearts and nothing in their minds, no memory of their mason and builder. They just went and walked wherever they wanted. Now they did not remember the Heart of Sky. And so they fell, just an experiment and just a cutout for humankind. They were talking at first but their faces were dry. They were not yet developed in the legs and arms. They had no blood, no lymph. They had no sweat, no fat. Their complexions were dry, their faces were crusty. They flailed their legs and arms, their bodies were deformed.

And so they accomplished nothing before the Maker, Modeler who gave them birth, gave them heart. They became the first numerous people here on the face of the earth.

AGAIN THERE COMES A HUMILIATION, destruction, and demolition. The manikins, woodcarvings were killed when the Heart of Sky devised a flood for them. A great flood was made; it came down on the heads of the manikins, woodcarvings.

The man's body was carved from the wood of the coral tree by the Maker, Modeler. And as for the woman, the Maker, Modeler needed the pith of reeds for the woman's body. They were not competent, nor did they speak before the builder and sculptor who made them and brought them forth, and so they were killed, done in by a flood:

There came a rain of resin from the sky.

There came the one named Gouger of Faces: he gouged out their eyeballs.

There came Sudden Bloodletter: he snapped off their heads.

There came Crunching Jaguar: he ate their flesh.

There came Tearing Jaguar: he tore them open.

They were pounded down to the bones and tendons, smashed and pulverized even to the bones. Their faces were smashed because they were incompetent before their mother and their father, the Heart of Sky, named Hurricane. The earth was blackened because of this; the black rainstorm began, rain all day and rain all night. Into their houses came the animals, small and great. Their faces were crushed by things of wood and stone. Everything spoke: their water jars, their tortilla griddles, their plates, their cooking pots, their dogs, their grinding stones, each and every thing crushed their faces. Their dogs and turkeys told them:

"You caused us pain, you ate us, but now it is you whom we shall eat." And this is the grinding stone:

"We were undone because of you.

Every day, every day,
in the dark, in the dawn, forever,
r-r-rip, r-r-rip, r-r-rub, r-r-rub,
right in our faces, because of you.

This was the service we gave you at first, when you were still people, but today you will learn of our power. We shall pound and we shall grind your flesh," their grinding stones told them.

And this is what their dogs said, when they spoke in their turn:

"Why is it you can't seem to give us our food? We just watch and you just keep us down, and you throw us around. You keep a stick ready when you eat, just so you can hit us. We don't talk, so we've received nothing from you. How could you not have known? You did know that we were wasting away there, behind you.

"So, this very day you will taste the teeth in our mouths. We shall eat you," their dogs told them, and their faces were crushed.

And then their tortilla griddles and cooking pots spoke to them in turn:

"Pain! That's all you've done for us. Our mouths are sooty, our faces are sooty. By setting us on the fire all the time, you burn us. Since we felt no pain, you try it. We shall burn you," all their cooking pots said, crushing their faces.

The stones, their hearthstones were shooting out, coming right out of the fire, going for their heads, causing them pain. Now they run for it, helter-skelter.

They want to climb up on the houses, but they fall as the houses collapse.

They want to climb the trees; they're thrown off by the trees.

They want to get inside caves, but the caves slam shut in their faces.

Such was the scattering of the human work, the human design. The people were ground down, overthrown. The mouths and faces of all of them were destroyed and crushed. And it used to be said that the monkeys in the forests today are a sign of this.

They were left as a sign because wood alone was used for their flesh by the builder and sculptor.

So this is why monkeys look like people: they are a sign of a previous human work, human design, mere manikins, mere woodcarvings.

SEVEN MACAW

THIS WAS WHEN THERE WAS JUST A TRACE OF EARLY DAWN on the face of the earth, there was no sun. But there was one who magnified himself; Seven Macaw is his name. The sky-earth was already there, but the face of the sun-moon was clouded over. Even so, it is said that his light provided a sign for the people who were flooded. He was like a person of genius in his being.

"I am great. My place is now higher than that of the human work, the human design. I am their sun and I am their light, and I am also their months.

"So be it: my light is great. I am the walkway and I am the foothold of the people, because my eyes are of metal. My teeth just glitter with jewels, and turquoise as well; they stand out blue with stones like the face of the sky.

"And this nose of mine shines white into the distance like the moon. Since my nest is metal, it lights up the face of the earth. When I come forth before my nest, I am like the sun and moon for those who are born in the light, begotten in the light. It must be so, because my face reaches into the distance," says Seven Macaw.

It is not true that he is the sun, this Seven Macaw, yet he magnifies himself, his wings, his metal. But the scope of his face lies right around his own perch; his face does not reach everywhere beneath the sky. The faces of the sun, moon, and stars are not yet visible, it has not yet dawned.

And so Seven Macaw puffs himself up as the days and the months, though the light of the sun and moon has not yet clarified. He only wished for surpassing greatness. This was when the flood was worked upon the manikins, woodcarvings. And now we shall explain how Seven Macaw died, when the people were vanquished, done in by the mason and sculptor.

HERE IS THE BEGINNING OF THE DEFEAT AND DESTRUCTION OF THE DAY OF SEVEN MACAW by the two boys, the first named Hunahpu and the second named Xbalanque. Being gods, the two of them saw evil in his attempt at self-magnification before the Heart of Sky. So the boys talked:

"It's no good without life, without people here on the face of the earth."

"Well then, let's try a shot. We could shoot him while he's at his meal. We could make him ill, then put an end to his riches, his jade, his metal, his jewels, his gems, the source of his brilliance. Everyone might do as he does, but it should not come to be that fiery splendor is merely a matter of metal. So be it," said the boys, each one with a blowgun on his shoulder, the two of them together.

And this Seven Macaw has two sons: the first of these is Zipacna, and the second is the Earthquake. And Chimalmat is the name of their mother, the wife of Seven Macaw.

And this is Zipacna, this is the one to build up the great mountains: Fire

Mouth, Hunahpu, Cave by the Water, Xcanul, Macamob, Huliznab, as the names of the mountains that were there at the dawn are spoken. They were brought forth by Zipacna in a single night.

And now this is the Earthquake. The mountains are moved by him; the mountains, small and great, are softened by him. The sons of Seven Macaw did this just as a means of self-magnification.

"Here am I: I am the sun," said Seven Macaw.

"Here am I: I am the maker of the earth," said Zipacna.

"As for me, I bring down the sky, I make an avalanche of all the earth," said Earthquake. The sons of Seven Macaw are alike, and like him: they got their greatness from their father.

And the two boys saw evil in this, since our first mother and father could not yet be made. Therefore deaths and disappearances were planned by the two boys.

AND HERE IS THE SHOOTING OF SEVEN MACAW BY THE TWO BOYS. We shall explain the defeat of each one of those who engaged in self-magnification.

This is the great tree of Seven Macaw, a nance, and this is the food of Seven Macaw. In order to eat the fruit of the nance he goes up the tree every day. Since Hunahpu and Xbalanque have seen where he feeds, they are now hiding beneath the tree of Seven Macaw, they are keeping quiet here, the two boys are in the leaves of the tree.

And when Seven Macaw arrived, perching over his meal, the nance, it was then that he was shot by Hunahpu. The blowgun shot went right to his jaw, breaking his mouth. Then he went up over the tree and fell flat on the ground. Suddenly Hunahpu appeared, running. He set out to grab him, but actually it was the arm of Hunahpu that was seized by Seven Macaw. He yanked it straight back, he bent it back at the shoulder. Then Seven Macaw tore it right out of Hunahpu. Even so, the boys did well: the first round was not their defeat by Seven Macaw.

And when Seven Macaw had taken the arm of Hunahpu, he went home. Holding his jaw very carefully, he arrived:

"What have you got there?" said Chimalmat, the wife of Seven Macaw.

"What is it but those two tricksters! They've shot me, they've dislocated my jaw. All my teeth are just loose, now they ache. But once what I've got is over the fire hanging there, dangling over the fire, then they can just come and get it. They're real tricksters!" said Seven Macaw, then he hung up the arm of Hunahpu.

Meanwhile Hunahpu and Xbalanque were thinking. And then they invoked a grandfather, a truly white-haired grandfather, and a grandmother, a truly humble grandmother, just bent-over, elderly people. Great White Peccary is the name of the grandfather, and Great White Tapir is the name of the grandmother. The boys said to the grandmother and grandfather:

"Please travel with us when we go to get our arm from Seven Macaw; we'll just follow right behind you. You'll tell him:

" 'Do forgive us our grandchildren, who travel with us. Their mother and father are dead, and so they follow along there, behind us. Perhaps we should give them away, since all we do is pull worms out of teeth.' So we'll seem like children to Seven Macaw, even though we're giving you the instructions," the two boys told them.

"Very well," they replied.

After that they approached the place where Seven Macaw was in front of his home. When the grandmother and grandfather passed by, the two boys were romping along behind them. When they passed below the lord's house, Seven Macaw was yelling his mouth off because of his teeth. And when Seven Macaw saw the grandfather and grandmother traveling with them:

"Where are you headed, our grandfather?" said the lord.

"We're just making our living, your lordship," they replied.

"Why are you working for a living? Aren't those your children traveling with you?"

"No, they're not, your lordship. They're our grandchildren, our descendants, but it is nevertheless we who take pity on them. The bit of food they get is the portion we give them, your lordship," replied the grandmother and grandfather. Since the lord is getting done in by the pain in his teeth, it is only with great effort that he speaks again:

"I implore you, please take pity on me! What sweets can you make, what poisons can you cure?" said the lord.

"We just pull the worms out of teeth, and we just cure eyes. We just set bones, your lordship," they replied.

"Very well, please cure my teeth. They really ache, every day. It's insufferable! I get no sleep because of them and my eyes. They just shot me, those two tricksters! Ever since it started I haven't eaten because of it. Therefore take pity on me! Perhaps it's because my teeth are loose now."

"Very well, your lordship. It's a worm, gnawing at the bone. It's merely a matter of putting in a replacement and taking the teeth out, sir."

"But perhaps it's not good for my teeth to come out since I am, after all, a lord. My finery is in my teeth and my eyes."

"But then we'll put in a replacement. Ground bone will be put back in." And this is the "ground bone": it's only white corn.

"Very well. Yank them out! Give me some help here!" he replied.

And when the teeth of Seven Macaw came out, it was only white corn that went in as a replacement for his teeth—just a coating shining white, that corn in his mouth. His face fell at once, he no longer looked like a lord. The last of his teeth came out, the jewels that had stood out blue from his mouth.

And then the eyes of Seven Macaw were cured. When his eyes were trimmed back the last of his metal came out. Still he felt no pain; he just looked on while the last of his greatness left him. It was just as Hunahpu and Xbalanque had intended.

And when Seven Macaw died, Hunahpu got back his arm. And Chimalmat, the wife of Seven Macaw, also died.

Such was the loss of the riches of Seven Macaw: only the doctors got the jewels and gems that had made him arrogant, here on the face of the earth. The genius of the grandmother, the genius of the grandfather did its work when they took back their arm: it was implanted and the break got well again. Just as they had wished the death of Seven Macaw, so they brought it about. They had seen evil in his self-magnification.

After this the two boys went on again. What they did was simply the word of the Heart of Sky.

ZIPACNA*

Here now are the deeds of Zipacna, the elder son of Vucub-Caquix.

"I am the creator of the mountains," said Zipacna.

Zipacna was bathing at the edge of a river when four hundred youths passed, dragging a log to support their house. The four hundred were walking, after having cut down a large tree to make the ridge-pole of their house.

Then Zipacna came up, and going toward the four hundred youths, said to them: "What are you doing, boys?"

"It is only this log," they answered, "which we cannot lift and carry on our shoulders."

"I will carry it. Where does it have to go? What do you want it for?"

"For a ridge-pole for our house."

"All right," he answered, and lifting it up, he put it on his shoulders and carried it to the entrance of the house of the four hundred boys.

"Now stay with us, boy," they said. "Have you a mother or father—"

"I have neither," he answered.

"Then we shall hire you tomorrow to prepare another log to support our house."

"Good," he answered.

The four hundred boys talked together then, and said:

"How shall we kill this boy? Because it is not good what he has done lifting the log alone. Let us make a big hole and push him so that he will fall into it. 'Go down and take out the earth and carry it from the pit,' we shall tell him, and when he stoops down, to go down into the pit, we shall let the large log fall on him and he will die there in the pit."

*From Recinos, op. cit., pp. 99–106.

So said the four hundred boys, and then they dug a large, very deep pit. Then they called Zipacna.

"We like you very much. Go, go and dig dirt, for we cannot reach [the bottom of the pit]," they said.

"All right," he answered. He went at once into the pit. And calling to him as he was digging the dirt, they said: "Have you gone down very deep yet?"

"Yes," he answered, beginning to dig the pit. But the pit which he was making was to save him from danger. He knew that they wanted to kill him; so when he dug the pit, he made a second hole at one side in order to free himself.

"How far [have you gone]?" the four hundred boys called down.

"I am still digging; I will call up to you when I have finished the digging," said Zipacna from the bottom of the pit. But he was not digging his grave; instead he was opening another pit in order to save himself.

At last Zipacna called to them. But when he called, he was already safe in the second pit.

"Come and take out and carry away the dirt which I have dug and which is in the bottom of the pit," he said, "because in truth I have made it very deep. Do you not hear my call? Nevertheless, your calls, your words repeat themselves like an echo once, twice, and so I hear well where you are." So Zipacna called from the pit where he was hidden, shouting from the depths.

Then the boys hurled the great log violently, and it fell quickly with a thud to the bottom of the pit.

"Let no one speak! Let us wait until we hear his dying screams," they said to each other, whispering, and each one covered his face as the log fell noisily. Zipacna spoke then, crying out, but he called only once when the log fell to the bottom,

"How well we have succeeded in this! Now he is dead," said the boys. "If, unfortunately, he had continued what he had begun to do, we would have been lost, because he already had interfered with us, the four hundred boys."

And filled with joy they said: "Now we must make our chicha [drink] within the next three days. When the three days are passed, we shall drink to the construction of our new house, we, the four hundred boys." Then they said: "Tomorrow we shall look, and day after tomorrow, we shall also look to see if the ants do not come out of the earth when the body smells and begins to rot. Presently we shall become calm and drink our chicha," they said.

But from his pit Zipacna listened to everything the boys said. And later, on the second day, multitudes of ants came, going and coming and gathering under the log. Some carried Zipacna's hair in their mouths, and others carried his fingernails.

When the boys saw this, they said, "That devil has now perished. Look how the ants have gathered, how they have come by hordes, some bringing his hair and others his fingernails. Look what we have done!" So they spoke to each other.

Nevertheless, Zipacna was very much alive. He had cut his hair and gnawed off his fingernails to give them to the ants.

And so the four hundred boys believed that he was dead, and on the third day they began the orgy and all of the boys got drunk. And the four hundred being drunk knew nothing any more. And then Zipacna let the house fall on their heads and killed all of them.

Not even one or two among the four hundred were saved; they were killed by Zipacna, son of Vucub-Caquix.

In this way the four hundred boys died, and it is said that they became the group of stars which because of them are called Metz, but it may not be true.

Now we shall tell how Zipacna was defeated by the two boys, Hunahpu and Xbalanque.

Now follows the defeat and death of Zipacna, when he was overcome by the two boys, Hunahpu and Xbalanque.

The boys' hearts were full of rancor because the four hundred young men had been killed by Zipacna. And he only hunted fish and crabs at the bank of the river, which were his daily food. During the day he went about looking for food, and at night he carried mountains on his back.

With a leaf of the ec plant [a large-leafed grass] which is found in the forest, Hunahpu and Xbalanque quickly made a figure to look like a very large crab.

With this they made the stomach of the crab; the claws, they made of pahac, and for the shell, which covers the back, they used a stone. Then they put the crab at the bottom of a cave at the foot of a large mountain called Meaguan, where he was overcome.

Then the boys went to find Zipacna on the river bank. "Where are you going, young man?" they asked him.

"I am not going anywhere," Zipacna answered, "only looking for food, boys."

"And what is your food?"

"Fish and crabs, but there are none here and I have not found any; I have not eaten since day before yesterday, and I am dying of hunger," said Zipacna to Hunahpu and Xbalanque.

"Over there in the bottom of the ravine there is a crab, a really large crab, and it would be well if you would eat it! Only it bit us when we tried to catch it and so we were afraid. We wouldn't try to catch it for anything," said Hunahpu and Xbalanque.

"Have pity on me! Come and show it to me, boys," begged Zipacna.

"We do not want to. You go alone, you will not get lost. Follow the bank of the river and you will come out at the foot of a large hilt; there it is making a noise at the bottom of the ravine. You have only to go there," said Hunahpu and Xbalanque.

"Oh, unfortunate me! Won't you accompany me, boys? Come and show it to me. There are many birds which you can shoot with your blowguns and I know where to find them," said Zipacna.

His meekness convinced the boys. And they asked him: "But, can you really catch him? Because it is only for you that we are returning; we are not going to try to get it again because it bit us when we were crawling into the cave. After that we were afraid to crawl in, but we almost caught it. So, then, it is best that you crawl in," they said.

"Very well," said Zipacna, and then they went with him. They arrived at the bottom of the ravine and there, stretched on his back, was the crab, showing his red shell. And there also in the bottom of the ravine was the boys' hoax.

"Good! Good!" said Zipacna happily. "I should like to have it in my mouth already!" And he was really dying of hunger. He wanted to try to crawl in, he wanted to enter, but the crab was climbing. He [Zipacna] came out at once and the boys asked, "Did you not get it?"

"No," he answered, "because he was going up and I almost caught him. But perhaps it would be good if I go in from above," he added. And then he entered again from above, but as he was almost inside, with only the soles of his feet showing, the great hill slid and fell slowly down on his chest.

Zipacna never returned and he was changed into stone.

In this way Zipacna was defeated by the two boys, Hunahpu and Xbalanque; he was the elder son of Vucub-Caquix, and he, according to the ancient legend, was the one who made the mountains.

At the foot of the hill called Meaguan he was vanquished. Only by a miracle was he vanquished, the second of the arrogant ones. One was left, whose history we shall tell now.

CABRACAN

The third of the arrogant ones was the second son of Vucub-Caquix who was called Cabracan.

"I demolish the mountains," he said.

But Hunahpu and Xbalanque also defeated Cabracan. Huracan Chipi-Caculha and Raxa-Caculha talked and said to Hunahpu and Xbalanque:

"Let the second son of Vucub-Caquix also be defeated. This is our will, for it is not well what they do on earth, exalting their glory, their grandeur, and their power, and it must not be so. Lure him to where the sun rises," said Huracan to the two youths.

"Very well, honored sir," they answered, "because what we see is not right. Do you not exist, you who are the peace, you, Heart of Heaven?" said the boys as they listened to the command of Huracan.

Meanwhile, Cabracan was busy shaking the mountains. At the gentlest tap of his feet on the earth, the large and small mountains opened. Thus the boys found him and asked Cabracan:

"Where are you going, young man?"

"Nowhere," he answered, "here I am moving the mountains, and I am leveling them to the ground forever," he answered.

Then Cabracan asked Hunahpu and Xbalanque, "What did you come to do here? I do not recognize you. What are your names?" said Cabracan.

"We have no names," they answered, "we are nothing more than shooters of blowguns and hunters with bird-traps on the mountains. We are poor and we have nothing, young man. We only walk over the large and small mountains, young man, and we have just seen a large mountain, over there where you see the pink sky. It really rises up very high and overlooks the tops of all the hills. So it is that we have not been able to catch even one or two of the birds on it, boy. But, is it true that you can level all the mountains?" Hunahpu and Xbalanque asked Cabracan.

"Have you really seen the mountain of which you speak? Where is it? If I see it, I shall demolish it. Where did you see it?"

"Over there it is, where the sun rises," said Hunahpu and Xbalanque.

"Very well, show me the road," he said to the two boys.

"Oh no!" they answered. "We must take you between us. One shall go at your left and the other at your right, because we have our blowguns, and if there should be birds we can shoot them." And so they set out happily, trying out their blowguns. But when they shot with them, they did not use the clay pellets in the tube of the blowgun; instead they felled the birds only with the puff of air when they shot them, which surprised Cabracan very much.

Then the boys built a fire and put the birds on it to roast, but they rubbed one of the birds with chalk, covering it with a white earth soil.

"We shall give him this," they said, "to whet his appetite with the odor which it gives off. This bird of ours shall be his ruin, as we cover this bird with earth so we shall bring him down to the earth and bury him in the earth.

"Great shall be the wisdom of a created being, of a being fashioned, when it dawns, when there is light," said the boys.

"As it is natural for man to wish to eat, so Cabracan desires food," said Hunahpu and Xbalanque to each other.

Meanwhile the birds were roasting, they were beginning to turn golden brown, and the fat and juice which dripped from them made an appetizing odor. Cabracan wanted very much to eat them; they made his mouth water, he yawned, and the saliva and spittle drooled because of the smell which the birds gave off.

Then he asked them: "What is that you eat? The smell is really savory. Give me a little piece," he said to them.

Then they gave a bird to Cabracan, the one which would be his ruin; and when he had finished eating it, they set out toward the east where the great mountain was. But already Cabracan's legs and hands were weakening and he had no strength because of the earth with which the bird he had eaten was rubbed, and he could do nothing to the mountains. Neither was it possible to level them.

Then the boys tied him, they tied his hands behind him and also tied his neck and his feet together. Then they threw him to the ground and there they buried him.

In this way Cabracan was overcome by Hunahpu and Xbalanque. It would be impossible to tell of all the things they did here on earth.

Now we shall tell of the birth of Hunahpu and Xbalanque, having first told of the destruction of Vucub-Caquix and that of Zipacna and of Cabracan, here on earth.

SUFFERING FOR ART*

And One Monkey and One Artisan were great flautists and singers, and as they grew up they went through great suffering and pain. It had cost them suffering to become great knowers. Through it all they became flautists, singers, and writers, carvers. They did everything well. They simply knew it when they were born, they simply had genius. And they were the successors of their fathers who had gone to Xibalba, their dead fathers.

THE CALABASH TREE†

Now we shall also tell the name of the father of Hunahpu and Xbalanque. We shall not tell his origin and we shall not tell the history of the birth of Hunahpu and Xbalanque. We shall tell only half of it, only a part of the history of his father.

Here is the story. Here are the names of Hun-Hunahpu [and Vucub-Hunahpu], as they are called. Their parents were Xpiyacoc and Xmucane.

---

*From Tedlock, op. cit., p. 119.
†From Recinos, op. cit., pp. 107–23, 142–64.

During the night Hun-Hunahpu and Vucub-Hunahpu were born of Xpiyacoc and Xmucane.

Well now, Hun-Hunahpu had begotten two sons; the first was called Hunbatz and the second Hunchouen.

The mother of the two sons was called Xbaquiyalo. Thus was the wife of Hun-Hunahpu called. As for the other son, Vucub-Hunahpu, he had no wife, he was single.

By nature these two sons were very wise, and great was their wisdom; on earth they were soothsayers of good disposition and good habits. All the arts were taught to Hunbatz and Hunchouen, the sons of Hun-Hunahpu. They were flautists, singers, shooters with blowguns, painters, sculptors, jewelers, silversmiths; these were Hunbatz and Hunchouen.

Well, Hun-Hunahpu and Vucub-Hunahpu did nothing but play dice and ball all day long; and when the four got together to play ball, one pair played against the other pair.

And Voc, the messenger of Huracan, of Chipi-Caculha, of Raxa-Caculha came there to watch them, but Voc did not stray far from the earth nor far from Xibalba, and in an instant he went up to heaven to the side of Huracan.

They were still here on earth when the mother of Hunbatz and Hunchouen died.

And having gone to play ball on the road to Xibalba, they were overheard by Hun-Came and Vucub-Came, the lords of Xibalba.

"What are they doing on earth? Who are they who are making the earth shake, and making so much noise? Go and call them! Let them come here to play ball. Here we will overpower them! We are no longer respected by them. They no longer have consideration, or fear of our rank, and they even fight above our heads," said all the lords of Xibalba.

All of them held a council. Those called Hun-Came and Vucub-Came were the supreme judges. All the lords had been assigned their duties. Each one was given his own authority by Hun-Came and Vucub-Came.

They were, then, Xiquiripat and Cuchumaquic, lords of these names. They were the two who caused the shedding of blood of the men.

Others were called Ahalpuh and Ahalgana, also lords. And their work was to make men swell and make pus gush forth from their legs and stain their faces yellow, what is called Chuganal. Such was the work of Ahalpuh and Ahalgana.

Others were Lord Chamiabac and Lord Chamiaholom, constables of Xibalba, whose staffs were of bone. Their work was to make men waste away until they were nothing but skin and bone and they died, and they carried them with their stomach and bones stretched out. This was the work of Chamiabac and Chamiaholom, as they were called.

Others were called Lord Ahalmez and Lord Ahaltocob; their work was to bring disaster upon men, as they were going home, or in front of it, and they would be found wounded, stretched out, face up, on the ground, dead. This was the work of Ahalmez and Ahaltocob, as they were called.

Immediately after them were other lords named Xic and Patan whose work it was to cause men to die on the road, which is called sudden death, making blood to rush to their mouths until they died vomiting blood. The work of each one of these lords was to seize upon them, squeeze their throats and chests, so that the men died on the road, making the blood rush to their throats when they were walking. This was the work of Xic and Patan.

And having gathered in council, they discussed how to torment and wound Hun-Hunahpu and Vucub-Hunahpu. What the Lords of Xibalba coveted were the playing implements of Hun-Hunahpu and Vucub-Hunahpu—their leather pads and rings and gloves and crown and masks which were the playing gear of Hun-Hunahpu and Vucub-Hunahpu.

Now we shall tell of their journey to Xibalba and how they left behind them the sons of Hun-Hunahpu, Hunbatz, and [Hun]chouen, whose mother had died.

Then we shall tell how Hunbatz and Hunchouen were overcome by Hunahpu and Xbalanque.

THE HEAD OF HUN-HUNAHPU

The messengers of Hun-Came and Vucub-Came arrived immediately.

"Go, Ahpop Achih!" they were told. "Go and call Hun-Hunahpu and Vucub-Hunahpu. Say to them, 'Come with us. The lords say that you must come.' They must come here to play ball with us so that they shall make us happy, for really they amaze us. So, then, they must come," said the lords. "And have them bring their playing gear, their rings, their gloves, and have them bring their rubber balls, too," said the lords. "Tell them to come quickly," they told the messengers.

And these messengers were owls: Dhabi-Tucur, Huracan Tucur, Caquix-Tucur and Holom-Tucur. These were the names of the messengers of Xibalba.

Dhabi-Tucur was swift as an arrow; Huracan-Tucur had only one leg; Caquix-Tucur had a red back; and Holom-Tucur had only a head, no legs, but he had wings.

The four messengers had the rank of Ahpop-Achih. Leaving Xibalba, they arrived quickly, bringing their message to the court where Hun-Hunahpu and Vucub-Hunahpu were playing ball, at the ball-court which was called Nim-Xob Carchah. The owl messengers went directly to the ball-court and delivered their message exactly as it was given to them by Hun-Came, Vucub-Came, Ahalpuh, Ahalgana, Chamiabac, Chamiaholom, Xiquiripat, Cuchumaquic, Ahalmez, Ahaltocob, Xic, and Patan, as the lords were called who sent the message by the owls.

"Did the Lords Hun-Came and Vucub-Came really say that we must go with you?"

"They certainly said so, and 'Let them bring all their playing gear,' the lords said."

"Very well," said the youths. Wait for us, we are only going to say good-bye to our mother."

And having gone straight home, they said to their mother, for their father was dead: "We are going, our mother, but our going is only for a while. The messengers of the lord have come to take us. 'They must come,' they said, according to the messengers.

"We shall leave our ball here in pledge," they added. They went immediately to hang it in the space under the rooftree. "We will return to play," they said.

And going to Hunbatz and Hunchouen they said to them: "Keep on playing the flute and singing, painting, and carving; warm our house and warm the heart of your grandmother."

When they took leave of their mother, Xmucane was moved and burst into tears. "Do not worry, we are going, but we have not died yet," said Hun-Hunahpu and Vucub-Hunahpu as they left.

Hun-Hunahpu and Vucub-Hunahpu went immediately and the messengers took them on the road. Thus they were descending the road to Xibalba, by some very steep stairs. They went down until they came to the bank of a river which flowed rapidly between the ravines called Nuzian cul and Cuzivan, and crossed it. Then they crossed the river which flows among thorny calabash trees. There were very many calabash trees, but they passed through them without hurting themselves.

Then they came to the bank of a river of blood and crossed it without drinking its waters; they only went to the river bank and so they were not overcome. They went on until they came to where four roads joined, and there at the crossroads they were overcome.

One of the four roads was red, another black, another white and another yellow. And the black road said to them: "I am the one you must take because I am the way of the Lord." So said the road.

And from here on they were already overcome. They were taken over the road to Xibalba and when they arrived at the council room of the Lords of Xibalba, they had already lost the match.

Well, the first ones who were seated there were only figures of wood, arranged by the men of Xibalba. These they greeted first:

"How are you, Hun-Came?" they said to the wooden man. "How are you, Vucub-Came?" they said to the other wooden man. But they did not answer. Instantly the Lords of Xibalba burst into laughter and all the other lords began to laugh loudly, because they already took for granted the downfall and defeat of Hun-Hunahpu and Vucub-Hunahpu. And they continued to laugh.

Then Hun-Came and Vucub-Came spoke: "Very well," they said. "You have come. Tomorrow you shall prepare the mask, your rings, and your gloves," they said.

"Come and sit down on our bench," they [the Lords] said. But the bench which they offered them was of hot stone, and when they sat down they were burned. They began to squirm around on the bench, and if they had not stood up they would have burned their seats.

The Lords of Xibalba burst out laughing again; they were dying of laughter; they writhed from pain in their stomach, in their blood, and in their bones, caused by their laughter, all the Lords of Xibalba laughed.

"Go now to that house," they said. "There you will get your sticks of fat pines and your cigar and there you shall sleep."

Immediately they arrived at the House of Gloom. There was only darkness within the house. Meanwhile the Lords of Xibalba discussed what they should do.

"Let us sacrifice them tomorrow, let them die quickly, quickly, so that we can have their playing gear to use in play," said the Lords of Xibalba to each other.

Well, their fat-pine sticks were round and were called zaquitoc, which is the pine of Xibalba. Their fat-pine sticks were pointed and filed and were as bright as bone; the pine of Xibalba was very hard.

Hun-Hunahpu and Vucub-Hunahpu entered the House of Gloom. There they were given their fat-pine sticks, a single lighted stick which Hun-Came and Vucub-Came sent them, together with a lighted cigar for each of them which the lords had sent. They went to give them to Hun-Hunahpu and Vucub Hunahpu.

They found them crouching in the darkness when the porters arrived with the fat-pine sticks and the cigars. As they entered, the pine sticks lighted the place brightly.

"Each of you light your pine sticks and your cigars; come and bring them back at dawn, you must not burn them up, but you must return them whole; this is what the lords told us to say." So they said. And so they were defeated. They burned up the pine sticks, and they also finished the cigars which had been given to them.

There were many punishments in Xibalba; the punishments were of many kinds.

The first was the House of Gloom, Quequma-ha, in which there was only darkness.

The second was Xuxulim-ha, the house where everybody shivered, in which it was very cold. A cold, unbearable wind blew within.

The third was the House of Jaguars, Balami-ha, it was called, in which there were nothing but jaguars which stalked about, jumped around, roared, and made fun. The jaguars were shut up in the house.

Zotzi-ha, the House of Bats, the fourth place of punishment was called. Within this house there were nothing but bats which squeaked and cried and flew around and around. The bats were shut in and could not get out.

The fifth was called Chayim-ha, the House of Knives, in which there were only sharp, pointed knives, silent or grating against each other in the house.

There were many places of torture in Xibalba, but Hun-Hunahpu and Vucub-Hunahpu did not enter them. We only mention the names of these houses of punishment.

When Hun-Hunahpu and Vucub-Hunahpu came before Hun-Came and Vucub-Came, they said: "Where are my cigars? Where are my sticks of fat pine which I gave you last night?"

"They are all gone, Sir."

"Well. Today shall be the end of your days. Now you shall die. You shall be destroyed, we will break you into pieces and here your faces will stay hidden. You shall be sacrificed," said Hun-Came and Vucub-Came.

They sacrificed them immediately and buried them in the Pucbal-Chah,[4] as it was called. Before burying them, they cut off the head of Hun-Hunahpu and buried the older brother together with the younger brother.

"Take the head and put it in that tree which is planted on the road," said Hun-Came and Vucub-Came. And having put the head in the tree, instantly the tree, which had never borne fruit before the head of Hun-Hunahpu was placed among its branches, was covered with fruit. And this calabash tree, it is said, is the one which we now call the head of Hun-Hunahpu.

Hun-Came and Vucub-Came looked in amazement at the fruit on the tree. The round fruit was everywhere; but they did not recognize the head of Hun-Hunahpu; it was exactly like the other fruit of the calabash tree. So it seemed to all of the people of Xibalba when they came to look at it.

According to their judgment, the tree was miraculous, because of what had instantly occurred when they put Hun-Hunahpu's head among its branches. And the Lords of Xibalba said:

"Let no one come to pick this fruit. Let no one come and sit under this tree!" they said, and so the Lords of Xibalba resolved to keep everybody away.

The head of Hun-Hunahpu did not appear again, because it had become one and the same as the fruit of the gourd tree. Nevertheless, a girl heard the wonderful story. Now we shall tell about her arrival.

THE STORY OF THE MAIDEN

This is the story of a maiden, the daughter of a lord named Cuchumaquic. A maiden, then, daughter of a lord heard this story. The name of the fa-

[4]See Glossary.

ther was Cuchumaquic and that of the maiden was Xquic. When she heard the story of the fruit of the tree which her father told, she was amazed to hear it.

"Why can I not go to see this tree which they tell about?" the girl exclaimed. "Surely the fruit of which I hear tell must be very good." Finally she went alone and arrived at the foot of the tree which was planted in Pucbal-Chah.

She exclaimed, "What fruit is this which this tree bears? Is it not wonderful to see how it is covered with fruit? Must I die, shall I be lost, if I pick one of this fruit?" said the maiden.

Then the skull which was among the branches of the tree spoke up and said: "What is it you wish? Those round objects which cover the branches of the trees are nothing but skulls." So spoke the head of Hun-Hunahpu turning to the maiden. "Do you, perchance, want them?" it added.

"Yes, I want them," the maiden answered.

"Very well," said the skull. "Stretch your right hand up here."

"Very well," said the maiden, and with her right hand reached toward the skull.

In that instant the skull let a few drops of spittle fall directly into the maiden's palm. She looked quickly and intently at the palm of her hand, but the spittle of the skull was not there.

"In my saliva and spittle I have given you my descendants," said the voice in the tree. "Now my head has nothing on it any more, it is nothing but a skull without flesh. So are the heads of the great princes, the flesh is all which gives them a handsome appearance. And when they die, men are frightened by their bones. So, too, is the nature of the sons, which are like saliva and spittle, they may be sons of a lord, of a wise man, or of an orator.

"They do not lose their substance when they go, but they bequeath it; the image of the lord, of the wise man, or of the orator does not disappear, nor is it lost, but he leaves it to the daughters and to the sons which he begets. I have done the same with you. Go up, then, to the surface of the earth, that you may not die. Believe in my words that it will be so," said the head of Hun-Hunahpu and Vucub-Hunahpu.

And all that they did together was by order of Huracan, Chipi-Caculha, and Raxa-Caculha.

After all of the above talking, the maiden returned directly to her home, having immediately conceived the sons in her belly by virtue of the spittle only. And thus Hunahpu and Xbalanque were begotten.

And so the girl returned home, and after six months had passed, her father, who was called Cuchumaquic, noticed her condition. At once the maiden's secret was discovered by her father when he observed that she was pregnant.

Then the lords, Huracan and Vucub-Hunahpu, held council with Cuchumaquic.

"My daughter is pregnant, Sirs; she has been disgraced," exclaimed Cuchumaquic when he appeared before the lords.

"Very well," they said. "Command her to tell the truth, and if she refuses to speak, punish her; let her be taken far from here and sacrifice her."

"Very well, Honorable Lords," he answered. Then he questioned his daughter:

"Whose are the children that you carry, my daughter," and she answered, "I have no child, my father, for I have not yet known a youth."

"Very well," he replied. "You are really a whore. Take her and sacrifice her, Ahpop Achih; bring me her heart in a gourd and return this very day before the lords," he said to the two owls.

The four messengers took the gourd and set out carrying the young girl in their arms and also taking the knife of flint with which to sacrifice her.

And she said to them: "It cannot be that you will kill me, oh, messengers, because what I bear in my belly is no disgrace, but was begotten when I went to marvel at the head of Hun-Hunahpu which was in Pucbal-Chah. So, then, you must not sacrifice me, oh, messengers!" said the young girl, turning to them.

"And what shall we put in place of your heart? Your father told us: 'Bring the heart, return before the lords, do your duty, all working together, bring it in the gourd quickly, and put the heart in the bottom of the gourd.' Perchance, did he not speak to us so? What shall we put in the gourd? We wish too, that you should not die," said the messengers.

"Very well, but my heart does not belong to them. Neither is your home here, nor must you let them force you to kill men. Later, in truth, the real criminals will be at your mercy and I will overcome Huracan and Vucub-Hunahpu. So, then, the blood and only the blood shall be theirs and shall be given to them. Neither shall my heart be burned before them. Gather the product of this tree," said the maiden.

The red sap gushing forth from the tree fell in the gourd and with it they made a ball which glistened and took the shape of a heart. The tree gave forth sap similar to blood, with the appearance of real blood. Then the blood, or that is to say the sap of the red tree, clotted, and formed a very bright coating inside the gourd, like clotted blood; meanwhile the tree glowed at the work of the maiden. It was called the "red tree of cochineal," but [since then] it has taken the name of Blood Tree because its sap is called Blood.

"There on earth you shall be beloved and you shall have all that belongs to you," said the maiden to the owls.

"Very well, girl. We shall go there, we go up to serve you; you, continue on your way, while we go to present the sap, instead of your heart, to the lords," said the messengers.

When they arrived in the presence of the lords, all were waiting.

"You have finished?" asked Hun-Came.

"All is finished, my lords. Here in the bottom of the gourd is the heart."

"Very well. Let us see," exclaimed Hun-Came. And grasping it with his fingers, he raised it, the shell broke and the blood flowed bright red in color.

"Stir up the fire and put it on the coals," said Hun-Came.

As soon as they threw it on the fire, the men of Xibalba began to sniff and drawing near to it, they found the fragrance of the heart very sweet.

And as they sat deep in thought, the owls, the maiden's servants, left, and flew like a flock of birds from the abyss toward earth and the four became her servants.

In this manner the Lords of Xibalba were defeated. All were tricked by the maiden.

BAT HOUSE

This was the first test of Xibalba. The Lords of Xibalba thought that [the boys'] entrance there would be the beginning of their downfall. After a while [the boys] entered the House of Gloom; immediately lighted sticks of fat pine were given them and the messengers of Hun-Came also took a cigar to each one.

" 'These are their pine sticks,' said the lord; 'they must return them at dawn, tomorrow, together with the cigars, and you must bring them back whole,' said the lord." So said the messengers when they arrived.

"Very well," [the boys] replied. But they really did not [light] the sticks of pine, instead they put a red-colored thing in place of them, or some feathers from the tail of the macaw, which to the night watches looked like lighted pine sticks. And as for the cigars, they attached fireflies to their end.

All night [everybody] thought they were defeated. "They are lost," said the night watchmen. But the pine sticks had not been burned and looked the same, and the cigars had not been lighted and looked the same as before.

They went to tell the lords.

"How is this? Whence have they come? Who conceived them? Who gave birth to them? This really troubles us, because it is not well what they do. Their faces are strange, and strange is their conduct," they said to each other. Soon all the lords summoned [the boys].

"Eh! Let us play ball, boys!" they said. At the same time they were questioned by Hun-Came and Vucub-Came:

"Where did you come from? Tell us, boys!" said the Lords of Xibalba.

"Who knows whence we came! We do not know," they said, and nothing more.

"Very well. Let us play ball, boys," said the Lords of Xibalba.

"Good," they replied. "We shall use our ball," said the Lords of Xibalba.

"By no means shall you use [your ball], but ours," the boys answered.

"Not that one, but ours we shall use," insisted the Lords of Xibalba.

"Very well," said the boys.

"Let us play for a worm, the chil [caterpillar]," said the Lords of Xibalba.

"No, but instead, the head of the puma shall speak," said the boys.

"Not that," said those of Xibalba. "Very well,' said Hunahpu.

Then the Lords of Xibalba seized the ball; they threw it directly at the ring of Hunahpu. Immediately, while those of Xibalba grasped the handle of the knife of flint, the ball rebounded and bounced all around the floor of the ball-court.

"What is this?" exclaimed Hunahpu and Xbalanque. "You wish to kill us? Perchance you did not send to call us? And your own messengers did not come? In truth, unfortunate are we! We shall leave at once," the boys said to them.

This was exactly what those of Xibalba wanted to have happen to the boys, that they would die immediately, right there in the ball-court and thus they would be overcome. But it did not happen thus, and it was the Lords of Xibalba who were defeated by the boys.

"Do not leave, boys, let us go on playing ball, but we shall use your ball," they said to the boys.

"Very well," the boys answered and then they drove their ball through [the ring of Xibalba], and with this the game ended.

And offended by their defeat, the men of Xibalba immediately said: "What shall we do in order to overcome them?" And turning to the boys they said to them: "Go gather and bring us, early tomorrow morning, four gourds of flowers." So said the men of Xibalba to the boys.

"Very well. And what kind of flowers?" they asked the men of Xibalba.

"A branch of red chipilin, a branch of white chipilin, a branch of yellow chipilin, and a branch of carinimac," said the men of Xibalba.

"Very well," replied the boys.

Thus the talk ended; equally strong and vigorous were the words of the boys. And their hearts were calm when they gave themselves up to be overcome.

The Lords of Xibalba were happy, thinking that they had already defeated them.

"This has turned out well for us. First they must cut them [the flowers]," said the Lords of Xibalba. "Where shall they go to get the flowers?" they said to themselves.

"Surely you will give us our flowers tomorrow early; go, then, to cut them," the Lords of Xibalba said to Hunahpu and Xbalanque.

"Very well," they replied. "At dawn we shall play ball again," they said upon leaving.

And immediately the boys entered the House of Knives, the second place of torture in Xibalba. And what the lords wanted was that they would be cut to pieces by the knives, and would quickly be killed; that is what they wished in their hearts.

But the [boys] did not die. They spoke at once to the knives and said to them:

"Yours shall be the flesh of all the animals," they said to the knives. And they did not move again, but all the knives were quiet.

Thus they passed the night in the House of Knives, and calling all the ants, they said to them: "Come, Cutting Ants, come, zompopos [black or red nocturnal ants], and all of you go at once, go and bring all the kinds of flowers that we must cut for the lords."

"Very well," they said, and all the ants went to bring the flowers from the gardens of Hun-Came and Vucub-Came.

Previously [the lords] had warned the guards of the flowers of Xibalba: "Take care of our flowers, do not let them be taken by the boys who shall come to cut them. But how could [the boys] see and cut the flowers? Not at all. Watch, then, all night!"

"Very well," they answered. But the guards of the garden heard nothing. Needlessly they shouted up into the branches of the trees in the garden. There they were all night, repeating their same shouts and songs.

"Ixpurpuvec! Ixpurpuvec!" one shouted.

"Puhuyu! Puhuyu!" the other answered.

Puhuyu was the name of the two who watched the garden of Hun-Came and Vucub-Came. But they did not notice the ants who were robbing them of what they were guarding, turning around and moving here and there, cutting the flowers, climbing the trees to cut the flowers, and gathering them from the ground at the foot of the trees.

Meanwhile the guards went on crying, and they did not feel the teeth which were cutting their tails and their wings.

And thus the ants carried, between their teeth, the flowers which they took down, and gathering them from the ground, they went on carrying them with their teeth.

Quickly they filled the four gourds with flowers, which were moist [with dew] when it dawned. Immediately the messengers arrived to get them. " 'Tell them to come,' the lord has said, 'and bring here instantly what they have cut,' " they said to the boys.

"Very well," the [boys] answered. And carrying the flowers in the four gourds, they went, and when they arrived before the lord [of Xibalba] and the other lords, it was lovely to see the flowers they had brought. And in this way the Lords of Xibalba were overcome.

The boys had only sent the ants [to cut the flowers], and in a night the ants cut them and put them in the gourds.

Instantly the Lords of Xibalba paled and their faces became livid because of the flowers. They sent at once for the guardians of the flowers: "Why did you permit them to steal our flowers? These which we see here are our flowers," they said to the guardians.

"We noticed nothing, my lord. Our tails also suffered," they answered. And then the [lords] tore at their mouths as a punishment for having let that which was under their care be stolen.

Thus were Hun-Came and Vucub-Came defeated by Hunahpu and Xbalanque. And this was the beginning of their deeds. From that time the mouth of the owl is divided, cleft as it is today.

Immediately they went down to play ball, and also they played several tie-matches. Then they finished playing and agreed to play again the following day at dawn. So said the Lords of Xibalba.

"It is well," said the boys upon finishing.

Afterward they entered the House of Cold. It is impossible to describe how cold it was. The house was full of hail; it was the mansion of cold. Soon, however, the cold was ended because with [a fire of] old logs the boys made the cold disappear.

That is why they did not die; they were still alive when it dawned. Surely what the Lords of Xibalba wanted was that they would die; but it was not thus, and when it dawned, they were still full of health, and they went out again, when the messengers came to get them.

"How is this? They are not dead yet?" said the Lords of Xibalba. They were amazed to see the deeds of Hunahpu and Xbalanque.

Presently the [boys] entered the House of Jaguars. The house was full of jaguars. "Do not bite us! Here is what belongs to you," [the boys] said to the jaguars. And quickly they threw some bones to the animals, which pounced upon the bones.

"Now surely they are finished. Now already they have eaten their own entrails. At last they have given themselves up. Now their bones have been broken," so said the guards, all happy because of this.

But they [the boys] did not die. As usual, well and healthy, they came out of the House of Jaguars.

"What kind of people are they? Where did they come from?" said all the Lords of Xibalba.

Presently they [the boys] entered into the midst of fire in the House of Fire, inside which there was only fire; but they were not burned. Only the coals and the wood burned. And, as usual, they were well when it dawned. But what they [the Lords of Xibalba] wished was that [the boys] would die rapidly, where they had been. Nevertheless, it did not happen thus, which disheartened the Lords of Xibalba.

Then they put them into the House of Bats. There was nothing but bats inside this house, the house of Camazotz, a large animal, whose weapons for killing were like a dry point, and instantly those who came into their presence perished.

They [the boys] were in there, then, but they slept inside their blowguns. And they were not bitten by those who were in the house. Nevertheless, one of them had to give up because of another Camazotz that came from the sky, and made him come into sight.

The bats were assembled in council all night, and flew about: "Quilitz, quilitz," they said: So they were saying all night. They stopped for a little while, however, and they did not move and were pressed against the end of one of the blowguns.

Then Xbalanque said to Hunahpu: "Look you, has it begun already to get light?"

"Maybe so. I am going to see," Hunahpu answered.

And as he wished very much to look out of the mouth of the blowgun, and wished to see if it had dawned, instantly Camazotz cut off his head and the body of Hunahpu was decapitated.

Xbalanque asked again: "Has it not yet dawned?" But Hunahpu did not move. "Where have you gone, Hunahpu? What have you done?" But he did not move, and remained silent.

Then Xbalanque felt concerned and exclaimed: "Unfortunate are we. We are completely undone."

They went immediately to hang the head [of Hunahpu] in the ball-court by special order of Hun-Came and Vucub-Came, and all the people of Xibalba rejoiced for what had happened to the head of Hunahpu.

Immediately he [Xbalanque] called all the animals, the coati, the wild boar, all the animals small and large, during the night, and at dawn he asked them what their food was.

"What does each of you eat? For I have called you so that you may choose your food," said Xbalanque to them.

"Very well," they answered. And immediately each went to take his [own food] and they all went together. Some went to take rotten things; others went to take grasses; others went to get stones. Others went to gather earth. Varied was the food of the [small] animals and of the large animals.

Behind them the turtle was lingering, it came waddling along to take its food. And reaching at the end [of Hunahpu's body] it assumed the form of the head of Hunahpu, and instantly the eyes were fashioned.

Many soothsayers came, then, from heaven. The Heart of Heaven, Huracan, came to soar over the House of Bats.

It was not easy to finish making the face, but it turned out very well; the hair had a handsome appearance and [the head] could also speak.

But as it was about to dawn and the horizon reddened: "Make it dark again, old one!" the buzzard was told.

"Very well," said the old one, and instantly the old one darkened [the sky]. "Now the buzzard has darkened it," the people say nowadays.

And so, during the cool of dawn, the Hunahpu began his existence. "Will it be good?" they said. "Will it turn out to look like Hunahpu?"

"It is very good," they answered. And really it seemed that the skull had changed itself back into a real head.

Then they [the two boys] talked among themselves and agreed: "Do not play ball; only pretend to play; I shall do everything alone," said Xbalanque.

At once he gave his orders to a rabbit: "Go and take your place over the ball-court; stay there within the oak grove," the rabbit was told by Xbalanque; "when the ball comes to you, run out immediately, and I shall do the rest," the rabbit was told, when they gave him these instructions during the night.

Presently day broke and the two boys were well and healthy. Then they went down to play ball. The head of Hunahpu was suspended over the ball-court.

"We have triumphed! [said the Lords of Xibalba]. You worked your own destruction, you have delivered yourselves," they said. In this way they annoyed Hunahpu.

"Hit his head with the ball," they said. But they did not bother him with it; he paid no attention to it.

Then the Lords of Xibalba threw out the ball. Xbalanque went out to get it; the ball was going straight to the ring, but it stopped, bounced, and passed quickly over the ball-court and with a jump went toward the oak grove.

Instantly the rabbit ran out and went hopping; and the Lords of Xibalba ran after it. They went, making noise and shouting after the rabbit. It ended by all of the Lords of Xibalba going.

At once Xbalanque took possession of the head of Hunahpu; and taking the turtle he went to suspend it over the ball-court. And that head was actually the head of Hunahpu and the two boys were very happy.

Those of Xibalba ran, then, to find the ball and having found it between the oaks, called them, saying:

"Come here. Here is the ball. We found it," they said, and they brought it.

When the Lords of Xibalba returned, they exclaimed, "What is this we see?"

Then they began to play again. Both of them tied.

Presently Xbalanque threw a stone at the turtle, which came to the ground and fell in the ball-court, breaking into a thousand pieces like seeds, before the lords.

"Who of you shall go to find it? Where is the one who shall go to bring it?" said the Lords of Xibalba.

And so were the Lords of Xibalba overcome by Hunahpu and Xbalanque. These two suffered great hardships, but they did not die despite all that was done to them.

THE DEATH OF THE TWINS

Here is the account of the death of Hunahpu and Xbalanque. Now we shall tell of the way they died.

Having been forewarned of all the suffering which the [Lords of Xibalba] wished to impose upon them, they did not die of the tortures of Xibalba, nor were they overcome by all the fierce animals which were in Xibalba.

Afterward they sent for two soothsayers who were like prophets; they were called Xulu and Pacam and were diviners, and they said unto them:

"You shall be questioned by the Lords of Xibalba about our deaths, for which they are planning and preparing because of the fact that we have not died, nor have they been able to overcome us, nor have we perished under their torments, nor have the animals attacked us. We have the presentiment in our hearts that they shall kill us by burning us. All the people of Xibalba have assembled, but the truth is, that we shall not die. Here, then, you have our instructions as to what you must say:

"If they should come to consult you about our death and that we may be sacrificed, what shall you say then, Xulu and Pacam? If they ask you: 'Will it not be good to throw their bones into the ravine?' 'No, it would not be well,' tell them, 'because they would be brought to life again, afterward!' If they ask you: 'Would it not be good to hang them from the trees?' you shall answer: 'By no means would it be well, because then you shall see their faces again.' And when for the third time they ask you: 'Would it be good to throw their bones into the river?' If you were asked all the above by them, you should answer: 'It would be well if they were to die that way; then it would be well to crush their bones on a grinding stone, as corn meal is ground; let each one be ground [separately]; throw them into the river immediately, there where the spring gushes forth, in order that they may be carried away among all the small and large hills.' Thus you shall answer them when the plan which we have advised you is put into practice," said Hunahpu and Xbalanque. And when they [the boys] took leave of them, they already knew about their approaching death.

They made, then, a great bonfire, a kind of oven; the men of Xibalba made it and filled it with thick branches.

Shortly afterward the messengers arrived who had to accompany [the boys], the messengers of Hun-Came and Vucub-Came.

" 'Tell them to come. Go and get the boys; go there so that they may know we are going to burn them.' This the lords said, oh, boys!" the messengers exclaimed.

"It is well," they answered. And setting out quickly, they arrived near the bonfire. There [the Lords of Xibalba] wanted to force the boys to play a mocking game with them.

"Let us drink our chicha and fly four times, each one, [over the bonfire] boys!" was said to them by Hun-Came.

"Do not try to deceive us," [the boys] answered. "Perchance, we do not know about our death, oh lords! and that this is what awaits us here?" And embracing each other, face to face, they both stretched out their arms, bent toward the ground and jumped into the bonfire, and thus the two died together.

All those of Xibalba were filled with joy, shouting and whistling they exclaimed: "Now we have overcome them. At last they have given themselves up."

Immediately they called Xulu and Pacam, to whom they [the boys] had given their instructions, and asked them what they must do with their bones, as they [the boys] had foretold. Those of Xibalba then ground their bones and went to cast them into the river. But the bones did not go very far, for settling themselves down at once on the bottom of the river, they were changed back into handsome boys. And when again they showed themselves, they really had their same old faces.

THE DEFEAT OF XIBALBA

On the fifth day they appeared again and were seen in the water by the people. Both had the appearance of fishmen;[5] when those of Xibalba saw them, after having hunted them all over the river.

And the following day, two poor men presented themselves with very old-looking faces and of miserable appearance, [and] ragged clothes, whose countenances did not commend them. So they were seen by all those of Xibalba.

And what they did was very little. They only performed the dance of the puhuy [owl or churn-owl], the dance of the cux [weasel], and the dance of the [armadillo], and they also danced the [centipede] and the chitic [that walks on stilts]. Furthermore, they worked many miracles. They burned houses as though they really were burning and instantly they were as they had been before. Many of those of Xibalba watched them in wonder.

Presently they cut themselves into bits; they killed each other; the first one whom they had killed stretched out as though he were dead, and instantly the other brought him back to life. Those of Xibalba looked on in amazement at all they did, and they performed it, as the beginning of their triumph over those of Xibalba.

[5]The Quiche word here is *vinac-ear*, literally, "fish man," but also the name for a variety of large fish; hence a pun.

Presently word of their dances came to the ears of the lords Hun-Came and Vucub-Came. Upon hearing it they exclaimed: "Who are these two orphans? Do they really give you so much pleasure?"

"Surely their dances are very beautiful, and all that they do," answered he who had brought the news to the lords.

Happy to hear this, the [lords] then sent their messengers to call [the boys] with flattery. " 'Tell them to come here, tell them to come so that we may see what they do; that we may admire them and regard them with wonder,' this the lords said. 'So you shall say unto them,' " this was told to the messengers.

They arrived at once before the dancers and gave them the message of the lords.

"We do not wish to," the [boys] answered, "because, frankly, we are ashamed. How could we not but be ashamed to appear in the house of the lords with our ugly countenances, our eyes which are so big, and our poor appearance? Do you not see that we are nothing more than some [poor] dancers? What shall we tell our companions in poverty who have come with us and wish to see our dances and be entertained by them? How could we do our dances before the lords? For that reason, then, we do not want to go, oh, messengers," said Hunahpu and Xbalanque.

Finally, with downcast faces and with reluctance and sorrow they went; but for a while they did not wish to walk, and the messengers had to beat them in the face many times, when they led them to the house of the lords.

They arrived, then, before the lords, timid and with head bowed; they came prostrating themselves, making reverences and humiliating themselves. They looked feeble, ragged, and their appearance was really that of vagabonds when they arrived.

They were questioned immediately about their country—and their people; they also asked them about their mother and their father.

"Where do you come from?" [the lords] said.

"We do not know, Sir. We do not know the faces of our mother and father; we were small when they died," they answered, and did not say another word.

"All right. Now do [your dances] so that we may admire you. What do you want? We shall give you pay," they told them.

"We do not want anything; but really we are very much afraid," they said to the lord.

"Do not grieve, do not be afraid. Dance! And do first the part in which you kill yourselves; burn my house, do all that you know how to do. We shall marvel at you, for that is what our hearts desire. And afterwards, poor things, we shall give help for your journey," they told them.

Then they began to sing and dance. All the people of Xibalba arrived and gathered together in order to see them. Then they performed the dance of the cux, they danced the puhuy, and they danced the iboy.

And the lord said to them: "Cut my dog into pieces and let him be brought back to life by you," he said to them.

"Very well," they answered, and cut the dog into bits. Instantly they brought him back to life. The dog was truly full of joy when he was brought back to life, and wagged his tail when they revived him.

The lord said to them then: "Burn my house now!" Thus he said to them. Instantly they put fire to the lord's house, and although all the lords were assembled together within the house, they were not burned. Quickly it was whole again, and not for one instant was the house of Hun-Came destroyed.

All of the lords were amazed, and in the same way the [boys'] dances gave them much pleasure.

Then they were told by the lord: "Now kill a man, sacrifice him, but do not let him die," he told them.

"Very well," they answered. And seizing a man, they quickly sacrificed him, and raising his heart on high, they held it so that all the lords could see it.

Again Hun-Came and Vucub-Came were amazed. A moment afterward the man was brought back to life by them [the boys], and his heart was filled with joy when he was revived.

The lords were astounded. "Sacrifice yourselves now, let us see it! We really like your dances!" said the lords. "Very well, Sirs," they answered. And they proceeded to sacrifice each other. Hunahpu was sacrificed by Xbalanque; one by one his arms and his legs were sliced off; his head was cut from his body and carried away; his heart was torn from his breast and thrown onto the grass. All the Lords of Xibalba were fascinated. They looked on in wonder, but really it was only the dance of one man; it was Xbalanque.

"Get up!" he said, and instantly [Hunahpu] returned to life. They [the boys] were very happy and the lords were also happy. In truth, what they did gladdened the hearts of Hun-Came and Vucub-Came, and the latter felt as though they themselves were dancing.

Then their hearts were filled with desire and longing by the dances of Hunahpu and Xbalanque; and Hun-Came and Vucub-Came gave their commands.

"Do the same with us! Sacrifice us!" they said. "Cut us into pieces, one by one!" Hun-Came and Vucub-Came said to Hunahpu and Xbalanque.

"Very well; afterward you will come back to life again. Perchance, did you not bring us here in order that we should entertain you, the lords, and your sons, and vassals?" they said to the lords.

And so it happened that they first sacrificed the one, who was the chief and [Lord of Xibalba], the one called Hun-Came, king of Xibalba.

And when Hun-Came was dead, they overpowered Vucub-Came, and they did not bring either of them back to life.

The people of Xibalba fled as soon as they saw that their lords were dead and sacrificed. In an instant both were sacrificed. And this they [the boys] did in order to chastise them. Quickly the principal lord was killed. And they did not bring him back to life.

And another lord humbled himself then, and presented himself before the dancers. They had not discovered him, nor had they found him. "Have mercy on me!" he said when they found him.

All the sons and vassals of Xibalba fled to a great ravine, and all of them were crowded into this narrow, deep place. There they were crowded together and hordes of ants came and found them and dislodged them from the ravine. In this way [the ants] drove them to the road, and when they arrived [the people] prostrated themselves and gave themselves up; they humbled themselves and arrived, grieving.

In this way the Lords of Xibalba were overcome. Only by a miracle and by their [own] transformation could [the boys] have done it.

SUN, MOON AND STARS

Immediately [the boys] told their names and they extolled themselves before all the people of Xibalba.

"Hear our names. We shall also tell you the names of our fathers. We are Hunahpu and Xbalanque; those are our names. And our fathers are those whom you killed and who were called Hun-Hunahpu and Vucub-Hunahpu. We, those whom you see here, are, then, the avengers of the torments and suffering of our fathers. That is the reason why we resent all the evil you have done to them. Therefore, we shall put an end to all of you, we shall kill you, and not one of you shall escape," they said.

Instantly all the people of Xibalba fell to their knees, crying.

"Have mercy on us, Hunahpu and Xbalanque! It is true that we sinned against your fathers as you said, and that they are buried in Pucbal-Chah," they said.

"Very well. This is our sentence, that we are going to tell you. Hear it, all you of Xibalba:

"Since neither your great power nor your race any longer exist, and since neither do you deserve mercy, your rank shall be lowered. Not for you shall be the ball game. You shall spend your time making earthen pots and tubs and stones to grind corn. Only the children of the thickets and desert shall speak with you. The noble sons, the civilized vassals shall not consort with you, and they will forsake your presence. The sinners, the evil ones, the sad ones, the unfortunate ones, those who give themselves up to vice, these are the ones who will welcome you. No longer will you seize men suddenly [for sacrifice]; remember your rank has been lowered."

Thus they spoke to all the people of Xibalba.

In this way their destruction and their lamentations began. Their power in the olden days was not much. They only liked to do evil to men in those times. In truth, in those days, they did not have the category of gods. Furthermore, their horrible faces frightened people. They were the enemies, they incited to evil, to sin and to discord.

They were also false in their hearts, black and white at the same time, envious and tyrannical, according to what was said of them. Furthermore, they painted and greased their faces.

In this way, then, occurred the loss of their grandeur and the decadence of their empire.

And this was what Hunahpu and Xbalanque did.

Meanwhile, the grandmother was crying and lamenting before the reeds which they had left planted. The reeds sprouted, then they dried up when [the boys] were consumed in the bonfire; afterward [the reeds] sprouted again. Then the grandmother lighted the fire and burned incense before the reeds in memory of her grandchildren. And the grandmother's heart filled with joy when, for the second time, the reeds sprouted. Then they were worshiped by the grandmother, and she called them the Center of the House, Nicab [the Center] they were called.

Green reeds growing in the plains was their name. And they were called the Center of the House and the Center, because in the middle of the house they planted the reeds. And the reeds, which were planted, were called the plains, Green Reeds growing on the plains. They also were called Green Reeds because they had resprouted. This name was given them by Xmucane [given] to those [reeds] which Hunahpu and Xbalanque left planted in order that they should be remembered by their grandmother.

Well, now, their fathers, those who died long ago, were Hun Hunahpu and Vucub-Hunahpu. They also saw the faces of their fathers there in Xibalba and their fathers talked with their descendants, that is the ones who overthrew those of Xibalba.

And here is how their fathers were honored by them. They honored Vucub-Hunahpu; they went to honor him at the place of sacrifice of the ball-court. And at the same time they wanted to make Vucub-Hunahpu's face. They hunted there for his entire body, his mouth, his nose, his eyes. They found his body, but it could do very little. It could not pronounce his name, this Hunahpu. Neither could his mouth say it.

And here is how they extolled the memory of their fathers, whom they had left there in the place of sacrifice at the ball-court: "You shall be invoked," their sons said to them, when they fortified their heart. "You shall be the first to arise, and you shall be the first to be worshiped by the sons of the noblemen, by the civilized vassals. Your names shall not be lost. So it shall be!" they told their fathers and thus consoled themselves. "We are the avengers of your death, of the pains and sorrows which they caused you."

Thus was their leave-taking, when they had already overcome all the people of Xibalba.

Then they rose up in the midst of the light, and instantly they were lifted into the sky. One was given the sun, the other, the moon. Then the arch of heaven and the face of the earth were lighted. And they dwelt in heaven.

Then the four hundred boys whom Zipacna had killed also ascended, and so they again became the companions of [the boys] and were changed into stars in the sky.

ADVENT OF HUMANS AND THE END OF OMNISCIENCE*

AND HERE IS THE BEGINNING OF THE CONCEPTION OF HUMANS, and of the search for the ingredients of the human body. So they spoke, the Bearer, Begetter, the Makers, modelers named Sovereign Plumed Serpent:

"The dawn has approached, preparations have been made, and morning has come for the provider, nurturer, born in the light, begotten in the light. Morning has come for humankind, for the people of the face of the earth," they said. It all came together as they went on thinking in the darkness, in the night, as they searched and they sifted, they thought and they wondered.

And here their thoughts came out in clear light. They sought and discovered what was needed for human flesh. It was only a short while before the sun, moon, and stars were to appear above the Makers and Modelers. Broken Place, Bitter Water Place is the name: the yellow corn, white corn came from there.

And these are the names of the animals who brought the food: fox, coyote, parrot, crow. There were four animals who brought the news of the ears of yellow corn and white corn. They were coming from over there at Broken Place, they showed the way to the break.

And this was when they found the staple foods.

And these were the ingredients for the flesh of the human work, the human design, and the water was for the blood. It became human blood, and corn was also used by the Bearer, Begetter.

And so they were happy over the provisions of the good mountain, filled with sweet things, thick with yellow corn, white corn, and thick with pataxte and cacao, countless zapotes, anonas, jocotes, nances, matasanos, sweets— the rich foods filling up the citadel named Broken Place, Bitter Water Place.

*From Tedlock, op. cit., pp. 163–67, 172–75.

All the edible fruits were there: small staples, great staples, small plants, great plants. The way was shown by the animals.

And then the yellow corn and white corn were ground, and Xmucane did the grinding nine times. Corn was used, along with the water she rinsed her hands with, for the creation of grease; it became human fat when it was worked by the Bearer, Begetter, Sovereign Plumed Serpent, as they are called.

After that, they put it into words: the making, the modeling of our first mother-father, with yellow corn, white corn alone for the flesh, food alone for the human legs and arms, for our first fathers, the four human works. It was staples alone that made up their flesh.

THESE ARE THE NAMES OF THE FIRST PEOPLE WHO WERE MADE AND MODELED.
This is the first person: Jaguar Quitze.
And now the second: Jaguar Night.
And now the third: Mahucutah.
And the fourth: True Jaguar.
And these are the names of our first mother-fathers. They were simply made and modeled, it is said; they had no mother and no father. We have named the men by themselves. No woman gave birth to them, nor were they begotten by the builder, sculptor, Bearer, Begetter. By sacrifice alone, by genius alone they were made, they were modeled by the Maker, Modeler, Bearer, Begetter, Sovereign Plumed Serpent. And when they came to fruition, they came out human:
They talked and they made words.
They looked and they listened.
They walked, they worked.
They were good people, handsome, with looks of the male kind. Thoughts came into existence and they gazed; their vision came all at once. Perfectly they saw, perfectly they knew everything under the sky, whenever they looked. The moment they turned around and looked around in the sky, on the earth, everything was seen without any obstruction. They didn't have to walk around before they could see what was under the sky; they just stayed where they were.

As they looked, their knowledge became intense. Their sight passed through trees, through rocks, through lakes, through seas, through mountains, through plains. Jaguar Quitze, Jaguar Night, Mahucutah, and True Jaguar were truly gifted people.

And then they were asked by the builder and mason:

"What do you know about your being? Don't you look, don't you listen? Isn't your speech good, and your walk? So you must look, to see out under the sky. Don't you see the mountain-plain clearly? So try it," they were told.

And then they saw everything under the sky perfectly. After that, they thanked the Maker, Modeler:

"Truly now,
double thanks, triple thanks
that we've been formed, we've been given
our mouths, our faces,
we speak, we listen,
we wonder, we move,
our knowledge is good, we've understood
what is far and near,
and we've seen what is great and small
under the sky, on the earth.
Thanks to you we've been formed,
we've come to be made and modeled,
our grandmother, our grandfather,"

they said when they gave thanks for having been made and modeled. They understood everything perfectly, they sighted the four sides, the four corners in the sky, on the earth, and this didn't sound good to the builder and sculptor:

"What our works and designs have said is no good:

'We have understood everything, great and small,' they say." And so the Bearer, Begetter took back their knowledge:

"What should we do with them now? Their vision should at least reach nearby, they should see at least a small part of the face of the earth, but what they're saying isn't good. Aren't they merely 'works' and 'designs' in their very names? Yet they'll become as great as gods, unless they procreate, proliferate at the sowing, the dawning, unless they increase."

"Let it be this way: now we'll take them apart just a little, that's what we need. What we've found out isn't good. Their deeds would become equal to ours, just because their knowledge reaches so far. They see everything," so said

the Heart of Sky, Hurricane,
Newborn Thunderbolt, Raw Thunderbolt,
Sovereign Plumed Serpent,
Bearer, Begetter,
Xpiyacoc, Xmucane,
Maker, Modeler,

as they are called. And when they changed the nature of their works, their designs, it was enough that the eyes be marred by the Heart of Sky. They were blinded as the face of a mirror is breathed upon. Their eyes were weakened. Now it was only when they looked nearby that things were clear.

And such was the loss of the means of understanding, along with the means of knowing everything, by the four humans. The root was implanted.

And such was the making, modeling of our first grandfather, our father, by the Heart of Sky, Heart of Earth.

AND THEN THEIR WIVES AND WOMEN CAME INTO BEING.
Again, the same gods thought of it. It was as if they were asleep when they received them, truly beautiful women were there with Jaguar Quitze, Jaguar Night, Mahucutah, and True Jaguar. With their women there they became wider awake. Right away they were happy at heart again, because of their wives.

Celebrated Seahouse is the name of the wife of Jaguar Quitze. Prawn House is the name of the wife of Jaguar Night.

Hummingbird House is the name of the wife of Mahucutah. Macaw House is the name of the wife of True Jaguar.

So these are the names of their wives, who became ladies of rank, giving birth to the people of the tribes, small and great.

THEY WALKED IN CROWDS WHEN THEY ARRIVED AT TULAN, AND THERE WAS NO FIRE. Only those with Tohil had it: this was the tribe whose god was first to generate fire. How it was generated is not clear. Their fire was already burning when Jaguar Quitze and Jaguar Night first saw it:

"Alas! Fire has not yet become ours. We'll die from the cold," they said. And then Tohil spoke:

"Do not grieve. You will have your own even when the fire you're talking about has been lost," Tohil told them.

"Aren't you a true god!
Our sustenance and our support!
Our god!"

they said when they gave thanks for what Tohil had said.

"Very well, in truth,
I am your god: so be it.
I am your lord: so be it,"

the penitents and sacrificers were told by Tohil.

And this was the warming of the tribes. They were pleased by their fire.

After that a great downpour began, which cut short the fire of the tribes. And hail fell thickly on all the tribes, and their fires were put out by the hail. Their fires didn't start up again. So then Jaguar Quitze and Jaguar Night asked for their fire again:

"Tohil, we'll be finished off by the cold," they told Tohil.

"Well, do not grieve," said Tohil. Then he started a fire. He pivoted inside his sandal.

After that, Jaguar Quitze, Jaguar Night, Mahucutah, and True Jaguar were pleased.

After they had been warmed, the fires of the other tribes were still out. Now they were being finished off by the cold, so they came back to ask for their fire from Jaguar Quitze, Jaguar Night, Mahucutah, and True Jaguar. They could bear the cold and hail no longer. By now they were chattering and shivering. There was no life left in them. Their legs and arms kept shaking. Their hands were stiff when they arrived.

"Perhaps we wouldn't make ourselves ashamed in front of you if we asked to remove a little something from your fire?" they said when they arrived, but they got no response. And then the tribes cursed in their thoughts. Already their language had become different from that of Jaguar Quitze, Jaguar Night, Mahucutah, and True Jaguar.

"Alas! We left our language behind. How did we do it? We're lost! Where were we deceived? We had only one language when we came to Tulan, and we had only one place of emergence and origin. We haven't done well," said all the tribes beneath the trees and bushes.

And then a person showed himself before Jaguar Quitze, Jaguar Night, Mahucutah, and True Jaguar, and he spoke as a messenger of Xibalba:

"Truly, since you have your god, your nurturer, and he is the representation, the commemoration of your Maker and your Modeler, don't give the tribes their fire until they give something to Tohil. You don't want them to give anything to you. You must ask for what belongs to Tohil; to him must come what they give in order to get fire," said the Xibalban. He had wings like the wings of a bat.

"I am a messenger of those who made you and modeled you," said the Xibalban. So now they were happy; now they thought all the more of Tohil, Auilix, and Hacauitz. When the Xibalban had spoken he made himself vanish right in front of them, without delay.

And so again the tribes arrived, again done in by the cold.

Thick were the white hail, the blackening storm, and the white crystals. The cold was incalculable. They were simply overwhelmed. Because of the cold all the tribes were going along doubled over, groping along when they arrived in the presence of Jaguar Quitze, Jaguar Night, Mahucutah, and True Jaguar. There was great pain in their hearts; they had covetous mouths and covetous faces.

And now they were coming as thieves before Jaguar Quitze, Jaguar Night, Mahucutah, and True Jaguar:

"Wouldn't you take pity on us if we asked to remove a little something from your fire? Wasn't it found and wasn't it revealed that we had just one home and just one mountain when you were made, when you were modeled? So please take pity on us," they said.

"And what would you give us for taking pity on you?" they were asked.

"Well, we'd give you metal," said the tribes.

"We don't want metal," said Jaguar Quitze and Jaguar Night.

"Whatever might you want, if we may ask?" the tribes said then.

"Very well. First we must ask Tohil, and then we'll tell you," they were told next. And then they asked Tohil:

"What should the tribes give you, Tohil? They've come to ask for your fire," said Jaguar Quitze, Jaguar Night, Mahucutah, and True Jaguar.

"Very well. You will tell them:

" 'Don't they want to be suckled on their sides and under their arms? Isn't it their heart's desire to embrace me? I, who am Tohil? But if there is no desire, then I'll not give them their fire,' says Tohil. 'When the time comes, not right now, they'll be suckled on their sides, under their arms,' he says to you, 'you will say,' " they were told, Jaguar Quitze, Jaguar Night, Mahucutah, and True Jaguar, and then they spoke the word of Tohil.

"Very well. Let him suckle. And very well, we shall embrace him," said the tribes, when they answered and agreed to the word of Tohil. They made no delay but said "very well" right away, and then they received their fire.

After that they got warm, but there was one group that simply stole the fire, there in the smoke. This was the Bat House. Calm Snake is the name of the god of the Cakchiquels, but it looks like a bat. They went right past in the smoke then, they sneaked past when they came to get fire. The Cakchiquels didn't ask for their fire. They didn't give themselves up in defeat, but all the other tribes were defeated when they gave themselves up to being suckled on their sides, under their arms.

And this is what Tohil meant by being "suckled": that all the tribes be cut open before him, and that their hearts be removed "through their sides, under their arms." This deed had not yet been attempted when Tohil saw into the middle of it, nor had Jaguar Quitze, Jaguar Night, Mahucutah, and True Jaguar received fiery splendor and majesty.

OUT OF TULAN*

There was nevertheless a tribe who stole the fire in the smoke; and they were from the house of Zotzil. The god of the Cakchiquel was called Chamal-can and he had the form of a bat.

When they passed through the smoke, they went softly and then they seized the fire. The Cakchiquel did not ask for the fire, because they did not want to give themselves up to be overcome, the way that the other tribes had been overcome when they offered their breasts and their armpits so that they would be opened. And this was the opening [of the breasts] about which

*From Recinos, op. cit., pp. 179–92.

Tohil had spoken; that they should sacrifice all the tribes before him, that they should tear out their hearts from their breasts.

And this had not yet begun when the taking of power and sovereignty by Balam-Quitzé, Balam-Acab, Mahucutah, and Iqui-Balam was prophesied by Tohil.

There in Tulan-Zuiva, whence they had come, they were accustomed to fast, they observed a perpetual fast while they awaited the coming of dawn and watched for the rising sun.

They took turns at watching the Great Star called Icoquih [Venus], which rises first before the sun, when the sun rises, the brilliant Icoquih, which was always before them in the East, when they were there in the place called Tulan-Zuiva, whence came their god.

It was not here, then, where they received their power and sovereignty, but there they subdued and subjected the large and small tribes when they sacrificed them before Tohil, and offered him the blood, the substance, breasts, and sides of all the men.

In Tulan power came instantly to them; great was their wisdom in the darkness and in the night.

Then they came, they pulled up stakes there and left the East. "This is not our home; let us go and see where we should settle," Tohil said then.

In truth, he was accustomed to talk to Balam-Quitzé, Balam Acab, Mahucutah, and Iqui-Balam: "Give thanks before setting out; do what is necessary to bleed your ears, prick your elbows, and make your sacrifices, this shall be your thanks to God."

"Very well," they said, and took blood from their ears. And they wept in their chants because of their departure from Tulan; their hearts mourned when they left Tulan.

"Pity us! We shall not see the dawn here, when the sun rises and lights the face of the earth," they said at leaving. But they left some people on the road which they followed so that they would keep watch.

Each of the tribes kept getting up to see the star which was the herald of the sun. This sign of the dawn they carried in their hearts when they came from the East, and with the same hope they left there, from that great distance, according to what their songs now say.

They came at last to the top of a mountain and there all the Quiche people and the tribes were reunited, There they all held council to make their plans. Today this mountain is called Chi-Pixab, this is the name of the mountain.

There they reunited and there they extolled themselves: "I am, I, the people of the Quiche! And thou, Tamub, that shall be thy name." And to those from Ilocab they said: "Thou, Ilocab, this shall be thy name. And these three Quiche [peoples] shall not disappear, our fate is the same," they said when they gave them their names.

Then they gave the Cakchiquel their name: Gagchequeleb was their name. In the same way they named those of Rabinal, which was their name, and they still have it. And also those of Tziquinaha, as they are called today. Those are the names which they gave to each other.

There they were come together to await the dawn and to watch for the coming of the star, which comes just before the sun, when it is about to rise. "We came from there, but we have separated," they said to each other.

And their hearts were troubled; they were suffering greatly; they did not have food; they did not have sustenance; they only smelled the ends of their staffs and thus they imagined they were eating; but they did not eat when they came.

It is not quite clear, however, how they crossed the sea; they crossed to this side, as if there were no sea; they crossed on stones, placed in a row over the sand. For this reason they were called "Stones in a Row, Sand Under the Sea," names given to them when they [the tribes] crossed the sea, the waters having parted when they passed.

And their hearts were troubled when they talked together, because they had nothing to eat, only a drink of water and a handful of corn they had.

There they were, then, assembled on the mountain called Chi-Pixab. And they had also brought Tohil, Avilix, and Hacavitz. Balam-Quitze and his wife Caha-Paluna, which was the name of his wife, observed a complete fast. And so did Balam Acab and his wife, who was called Chomiha; and Mahucutah and his wife, called Tzununiha, also observed a complete fast, and Iqui-Balam with his wife, called Caquixaha, likewise.

And there were those who fasted in the darkness, and in the night. Great was their sorrow when they were on the mountain called Chi-Pixab.

And their gods spoke to them again. Thus Tohil, Avilix, and Hacavitz spoke to Balam-Quitzé, Balam-Acab, Mahucutah, and Iqui-Balam: "Let us go, let us get up, let us not stay here, take us to a secret place! Already dawn draws near. Would it not be a disgrace for you if we were imprisoned by our enemies within these walls where you, the priests and sacrificers, keep us?

Put each of us, then, in a safe place,' " they said when they spoke.

"Very well. We shall go on, we shall go in search of the forests," all answered.

Immediately after, they took up their gods and put them on their backs. In this way they carried Hacavitz to the ravine called Euabal-Zivan, so named by them, to the large ravine of the forest, now called Pavilix, and there they left him. In this ravine he was left by Balam-Acab.

They were left one by one. The first one left was Hacavitz, he was left on a large red pyramid, on the mountain now called Hacavitz. There they founded their town, there in the place where the god called Hacavitz was.

In the same way, Mahucutah left his god, who was the second one hidden by them.

Hacavitz was not in the forest, but on a hill cleared of trees, Hacavitz was hidden.

Then Balam-Quitzé came, he came there to the large forest; Balam-Quitzé came to hide Tohil at the hill which is today called Patohil. Then they celebrated the hiding of Tohil in the ravine, in his refuge. A great quantity of snakes, jaguars, vipers, and cantiles were in the forest where they were hidden by the priests and sacrificers.

Balam-Quitzé, Balam-Acab, Mahucutah, and Iqui-Balam were together; together they awaited the dawn, there on the mountain, called Hacavitz.

And a short distance away was the god of the people of Tamub and of the people of Ilocab. Amac-Tan, the place is called, where the god of the Tamub [people] was, and there dawn came to the tribes. The place where those from Ilocab awaited the dawn was called Amac-Uquincat; there was the god of those of Ilocab, a short distance from the mountain.

There, too, were all the people of Rabinal, the Cakchiquel, the Tziquinaha, all the small tribes, and the large tribes. Together they stayed, awaiting the coming of the dawn and the rising of the large star called Icoquih, which rises just before the sun, when it dawns, according to the legend.

There they were together then; Balam-Quitzé, Balam-Acab, Mahucutah, and Iqui-Balam. They did not sleep; they remained standing and great was the anxiety of their hearts and their stomachs for the coming of dawn and the day. There, too, they felt shame; they were overcome with great sorrow, great suffering, and they were oppressed with pain.

They had come that far. "Oh, we have come without joy! If only we could see the rising of the sun! What shall we do now? If we lived in harmony in our country, why did we leave it?" they said to each other, in the midst of their sadness and affliction, and with mournful voices.

They talked, but they could not calm their hearts which were anxious for the coming of the dawn. "The gods are seated in the ravines, in the forests, they are among the air-plants, among the mosses, not even a seat of boards were they given," they said.

First there were Tohil, Avilix, and Hacavitz. Great was their glory, their strength, and their power over the gods of all the tribes. Many were their miracles, and countless their journeys, and their pilgrimages in the midst of the cold; and the hearts of the tribes were filled with fear.

But calm were the hearts of Balam-Quitzé, Balam-Acab, Mahucutah, and Iqui-Balam with respect to them [the gods]. They felt no anxiety in their hearts for the gods whom they had received, and had carried on their backs when they came there from Tulan-Zuiva, from there in the East.

They were there, then, in the forest, now called Zaquiribal, Pa-Tohil, P'Avilix, Pa-Hacavitz.

And next came the dawn, and light shone for our grandparents and our parents.

Now we shall tell of the coming of the dawn and the appearance of the sun, the moon, and the stars.

Here, then, is the dawn, and the coming of the sun, the moon, and the stars.

Balam-Quitzé, Balam-Acab, Mahucutah, and Iqui-Balam were very happy when they saw the Morning Star. It rose first, with shining face, when it came ahead of the sun.

Immediately they unwrapped the incense which they had brought from the East, and which they had planned to burn, and then they untied the three gifts which they had planned to offer,

The incense which Balam-Quitzé brought was called Mixtan Pom; the incense which Balam-Acab brought was called Cavixtan Pom; and that which Mahucutah brought was called Cabauil-Pom. The three had their incense and burned it when they began to dance facing toward the East.

They wept for joy as they danced and burned their incense, their precious incense. Then they wept because they did not yet behold nor see the sunrise.

But, then, the sun came up. The small and large animals were happy; and arose from the banks of the river, in the ravines, and on the tops of the mountains, and all turned their eyes to where the sun was rising.

Then the puma and the jaguar roared. But first the bird called Queletzu [a kind of parrot] burst into song. In truth, all the animals were happy, and the eagle, the white vulture; the small birds and the large birds stretched their wings.

The priests and the sacrificers were kneeling; great was the joy of the priests and sacrificers and of the people of Tamub and Ilocab and the people of Rabinal, the Cakchiquel, those from Tziquinaha, and those from Tuhalha, Uchabaha, Quibaha, from Batena, and the Yaqui Tepeu, all those tribes which exist today. And it was not possible to count the people. The light of dawn fell upon all the tribes at the same time.

Instantly the surface of the earth was dried by the sun. Like a man was the sun when it showed itself, and its face glowed when it dried the surface of the earth.

Before the sun rose, damp and muddy was the surface of the earth, before the sun came up; but then the sun rose, and came up like a man. And its heat was unbearable. It showed itself when it was born and remained fixed [in the sky] like a mirror. Certainly it was not the same sun which we see, it is said in their old tales.

Immediately afterward Tohil, Avilix, and Hacavitz were turned to stone, together with the deified beings, the puma, the jaguar, the snake, the cantil, and the hobgoblin.[6] Their arms became fastened to the trees when the sun,

---

[6]Tedlock translates "the snake, the cantil" as "the rattle snake, the Yellowbite, the snake generally known as fer de lance."

the moon, and the stars appeared. All alike were changed into stone. Perhaps we should not be living today because of the voracious animals, the puma, the jaguar, the snake, and the cantil, as well as the hobgoblin; perhaps our power would not exist if these first animals had not been turned into stone by the sun.

When the sun arose, the hearts of Balam-Quitzé, Balam-Acab, Mahucutah, and Iqui-Balam were filled with joy. Great was their joy when it dawned. And there were not many men at that place; only a few were there on the mountain Hacavitz. There dawn came to them, there they burned their incense and danced, turning their gaze toward the East, whence they had come. There were their mountains and their valleys, whence had come Balam-Quitzé, Balam-Acab, Mahucutah, and Iqui-Balam, as they were called.

But it was here where they multiplied, on the mountain, and this was their town; here they were, too, when the sun, the moon, and the stars appeared, when it dawned and the face of the earth and the whole world was lighted. Here, too, began their [farewell] song, which they call camucu; they sang it, but only the pain in their hearts and their innermost selves they expressed in their song. "Oh pity us! In Tulan we were lost, we were separated, and there our older and younger brothers stayed. Ah, we have seen the sun! but where are they now, that it has dawned?" so said the priests and the sacrificers of the Yaqui.

Because, in truth, the so-called Tohil is the same god of the Yaqui, the one called Yolcuat-Quitzalcuat.

"We became separated there in Tulan, in Zuyva, from there we went out together, and there our race was created when we came," they said to each other.

Then they remembered their older brothers and their younger brothers, the Yaqui, to whom dawn came there in the land which today is called Mexico. Part of the people remained there in the East, those called Tepeu Oliman, who stayed there, they say.

They felt much grief in their hearts, there in Hacavitz; and sad, too, were the people from Tamub and Ilocab, who were also there in the forest called Amac-Tan where dawn came to the priests and sacrificers of Tamub and to their god, who also was Tohil, because one and the same was the name of the god of the three branches of the Quiche people. And this is also the name of the god of the people of Rabinal, for there is little difference between that and the name of Huntoh, as the god of the people of Rabinal is called; for that reason, it is said, they wanted to make their speech the same as that of the Quiche.

Well, the speech of the Cakchiquel is different, because the name of their god was different when they came from there, from Tulan-Zuiva. Tzotz-iha Chimalcan was the name of their god, and today they speak a different tongue; and also from their god the families of Ahpozotzil and Ahpoxa, as they are called, took their names.

The speech of the god was also changed when they were given their god there, in Tulan, near the stone; their speech was changed when they came from Tulan in the darkness. And being together, dawn came to them and the light shone on all the tribes, in the order of the names of the gods of each of the tribes.

And now we shall tell of their stay and abode there on the mountain, where the four called Balam-Quitzé, Balam-Acab, Mahucutah, and Iqui-Balam were together. Their hearts mourned for Tohil, Avilix, and Hacavitz, whom they had placed among the air-plants and the moss.

We shall tell now how they made the sacrifices at the foot of the place where they had carried Tohil, when they arrived in the presence of Tohil and Hacavitz. They went to see them, to greet them, and also to give them thanks for the arrival of the dawn. They were in the thicket amidst the stones, there in the woods. And only by magic art did they speak when the priests and sacrificers came before Tohil. They did not bring great gifts, only resin, the remains of the gum, called noh, and pericon, they burned before their gods.

Then Tohil spoke; only by a miracle he gave counsel to the priests and sacrificers. And they [the gods] spoke and said:

"Truly here shall be our mountains and our valleys. We are yours; great shall be our glory and numerous our descendants, through the work of all men. Yours are all the tribes and we, your companions. Care for your town, and we shall give you your learning.

"Do not show us before the tribes when we are angered by the words of their mouths, or because of their conduct. Neither shall you permit us to fall into a snare. Give us, instead, the creatures of the woods and of the fields, and also the female deer, and the female birds. Come and give us a little of your blood, have pity upon us. You may have the skins of the deer and guard us from those whose eyes have deceived us.

"So, then, [the skin of] the deer shall be our symbol which you shall show before the tribes. When they ask 'Where is Tohil?' show the deerskin before their eyes. Neither shall you show yourselves, for you shall have other things to do. Great shall be their position; you shall dominate all the tribes; you shall bring your blood and their substance before us, and those who come to embrace us, shall be ours also," thus spoke Tohil, Avilix, and Hacavitz.

They had the appearance of youths, when those who came to offer gifts saw them. Then the persecution of the young of the birds and of the deer began, and the fruit of the chase was received by the priests and sacrificers. And when they found the young of the birds and the deer, they went at once to place the blood of the deer and of the birds in the mouths of the stones, that were Tohil and Hacavitz.

As soon as the blood had been drunk by the gods, the stones spoke, when the priests and the sacrificers came, when they came to bring their offerings. And they did the same before their symbols, burning pericon and holom-ocox.

The symbols of each one were there where they had been placed on the top of the mountain. But they [the priests] did not live in their houses by day, but walked over the mountains, and ate only the young horseflies, and the wasps, and the bees which they hunted; they had neither good food nor good drink. And neither were the roads from their homes known, nor did they know where their wives had remained.

CRY OF THE HEART*

AND THIS IS THE CRY OF THEIR HEARTS, here it is:

> "Wait! On this blessed day,
> thou Hurricane, thou Heart of the Sky-Earth,
> thou giver of ripeness and freshness,
> and thou giver of daughters and sons,
> spread thy stain, spill thy drops
> of green and yellow;
> give life and beginning
> to those I bear and beget,
> that they might multiply and grow,
> nurturing and providing for thee,
> calling to thee along the roads and paths,
> on rivers, in canyons,
> beneath the trees and bushes;
> give them their daughters and sons.
>
> "May there be no blame, obstacle, want or misery;
> let no deceiver come behind or before them,
> may they neither be snared nor wounded,
> nor seduced, nor burned,
> nor diverted below the road nor above it;
> may they neither fall over backward nor stumble;
> keep them on the Green Road, the Green Path.
>
> "May there be no blame or barrier for them
> through any secrets or sorcery of thine;
> may thy nurturers and providers be good

*From Tedlock, op. cit., pp. 220–23.

before thy mouth and thy face,
thou, Heart of Sky; thou, Heart of Earth;
thou, Bundle of Flames;
and thou, Tohil, Auilix, Hacauitz,
under the sky, on the earth,
the four sides, the four corners;
may there be only light, only continuity within,
before thy mouth and thy face, thou god."

So it was with the lords when they fasted during nine score, thirteen score, or seventeen score days; their days of fasting were many. They cried their hearts out over their vassals and over all their wives and children. Each and every lord did service, as a way of cherishing the light of life and of cherishing lordship.

Such were the lordships of the Keeper of the Mat, Keeper of the Reception House Mat, Minister, and Crier to the People. They went into fasting two by two, taking turns at carrying the tribes and all the Quiche people on their shoulders.

At its root the word came from just one place, and the root of nurturing and providing was the same as the root of the word. The Tams and Ilocs did likewise, along with the Rabinals, Cakchiquels, those of the Bird House, Sweatbath House, Talk House. They came away in unity, having heard, there at Quiche, what all of them should do.

It wasn't merely that they became lords; it wasn't just that they gathered in gifts from nurturers and providers who merely made food and drink for them. Nor did they wantonly falsify or steal their lordship, their splendor, their majesty. And it wasn't merely that they crushed the canyons and citadels of the tribes, whether small or great, but that the tribes paid a great price:

There came turquoise, there came metal.

And there came drops of jade and other gems that measured the width of four fingers or a full fist across.

And there came green and red featherwork, the tribute of all the tribes. It came to the lords of genius, Plumed Serpent and Cotuha, and to Quicab and Cauizimah as well, to the Keeper of the Mat, Keeper of the Reception House Mat, Minister, and Crier to the People.

What they did was no small feat, and the tribes they conquered were not few in number. The tribute of Quiche came from many tribal divisions.

And the lords had undergone pain and withstood it; their rise to splendor had not been sudden. Actually it was Plumed Serpent who was the root of the greatness of the lordship.

Such was the beginning of the rise and growth of Quiche.

The Books of Chilam Balam

Chumayel, Mani, and Tizimin are small villages in northern Yucatan. Maya priests, known as chilams, lived in these as well as many other small villages. The chilams were expert in the reckoning of time and its astrological implications. After the Spanish invasion, a few of them who survived were taught the art of alphabetic writing by the Christian friars, who adapted it to represent the phonemes of the Maya language. One of the chilams, whose name was Balam—"Jaguar"—became famous for writing the Book of the Chilam Balam of Chumayel. In all, fourteen books received a designation indicating their village of origin.

The books of the chilams appear in two sections here: the book from Chumayel is part of section 1 on Sacred Narrative, while material from those of Mani and Tizimin appears in section 4, devoted to Prophetic and Historical Literature. Since there is both history and prophecy in the Chumayel, it could also have been included with historical and prophetic works. The chilams were not concerned with such arbitrary categorizations when composing their works.

The plural, chilams, applies not only to the group of works but to each individually, for upon closer examination it is apparent that each of these books was written by more than one chilam. In reality, like the cycles of time they register, the contents of each book are renewed again and again to tell about happenings which link a past (not the past, but a specific past period) with a present or a future. This explains why even if the writing of these books began in the sixteenth century, they incorporate accounts and prophetic statements that have to be placed in later times, including the years following Mexican independence.

We have mentioned the great surprise of the anthropologist Alfonso Villa Rojas, who was reading to a group of Mayas in the town of Tusik in 1936 from the Chilam Balam of Chumayel when he was suddenly interrupted by an elderly Maya who began to recite a parallel text from another book in their possession to which they kept adding new texts. Thus the existence of another book of Chilam Balam came to light. It is, of course, now known as the Book of the Chilam Balam of Tusik.

Religious, historical, poetic, calendric, and astrological compositions, some of them closely related to what we know of the contents of the extant pre-Hispanic Maya codices, are at the core of these books. Some of the religious texts include expressions of the purest Maya tradition; others are mixed with elements brought in by invading peoples who came into Yucatan from the central plateau of Mexico. The preachings of the Catholic friars also filtered into some of the ancient Maya prayers as they are recorded. The historical accounts, too, are a mixture of pre-Hispanic, colonial, and even modern recollections of occurrences interpreted as *part of the Maya conception of the recurrent cycles of time. Poetry, for its part, permeates much of these texts.*

Excerpts from the Chilam books of Chumayel, Mani, and Tizimin are given here, including the ceremonies of the May or cycles of time. This text can be read as if it were a drama distributed in thirteen acts, in which the histories of all eighteen katuns (cycles of twenty years) are provided. The text, rich in metaphors, tells about those who impersonated the cycles of time, the gods related to them, the rituals, the foods and drinks consumed, the fates that were to be anticipated, cosmic performances, and a variety of esoteric speeches.

Prophetic words about the arrival of the bearded people, "lustful faces, lustful people," those who would be governors, anticipate or— playing with the cycles of time—recall the coming of the Spaniards. All this is accompanied by allusions to the raising of "the standing tree" (the Christian Cross), the preaching of the One God, a time of crazy days and nights, "of the monkeys of the world."

From The Book of the Chilam of Tizimin, *several excerpts are offered. One, "The Flower Katun of the Xiu" (p. 507), marked the beginning of an Itza cycle: the Maya-Itza, or "Water Witches," who ruled the eastern half of Yucatan during the post-Classic period and that of the Spanish colony. According to the Itza tradition, they established the siege of the Katuns in Chichen-Itza at a date corresponding to the year 672 B.C.*

During the "Flower Katun," the Itza had to resist the Spanish presence and that of the Xius, Mayanized people of Nahuatl origin. To the Itza, this was a time of suffering, "crying for food, crying for drink." Another, later katun was even worse for the Itza, when "there was the beginning and rise of Christianity . . . and there was great theft and tribute."

Cycles of time moving forward and coming back are both recalled and anticipated here. Prominent rulers are described, those who triumphed in battle and those who were defeated: "There—as is mysteriously expressed—came the time of the seven day rule, of the instant rule, and fallen rule . . . by the people, ending the count."

More prophecies about what will happen, and also about a past that will return, tell the story of the Itza nation in the Chilam Book of Tizimin. *In dates given always in accordance to the Maya calendar, "the word of the glyph" conveys voices of deep concern and suffering but also of hope. The Itza, playing with the cycles of time, give their own version of what has happened to them, above all, with the arrival and dominance of the Spaniards. And then with a historical leap, they tell of the Caste War and predict the end of the rule of the bearded whites.*

Chilam Balam of Chumayel*

THE RISE OF HUNAC CEEL

The sorcerer, Tzim Thul the rain priest, ruled in Heaven Born Merida. Uayom Ch'ich' the Strong was their sun priest, and Can Ul was the counselor to the Jaguar. There were two sun priests: Chable was their lord (in Mayapan) and Cabal Xiu was their sun priest; Uxmal Chac was their ruler (in Uxmal). This was the sun priest office.

Then Hapay Can was brought to Chem Chan. This was the piercing; then bloodletting occurred on the walls there at Uxmal.

The yearbearers were seized: the East priest Xib Chac and the North priest Xib Chac, and the West necklaced rain priest was also seized. And the name of the mother's mother of the rain priests was the North priest Bel Iz. The West necklaced rain priest was their father. A certain (other) necklaced rain priest was their youngest brother. His name was Uoh Puc. It was written as a glyph on the palm of his hand. There was also a glyph written on his neck and on the sole of his foot, and on the ball of his thumb.

They were not gods: The rain priests were chiefs. The True God is our Father Who is God. They worshiped him in the words according to the wisdom of Mayapan. The sun priest of Coba was the priest there in the fort. Zulim Chan was in the west. Nahuat was the guardian of the spirit of the fort to the south. Co Uoh was the guardian of the spirit of the fort to the east. Ah Ek was the other one; these were their lords. Cau Ich of the Embroidered Mantle was the name of their governor.

Hunac Ceel was the sacrificer of Mex Cuc. Then he demanded one yam blossom, a white mat, two-faced mantles, a green turkey, a mottled snail and white drinking gourds.

These are the names of the towns of the dam people and the names of the wells, so that it may be known where they passed when they explored to see whether this country was good, whether it was really suitable to live here.

The Ordered Country was its name, they told Our Father Who is God. It was he who ordered the country; it was he who created the whole earth around. But really it was they who named the lands, the wells, the villages,

---

*These excerpts from Munro Edmonson, *Heaven Born Merida and Its Destiny, The Book of Chilam Balam of Chumayel* (Austin, TX: University of Texas Press, 1986), follow the order preferred by Edmonson, with sixteenth-century material preceding that ascribed to the following century. The excerpts are English only from pp. 79–99, 120–26, 152–67, and 168–93. The material has been converted to block prose with the permission of the author here and in excerpts from the *Chilam Balam of Tizimin*, which follows.

and the fields of their towns, because no one had come here, to the neck of the country, before we came here:

[The list of 171 place names describing two complete tours of Yucatan has been omitted.]

ACT 10[7]
And then they settled Heaven Born Merida and went down to the Hol Tun Ake people. Then the Zabac Na people went down and they appeared together with their fellow lords. These were the Zabac Na, the root of the people of the Na lineage. They gathered together there in Heaven Born Merida, which also had the mat for the Jaguar, which was like the lordship, the Jaguar Spring throne. . . . (Which was the) generation of the lordship (of Pochek Ix) Tz'oy, who was the head of the people of Copo, a Xiu and Spokesman as well. Chac Te was the lord; Chac Te's land was where their lordship occurred.

ACT 13
Then their throwing sacrifice began, their throwing people into the well. Their words were to be used up for the lordship, but their words were not used: It was "Cau Ich and a certain Hunac Ceel." This Cau Ich was the name of the man who was being seated at the head of the well to the south.

ACT 14
So then he went to create it. He asked to speak his word. Then he began to speak it when the lordship was seated in the burden of the lords by them. Then the speeches of the governors began. But the lord was not seated, only the path of Mex Cuc. Then it was said that the lordship was the sacrifice of Mex Cuc.

His mother will be Eagle, then he will be found in disguise in the hills.

Then this lord began to create his word. The speech was sweet. Then the erection of the high house for the lordship began.

The use of steps began. And then he was seated in the high house in 13 Ahau, the sixth rule.

ACT 15
Then he began to come to speak the word of the day, the elevation of Mex Cuc by name, then his throwing. And they were close together—the two days of Mex Cuc. When he was elevated, the father of my pretended return, the homage to the name of Mex Cuc began. So then they honor him, they

---

[7]Edmonson notes that here the ceremonial business is completed and the distribution of the lands begins with Act 10. He has omitted the earlier acts.

face toward the direction of the well, the mouth of the well of the Itza by name. Because it will be the Itza who then remove the stones of the earth, the stones of the moon. The burden of the Itza will be removed when he is in the water.

ACT 16
So then the entrance of suffering began there at the well mouth of the Itza.

And then they will go there to the east, the two gods together with the sun priest of Coba, coming to begin *katun* 8 Ahau. The name of the make-believe *katun* was tiny little 8 Ahau. And then the change of the *katun* appeared, and then the change of the lords. . . .

ACT 17
. . . They say, this is the coming of this calendar round which burns; it is a cycle which burns the edge of the sea and the sea itself: that is the suffering. It was just the judgment of Heaven, just their judgment. Then the burden of the sun was set down.

Perhaps the face of the sun departed then. Its high face was quenched. Then the sun priests told them the burning orbs of heaven were strangled. "That has ended the word of our lordship," the sun priests told them.

ACT 18
Then they began thinking of writing the past sun. They listened and they saw the moon.

ACT 19
Then the lordships, the stalks, came, and they were Centipedes and Gnats. That was what brought sin to us, the slavery of the land, which comes when the word of the *katun*, the curse of the *katun* is accomplished. That is what will be brought about, just as you say: You, Your lordships, and your lands.

So goes then the word, the nature of the *katun*. The *katun* is finished and accomplished. And the Centipedes and Gnats.

ACT 20
Then thousands of their soldiers were seen, and the slaughter of them began. Then they were weakened by the white stick and clubbing to death. Shooting with three-pronged arrowheads began then. The division of the lordships and their lands commenced.

There will be bloodshed when it is seized by the deer people. It will strangle their will. . . .

[The next fourteen lines are missing.]

THE BIRTH OF THE UINAL

Thus it was read by the first sage, Melchisedek, and the first prophet, Puc Tun, the priest, and the first sun priest. This is the sermon of the birth of the *uinal,* which occurred before the world awakened and began to run by itself alone. His mother's mother, his mother's sister, father's mother, and his sister-in-law said, "What is to be said when a man is seen on the road?"

They said this while they were going along, but no man occurred. And then they arrived there at the east, and they began to say: "Who is it that passed by here now? Here are his tracks, right here. Measure them with your foot according to the word of the planter of the world."

Then they were to measure the footprint of our Father who is the holy God. This was the beginning of saying the count of the world by footsteps. This was 12 Oc.

This is the account of his birth. In 13 Oc they matched each other's paces and arrived there at the east. They said his name, since the days had no name then, and he traveled on with his mother's mother, his mother's sister, his father's mother, and his sister-in-law. The month was born and the day name, and the sky and the earth; the pyramid of water and land, stone and tree. The things of sea and land were born.

On 1 Monkey (Chuen) he manifested himself in his divinity and created heaven and earth.

On 2 Peak (Eb) he made the first pyramid. He descended, coming from the heart of heaven, there in the heart of the water.

For there was nothing of earth, or stone, or tree.

On 3 Ben he made all things, each and every thing, the things of the heavens and the things of the sea and the things of the land.

On 4 Ix the separation of heaven and earth occurred.

On 5 Men the working of everything began.

On 6 Cib the first candle was made, and illumination occurred then, for there was no sun or moon.

On 7 Caban the earth, which we didn't have before, was born.

On 8 Etz'nab he planted his hands and feet and made birds upon the earth.

On 9 Cauac Hell was first tasted.

On 10 Ahau evil men went to hell, because the holy God had not yet appeared.

On 11 Imix the stones and trees were shaped. This was what was done on this day.

On 12 Wind (Ik) breath was born. This was the beginning of what is called breath, because there is no death on it.

On 13 Akbal the taking of water occurred. Then he moistened earth and shaped it and made man.

On 1 Kan he was first disturbed at heart by the evil that had been created.

On 2 Chicchan everything evil first appeared, and he saw it even within the towns.

On 3 Death (Cimi) he invented death. It happened then: The first death was invented by our Father who is God. . . .

On 5 Lamat the seven floods of rain, water, and sea were invented.

On 6 Muluc all caves were buried, and this was before the awakening of the world. This occurred by the commandment of our Father Who is God. Everything that did not exist was then spoken in heaven, for until then there had been no stones and trees.

And then they went and tested each other, and he spoke as follows: "Thirteen heaps and seven heaps make one."

He said for speech to emerge, for they had no speech. Its origin was requested by the first lord day, for their organs of speech were not yet opened enabling them to speak to each other.

They went there to the heart of the sky and took each other by the hand. And then they stood there in the middle of the country and divided it up, and they divided the Burners, the four of them:

4 Chicchan the Burner, 4 Oc the Burner, 4 Men the Burner, and 4 Ahau the Burner. These are the lords: the four of them.

This was the birth of the *uinal*, the awakening of the world.

Heaven and earth were finished, as were the trees and stones. Everything was born through our Father Who is God, Who is holy.

There was no heaven or earth, so there he was in his divinity, in his nebulousness, by himself, alone. And everything that was invented he caused to be born. In his divinity he moved to heaven, which was thus a great event. And he was the ruler.

The account of all the days through which the beginning is counted was in the east, as has been told.

THE CEREMONIAL OF THE BAKTUN[8]

It is very necessary to know the path that is the introduction to the heart. This is the *tun* period when it was shaped by our Father, the remote one.

ACT 1
This is the taking of the occasion. This is the balche [mead] ceremony in which we honor him here.

---

[8]The ceremonies required twenty acts, one for each of the *katuns* in a *baktun*. See *tun* in the Glossary.

We, the rulers, spread in many separate parts, worship them, the true Gods. There they are as stones, the established representation of the True God, Our Father Who is God, the Father of heaven and earth. However, the first gods were leprous gods, the word of their worship is finished. They have been done in by the benediction of the Father of heaven.

Then it ends. The redemption of the world, the twice-born life of the True God, the True *Dios* is over. When they sweetly prayed to heaven and earth, that put an end to the gods of you Mayan people.

This is the account of the land at the time when the belief in your god was shattered. That is because it was written there, because it wouldn't have happened at the time of the making of these books. These are millennial words for the examination of the Mayan people here so they may know how they were born and settled the land here in this country.

ACT 2

In 11 Ahau the Muzen Cabs began to tie the faces of the 13 Gods, but they did not know their true names. For their older sisters and their engendered sons, their offspring and those who are not grown—perhaps even their faces and their voices are gone.

ACT 3

They didn't know about the dawning of the land either, the going and coming.

And then the 13 who are Gods were finished by the 9 who are Gods. They brought down fire; then they brought down the rope; then they brought down stones and sticks. Then came beating with sticks and stones. And then the 13 who are Gods were finished. And so then their heads were beaten, and then their faces were flattened, and then they were forgotten, and then they were carted away.

ACT 4

And then the four changers were planted together with the Soot Heads.

ACT 5

Then the quetzal and the blue bird were created.

ACT 6

And then they created the placenta of breast plants, the heart of breast squash, breast pumpkin and breast beans, and the wrapping of the seed of the first nine steps. Then they went to the thirteenth level of heaven, and established his membranes, his nose, and his skeleton here in the world.

So there went his heart because of the 13 who are Gods. But they didn't know his heart was to be a plant.

ACT 7

And then they all arrived, even the fatherless, the suffering poor, and the widows—the living and those without hearts. And they began to wait for the direction of thatch grass, the direction of the sea.

Then a deluge of water, a storm of water reached the hearts of the four changers, who radiated in heaven and radiated also on the land.

The 4 who are Gods, the 4 who are Fathers of the Land, said, "This water shows their faces to them. Then let us finish the flattening of the lands. This is the initiation of the future of our count."

ACT 8

Then the South priest Xib Yuy bore the north alligator tree in the north. And then he bore the entrance to heaven, the sign of the flattening of the lands. That is the north alligator tree, said to be carried.

Then he bore the west alligator tree to seat the black-breasted weaver bird.

Then he bore the south alligator tree, the sign of the flattening of the lands to seat the yellow-breasted weaver bird,

And the South priest Xib Yuy and the South priest Oyal Mut were seated.

And then he bore the center alligator tree to the middle, signifying the flattening of the land. It is seated.

ACT 9

Being raised establishes the town; and the same when the return of the *katun* is fulfilled.

ACT 10

The leaders of the hand (and) the leaders of the foot were its fathers:

They established the town of the red noble in the eastern lands, with the leader of the foot as its father; they established the town of the white noble in the northern lands, with the leader of the foot as its father; they established the town of Lahun Chan, with the leader of the hand as its father; and they established the town of the yellow noble, with the leader of the hand as its father. And that is the heart of the lands, it is said.

ACT 11

The 7 Pacers have come to the seven levels of the land. Then the pacing pole comes down on the back of Itzam Cab Ain.

He then descended with the strength to bury earth and heaven, walking through the villages to light candles, to light lamps in the dark, obscure lands.

ACT 12

To one who has no day, to one who has no night, to one who has no moon, he is their painter and he has the dawn.

So then it dawned, if that is indeed he, the dawn. Thirteen thousand steps and seven is the count of the dawn.

So then the landowners among them say to themselves, "Two-day thrones; three-day thrones." And then they begin to be over the 13 who are Gods, over the towns in the lordship, reddening the stone of rule, reddening the mat, reddening the lamentation of the Ceiba Land. The oppressed land is reddened because of them.

The seven priest Ol Zip (appeared), but it was not time for his rule—that is when they raised up the 9 who are Gods there. What then came was the counting of mats, and it reddened the mats to seat the 9 who are Gods.

And the ass that sat upon the mat, haggling and trading, brought down envy from the center of heaven; that was the envy of the ruler, the envy of the lordship.

ACT 13

And then the red-placed and the white-placed lords were established. The place then established was black and then yellow.

The Red Death Lord was then established as lord of the death mat, Lord of the death throne. Then the Black Death Lord was established as lord of the death mat, Lord of the death throne.

Then the Yellow Death Lord was established as lord of the death mat, Lord of the death throne. And he was a god, he said. And it may be too that he was not a god.

ACT 14

And he had no food, he had no water. When he ordered a pile of shoots one fragment spread out. There was nowhere to get his fruit as he liked it.

Harsh news was seated. Harsh times, harsh suffering were what came during the lordship when he arrived to sit upon the mat: fornication on high, fires being set, the face of the sun was snatched away; the judgment on the lordship was burned on the land. That was its foundation as his rule became known. It was a time to suffer fists, to suffer shoulders. It was a time for the riddles of the lords, teaching him to say wooden lance (for) the track to the sun: he forgets everything.

Teaching him to say the tree for the crier at the four crossroads, for the four changers.

The bowl is come—seated in the time of the swarming of butterflies. What is coming is a great plague of suffering, since there came three kinds of folds in the time of *katun* 3 Ahau, threefold in a year. That will be the closing up of *katun* 3 Ahau.

Then the nature of the *katun* will be established. Its food is gourdroot, its water is gourdroot. Its food is breadnut, its water is breadnut. He will eat that; he will drink that. And what then?

Scrounged cabbage to eat for him who is seated here in the city that was to suffer the fathers.

In the ninth *tun* there was haggling over wanting to settle the burden of the *katun* for the whole period of 13 Ahau. Which (two by two) broke up the entry of 11 Ahau. That then brought down the word of the nine steps. The tip of his tongue then came down, wanting to settle the burden of the *katun*, a *katun* which was his ninth burden.

ACT 16

Then he came down from heaven. And Kan was the day he tied his burden, which then brought water coming from the heart of heaven, ordaining second birth, the nine bowers and homes, and bringing down the nine cycle dripping at the mouth. The tip of his tongue dripping, perhaps his brains. Then the four rain gods, the naguals descended.

ACT 17

It was clear that those were the lands of Flowers. He who then appeared also was Red Hoch Kom, who was also with White Hoch Kom, who was also with Black Hoch Kom, and Yellow Hoch Kom, and Hau Nal, and Huk Nab. These also appeared: Ci Tun, Oyal Nicte, Ho Nicte, Ninich' Cacau, Chac Uil Tok, Bac Nicte, Macuilxuchit, Hobon y Ol Nicte, Laul Nicte, Kou Ol Nicte, and Octah Nicte. These were the appearances of the flowers, the madmen of the cycles. When they appeared, their mother was Nicte. The burden of the Flower lords is the scent of the sun priest, the scent of the lord, the scent of the commander.

When they came down and had no existence, this was the end they said. But they bore no food when they appeared and sacrificed flowers, entering into the sin of the 9 who are Gods; they bore the burden three times in a year. But they did not come to create the rise of God or hell. There were nine steps when they descended to the founding of the Flowers. P'izlim Te, the Green Bird, and Hummingbird were the spirit seeds that descended. They sucked the nectar of the nine children of Flowers, and in just that way they got mates and little Flowers. So then the heart of the Flower with four branches appeared, moving itself along. That was the Flower then.

ACT 18

She was seated as sun priest, counting the *tuns* in the middle, which she did for each of the middle ones of the 13 who are Gods. She is the god you have spoken of, but she didn't know the origin of the sin of the mat, and Flower is her mat, Flower her bench, Flower her descent.

ACT 19

Envy was seated: his walk Envy, his bowl Envy, his gourd Envy, his heart Envy, his mind Envy, his thought Envy, his mouth Envy; his word in the lordship was Crazy. The voice of hunger was in his time, the voice of thirst was in his time. It was divided, like his eating after he got dizzy, as the need occurred.

No sticks and no stones.

The rain priest, in the person of Lahun Chan, who seated the person of Spite, was his wife. His word was Spite, his teaching was Spite, his knowledge was Spite, Spite was his gait.

The face which was seated was tied; the mat to be seated during the lordship was a big city.

His father was dropped, his mother was dropped, and his mother, her heart burning by itself, didn't know what she was to have borne. In being fatherless the Death Lord was his father; in being motherless he will be a vagabond. Through his father and through his mother, his message was hardened, his mind was furtive.

He had no fear; there was no good in his heart. Truly it is stone, and his tongue is plaster. He doesn't know what will end his sins, and he doesn't know he has them. The lordship is over; that is what will terminate his time and his rule.

These are the 9 who are Gods; these are the nine little faces of the lordship: commoners, those of the two-day mat, those of the two-day throne. This comes in *katun* 3 Ahau. And it will be his nature, the nature of the fatherhood of the country, the incumbent receiver of the word, the nature of the *katun*.

ACT 20

Then the word of *katun* 3 Ahau will be finished. At a time of very few sons, this will be the lamentation of the stupid Itza. If one is clever, if one is strong, one part of a *tun* will change the sin, the stupidity of the Itza; that is, the 9 who are Gods. That will be the ending of the word of *katun* 3 Ahau.

That is the riddle of the lordship of the lands, the termination of the word of the *katun;* that is the manifestation of the descent of born and engendered children and chiefs, and the existence of living souls, and the lineage of the chiefs. That is the secret pacing of the lands in the sight of our poor, because of the madness of the time, the madness of the *katun*. The wicked son, the stupid child—that is their birth when they are awakened in *katun* 3 Ahau.

Thus will be the termination of the rulers, the two-faced people by our Father who is God. And he then will bring about the end of the word of this *katun*. So then God will be given the achievement of a flood for the second time. That will flood the lands; that then will finish it. So then Our Father who is Jesus Christ will descend over the pit of Jehoshaphat beside the city of Jerusalem, succeeding in redeeming us with his holy blood.

And that will be the descent in a great storm, being given the right to heavenly truth.

He will be made to pass in subjection to the wooden cross he bore, which then is the descent to the great event, and to the great rule also of the True *Dios,* that is, the True God. That will bring to birth heaven and earth and the entire world. And that will be the descent that flattens the surface of the earth too, for good or evil, sheltering the weak and frightened and the stupid.

THE LANGUAGE OF ZUYUA

Indeed this is in Zuyua language! This will be the language, these will be the questions of the governing people of this town when the time comes to finish the speech of 3 Ahau *Katun* and we arrive at the *katun* period of the 1 Ahau *Katun.* . . .

This comes at the time of questions and answers of the village officials: whether they know how the people and the lords came; whether they recount the coming of the officials and the governors; whether the lineages of the lords or the officials of the lineages are cited correctly.

1 This is the first basic phrase to be asked of them: They will ask them for food. . . .

"Bring the sun, my son, and stack it on my plate, which is pierced by the lance of the high cross that is in the middle of its heart, and with a green jaguar seated over the sun drinking its blood there."

The meaning is Zuyua.

So the sun they will be asked for is the lord's fried egg. And the lance with the high cross piercing its heart is just like saying these are the holy words. And the green jaguar piled over it drinking its blood is green chile, the jaguar that is there.

This language is Zuyua.

2 The second secret word that is to be asked of them is that they go get the brains of heaven to be seen by the headman wherever he lives. Perhaps they will be told, "I wish it to be seen; let it be seen." For these brains of heaven are incense (in) Zuyua. And fatherless who come there.

3 The third secret word that is to be asked of them is that they tie together a great house six rows high and one jump wide. . . .

It is the lord's hat and hair. He should be told to mount the lord's all-white horse. His clothes and appearance are all white, as is the rope held in his hand while he is roping the horse which has a ball of rubber on the blossom of the rope which bounces when it is moved.

So the white horse is the sole of a maguey fiber sandal and the all-white rope is the flower of the white branch. The ball of rubber on the blossom of the rope is money that is in the middle there, because of pain arising from the blood, and the motherless and fatherless who come there.

4 . . . "When you have come you should be seen in the fire of high noon then. Appear double, proceeding jointly, and when you arrive have your puppy behind you. So your puppy may then be burning the commandment of our blessed lady which he shall bring with him." And the double appearance that is mentioned to him is that exactly at noon he will clear his darkness: He will have no shadow, which is like saying going jointly. Then he arrives at the governor.

So the puppy that he is asked for is his wife, and the commandment of our blessed lady is the lord's candles of sweet wax.

This language is Zuyua.

5 . . . They are told to go and get the heart of the blessed God in heaven: "Go then and bring me thirteen covered folds which are wrapped behind you with white cord."

This is the heart of God the blessed; it is cordage. The cover and the thirteen folds are the lord's tortillas, with thirteen "folds" of beans in it. And the all-white cord is an all-white cloth.

This is what is to be asked them and the answer, in Zuyua.

6 . . . "I eat tomorrow; I wish to be fed then. It is not necessary that this ceiba root be chewed," so they are told.

So the ceiba branch is a chuckawalla, the twisted bamboo is iguana tail, the living vine is a pig's intestines, and the ceiba root is the root of a chuckawalla tail: Zuyua language.

7 . . . "Go gather me the man of the well bottom, two bright white and two bright yellow. I want to eat then."

The man of the well bottom that is asked of them is bright white gourdroot and two bright yellow ones.

The village official completes the explanation, then throws it before the lord, the new governor there. These are the words then. If they have not been understood by the officials of the village, then the myriad stars adorning the abyss of night, seizing the forest and the sanctity of home are gone. The myriads of the deep are gone and the dark whales [black beans-a pun?] which are in the middle of the half earth among the nobles are also gone.

The dead do not understand; the living will.

This is to be placed above the officials of the villages. This examination will be concerted and precise knowledge will finally unite the lordship here. Then, tying their hands before them with a swaying log and taking the rope separately, they will be brought to the village before the lord, the new governor. This was the end of the village chieftainship.

It is to be done on the mad day, the mad *katun*. They will come to hear exactly when it will be the end of the property of the officials of the villages. This is to be done on that day, the ending of the word of the *katun*. Then it will be over, the 3 Ahau *katun*, ending the office of the villages because of their lack of understanding.

Thus will occur the completion of the village offices. This is the record of what occurs. They give food to the new governor; then they ask for their dinners. Knotting their necks, cutting off the tips of their tongues, ripping out their eyes, that very day will be the end then.

And so the lineages there which just present themselves before the father and kneel will achieve knowledge and be encouraged while he is seated on his mat and throne by them also. This is the convocation and review, the examination and correct review of the lineages of the governors in the land here.

This is to be the experience of the time. This is also to be the taking of new staffs. Thus then will be the seating of lands and houses of the lineages of the Mayan people here in the region of Yucatán. . . .

   8   "Son, go get the flower of night for me here," might just be said.

So then he went and knelt before the governor who asked him: "Father, here then is the flower of night as you have asked of me. It comes together with the evil of night here which is with it."

He just says, "What's that, son! If you have it with you, if you do have it, it is the tender wasting vine on your back and a large fig branch, then."

"Father, they are with me; they came together."

"What's that, son! If you came together then, go separate your companions for me. There is one big man there with nine sons and one fat woman with nine children there."

. . . Zuyua language.

So the night flower that he is asked for then is a star in the sky, and the evil of night is the moon. The tender wasting vine and the large fig branch are the bearers of the earth, the filling of the earth, as it was called then. And the big man is asked for who has nine sons then—that is the big toe. And the fat woman that he is asked for, that is the thumb. . . .

   10   "Son, you are a governor and you are a ruler as well. Go then and bring me your green beads as you are praying."

And the green beads asked of him—that is a hammock.

So then he is to be asked how many days he prays.

"Father," he says, "I pray for one day and I pray for ten days."

"What then are the days when you raise your prayer?"

"Father, the ninth day and the thirteenth day, to the nine gods and the thirteen spirits. That is when I count my beads perhaps."

11 "Son, go bring me your pants that I might smell their scent and the burning of their scent, the scent of my pants, the scent of my clothes, the scent of my incense vine, the great scent at the center of heaven, at the center of the clouds. And my green nance plants which have white seeds. If you are a governor so be it."

"Father, I shall bring it," he says.

The scent of pants that he is asked for is the great scent at the center of heaven: It is incense there in the fire beginning to burn. And the green nance plants requested: That is ground cacao in cocoa then.

12 "What's this, son? Bring me the fresh blood of my daughter and her head and her entrails, and her thigh, her arm; lay out your persons there who are virgin descendants. Show them to me together, also the new throne of my daughter. I want to see them. As I have been given it by you while you stood before me as I cursed and wept."

"Wherefore even so, father."

"And the next day, when it is clear, bring with it the left ear of a wild bee."

The fresh blood of his daughter, which he may ask for, is Mayan wine. And his daughter's entrails—that is the honeycomb. The head of his daughter is a virgin jar to steep the wine and his daughter's new throne is the contained glyph stone of the land. The left ear of the wild bee is the dregs of the wine that is the last of the mead. And the thigh that is mentioned is the balche tree, while the arm of his daughter is a branch of balche. . . .

14 "Son, go bring me the birds of night and spoons of night and let the brains of heaven come with it. I have a great desire that they be seen here."

"Then it will be so served, father."

What he requests is sprinkling and burning incense. The spoons of night he asks for is cordage and the brains of heaven is incense.

Zuyua language.

15 "Son, go bring me the bones of your father that you buried three years ago. I have a great desire that they be seen."

"Then it will be so served, father."

What he is asking for is baked manioc. Then it will be served to the governor.

16 "Son, go bring me a grown man without grabbing his high balls, his water sac; his name is sunk and impotent."

"Then it will be so served, father."

What he is asking for is armadillo and armadillo meat.

17 "Son, go bring me three slices of heaven. I have a desire to eat it."

"Then it will be so served, father."

What he is asking for is bowls of corn gruel—that is corn gruel foam.

In Zuyua language everything is requested.

18 "Son, go bring me maguey root, the bottom of the maguey that has no hands. Don't remove its heart. Also bring line-paw, sliced-foot."

"Then it shall be so served, father."

What he is asking for is a boar's head, baked. Then he will go and bring it to him. And the heart, as he calls it, that is the tongue, because that is a symbol for his heart.

Zuyua.

19 "Son, go bring me hawks of the night for me to eat."

"Then it will be served, father."

What he is asking for is chickens, cocks.

Zuyua.

20 "Son, go speak to the first little old lady named Fallen to the Ground that she might bring me a large basket of blackbirds which are all under the big fig tree, piled up in the shadow of the fig tree."

"It will be served, father."

What he is asking for is black beans that are in the house of the owner of the lands; that is the first little old lady, and Fallen to the Ground as he mentions—Zuyua language.

21 "Son, go and get the jaguars of the spring so that you can sweeten my food. I have a desire to eat jaguar."

"It shall be so served, father."

The jaguar that he asks for is agouti.

Zuyua language.

22 "Son, go bring me seven knee babies and orphans. I have a desire to eat them at the beginning and end of my dinner."

"It shall be served, father."

What he is asking for is stuffed leaves of cabbage.

23 "Son, go bring me green dandies here. Let them come dancing so I can watch it. And bring drums and rattles and fans and drumsticks with them. These are my expectations."

"It shall be served, father."

What he is asking for is turkeys; their drums are their pouches, their rattles are their crests, their fans are their tails, and their drumsticks are their thighs.

Zuyua language.

24 "Son, go bring me the stink of the country. I want to eat it."
"It shall be served, father."
What he is asking for is the juice of honey:
Zuyua. . . .

26 "Son, go bring me the night firefly that is far to the north. Its odor passes far to the west. And bring with it the signal of the tongue of the jaguar."
"It shall be served, father."
What he is asking for is tobacco. And the signal of the tongue of the jaguar that he asks for is fire.

27 "Son, go bring me your daughter for me to see. Have her face wrapped all in white. She is very beautiful. Her shawl and her sash are brilliant white. I very much want some."
"It shall be served, father."
What he is asking for is a white bowl with chicken in corn gruel.
Zuyua.

28 "Son, go bring me a swollen bald, as it is called, and it should be redolent in odor."
"It shall be served, father."
What he is asking for is a melon. . . .

30 "Son, go bring me a woman with very white well-rounded knees. Here I'll roll up her petticoat to her knees."
"It shall be served thus, father."
What he is asking for is gourdroot. And to roll up her petticoat is to peel its rind.

31 "Son, go bring me a woman who is very pretty with a very white face. I very much want one. Here I'll throw down her petticoat and blouse in front of me."
"It shall be served so, father."
What he is asking for is a hen and a hen turkey to eat. To throw down her petticoat and blouse is the plucking of its pin feathers. And then the meat is cooked for eating.
Zuyua language.

32 "Son, go bring me a guardian of the fields, a grown man here. I want his face to be seen."

"It shall be served so, father."

What he is asking for is the body of a yam to eat, giving the explanation.

33 "Son, go bring me also a keeper of fields, a black old lady, then all her people, seven palms across the bottom. I want it to be seen."

What he is asking for is the green fruit

Of the squash.

Zuyua language. . . .

⟲ 2 ⟲

Dramatic Literature

The *Rabinal Achí*

Several sixteenth-century chroniclers speak of dramatic and comic performances among the Maya. While some of these took place at the customary feasts during the year, others were sponsored by the local rulers for the entertainment of the people on special occasions. One dramatic piece has survived which is of probable pre-Hispanic origin. In the mid-nineteenth century, a French priest and researcher, Etienne Brasseur de Bourbourg, who was in charge of the parish of the town of San Pablo Rabinal in the department of Baja Verapaz, Guatemala, heard about it from a Quiche Indian elder, Bartolomé Ziz. Brasseur had actually transcribed such a piece in Quiche. The work, of course, was part of the oral tradition. Moreover, he convinced Ziz to arrange a performance of the pageant play—a drama including dance and music—in the main plaza of the village on January 25, 1856.

The play is known today as the Rabinal Achí or Warrior of Rabinal. *To the contemporary reader, the form will seem strange, for there appears to have been little Occidental influence on the manner of the dialogue and presentation. Even the plot itself is Mesoamerican in character. A Nahua story records a similar tale of a warrior who, as we might say in modern terms, prefers death to dishonor.*

The Rabinal Achí *was probably based on historical events, although we do not know when they may have occurred since the calendrical elements that most likely accompanied the play have either been forgotten or perhaps lost, like those of the Popol Vuh.*

For the Quiche audience, the play had functions other than mere entertainment. First, it recalls events that occurred offstage, among them, the capture of the ruler of Rabinal (who appears by his calendrical name, Ahau Hobtoh or Chief Five-Rain). Then his daring rescue by the Warrior of Rabinal.

Long wars of shifting alliances, and attempts to expand the territory of one city-state, are evident in the incidents connected with the placing of boundary markers, all included in the dialogue. There are also references to the products of the milpa (small farm), to the collection of honey, and other aspects of Maya life that were of great economic, political, and religious importance.

Another possibly didactic aspect of the play is the reenactment of fundamental attitudes toward war, sacrifice, and above all, loyalty to the code. The participants recite old affronts to their honor, repeating the words of their antagonists and then commenting on them in an almost dialectical process. Everything in the work is highly stylized, as was warfare itself in Mesoamerica, which almost always began with the presentation of weapons by the aggressor to the nation to be engaged in battle. Like these rituals of war, one must assume that the play took form over decades, perhaps centuries, slowly developing the eloquent language of the speakers as it shed naturalistic details of a history that had become common knowledge for the audience.

The plot of the Rabinal Achí is similar to the Nahua story of Tlahuicole of Tlaxcala, who was captured by the Mexica and made to participate in the gladiatorial sacrifice. In this ritual death, the captured warrior was tethered by a short cord, armed only with a feathered club and a flimsy shield, and given the chance to fight a series of Mexica warriors bearing flint-edged war clubs and protected by shields of woven branches, skins, and cotton padding. After defeating a good number (we do not know exactly how many) of the heavily armed warriors, Tlahuicole was offered the opportunity to join the Mexica and live on as an honored warrior. He chose instead to die.

In the Rabinal Achí, the Warrior of Quiche has the opportunity to save his life by joining the family of Five-Rain. His response is not only negative, it is ferocious. Hence the code of the warrior, the loyalty of the citizen to the state—the grand gesture and ultimate tragedy of the Warrior of the Cavek Quiche.

RABINAL ACHI—The Warrior of Rabinal

A Ballet-Drama of the Quiche Indians of Guatemala[1]

Cast of Characters

Chief Five-Rain—Calendrical name of the ruler of the city of Rabinal
The Warrior of Rabinal—High Chief of the Warriors, son of Chief Five-Rain
The Quiche Warrior—Ruler of the Foreigners[2] who lived in the cities of Cunen and Chajul, son of the Priest of the Warriors, Priest and Ruler of the Men of Quiche
The Wife—Wife of Chief Five-Rain
Precious Gems—Wife of the Warrior of Rabinal
A Manservant of the Warrior of Rabinal
A Woman Servant
The Mother of the Plumes—A Virgin of Rabinal
Twelve Yellow Eagles (warriors who have earned the right to wear the head and skin of the Yellow Eagle)
Twelve Yellow Jaguars (warriors who have earned the right to wear the head and skin of the Yellow Jaguar)
Many servants and women of the Warrior of Rabinal. Dancers
White Boys, White Sons (ordinary soldiers)
[Musicians]

---

[1]The reader can enjoy the form, plot, language, and general aspect of the pageant-drama from this translation. However, it has passed through many languages over the centuries, blurring or even confusing some of the details.

To remove some repetition in the work without creating "a tomb for metaphors," as has so often been done with Mesoamerican work, several of the metaphors appear the first few times, then in more direct language thereafter:

your mouth, your face—you
beneath the sky, upon the earth—here
thus spoke my word—I said
inside the great walls, inside the great fort—in the fort.

[2]The word "foreign" also refers to kinds of weapons brought into the south of Mesoamerica from central Mexico and perhaps even further north.
Place names when translated from Quiche appear in parentheses in English.

PART I

In front of Fort Cak-Yuc-Zilic-Cakacaonic-Tepecanic[3]

(A chorus performs for the Warrior of Rabinal and his people. The Quiche Warrior enters the circle suddenly and dances in the center, brandishing his lance and menacing the head of the Warrior of Rabinal. The circle begins to move more quickly. In this dialogue, the audience is made aware of actions that took place earlier, including the challenge by the Quiche and his capture.)

The Quiche Warrior

Come on, chief lancer, chief cocksman!

This is my word to the face of the sky, to the face of the earth: He is the first one whose lineage I will put an end to, this chief of the Chacach, of the Zamen, of the environs of Rabinal.

And therefore, I will not say many words to you.

May the sky and the earth be with you, distinguished warrior, Warrior of Rabinal.

The Warrior of Rabinal

(Dances, brandishing his bow, with which he menaces his adversary.)

Truly, Brave One, Chief Warrior of the Cavek Quiche. This was your word before the sky, before the earth. "Come on, chief lancer, chief cocksman!"

Were these your words? Of course, yes, behold the sky! behold the earth! You gave yourself up to the point of my arrow, to my shield, to my foreign mace, to my foreign ax, to my coat of mail, to my bonds, to my white earth, to my magical herbs, to my strength, to my daring.

So it would be or so it would not be. I will cast my good rope, my good lariat, before the sky, before the earth. May the sky and the earth be with you, brave, chief warrior, prisoner and captive!

(Having roped him, he brings him closer. The music and dancing stops. A long silence, during which both warriors look furiously at each other. There is neither music nor dancing during the following discussion.)

Greetings, brave, chief warrior, prisoner and captive. I have lassoed you, the one from your sky, from your land. Yes, surely the sky, yes, surely the earth, have hurled you at the point of my arrow, at my shield, at my foreign mace, at my foreign ax, at my coat of mail, at my bonds, at my white earth, at my magical herbs.

Speak, declare yourself! Where are your mountains? Where are your valleys, if you were born on the slope of a mountain, on the slope of a valley? Are you not the son of the clouds, the son of that big black cloud? Have you not come because you were driven out by the lances, by the war?

This is my word to the face of the sky, to the face of the earth. May the sky and the earth be with you, imprisoned chief, captive!

---

[3]The ruins of this city are still visible from Rabinal.

The Quiche Warrior

Ay! Oh sky! Ay! Oh earth! Is it true, as you said, the grotesque word that you used to my face, to the face of the sky, to the face of the earth, to my mouth, to my face? "I am a brave, I am a warrior."

Let's go! I would be a brave. Let's go! I would be a warrior! And I have come here, driven out by the lance, by the war.

Furthermore, you also said, "Say it, speak, to the face of my mountains, to the face of my valleys."

Let's go! I could be a brave. Let's go! I could be a warrior!

And I could have said, I could have declared, before the face of my mountains, the face of my valleys, "Is it not apparent that I was born on the slope of a mountain, on the slope of a valley, I the son of the clouds, the son of the big black cloud?"

Let's go! I could say, I could proclaim them, my mountains, my valleys. Ah, how they surpass the sky, how they surpass the earth!

And so I will not say many words to you, distinguished warrior, warrior of Rabinal. May the sky, may the earth be with you!

(*Music and dancing resume.*)

The Warrior of Rabinal

Eh! brave, warrior, imprisoned chief, captive!

If you do not say, if you do not declare, the face of your mountains, the face of your valleys, then the sky and the earth will desire that I make you go in, be tied up, and cut to pieces, before my Ruler, before my Chief, in front of my walls, in front of my great fort.

The Quiche Warrior

Oh sky! Ay! Oh earth! To whom shall I speak, to whom shall I declare myself before the mountains, before the valleys? To your nightingales, to your birds? I the brave, I the warrior, Chief of the Foreigners from Cunen, of the Foreigners of Chajul! Surely the Head Priest of the Warriors, Priest of the Bundle descended the slope ten times into my mountains and into my valleys. How shall I make them fall, how shall I make them rise, these words, these terms, that I will speak with you beneath the sky, upon the earth?

The Warrior of Rabinal

Brave, Chief Warrior of the Cavek Quiche, are you my aide, are you my older brother, are you my younger brother? Admirable One! My spirit could have forgotten that I saw you, could have forgotten that I looked at you inside the great walls, inside the great fort.

It was surely you who imitated the cry of the coyote, who imitated the cry of the fox, the cry of the weasel, of the jaguar to those behind the great walls of the great fort, daring the white boys, the white sons, to come out, luring them out in front of the great walls, in front of the great fort, to nourish us with the richness and the excellence of wild honey, the food of our Ruler, our Chief, the grandfather Five-Rain.

Why make this display, inciting, as you have done, my daring and my bravery? It was not the cries that provoked, that drew out, the twelve chiefs, each and every one a chief inside his own wall, his own fort.

In truth, did you not tell us: "You free men, the twelve Braves, the twelve Warriors, come! listen to what is arranged for you, because every one of your meals, your beverages, is liquified, consumed, destroyed, absorbed by a porous stone. Only the grasshopper, only the crickets sing behind the walls of the fort, because no one else is left, except for nine or ten of these white boys, these white sons. This is the reason why we've stopped devouring the white boys, the white sons, because we have eaten them like a fried dinner of beans, lobster, and parrot, like a stew."

Wasn't this the warning to us, the chiefs and the warriors? In this, didn't you even go beyond the desires of your daring and your courage? At the Belehe Mokoh (Nine Occasions), at the Belehe Chumay (Nine Knolls), this daring, this bravery, were they not the reason for the covering up, the burying by our warriors in Qoton (Carved Sculpture), in Tikiran (Beginning), as they are called?

Here is where you will pay now for this disruption, beneath the sky, upon the earth. You have said, then, good-bye to your mountains, your valleys, because here we shall cut off your sprouting, your lineage. You will not have the occasion again in the day, in the night, to descend from, to go out of your mountains, your valleys. It is necessary that you die here, that you disappear. That is why I will announce this news to my ruler in the great fort.

The Quiche Warrior

Did you speak this way to the face of the sky, to the face of the earth? "Why make a display of my daring, make a display of my bravery?" In truth, there was a dare at the beginning, taunting my ruler, my chief. This is the only cause of my arrival, of my journey from my mountains, from my valleys. The message of daring came from here, inside the walls under the command of Cak-Yuc-Zilic-Cakacaonic-Tepecanic; which is the name, the mouth, the face of these walls, of this fort. Was it not from here that the ten loads of cacao (money), the ten loads of (fine) cacao were bound to be presented before my ruler, before my leader, wizard chief, wizard of the warriors, wizard of the bundle; so great is your name, your mouth, your face, within my walls, within my fort?

Since this had been presented, and because of this, the chief, wizard chief, wizard of the bundle, desired the immediate death of the chief of the Chacachs, of the Zaman, of the Cauk, of Rabinal, before the face of those of Ux, of those of Pokomam.

"We should do it brilliantly. May you go and say that you want to see the daring, the bravery of the chief of the Quiche mountains, of the Quiche valleys. May he come to take possession of the beautiful mountains, of the beautiful valleys. May my younger brother, my older brother come. May he come to take possession here, of these beautiful mountains, of these beautiful valleys. May he come to plant, to make seedbeds, in the place where the blooms of our cucumbers, of our fine squashes, of our beans are nurtured." So you spoke your challenge, your cry of daring, to the face of my ruler.

Here is how the boldness, the cry of my ruler was quickly launched: "Greetings! greetings! my brave, my warrior, go and answer and (then) return, because a message of challenge has arrived here. Gather your strength, your courage here; the point of my arrow, my shield, and return to the slope of my mountain, the slope of my valley."

Thus came the challenge, the cry of my ruler, my chief. I had already gone. I was placing the boundary markers over there where the sun sets, where the night begins, where the cold oppresses, where chill oppresses, in Pam-Ezahao-cak as it is called. Then I took out the point of my arrow, my shield, and I returned over the side of the mountain, the side of the valley. Over there, for the first time, I delivered my challenge, my cry, before Cholochic-Huyu, Cholochic-Chah, as they are called. I left there, going to deliver my challenge, my cry for the second time at Nim-che Paraveno, and at Cabracan, as they are called. I left from over there, going to deliver my challenge, my cry, for the fourth time, at Xol Chacah, as it is called. Over there I knew that the (great) sacred drum, the (small) sacred drum, were played by the twelve Yellow Eagles, the Yellow Jaguars. The sky shook, the earth shook, from the great noise, from the great tumult of the twelve Yellow Eagles, the Yellow Jaguars, with the warrior's servants.

Over there I began my song. "Come, chief lancer! chief cocksman!

"Is he the first whose lineage I will put an end to by cutting off his root, his stalk, this chief of the Chacach, of the Zaman. This Cauk of Rabinal"; so I said. What must you do, oh chief, since I have not been able to ruin you, to tear you apart, but only to speak my word, only to sing to the face of the sky, to the face of the earth, distinguished warrior, Warrior of Rabinal? Speak, then, you too, one time.

The Warrior of Rabinal

(Here again, the actors in the dance are speaking of events that took place offstage.)

Ah! Surely it is not a defect, it is not a wrong, making a challenge for the ears of the chief, the chief wizard of the bundle, when he wanted the death, the disappearance, of the chief of the Chacach, of the Zaman, of the Cauk of Rabinal, by those of Ux, by those of Pokomam here. "We should do it brilliantly so that the chief from the Quiche mountains, from the Quiche valleys, comes with his boldness, his bravery. May he come to take possession of the beautiful mountains, of the beautiful valleys. May he come to plant, may he come to make seedbeds, in the place where the blooms of our cucumbers, of our fine squashes, of our beans are nurtured."

Good! We shall plant, we shall make our seedbeds, over there where the blooms of our fine cucumbers, our fine squashes, our fine beans, are nurtured! Thus, our word was spoken. It is because of this that you came in vain, uselessly, to dare us, to menace us.

"Thanks to the sky, thanks to the earth, you came to make yourself known, in front of our walls, in front of our fort. It is for this that we shall accept the dare, we shall accept the war, we shall fight those from Ux, those from Pokomam. I shall give you, then, the task of making the dare. Go, run in front of Nim-Be where the bird drinks the water, in front of Cholochic-Zakehun, as it is called. Do not grant what the hearts of those of Ux, of those of Pokomam, desire. Do not abandon the struggle in their mountains, in their valleys. Rip apart! Destroy!"; so I spoke, in the beginning.

"But you do not have to look at, to see, those from Ux, those from Pokomam, because they will be turned into flies, into butterflies, into big ants, into tiny ants; and your ranks, your columns, will scale the slope of the mountain called Equempek Gamahal (Under the Cavern of the Dry Yellow Ears)."

Then I directed my vision, my glance to the face of the sky, to the face of the earth; at the same time I saw those from Ux, those from Pokomam; my heart grew faint, my heart was wounded by the sight of you, by looking at you, because you had granted what they wanted, those of Ux, those of Pokomam.

Then I hurled my cry, my dare at you. "Hail! Brave, warrior, Chief of the Cavek Quiche. Why are you giving up your struggle against those of Ux, against those of Pokomam, in their mountains, in their valleys? Ay! oh sky! Ay! oh earth! Surely, it was expected in our mountains, in our valleys, that you should hurl your boldness, your cry, against those of Ux, those of Pokomam. Have you answered those from Ux, those from Pokomam, who have hurled their boldness, their cry?

"Ah! Ah! come back, oh you of Ux, you of Pokomam, to listen here to the orders"; so you spoke your word. Then they answered: "Abandon the struggle in our mountains, in our valleys. Were we not born here with our dependents, our children, in the place where the black clouds, the white clouds descend, where the cold, the chill oppresses? Below the branches, the green branches, are the yellow cacao (money), the (fine) yellow cacao, the gold, the silver, the embroidery, the goldsmith's work, with my dependents, my children (my clan). Here are my dependents, here are my children; where they need not suffer deeply or even a little in order to survive; while they sleep the load of cacao (money), the load of (fine) cacao, arrives, because they are embroiderers, goldsmiths and silversmiths, and have been so since the first dawn.

"But look at the dependents, the children, of the distinguished warrior, of the Warrior of Rabinal; since the first dawn they have not gotten their subsistence in all or in part, without great pain, without great suffering. They have one leg looking forward, (one leg) looking back; but since the first dawn there are no cripples, no one-armed ones, among the nephews, the grandchildren of the distinguished warrior, the Warrior of Rabinal." Thus he answered the daring, the cry, of those of Ux, of those of Pokomam, because of the envy in their hearts.

And you answered them: "Hail! oh, you of the Ux, oh, you of the Pokomam! Did you speak this way to the face of the sky, to the face of the earth? Concerning these dependents, these children of the Warrior of Rabinal, you do not have to touch their faces, be concerned with their means of survival, because they are strong, because they are brave. As far as your children, on the contrary, they get lost, they disperse, they come and go, they arrange themselves, they go to their mountains, their valleys. Perhaps no more than one or two return to their walls, their fort, because they are destroyed, they are pursued, while they look for sustenance, for their means of survival. In regard to the children of the brave, the warrior, the distinguished warrior, the Warrior of Rabinal, if one or two depart, one or two return to their walls, to their fort."

But this is what I said: "The challenge, the cry, that have been hurled by those from Ux, those from Pokomam, has been heard. Ay! oh sky! Ay! oh earth! It was necessary that you should have been furious at the abandonment there of my dependents, my children. It must be told that they were unable to take possession of those beautiful mountains, those beautiful valleys. It is a wonder that you have come to end many days, many nights here, that you have come to end the point of your arrow, of your shield, that you have come to end the face of your strength, of your power. You have gained nothing, and it has to be said that you have not been able to take possession yourself here. You knew the boundaries of your land were next to the slopes of the mountains, to the slopes of the valleys. It must be said that I am the one who has gained renown with my dependents, my children here."

The Quiche Warrior

Your word is true when you say that I was unable to take possession here, of the beautiful mountains, of the beautiful valleys. Was it in vain, uselessly, that I came here to end many days, many nights here? Then was it my daring, my bravery, that did not serve me?

Ay, oh sky! Ay, oh earth! I went then, to my mountains, to my valleys. I scaled the slopes; there, on the point known as Camba, I placed my signs. This is my word: "Was I not able to draw out the chief of Camba to put my sandals on the heads of the dependents, the heads of the children of the foremost warrior, the Warrior of Rabinal?" Thus I spoke the grieving of my heart. But even though the sky itself wished to rebuke me, if the earth wished to rebuke me, I gave my word. From there I went to place my signs on the peak of Zaktihel (Limestone) mountain, in the valley of Zaktihel; I hurled my challenge, my cry.

Is it true that I did not take possession here? From there I soon descended to the riverbank and then I saw the new lands, ancient ones, the land of the yellow ears, of the yellow beans, of the white beans, of the birds with talons.

Then I said: "Could I not take a little of this new land, this ancient land, with the help of the point of my arrow, my shield?" Then I placed my sandals onto the new land, the ancient land. From there I soon went to place my signs on Xtincurum (House of Bonds) peak, in front of Ximbal Ha (Prison), as they are called. I also left from there, I went to plant my signs on the peak called Quezentun; there I beat the drum to my heart's content (for) two hundred and sixty days, two hundred and sixty nights,[4] because I had not been able to take possession here, of the beautiful mountains, of the beautiful valleys."

Ay, oh sky! Ay, oh earth! Truly I was not able to take possession here, for I came in vain, uselessly, to end many days, many nights. I came to complete the face of my strength, the face of my power; but my daring, my bravery, have not sufficed. Thus I spoke. I went to my mountains, my valleys. Soon I scaled the slope of the mountains, the slope of the valleys.

The Warrior of Rabinal

Why have you lured out my dependents, my children? You did not have anything to do with them. Leave them to their mountains, to their valleys. If you do not leave them, the sky wishes, the earth wishes, that I throw the sky into disarray, that I throw the earth into disarray. Thus I spoke my challenge, because I had gone out; I was dedicated to placing the signs of the lands on the peak called Mucutzunun (Hidden Hummingbird), when you abducted the white boys, the white sons, aided by the point of your arrow, aided by your shield, without the echo of your heart hearing my challenge, my cry. Then I scaled the slope of the mountains, the slope of the valleys, and I placed my signs on Pan-Ahachel (Place of the Magical Grandmother), as it is called. There I hurled my challenge, my cry, against you. Until then you left the white boys, the white sons, there on Nim-Che, on Cabrakan Paraveno, as they are called, certainly a short distance from the Quiche mountains, the Quiche valleys. They came back from there, they scaled the slopes of the mountains, the slopes of the valleys; with the gut hollow, the belly empty, they came back; nevertheless, they did not break up the walls they had built in Panamaka (Hot Springs), as it is called.

Then you came opposing my ruler, my chief, there in the Baths [Lake Atitlan], as it is called. I had not left, I was not at the point where the signs were placed on the lands over there in Tzam-Ha (House of the Point), in front of Quilavach-Abah (Facing Rocks), as they are known. Then I abandoned my view, my lookout, to the face of the sky, to the face of the earth. There was a great space where the clouds went, where the great clouds passed, before the great walls, before the great fort; there I hurled my challenge, my cry, to the face of the sky, to the face of the earth:

"Hail! brave, warrior, Chief of the Cavek Quiche! Why did you come to abduct my ruler? You have nothing to do with him. Leave him alone, then,

---

[4]The ritual and astrological calendar, consisting of thirteen months of twenty days each.

to return to the great walls, to the great fort!" So I spoke. But my challenge, my cry, did not enter your heart. Then I spoke again: "If you do not let my ruler, my chief, go, If you do not leave him, the sky wishes, the earth wishes, that I put the sky in disarray, that I put the earth in disarray."

But my challenge, my cry, did not enter your heart. Then I scaled the slopes of the great, beautiful mountains, of the great, beautiful valleys, and I went to place my signs (inside the great walls), inside the great fort. However, I did not see anything but the horizon, where the clouds went by, where the great clouds went by, in front of the great walls, in front of the great fort. Only the grasshopper, (only) the cricket, came to drum, to sing, in the fort.

But my heart grew faint, my heart grew weak, and I climbed the slopes of the valleys, the slopes of the mountains, until I had ascended to the Quiche mountains, to the Quiche valleys, until I had reached my ruler, my chief, who was walled in front and back, in the rock, in the limestone. I struck there with the point of my arrow, with my shield, my foreign mace, my foreign ax, my boldness, my bravery. Then I saw my ruler, my chief, completely abandoned in the rock, the limestone. I carried him from there with the help of the point of my arrow, my shield. I must say that if I had not been there, in truth, they would have cut off the stalk, the root of my ruler, of my chief, at the Quiche mountain, at the Quiche valley. It was this way that I came back to see him, with the help of the point of my arrow, of my shield; I conducted him back to the walls, to the fort, of my ruler, my chief.

Did you not destroy two, three villages, the cities with moats of Balamvac (Wizard Hawk) whose sandy soil resounds (under one's feet), of Chi-Calcaraxah (On the Coast of Green Reeds), of Chi-Cunu (The Pudenda), from Chi-Gozibal Tagah Tulul (Valley Filled with Grass and Red Sapodilla), as they are called. When will your heart stop being intensely jealous of my daring, of my bravery?

But you are going to pay here. I will announce the news of your presence in the fort, to my ruler, to my chief. You have said good-bye to your mountains, to your valleys, because we shall put an end to your lineage here.

The Quiche Warrior

Hail! brave, Warrior of Rabinal! Did you speak this way? You do not have to change the words you have said to me. It has to be said that at the beginning I failed to carry out the orders of our ruler, our chief.

"Those we dare, those we challenge," so said our ruler, our chief, the chief of Teken Toh (Gathered Rains), the chief of Teken Tohax (?), of Gumarmachi (Incised Gourds), in Taktazib (Cut-down Forests), Taktazimah (Arranged Posts), Cuxama Ah (Array of Reeds), of Cuxama Cho (Array of Lakes), of Cuxama Civan (Array of Gorges), of Cuxama Cab (Array of Lands), of Cuxuma Tziquin (Array of Eagles), which are the names, the mouths, the faces of our ruler, of our chief.

"Come, oh! twelve warriors, come to hear the orders, such was the word given to them in the beginning, and in turn to you, at the start of the waste, of the disorder, there in the employment, in the public duties, inside the walls, inside the great fort, where there were but nine white boys, but ten white children." So the words were spoken to them and to you.

It is because you were not able to capture me, because of the desire of my heart, that I made the white boys, the white sons, come back, return, though they had been diverted in Iximche (Great Bamboo), seeking the bees of the yellow honey, of the green honey. When I saw them, I said this: "Were you unable to abduct those white boys, those white sons, because they had established themselves in my mountains, on my plains?"

I said, "I will bring them to my ruler, in the Quiche mountains, in the Quiche valleys. Here, then, a little of these new lands, ancient lands, of the white, open ears, of the yellow beans, of the white beans." From there I went to Pan Cakil (In the Fire), as it is called, because my heart was with the white boys, with the white children.

It was because of this, then, that you hurled your challenge, your cry; then my heart (wept), my heart howled, hearing your challenge, your cry. But soon I let them go free, there in Nim-Che, in Cabrakan Paraveno, as they are called. It was not long before the white boys, the white sons, arrived at my mountains, at my valleys, at the Quiche mountains, at the Quiche valleys. As they went, so they returned, the white boys, the white sons, the inside of their guts dry, the inside of their bellies empty. They continued the trek over the slopes of the mountains, the valleys. Nevertheless, they did not arrive at their walls, their fort; since they established themselves in Panamaka, as it is called.

Meanwhile, I was the one who carried out the evil abduction of your ruler, your chief, there in the Baths, as it is called. I captured him while he was bathing, helped by the point of my arrow, helped by my shield. I then put him in my mountains, in my valleys, Quiche mountains, Quiche valleys, because of the desire of my heart, because he was unable to take possession of me here. I closed him up, then, inside the walls of limestone and song, I walled up his face in the limestone, in the rock.

I must say that I have done wrong, because you said, "You destroyed two, three villages, the cities with moats, of Balamvac, where the sandy ground resounds (under one's feet), of Chi Calcaraxah, of Chi Cunu, of Gozibal-Tagah-Tulul, as they are called." In truth then, I did wrong, because of the desire of my heart, with which I will pay now.

Now I have no more words in my mouth, in my face. Only the squirrel, only the bird here before, perhaps will whistle at you, oh chief!

Did you not also say: "I am going to announce the news of your presence to the face of my ruler, of my chief, in the great walls, in the great fort? You have said good-bye to your mountains, to your valleys, for here we shall cut off your stalk, your root"?

Can we not proceed splendidly, as if I were your older brother, your younger brother? I will adorn you. I will bedeck you with my gold, with my silver, with the point of my arrow, with my shield, with my foreign mace, my foreign ax, even with my armor, my sandals; and then I will work here, I will occupy myself as if I were your child, your son, as the ultimate sign that you will not allow me to go to my mountains, to my valleys.

The Warrior of Rabinal

But then I would have to go and say to the face of my ruler, my chief: "We have had a fight with a brave, a warrior, lasting two hundred and sixty days, lasting two hundred and sixty nights; our sleep has not been restful, and now I have adorned myself with his gold, with his silver, with his foreign mace, with his foreign ax, even his armor, his sandals."

And I should go to say to the face of my ruler, to the face of my chief, that right now he must allow you to return to your mountains, to your valleys. Will I go to say this to my ruler?

But I am already provided for, fulfilled, by my ruler, my chief; I have gold, silver; I have the point of my arrow, my shield, my foreign mace, my foreign ax; I am provided for by my ruler, my chief, here in the fort. Therefore I am going to announce the news of your presence to my ruler.

If he allows you to go to the mountains, to the valleys, if my ruler says this, then I shall allow you to go. Yes, if my ruler says so, I will allow you to go. But if my ruler, my chief, says: "Bring him before my mouth, my face, so that I can examine his mouth, his face, from up close to see if they are the mouth, the face of a brave, a warrior."

If my ruler, my chief, says this, I will announce it to you.

The Quiche Warrior

Good! Let it be so!

PART II

Inside the fort

(*In the presence of Chief Five-Rain. He occupies a low seat, with a back-rest, adorned with ancient cords. Near him, his wife, surrounded by manservants and woman servants, warriors, Eagles and Jaguars.*)

The Warrior of Rabinal

Hail! oh chief! Greetings to your wife! I give thanks to the sky, I give thanks to the earth. Here you offer protection, you give shelter, beneath the canopy made of feathers of green birds, inside the fort. As I am your brave, your warrior, I have brought before you a brave, a warrior, that we fought during two hundred and sixty days, during two hundred and sixty nights, in which our sleep was not restful.

The sky has given him to us, the earth has given him to us, hurling the point of my arrow, my shield at him. I have tied him up, I have lassoed him, with my good rope, with my good lasso, with my foreign mace, with my foreign ax, with my net, with my strings, with my magical herbs. He now goes to speak calmly, not foaming at the mouth. This is the brave, the warrior, who imitated the cry of the coyote, the fox, the weasel in front of the walls of the fort, to dare, to draw out the white boys, the white sons.

This is the brave, this warrior, who has destroyed nine or ten white boys, white sons. He is also the brave who abducted you in the Baths. He is the brave, this warrior, who destroyed two or three villages, the city with moats of Balamvac where the sandy ground resounds beneath your feet, as it is called. Will your heart's desire, then, not impose an end to this boldness, this bravery? Were we not prepared by our rulers, our leaders, every ruler from the walls, from the fort, the chief of Teken Toh, the chief of Teken Tihax, Gumarmachi Tactazib, Tactazimah, Cuxuma Ah, Cuxuma Zivan, Cuxuma Cho, Cuxuma Cab, Cuxuma Tziquin? Those are their names, their mouths, their faces. It is here that he comes to pay. Here we shall cut off his root, his stalk.

Chief Five-Rain

My brave, my warrior, thanks to the sky, thanks to the earth, you have arrived at the great walls, at the great fort, before me, your ruler, I Chief Five-Rain. Therefore thanks to the sky, thanks to the earth, that the sky has given you, that the earth has given you, this brave, this warrior, that you have tied up, that you have lassoed. Surely he is the one whom you have announced.

Yet let him not make noise, yet let him not make a disturbance when he comes to the entrance of the great walls, of the great fort, because he must be loved, because he must be admired in the fort; because here there are his twelve older brothers, his twelve younger bothers, those of the precious metals, those of the precious stones.

Their mouths, their faces, are not yet finished; perhaps he has come to complete your group in the fort. Here there are twelve Yellow Eagles, twelve Yellow Jaguars; their mouths, their faces, are not yet finished; perhaps this brave, perhaps this warrior, has come to complete them. Here there are mats of precious metals, seats of precious metals; one may be seated there, one may not be seated there; perhaps this brave, this warrior, has come to seat himself. Here there are twelve drinks, twelve intoxicating liquors, called Ixtatzunun (We Await the Hummingbirds), sweet, fresh, sleep-inducing, agreeable, appetizing, that are drunk before retiring, here in the fort, beverages of chiefs; perhaps this brave has come to drink them.

There are very fine cloths, well woven, brilliant, resplendent, the work of my Mother,[5] of my Wife; perhaps this brave, this warrior, has come to use the

---

[5]A sign of respect, no relation, as in describing the chief as "grandfather."

finery for the first time. There is also the Mother of the Plumes, the Mother of the Green Birds, from Tzam-Gam-Carchag; perhaps this brave, perhaps this warrior, has come to use her mouth, her face, for the first time; perhaps he has come to dance with her, in the fort. Perhaps this brave has come to make himself into a son-in-law, brother-in-law, in the fort. If he is obedient, if he is humble, if he defers, if he bows his face, then may he enter.

The Warrior of Rabinal

Chief Five-Rain, approve of me to the face of the sky, to the face of the earth. This is my word: "Here is my strength, my bravery that you have given me, that you have furnished to me. I will leave my arrow, my shield. Watch over them, then, close them up in your bundle, in your arsenal; may they rest there; I shall also rest; they were the reason why we could not sleep when we were in need of it. I leave them to you, then, inside the great fort."

Chief Five-Rain

But how will you guard them, how will you close them up, in your bundle, in your arsenal? Did you not say, "Here is my strength, here is my bravery, here my arrow, my shield, that you had given to me, that you have furnished to me. I leave them to you so that you can watch them, so that you can close them up in your bundle, your arsenal"? Which will you have then, against those that may come to show themselves to the head of the lands, to the feet of the lands? What arms, also, for our boys, our sons, when they come to seek, to find (their food), in the four corners, on the four sides? It is here, then, that once, twice, you must take your strength, your bravery, your arrow, your shield, which I give to you.

The Warrior of Rabinal

Very well! Then I shall return here to take my strength, my bravery, that you have given me, that you have conformed, to my mouth, to my face. Thus, I will take them once, twice. Thus I spoke. Therefore I will leave you for a moment in the fort.

Chief Five-Rain

Very well. Be prudent, do not fall, do not hurt yourself.

PART III

In front of the fort
The Warrior of Rabinal

(He takes the Quiche Warrior from the tree where he was tied up.)

Hail! Chief of the Cavek Quiche. I have announced you in the fort, before the face of my ruler, my chief.

And he said to warn us of your boldness, of your bravery: "Let him not make noise, let him not make a scandal when he comes to the entrance of the fort, because he must be loved, because he must be admired inside the fort; because here he is complete, here he is fulfulled; here there are your twelve older brothers, your twelve younger brothers, those of the precious metals, those of the precious stones; perhaps this brave comes to complete the group?

"Perhaps their mouths, their faces, are not yet finished; perhaps he has come to complete your group in the fort. Here there are twelve Yellow Eagles, twelve Yellow Jaguars; their mouths, their faces, are not yet finished; perhaps this brave, perhaps this warrior, has come to complete them? Here there are mats of precious metals, seats of precious metals; perhaps this brave, this warrior, has come to seat himself. Here there are twelve drinks, twelve intoxicating liquors, sweet, fresh, beverages of chiefs; perhaps this brave has come to drink them?

"There are very fine cloths, well woven, brilliant, resplendent, the work of my Mother, of my Wife, for which, perhaps, this brave, this warrior has come to use the finery for the first time. Here also are the Mother of the Plumes, the Mother of the Green Birds, the precious gem which comes from Tzam-Gam-Carchag; her mouth is about to be used for the first time; her mouth has not been used before; perhaps this brave, this warrior, comes to use her mouth, her face for the first time?" Thus spoke my ruler, my chief.

I come, then, to warn you not to make noise, not to make a disturbance. When you arrive at the entrance to the great walls, to the great fort, bow, bend your knee, at the entrance in front of my ruler, my chief, the chief, Five-Rain. Our conversations will not go on any longer. May the earth, may the sky be with you!

The Quiche Warrior

Eh! Brave, warrior, warrior of Rabinal! Did you not say, "I announced the news of your presence to the face of my ruler, to the face of my chief, in the fort"?

You also said: "It is for this that I come to warn you, brave, warrior. Now begins the appraisal, in order that I see in his mouth, in order that I see in his face, how brave he is, how warlike he is. I come to warn him not to make noise, not to make a scandal. When he comes before my mouth, before my face, he must defer, he must bow his face, because if he is a brave, if he is a warrior, he is obedient, submissive, so that he will be loved, admired, here inside the fort"; so said my ruler, my chief.

Did you not say this?

Let's go! Would I be a brave, would I be a warrior, if I deferred, if I bowed my face? Here is what I will defer with: here is my arrow, here is my shield, here is my foreign mace, my foreign ax; there are my instruments for bowing, for bending my knee, when I come to the entrance of the great walls, of the great fort. I pray to the sky, to the earth, that I may devastate the greatness, the day of the birth, of your ruler, of your chief. I pray to the sky, to the earth, that I may strike the lower part of his mouth, the upper part of his mouth, in the fort, but first, you will suffer this.

(With these words he moves closer, menacing the Warrior of Rabinal.)

A Woman Servant

(Comes between the two warriors, saying:)

Brave, warrior, Chief of the Cavek Quiche, do not kill my brave, my warrior, the Warrior of Rabinal.

PART IV

Inside the fort

The Quiche Warrior

(He comes before Chief Five-Rain.)

Greetings, Chief Five-Rain! I am the one who just entered the gates of the great walls, of the great fort, where you extend your hands, where you extend your shade.

They came to announce the news of my presence to your mouth, to your face.

The Warrior of Rabinal

I have announced the news of your presence to the face of my ruler, my chief, inside the great walls. My ruler has said this:

"Bring this brave, this warrior before me so that I can see from his mouth, from his face, what kind of brave he is, what kind of warrior he is. Advise this brave, this warrior, not to make noise, not to cause a scandal, to defer, to bow his face, when he arrives at the gates of the great walls, the gates of the great fort."

The Quiche Warrior

Very well! I am a brave, I am a warrior, and if I must defer and bow my face, here is that upon which I must bow, upon which I must bend my knee. Here is my arrow, here is my shield with which I shall bring down your destiny, your day of birth. I shall smash the part below your mouth, the part above your mouth, and you are going to suffer, oh chief!

(Menaces Chief Five-Rain with his mace.)

Woman Servant

Brave, warrior, Chief of the Cavek Quiche, do not kill my ruler, my chief, the Chief Five-Rain.

The Quiche Warrior

Then do it, prepare my mat, my seat, because it was so in my mountains, in my valleys, it showed my destiny, it showed the day of my birth. My mat was over there, my seat was over there. In this place shall I be exposed to the ice, shall I be exposed to the cold? So I say to the face of the sky, to the face of the earth.

Chief Five-Rain

Brave, warrior, Chief of the Cavek Quiche, thanks to the sky, thanks to the earth, you have arrived at the great walls, at the great fort, where I extend my hands, where I extend my shade, I the grandfather, the Chief Five-Rain. Therefore, tell, declare, Why do you imitate the cry of the coyote, the cry of the fox, the cry of the weasel, across the great walls, across the great fort, to call, to attract, my white boys, my white sons, to bring them out in front of the great walls, in Ixmiche, to seek, to find, the yellow honey, the green honey of the bees, my food for me, the grandfather, the Chief Five-Rain?

It was you who abducted the nine, the ten white boys, white sons, and it was not long before they would have been carried off to the mountains of the Quiche if my boldness, my daring, had not been on the alert; because there you would have cut off the root, the stalk, of the white boys, the white sons.

You came also to abduct me over there in the Baths. Over there I was the prisoner of the point of your arrow, of your shield. You enclosed me in the stone, in the lime, in the mountains of the Quiche, in the valleys of the Quiche; over there; you would have ended up cutting off my root, my stalk, in the mountains of the Quiche, in the valleys of the Quiche.

But my brave, my warrior, the distinguished warrior, the Warrior of Rabinal, freed me from there, tore me loose, with the help of the point of his arrow, his shield. If my brave, my warrior, had not existed, surely over there they would have cut off my root, my stalk. So I was brought back to the great walls, to the great fort.

You also destroyed two or three villages, cities with moats, in Balanvac, where the sandy ground resounds beneath one's feet, in Calcaraxah, Cunu, Gozibal-Tagah-Tulul, as they are called.

When will you stop conquering according to your heart's desire, your boldness, your daring? When will you stop using them, exciting them? This boldness, this daring, were they not sealed up, buried, in Qotom, in Tikiram? In Belehe Mokoh, in Belehe Chumay, this boldness, this daring, were they not buried, were they not sealed up, by us the rulers, us the leaders, every one from the walls of the fort? But you shall pay for this here. Have you said goodbye to your mountains, to your valleys, because you shall die, you shall disappear here?

The Quiche Warrior

Chief Five-Rain, give me your approval before the face of the sky, the face of the earth. These are certainly the words, these are certainly the opinions that you have spoken to the face of the sky, to the face of the earth; surely I have done wrong. You also said, "Have you not lured, drawn out, the white sons, the white boys, to induce them to the search, to the discovery of the yellow honey, the green honey of the bees, my food for my grandfather, the Chief Five-Rain?" Surely I have done wrong because of my heart's desire, because I have not been able to take possession of these beautiful mountains, of these beautiful valleys, here below the sky, upon the earth.

You also said, "You were the one who came to abduct me. You were the one who was going to overpower me in the Baths."

Surely I have done wrong because of my heart's desire. You also said: "You destroyed two, three villages, the cities with moats of Balanvac, where the sandy ground resounds beneath one's feet, Calcaraxah, Cunu, Gozibal-Tagah-Tulul."

You also said, "Say good-bye to your mountains, to your valleys, speak your word, because here you will die, here you will disappear, here we shall cut off your root, your stalk."

But surely I must deny your word, your orders, because my heart desires it, here before the face of the sky, before the face of the earth. If it is necessary that I die, that I disappear here, then I have here the words which I spoke to you: "Since you are provisioning, you are stocking up, inside the great walls, inside the great fort, I shall lend you your food, your drink, those drinks of the chiefs named Ixtatzunin, the twelve drinks, the twelve intoxicating liquors, sweet, fresh, sleep-inducing, appetizing, that you drink before retiring, inside the great walls, inside the great fort, and also the marvels of my Mother, of my Wife. I shall taste them right now as the ultimate sign of my death, of my disappearance, beneath the sky, upon the earth"; thus I spoke my words. May the sky, may the earth, be with you, Chief Five-Rain!

Chief Five-Rain

You said: "Give me your food, your beverages. I will lend them to you to taste"; so you spoke. "This shall be the ultimate sign of my death, of my disappearance." Here I give them to you, here I lend them to you. Servant, bring my food, my beverages. Give them to this brave, to this warrior, Chief of the Cavek Quiche, as the ultimate sign of his death, of his disappearance.

A Woman Servant

Very well, my ruler, my chief. I give them to this brave, to this warrior, Chief of the Cavek Quiche.

(*The servants bring a low table laden with food and drinks.*)

Taste a bit of the food, the drinks, of my ruler, my chief, the grandfather, Chief Five-Rain.

The Quiche Warrior

(*The Quiche Warrior eats and drinks disdainfully; later he goes to dance in the center of the courtyard. Soon he returns and speaks.*)

Is this your food? Is this your drink? Surely there is nothing to say about them, nothing distinctive about them to my mouth, to my face. If only you were to taste but briefly the appetizing drinks, agreeable, sleep-inducing, sweet, fresh, that I taste in my mountains, in my valleys!

I speak my word to the face of the sky, to the face of the earth! Is this your table of foods, is this your cup of drink?

But this is the skull of my grandfather, this is the head of my father, that I see, that I look upon! Will you not be able to do the same with the bones of my head, with the bones of my skull, incising my mouth, incising my face?

So when going from my mountains, from my valleys to barter five loads of cacao (money), five loads of fine cacao from my mountains, from my valleys, my dependents, my children will say: "Here is the skull of our grandfather, of our father," so my dependents, my children, shall say here from one day to the dawn of the next.

Here also, the bone of my arm, here is the handle of the gourd of precious metals that will clatter, that will make a clamor, in the fort. Here also, the bone of my leg, here the drumstick for the great drum, the small drum, that will make rhythms in the sky, on the earth, within the great walls, within the great fort. Here is what I also say: "I will lend you the splendid, smooth, beautifully woven thing, the work of my Mother, of my Wife, to adorn myself in the fort, in the four corners, on the four sides, as the ultimate sign of my death, of my disappearance, here."

Chief Five-Rain

What do you want, what do you ask for? Whatever it is, I will give it to you, the sign of your ultimate death, of your disappearance. Servant, bring the splendid, smooth, beautifully woven thing, the work you have made in the fort, and give it to this brave, this warrior, as the ultimate sign of his death, of his disappearance.

A Servant

Very well, my ruler, my chief. I am going to give him what he asks for.
(*The servant gives the warrior a shawl, which he puts on.*)
Brave, warrior, here is the finely woven work that you desire, that you ask for. I give it to you, but do not unravel it, do not damage it.

The Quiche Warrior

Your flutes, your drums, would you agree to sound them now, as if they were my flute, my drum? Play, then, the grand melody, the delicate melody. Play my foreign flute, my foreign drum, my Quiche flute, my Quiche drum, the dance of my prisoner, of my captive in my mountains, in my valleys, so as to make the sky shake, to make the earth shake; that our faces, our heads are bowed, when we make our turns (*stamping his foot*), when we dance (*rhythmically, he stamps on the ground*) with the manservants, woman servants here. May the sky, may the earth, be with you, oh flutes! oh drums!

(*The warrior dances in a circle in the center of the courtyard and goes to every corner to hurl his war cry.*)

Greetings, Chief Five-Rain. Give me your approval. Here is what you have lent to me, what you have bestowed upon me. I come to return it, I come to hang it at the entrance to the great walls, to the great fort. Guard it, close it up, in your bundle, in your box, in the fort. You have agreed with my desire, my petition, and I have displayed it in the fort, in the four corners, on the four sides, as the ultimate sign of my death, my disappearance here.

If, however, it is certain that you are supplied, that you are satisfied, in the fort, allow me to lend you the Mother of the Plumes, the Mother of the Green Birds, the Precious Gem, come from Tzam-Gam-Carchag, whose mouth is to be used the first time, whose face has not been used, so that I can use her mouth for the first time, so that I can use her face for the first time, may I dance with her, may I show her inside the great walls, the great fort, in the four corners, on the four sides, as the ultimate sign of my death, of my disappearance?

Chief Five-Rain

What do you desire, then, what are you asking for? Nevertheless, I grant what you desire, because the Mother of the Plumes, the Mother of the Green Birds, the Precious Gem, come from Tzam-Gam-Carchag, whose mouth is to be used for the first time, whose face has not been used, is inside here; so I grant this to you, as the ultimate sign of your death, your disappearance. Servants, bring the Mother of the Plumes, the Mother of the Green Birds, give to this brave, this warrior, what he desires, what he asks for, as the ultimate sign of his death, of his disappearance.

A Servant

Very well, my ruler, my chief. I am going to give her to this brave, this warrior.

(*They bring the Mother of the Plumes and convey her to the Quiche Warrior.*)

Here she is, brave, warrior, Chief of the Cavek. I give you what you desire, what you ask for; but do not offend, do not hurt, the Mother of the Plumes, the Mother of the Green Birds. Let her only be seen dancing inside the walls of the great fort.

(*The Quiche Warrior greets the young girl, who withdraws from before him, dancing, continually turning her face. He follows in the same way, swaying before her, like a curtain; in this manner they do a turn around the courtyard, to the sound of the trumpets, and then return to the place near Chief Five-Rain.*)

The Quiche Warrior

Chief Five-Rain, give me your approval. Here is the one whom you have lent me, whom you have bestowed upon me, as a companion. I went to show her, I went to dance, in the four corners, on the four sides, within the great walls, within the great fort. Now, watch over her, enclose her in the fort.

I also said: Agree to lend me the twelve Yellow Eagles, the twelve Yellow Jaguars, that I have encountered in the day, in the night, armed, with spears at the ready. Lend them to me so that with them I am going to launch the point of my arrow, my shield, in the four corners, on the four sides of the great walls, in the great fort, only as the ultimate sign of my death, of my disappearance, here. May the sky, may the earth, be with you, Chief Five-Rain!

Chief Five-Rain

I lend to you, I bestow upon you, the twelve Yellow Eagles, the twelve Yellow Jaguars, that you desire, that you solicit from me. Go, then, oh my Eagles, my Jaguars, proceed like this brave, this warrior, so that he is able go out with you to brandish the point of his arrow, his shield, in the four corners, on the four sides.

The Quiche Warrior

(The Quiche Warrior goes out with the Eagles and Jaguars and performs a war dance around the courtyard with them. Soon they return to the gallery where Five-Rain is with his family.)

Chief Five-Rain, give me your approval. You have given me what I desired, what I asked for, the Yellow Eagles, the Yellow Jaguars, and I went with them to brandish the point of my arrow, my shield. Are these, then, your Eagles, are these, then, your Jaguars? It is not possible to speak of them in my presence, because some of them come, some of them do not come; they do not have teeth, they do not have claws. If you were to come and look for just a moment, you would see that those of my mountains, of my valleys, look intently, watch intently, they fight, they struggle, with tooth and claw.

Chief Five-Rain

Brave, warrior, Chief of the Cavek Quiche, we see the claws, the teeth, of the Eagles, of the Jaguars, that are in your mountains, in your valleys.

What then is the sight, the vista of your Eagles, your Tigers, who are in your mountains, who are in your valleys?

The Quiche Warrior

Chief Five-Rain, give me your approval before the face of the sky, before the face of the earth. Thus I speak to you: Give me two hundred sixty days, two hundred sixty nights, to go to say farewell to the face of my mountains, to the face of my valleys, where I was going to the four corners, to the four sides, to seek, to find, how to provide my food, my meals.

(No one answers him. Then, dancing, he disappears for a moment; soon, without returning to the gallery where Five-Rain is sitting, he approaches the Eagles and the Jaguars, who are in the center of the courtyard, close to a kind of altar.)

Oh Eagles! Oh Jaguars! "He has run away," you said just now. I was not running away, I was only going to say farewell to the face of my mountains, to the face of my valleys, where I was to seek something to provide my food, my meals, in the four corners, on the four sides.

Ay! oh sky! Ay! oh earth! My daring, my bravery did not serve me. I am trying out my road under the sky, my road upon the earth, parting the grasses, parting the cactus. My daring, my bravery, have not served me.

Ay! oh sky! Ay! oh earth! Must I really die here, disappear here?

Oh my gold! oh my silver! oh the points of my arrows, my shield, my foreign mace, my foreign ax, my coat of mail, my sandals, go to our mountains, to our valleys. Carry our news to the face of our ruler, of our leader; because he said: "It has been a long time since my daring, my bravery sought, and found, our food, our meal"; so my ruler, my chief spoke; may he say it no more, although I have no expectation but my death, my disappearance, here.

Ay! oh sky! Ay! oh earth! Although it is necessary that I die, that I disappear here, I cannot change myself into a squirrel, a bird, that dies on the branch of the tree, on the limb, where it finds its food, its meals, beneath the sky, upon the earth. Oh Eagles! Oh Jaguars! come, then, to fulfill your mission, to fulfill your duty; kill me with your teeth, kill me with your claws, kill me, for I am a warrior come from my mountains, from my valleys. May the sky, may the earth, be with you, oh Eagles! oh Jaguars!

(Eagles and Jaguars surround the Quiche Warrior. They lay him on the sacrificial stone and open his chest. Then the assistants perform a grand chorus.)

Spanish version by L. Cardoza y Aragon, based on Charles Etienne Brasseur de Bourbourg's mid-nineteenth-century work with the original Quiche document (Guatemala, 1929; National Autonomous University of Mexico, ca. 1960). English version by Sylvia and Earl Shorris.

⚬ 3 ⚬

Political Literature

Title of the Lords of Totonicapan

*History and legend are intertwined in this narrative whose subject runs
parallel in many respects to that of the* Popol Vuh, *corroborating the latter's authenticity. Derived from oral tradition and probably from the
contents of one or several indigenous codices, the title was transcribed
by the native scribe Diego Reynoso around 1554.*

*Although the original manuscript in Maya Quiche was thought to
have been lost, this text survived in a Spanish translation done in 1834
by the parish priest of Sacapulas, who was asked to prepare it for the Indians of Totonicapan. They were in need of such translation as a title in
support of their claims to their communal land.*

*Better than a legal document, this is the story of the journey of the
Quiche nobles to where Nacxit Quetzalcoatl resided in order to obtain
the insignia of authority from him, followed by their roamings until they
reached the place where they finally settled. Such a journey was common
practice in Mesoamerica, based on the belief that Quetzalcoatl was the
ultimate source of authority, since all noble lines derived from him. The
two excerpts offered here deal with affairs of the Quiche nation and
some admonishments to their chiefs.*

1. Affairs of State: Tale of the Beautiful Young Girls

These are the names of the enemy chiefs: Rotzhaib, Quibaha, Uxcab, Bakah,
and Quebatzunuha. These met again for a third time to consult together on
how they could kill our fathers Balam-Qitze, Balam-Agab, and Mahucutah.
They learned that every seven days our fathers went to bathe at a certain pool
of warm water, and said: "Perhaps because they do not know other women,

they are valiant and as if filled with a divine fire. Let us choose and adorn three beautiful young girls: if they fall in love with them, their nahuales[1] will hate them, and lacking this help, we will be able to kill them."

Approving the plan, they chose three beautiful maidens whom they adorned, perfumed, and advised what they were to do in the bath. Balam-Qitze, Balam-Agab, and Mahucutah arrived, to whom the young girls said: "God keep you, lords and chiefs of these heights! Our fathers and lords order us to greet you in their name and to obey whatever it shall please you to order us, or if it should be your desire to marry us, to consent gladly. This say our fathers Rotzhaib, Uxab, Qibaha, and Quebatzunuha." "Very well," said Balam-Qitze, "but do us the favor of telling your fathers that you have not seen us or spoken with us." "That cannot be," the girls replied, "for the purpose of our mission is to speak to you, and our fathers told us: 'Bring back proof that you have surely spoken to these lords to whom we sent you, otherwise you will be the victims of our anger.' Have compassion on us, then, give us some token that we have done so, that we may not perish." "Wait, then, for the token we can give you," said Balam-Qitze.

And he went to consult the nahuales and, having explained the case, said: "Tell us, Tohil, Avilix, Hacavitz, what we must do or what token we can give these young daughters of the peoples of Vukamag." "Take three blankets," said Tohil: "on one paint a wasp, on another an eagle, and on another a tiger, and, giving them to the girls, tell them it is the token and also a gift that you send for the principal lords of those peoples."

Having had three white blankets painted, Balam-Qitze gave them to the girls, whose names are Puch, Taz, and Qibatzunah, who returned very happy to their lords, to whom they said: "We have accomplished our mission, and, in proof, here are the presents that those lords send you." Much pleased, the princes of Vukamag examined the presents, distributed them, and immediately covered themselves; but at once the paintings came alive and so tormented the lords of Vukamag that they said to their daughters: "Infernal women, what kind of scourge is this that you have brought us?"

Thus was dissipated the opposition that had been raised against our fathers. Thus they became feared and respected by all their enemies. There in Hacavitz was where our fathers made known the dignity and majesty in which they were cloaked, and where they lived a long time.

2. Admonishments to the New Chiefs

Expedition of the chiefs newly elected and appointed, Agalel and Ahpop; and they were thirteen of Culaha, twelve of Tzihbachah, and eight of those who were called Tzalam-Coxtum.

[1]See Glossary under "nagual."

When the new chiefs were about to leave at the head of an infinity of men, the old chiefs made this exhortation to them: "On seeing you off, our hearts are moved; but you should pay no attention to this, you to whom we have transmitted our valor and who are our hope. Go to seek and subdue all the enemy peoples, to fight those of Ahpozotzil and those of Ahpoxahil and the Ahporamoner. Show valor and steadfastness in all dangers, remember that on you depends the happiness of so many people; go, then, to inspect and take possession of the mountains and valleys that seem good to you."

This said, they embraced and took leave of one another. They took their weapons and went away, [these] men who did not aspire to or covet the offices and destiny that were entrusted to them. They were chosen for their known valor and disinterestedness.

Dionisio José Chonay and Delia Goetz, *Title of the Lords of Totonicapán* (Norman, OK: University of Oklahoma Press, 1953), pp. 174–75, 190.

🌀 4 🌀

Prophetic and
Historical Literature

*G*iven the Maya sense of time occurring in cycles, the literature containing Maya history is also prophetic. As the Maya documents say,
"What could have happened before could happen again." In the Chilam
Balam of Mani, *for example, one reads of the tragic acts of Conquest,
but in the future tense. It has a more prophetic tone than the* Chilam
Balam of Tizimin, *which is the most historical of the books of the Chilam
Balams. The* Tizimin *covers the period from the seventh to the nineteenth century, concentrating on each* katun *by period, from 1441 to
1848.*

*The Maya priests who wrote the books of the Chilam Balams were ex-
pected to predict the future based on the past, then to record what happened during the predicted period. Readers should realize that there is
no linear history, as we know it, in Maya literature. The linear sense we
have in the arrangement of these compositions comes largely from the
order imposed upon them by such translators as Munro Edmonson,
whose work has made these books, all of them far more difficult than the
storytelling of the* Popol Vuh, *accessible to the non-professional reader.*

The Tizimin *is mainly the story of the Itza (Water Witches) of the Yucatan and the Xiu (a Toltec people) who came later to the peninsula.
Much of it has to do with the seating of a cycle (a period of 260 tuns,
approximately 256 years) in a single city. The importance of the choice
of the city devolves from the religious and dynastic advantages accompanying the seating of the cycle. However, at the end of the cycle, the city
was destroyed, and the new cycle was seated in another city. The last such
cycle begins with a deal made by Hunac Ceel (whom readers first encountered in the* Chumayel), *which leads to the ultimate destruction of
Mayapan.*

One can read in the Tizimin *of the way in which the arrival of the
Spaniards exacerbated the rivalries among the Maya. From the outset,*

such Spanish notions as the seven-day week, which conflicted with the Maya calendar, made for all but insurmountable cultural and religious problems. Syncretism was much more difficult for the Maya than the Nahuas. In fact, the Maya history largely ignores much of what the Spaniards did during the early colonial period, confining their comments to insults. This is a Maya history about the Maya, and thus, as Edmonson said, a kind of secret history.

The Last Flight of the Quetzal Prince is the story of Tecum, the national hero of Guatemala, as he went to war against the Spaniards. The Death of Cuauhtemoc records the death of the glorious Mexica prince. Finally, the Crónica de Chac-Xulub-Chen tells of the Spanish demands and the tribute paid them as they enslaved the people and took the product of their labors. It is tragic history, raised from a mere litany of woes to the level of literature by the beauty of the telling and the character of the heroic resistance.

1. Conquest — *Chilam Balam of Mani*

THE PROPHECY AND ADVICE OF THE PRIEST XUPAN NAUAT

"My brothers, prepare yourselves. Our brothers the white men will be coming now. The eternal God will come on the day 13 Cauac in the eighth year of the Katun 13 Ahau, of the Maya rule. The tiger and the eagle will be humiliated by the powerful white man who has a visor, large mouth, and bloody teeth and fingernails. There will be a plague of army ants. It will be necessary to move rapidly with your burden on your back. Your white clothes will be changed permanently. Crazed children do not respect their parents and are very lazy. Those who will remove us will come with great noise and strange rulers will enter in place of those we have had since the creation of the world. They shall come with visors, travel on carpets, sit on their beds with sleepy faces, and later they will do harm. The priests, the seers, and the prophets will be changed, and there will be many miracles from the first year of the Katun 11 Ahau. The capital city will be in the middle of Peten, and in the capital city the house and worship of the holy virgin will be established. Thus it is written in the holy book and in the papers that they will give to the priests so that they might read the number and the order of the Katun. The holy book was given to them because, according to the book of *Ah Uuc Zatay*, it was taken from *Chun-caan*, in Ichcaanziho [Merida]. The *Nicte Katuns* are collected in the book of Hunab Ku, and there the priests will look for the day and the order of the coming Katun. There [in Ichcaanziho] where houses built of rubble and houses of stone are seen, the worship of the virgin queen will be established. The people do not know anything about this. After 13 groups of *Nicte Katuns* have passed it will be seen that the sacred house comes to an end, it will be razed.

"The day 10 Cauac will mark the beginning of the Katun 11 Ahau, and the clamor of war will be heard in the western part of the Peten. The time shall come when the bud of the flower will sprout, a time of handsome nights, much madness, and much lust. Many who look like turtledoves will be born, and because there will be no youth, old dissolute women and the old libertines will have children. The ship at sea, now old and without strength to navigate be it with two or three masts, will list and turn over. The people [Mayas] will be required to go without sandals; they will be asked to wear short pants with a cord at the waist, and many other things will be required [of them]. They will be spied upon even though they be pierced with arrows. [The Katun 11 Ahau] will bring panting with the mouth open; a lack of strength; an age in which the small serpent, the lizard, bites; an age in which the ferret hides and in which the tiger and the lion [the governors] fight. Trees will bear very little fruit in the Katun 11 Ahau, the Katun in which the tiger and the lion shall fight each other."

THE PROPHETIC WORDS OF THE GREAT PROPHETS, THE PRINCIPAL GODS OF THE UNDERWORLD, AND THE GREAT PRIESTS

. . . After reading the books in which the ages are accounted, the priests and the prophets advised the nobles and the warriors to pay tribute to the Spaniards and not to make war against them. Three years passed after the arrival of the foreigners when God spoke to the prophets. *Uuc Zatay,* the chief of the demons and the one who was on Mount *Chun-caan,* in Ichcaanziho, always told the warriors to war against the Spaniards. Because of the arrival of the foreigners, *Uuc Zatay* was suffering and his power was ending. Hun Ahau was angry, and for this reason the priests and the prophets, displaying the papers in which the arrival of the enemy was forecast, preached that for some time they had known all that was going to take place. They also said that, although the Itza would suffer greatly in the future, their souls would benefit from all of these misfortunes. . . .

The Katun 11 Ahau was being counted when the foreigners arrived in this country and Christianity came to us. Then the prophecies of the great priest Chilam Balam began to be fulfilled. . . .

There are thirteen Ahau-Katuns of twenty years each. Ichcaanziho will establish Katun 11 Ahau and [Yaxal Chal will be its countenance]. He holds his hand on high, in his palm a bouquet of fragrant flowers; when he moves, the bells he wears on his boots tinkle. It is the time of the peacock, the catfish [Zulim Chan], and [Chakanputun]. We shall find our food among the trees and among the rocks. We shall pray for bread from heaven, for there shall be death from starvation, and we will be scattered throughout the world. There will be great weeping; there will be no one who does not weep. Children, old men, and old women will cry out, "Your brothers are coming now, they are coming now to change your white clothes." The invading foreigners will establish their quarters in Ichcaanziho. In the times that will be ending, the True God will be worshipped in the entire world. Your government will tumble down, evil son, tiger head with the body of a deer; this will be because of the bad government [Spaniards] in Ichcaanziho. These are the predictions for Katun 11 Ahau, which will end in the year 1548.

Uucil Abnal will establish the Katun 9 Ahau. In the days that follow, the governor will be the only one who has not been removed from power, but he will have to share his power with the priest and the Nacom. In this Katun 9 Ahau the ruler offends with his words, tyrannizes his subjects, and abuses his power. There will be many diseases, no salt, and the corn bread that is eaten daily will be black. We shall be frightened by war on all sides and there will hardly be sufficient spirit to take away the governor who abuses his power and commits many nocturnal misdeeds during this Katun 9 Ahau. [The lords and the warriors will be vanquished] and there will be much praying as they lay stretched out on their mats. There will also be much adultery. The great priest Chilam Balam says that this will all take place in the Katun 9 Ahau, which will end in the year 1572.

Mayapan will establish Katun 7 Ahau. [Ek Chuah] will govern from his mat in his bed and at noon will look toward the sky. In his reign the *bud of the flower* on whose petals the future is written, will begin to sprout. The prophet will lose his senses because of this flower; and, as no one will be able to redeem him, he will become sorrowful because his heart and his mind are prisoners of lust. There will be much adultery; that is the direction his steps will lead, that will be what he thinks about day and night, and that will be his sin. He will show his staff and his stone to the governors and to the priests. Everyone in Ichcaanziho will be persecuted in the Katun 7 Ahau, and there will be vulgar language, much eating, drinking, and carousing with pretty women who are content to destroy their beauty. But the time will come when power will be confounded. The men, like foxes and iguanas, rule in vain. Sometimes, in order to govern in the Peten, they will have to dress in the skin of the tiger and, at others, in the skin of the deer or the rabbit. They will govern on borrowed mat [power] and their governing will be buried [ended] at the beginning of the Katun 7 Ahau, which will end in the year 1596.

Zodzil will establish a Katun 5 Ahau. The queen of bees will be a prisoner and the drones will enter in a row. Beehives, previously cared for by the rulers, shall be perforated in order to rob them of their honey. No longer will anyone have confidence in the rulers who walk alone. The rulers will forget about nourishment and quarrel among themselves, as foxes, forever devoured by envy. So Chilam Balam said it. The Katun 5 Ahau will end in the year 1621.

Zuyua will establish a Katun 3 Ahau in which the tiger changes his skin. Yaxcocahmut [Itzamna?] will be the countenance of the Katun 3 Ahau during its reign. The year that will pass will be calamitous. The governor will rule with his eyes toward heaven and, although dying, will always be content to be seen stretched out on his carpet in his bed. Animals such as the tiger, the lion cub, and the mountain lion with white spots will howl lugubriously in the vicinity. When envy comes to an end, the poor, deteriorated and disrespectful sons, lacking in education, will have wisdom. The Mayas will be scattered over all the Peten with faces uncovered and hands and feet tied. If they return, there will be great slaughter among them or some great cataclysm will finish them off. This, says the Chilam Balam, is what will happen in the Katun 3 Ahau. Although they will be content on their carpets and in their beds, they will vomit everything they swallowed when the priest pokes in their throat. What they swallowed with such gusto, with sorrow they will vomit. He [the Itza?] is envious, miserly, importunate, and an impoverisher. By the side of the road he will weep over his lost bed, his lost carpet, and he will not know his father or his mother: he is the one who destroyed what Ah Kin Chel established in Dzilam. The Chilam Balam said that the son of the country who engraved the stones of Dzilam will faint and be conquered in order that the prophecies may be fulfilled. Misfortunes increase in the years in which envy reigns. It will be very grievous; perhaps a cataclysm will be that which will fulfill the prophecies of the Chilam Balam concerning this Katun 3 Ahau.

Emal will establish a Katun 1 Ahau and [Amaite Kauil will be its countenance]. The cord descends and these will be days in which the owls will come down from the ruined buildings. Those who will live in this Katun 1 Ahau will see filth, shame, ill will in government, small talent for governing, and kings come to naught. The base of power will be moved to Ichcaanziho. The ruler who has borrowed bed, rug, and kingdom will be cast out of it when the rivalries of the government end. The people of the country will be tied up and shaken, and we shall be filled with sadness since everything will be razed and destroyed. The day will come when, after suffering the sorrows of war, the Peten will no longer be a Maya province. The curse will fall upon the Mayas for having transgressed, and the knife will annihilate them, spilling their blood. When rivalries end in this Katun 1 Ahau, brotherhood will return. Throughout the world it is said that in a year when there are rivalries among children these shall be as turtledoves who weep for the loss of their kingdom and their language. This is what the priest Chilam Balam says will happen in Katun 1 Ahau.

Zaclactun, Mayapan will establish a Katun 12 Ahau and [Yaxhal Chuen will be its countenance during its reign]. The priest will be surprised in his bed, on his mat, by those who will come from Tibalam where they had reigned. Kings, caciques, nobles, and subjects were contented there. Everybody, with the fox on his back, will take his bed and rug and go to the mountain. Impoverished, the people will establish themselves where there are no lions, wildcats, nor jaguars to suck their blood and no governors to insult or wound them. Thus it will happen in this Katun 12 Ahau. There will be government and obedience, but destruction will not cease. With the slaughter of the Mayas there will be no one to make war against those who killed them. Six good years and six bad years will pass before the knife of war will settle them and well-being returns. Respect for the king will be preached, and there will be no wildcat and no jaguar, for the tiger's claws will have been pulled. The country will still live, the Peten will continue to exist, but in the future the descendants will be cowardly. . . .

Kinchil Coba will establish a Katun 13 Ahau. The stone on which it will be written will be in Mayapan. Itzamna, Itzamna-tzab will be its countenance. There shall be much famine. For five years bread made of the cup shall be eaten because there will be three years when a plague of locusts will devour the plants and flowers and lay their larvae by the millions. The ruler will have his eyes on the heavens and the stars, and there shall be eclipses of the sun and the moon. Rulers, prophets, and wise men will be lost according to the prophecy of the petal of the flower. There will be much madness and adultery in the kingdom. The cornfield worker, talking to himself, will bury the ruler and his children will not receive their bread. After the creation of the [new] world [of the Spaniard] the son will always be disrespectful to his parents and immoral. The men with the big boots [the Spaniards] will be on their mats on their beds all day, and their children [the Mayas], without education, crazed, will bite with their big mouths all year long. The tiger will roar, and the deer that fell into the trap will be heard agonizing until he dies.

I wrote this not to speak of our poverty but to make known the events that happened in the life of our ancestors. That past may be blamed on the prophecies which are not true and should not be believed. One should always believe in God our Lord, who is the One who orders this.

THE PROPHECY OF OXLAHUN-TI-KU FOR
KATUN 13 AHAU: RECITAL OF THE PRIEST
CHILAM BALAM

"Eat, eat, thou hast bread:
Drink, drink, thou hast water;
On that day, dust possesses the earth,
On that day, a blight is on the face of the earth,
On that day, a cloud rises
On that day, a mountain rises,
On that day, a strong man seizes the land.
On that day, things fall to ruin,
On that day, the tender leaf is destroyed,
On that day, the dying eyes are closed,
On that day, three signs are on the tree,
On that day, three generations hang there,
On that day, the battle flag is raised,
And they are scattered afar in the forests."

It will be a time when the catastrophes of war will be seen; a time when everything, everywhere, shall be swept away. Children, disconcerted, will walk through deserted fields; and the misfortunes of the Maya will be greatly augmented, as everything shall burn. [In the time of Katun 13 Ahau], Lahun Chan will seize the earth. He shall come with a branch of the ceiba tree, a branch of the plumeria flower, and the wing of the turtledove in his hand. In the time of the Katun 13 Ahau, everything in Chichen Itza shall be swept away and fire will burn in the middle of the city. It will be a time when the priests will disagree among themselves. The fortune tellers will say that the rains will change; and the priests will say there will be no rain, because the pheasant [quetzal?] will fly toward the east, and the bouquet of flowers [power] will move toward Chactemel. The country will appear yellow [where there will be a great drought]. It will be the time to count the calendar, a time when agonizing death for the Mayas will be the greatest since the descent from Holtun Zuyua. These are the portents for Katun 13 Ahau.

[The descent from Holtun Zuyua falls in this Katun 13 Ahau. It was a time when five small groups left their fields; a time when the Canul left their fields which were in the wide part (on an island?) of the channel with running water which forms at the entrance to seaports, to begin the climb to Zaclactun. The cold Ah Ek makes the necessary and perhaps wearisome climb to the mountain peak] and, with the rapacious Ah Canul, brings to the Mayas in the heart of Cuzamil Peten seven years of suffering and death. The government of Ah Kin Uoob was ended. [In the reign of 13 Ahau and 1 Ahau were the days and nights that fell without order, and pain was felt throughout the land. Because of this] Oxlahun ti Ku [the Thirteen Gods] and Bolon ti Ku [the Nine Gods] created the world and life; there was also born Itzam Cab Ain [Iguana Earth Crocodile]. [Ah Mesencab] turned the sky and the Peten upside down, and Bolon ti Ku raised up Itzam Cab Ain; there was a great cataclysm, and the ages ended with a flood. The 18 Bak Katun was being counted and in its seventeenth part. Bolon ti Ku refused to permit Itzam Cab Ain to take the Peten and to destroy the things of the world, so he cut the throat of Itzam Cab Ain and with his body formed the surface of Petén.

Behold, the one called Ah Uooh Puc who refused to confess his name to them. It is the face of the Katun which governs now. [Ah Mesencab], the one who laid waste to the earth, rose up in the Katun 11 Ahau and bandaged the face of Oxlahun ti Ku; but they did not know his name and they were told he was called Father, Son, and Holy Ghost. . . .

2. Character Predictions — *Chilam Balam of Mani*

CHARACTER PREDICTIONS FOR INDIVIDUALS BORN ON CERTAIN DAYS

South:
  Cauac, tanner, cacao cane, noble.
  Ahau, wild bee, eaglet, pheasant, wealthy.
  Imix, rosewood, comet, uncertain fame.
  Ik, sufferers from air, comet, rosewood, lust.
  Akbal, little fame, poor, deer hunter.

East:
  Kan, yellowish, poisonous snake, singer, wise man.
  Chicchan, demanding, *habin* cane, scary.
  Cimi, moth, carries a cane, homicidal.
  Manik, bewildered, cacao cane, sanguinary.
  Lamat, dog's fame, and of the tiger that bites.

North:
  Muluc, reader, noble heir, wealthy.
  Oc, delicate, wand of authority, sickly, ignorant.
  Chuen spinner, also wealthy.
  Eb, cotton raiser given to borrowing, wealthy.
  Ben, orphan's fame, unfortunate, poor.

West:

Ix, tiger soldier, bloody claws, bloody mouth.

Men, miser, entangled noble.

Cib, delinquent, thief, assassin.

Caban, cornfield worker, good businessman.

Eznab, truthful, bleeder, medicine man, valiant.

Eugene R. Craine and Reginald C. Reindorp, *The Codex Perez and the Book of Chilam Balam of Mani* (Norman, OK: University of Oklahoma Press, 1979), pp. 70–88, 116–19, 91.

3. The Secret History of the Itza — *Chilam Balam of Tizimin*

The following notes by Munro Edmonson offer excellent insight into the language, complexity, and history of the Maya, and make the Chilam Balam of Tizimin *more accessible:*

This text, together with the two other early chronicles in the Mani *and the* Chumayel *(Barrera, 1948: 68 ff.; Roys, 1967: 139 ff.), is unquestionably the oldest sketch of Mayan history we have. While the* Chumayel *contains one text that can be dated to 1556 (Edmonson, 1976), it is likely that nothing in the* Tizimin *was transcribed from glyphs before 9 Ahau (1559). A glyphic version of this chronicle could have been composed in 13 Ahau (1539) but could also have drawn on glyphic predecessors. I consider the claim of the Itza to have ruled Chichen Itza (and that of the Xiu to have come from Tula) in 8 Ahau (692) to be legend or myth, but the tale seems to be substantially historical from the following 8 Ahau (948) on.*

All the earliest chronicles are preoccupied with the sequence and dates at which various cities became the seats of the cycle. Taken together, the sources provide us with the following outline.

Date	*Xiu*	*Itza*	*Other*
8 Ahau (692)	*Tula*	*Chichen Itza*	*Bacalar*
8 Ahau (948)		*Champoton*	
2 Ahau (1263)	*Uxmal*	*Mayapan*	
8 Ahau (1461)			*Tayasal*
11 Ahau (1539)	*Merida*		
4 Ahau (1752)		*Valladolid*	

Tutul Xiu "Toltecs" were traditionally the rulers of Uxmal "windfall." The name is significantly bilingual: Nahuatl totollin, "many reeds," with the Mayanized Nahuatl explanation xiu, "grasses." It identifies an elite ethnic group rather than a lineage or a person. The Xiu were the nobility of the western half of the Yucatan Peninsula and were more influenced by Nahua and Spanish ideology than were the eastern Itza. They claimed identification with Nonohualco, Zuyua, Chiconauhtla, and "the great city of Tula" (Barrera, 1948: 57–58).

Chi Ch'en Itza, "mouth of the well of the witches of water," is the best known of the Mayan cities and the traditional seat of the Itza. Like the Xiu, the Itza were an elite ethnic group. Together they dominate the history of Yucatan in an east-west, quasi-moiety political system.

The mats were counted at the end of the (Itza) katun cycle. Since mats were symbols of authority, frequently paired with thrones, counting them was a ritual confirmation of inherited ranks. Succession was not automatic; it involved an examination in ritual knowledge.

A Hal ach uinic, "true virile man," [was] the governor of a province or city, in this case the rain priest Xib Chac of Chichen Itza.

The fall of Mayapan was the epochal event of the preconquest period. Two different versions put the blame on Hunac Ceel and on Can Ul, the usurping Itza governor of Izamal. The primacy of the katun cycle was at stake. The sequence of events is far from clear, but it involved the elimination of Xib Chac (who was succeeded by Kukul Can as governor of Chichen Itza) and a related dynastic dispute in Izamal. It culminated in an internal rebellion within the walls of Mayapan by seven Xiu lords, and Mayapan was destroyed in accordance with the Xiu time schedule. The Mani gives the most precise date for the destruction of Mayapan: 1451 (Barrera, 1948: 71). All sources agree that it occurred in katun 8 Ahau, though Barrera (1948: 62) puts Hunac Ceel in 1204. Tozzer (1941: 32–34) identifies Hunac Ceel with Kukul Can.

Mayapan: Mayan may "cycle" plus Nahuatl -apan "water place," the holy and primate city of the Itza from the end of the Classic period (ca. 987–1007), when it was first called Born of Heaven, to 1752, and perhaps to 1824 for at least some Itzas. Barrera (1948: 99) translates the name as "deer standard." It was the largest walled city of the post-Classic period; hence it is often referred to as Pa Cabal, "fort of the lands," or just as Pa "fort." After its destruction in 1451, it continued to be a ceremonial center, but the ceremonies were often held "outside the walls," and it acquired a new nickname: Tzucub Te, or Sacred Grove. Centrally located, it was the storm center of Mayan politics during the post-Classic and colonial periods. The modern name of the Maya may be derived from Mayapan but does not appear in the Tizimin until 4 Ahau (1737), despite the fact that it was known to Columbus and used constantly in the Chumayel.

INTRODUCTION

The East priest Bi Ton, the chief of the Tutul Xiu, arrived one year before it was one hundred years.

8 Ahau (692) had been revealed; Chichen Itza had been manifested as the grove Born of Heaven there. Chichen Itza ruled for two hundred years. Then it was destroyed. Then they went to the settlement of Champoton, to the homes of the Itza, the gods who own men.

6 Ahau (968) completed the seating of the lands of Champoton.

. . . 8 Ahau (1204). Champoton was destroyed. Champoton was ruled by the Itza people for two hundred sixty years. Then they returned to their homes for the second time. They destroyed the road of Champoton. For two parts of the *katun* cycle the Itza went on beneath the trees, beneath the bushes, beneath the vines, where they suffered.

6 Ahau (1224), 4 Ahau (1244): Forty years passed, then they came and established their homes again. Then they destroyed the road of Champoton.

. . . 10 Ahau (1441). They established the land of Zuy Tok, a Tutul Xiu of Uxmal. Two hundred years had passed since they established the land of Uxmal.

. . . 8 Ahau (1461). They destroyed the governors of Chichen Itza by the sinful words of Hunac Ceel.

Cinteotl Chan, Tzontecome, Tlaxcallan, Pantemitl, Xochihuehuetl, Itzcoatl, and Cacalacatl are the names of the people there, the seven of them, because they were patting tortillas with Izamal and Ul Ahau. After thirteen folds of the *katun* cycle, they were destroyed by Hunac Ceel because of the giving away of their knowledge.

6 Ahau (1480).

4 Ahau (1500). Forty years.

Then the land within the walls of Mayapan was completed by the Itza people and Ul Ahau because of the sinful words of Hunac Ceel. . . .

8 Ahau (1461). There was crushed stone inside the walls of Mayapan because of the seizure of the walls by crowd rule in the city.

6 Ahau (1480),

(4 Ahau) (1500),

Second Ahau (1520), the thirteenth *tun*. The foreigners came and first saw the lands of Yucatan and the grove, eighty years (after the fall of Mayapan),

And then was the thirteenth measure.

THE FLOWER KATUN OF THE XIU

In 11 Ahau the priest of Muzen Cab arose and tied the faces of the 13 Gods, but they didn't know their names. They called them "The Holy," and

"The Remote." And they also didn't show their faces to them either. At last it dawned, and they didn't know their going or their coming, and then the 13 Gods spoke to the 9 Gods: "Bring down fire. Bring down the rope. Bring down stones and trees."

There was a pounding of sticks and stones. And then the 13 Gods appeared and beat their heads and flattened their faces. The four yearbearers and the 5 priest Za Bac were spat on and snatched away. The quetzals were taken and blue birds, crushing the Zic, crushing the Top and wrapping the seeds of the first nine steps which went to the thirteen levels of heaven.

Then the membrane and the nose of the skeleton were cut. Then on account of the 13 Gods the heart went, but they didn't know what was going on. The heart of the moon there was dropped flat. And the fatherless, the miserable, and those without spouses or living relatives, and those that don't have hearts began to rot upon the sand, upon the beaches.

The yearbearers released a torrent of water. That was the clearing of heaven and also the clearing of the lands for the period opposite the fold, killing youngest sons. That is the fold of the *katun* cycle; it arrived here at the time of 3 Oc.

The word of the returned *katun* ended in 1 Cimi. The four gods—the four Fathers of the Land—that is their flattening of the land. When the lands have been flattened, the red Imix tree returns, proceeding to pass the four. That is the sign of the flattening of the land. That is the toppling of the tree of the Fathers of the Land, called the East priest Xib Yuy.

Then the white Imix tree returns to the north. He is called the North priest Hic, the sign of the flattening of the lands. Then the black Imix tree returns to the west of the country, the sign of the flattening of the lands: That is the black Imix tree, seating the West priest Tam Pic the Weak.

Seating the yellow Imix tree to the south of the country, the sign of the flattening of the lands seating the South priest Oyal Mut.

Then the green Imix tree is seated in the middle of the land, the reminder of the flattening of the lands. The whole of the existence of this *katun* is piled in its place.

11 Ahau is the time of the coming of the word of the nine steps of sages who folded and asked for the burden of the *katun*, the ninth of his burdens that came down on 4 Kan, the time of the return that ended the burden. Then it descended and came before the center of the sky; this was the second birth of the nine bush houses.

The nine cycles, dripping at the mouth, dripping at the nose, the tongue, dripping its brains also descended. Then the two descended: The Red Were Bats who suck the nectars of the Flowers.

And then the Flowers, the sellers of the cycles appeared: the red Hoch'Kom, the white Hoch'Kom, the black Hoch'Kom, the yellow Hoch'Kom,

Hau Nab, Hutz' Nab, Kuk Nab, Oyal Nicte, Ninich Cacau, Chabi Tok, Macuilxochitl, Hobon y Ol Nicte, and Kouol y Ol Nicte.

These Flower Houses appeared: the blossom of the sun priest, the blossom of the lord, and the blossom of the captain. That is the burden of the Flower lords when they descend. And "there is no food" is the burden of the Flower *katun*.

The creation of the Gods of hell, the nine steps that descend, the creation of the Flowers of the measuring stick does not come in his time. Blue bird and hummingbird are also the spirits who come down when they suck the nectars of the Flowers, the nine children of Flowers. Then the heart of the Flower appears—four branches and all the Flowers—and the sun priest is seated there for the counting of the *tun*.

When that is done, the 13 Gods appear, descending to the unfolded mat, arriving at the word, bearing the Flower and the mat of the Flower, and the yellow throne. But they do not know them.

Za Uin is seated: his gourd is envy, his plate is envy; his heart is envy; his mouth is envy. His madness is great; his word in the lordship at the time cries for food and drink; he opens his mouth as though eating and afterward gets dizzy, fasting and crying for drink.

The word of him who is seated is blame, his teaching is blame. The face of him who is seated is tied. He takes his place, demands his mat place, and sits as the lord, as if forgetting his father, forgetting his mother. He does not know the father who engendered him and does not know the mother who bore him, for truly it was by nose and tongue he was born, crier of the burden he did not ask for. The 7 priest Sat Ay descended from the 9 Gods.

Their spirit was destroyed and then their breath was destroyed. Then their throats were cut; their throats were tied, by themselves, alone. The word of that prophet was blamed and that sun priest was blamed. The lord was twice blamed and those captains were blamed who rested in the bottoms of the hammocks—who had dropped the shields and the lances of the ten born children, the enemies, there, and then turned back and didn't know about the coming of the ending of the word of the war and soldiers. They may have raised their hangings and tying by the hands, and they did not tie the face of the *katun;* they gave up their fronts to the stabbing Flower and died.

The sun priests, the sages, the lords, and the captains entered and spoke in the period of the war, in the ninth *tun,* in the moon when the chiefs in the lordship, the born and engendered children of Kin Chil of Coba and Miz Cit again were judged.

This is the word of the 13 Gods; it is not in my words. It happened on three occasions to these people again on earth, and it happened three times in this *katun*'s return: On the day of Naclah Uitz bearing the load and on the day of red stone suffering of the born and engendered children of the sufferers, the Itza; otherwise the Flower people, the Flower *katun* will be ending on Christianity's return.

THE INQUISITION FROM THE BOOK OF THE JAGUAR PRIEST

Little by little we began to grow weary of the maiming of the people by the Christians, when I should have liked to protect the people and guard the country. They gradually began to plant a church in the middle of Tiho. This did not do much harm to the *katun* treasure.

Gradually, they began the hangings again for the second time, and they kindled the fire on the stone. The offenses of the white people are all alike, even against those who surrender themselves or their relatives, everywhere they go. Brothers plead for justice in their throats. Gradually we discover that the Christians are great liars. Little by little we realize that they are great cheats.

Little by little, whether they take seven sacraments or not, their prayers are heard by their powerful God. You cast your lots. The people come. You set in order the enchantments.

DEMORALIZATION

Mayapan was the seat of the *katun* in 7 Ahau. The West priest Chu Uah was the person in the lordship of mat and throne. Amayte Kauil was the person on high in the lordship, who began and ended the sprouting of the nine-heart flower, the painted-heart flower. Its juice was flowery bread, flowery water.

(He was) acting like the governor of the world, acting like a sun priest, acting like a prophet. Nobody will escape from the true teaching of the lordship, which is its face and its heart. He will gather lust in the land.

There was lust and adultery, which was carried and sprouted everywhere. That was the thought by day; that was the thought by night: the sin of day; the sin of night, enslaving the hearts of the governors, the prophets and blackening the trees and the stones, the motherless and fatherless.

The people of *katun* 7 Ahau demeaned themselves to crawling on all fours. Their words were mad words. The behavior of Heaven Born Merida was very mad from start to finish, covering the world entirely.

Nine-step bread: Nine-step water—born of the quetzal, born of the blue bird.

Food was raised to be sucked, to be crammed down; and goodness—the beauty of girls—being beautified is not beauty. Who should be awake is not awake. There came the time of the seven-day rule, of instant rule and fallen rule. Seven-day rules took place by the people, ending the count.

And the farmers will rule over them. They will be robed as Strong Skunks, Jaguars, masked as Deer and Rabbit people with wooden faces in the land, in the country, in the rule, in the lordship: borrowers of the mat, borrowers of the throne, borrowers of the rule.

That is who was beginning to speak and will pile up the pacing of the governors of the towns. The coveting of the lordship—that will be the lordship there in this 7 Ahau.

THE COUNCIL OF MERIDA

The 7 Ahau *katun* was the third *katun* to be counted. Heaven Born Merida was the seat of the *katun*. Yax Chac was the person in the lordship. There was the breaking of the lands; there was the shaking of the heavens. Flower food and flower water were the burden of the *katun*. And there was the beginning of the gatherings of the sages, rolling their eyes at what was spread in the world: These fathers of the waning moon, Quetzal and blue bird.

Amayte Uitz was the leader, and lies and madness will be the word of the Jaguar Possums, the Jaguar Foxes. Nowhere is the word of the *katun* given.

And there is the beginning of the asshole boils *katun* and the beginning of the Bech' Kab Flowers.

The right is to be accepted: Welcome it! The pairs will come to your towns. Come to the towns to desire that you be Christian at midday again.

THE *ANNALS OF BACALAR*—2 IX (1595)

The time of the guns returns on 2 Ix. The removal of bullets returns. It is the time of flaming fires before the heart of the country, burning on earth, burning in heaven. In the time of the seizure of food plants, in the time of dances on high, the bread was destroyed, the gods were destroyed.

Gone is the witch, gone the owl at the four crossroads; the one spread over the earth, the other over the sky. The bees will have been moved; the poor will have been moved at the word of the nine trunks and the nine branches. The face of the field is fallen, the face of the fort is fallen at the time of the posting of the judgment. . . .

THE *ANNALS OF BACALAR*—5 IX (1611)

This is the return from the north country to the south country that is the capital, Mayapan, in the moon of the self-transformation of the 7 priest Cha Pat. That was also the moon of the self-transformation of the 7 priest Ol Zip again. (It happened) on the arrival of the burden of the time of 5 Ix in the eighteenth *tun,* the ending of the *katun* again on the day of the tying of the burden of 5 Ahau.

(This was) in the *tun* of his slavery, in the *tun* of the slavery of the stuffer of tamales, *Tun* of completion of the filling of pain, lamented by the wooden drum spoken in the middle of the water.

They hurt and beat each other greatly, and the impersonators started and came and finally closed the word, the inauguration into the lordship of Uuc Het. That is the word on the eighteenth measure which is the return back to the country: the chastisement of the Itza.

There will have been the parading of the mask, the human figure of wax that may be worshiped in the middle of the water or whose place may be abandoned, needing the lordship, broadcasting the word that is coming. (Also broadcasting) the goodness of the lordship standing in the place of the change of the gourd, the change of the clothes. The beating, the end of the wooden mask, may occur there . . . on 11 Ahau, on the day of the dried mat, the pounded flat look at the wooden mask, the hammered wooden mask of metal, because it is the second day of wine, the third day of rioting.

At the time of the return to the wells, to the springs the honored sons seized each other—that is beating on the legs, the reseeding of water, the speaking of lamentation for the arrival of the time of the return of the Itza, arising at the pass of pain, the pass of thirst.

Thus is the return or else the fulfillment of the desire of the burden of his existence; also of the springs which occurred moving heaven and earth.

Both Chacs hummed, and Chu Uahs at the wells, at the springs, he just sat on his ass, the wooden mask, because of red sleep madness, white sleep madness—chest knife and tooth of the *katun.*

ASSIMILATION OF THE ITZA

These are the lords who are going to be approaching then. On the first of Pop, Cauac is the dawn, and the second day of the year is the seating of 4 Ahau. Third Cauac is seated; 4 Ahau is the *katun.*

1752 3 Cauac
1753 4 Kan . . .
1771 9 Ix

The burden of *katun* 4 Ahau ends and then four years without names are seated to complete the *katun:*

Then 2 Ahau the full cask of the *katun* is to be seated:

1772 10 Cauac

1773 11 Kan

1774 12 Muluc

1775 13 Ix

And this is 2 Ahau who is seated.

1 Cauac is the dawn; it is the second of the days. The first of Pop. This is the word that is in its burden and the road that is the burden of the year. The seat of the *katun* is Valladolid, which is 2 Ahau. Valladolid is the seat of the cycle, and City of the cycle, establishing the *katun* for itself.

At the time there is the descent of the rope, the descent of venom, the descent of pain, painless death, the three pyramids. That is the burden, that is the appearance of the *katun* 2 Ahau. The burden of the 11 priest Ch'ab Tan is tied.

Then Hun y Op Oc Ik is born. His food is breadnut and gourdroot.

Half of the burden of the year is good. There is food; there is drink, and the glory of the lordship; and half is red stone and suffering. There is his throne, his mat. There is his honor on the mat, in the lordship of the lands, which is the pacing off of the existing lands. This is so they will be informed of the days of the white people, the bearded people as has been manifested by me, the sun priest spokesman.

The time of arrival of their older brothers thus is coming to the poor Itza. You will intermarry with them; you will wear their clothes; you will put on their hats, and you will speak their language.

Nevertheless there will be trade, war trading at the time of the sprouting flowers, of the flowers of the cross; but no one of us will rest, and their lamentation will be on the day of painted flowers of the count of 3 Ahau again.

We shall have half filled the cask of the *katun* cycle of 11 Ahau. 2 Ahau is seated there. He is seated on first Cauac.

1776 1 Cauac

1777 2 Kan . . .

1795 7 Ix

It ends, and the burden of 2 Ahau ends, seating the ending of the *katun.* The(n come) four years without names, and 13 Ahau is to be seated.

1796 8 Cauac

1797 9 Kan

1798 10 Muluc

1799 11 Ix

Munro Edmonson, *The Ancient Future of the Itza* (Austin, TX: University of Texas Press, 1982), pp. 3–11, 45–54, 61–64, 73–75, 103–06, 172–75.

4. A Spanish Raid: *Maya Chronicles*

Written in Yucatec Maya, this account belongs to the dramatic narrative which conveys the so-called Vision of the Vanquished.

Nakuk Pech's words tell of the Spanish Conquest of the Yucatan from the arrival of the Spaniards who first landed on the peninsula in 1511, 1517, and 1519, and then invaded it in force years later, in 1541, until the surrender of the Maya to their new rulers. Nakuk's story describes events in which he took part or knew of from qualified witnesses: battles, humiliations, servitude, tribute, and forced conversion to Christianity.

The Chronicle of Nakuk Pech, Ruler of Chac-Xulub-Chan

1. The fifth division of the 11th Ahau Katun was placed when the Spaniards arrived and settled the city of Merida; it was during the 9th Ahau that Christianity was introduced; the year in which first came our lords the Spaniards here to this land was the year 1511.

2. I, who am Nakuk Pech, of the first hidalgos conquistadores here in this land in the district Maxtunil, I am placed in the first town in the district Chac Xulub Chen. As thus it is given me to guard by my lord Ah Naum Pech, I wish to compose carefully the history and chronicle of the district of Chac Xulub Chen here, my first command, the town having two districts, Chichinica and, here, Chac Xulub Chen.

3. My name was Nakuk Pech before I was baptized, son of Ah Kom Pech, Don Martin Pech, of the town of Xul Kum Chel; thus we were given the districts to guard by our lord Ah Naum Pech from the town Mutul, and I was promoted to guard the district Chac Xulub Chen; when our lords, the Spaniards, did not pass nor come here to this land Yucatan, I was then governor here in this town, here in this land, Chac Xulub Chen. When our lord, the Señor Adelantado came here to this province in the year 1519, I was head chief; when the Spaniards came here to the land of Maxtunil we received them with loving attention; we also first gave them tribute and respect, and then we gave to eat to the Spanish captains; he who was called Adelantado came here to Maxtunil to the dwelling of Nachi May; then we went to see that they should be given pleasures; they did not even enter the towns, not even visited the towns; they were here in this land for three months, being placed here in the district of Maxtunil; then they departed and went to begin a seaport, the seaport Dzilam, and remained there three years and a half.

4. They were there when my father went to make delivery to them; he called the Adelantado [military commander appointed by the crown] returned here to this land; the maid servant named Ixkakuk was presented to them by

my father to give them food and wait upon them; and they were there when they were attacked by the Cupuls; and they departed, and went to live at Ecab Kantanenkin, as is called the land where they settled; they were there when they were attacked by those of Ecab, and they departed and arrived at Cauaca, which they entered, and passed to the town Dzekom, as the town is called; they passed it and arrived at the town Tixcuumcuuc, so-called; and they departed from there and arrived at the town called Tinuum; and then they all set out in search of Chichen Itza, so-called; there they asked the King of the town to meet them, and the people said to them; "There is a king, O Lord," they said, "there is a king, Cocom Aun Pech, King Pech, Namox Chel, King Chel, of Dzidzantun; foreign warrior, rest in these houses," they said to them, by the Captain Cupul. They departed from Chichen Itza and arrived with King Ixcuat Cocom of Ake; "Lords, you cannot go, you will lose yourselves," was said to them by the King Ixcuat Cocom, and they turned back again, and went and arrived at Cauaca for the second time, and they reached the seaport called Catzun, where they marched by the sea, and went and returned to Dzelebnae, as it is called, where they first settled when they first came to this land.

5. They remained in Chanpatun six years, when they went forth to Campeche; he, called the Adelantado, the first Spaniard, passed here to this land; they were at Campeche when they asked tribute; according to orders by the chiefs to all the villages there was tribute. They passed on by the sea (asking) for tribute to be brought to them. Then I went with my companions Ah Macan Pech and his younger brother Ixkil Ytzam Pech, the king of the town Cumkal, and my father, who was in the town Xulcumcheel; these were my companions when I went back for the tribute; they saw it; also Nachi May accompanied us, because he knew that he (the Adelantado) did not know the language; because they first stayed at his house when they came, and for this reason they spoke to him to accompany them when they went after the tribute, because he was a friend to the Spaniards when it (the tribute) was delivered to the captains; from them we received coats and cloaks and shoes and rosaries and hats, and had much pleasure from the captains; we left when the Spaniards had ended giving these gifts; already we had our clothes when we arrived, the coats and cloaks (we) Ixkil Ytzam Pech of Conkal, our companions Ah Macan Pech of Yax Kukul, and my father Ah Kom Pech, who were the greatest of us.

6. And I Nakuk Pech by name was head chief when they first delivered tribute, when we went to Campech to deliver tribute, and we came back when the Spaniards coming on the road from Campech came to the towns to dwell at Ichcanzihoo, the city of Merida; and when it was heard that the Spaniards were coming on the road from Campech we went to give them gifts, and I went the second time to deliver tribute. And I Nakuk Pech of this

district of Chac Xulub Chen, and Ah Macom Pech of the district Yan Kukul, and Ixkil Ytzam Pech the head chief of Conkal, and also I Nakuk Pech, chief here in the town Chac Xulub Chen, entered into giving gifts to them a second time at Dzilbikal, and they wished an abundance a second time, and they were given gifts, pheasants, and honey, and sweet food at Dzibilkal, when they came to settle at Merida; Don Francisco de Montejo, first Captain General, first came here to this land, to Merida, with Don Francisco de Bracamonte and Francisco Tamayo and Juan de Pacheco and Perarberes; these captains came in the year 1541. . . .

17. In the year 1521, on the 13th day of August, the territory of Mexico was taken by the Spaniards. The third attack on the same Spaniards took place by all the towns here in the town of Cupul, when they asked Ah Ceh Pech about the killing at Zalibna, and his companion-king Cen Pot of Tixkokhoch of the province of Ticanto, with the priest Ich Kak Mo of Itzmal the companion of Holtun Ake. The year in which the Spaniards arrived at Chichen Itza for the second time to settle at Chichen Itza was that when arrived the captain Don Francisco de Montejo, the just one, leader of the Cupuls. They arrived at the town twenty years after they arrived at Chichen Itza (the first time), where they were called eaters of anonas, biters of anonas.

18. In the year 1542, the Spaniards settled the territory of Merida; the first speaker, the companion priest Kinich Kakmo and the king of the Tutulxiu of the capital Mani humbled their heads, and the first families were settled; then first they came under tribute the third time (the Spaniards) came to this land, and they established themselves permanently, and stopped here. The first time when they came here to Chichen Itza they began to eat anonas; never before had anonas been eaten, and when the Spaniards ate them they were called anona-eaters; the second time they came to Chichen they stopped at the house of the Captain Cupul; the third time they arrived they settled permanently, in the year 1542 they settled permanently in the territory of Merida, the 13th Kan being the yearbearer, according to the Maya reckoning.

19. In the year 1543 the Spaniards went north of the Chels to procure Maya men for servants because there were no men for servants at Merida; they came to procure men for servants for their bidding; when they reached Popce the tribute was increased by those from Merida, when those who command arrived at Popce, and they went on to Tikom, and the Spaniards remained at that time in Tikom more than twenty days before they departed.

Daniel G. Brinton, *The Maya Chronicles* (Philadelphia, 1882), pp. 216–20 and 228–29.

5. A Cakchiquel History

As with Nahua literature, the colonial Maya have left us compositions of great historical interest. We have seen already that the books of the Chilam Balam deal in part with the history of the Yucatec Maya. The same can be said of the Popol Vuh *and the* Title of the Lords of Totonicapan, *which, among other things, include historical and legendary narrations concerning the Quiche Maya.*

Beginning with the remote and mythic origins of the Cakchiquel nation, these annals, which were written in Solola, the Cakchiquel capital, on or around 1601 by an anonymous scribe, recount many events concerned with the Spanish invasion. In this respect they provide another dramatic chapter of the "Vision of the Vanquished."

Annals of the Cakchiquels

"And setting out, we arrived at the gates of Tulan. Only a bat guarded the gates of Tulan. And there we were engendered and given birth; there we paid the tribute in the darkness and in the night, oh, our sons!" said Gagavitz and Zactecauh. And do not forget the saying of our elders, our forefathers. These were the words which they bequeathed to us.

HERE IS THE BEGINNING OF THE REVOLT AGAINST QIKAB

Then began the revolt of the Quiches against the king Qikab and also against the clan [*chinamital*] of the king. The revolt spread, and the king's clan was destroyed together with the principal chiefs. The Quiches did not wish the vassals to serve [the king]. They wanted the Quiche people to travel [freely] on the roads, but the king did not wish this. The principal chiefs became angry with the king and refused to pay him homage. For this reason the Quiche people rose against the king and so his glory diminished.

The two sons of the king had become arrogant. One was called *Tatayac* and the other *Ah Ytza*. The king's two sons also held the titles of *Chituy* and *Quehnay*. The Quiches then gathered to confer; the sons had turned them against the king so that they should not pay him tribute, now that they were angered by having to render him services. In this way the sons turned against the king. In addition, the two called Tatayac and Ah Ytza had a grudge against their father because they coveted the royal power and also the precious stones, the metal, the slaves, and their father's people. Then the Quiches gathered in council to plot against the principal chiefs who served the king, and they killed those of the first rank in the sovereign's service.

These were the names of those lords and principal chiefs: *Herech, Tagunun, Ixhutzuy, Eventec, Azacot,* and *Camachal.* So they were called. The sons

did certainly join in counsel with the different groups, but they did not decide to kill the king. After the soldiers entered the houses of the lords, these
were slain by the soldiery and not by order of the king. The king at the time
was in the city of *Panpetak*. The soldiers wished to kill the king also, but by
order of his sons his house in Panpetak was well guarded. King Qikab humbled himself before the soldiers, and they returned then with the intention
of destroying and killing the lords of the house of Xahil. After the king had
humbled himself before the soldiers, he arranged to deliver to them the precious stones and the metal, as well as the government and the supreme command, and he delivered the power and the majesty to the soldiers. The heart
of King Qikab was full of bitterness because of the wrong his sons had done
him, the two called Tatayac and Ah Ytza. Thus the soldiers and the people
seized the government and the power. Afterwards, and by order of the tribes,
they assigned their dwellings to the thirteen lords, the principal chiefs who
initiated the revolt, and the greatness of the Quiche was ended after this act
of King Qikab. Thus it was that the tribes seized command of old, oh, our
sons! Since that time, because of this act of the soldiers, the people and the
vassals have ceased to exalt the kings. In truth they had pity on the king, in
the same manner as the thirteen divisions of warriors had pity when the revolt of the Quiches against the king was ended. But when the revolt was
about to end, it began once more against our grandfathers.

ANOTHER REVOLT BEGINS

Immediately another revolt started against the kings *Huntoh, Vukubatz,
Chuluc,* and *Xitamal Queh,* who were the four kings. A woman was the cause
of this other revolt against the Zotzils and the Tukuchs. The woman who
caused the revolt was called *Nimapam Ixcacauh*. This woman had gone to the
city of Gumarcaah to sell bread, and a soldier of the king's guard wished to
snatch it from her. The woman refused to let him take the bread by force, and
the soldier was driven away with a stick by the woman. They wished to hang
the soldier then, they wished to hang him on account of the woman called
Nimapam Ixcacauh. For this reason the revolt of the Quiches was resumed.
These people wished to have the woman killed, but our grandfathers Huntoh
and Vukubatz refused to give her up to the Quiches or to the soldiers.

The Quiches then desired to humiliate the [Cakchiquel] kings and they
wished King Qikab to be the one to do this. Furious, the Quiches gathered
in council and they said: "Only the Ahpozotzil and the Ahpoxahil have received greatness and majesty; let us kill Huntoh and Vukubatz because they
are becoming great." Thus said the soldiers about our grandfathers. They
wished to persuade King Qikab to consent to having the Zotzils and the
Tukuchs slain, but the king did not listen to the words of the Quiches. In
truth, in his heart the king favored Huntoh and Vukubatz. Because the wisdom of Qikab, a wonderful king, was truly great. Not only was he an illus-

trious king, but his judgment and wisdom, brought from Tulan, aroused admiration. But the soldiery were ignorant, they were only the common people; and because, in addition, they coveted power, they did not obey the king's orders and they continued to carry on the war.

THE DESTRUCTION OF THE QUICHES

When the sun rose on the horizon and shed its light over the mountain, the war cries broke out and the banners were unfurled; the great flutes, the drums, and the shells resounded. It was truly terrible when the Quiches arrived. They advanced rapidly, and their ranks could be seen at once descending to the foot of the mountain. They soon reached the bank of the river, cutting off the river houses. They were followed by the kings Tepepul and Iztayul, who accompanied the god. Then came the encounter. The clash was truly terrible. The shouts rang out, the war cries, the sound of flutes, the beating of drums and the shells, while the warriors performed their feats of magic. Soon the Quiches were defeated, they ceased to fight and were routed, annihilated, and killed. It was impossible to count the dead.

As a result, they were conquered and made prisoner, and the kings Tepepul and Iztayul surrendered and delivered up their god. In this manner the *Galel Achih*, the *Ahpop Achi*, the grandson and the son of the king, the *Ahxit*, the *Ahpuvak*, the *Ahtzib*, and the *Ahqot*, and all the warriors were annihilated and executed. The Quiches whom the Cakchiquels killed on that occasion could not be estimated at eight thousand nor at sixteen thousand. Thus our fathers and grandfathers related, oh, my sons! This is what they did, the kings Oxlahuh Tzii and Cablahuh Tihax, together with *Voo Ymox* and *Rokel Batzin*. And not otherwise did the place of Yximch become great.

ARRIVAL OF THE SPANIARDS AT XETULUL

DURING this year the Spaniards arrived. Forty-nine years ago the Spaniards came to *Xepit* and *Xetulul*.

On the day I Ganel [February 20, 1524] the Quiches were destroyed by the Spaniards. Their chief, he who was called *Tunatiuh Avilantaro*[Pedro de Alvarado], conquered all the people. Their faces were not known before that time. Until a short time ago the wood and the stone were worshiped.

Having arrived at *Xelahub*, they defeated the Quiches; all the Quiches who had gone out to meet the Spaniards were exterminated. Then the Quiches were destroyed before Xelahub.

Then [the Spaniards] went forth to the city of Gumarcaah, where they were received by the kings, the Ahpop and the Ahpop Qamahay, and the Quiches paid them tribute. Soon the kings were tortured by Tunatiuh.

On the day 4 Qat [March 7, 1524] the kings Ahpop and Ahpop Qamahay were burned by Tunatiuh. The heart of Tunatiuh was without compassion for the people during the war.

Soon a messenger from Tunatiuh came before the [Cakchiquel] kings to ask them to send him soldiers: "Let the warriors of the Ahpozotzil and the Ahpoxahil come to kill the Quiches," the messenger said to the kings. The order of Tunatiuh was instantly obeyed, and two thousand soldiers marched to the slaughter of the Quiches.

Only men of the city went; the other warriors did not go down to present themselves before the kings. The soldiers went three times only to collect tribute from the Quiches. We also went to collect it for Tunatiuh, oh, my sons!

HOW THEY CAME TO YXIMCH

On the day I Hunahpu [April 12, 1524] the Spaniards came to the city of Yximch; their chief was called Tunatiuh. The kings Beleh Qat and Cahi Ymox went at once to meet Tunatiuh. The heart of Tunatiuh was well disposed toward the kings when he came to the city. There had been no fight and Tunatiuh was pleased when he arrived at Yximch. In this manner the Castilians arrived of yore, oh, my sons! In truth they inspired fear when they arrived. Their faces were strange. The lords took them for gods. We ourselves, your father, went to see them when they came into Yximch.

Tunatiuh slept in the house of *Tzupam*. On the following day the chief appeared, frightening the warriors, and went toward the residence where the kings were. "Why do you make war upon me when I can make it upon you?" he said. And the kings answered: "It is not so, because in that way many men would die. You have seen the remains there in the ravines." And then he entered the house of the chief *Chicbal*.

Then Tunatiuh asked the kings what enemies they had. The kings answered: "Our enemies are two, oh, Lord: the Zutuhils and [those of] *Panatacat*." Thus the kings said to him. Only five days later Tunatiuh left the city. The Zutuhils were conquered then by the Spaniards. On the day 7 Camey [April 18, 1524] the Zutuhils were destroyed by Tunatiuh.

Twenty-five days after his arrival in the city, Tunatiuh departed for *Cuzcatan*, destroying *Atacat* on the way. On the day 2 Queh [May 9] the Spaniards killed those of Atacat. All the warriors and their Mexicans went with Tunatiuh to the conquest.

On the day 10 Hunahpu [July 21, 1524] he returned from Cuzcatan; it was two months after he left for Cuzcatan when he arrived at the city. Tunatiuh then asked for one of the daughters of the king and the lords gave her to Tunatiuh.

THE DEMAND FOR MONEY

Then Tunatiuh asked the kings for money. He wished them to give him piles of metal, their vessels and crowns. And as they did not bring them to him immediately, Tunatiuh became angry with the kings and said to them:

"Why have you not brought me the metal? If you do not bring with you all of the money of the tribes, I will burn you and I will hang you," he said to the lords.

Next Tunatiuh ordered them to pay twelve hundred pesos of gold. The kings tried to have the amount reduced and they began to weep, but Tunatiuh did not consent, and he said to them: "Get the metal and bring it within five days. Woe to you if you do not bring it! I know my heart!" Thus he said to the lords.

They had already delivered half of the money to Tunatiuh when a man, an agent of the devil, appeared and said to the kings: "I am the lightning. I will kill the Spaniards; by the fire they shall perish. When I strike the drum, depart [everyone] from the city, let the lords go to the other side of the river. This I will do on the day 7 Ahmak [August 26, 1524]." Thus that demon spoke to the lords. And indeed the lords believed that they should obey the orders of that man. Half of the money had already been delivered when we escaped.

THEN WE FLED FROM THE CITY

On the day 7 Ahmak we accomplished our flight. Then we abandoned the city of Yximch because of the agent of the devil. Afterwards the kings departed. "Tunatiuh will surely die at once," they said. "Now there is no war in the heart of Tunatiuh, now he is satisfied with the metal that has been given him."

Thus it was that, because of the wicked man, we abandoned our city on the day 7 Ahmak, oh, my sons!

But Tunatiuh knew what the kings had done. Ten days after we fled from the city, Tunatiuh began to make war upon us. On the day 4 Camey [September 5, 1524] they began to make us suffer. We scattered ourselves under the trees, under the vines, oh, my sons! All our tribes joined in the fight against Tunatiuh. The Spaniards began to leave at once, they went out of the city, leaving it deserted.

Then the Cakchiquels began hostilities against the Spaniards. They dug holes and pits for the horses and scattered sharp stakes so that they should be killed. At the same time the people made war on them. Many Spaniards perished and the horses died in the traps for horses. The Quiches and the Zutuhils died also; in this manner all the people were destroyed by the Cakchiquels. Only thus did the Spaniards give them a breathing spell, and thus also all the tribes made a truce with them [the Spaniards].

In the ninth month after our flight from Yximche, the twenty-ninth year was ended.

On the day 2 Ah [February 19, 1552] the twenty-ninth year after the revolution was ended.

During the tenth year [of the second cycle] the war with the Spaniards continued. The Spaniards had moved to Xepau. From there, during the tenth year, they made war on us and killed many brave men.

Then Tunatiuh left Xepau and began hostilities against us because the people did not humble themselves before him. Six months had passed of the second year of our flight from the city, or [from the time] when we abandoned it and departed, when Tunatiuh came to it in passing and burned it. On the day 4 Camey [February 7, 1526] he burned the city; at the end of the sixth month of the second year of the war he accomplished it and departed again.

On the day 12 Ah [March 26, 1526] ended the thirtieth year after the revolution.

During the course of this year our hearts had some rest. So also did the kings Cahi Ymox and Beleh Qat. We did not submit to the Spaniards, and we were living in *Holom Balam,* oh, my sons!

One year and one month had passed since Tunatiuh razed [the city], when the Spaniards came to *Chij Xot.* On the day I Caok [March 27, 1527] our slaughter by the Spaniards began. The people fought them, and they continued to fight a prolonged war. Death struck us anew, but none of the people paid the tribute. The thirty-first year after the revolution had almost ended when they arrived at Chij Xot.

On the day 9 Ah [April 30, 1527] ended the thirty-first year after the revolution.

During this year, while we were busy with the war against the Spaniards, they abandoned Chij Xot and went to live at *Bulbuxya.*

During that year the war continued. And none of the people paid the tribute.

THEN OUR INSTRUCTION BEGAN

During the eighth month after the landslide there came to our church the Fathers of St. Dominic, Fray Pedro de Angulo and Fray Juan de Torres. They arrived from Mexico on the day 12 Batz [February 10, 1542]. The Fathers of St. Dominic began our instruction. The Doctrine appeared in our language. Our fathers Fray Pedro and Fray Juan were the first who preached the word of God to us. Up to that time we did not know the word nor the commandments of God; we had lived in utter darkness. No one had preached the word of God to us.

The Fathers of St. Francis, Father Alamicer, the Father Clerico, and the Fathers of St. Dominic were there also and preached to us. They translated the Doctrine into our tongue, and thus we were quickly instructed by them.

THE YEAR 1601

On the day Hunahpu, Friday [September 5, 1601], seventy years were completed after the arrival of the Spaniards.

In the month of October a deadly epidemic began, attacking the throat of the women and men, who died after two days.

Adrián Recinos and Delia Goetz, *The Annals of the Cakchiquels* (Norman, OK: University of Oklahoma Press, 1953), pp. 47–48, 94–97, 103–04, 119–27, 134–35, 159.

6. Last Flight of the Quetzal Prince — *Titles from the House of Ixquim-Nehaib*

Curiously, the dramatic story of a hand-to-hand fight between two well-known personages during the Spanish Conquest of Guatemala is a part of a Maya Quiche legal document, the Titles from the House of Ixquim-Nehaib. *The combatants were Pedro de Alvarado, who had fought at Cortés's side against the Mexicas, and the courageous Quiche prince Tecum Uman.*

The contest took place in Pachah, near the town now known as Quetzaltenango. After a three-hour battle, many Quiche warriors had been killed by the Spaniards and their native allies. Then Prince Tecum, flying like an eagle, hurled himself against Alvarado. The outcome is the tragic story of Guatemala's great hero. From this encounter comes the name of the nearby town, Quetzaltenango, meaning "The place defended by the quetzal bird," the national bird of Guatemala and the name of its currency.

And then the Spaniards began to fight with the ten thousand Indians who had with them this captain, Tecum. At first nothing happened; they only turned each other aside. Then they withdrew half a league and came together again. They fought three hours and the Spaniards killed many Indians. It was impossible to count how many were killed. Not a single Spaniard died; only the Indians, led by the captain, Tecum. Much blood was spilled from all the Indians that the Spaniards killed; and this happened in Pachah.

Then the captain Tecum appeared flying like an eagle; the eagle was covered with feathers which grew from it; they were not false; it had wings which grew from its body and it had three crowns; one was of gold, one of pearls, and one of diamonds and emeralds. This captain Tecum was determined to kill Tunadiú [Alvarado], who came riding on a horse; he struck the horse so as to strike Alvarado; and he cut off the horse's head with a bludgeon. It was not an iron bludgeon but a wooden one with obsidian knives; the captain Tecum did this by magic. And when he saw that he had not killed Alvarado but the horse, he returned again, flying like an eagle, so that from above he could kill Alvarado. Then Alvarado waited with his lance and ran it right through the middle of this captain, Tecum.

Then came two dogs; they did not have any hair, they were bald. These dogs seized the aforementioned Quiche to tear him to pieces; but as Alvarado saw that this Quiche who wore the three crowns of gold, silver, and diamonds and emeralds and pearls was very noble, he went to protect him from the dogs and he looked at him carefully. The Quiche was covered with very beautiful plumage; and because of this, the name of this village is Quetzaltenango, the place defended by a quetzal bird, because here was the death of this captain Tecum. And then Alvarado called all his soldiers that they should come to see the beautiful Indian quetzal. Then he told his soldiers that he had never seen in Mexico, nor in Tlaxcala, nor in any of the villages he had conquered, an Indian so noble, such a prince, so covered with quetzal plumage and so handsome; and for that reason he said that the name of this village should be Quetzaltenango. Therefore this village has the name of Quetzaltenango.

Miguel León-Portilla, ed., *Pre-Columbian Literatures of Mexico* (Norman, OK: University of Oklahoma Press, 1969), pp. 143–44.

7. The Death of Cuauhtemoc —
A Chontal Story

The Spaniards came to this land in the year 1525. The captain was called Don Martín [Hernán] Cortés. They came in from Tanocic and passed through the village of Taxich where the Xacchute land begins. They took provisions in the village of Tazahhaa. And being there with all his people, he [Cortés] sent to call Paxbolonacha who was, as we have already said, the king; this one brought together all the leaders from all his villages, from the village of Taxunum and the leaders from the village of Chabte and the leaders from the village of Atapan and the leaders from the village of Tatzanto, because he was not able to do anything without consulting these leaders. He told them what the thing was about. . . . And they said it was not right that their king should be called by the Spaniards because they did not know what they wanted.

Then one of the leaders, called Chocpaloquem, stood up and said: "Oh King and Lord, you remain in your domain and your city; I would go and see what the Spaniards want." And thus he went, in the name of the king, with other leaders who were called Pazinchiquigua and Paxguaapuc and Paxchagchan, companions from Paloquem. And coming into the presence of the Captain del Valle [Cortés] and of the Spaniards, those did not believe them; they must have had among them the one who told them that the king who was summoned would not come. And thus the captain said to them: "The king must come, for I wish to see him; for I do not come for war nor to do evil; for I only wish to pass through to see the land, whatever there is to see; for I will do him much good if he receives me well."

And having understood this, those who came in the name of the king went back and told Paxbolonacha their king, who was waiting in the village. And after they had returned, all the chiefs came together, and the king said to them: "I wish to go myself to see the captain and the Spaniards, for I wish to see them and to know what they want and why they have come." And thus Paxbolonachá went.

The Spaniards, knowing this, went out to receive him, and the Captain del Valle with them. And the Chontals had brought many presents for them: honey, wild chickens, maize, copal, and much fruit. And the captain said: "King Paxbolonacha, I have come here to your land, for I am sent by the lord of the world, the emperor, who is on his throne in Spain, who sent me to see the land and what kind of people populate it; for I do not come for war, but only to ask you to show me the way to Ulua which is also Mexico, the land where one finds silver and plumage and cocoa; all this I would see as I pass through." And thus Paxbolonacha replied to him that he would let him pass in good time and that he should go with him to his place and his land and that there they would discuss whatever was necessary. And the captain replied to him that he should be at ease, that indeed he would go. And so they were resting there for twenty days.

And there was Cuauhtemoc, king of Mexico, who came with the captain Cortés, and Cuauhtemoc spoke secretly with Paxbolonacha, the king: "Oh King, there will come a time when these Spaniards will give us much trouble and do us much harm and they will kill our people. To me it seems that we should kill them, since I bring many people and you are many." And this said Cuauhtemoc to Paxbolonacha, king of the Chontals. Having heard this reason, Paxbolonacha replied: "I will see about this, leave it for now, that we may consider it." And thinking about the matter, he saw the Spaniards had done nothing evil, they had not beaten nor killed any Indian, and they only asked for honey, chickens, and maize and some fruits, which they gave them each day; and since they had done them no harm, he could not have two faces toward them nor be of two hearts towards the Spaniards. And Cuauhtemoc was constantly molesting him because he wanted to kill all the Spaniards; and seeing that he was molested, Paxbolonacha went to the Captain del Valle and said to him: "Captain del Valle, this leader and captain of the Mexicans you have brought, treat him with care, that he should not be treacherous with you, because three or four times he has suggested to me that we kill you."

Having heard this, the Captain del Valle took Cuauhtemoc and threw him in prison, and the third day that he was prisoner they took him out and baptized him, and it is not verified whether they gave him the name Don Juan or Don Fernando; and having finished baptizing him, they cut off his head and it was nailed to a silk cotton tree in front of the house of the gods in the village of Yaxzam.

Frances V. Scholes and Ralph Roys, *The Maya Chontal Indians of Acalan-Tixchel* (Washington, DC: Carnegie Institution, 1948), pp. 143–44.

8. From the *Crónica de Chac-Xulub-Chen*

The year 1542 was when the men of Castile settled down in the land of Ichcaansiho. . . . It was then that tribulations came and entered there for the first time, when, it is known, the men of Castile came for the third time to this land and established themselves forever, that is to say, they settled down. The first time when they came to Chichen Itza, then was when they ate custard apples for the first; since no one ate these custard apples, when they ate them, they were called "eaters of custard apples." The second time they came to Chichen Itza was when they overthrew Nacon Cupul. The third time they came was when they established themselves forever, and that, it is known, was in the year 1542, the year in which they settled down forever here in the land of Ichcaansiho. It was the 13-Kan, the year-bearer, according to Maya count.

The year 1543 was the year in which the men of Castile were in the north, near the land of the Cheeles, looking for Maya men to be slaves, because there were no men slaves in T-Ho. They came suddenly, looking and searching for men slaves. When they came to Popoce, after having left T-Ho, they imposed heavy tribute there in Popoce. And then they left and came to Tikom for many days; and after they arrived in Tikom, it is known, it was twenty days before the men of Castile left there.

It was in 1544, it is known, the year in which Cauacan was given over to the foreign lord, the captain Asiesa. In Cauacan the lords were gathered together and as tribute they gave honey, wild turkeys, and maize. It was in Cauacan, later on, that they shut up in prison the counselor Caamal of Sisal and demanded tribute and the records from all the villages. . . .

Hector Pérez Martínez, reprinted in Miguel León-Portilla, ed., *Pre-Columbian Literatures of Mexico*, pp. 143–44.

☙ 5 ☙

Songs and Incantations

*E*xisting *somewhere between eroticism, magic, and traditional medicine, the ancient Yucatec Maya recitations known as the* Rituals
of the Bacabs, *at times sung or chanted, were redacted in the Roman
alphabet at the end of the eighteenth century. The manuscript, which
was found in Merida, Yucatan, in the winter of 1914, is now in the Library of Princeton University.*

Here are nine out of the forty-two ritual chants or incantations.

*The diseases that are personified in these incantations are attacked
in various ways by the shaman who performs the curing ritual. A great
variety of metaphors and many religious, cosmic, and botanical references appear. Thus, while the shaman asks questions, he describes the illness under consideration, along with chants invoking the four cosmic
quadrants, with their deities, sacred trees and varicolored flowers, birds
and animals, as well as the winds and other evanescent sources of vital
influence.*

*While the texts reflect ancient Maya beliefs, they also include Chris-
tian interpolations, proof of the uninterrupted line of recitation into
colonial days. Since they still survive in some form to the present day,
they serve as yet another proof that Maya culture is far from dead.*

1. *Rituals of the Bacabs**

FEVER

To cure fever this is your tree, this is your plant.
Then he was born there.
Making a clamorous noise
his mother descended from the center of the skies.
It was frenzy that gave you birth.
The other frenzies appear from the center of the skies,
accompanying me deep into the ocean.
The water in the center of the ocean swelled
because the mangrove grew,
because the fish puffed itself up,
because the fish augmented,
because the river swelled;
that is the reason.
Frenzy arrived
together with the god,
because of *Uaxac Yol,* "Eight-Heart."
Thus *Chac,* "Great Fever" grew
because of it.
Fever increased
because of it.
Thus the tobacco in the underground pit increased
because of it.
Thus the tobacco for initiation into witchcraft increased
because of it.
Thus the four *mojarras* [fishes] increased
because of it.
For four days, it is said,
the tobacco swelled up,
the white tobacco.
Then there was sleeping,
then there was curling up,
and thus the abode of the god *Chac*
with the swollen heel was reached.
Thus his white heel swelled up

*The first seven incantations are taken from Ruth Gubler's English renderings of the Spanish version by the Mexican-Maya scholar Ramón Arzápalo; the last two were translated into English by the American Mayanist Ralph L. Roys.

because of it.
What is occurring,
Frenzy?
must be asked.
"You moan all the time,
as with birth pangs,"
must be said.
Thus the mat of authority expanded,
the tightly-woven mat;
because of Frenzy's arrival at the abode of "Foreign Goddess";
because of his arrival at the abode of "Custodian of the Entrance to the
Earth."
Together they obstruct her buttocks;
four times it will be done.
My red hail, my white hail,
at the beginning of the rains.
The chill will numb my arm,
it will numb my leg.
Here I trample and curse
the wooden man,
the stone man.
Oh, *Hun Can Ahau,* "Unique Four Ahau"!
Amen.

EROTIC FRENZY

This text is to cure the wind of *Nicte Tancas,* "Erotic Frenzy," which afflicts a person.

Entirely free of the wooden man,
entirely free of the stone man,
tightly embracing the clouds,
ardently embracing the wind,
thirteen times I raised myself
and stood up to call the malignant wind.
Three times I summoned you with my flute,
oh, *Bacabs,* who are in the center of the skies.
Three times I summoned you with my flute,
oh, *Bacabs.*
I summoned you from the center of the earth,

oh, lords, oh gods!
Chac Pauahtun, "Magnificent Red *Pauahtun"* is your symbol.
You must surmise that the wind is in the center of the flower,
in the center of the skies,
in the center of the underworld,
in the caverns of the skies,
in the caverns of the earth.
That is why I stood up to seize the wind
in the center of the flower.
I have hurled you to the center of the skies,
to the center of the underworld.
Thirteen times I seized *Kakal Moson,* "Whirlwind."
Countless times you fell into my power
and embraced me, oh, wind!
You who are in the seven innermost parts of the flower,
you must cast him to the center of the underworld.
Thirteen times I seized [the wind]
and countless times I pounced on him.
That is how I kicked that wind.
The flower that is in the center of the earth has twelve pistils.
Thirteen days I spent fasting for *Chac Ualom Kin,* "Sun-God on the
    Summit,"
imbibing *Yikal Nicte,* "Wind of the Flower of Lust"
and the wind of the fourteen times lustful one.
Then I turned to cover the mouth of *Ix Yan Coil,* "Goddess of
    Madness,"
[and] the genitals of *Chac*
and of *Ix Hun Ahau,* "Goddess One Ahau."
The symbol is *Ix Yan Coil,* "Goddess of Madness."
Thirteen times I swept,
that is how I had to sweep the wind of madness,
to reach its heart and arm,
using my axe as a sweeper.
It was thirteen times,
and not twice that I covered her mouth;
that is, the mouth of *Ix Yan Coil,* "Goddess of Madness."
That is where I covered her.
She is then penetrated; penetrated in her hidden parts.
Thirteen [days] I spent fasting,
so I could represent *Tzootz Bacab,* "Hairy Bacab,"
and could frighten away the wind.
[Holy] Jesus and Mary.
Amen.

DEADLY GODDESS

The text for a frenzy called *Ix Hun Pedz Kin,* "Deadly Goddess."

It was on *Hunuc Can Ahau,* "Unique Four Ahau"
that she was born.
It was in a single day;
it was in a single night;
it took an entire day.
The entire day she moved in her mother's womb.
Who is her mother?
One must say that it is *Ix Hun You Ta,* "Well-aimed Lance."
Ix Hun You Ton, "Well-aimed Member,"
Ix Hun Tah Dzib, "Goddess of Sacred Writing,"
"Goddess of Glyphs."
Who is her mother? is asked.
Ix Hun Dzalab Caan, "Goddess of the Layered Skies,"
Ix Hun Dzalab Munyal, "Goddess of the Layered Clouds."
Ix Hun Tzelep Kin, "Goddess of Shortly-After-Midday,"
Ix Hun Tzelep Akab, "Goddess of Shortly-After-Midnight."
Who are the others? must be asked.
The primogenial iguana,
the primogenial crocodile,
the primogenial deluge,
the primogenial lizard;
Where did the rest come from?
They came from her father's abode,
from the sun, *Chac Ahau,* "Magnificent Red God," *Itzamna.*
Where did he acquire the strength in his back?
He spent one day coiled up in the center of the flower,
right there, in the center of the flower.
Where did he acquire his powers of divination?
From the abode of *Ix Yaxal Chueen,*
"Primogenial Green Howler Monkey";
it was there he acquired
Chacal Yax Cab, "Great Primogenial World."
Where did he get the pellagra on his face?
He got it from there, from the abode of *Sac Bat,* "White Batz-Monkey,"
from the heart of *Chuuen,* "Howler Monkey."
From there he got the red ink,
the white ink,
the black ink,
the yellow ink.

This is where he is afflicted with pellagra on his face.
Golden beads were inserted into his anus,
and also sacred spindles.
This is where his tail is afflicted.
Rings are inserted into his anus;
tense strands, strong as ropes,
are inserted into his intestines.
Who are the others? must be asked.
Ix Hun Pedz Kin Caan, "Deadly Sky Goddess,"
Ix Hun Pedz Kin Calam, "Deadly Calam Goddess,"
Ix Hun Pedz Kin Kokob, "Deadly Kokob Goddess,"
Ix Hun Pedz Kin Taxinchan, "Deadly Taxinchan Goddess,"
Ix Kokob Tii Calam, "Kokob-Calam Goddess,"
Ix Paclah Actun, "Goddess Who Fornicates in Caves,"
Ix Mumuc Sohol, "Goddess Hiding in Piles of Fallen Leaves."
Who are the others?
Here the writing ends,
behind the red page,
where *Ix Hun Pedz Kin,* "Deadly Goddess" is depicted.
The mother of the sun was depicted behind *Hun Pedz Ac,* "Trapping
    Turtle."
The mother of the sun was also depicted behind *Hun Pedz,* "Great
    Trap."
The mother of the night was depicted in the back.
Which were her symbols?
They were the red wasps,
the white wasps,
the black wasps,
Kan Pet Kin, "Deep Orange Yellow Sun."
The person's red face,
the person's white face,
the person's black face,
the person's yellow face.
Chacal Tup Chac, "Magnificent Chac of the Red Ear-Spools."
Kanal Tup Chac, "Chac of the Yellow Ear-Spools."
Here their meanings were taken.
It is also where *Hunah Ah Chibal,* "God of Painful Bites," was seized.
The meanings are
the red ant,
the white ant,
the black ant,
the yellow ant,
the red *hoch'* snake,

the white *hoch'* snake,
the black *hoch'* snake,
the yellow *hoch'* snake.
Here the *hoch'* snakes penetrate him
and also *Ix Hun Pedz Kin,* "Deadly Goddess."
These are their meanings:
the red *calam* snake,
the white *calam* snake,
the black *calam* snake,
the yellow *calam* snake.
What was the last thing written on the back of the page?
Did you notice when they bit?
I did not notice,
I was not aware
when they bit.
My back will be bitten.
Which was [the deity's] tree?
which was its plant,
when it was born?
The red *hun pedz kin,* "deadly" tree,
and the *hun pedz kin,* "deadly" plant
Its lineage was destroyed.
What is its lineage?
The *ix hun pedz kin,* "deadly" tree
and the *hun pedz kin,* "deadly" plant.
One day [the deity] spent coiled up
at the very origin of the lineage.
It spent an entire day walking around the plant
in the center of the sky.
It destroyed its father's nest.
It spent an entire day lying in its father's nest.
There it was that the sun's face was destroyed,
and the face of the moon.
[The deity] spent an entire day biting the moon's face.
It moved on high [in the sky] because of this.
Then its tail was struck,
its head was struck.
How was that? must be asked.
By no means is its heart to pound,
nor is its head to be cut off.
Then it destroyed the primogenial wooden man,
the primogenial stone man.
Their very being was destroyed.

At a single stroke *chuuen,* "chuuen monkey," was dismembered;
it was a single time,
just once.
It was done only once near the *Acantun,* "Precious Babbling Stone,"
near the *Acante,* "Precious Babbling Wood";
one drop of blood behind the *Acante,* "Precious Babbling Wood,"
behind the *Acantun,* "Precious Babbling Stone."
It came suddenly,
the pouring rain,
the hurricane-strength rain.
Which are my symbols?
It is I who stood up.
The great *ek pip,* "black *pip"* is the symbol.
Max in [uaesba] <uayasba>.
that look like bloody spiders
Which are my symbols?
It is I who stood up.
Therefore the red *ek pip* is the symbol,
the white *ek pip* is the symbol,
the red *hun kuk* is the symbol,
the white *hun kuk* is the symbol.
What are its symbols?
My red nails
and with which I scratched you.
It is I who arrived to seize the primogenial iguana,
the primogenial crocodile.
It is I who stand up to seize
the primogenial iguana.
It is I who stand up to break the code of the *bob*
which he carried on his back.
It [the code] was broken.
The bloody red *pap* is my symbol,
so I broke it in the sun's face.
I broke it in the moon's face,
on *Yaxal Chac,* "Primogenial Rain-god,"
who is my symbol.
Which is my symbol?
It is I who have just arrived,
the wooden remedy,
the stone remedy.
Move it from there
[and] administer it
to the primogenial wooden man,

the primogenial stone man.
It was exactly the day *four Ahau*
when it was born,
when it was created
by its father,
by its mother.
Amen.

GOUT

The text for curing gout.

I stand up to disperse
the red ants,
the white ants,
the black ants,
the yellow ants.
I stand up to undo
the red conflicts,
the white conflicts,
the black conflicts,
the yellow conflicts.
They are the symbolic blankets
of the primogenial wooden man,
of the primogenial stone man.
I proceed to remove
the red hooch' snake,
the white hooch' snake,
the black hooch' snake,
the yellow hooch' snake.
This is where the hooch' snakes
and the ix hun pedz kin, "the deadly one," penetrate.
I proceed to remove
the red nettles,
the white nettles,
the black nettles,
the yellow nettles
from the back of the primogenial wooden man,
of the primogenital stone man.
I proceed to remove the red nettle

from the blanket of *Acantun,* "Precious Babbling Wood,"
from the blanket of the night where it was born.
Has it been long since I changed your symbolic blankets?
What is meant by changing your symbolic blankets?
They are the layers of the *yaxum* bird's tail,
the layers of the *ix op* bird's tail.
How many must be mentioned?
Nine layers.
Thirteen are the layers
of the *kubul* bird's tail
of the *yaxum* bird's tail.
I have already placed my symbolic blankets
on the wooden man
on the stone man.
I now proceed to leave *Hunac Ah Chibal,* "Great God of Painful Bites."
What is meant by *Ah Chibal,* "Biting God"?
[It is] a man's red part,
loaded with the white substance.
How did it manifest itself
when it attacked
the red stick,
the white stick,
the black stick,
the yellow stick?
This is when the member is penetrated, when it attacks.
I now stand up to destroy the illness of *Ah Bolon Paaben,*
"The Great Destroyer,"
with terrestrial fire,
with celestial fire.
I smashed *Hunac Ah Chibal,* "Great God of Painful Bites,"
on top of the primogenial wooden man,
the primogenial stone man.
I smashed him in the sun's face, in the moon's face.
Red sky perforator,
sac white sky perforator,
red fire perforator,
white fire perforator,
red *calam* snake perforator,
white *calam* snake perforator.
This is when his illness began.
I now stand up to seize *Hunac Ah Chibal,* "Great God of Painful Bites."
I now stand up to shake his hammock.
I now stand up to destroy him.

What is the link with *ix hun pedz kin*
"deadly" snake tied up in the sky?
[the one that was] seized,
I mean the red *hun pedz kin*.
Four were my red destructions,
my white destructions.
What was my symbol when I stood up?
The red *ek pip*
the red *hun kuk;*
white is my symbol.
It is I who have arrived,
says the wooden curer,
the stone curer.
But, oh, how could that have come about?
With him came *Hunuc Kuenel,* "Unique God,"
carrying the primogenial wooden man,
together with *Hunac Tii Balam Caan,*
"Great God of the Hidden Sky,"
carrying the wooden man,
carrying the stone man.
What part does *Hunac Ah Uenel,* "God of Deep Sleep,"
play in this?
Once and for all
I destroyed the one who attacked the primogenial stone man,
the primogenial wooden man.
Some time has passed
since I spread out the other symbolic blankets.
Come, *Ix Hay,* "Yawning Goddess,"
come *Ix Mudz,* "Goddess with the Closed Eyes,"
come, *Ix Nook,* "Snoring Goddess,"
come, *Ix Lam,* "Fainting Goddess,"
come, *Ix Nath,* "Bashful Goddess."
Yax Hun Can Ahau, "Primogenial Four Ahau"!
It was during One Ahau that it was born
and created by its father,
by its mother.
The first layer of the *yaxum* bird's tail,
the first layer of the *kubul* bird's tail.
I gave them blankets so they could lay their eggs.
This is what I did:
I destroyed *Hunac Ah Uenel,* "Great God of Profound Sleep,"
and he chased out *Hunac Ah Chibal,* "Great God of Painful Bites."
Come, *Ix Hay,* "Yawning Goddess,"

come, *Ix Mudz,* "Goddess with the Closed Eyes,"
come *Ix Nic,* "Deadly Goddess,"
come *Ix Lam,* "Fainting Goddess,"
come *Ix Nath,* "Bashful Goddess,"
come, *Ix Nook,* "Snoring Goddess."
Hunuc Can Ahau, "Unique Four Ahau."
Can Ahau, "Four Ahau."
Amen.

SMALLPOX

The cure for smallpox with fever; the seizure of these evil frenzies.

It is I who will undo your spell, Frenzy's younger brother.
They are human beings.
Could they be cases of smallpox?
Can they be destroyed?
Ah! who are you?
Chac Mul Ah Kakob, "Red-Hill Smallpox,"
Ocom Kakob, "Penetrating Smallpox,"
Holob Kakob, "Perforating Smallpox,"
Chacuil Kakob, "Feverish Smallpox":
these are their names.
Here they are scolded
by their respective mothers,
by their respective fathers.
Who by-passed you, *Ix Hun You Ta,* "Well-aimed Lance,"
"Well-aimed Member"?
He spent four days erring around on the path,
until he finally found his way
to the wooden man,
to the stone man.
It has been a while since the path was cleared
so I could smash the illness of *Hunac Ah Kinambe,* "Great Patient."
Here he was put to sleep.
Alas! not you!
he still has not fallen asleep;
he still is not resting, alas! not at all!
Fiery blaze, roast them!
Ah! now it is clear.

Three piles of wood-shavings were cast into the hearth.
What must be said so they will vanish to the fiery caves? ah . . . What
  about the
bones that must be [thrown] into the bonfire? woe to his bones!
What happens to the blood that must be taken
to the gigantic opening that leads to the bonfire? alas!
Woe! there could be six foldings of the sky,
six foldings of the underworld
that consume them slowly,
that fling them slowly
far beyond the north. Alas!
His pustules dried up completely at the side of the *actun,* "cave."
His pustules dried up completely at the seashore.
Then it happened that they returned,
becoming men,
because of their mothers,
because of their fathers,
Ah! they are human beings!
The perversity of birth,
the perversity of creation.
What is the meaning of all this?
Oh! I see! it is now clear that this concerns their progenitors.
Oh! they are not totally evil.
Alas! wounded smallpox!
Which are the symbolic birds,
the symbols of smallpox? Oh!
Woe! here they are seized by their plants:
Chac Tan Mo, "Red *Tan Mo,*"
Sac Tan Mo, "White *Tan Mo,*"
Ek Tan Mo, "Black *Tan Mo.*"
You plants, you are created by *Chac Tan Dzidzib,* "Red Cardinal,"
by *Sac Tan Dzidzib,* "White Cardinal,"
by *Ek Tan Dzidzib,* "Black Cardinal." Alas!
They are created by *Chac Tan Mo,* "Red Tan Mo,"
by *Sac Tan Mo,* "White Tan Mo,"
by *Chac Tan P'ocinbe,* "Red-crested Bird,"
by *Sac Tan P'ocinbe,* "White-crested Bird."
These are the symbolic birds,
these are the symbols of smallpox, alas!
Is it smallpox?
Can it be destroyed? Ah!
Which will be the plant,
and which the herb

for curing smallpox? Ah!
Alas! it is created by the red woodpecker.
It is created by *Chacal Nix Che*
Woe! it is coming.
Woe! it is the red *chacah*
It is coming,
woe! smallpox [is coming].
Oh! I see. They [the smallpox spirits] were spun around
by their mothers,
by their fathers.
Woe! who can they be?
Woe! my arm is getting numb.
I just succeeded in destroying *Ah Kinam,* "Great Patient." Ah!
All arrived together,
my red spring,
my white spring,
in which I cooled down his illness.
All arrived together,
my red cenote,[1]
my white cenote,
my black cenote
in which I cooled down his illness.
All arrived together,
my narrow red path,
my narrow black path,
where I calmed down this very illness.
Oh! they all arrived together,
my red hail,
my white hail,
my black hail.
I calmed
his illness.
Amen.

The potion must be made with *chacah,* two chiles, and a bit of honey and tobacco juice. Just a small amount must be taken, and it must be liquid.

---

[1]An area in which the limestone has collapsed, opening to the underlying water table, which may be hundreds of feet deep, like the cenote at Chichen Itza, often erroneously said to be a well.

RATTLESNAKE BITES

For curing parasites (called) rattlesnakes.

Can Ahau, "Four Ahau," *Hunuc Can Ahau,* "Unique Four Ahau."
Has it been long since you emerged from the snakes' mating, mating in
    the darkness?
Has it been long since the lord's red piece of flesh appeared?
Has it been long since the lord's white piece of flesh appeared?
Has it been long since the lord's black piece of flesh appeared?
Has it been long since the lord's yellow piece of flesh appeared?
Four times it slid,
four times the precious stone moaned.
Immense pain and weakness of the world,
immense pain and weakness of the engenderer of humanity.
His head must be cut into four pieces,
because of his mother,
because of lechery.
Blood is dripping, it is said,
that is how they penetrate,
and blood gushes out;
They penetrated, it is said;
the *ix buhumil* snakes, the *ix cuyum* snakes,
the tranquil *ix cuyum* of the plains [penetrated].
Ix Ho Tii Tzab, "Five Rattle Goddess,"
daughter of servants,
daughter of slaves.
Ix Catil Ahau, "Goddess of Vessels,"
Ix Madzil Ahau, "Goddess of Dregs,"
Ix Pokol Pic, "Goddess of Countless Wounds,"
Ix Hun Pudzub Kik, "Goddess of the Blood-drawing Needle."
It is said that she falls with wide-open legs to the abode of the sun,
shaped like a small figurine.
He licks himself, it is said,
he is licking his foam and moaning.
He falls, it is said,
to the abode of *Ix Bolon Ahau,* "Glorious Nine Goddess."
He falls, it is said,
to the abode of *Sac Dzam Pul Acat,* "Goddess Who Soaks and Hurls
    Buds."
He falls, it is said,
to the abode of *Ix Bolon Sut Ni,* "Glorious Disdainful Nine Goddess."
Uttering piercing cries,

the intestinal parasites penetrate, it is said,
they penetrate deeply until they are hoarse.
They penetrate, it is said, to the sacred caries in the teeth.
They penetrate, it is
said, until they cut, the frenum.
They jump with joy,
spinning their tails like spindles,
as though they were spinning with their fingers.
Ix Hun Ahau, "Goddess One Ahau,"
is helping them penetrate deeply to the hidden stench of the intestines.
Like brilliant cochineals is his blood.
Then his heart is opened,
and his understanding as well,
and he will surely remember.
They must penetrate to the surface of *Yaax Cab,* "Primogenial World,"
and they must be tied up on the mountain top,
at the entrance to the village.
They begin moaning loudly.
They are tied up on the mountain
and in the lechery of fornication their necks are twisted.
Cast them far away, to the east,
far away, to the west.
They must be tied up on the sea-shore.
They begin gurgling and allowing themselves to be tied up quietly
in the lechery of birth,
in the lechery of fornication,
in the lechery of darkness.
They fall far away, to the south.
They burn,
the malevolent ones burn and vanish.
The masts begin to creak,
and the poles begin to creak.
Uuc Can Ahau, "Lascivious Four Ahau."
Hun Ahau, "One Ahau."
Amen.

WASP BITES

[For curing] *kan pedz kin,* wasp bites on a person's head.

Take the plant called yellow *dzu to.*
Boil it with four chile peppers and drink the potion.

Hun Ahau, "One Ahau." *Can Ahau,* "Four Ahau."
His mother was standing when he was born,
his father was standing when he was engendered;
four times he was engendered,
during four nights.
Whom did you engender?
Whom did you impregnate?
The meaning is *Yum Tii Kin,* "Sun Lord," *Chac Ahau,* "Magnificent Red
    God,"
Kolop U Uich Kin, "Sun-God with the Flayed Face,"
Kolop U Uich Akab, "Nocturnal Sun-God with the Flayed Face"
in the center of the sky,
in the center of the underworld.
Meanwhile he will be born,
meanwhile he will be engendered.
Who is his mother?
Who is the lecherous one?
The answer is: *Ix Hun Acay Kik,* "Blood-drawing Goddess,"
Ix Hun Acay Olom, "Coagulated Blood-drawing Goddess" from the
    center of the sky.
Your mother's cunt, penis!
From the four fornications,
from the four nights,
man's severe pains will originate,
the sharp pains of primogenial man.
Then he awoke.
Cut off their heads,
chop them into pieces,
you, *Bolon Tii Ku,* "Nine Deity,"
you, *Oxlahun Tii Ku,* "Thirteen Deity."
This is the purpose of their cunt;
their cunt is for fornicating,
for the lechery of fornication in the lechery of darkness.
It has been a while since the wooden man,
the stone man were destroyed.
Your mother's cunt, penis!
Is it to be burned?
Is it to be cut?
This must be shouted.
Ix Hun Tah Kik, "Goddess of Abundant Blood"!
Ix Hun Tah Olom, "Goddess of Abundant Coagulated Blood"!
Here she is, the mother,
here is the lechery of fornication of our *Yum Kin,* "Sun-God,"

Kolop U Uich Kin, "Sun-God with the Flayed Face."
Can it be *Kolop U Uich Akab,* "Nocturnal Sun-God with the Flayed
    Face"?
Is his heart fiery?
The flint drills will be burning,
but hopefully not.
I address you, *Bolon Tii Ku,* "Nine Diety."
Slap them around, embrace them
in the lechery of fornication,
in the lechery of darkness.
Is it to be burned?
is it to be cut?
Could it have worsened?
Could the illness have become worse?
Could the fever have increased?
Your mother's cunt, penis!
He has already burned her soft parts;
he has already burned his testicles until they turned black.
Red lance, white lance.
That is why his red testicles burned,
his white testicles burned;
because of the red *kanal* wasps,
and also because of the white *kanal* wasps.
Because of this *Ix Hun Pet Ah Kin,* "Perfectly Round Sun,"
Ix Hun Pet Akab, "Perfectly Round Night,"
Kin Chac Ahau, "Magnificent Sun-God"
of the sky will be invoked.
It was then that he was humiliated.
Was it then that he licked the red talisman, the white talisman?
He licked the red amulet, the white amulet.
It was then that hoarseness began;
it was then that expectoration began;
it was then that fainting began.
It was then that aphonia began, the broken voice.
Your mother's cunt, penis!
Then the fever burned, red flames,
then the fever cooled, white flames,
because of the hoarse and hollow voice,
because of the night full of holes made by the flint drill, made by the
    leaping flame's fire.
Because of the four fornications during the four days he suffers pain
    for four days.
Your mother's cunt, penis!

Hack off their entrails, chop them up;
so [they] are commanded:
Chacal Kanal, "Magnificent Red *Kanal,"*
Sacal Kanal, "White *Kanal," Chacal Kan Pet Kin,* "Magnificent Wholly
    Orange Sun-God,"
Sacal Kan Pet Kin, "Tiny Wholly Orange Sun-God,"
Chacal Tup Chac, "Magnificent Chac of the Red Ear-spools,"
Sacal Tup Chac, "Chac of the White Ear-spools."
They are dragged to the red ditch, to the white ditch.
It was then that your ailment began.
It was not burned; it was not stopped either.
Who is his mother?
Who is the lecherous mate of *Ix Hun Pet Ah Kin,* "Perfectly Round
    Sun"?
Ix Hun Pet Ah Akab, "Perfectly Round Night," must be asked.
What is his symbol, what is his omen?
It is *Sac Pauahtun,* "White God of Wind."
I stand up,
I who am your mother,
I who am your father.
I curse you and send you to the accursed underworld.
I have already confounded you,
who are in your tree, who are in your plant.
You, *Chacal Kanal,* "Magnificent Red *Kanal."*
you, *Chacal Kan Pet Kin,* "Magnificent Wholly Orange Sun,"
you, *Sacal Kan Pet Kin,* "Tiny Wholly Orange Sun,"
you *Chacal Tup Chac,* "Magnificent Chac of the Red Ear-spools,"
you *Sacal Tup Chac,* "Chac of the White Ear-spools."
You are the trees, you are the plants:
chacal dzooc, red *dzooc,*
and *sacal dzooc,* white are your trees, are your plants.
I mean you.
It is on top of you that he slept,
I mean you.
It is on top of you that he coiled up,
on top of the wooden man,
on top of the stone man.
Can it be that thirteen jars of cold water,
of refreshing water,
of refreshing hail,
of red hail,
of white hail,
of white leaks, are needed to slowly increase the intensity of my chills?

It is I who am your mother,
it is I who am your father,
Kin Chac Ahau, "Great Sun-God" of the sky.
Thirteen times water must be applied for the swelling;
my sky-water, my fog-water, to cool the ailment of the lechery of
    fornication,
the lechery of darkness.
Amen.

ASTHMA*

The words for asthma; an incantation for asthma

Unique Can ("four") Ahau! Can Ahau would be the creation, Hun Ahau would be the darkness, during his birth. Four days would he ruffle his arbor; four days would he ruffle the *maxcal*-plant; four days would he ruffle his *acantun,* during his birth, during his creation, by means of Oxlahun-ti-ku, by Bolon-ti-ku ("nine gods").

Who is his mother? The *uoh* in the sky, the *uoh* in the clouds. The biter in the sky, the biter in the clouds.

He would be cast down by Ix Hun-sipit-caan ("lady unique-discharged-from-the-sky"), Ix Hun-sipit-muyal ("from-the-clouds"). He would fall to the east shore, to the east lagoon.

Four days he ruffles the red wooden trough; four days he ruffles the red lake *(koba)*; four days he ruffles the face of the red Ix Chel, the white Ix Chel, the yellow Ix Chel; four days he ruffles the face of the red Itzamna.

Who was his creator, who was his darkness, when he was born? The throbbing of birth would be the creation of the asthmatic one, when he was born, shortly before he was born.

Alas for chest-asthma! Alas for throat-mucus! Alas for biting-chest asthma! Alas for the time shortly before his birth! Alas for hollow tree-fire-asthma! Alas for head-asthma, nose-pinching-asthma, severe asthma, yellow-dove-asthma! Alas for brush-fence-asthma! Alas for consumptive asthma! Alas for granary-asthma! Alas for wild-gourd-rattle-asthma! Alas for rattle-asthma! Alas for gasping-asthma! Alas for purging(?) asthma! Alas for *cuyum*-snake-asthma! Alas for nose-obstructing asthma! Great causer of pain! Great fearsome one!

He would fall at the place of flat-stone-asthma, at the place of nose-obstructing asthma, speechless asthma. This then would be his mother. Alas, venom-fire-asthma! So he would fall at the place of the *hunpedzkin*-reptile. Then fell *dzi*-blood, *dzi*-vein.

*Ralph Roys, *Ritual of the Bacabs* (Norman, OK: University of Oklahoma Press, 1965), pp. 23–29, 56–57.

Then he licked the poison on the back of the *hunpedzkin*-reptile. Thereupon he took the pain of its force, four days stretched out, four days curled up. He would fall to the place of *sinic*-ant-blood, *sinic*-ant-humor; there he took their poison. This would be [from] the back of their mother [or "bedroom," a pun].

He would fall to the place of the red *xulab*-ant; he would fall to the place of the red flint knife; he would fall to the place of the red[-hot] coal; he would fall to the place of the red trough. There would be turning back and forth. So I grasp the bowl, then, of the fire of my foot. So I would stand, then, erect over the red wooden man, the white stone man.

Thirteen (or supreme) are the sprinklers, with which I sprinkle the seashore. Whose is all the water? My property, it is said. Suck up the asthma, is the reply, behind his *acan*-plant, behind his *maxcal* plant, at the opening to his *acantun*. Cast ye him, is the command of his bird. This is the reply: he is cast to the place of Ix Macanxoc.

He would have taken for his mother the red *puhuy*-bird, his bird, the *ix-huytok*, when he suffers from diarrhea. This is the cry of his bird.

I stand erect. This is what stops his nostril. This is the lewdness of creation, the lewdness of darkness.

Thirteen are the stoppers, with which I stop the nostril of [the lewdness of] creation, the lewdness of darkness.

What is his bird? Who is his bird of tidings? The red *coco-can*-trogon, the white *coco-can*, the black *coco-can*, the yellow *coco-can*, the red *coc-ye*-bird, the white *coc-ye*, the black *coc-ye*, the yellow *coc-ye*.

Who created him? His creator is my *coc bal tun*, the offspring of Ix Uoh in the sky, the offspring of Ix Culum-can, the offspring of Ix Co-pauah-ek, the offspring of Ix Hun-meklah ("lady unique-all-embracer"), the offspring of Ix Hun-sipit-muyal ("lady cloud-releaser"), the offspring of Ix Oc-tun-xix ("lady cement-pillar"?), Ix Ocom-tun ("lady stone-pillar") in the Tzab ("snake-rattles-constellation"), in the *ko* in the clouds. Who created him, when he was born? Ye four gods! Ye four Bacabs! Behead him, husk his shell! He would be beheaded by the four gods, the four Bacabs.

Then he would enter into fire-eruption-phthisis. Then he would enter into the vault, its slippery part. Then he would enter into the vault, its door. Then he would enter into the vault, its front. Then he would enter into the vault, its rear. Then he would enter into the buried part of the vault. Then he would enter into the base of the vault, its base.

The gold spindle would be the tail of the gold turtle. It enters into the front of the gold shell (or scab?); it enters into the back of his eye. Cast down is the bad crystal. It enters into his face. Cast down would be the white *bob*. This would enter into the circle of his eye. It would be cast down the white gullet, the red gullet. It would enter to the upper tooth, to the lower tooth.

The viscous poison of the yellow phlegm is to be cast out. There he would take its force (or poison). There it would be cast into the [white] opening, the red opening. There he took the slippery substance of the throat. There he took the froth of the mouth. There he took the burden of the pain, when he was seized.

Who is his tree? Who is his bush? The red spasm asthma, the red extreme asthma, the red *bacal-ac*-tree, *xich'il-ac*-plant. These would be his tree; these would be his bush. Four days he ruffles the red much ruffled, the red *bilim-coc*, the red *bacal-ac*, the red asthma-tree, the red *xich'il-ac*, the red *sihom-che*-tree, gold is its fruit.

There is a change in the opening of his throat. The tongue of the butterfly-(bead) would clack; it would enter his heart. The imitation jewel would enter his gall. A cord of strong thread would enter into his bowels. A finger-ring (or thimble) would enter into his rectum. A garment, a mantle, would enter to his back. A white mat would enter to his front (or breast). . . . Tix-pic-dzacab ("lady 8,000-generations"), Tix-ho-dzacab ("lady five-generations").

[Like] a puma is his mouth, when it pains. It enters into the virgin-needle when it pains, when he is sleepless, when he does not curl up, the wooden man, the stone man, because of it. I cast you out by the power of the fan, by the power of the staff. Oh, ye Bolon-ti-ku ("nine Gods")!

He would arrive at the north shore, the north estuary. Four days would he ruffle the red beaten water; four days he ruffles the white beaten water, the black beaten water, the yellow beaten water. Four days he ruffles the red broth; four days he ruffles the white broth, the black broth, the yellow broth. Four days would he ruffle the face of White Ix Chel; four days would he ruffle the face of White Itzamna.

Who, then, are his birds? What, then, are his birds of tidings? The red *coco-chan*-trogon, the white *coco-chan*, the black *coco-chan*, the yellow *coco-chan*; the red *coc-ye* [-bird?], the white *coc-ye,* the black *coc-ye.*

He would arrive at the west shore, the west estuary. Four days he would ruffle the face of Black Ix Chel. Four days he would ruffle the face of Black Itzamna. He would fall to the place of The Middle of the White Savannah. Four days he would ruffle the face of Ix Bolon-puc ("lady nine" or "many-hills"). Four days he would ruffle [the face of] Ah Tabay; four days would he ruffle [the faces of] Hun-pic-ti-ku ("8,000 gods").

Then he would be beheaded by Hun-pic-ti-ku. He would enter the vault to arrive at the place of Lord-high-savannah, at the place of Lord-high-clump-of-trees. Then he would be beheaded by Ah Can-chakan, by Ah Can-tzuc-che.

Then he would enter the stalks of *ac*-grass. Four days would he be at the place of Ix Kan-kinim-tun, Ix Kan-kinim-te. He would arrive at the place of Sudden Caster, Sudden Thrower. There he took the shoots of the *chi*-plum; there he took the shoots of the *pul*-guava. There he took his force (or pain).

Four days he took the red Hiccough-groaning, the white *tukbil-acan,* the black *tukbil-acan,* the yellow *tukbil-acan.* Then he took his faint sighing. Then he took the flatulence of your asthma. Then he took his white saliva, his faint yawning, his white (pathological?) sweat. Then he took his fainting, when he suffered, when he was seized [by the attack].

He would arrive at the south shore, at the south estuary. Four days he would ruffle the yellow beaten water. Four days he would ruffle the face of Yellow Ix Chel, Yellow Itzamna, when he would arrive at the place of Ah Bolonte Uitz ("lord-nine-mountains").

Then he was beheaded; then he entered to the open chest-trough, its opening. Then he entered to the bottom of the trough, then to the back of the trough, its back. Then he entered to the front of the trough, its front.

For four days he would drink the juice of the red tobacco, the white tobacco, the black tobacco. Then he would be asleep; then he would be curled up. He would arrive at the place of the unique planting-stake. He would arrive at the. . . . There he would crunch its leg; there he would eat its arm.

He would arrive at the place of Chac-uayab-cat. He would arrive at the place of Red Ix Chel, White Ix Chel, Black Ix Chel, Yellow Ix Chel. Then he damaged the wooden man, the stone man.

He is thrust, falls, into the left eye, how? of seizure, submerging asthma. This is to be recited. The left of the mat. The submerging ended; virginal was the submerging. Raised was the left of the mat by him.

He would arrive at the place of Lady-detrimental-one, the stopper of the opening in the earth, the guardian of the rear of Yaxal Chac. The coolness of my foot, the coolness of my hand, when they were seized, the wooden man, the stone man.

Unique Can Ahau! Amen.

TEETH

This is also a worm, in the tooth also

Unique Can Ahau! Curses upon you! [Addressed to the worm in the tooth.]

Shortly ago, how? a new worm was born, a night worm, a deadly poisonous worm, a fiery worm, an awakening worm, a *sibis*-worm. I curse you!

Hollowly resounding in the *copo*-tree, hollowly resounding in the *tzalam*-tree, hollowly resounding in the *yaxnic*-tree, hollowly resounding in the *kulimche*-tree, hollowly resounding in the yellow-budding-shoot, hollowly resounding in the *chacah*-tree.

Spread about, they [the worms] move, to be seen by the red woodpecker, the white woodpecker. Oh, this would be sudden forcible biting. This would be seen by the blacktail-snake; this would be seen by he-who-cleaves-in-the-middle [snake?]. He would arrive in the midst of the foliage.

The *yaxche*-tree is its sign to release what is known. It would not come to pass, it would not ascend, its sign. It would be on the bean-vine. These, then, are corded faggots to be dragged in because of the food.

Four days, and he would return shortly to the forest, to the belly of the food, to the forest, to the heart of the food. *Uakeh*[-bird?], *uakeh!* What *uakeh!* The paternal *uakeh*, the father *uakeh*, the *uakeh*. The unripe food, the unripe breadstuff. Oh, not pleasing is his command to my heart.

What do ye still cut? [What] do ye still husk? [What] do ye still mangle?

He does not sleep, he does not curl up. The lust of birth, the lust of creation. So it is. *Uakeh* of the water.

Now he goes. He would ascend to the sky, to the place of his father, the thirteen[-gods].

Firmly set would be the virgin dry-stone wall; and then he goes to the door of the wasps' nest. There his evil would be shut in. He is thrown, to be crammed into the interior of the conch-shell, the place of Hub-tun Ahau.

Set up, then, is my red cooking stone, where I roast him. Then I roast my red breath, my white breath, my black breath, my yellow breath.

Then, how? I drag in my red *tuncuy*-tree, my white *tuncuy*. This, then, is to kindle the fire, where I roast my red breath, my white breath.

What is his bush? The red *chacah*-tree, the red *kutz*-tobacco, the white *kutz*.

This was his mother, the *ul*-snail, in a way, your father. You are the great substitute (or mask). I bite you; I bite the back of your claw. Hun Ahau. I curse you, seizure!

First scattered there, first scattered then!

On Unique 4 Ahau was he born, was he created, by his mother, by his father, Kin Colop-u-uich-kin.

I curse you, seizure! It ends now, finally.

2. The *Songs* of *Dzitbalche*

The songs and poems of the Mayas, although less abundant than those in Nahuatl, were until recently known only through the few poetic compositions in books like those of the Chilam Balam or in the Popol Vuh.

In 1942, however, a fortunate discovery was made in Merida, the capital of the state of Yucatan, revealing the existence of an old manuscript written in Yucatec Maya that contained fifteen ancient songs from the town of Dzit-balche. As the first editor and translator of the work, the Mayanist Alfredo Barrera Vásquez, said, we have here magnificent examples of the poetry that accompanied the dances performed during Maya religious celebrations. Four of these compositions follow: "The Watcher," a poem or song to accompany a dance of sacrifice; "The Birds," homage to the birdsong that honors the gods; the beautiful, erotic, and famous "Flower Song" (Kay Nicte); and the lamentation of an orphan dancing to the sound of a drum.

There are some interesting questions about the extent of Christian influence in these songs, such as those raised by the "Orphan Song." It uses the word Yum, which can mean "Father" or "Lord." Does the song refer to the father of the orphan or to one abandoned by God? And if it refers to God, is this comparable to the Nahua notion of abandonment or to the Christian notion?

THE WATCHER*

Oh watcher, watcher from the trees,
with one, with two,
we go to hunt at the edge of the grove,
in a lively dance up to three.
Raise your head high,
do not mistake,
instruct well your eyes
to gather the prize.

Make sharp the tip of your arrow,
make taut the cord
of your bow; now you have good
resin of *catsim* on the feathers
at the end of the arrow's rod.
You have rubbed well
the fat of a male deer
on your biceps, on your muscles,
on your knees, on your twin muscles,
on your shoulders, on your chest.

Go nimbly three times round
about the painted stone column,
where stands that virile lad,
unstained, undefiled, a man.
Go once, on the second round
take up your bow, put in the arrow,
point it at his chest; you need not

---

*The first two songs are from Miguel Leon-Portilla, ed., *Pre-Columbian Literatures of Mexico*, pp. 72–73, 90. The remaining two are from Munro S. Edmonson, *Tlalocan*, vol. IX (1982), pp. 181–83.

use all your strength
so as to kill him,
or wound him deeply
Let him suffer
little by little,
as He wishes it,
the magnificent Lord God.

The next time you go round
this stony blue column, the next time
you go round, shoot another arrow.
This you must do without
stopping your dance, because
thus it is done by well-bred
men, fighters, those who
are sought after, pleasing
in the eyes of the Lord God.

And as the Sun appears
over the forest to the east,
the song of the bowman begins.
These well-bred men, fighters,
do their utmost.

THE BIRDS

You are singing, little dove,
on the branches of the silk-cotton tree.
And there also is the cuckoo,
and many other little birds.
All are rejoicing,
the songbirds of our god, our Lord.
And our goddess
has her little birds,
the turtledove, the redbird,
the black and yellow songbirds, and the hummingbird.
These are the birds of the beautiful goddess, our Lady.
If there is such happiness
among the creatures,
why do our hearts not also rejoice?

At daybreak all is jubilant.
Let only joy, only songs,
enter our thoughts!

FLOWER SONG (*Kay Nicte*)[2]

The sweet,
The beautiful moon
Has risen
Over the forest,
And begun
Its start
To the middle of the sky—
The sky where
It will suspend
Its radiance
Over the earth
And all the forest.

Only fragrant is the passing breeze
And its sweet perfumed smell.
Its center comes
To the middle of the sky,
Just lighting the earth
With its glow.
Over everything there is happiness
For all good men.

One has arrived inside
The womb of the forest,
Where there is not even anyone stirring
Who can counterspy
On anything
Whatever
We may come
To do.

One has brought rose blossoms,
First flower blossoms,
Dog jasmine blossoms,

[2]Flower song is the Maya kenning (*difrasismo*) meaning "poetry."

Tangleflower blossoms;
One has brought copal
And cane vine;
Likewise black tortoise shell;
Likewise new quartz and flint
And new cotton,
New spinning sockets,
Great green flints,
New weights,
Fresh conch;
Likewise a quantity of turkeys,
And new sandals:
Everything is new, even the ties for our heads,
So that we can gather nectar,
And thus we can skim the flowers.

Thus is ancestry ended;
It is done.
We are here then in the heart of the forest
At the edge of the stone pool
To await the appearance
Of the beautiful smoking star over the forest.
Shed your clothes!
Remove your hair stays!
'Til you are
As you arrived
Here
On this earth,
Oh virgins,
Maidens of the changing moon.

ORPHAN SONG[3]

The lamentation song of the poor, the motherless
—A drumbeat dance

---

[3]The concept of orphanhood is complex in Mesoamerica. The subject was very important to the Nahuas, for whom it may have represented what we would now describe as a kind of existential loneliness. Such may also be the case here. To be described as fatherless, however, was an insult, and a person who is said to be fatherless and motherless in contemporary Yucatan is merely a poor person, a pauper.

I was very little
When my mother died
And my father died;
Oh alas, I am my father!
I was just left in the hands
And company of my fellows.
I have nobody here on earth:
Oh alas, I am my parents!

Two days pass
And my fellows may have died.
I shall be left groping,
groping and alone, oh alas!
That time passed
When I was left alone,
When I was wet
And dripping,
And taken in fright by a stranger in his arms:
Oh alas, I am my parents!

A man of evil, too much so,
Enormous evil
Have I been subjected to
Here on earth.
Perhaps never
Will my weeping end.
I have no relatives:
I am just very much alone.

Just so do I pass here
In my land
Day
And night.
Just weeping, Weeping
Consumes my eyes,
And that consumes my soul.
So hard a period of evil,
Oh my father!
Take me poor.
Give me an outlet
For this pain
And hard suffering.
Give me the ending of death,

Or give me truth of soul, my blessed father.
Poor, poor and abandoned
And alone on earth.

If it is that one begs,
Groping and alone,
Begs
And begs
At the doors
Of houses
Of everyone
He sees,
Surely
He will be given love.

He has no home;
He has no clothes;
He has no fire,
Oh my father!
Take me poor.
Grant me a true spirit,
So that it will be possible
For me to suffer the pain.

3. Prayers for Rain

In contemporary Yucatan the most important and frequently practiced Maya ceremony is the Chaa Chac, a prayer to Chac, the god of rain. It is frequently described by the Maya as the second stage in praying for rain. In the first stage, the Maya pray to San Isidro (St. Isidore), but should those prayers not produce rain, they pray to Yum Chac (Lord Chac). Since the topsoil is very thin across most of the peninsula, the slash-and-burn method is used. Corn, beans, and squash are planted in the ash-laden field, after which the Maya must pray that rain comes before the wind carries off the nutrient-rich ashes.

Some Maya fields now benefit from electric or diesel powered pumps that bring water up from under the limestone, enabling the farmers to irrigate their fields. There are no rivers of importance in Yucatan, which made irrigation impossible until late in the twentieth century.

The Chaa Chac lasts twenty-four hours or more, and is conducted

partly in caves. The ceremony is rich in symbolism. For example, the role
of small boys is to hop along imitating the sound of frogs.

I go now to pray that they may descend,
all those beautiful saints who shower us with rain,
Lords who govern,
Lords who send showers,
My Lord.
To the beautiful Holy Chaak,
keeper of the celestial source,
my Lord.
Beautiful Holy Keeper of the Earth,
my Lord.
Beautiful Holy Keeper of the Clouds,
my Lord.
Beautiful Holy Dancer among the Clouds,
my Lord.
Beautiful Holy Dragonfly of the Rain,
my Lord.
Beautiful Holy Heavenly Engraved Stone of the Rain,
my Lord.
Beautiful Holy Heavenly Stone that Gives the Rain to Blossom,
my Lord.
Beautiful Holy Heavenly Stone that Collects Rain,
my Lord.
Beautiful Holy Heavenly Thunder of the Rain,
my Lord.
Beautiful Holy Lightning of the Rain,
my Lord.
Beautiful Holy Sprinkling of the Rain,
my Lord.
Beautiful Holy Rumbler of the Rain,
my Lord.
To the Beautiful Holy Thunderbolt
that precedes
the Beautiful Holy Lords
to cleanse of all evil
the road to the Beautiful
Holy Saints who Sprinkle the Rain,
my Lord.
For this reason I delicately deliver
the Beautiful Holy White Offering
to your Beautiful Right Hand,

my Lord.
Thirteen then I deliver
to your Beautiful Right Hand,
my Lord.
Beautiful Father,
the Beautiful Holy White Offerings
are hanging
in this Beautiful Holy Circle
in which I am also delivered
to your Beautiful Right Hand.
These Beautiful
Holy Dependents on the Rain,
my Lord,
are thirteen and I deliver them
to your Beautiful Holy Right Hand
in this Holy hour
of this Holy day,
my Beautiful Father,
Heavenly Father,
my Lord.

Carlos Montemayor, *Rezos Sacerdotales Mayas II,* Instituto Nacional Indigenista, Mexico City, pp. 19–21; English version, Sylvia and Earl Shorris.

4. A Lancandon Song

WHEN COPAL AND POSOLE ARE DISTRIBUTED IN THE CEREMONY OF RENEWING THE INCENSE-BURNERS

I am restoring it, my offering of copal [incense] to you, for you to restore it, Father, for you to raise it up to the Father. I will pay it to you, my offering of posole [cornmeal porridge] to you, again (for) your welfare, for you to restore it to the father. I will pay it to you, my offering of posole to you, for you yourself. I am making it my gift to you again (for) your welfare.

I am about to dry my gifts to you, may they not be affected by crumbling, may they not separate (as to) their heads, my gifts to you. May they not crack, my gifts to you. May they not break, my gifts to you.

See me making them, my gifts to you, oh Father. May I not be affected by a fall fever.

I am about to place you (the idol) in the new brasero [brazier].

See me making them, my gifts to you, again (for) your welfare. See me making them, my gifts to you, for the health of my children. May harm not trample them under foot, may cold not trample them under foot, may fever not trample them under foot.

Enter, walk. You see my son, cure my son.

Alfred M. Tozzer, *A Maya Grammar* (Cambridge, MA: Peabody Museum, 1921).

5. A Chorti Curing Ritual

When the curers are curing, they proclaim, name by name, everything found in the divining.

They speak like this: you judgements from above, where you are coming to play in the blue ring, the white ring, of San Gregorio of Water, with the rainbow of your appearance, the rainbow of your expression, the warmth of your appearance, the warmth of your expression, the heat of your appearance, the heat of your walking.

Where you pile yourselves up, coming into the blue basin, the white basin, the child San Gregorio is playing there, with the reflection of his appearance, the reflection of his expression, the beams of his appearance, the beams of his walking, the warmth of his appearance, the warmth of his expression.

Where you have come to play, with the water-dam of your walking, the water-dam of your running, the *lam?pat* of your hands, the *lam?pat* of your feet, the numbness of your hands, the numbness of your feet, the hallucination of your appearance, the hallucination of your expression.

With the hardening of your walking, the hardening of your running, the lassitude of your expression; with the jaundice of your walking, the jaundice of your running, the jaundice-ghost, the bone-breaker ghost, the dizziness ghost, the water-drip ghost, the water-slosh ghost.

You come with the trembling of your running, the trembling of your walking, the vein-distension of your running, with the impaling of your walking, the impaling of your running, with the thick mucus of your presence, the thick mucus of your coming, with the bloating of your presence, the bloating of your coming, with the nausea of your walking, the nausea of your running, with the panting of your walking, the panting of your running, with the itching of your presence, the itching of your coming, the tickling of your presence, the tickling of your coming, with the body-burning of your presence, the body-burning of your coming, with the mucus-dripping of your presence, the mucus-dripping of your coming, the coldness of your hands, the coldness of your feet, with the body-draining of your walking, the body-draining of your running.

Where you are playing, you come and are playing your ghost beams, you are playing your ghost Hol Txan, the Hol Txan of your appearance, the Hol Txan of your expression, the jaundice of your appearance, the jaundice of your expression, with the desiccation of your presence, the desiccation of your coming, with the bone-bending of your walking, the bone-bending of your running.

Where you are tossing end over end the angel of this little creature, you are playing cat and mouse with his ghost, his spirit; you who are deceivers, deceiver your coming, deceiver your arrival, deceiver ghosts, deceiver spirits, where you are guiding the ghost of this little creature.

And now you are diminishing his ghost, you are diminishing his spirit, when you toy with it. You carry his ghost on a litter, you carry his spirit on a litter, there you are already metamorphosing over his head. You are becoming beasts of prey over his ghost's head, you are becoming beasts of prey over his spirit, like you who become beasts of prey over the head of this sick person.

You are clutching at his spirit, you are clawing at his ghost, you are softening his ghost, you are softening his bones when you waste away the healthiness of his appearance, the healthiness of his expression. You are trampling on his ghost, you are trampling on his vitality.

When you tug at this little creature, you are making his soul pant with the warmth of your appearance, the warmth of your walking, the sweat of your appearance, the sweat of your expression, with the roaring of your walking, the roaring of your running. As you are all crowding together, gnashing together over his head where he lies whipped and punished by you.

You make him unconscious where you crowd together, snorting beside this little creature. His appearance is made sorrowful, his expression is made sorrowful by you. He has no vitality, no protection because of you.

Truly, you are the kings of death, the kings of disease, the kings of all evil spirits. You are now hovering, sickening, casting your beams over mankind, over the earth, since you seek the Silent Day, the Silent Hour so as to transform yourselves, to Hol Txan over mankind, since your walking is like a thief's presence, your running is like a thief's presence.

But today, this is the hour, this is the day; in the name of all the gods which we are proclaiming over the head of this sick person here, this day let there be protective power over the head of this little creature, you will release his angel, release his spirit where it lies threatened and punished by you.

But today I deliver you spirits of disease into the hands of the angel Holy Spirit, and all the angels. So, they chase you running, throw you to the King Mountain. So, Lightning Aimer, Thunder Aimer carry you away.

Sarah S. Fought, *Chorti (Mayan) Texts* (Philadelphia: University of Pennsylvania Press, 1972), pp. 272–75.

6. A Song for His Wizard

I am a man of the earth and a man of the world,
but I tell my brothers:
I am the spirit of the thunderbolt, lightning spirit,
everything that I say happens;
I am going to speak to my spirit.
What I say, he says,
what he says, I also say;
we speak as one,
we have the same sentiments.
I conceal myself in cotton
and he conceals himself in mist.

7. Bright Star of Evening

I am going to sing to the bright star of evening,
brilliant as lightning;
I am going to wait until it comes out,
I am going to speak
and we are going to write down our words,
both the language and the home.
Ay, ay! I cry only to you in the sky:
One day a man of this world

is going to speak with Venus
or with the stars in the sky.
O my wretched heart! O my wretched language!
Listen and accept the voice
of the man of the earth,
of the man of the day.
The chatting is finished;
listen to what he sang,
what the enchanted man sang:
The last of the sky
is as far as the end of the beginning of the sky
—Heart is breath,
it is not purely heart, as we say.

Masanosuke Oguita/Taro Takano, *Cancion de Chontal* (Tokyo: Candelaria Sha Co. Ltd., 1983), pp. 118, 156; English version, Sylvia and Earl Shorris.

⚙ 6 ⚙

Maya Proverbs and Kennings

*T*he quotidian speech of the Mayas, as well as their writings, is rich
in the use of proverbs and metaphors. The latter often appear in the
form Munro Edmonson describes as kennings, a form related to the
difrasismos *used by the Nahuas.*

In translating work from Mesoamerican languages, there is a ten-
dency to convert prose to poetic form in order to make the linguistic parallels clear. Some translators, among them Edmonson and Dennis
Tedlock, agree that prose should appear in prose form for the general
reader, while Victoria Bricker holds that the form must emphasize the
parallelisms, even when the work is oral history.

The proverbs and kennings included here are not only interesting in
their own right, but will give the reader some sense of the richness of the
language. Nonetheless, readers should not take away the impression that
Mesoamericans speak poetry.

The proverbs were culled from hundreds compiled by Eleuterio Po'ot
Yah, a professor of the Maya language in Merida, and the co-author, with
Victoria Bricker, of The Dictionary of Hocabá. The kennings were selected from the work of Munro Edmonson, whose chief Maya language
informant was don Eleuterio.

In choosing the proverbs, an attempt was made to select those of pre-
Hispanic or early colonial origin, since Spanish proverbs now permeate
the daily language of Maya speakers in the state of Yucatan, as well as the
rest of Mayab or "Mayaland." Both cultural and linguistic criteria influenced the selection.

The Tzotzil work at p. 565 is from a book of photographs and creencias, or "beliefs of our ancestors," by Maruch Sántiz Gómez, a young
Chamula writer and photographer from Cruzton, Chiapas. The creencias included here have been edited to reflect the form of sayings or
proverbs in English while retaining the Chamula content.

Proverbs

You go about gleaning, and they are reaping your milpa (field).

There are those who do not see your road.

The small squash does not hang from the vine where the great squash grows.

Live together, demonize each other.

It could happen once, it could happen again.

Even an animal can be annoyed.

Everything has an end.

Where there is hunger, there are no bad tortillas.

He who has wants more.

Watch your way carefully so that you do not stumble.

There are no fat birds (*chachalaca*) in the forest.

The crying child is put to suck.

Even animals care for their cubs.

Sleep is the younger brother of death.

A poor man does not exceed his poverty.

Time measures all things.

He who knows, knows.

He who knows nothing is worth nothing.

Do not be proud of a small turd.

The armadillo, accustomed to his cave, does not stray.

Here the bones, here the hair.

You cannot speak of a place where you have not been.

When Kisne' (evil or the devil) can lie, he will.

Collected and translated into Spanish by Eleuterio Po'ot Yah; English version, Sylvia and Earl Shorris.

Kennings

Rope and cord or sticks and stones: war

Born and engendered: noble

Fatherless and motherless: poor peasants

Older and younger brothers: everybody

Gourdroot and breadnut: famine

Food and water: fate

Shot and shout: soon

Pants and sandals: religion

Munro Edmonson, *The Chilam Balam of Chumayel* (Austin, TX: University of Texas Press, 1986), p. 19.

Creencias

Till the soil in your sleep and over someone's death you'll weep.

If at night you hear the hummingbird trill someone will soon be ill.

One who eats straight from the pot is as sure to become a glutton as
   not.

Seat a child on a stone and it will be lazy to the bone.

Taste of the cat's first course and your voice will soon be hoarse.

When the pigs dance, rain's a good chance.

Comb your hair at close of day and your mother will pass away.

A girl who sews at night will often lose her sight.

Maruch Sántiz Gómez, *Creencias* (Mexico City: CIESAS [Centro de Investigaciones y Es-
tudio Superiores en Antropología Social], 1998); English version, Sylvia and Earl Shorris.

⚬ 7 ⚬

Myths, Legends, and Poems

*T*hese works deal with less well known stories, mainly outside the Yucatecan and Quiche Maya languages.

The Itza Maya language is now on the verge of extinction. Only a
hundred people, most of them old, still speak this variant of Yucatecan
Maya. The books of Chilam Balam tell us that the peninsula was at one
time divided between the Xiu in the west and the Itza in the eastern portion. During the fifteenth century, a group of Itza moved south to the
Lake Peten area. The majority of the Itza remained in Yucatan, where
they speak Yucatecan Maya, according to Charles Andrew Hofling, translator of the story of "A Faithful Husband" (p. 573). Although many contemporary Maya tales depend on irony, this one, recorded in 1988, has
a particularly sharp twist.

In "On the Human Condition and the Moral Order," the Maya of
Chiapas give their version of the basis for ethical behavior. "The Sweeper
of the Path" (p. 570) has a different function: It clearly raises the level
of self-esteem of the Chamula in the world. The Chorti tale, "What the
World Used to Be Like" (p. 569), with its amusing view of the United
States, is apparently a modern version of the Chorti Maya cosmogony.

Finally, the battle song (p. 575) belongs to the Yucatecan Maya Caste
War conflict, although it recalls much earlier wars.

1. On the Human Condition and the Moral Order—
The Chamula Origin Story

At the time when people first began to multiply,
Jaguars started to be born,
Coyotes started to be born.

Animals started to be born.

All the animals there are on the earth started to be born.

The jaguar was the first.

He emerged with the coyote,

With the lion,

With the bear.

The jaguar was the first one to come out.

You see, that is how they came to be the animal-soul companions of
    half the people.

The other half had the coyotes as their animal-soul companions.

This was because the large animals came first.

You see, the people were occupied in increasing their numbers.

So it was when the first people emerged.

Jaguars accompanied some of them;

Coyotes accompanied some;

Weasels accompanied others.

But those whom the jaguars accompany,

These are the richest.

Those whom the coyotes accompany,

These are not so rich.

Those whom the weasels accompany,

These people are poorer.

Those whom foxes accompany,

These are the poorest,

Just as poor as those of the weasel.

Furthermore, those human counterparts of both the fox and the weasel,

They do not live very long.

There was once a person whose baby chicks had been eaten by some
    animal.

Then the owner of the chicks saw this.

He shot the culprit, a weasel, with a shotgun.

After the weasel died,

It was only three days until the owner of the chicks died also.

[He had shot his own animal soul] and so died quickly himself.

So also with the fox.

He who has the fox as a soul companion does not live very long.

This one, the fox, likes to eat chickens.

When the owner of the chickens sees that the fox is catching his
    chickens,

The fox quickly meets his end at the point of a shotgun.

Then, when the fox dies of shotgun wounds,

He who has this fox as a soul companion lives for only three days.

The person who has the fox as a soul companion may be a man or a
   woman.
In this manner, whoever we are, we die just as our soul companions do.
You see, long ago it was Our Father who thought about all this.
Our Father long ago gave us dreams about our animal-soul
   companions.
That is why it remains the same even today,
That not all of us have jaguars as animal souls.
There are several kinds of animals which Our Father has given to us as
   soul companions.
For this reason it is often unclear what soul companion our Father has
   given us,
Whether it is a jaguar,
Whether it is a coyote,
Whether it is a fox,
Whether it is a weasel.
These, then, are the kinds of soul companions that Our Father
   provides.
That is our heritage, even into our time.
You see, long ago it was this that occurred to Our Father,
At the time when he started to prepare the earth.

Gary Gossen, *South and Mesoamerican Native Spirituality* (Crossroad, New York: 1997), pp.
428–29.

2. What the World Used to Be Like—A Chorti Origin Story

Because the people used to tell long ago that the sea, from time to time, rose
up, in its waves, and rose up standing like the clouds. And when it rose up
standing, then it let itself come down, and covered everything on the earth.
So they used to tell it, because long ago, they tell that the sea lay all around
the edges of the world, and that is why it immediately covered over the world
when it was rising in—the world.[1] So they used to tell it long ago.

   And they used to tell too that the sea was not all one. They say there was
one sea that was red, and one sea was white, and there was one sea that was
sticky like tar. And they say there was one sea that was pure blood, perfectly
red. But we did not get there to see. They say there was one sea which was
very large, and just like milk, perfectly white; they say that they were stuck
together, the sky and the sea.

[1]The author uses dashes to reproduce the rhythms of the speaker, who glosses the story as
it is told.

And there lived the gods. And they say that on that sea every day as every night, there was lightning. Because they say that there lived the gods. But we do not know if it is really true, what they tell. And they say that in the sea there were many animals, filling it.

And that is why there was a town whose name is Barrios—Guatemala—where—the sea lies—they tell that long ago that from time to time those animals tried to come out in ships, wanting to fall on the town. But they were not allowed by the soldiers; they shot and they turned and went. But we didn't get there to see.

But so they tell it. They tell that—they used to say that beyond the sea there are people who have horns. There are people with four eyes. They say that there are other people whose eyes are behind their heads, and some in front. They say they have four eyes. And then those people who—they eat. They eat people. But they said that beyond the sea they are. And they say there are people who—they have no heads. And there are—people—whose heads are flat. They used to tell all this. That beyond the sea there are no people like—where we live.

And that is why they told that—if they were allowed to go out, by the government, they would destroy the people, but—they say that—they were not given permission. No—the people who are beyond the sea wanted to go out and—they were feared.

They told that there was a place named the United States. They say that the people in that place, the people had hair, and—their arms were big around. And they say that when—they used to eat people, because they say that their hair grew. And that is why long ago, they were frightening, people who came from distant places who were not known, they were feared, and they hid the children from them and—all the women they hid when they saw them. Once they made a—a war in a place.

They used to tell that those people where there was a war, when bombs were dropped on their heads, they say that they went into the sea, and there they were protected, and for that reason they were not killed. But they say that there came a day when poison was dropped in the sea; then they all died. But they say that when shots were fired they were not killed, because they went into the sea; not until the poison was dropped in—the sea did they all die. So they used to tell it.

Sarah S. Fought, *Chorti (Mayan) Texts*, pp. 354–56.

3. *The Sweeper of the Path*

The great star appeared. The sky grew bright from end to end.

"I am the sweeper of the path. I sweep Our Lord's path so that when Our Lord passes by he finds the path already swept."

Venus is the morning star. She is a girl from Chamula.

The women didn't believe the Chamulan girl who said she was a star.

"She says she is a star! Could she be a star? She's an awful, ugly, black Chamulan. Isn't the star beautiful? It has rays of light. The star is a beautiful bright red," said the women.

"I am the one who fixes the path. When Our Lord disappears, the ocean dries up. The fish come out of the sea. When Our Lord disappears, there is a red sun, the monkey's sun.

"I am the sweeper of the house. I walk when it grows light. When night falls, I sweep beneath the world. When dawn comes, I appear and sweep again, because that is my work. That's why I am a star. Venus appears early in the dawn, say the people, but it's me. I sweep Our Lord's path. It isn't just anyone's path."

She sweeps the path off constantly. When she disappears, she is traveling inside the earth. When the star reappears the next morning, she sweeps the path again, the path of the holy sun.

We didn't believe it was a Chamulan girl. "It seems to be a star, but a Chamulan. I don't believe it!" we said.

But the poor girl heard us mocking her. If it weren't so, she wouldn't have heard. But she did hear, so it's true.

Tonik Nibak

4. The Famine

Our Sustenance suffers; it lies weeping. If we should not gather it up, it would accuse us before Our Lord. It would say "O Our Lord, this vassal picked me not up when I lay scattered upon the ground. Punish him!" Or perhaps we should starve.

—Aztec prayer

Long ago the famine came. The famine was a punishment from Our Holy Father.

The first year it rained and rained. It was raining then like it's raining now. The holy rain didn't let up at all.

The corn grew well. There was a good harvest.

The second year there was no rain at all. The lowlands were laid waste by the sun.

Those who had sold much of their corn nearly died. We had no tortillas. People ate tortillas made of banana roots, fern roots. As soon as the corn fields flowered, the poor people pulled all the tassels off to eat.

In San Cristobal there wasn't a tortilla for sale. You could buy a wheat bun for a peso. But that's if there were any, and there weren't.

The Ixtapanecs went mad. They sold corn for five pesos an almud.[2] Solid money, not paper like it is now. Five peso pieces, round silver pieces if there were any, but there weren't.

People were paid one quart of corn for a week's labor—enough to eat for one or two days. But that's if there was any work, and there wasn't.

The Chamulans would fill two ceremonial gourds with a ball of weed leaves, greens, and amaranth and go out looking for an employer. The Chamulans who weren't given jobs were stretched flat on their backs, dead on the road. It made no difference if they were old or young, man or woman, still they perished.

Once a Chamulan girl passed by our house. She was carrying two ceremonial gourds filled with amaranth greens and spider flowers. My mother offered her food. But she didn't want to fluff wool or weed in the field. She was too weak to work. She just lazed about.

There beneath the redberried hawthorn, in the tiny gully, she died.

Twice my parents ate banana root. Once my older brother and my father went scavenging as far as Cherry Trees. They walked all day, but they found only eight ears of dried corn!

I had a binful plus ten fanegas[3] of flailed corn. If I had sold it, we would have died.

"Never mind, father. I have some stored away. Don't go again! It costs so much effort," I told him. Since it pleased me, I supported my parents, my older brother, and my sister.

In return for three almuds of corn, my father gave me a piece of his land.

I had planted irrigated fields at Vunal. The holy corn was ripening. I guarded my corn with a shotgun and a machete. I stood guard with three friends, long-panted ones from Ixtapa.

When the corn was yellow, the four of us carried it up the mountain. Robbers were killing people. You couldn't travel alone during the famine.

There was no corn. There was no wheat. Everyone ate corn tassels. Some ate fern root. Some ate banana root. If you had any tortillas, you would eat secretly, yes indeed!

Not even in San Cristobal was it any better. It was a stiff punishment for everybody!

Now the Ladinos haven't taken it to heart. They step on the corn. They throw it out. They eat it on the cob.

We had grown arrogant because we offered them corn for the money we could get. The chastisement is yet to come, you'll see!

The famine will come again, some day, some year! The price of corn will rise, because people spill it and step on it all the time. The holy corn suffers so.

---

[2]See Glossary.
[3]See Glossary.

It is offered up for money. The money flows in San Cristobal. The people keep buying things.

But corn is so hard to raise. There is exhaustion. There are long trips to the fields where the corn is harvested. The holy corn takes so many days!

Xun Vaskis

Robert M. Laughlin, *The People of the Bat,* edited by Carol Karasik (Washington, DC: Smithsonian Institution Press, 1988), p. 249.

5. A Faithful Husband
Told by Fernando Tesúcun

There was, they say, long ago, a man and a woman. They were married. One day the man was talking with his wife. And he said to her, "Look, the day that you die, I am going to be buried together with you so that you see that I truly love you very much.

"If you die first, I am going to be buried together with you. But if I die first, you have to be buried with me."

Then they said: "Good, very good." They shook hands, (sealing the deal).

The man lived with his wife, and they talked every day, (he) with his wife. Then his wife got sick, and she died. And the man remained alone.

Then he asked that he be buried together with his wife. He was taken, and put into the tomb where his wife went.

Days pass, days come.

Days pass, days come.

And the man, there he is inside the tomb together with his wife. Every day he sees (cherishes) the face of his wife inside the tomb.

And then the day came when he saw it: a mouse! It appeared inside the tomb, it arrived with a small bough of flowers in its mouth.

And the man stayed to see it. And it came into his thoughts: "This little animal, from where does it bring this flower that it carries in its mouth?"

Then he grabbed it. He only grabbed the flower, and the mouse went away.

It came into the man's thoughts to pass the flower over the face of his wife, all over her body. He grasps it (the flower), he passes it from her head to the tips of her toes.

Then the man said: "I am going to pass the flower over my wife every day." And thus he did it. Only then he saw it: his wife began to move herself. And he, he is passing the flower, he is passing the flower over his wife. Until he noticed, she sat up.

When his wife sat up, they began to talk: "And you, where am I here?" they say the wife said to the man.

And the man said to her: "If you are dead, here we ourselves are buried. Aren't you remembering when you were alive we talked and we said (promised) that if you die first I am going to come to be buried together with you. And as you died first, therefore I am here with you, guarding you. But now you are already revived. And now let's see how we can leave here."

Then they began, they say, to dig out the tomb, to make a hole, until they escaped. And when they left, they walked a little. The woman is tired, like she is drunk, because it was a long time then she was buried inside the tomb. (After) a lot of walking then they arrived at the shore of a sea. Then they sat to rest.

And the woman, she felt drunk, and she lay down. The man sat down on a rock. And when the man sat down, the woman lay down, and the man put his head on his wife's thigh. And then there came a large canoe. When the men came out of the canoe, they saw the woman, she is very pretty; they liked her. They said to the woman: "Let's go. Why don't you come with us?"

And the woman said to the men: "I can't go because my husband is sleeping. On my thigh, there is his head."

And then said the man who came from the big canoe: "If you want, I'll bring you a stone. You put it underneath your husband's head and you go with us."

The woman wanted to. Then the man came, he put the stone beneath the head of the woman's husband. And then the woman entered into the big canoe, and they went. The woman fled. She left her husband sleeping on the shore of the sea. Then they went, they went.

Days pass, days come, until they arrived at a city. When they arrived at a city, they looked for a little house, where they were going to live.

There they came to know that a king had a dead child, a girl. And the king says that he will give his daughter in marriage to the man who revives his daughter.

This man (who has followed his errant wife) guarded the bough of flowers with which he revived his wife. He carries it. He has guarded it. And when he heard that it's being said that the child of the king was dead and whoever revives her will be given her to be his wife, then he took his branch of flowers and he went.

When he met with the king, he saw, it was true, there lay the corpse inside the king's home. Then he entered. Then he began to pass the flower over the dead woman. Then they saw the woman already moving herself. She revived. When the king saw that his child revived, he told the man: "You revived my child and now you are going to be her husband. You will marry her."

Then the man said that was fine. The king married them. And then the man was the husband of the child of the king. Then the man said: "Now, I'm going to say to the king that he should send all of the police that are with him to seek the woman, my former wife."

Then he gave his wife's name to the police. Then the police all spread out in the city to seek the woman that had fled from him, that he revived first. And when the woman was found, the man, her husband, put a big pot on the fire, full with oil. The oil was boiling when the woman was brought and she was put inside. Then the woman died.

And there ended the story of the woman who fled, who left her husband sleeping on the seashore.

Charles Andrew Hofling, *Itza Maya Texts* (Salt Lake City: University of Utah Press, 1991), excerpts from pp. 166–85. The original publication was by text line. It has been edited here into more conventional English prose.

6. Awaken the Flint! (A Battle Song)

Awaken the flint! Kukican sweats,
   he is sweating blood,
Ordering the Maya to go now to war,
And to launch from the steadfast bow
   the swift, sharp flint arrow.
Raise yourself up. Look at the fiery faces of
   Kinichkakamo, Kambul, and Kakupacat arrayed for battle.
Prepare from the "cauipil," the breastplate, the cape,
   and the collar,
The moment of combat has arrived,
   this is the time to fight!

(*chorus*)
We go to fight, we go,
It is time to go to war.

Awaken the flint! The cutting edge shines
   equally on lance and ax,
And the great, piercing sound of the shell
   is heard everywhere
And all the warrior peoples await the chance
   to show their courage.
Come on, Maya, crush the enemy like
   a terrifying hurricane
That uproots the world tree

and destroys its grandeur.
Show your spirit, remember that your daring
   is constantly challenged.

We go to fight, we go,
It is time to go to war.

Awaken the flint! The winds of war repeat
   without cease
And the flint clamors for the soldiers
   that give their blood,
And the eaglet squadron arrives,
   the eagle and pheasant,
Adding up to seven thousand, including the tigers
   of the royal guard.
Come, pheasant division,
   the 1,600 of the eagle,
Come, the 1,600 of the tiger, royal guards,
   and the 1,600 eaglets.
Those who consider themselves brave
   and carry flint
Go swiftly to war, to fight
   for the Maya people.

Manuel Rejón García, first published in *Supersticiones y leyendas mayas: Imprenta la Revista de Merida* (Merida, 1905); English translation, Sylvia and Earl Shorris.

☙ 8 ☙

Modern Historical and
Pragmatic Narratives

*T*he literature of the Maya continued after the colonial period as it
was written by Mayas in Roman letters or redacted by historians
and anthropologists from oral versions. Victoria Bricker produced,
among other works, The Indian Christ, the Indian King, in which the
Caste War in the Yucatan is described in detail, beginning with "The
Proclamation of Juan de la Cruz." This document, dated 1850, at the beginning of the Caste War, is elegantly constructed. It follows the Old Testament Ten Commandments in structure, although it is Maya in both
form and spirit.

The Caste War in the Bricker work was not the only war of resistance
fought by the Yucatecan Maya. In an earlier war centered on the east
coast of Yucatan, the Maya fought against their Spanish conquerors in
the sixteenth century—laying siege to the Spaniards in Valladolid, fighting them in the jungle and the cities, before the resistance was finally put
down by a small Spanish contingent from Merida aided by 500 indigenous troops.

On the west coast, in what is now the Mexican state of Chiapas, the
three main Maya language groups, Tzotzil, Tzeltal, and Chol, produced
similar resistance to Spanish domination. The wars of Chiapas became
more complicated as religious and ethnic issues mixed with the suffering of indigenous people under colonial rule. Unlike the eastern Maya,
the peoples of Chiapas were not united. Adherents of one religious belief and another, mestizos and Indians, pro- and anti-government groups
came into conflict again and again over the centuries.

Some observers believe that the roots of the problems in Chiapas may
be found in two major areas: distribution of wealth and maintenance of
indigenous culture. Chiapas is one of the richest of Mexican states in
natural resources, with an abundance of oil, timber, and rich grazing
land, yet the percentage of people living in what the Mexicans define as

extreme poverty (less than two dollars a day) is very high. A great number of people in Chiapas speak indigenous languages and follow a syncretic religion, despite centuries of cultural oppression by governmental and other groups, all of whom claimed to have the "best intentions."

Two works redacted and translated more recently by Gary Gossen refer to the long history of tensions between the Chamulas of Chiapas and the Ladinos, in the sense of non-indigenous persons. These pieces reflect some of the roots of the Zapatista conflict in Chiapas, including struggles between the authorities and the indigenous people. According to Gossen, "The Chamula civil conflict, which had been encouraged by pro-clerical Ladinos, was actually turned against the Ladinos to become a movement of ethnic separatism and revitalization. It is worth noting that no Ladinos live in Chamula. The last of the Ladino population was driven out during the anti-clerical movement of the 1930's."

The "Origin of the Ladinos" (p. 593) gives a clear conception of the ethnocentrism of the Chamulas. Long troubled by the Ladinos, they have had their revenge in this story.

In "The First Two Months of the Zapatistas" (p. 593), the history of the struggle for indigenous rights is brought to the end of the millennium with prose and poetry devoted partly to the effect of the Zapatista rebellion on the self-esteem of the Tzotzil Maya in Chiapas.

1. The Proclamation of Juan de la Cruz, 1850

[PROLOGUE]

Jesus,
  Mary.
In the name of God the Father,
  And God the Son,
And in the name of God the Holy Spirit,
  Amen Jesus.
It was the month,
  On the fifteenth
Of the count
  Of October
That I began to speak
  With my children here
In the world
  In the year
1850
  (Years).

I,
   John of the Cross,
I reside
   In the village,
In the village
   Of Jaguar House.

[I]

My very beloved,
   Ye Christian villagers,
Now is the hour;
   There have arrived
The day
   [And] the hour
For me to show you
   A sign
Upon the land of all my engendered people
   In the world;
To the end that
   It might be read to be heard by all the
   Commanders,
And to be heard by all the Captains,
   And by all the Lieutenants,
And by all the Sergeants,
   And to be heard by all my engendered people
In the world;
   To the end that
They might know it,
   All my children.
They have done so much more.
   I was passing it
Beneath my Father's right hand
   On behalf of my engendered people
Here,
   In the world.
Because truly it is I
   Whose heart is burdened
For you,
   Ye my engendered people.
Because I it was who caused you to be created;
   Because I it was who redeemed you;
Because I it was who spilled

My precious blood
On your behalf
   When I created you
To see
   In the world.
Thus, then,
   My beloved,
Ye men
   In the world,
In the very name of the Most Holy Crown of my
Father,
   Holy Jesus Christ,
I am making it known here,
   Before their eyes,
This paper,
   To the end that
They might know all my commandments,
   These my engendered people
In the world.
   Whoever is not believing in my commandments
Will have drunk a draught of suffering
   Without end.
Whoever will obey my commandments
   Will also win the fullness of my Grace.
They will also win my love;
   I will also shade them
Beneath my right hand;
   I will also give them my final Grace
That their souls might attain
   Final resurrection.

[II]

And another thing
   Is my Father's commandment,
Ye Christian villagers:
   Know ye
That not only did there arise the war of the whites
   And the Indians;
Because it has come
   The time
For an Indian uprising
   Over the Whites

For once and for all!
    It was so much better
That I was offering my blessing
    That the war of my Indian children might begin then.
It was only because not a single one of my Indian children
    Came here at my command
That it might be obeyed.
    This is the reason
Why my Indian children retreated
    Because of the Whites
For the second time.
    Because not a single order of the elder lords
Was obeyed
    By their subjects.
This is the reason
    Why the Whites did what they pleased
To you,
    Ye my descendants
In the world.
    Thus, then,
My beloved,
    Ye Christians
In the world,
    I command it
For the ears of small
    And great.
Already, then,
    Have arrived
The hour
    [And] the year
For the uprising of my Indian children
    Against the Whites
For the second time,
    In the way that
Wars used to arise.
    And I command it,
That there might be for me
    In the ears of all the troops under my command
These things I command;
    To the end that
They sanctify
    In their hearts
All these my commandments.

Because even though they are going to hear
The roar
  Of the firing
Of the Enemy's guns
  Over them,
Nothing is going to cast harm
  Upon them.
Because it has come,
  The time
For once and for all,
  For my fame
[And] my blessing
  Over the Whites
For the second time
  [For] whosoever
[Of] you shall desire it.
  Because know ye,
Ye Christian villagers,
  That it is I who accompany you;
That at all hours
  It is I who go in the vanguard
Before you,
  In front of the Enemies
To the end that
  There not befall you,
Not even a bit of harm,
  O ye my Indian children.

Victoria Bricker, *The Indian Christ, the Indian King* (Austin, TX: University of Texas Press, 1981), pp. 187–205, main English text only.

Editor's note: The proclamation is structured to follow the Ten Commandments. Nine more sections follow. The original was written in continuous prose form. The arrangement in couplets, which is apparent in Maya, is the translator's preference.

2. The War of Santa Rosa, 1868–70
as told by Mateo Mendez Tzotzek

This text refers to the so-called Cuscat Rebellion or War of Saint Rose, which was a Tzotzil political and religious movement that occurred in

1868–69. San Juan Chamula in the state of Chiapas was the center of this armed rebellion.

This is a story about the conscripted soldiers.

Well, the Chamulas were carrying on a war with the soldiers from San Cristóbal. The conscripted soldiers were called "frock coats." The Chamulas were called "Cuscateros."

Well, the Chamulas first celebrated their fiestas in their hamlet. There in Tsajalhemel hamlet. For there was a holy image in their houses. That is why they celebrated fiestas in their hamlet. Every time they celebrated the fiesta, they went to the river with their guitars and their sky rockets. They went there to dance in the river with the saint and their guitars. At night they went to celebrate the fiesta in the middle of the river. They carried the saint on their backs with a tumpline.

When they danced they carried the saint on their backs. They danced there in the river during the night. The musicians accompanied them as they sat there by the river playing their guitars. Others were setting off fireworks at the edge of the river.

While they were dancing they said: "Samataloma, Samatalu?isha [sic], Shalataperez, Shalatagomez," they said while they were dancing in the river. That is what they sang every time they were dancing. Then, afterward, the priest in San Cristobal found out that there was a saint in Tsajalhemel hamlet. He went to see because he wanted to find out about the saint. But the people of Chamula found out that the priest was going to Tsajalhemel. That he wanted to find out about the saint.

Well, the Chamulas knew that the priest was going there. Then they went to block his way by Nichtojtik, close to Jolpajalton hamlet. They waited for the priest there. But the people were waiting by the road with their guns and their machetes. They were waiting there in the road for the priest and his horse. Because the priest went on horseback when he went to see the saint at Tsajalhemel. But he didn't realize that there was someone hidden there by the road. For he was happy that he was going to see the saint.

Well, the people were hidden there above the road with their guns and their machetes. When the priest came to the place where the people were hidden, they quickly fired their guns when they saw the priest come along the road with his horse. He and his horse perished there in the road at Nichtojtik, close to Jolpajalton. The priest died there with his horse. He didn't ever get to see the saint where it lived with the people. He and his horse died there on the road.

Then the Chamulas, when they saw the priest and his horse die there, returned to their homes with their guns. The priest and his horse remained lying there on the road. But the soldiers of San Cristobal found out that the priest had died there on the road with his horse. They went to investigate. They went to find him and to bring him back to San Cristobal.

They buried the priest there in San Cristobal. Then, after they had buried the priest, they went to kill the Chamulas. But the Chamulas found out that the soldiers were coming. They went to wait for them by the road at Tsajalchen hamlet, on the road to Chamula. But it happened that the soldiers came to Tsajalchen first. The Chamulas arrived later. Then when the soldiers arrived at Tsajalchen, they started to eat there at the edge of the river.

They were sitting there eating. They didn't realize that anyone was coming. Well, the Chamulas arrived there at Tsajalchen. They saw the soldiers sitting there. They were eating there by the river. They quickly fired their guns at the soldiers because the soldiers were busy eating.

[You see,] as they began to eat, they put their guns down beside them on the ground. They put them down beside their cannons. When the [Cuscateros'] guns were fired, the [soldiers] started to flee at once. All their guns were left there at the edge of the river along with their cannons, their tortillas and their carrying bags. Those things remained there at the edge of the river at Tsajalchen, close to Chamula Center.

The Chamulas fought there with the soldiers. All of the soldiers fled. They went to San Cristobal. They were very scared.

Then the soldiers set out once more for another try. They went to fight with the Chamulas. But the Chamulas found out that the soldiers were coming again. They went to wait for them again at Tsajalchen. They went with their wives. The women went to help them. They went to chill the guns so that the soldiers' guns wouldn't fire. For indeed, they had ugly and powerful assholes.[1] They were very cold.

That is the way they were going to chill the guns. But when the soldiers arrived with their guns, the guns didn't become cold. The guns fired at once and were obviously not made powerless by the [women's] asses. The women had come in vain. All the women died there from the bullets. The bullets ripped right into their asses. [The bullets entered with such force that] they went through their bodies and ended up in the men's mouths [as they stood behind them]. They were still trying to fire their guns, but not so much now. They were no longer winning.

At the beginning they were indeed winning, but the second time they could not prevail. The fact was that the soldiers were winning. At the beginning they didn't win, but the second time they did win. They were no longer

---

[1]The use of unarmed women who bare their buttocks as a strategic defense requires some interpretation. Generally speaking, Chamula men and women both regard female genitalia as "cold" in their taxonomy of gender associations. At the same time, the earth itself is associated with the powerful, cold female.

scared. Now the poor Chamulas didn't run away. Many of them died. Men died; women died. They all died in like manner.

The soldiers did not die. They prevailed. As for the poor Chamulas, they could no longer return to their homes. They all died there, close to Tsajalchen. The soldiers returned to their homes in San Cristóbal.

3. At the Time of the Closing of the Churches, 1935

This was the time of President Lázaro Cárdenas's most extreme anticlerical policies, a culmination of the disestablishment of Catholicism as the official state religion, as dictated by the Mexican Constitution of 1917. The churches of Chiapas were indeed closed during this period (1934–36), and there was a great deal of local vandalism directed against church property, including contents of the buildings themselves. The churches were reopened in 1936, but with the proviso that the clergy could not wear religious garb. Nor was the church allowed to be the sole agent for performing marriages. To this day, there is no established church in Mexico, although there is virtually complete freedom of religious practice and affiliation, a policy which Chamulas have used to advantage in sustaining a highly traditional form of Maya/Christian public religious practice. Protestantism and reform Catholicism (post–Vatican II) have been summarily rejected by the Chamula central government. A nascent Protestant movement which began in 1965 was eventually crushed in the early 1970s by the wholesale expulsion of hundreds of Protestant converts from the community. It is therefore worth noting that the narrator classifies the anti-clerical secular policies of the state and federal government in the 1930s as being of Protestant inspiration. This interpretation makes absolute sense from the perspective of 1968, when this text was dictated, at a time when Protestantism was a palpable threat.

Heroic deeds spanning the period from the Mexican Revolution (1910–17) to the 1950s are attributed to Erasto Urbina.

An account of how the Protestants burned the images of the saints.

Well, the Protestants burned up the images of the saints in the church in a live flame. The reason for this was that they didn't want there to be any saints in the church. [According to them], these images were not gods. They were but carved wood. They did not know how to speak.

[They believed that] there indeed was a god, but only one god. Our Father Sun in Heaven was not the [true] god. He was nothing but light. [It was said that] we ought not pray to [Our Father Sun in Heaven]. [They said that] he was a demon.

There was a god who lived in a cave. [The Protestants] would pray to this god. He was the true god. Those in the church were different, They were not like gods. They were like demons. That is why they burned up the saints in the church. Truly, they burned up all of the images of the saints.

The church itself was closed. No longer could people even go in. The door of the church was covered over with cardboard so that the people could no longer go in. All the churches were closed. Then they took away the images of Our Lord San Juan and Our Lord San Mateo. They removed the images of all the saints.

They went to hide them in people's homes so that the Protestants couldn't see them. But when they removed the image of Our Lord San Juan, they put an old image in Our Lord San Juan's place. They removed all of the true images of the saints. They hid them in the people's homes. As for the old worn-out saints' images, these were left in the church. They were left in the very place of the real images of Our Lord San Juan [and others].

When the Protestants got to the church, they immediately seized the image of Our Lord San Juan. They thought that it was the true image of Our Lord San Juan sitting there. They took it out. They went and burned it up. But it was really only an old worn-out image. It was not the [true] image of Our Lord San Juan.

It seemed as though all the saints were right there inside the church. But there were no longer the true images of the saints. The Protestants had been taken in and deceived. These were nothing but old, worn-out images of the saints. So it was that the Protestants burned up all of the old images of the saints.

With that, therefore, they boarded up the church door. Not one saint's image remained in the church. With this, the Protestants believed that Our Lord San Juan was dead, That all of the saints were dead. But Our Lord San Juan and his companions were not dead. There they were hidden in a house. They were not dead.

Later on, after all of this had happened, Erasto Urbina resolved the problem. He drove out all of the Protestants. Indeed, when they burned the images of the saints, the priest couldn't even say the mass; Not even for the Ladinos, for the door of the church was boarded up. Then when Don Erasto finally resolved the problem, they opened the doors of the church. So it was that the images of the saints went back to reside in the church, all of the saints.

So it was that the priest once again could go in the church to say mass for the Ladinos. So it was that the Chamulas could go in to speak to the saints. They opened the doors of the church. And Our Lord San Juan returned once again with his companion saints.

The people of Chamula rejoiced, now that at last the doors of the church were opened. They began speaking to their saints. They opened all the churches. They opened all the churches in San Cristobal de las Casas and in Tuxtla Gutierrez. Indeed, all the churches opened, For Don Erasto had solved the problem. Once again they began to have fiestas, now they could have fiestas on each and every feast day.

Gary Gossen, "Translating Cuzcat's War: Understanding Maya Oral History," *Journal of Latin American Lore*, 3 (2) (Los Angeles, 1977), pp. 249–78.

4. Pajarito's War

The armed conflict of 1910 was led by Jacinto Peres Chixtot, who was known by the nickname "Pajarito." The goal of the uprising was the expulsion of the "Ladinos" or non-Indians. It is likely that the priest referred to in this tale is none other than the bishop of Chiapas, Francisco Orozco y Jiménez, or his representative, who is said to have used the Chamulas' religious zeal for his own political ends, thus precipitating Pajarito's armed rebellion against the anti-clerical, liberal elements of Tuxtla Gutierrez. The Captain was Jacinto Peres Chixtot, "Pajarito" himself.

Well, long ago the elders got themselves involved with the prayer-making cult. However, they were not the sole instigators. It came as an order from the priest, the President, the Juez [Judge], and the Alcaldes there in Chamula Center.

Now, when the Presidente of Chamula heard of the priest's wishes, he began assembling people to do the [the priest's bidding]. When some of the people heard this [request for assistance] they heeded it willingly. Mind you, though, not all the people heard and responded eagerly. To some, it seemed like a good idea. Others thought that the proposal that they join this new cult and learn new prayers was disgusting. Therefore, not everyone heeded the call [to join the new cult].

But, then, those who did like the idea set about eagerly to learn the prayers and tenets of the new cult. Every day they would go with their wives to the ceremonial center of Chamula to learn the new prayers. They would go to receive indoctrination right there in the Chamula church. Now, they received the indoctrination very eagerly. Every day they would go with their wives to learn the new faith. Now, in the midst of the indoctrination sessions, they set about organizing themselves, and named recruiters to enlist followers for the cult.

One of these was called the "Captain." One was called the "Lawyer." And one was called the "Judge." The Captain, the Lawyer and the Judge were the bosses. They gave orders. This was because they were the chief officers of the prayer-makers. They spoke with the same authority as the Presidente and the Alcaldes.

They now took to giving orders with the same authority [as the traditional officials]. This was because the Captain, the Lawyer and the Judge had become very powerful. It got to the point that they put those who did not want to join the new cult in jail. But putting them in jail was but the first step. Afterwards, they would go at night to take them out of jail. They would give transferral papers labeled "Tuxtla" to those who refused to join the cult. But this was really a grim joke. "Pajarito Prayer-makers" was what the cult members were called. And the Captain, the Lawyer and the Judge were the commanding officers of Pajarito's cult. Now, this gave [Pajarito's] commander officers the pretext to capture anyone they didn't like and put them in jail.

And then they would go at night to take them out of jail and give them their transferral papers labeled "Tuxtla." But, in reality, it was a lie that they were given transferral papers for Tuxtla. In truth they sent them to be executed in the hamlet of Kuchulumtik. That is why they said they were being sent to Tuxtla to deliver their documents.

In truth this meant that they sent people every night to be executed in Kuchulumtik. Now, at first the prayer-makers seemed to be winning. But right in the wake of their victories came a succession of casualties for the prayer-makers themselves. They were not destined to win. The winners in the conflict were going to be those who refused to join in with the prayer-makers.

At first those who refused to join the cult of the prayer-makers suffered casualties. But in rapid succession thereafter those who refused to join the cult of the prayer-makers started to prevail. They killed the prayer-makers. Some of the prayer-makers died because they did not realize that they were vulnerable to death. They did not realize that they could even be killed. They did not imagine how they could possibly die. Those who managed to survive were the ones who realized that they were indeed vulnerable to death. When they became aware of the threat to their own lives, they fled immediately. They refused to sleep in their own houses any longer. They fled with their wives. They went off to Rincon Chamula. They took their wives with them and went far away. However, these people had this hardship coming for they were the ones who had first tormented and fought with those who did not want to join the prayer-making cult.

For example, the prayer-makers would accost and tie up their enemies, forcing them to come along with them, beating them on the way. The prayer-makers arrested the men along with their wives. As for the man, they would beat him up brutally [as they dragged him along]. But they would not kill the woman [who was with him]. They would simply rape her, violently, right there on the path. Then they would take the woman to the ceremonial center. They would not kill her. They would simply rape her continuously [as they went] along the road.

But, as for the man, they would murder him in cold blood. He would never reach the Ceremonial Center. He would meet his death right there on the path. He would not even be sent to deliver his documents to Tuxtla [to be summarily executed]. But the poor women suffered horribly from having their bodies swell up with cramps. They could scarcely walk!

[Some of the men] had great long penises. Others had them long and slender. Still others had penises that were big around but short. That is why the women's bodies were swollen with irritation.

But, later on, the prayer-makers stopped imposing their will. It was those who refused to join the cult of the prayer-makers who won out in the end. As for the prayer-makers, they got a taste of their own medicine. They got a sample of what they themselves had done to others. They had been involved in the murder of many people. And many women had been raped by them on the road. Thus [the victors] engaged in some of the same behavior as [those who were defeated]. [The victors themselves] were responsible for frequent rapes of women along the road and in their own homes. Many prayer-makers met their end along the road. They, too, were sent to the woods to "deliver the documents to Tuxtla."

In this manner, the prayer-makers were having to pay dearly for what they had done to their own countrymen. This is why the "Judge" and "Lawyer" had to go to take refuge in Rincon Chamula. They fled with their wives. And thus they did not die. The Captain himself fled to San Cristobal. He went to hide out near the church of San Nicolas, which is close to the park in San Cristobal. Soon, the people who had opposed the prayer-making cult found out where the Captain was hiding. They went to search for him in San Cristobal.

When the people who were intent on killing him got to San Cristobal, they went to talk to the soldiers who were stationed in San Cristobal. "Please, let's be off to kill the Captain. He has been stirring up endless fighting and trouble for us in our town."

"He ran away!

"He's come here!

"He's there in hiding near the San Nicholas Church. Therefore, please, let's be off to kill him," insisted the Chamulas who had not joined the prayer-making cult.

"All right. Let's do it. Let's go find him. Why would he do such [things as he's done]?" replied the soldiers. So off they went to search for the Captain.

Lots and lots of soldiers armed with guns accompanied the Chamulas.

Sure enough, they found the Captain hiding there near the San Nicolas Church. Well, then, when they had flushed the Captain out they bound his hands. They marched him straight to the San Cristobal cemetery. They force-marched him there, pulling him along, his body bound up in a rope. When they got to the cemetery they stood the Captain up in front of a cross. Then they tied his hands to the cross there in the cemetery. In this manner they bound him to the cross with a rope. And they placed a black scarf over his eyes as a blindfold. Then they opened fire on the Captain. But he remained there, standing erect against the cross. And, with life still in him before he died, the Captain spoke:

"When I am dead, you should take care to bury me face down. As for me, [you will see that] I shall not die at your will. I will rise from the grave. Therefore, you should be sure to bury me face down," declared the Captain.

"Very well, that should be no problem," replied the soldiers and the Chamulas. And with that, they let him have it with their guns. He did not even seem to feel the lead pass through his body from the first shot of gun-fire. He remained standing erect. Well, when the second shot was fired, it was then that he felt the lead smash through him. It crushed his head and he seemed to die then and there. But it was only his head that was smashed. His body remained erect there on the cross. Now, when he died, they untied his body and proceeded to bury him.

But first they dug the grave.

Once they had dug the grave, they buried the Captain. But the soldiers and the Chamulas did not heed his request to bury him face down. They buried him face up. They did not heed his request that they bury him face down.

In truth, the soldiers really believed that the Captain would not die from the gunshot and that he would rise up alive from his grave. Every day the soldiers would go to check the place where he was buried. They were checking to see if he would rise from the dead. But after three days he remained there, buried. He did not escape [death].

The Captain of the Pajarito prayer-makers died right there in the San Cristobal cemetery. He did not come back to life. He got just what he had coming, just what he had done to others, just as he had gone about killing his own people. So it was now his turn to die, also.

The Chamulas who were opposed to the prayer-making cult went off in pursuit of the prayer-makers who had fled. They were determined to find the prayer-makers. They wanted to kill them all. In the first period of the conflict, it was the women who did not believe in the prayer-making cult who were raped.

Afterward, it was the women who were devoted to the prayer-making cult who were raped. Men were killed every day. They were flushed out from the woods and caves where they were hiding. If they found them in hiding, they would kill them. And they would rape the women. But this time the rapists and plunderers were the opponents of the prayer-making cult. So it turned out that some of the prayer-makers died in this conflict. Some [of the prayer-makers] survived. Those who survived found their way to Rincon Chamula as refugees. For that reason, those people who now live in Rincon Chamula are descendants of the prayer-makers. They were forced into exile for they were very evil and wicked. They killed. They raped. That is why they were forced into exile. Those who drove them out were those who did not believe in the prayer-making cult. But when the Captain was still alive and when he was still in league with the Judge and the Lawyer, they extended their campaign by seizing Ladinos, those Ladinos who lived in Indian communities. For there were indeed some Ladinos who lived right in the municipal territory of other Indian communities.

That is why they went to force them to leave. They didn't want them living in Indian communities. They wanted to force them to go back and live in their own towns, where they had come from in the first place. They went to drive the Ladinos out of San Pedro Chenalho, out of San Andres Larrainzar, out of San Pablo Chachihuitan, out of Magdalena, out of Tenejapa, out of Hot Country. They didn't want any of them living there in Indian communities. They wanted them to go and live in their own communities.

They succeeded in driving out all the Ladinos who lived in Indian communities. The Ladinos took refuge in San Cristobal. They went with their wives to live there. Then, when they found out that the leader of the Pajarito prayer-makers was dead, the Ladinos returned to their former homes, to where they had lived before. They returned for good. That is why, to this day, there are Ladinos who live in Indian communities. They live in San Pedro Chenalho. They live in San Andres Larrainzar. They live in Tenejapa. And they live in San Lorenzo Zinacantan.

But this [return of the Ladinos] did not occur until the leader of the Pajarito prayer-makers died. Not until the Captain himself died. And the Judge and the Lawyer had fled. While they were still pursuing their cause, the Captain, the Judge and the Lawyer were intent on going to Tuxtla Gutierrez to demand the return of San Juan's staff. This was because the staff was there in Tuxtla. The Ladinos had stolen it long ago. In particular, it was the Ladinos in Tuxtla Gutierrez who stole San Juan's staff. That is why the Pajarito prayer-makers were intent on going to Tuxtla Gutierrez to demand that San Juan's staff be returned.

The followers of Pajarito went on this campaign armed with guns, machetes and walking sticks. They were determined to reclaim San Juan's staff at gunpoint. These were indeed Chamulas who sought to reclaim San Juan's staff. But, being as they were, the Pajarito prayer-makers, they did not succeed in this mission. Now, the soldiers who were stationed in Tuxtla

Gutierrez found out about the Pajarito prayer-makers' plans to reclaim San Juan's staff.

"We are well-informed of their plans to steal back the staff. We shall be waiting for them right here," said the soldiers. "Or, even better, we will go to wait for Pajarito's troops over there at Jompana. When they show up, we will offer them something to eat right by the road. They won't make it this far [i.e., to Tuxtla]. When they get to Jompana, we will offer them something to eat. This will help to distract Pajarito's people. We will enlist some women to go and offer them free food there at Jompana. This is where all of Pajarito's troops will enjoy their noon meal," plotted the soldiers from Tuxtla.

With this, the soldiers went to enlist some Ladino women from Tuxtla [to stage the ambush]. They were supposed to offer a free meal at Jompana. It was just women, women alone, who would offer the free meal at Jompana. "Once you have given them their food, you should get out of the place as fast as you can," they said to the women.

So said the soldiers from Tuxtla. So it was that when Pajarito's troops reached Jompana, they found these women there with food all prepared. "Come now, rest here a little while. And perhaps a bit of coffee to drink will help you relax. Maybe you'd even like a little bit to eat so you won't get so tired on the road," said the Ladinas.

"Don't worry about paying for it," coaxed the Ladinas. "Fine, then, thanks very much," agreed Pajarito's men. With that, they accepted the invitation. They drank coffee and had something to eat. There at Jompana they stopped to rest. Little did Pajarito's unfortunate troops realize that they were about to be ambushed. They had no idea that there was anyone hiding there on the hillside by Jompana. And while Pajarito's poor men were still eating, the guns opened fire on them. They were right in the midst of their meal and drinking their coffee when they were fired upon. Pajarito's poor troops didn't even know what hit them. There they died at Jompana, every one of them.

The soldiers were hiding there in the forest on the hillside. Therefore Pajarito's poor men didn't even see where the gunfire was coming from. As for the women, as soon as they had served the meal to Pajarito's troop, they got out of there. They fled as fast as they could. Indeed, the soldiers had told the women to leave as soon as they had served the meal. So all of them fled and got away safely.

As for the soldiers, as soon as they saw that all of the women had gotten away from the place, they immediately opened fire. Right there at Jompana all of Pajarito's men died. They never made it to Tuxtla Gutierrez. They did not succeed. It was the soldiers from Tuxtla who won. They did not succeed in reclaiming San Juan's staff. San Juan's staff remained right there in Tuxtla Gutierrez. This is why the Ladinos are very rich. For San Juan's staff is there in Tuxtla Gutierrez.

You see, San Juan's staff magically produces a great deal of money. For it is the "mother of money." That is why Ladinos are very rich, and why the poor Indians are very poor indeed.

From a work in progress by Gary Gossen, with the permission of the author.

5. The Origin of the Ladinos

Well, long ago, the Ladinos had a dog for their father [and this account tells how it all came about]. It happened when a Ladino woman came along with her dog.

Now, long ago there were still meadows all over the earth. There were still no houses.

Whereupon, the dog started to fuck his mistress. Indeed, the Ladino woman encouraged him and helped him. Then and there, the dog fucked her. There was the Ladino woman waiting for him on her hands and knees. Well, they did it lots and lots of times. And sure enough, he got the Ladino woman pregnant.

Now, the Ladino woman had a baby. Her child was born. But it was already a modern-day Ladino who was born.

Well, as soon as the Ladino woman's child was born, she and her dog set up housekeeping. Slowly but surely the Ladinos began to multiply.

That is why Ladinos have no shame. They flirt and speak with each other on the road. They hug and put their arms around each other in public. They kiss each other in public. This is all because they had a dog for a father long ago.

Long ago the land was an expanse of grass. That is why they called their town Hobel [San Cristobal], for it means "grass." This [story] explains also why Ladinos have no fear, why they are powerful, why they harass and strike Chamulas.

The Chamulas do not have a dog as their father. That is why they are more self-conscious and proper in their behavior. They are also afraid of Ladinos. Perhaps it is because the Indians do not speak Spanish.

Gary Gossen, as told by Mateo Mendez Tzotzek, *Telling Maya Tales: Tzotzil Identities in Modern Mexico* (New York: Routledge, 1999), p. 127.

6. The First Two Months of the Zapatistas

EARLY JANUARY: PREPARATIONS AND VISITS
Before the invasion of San Cristobal, everyone always talked about how the soldiers at the army base overlooking the southern approach to the city

had spread booby traps all around their land, how they had fixed it so no one would ever dare attack them. If the poor Indians ever came to make trouble, everyone said, the soldiers would finish them off right there, before they even got out of the forest. The army officers are maestros of killing, they said, and all they have to do every day, their only chore, is teach the young soldiers how to kill. And as if all of that weren't enough to scare away a bunch of raggedy peasants, all the people said, the soldiers also have mounds of bombs stored behind their fort. Nothing but special bombs for killing Indians!

K'elavil, look here, according to what people said, the soldiers had strung a special wire around their barracks that was connected to a bomb every few steps. If the damn Indians ever did come around, they said, all the soldiers would have to do was lean out of their beds and touch the wire with a piece of metal—like, say, a beer can—and the bombs would all blow up. And if the Indians tried to cut the wire, it would also blow up.

But of course, the soldiers are famous for never sleeping, so the Indians would never even get close to the bombs in the first place. No one, the soldiers figured, would ever get past them. But after all those preparations, what happened? On January first, the soldiers were asleep when the Zapatistas arrived in San Cristobal! But snoring! They didn't see the Zapatistas go by their check-points with the other passengers on the second-class buses. They didn't notice the Zapatistas get out of their buses at the station and walk into the center of town. They didn't see anything! And when the soldiers woke up, the Zapatistas had already seized the Palacio de Gobierno—and set up their own guards around the city! After all, it was the army that was left outside of town, safely holed up in its barracks! The Zapatistas won by just ignoring them! Not until the next day, when they had finished their business in town, did the Zapatistas finally go to pay a visit on the soldiers![2]

The Zapatistas are only Indians but what the army officers forgot is that Indians too are men. And since they are men, they also could be armed and trained, just like the army. All they needed was the idea. And as it turned out, their thinking was better than the army's! They fooled the officers, who are maestros of killing! Since that day, all of us, even those who are not enemies of the government, feel like smiling down into our shirts.

If there is a sad part to all of this, it is that even though the Zapatistas are men, they will have to live in hiding from now on. They won't be able to sleep in their own beds in their own houses, but will have to stay hidden in caves in the jungle. If they want to make babies like everyone else, they'll even have to screw in the caves. Like armadillos!

---

[2]The Zapatistas attacked the army post at Rancho Nuevo on January 2, 1994, as they were retreating from San Cristobal.

EARLY JANUARY: UNCERTAINTY IN CHAMULA

When word first came that the Zapatistas had occupied San Cristobal, all the Chamulas said that they weren't afraid. But that was a lie; they were. Just to keep up appearances, though, everyone said that the only one who really had anything to be scared of, the single person responsible for all the bad things that have happened in Chamula, was the municipal president. In truth, of course, all of them knew that they too had participated in the round-ups and expulsions of their Protestant neighbors, and they were all afraid the Zapatistas were going to come and exact justice. They had heard that the Zapatistas were well armed and figured they wouldn't waste a lot of time listening to excuses, that they would just kill all the Chamulas who had beaten the Protestants and burned their property. And what could the Chamulas do about it? They didn't have any good weapons, just some rifles, a few pistols, and one or another old shotgun— enough to scare their unarmed neighbors, maybe, but against real soldiers they wouldn't have a chance. Instead of fighting, they all said, everyone in the whole town would be better off if they just stayed in bed and screwed one last time.

As you can imagine, however, if everyone else was worried, the municipal president himself was terrified. He was so scared about what the Zapatistas and Protestant exiles would do to him if they ever caught him that he walked around for a week with a hard-on. But stiff! He better than anyone knew all of the terrible things that had been done. But he wasn't alone. To tell the truth, the whole town was afraid.

Finally, since there was no other defense, the presidente announced that the whole town should offer candles and incense at the sacred caves and mountaintops and ask for the protection of God and the saints. Since Chamula's *j-iloletik* [shamans] are famed for their power, this seemed like such a good idea that the officials of the municipios of Zinacantan, Amatenango, Mitontic and Huistan decided to join in as well. Together, they thought, maybe their prayers would be powerful enough to keep the Zapatistas away.

On the appointed day, scores of officials and dozens of chanting shamans, all dressed in their ceremonial clothes and many carrying candles and *yavak'aletik* [braziers] of burning incense, assembled at the church in Zinacantan. From the church and sacred mountain of Zinacantan, they proceeded together to the sacred cave at the border of the municipio of San Andres, and then to the mountain of Chaklajun on the road between the *cabecera* of Chamula and San Cristobal. They prayed for more than an hour at each site. *Kajaval!* [Lord] There was so much incense it was like a fragrant fog, and the whole entourage seemed to hum like bees as each man murmured somberly in his own prayers.

Have Mercy, *Kajaval,*
Have Mercy, Jesus.
Make yourself present among us, *Kajaval,*
Make yourself present in our incense,
Jesus with us, your daughters,
With us, your sons.
We have brought you food, *Kajaval.*
We have brought you drink, Jesus.
To awaken your conscience,
To awaken your heart,
That you might lend us your feet,
That you might lend us your hands,
That you might discharge your rifle,
That you might discharge your cannon.
What sin have we, *Kajaval?*
What guilt have we, Jesus?
Don't you see that we are here, sacred lightning?
Don't you see that we are here, sacred thunder?
We beg that you close the roads to your sons who are coming,
We beg that you close the roads to your daughters who are coming,
That you bind their feet,
That you bind their hands,
That you silence their rifles,
That you stifle their cannons,
If only for an hour,
If only for two hours, *Kajaval,*
Although they come at night,
Although they come in the day,
Although they come at sundown,
Although they come at sunset.

Holy guardian of the earth,
Holy guardian of the sky,
Because we come on our knees,
Because we come bent over,
Accept this bouquet of flowers,
Accept this offering of leaves, *Kajaval.*
Accept this handful of incense,
Accept this offering of smoke,
That we come to offer at your feet,
That we come to offer to your hands,
Holy Father of sacred Chaklajun,
Holy Mother of sacred Chaklajun.

As the days passed and the Zapatistas never came, it seemed that the prayers had worked. . . .

EARLY JANUARY: THE EVANGELICALS' PRAYERS

The traditional officials and *j-iloletik* were not the only ones who were afraid during the siege of San Cristobal, however. The Chamula evangelicals—the *expulsados*—were also scared. Since they live in colonies on the outskirts of the city, it might even be true that at the beginning they were even more frightened than the traditionalists. But even later, when they saw that the Zapatistas meant them no harm, they continued praying because now they were afraid the national army was going kill them. Their prayers sound just the same as the traditionals, but if you listen to the words they say different things. Here's the prayer of the pastor of the colony *Paraiso*:

Our Lord Jesus Christ,
God, who is in Heaven,
Lord, we are your daughters,
We are your sons,
Look, Lord, at the thoughts of those who are invading,
Look at how they don't want the good you bring,
How they are coming with arms,
How they are coming with machetes,
But listen to our words, Eternal Father,
You alone decide what will be,
You alone prepare what will be.
We, Lord, without you can do nothing,
We, without you, are not complete.
Listen, Lord Jesus Christ,
You who accompany us on your path,
You who accompany us on our walk,
There is nothing we can do without you,
There is nothing we can start without you, Lord.
Look at us,
See us,
On your path,
On our trip, Lord.
We only ask your favor, Lord,
That they not come to hit us,
That they not come to fight us,
In our houses,
In our homes.
You, Father,
You, Lord,

Accept our thanks,
That what you say will be done,
That your children will do only what you have thought.
Look; Lord, pardon us,
That we do not know how to communicate with you more respectfully,
That we are not worthy to address you, Lord.
This is the only way we know,
Only like this,
In our own language,
With our heads bowed, Lord.
Hallelujah,
Hallelujah,
Hallelujah.

LATE JANUARY: TOWARD A FREE MARKET

For the first two weeks or so after the seizure of San Cristobal, not a single *kaxlan*[3] official showed his face in public, not a policeman, not a parking officer, not a collector of market fees. Not one. They disappeared! They were so terrified of the Zapatistas that they hid. But the moment they were sure the Zapatista Army was gone and wasn't coming back, Ha!, immediately the parking officers were back unscrewing license plates, the municipal police beating up drunks, and the market collectors chasing away poor women trying to sell tomatoes and lemons on street corners. With the Zapatistas gone, suddenly they were fearless again. But when the Zapatistas were here, they stayed in their bedrooms with the shades closed, quaking with fear. They couldn't even get it up with their wives they were so scared.

You see what that means? They were afraid of Indians—because that's what the Zapatistas were, Indians. When we other Indians realized that, we felt strong as well. Strong like the Zapatistas. The *kaxlanetik* of San Cristobal have always pushed us around just because we don't speak Spanish correctly. But now everything has begun to change.

One example of this is that in mid-January, when the *kaxlan* officials were all still hidden, the Indian charcoal sellers got together and formed the Organizacion Zapatista of Charcoal Sellers. Then, without asking anybody's permission, they moved from the vacant field where they had always been forced to sell in the past to the street right next to the main market. The thing is, *ak'al* [charcoal] is really dirty. Everything around it gets covered with black dust so the market officials had always kept it far away from the

---

[3]The word *kaxlan*, pronounced "kashlan," is a corruption of the Spanish *castellano*, "Castilian," and is the Tzotzil word for non-Indians.

part of the market frequented by "decent people" and tourists. With no one to stop them, however, the charcoal sellers came to be near everyone else.

But there are a lot of other Indians who have always been relegated to the edges of the market too. When these people saw that the charcoal sellers had changed their location without asking anyone's permission, they started coming around and asking if they could change as well. *Hijole!* Suddenly there were a couple of hundred people sitting in orderly rows selling vegetables and fruit and charcoal in what used to be the parking lot where rich people left their cars! The first day they gathered there, the leader of the charcoal sellers gave a speech. Brothers and sisters! he cried, Don't be afraid! There are too many of us selling here in this street now. Let all of those who have been forced to sell out of the backs of trucks, all of those who have been driven to the edges of the market, come sell right here in the center with us. Let them come and take a place here in these rows we have made and then we'll see if the *kaxlan* officials dare say anything! Only one thing to all of those who join us: I don't want to hear anyone talking about being afraid! If we remain united and firm, we have nothing to fear! All the Indian peddlers jumped to their feet. "We're with you!" they responded joyfully.

So every morning early all of these people came and formed themselves into neat rows and spread their goods out on the ground. But then the day finally came when the Market Administrator returned. Since he's the boss of the market and all the surrounding streets, he stomped up to the first charcoal seller he saw and demanded, Who gave you permission to sell here? No one had to give us permission because we belong to an organization. What fucking organization? Pick up all this shit and get the hell out of here before I lose my temper, the Administrator screamed, I don't want to hear another word from any of you assholes! Are you going to fucking obey or not? Mother of God! He seemed pretty mad. No, we're not going to move. We're poor and hung [humble] and we have to sell to eat, the Indian said stubbornly. Then the leader of the charcoal sellers spoke. "You sound brave now," he said evenly to the Administrator, "but when the Zapatistas were here you didn't say anything because you were hiding behind your wife's skirts. Not until now have you had the balls to talk. So who's the asshole? Maybe it would be better for you if you kept quiet, because if you run us off we're going to make sure the sub-comandante of the Zapatistas gets your name, and then we'll find out how much of a man you are. You might win today, but maybe you ought to think about what it's going to cost you in the long run."

Hijo! The Administrator had never been talked to like that by an Indian before! He started to tremble, who knows whether from fear or rage, and then he turned and fled without saying another word, taking all of his fee collectors with him.

And that's where things remain at the beginning of March. Thanks to the Zapatistas, the Indians are learning to stand up for themselves. . . .

Translation by Jan Rus of Marián Peres Tzu, *Indigenous Revolts* (Amsterdam: Grosnor & Ouweneel, Cedla, 1996), pp. 122–28.

⑥ 9 ⑥

Modern Stories, Fables, and Poems

*T*wo *forms dominate contemporary Maya written, as opposed to
redacted oral literature: poetry and fable. The provenance of the
fable in Maya literature is unclear. Although it is a common form in
the indigenous literature of North America, there are no fables per se
in the extant pre-Hispanic literature of Mayaland. The Popol Vuh
could be construed as a fable, but its form and content are far too
complex to be included in that category. It may be that fables existed
in pre-Hispanic and colonial Mayaland but were limited to the oral tradition; it is more likely that the form is a borrowing from North American and European work. In any event, Maya writers have adapted
with charm and wit to the form.*

*Miguel Angel May May, a professor of Maya and a very sophisticated
essayist as well as a fabulist, offers a tale of the jungle (p. 602) with a subtle moral. The moral of the fable of "The Little Bee" (p. 612), on the
other hand, is direct and affecting.*

*Many stories are now being redacted from the oral literature, but
fewer are as yet being written in Maya, although longer works, including novels, are being written in several indigenous Mesoamerican languages. One of the stories included here, "Butterflies of Four Colors" (p.
605), has something of the character of a fable. The other, "The Son Who
Came Back from the United States" (p. 604), is a comic story of the confusion of languages resulting from the globalization that has begun to affect Mesoamerican culture. A boy returns home from the United States
and addresses his parents in English. When he responds to a question
with "All right, yes," his parents, Maya speakers, interpret it as Spanish
for Ahorita, diez, meaning "Ten, now," and the confusion begins.*

*The great strength of contemporary work in Maya languages, how-
ever, has been in poetry. There is little doubt that the best of this work is
as sophisticated as any being produced in the world. The Yucatecan Bri-*

*ceida Cuevas Cob appears here with two poems. In one, "The Pitcher,"
a personified pitcher of water becomes a key to the sheer pleasure of existence of two lovers. The other is a selection from his best known work,
a series of poems about a dog. They are ironic, complex, yet made of ordinary language. While the form and style are clearly contemporary,
bearing witness to the poet's familiarity with the most sophisticated work
of other cultures, the foundation of the work is Mayan and utterly de-
pendent upon the subtleties of the Maya language. To translate such
work into English requires looking through the Spanish translation to
the original Maya, which is more successfully rendered into English
than Spanish.*

*The largest number of poems here, as well as a brief essay on the art
of writing entitled "At the Side of the Road," belong to Humberto Ak'a-
bal, who writes in Quiche Maya: brief, brilliant gems that resonate with
both personal and political experience. When Ak'abal speaks of buz-
zards, he is referring to military helicopters, and when he says that it is
better to carry a book than a gun, he is speaking about the overall political and educational situation for indigenous people in Guatemala.
But it is when he writes of the natural world that his work soars. In both
Ak'abal's work and that of Cuevas Cob, echoes of the Popol Vuh, the
Chilam Balam books, and the other great works of Maya literature can
be found.*

*Ak'abal, who translates his own work into Spanish, has been pub-
lished in many languages. He was born in 1952 in Momostenango, Totonicapan, Guatemala. The essayist Jorge Miguel Cocom Pech says that
"when Ak'abal writes poetry, he retrieves the music that underlies the language of both man and nature. More importantly, when he reads or re-
cites his poems, we feel that we are hearing the piccolo of a Vivaldi who
was not born in happy Italy, but in a land that unfortunately has suffered
the pain of military, economic and cultural repression, yet has resisted
the servitude imposed upon it by mestizos and foreigners." It is a notion
that applies to virtually all contemporary indigenous literature, but perhaps none more so than the work of Ak'abal.*

The Little Bird and the Monkey
by Miguel Angel May May

One day when the Monkey was going along in search of food in the forest,
he climbed a hill, and flushed a Little Bird that he found in its nest. Upon
seeing it, he stopped moving. And when he caught it in his hands he saw that
it was very thin, and he said:

"Aah, you are very little, you do not have much meat on you; in such a state you cannot provide me with anything, so what I'm going to do is to nourish you—so that when you are fattened up I will be able to eat you."

And that is what he did, he took him to his house to fatten him up.

When the day came to eat the Little Bird, he took him out of the cage. He was just about to put him in his mouth when the Little Bird asked:

"And . . . you are going to eat me?"

"Yes, why shouldn't I eat you? For this I raised you over a long time."

"Was there not a moment when it passed through your mind to ask why I was so thin when you found me?"

"No, not for a moment. Why do you ask?" said the Monkey, while he scratched his head.

"Did you not see that I had a very bad illness, and if you eat me you can catch it? Moreover, you must know that this sickness has no cure and that it kills in a very rapid manner." Seeing that this frightened him, the Little Bird went on speaking: "What is going to kill you is pure sadness, what you will see and what you will hear, this will cause you sadness and send you to weeping, and you will cry so much that you are going to become so thin you will die."

"Is what you are saying correct?" asked the Monkey, while swallowing his saliva.

"If you think I am tricking you, eat me, but you will only enjoy me for a little while, because it won't be long before you die."

The last thing said caused him to hesitate for a moment.

"Ay, ay," said the Little Bird, and fell over, "I am nauseated, I am going to die."

When the Monkey saw that the Little Bird had collapsed, he tossed him away, and at precisely that moment, the Little Bird began to fly. "Pok, pok, pok, pok, pok," he went.

"Son of the devil! You tricked me," said the angry Monkey.

While the Little Bird flew on, the Monkey followed him with his gaze and licked his chops, because he still had an appetite for the Little Bird.

One day a Tiger came to that place, and caught the Monkey, who spoke to him this way:

"No, don't eat me, because I have a very bad sickness and you could catch it."

Frances Ligorred Parramon, ed., *U Mayathanoob Ti Dzib/Las Voces de la Escritura* (Merida: Ediciones de la Universidad Autonoma de Yucatan, 1997), pp. 333, 335; English version, Sylvia and Earl Shorris.

The Son Who Came Back from the United States

A gentleman sent his son to study and work in the United States. He was a Maya who was sent there in order to help the family prosper. As the gentleman had money, he was able to send his son to work and study English.

And his son studied there. He came back home after six years.

When the boy came home, he asked his father, "What's to eat? What are you going to have?"

Well, they were going to eat eggs. And the son said, *"All right. Yes."*

"What is my son saying? Surely, he is saying that he is accustomed to eating ten eggs."[1]

And the father went to tell the boy's mother: "You have to cook ten eggs for my son, because he just told me *'awrait diez.'* " Later he went to tell his son that the ten eggs were ready.

And the son said again, "All right, yes."

"My God! you have to go buy another ten eggs," the father said to the mother of the boy who was accustomed to eating twenty eggs, the great glutton. "Since they have a lot of money in the United States, my son eats a lot. He wants to eat ten more eggs. You must get another ten eggs, because the boy said again, *'awrait diez.'* "

"Absolutely, absolutely," and the father was wondering if the twenty eggs were ready.

But the mother was getting angry with the boy [who had not eaten the first ten eggs]: "My son doesn't want to eat? What the devil! Let's keep the ten eggs. Tell the boy to come here so that I can talk to him."

The boy came, and his mother asked him if he was hungry or not and he said again, *"Awrait, diez,"* in English.

He was only pretending to be stupid; he did not want to speak in Maya, although he really speaks it.

The mother grabbed a stick to hit her son so that he would speak Maya. Then he spoke in Maya, and he did not go back to saying, *"Awrait, diez."*

"I know that you spoke Maya and Spanish very well when you left," she said. The mother understood that he only spoke English because he believed it showed that he comes from the United States.

Silvia Terán and Christian Rasmussen, eds., *Relatos del Centro del Mundo, Sixto Canul*, Instituto de Cultura del Estado de Yucatan, 1994; English version, Sylvia and Earl Shorris.

[1]"All right. Yes" is meant as a pun. Yes said with a Spanish/Maya accent sounds remarkably like *diez,* the number ten. "All right" can be understood as *Ahora,* or "Now," but could also be a pun for the Maya, "I say eat greedily."

Butterflies of Four Colors
by Feliciano Sánchez Chan

Once upon a time, a very rich man was buying and storing up great quantities of corn that were produced by the campesinos.

The day that the crop was lost in that place, he had his barns full, but when the people came to ask him if he would sell them a little corn, he always refused. He said that he was not keeping more than a little to feed his children. The truth was that he enjoyed watching the suffering of his neighbors and brothers: he refused to give a little corn even to his own mother for her daily sustenance.

One fine day, an old man dressed in white and carrying a cane arrived at his house, and said:

"Son, I only came to ask a favor of you, that you sell me a bushel of what you have kept; I am hungry and I have nothing to eat."

"Oh, little daddy," he answered, "my corn is just about used up. I have just kept a little bit for my own use."

"Even though it would be just a little, son," the old man repeated.

"Really, I have none, grandpa; if I did, why would I not have sold it?"

"It makes sense," the little old man said. "I was thinking that the five bushels that you have kept were full of corn but I see that there are only butterflies. So that takes care of me."

Having said that, the old man left. The greedy one smiled and said: "Your foolishness, old man."

Something provoked a kind of fear in him and he went running to look for the old man to tell him that he would sell him the corn he had asked for. Nevertheless, he could not find the old man anywhere. At the same time he said that he did not believe in curses and that it mattered little if the old man had uttered a curse. Much to his surprise, when he turned to look at the place where he had his baskets, thousands and thousands of butterflies, white, yellow, red and dark, were pouring out of them.

There were so many that in another moment they covered the surroundings with their shadows. The five baskets of corn that this greedy one was keeping were left empty. The grains of four colors had been changed into butterflies.

Sixto Sánchez Chan, Casa de los Escritores en Lenguas Indigenas. Spanish translation by the author; English version, Sylvia and Earl Shorris.

Seven Poems
by Humberto Ak'abal

STONES

It is not that the stones are mute:
they are only keeping silent.

ADVICE

Speak with anyone
so that you will not be taken for a mute,
my grandfather said to me.

And be careful that they
don't turn you into someone else.

EFFORT

The effort to forget
is also poetry.

NAVEL

The sun
is the navel of the day.

The moon,
that of the night.

FIREFLIES

The fireflies are stars
that come down from the sky,
and the stars are fireflies
that could not descend.

They turn their torches off and on
so that they will last the night.

WALKER

I walked all night
in search of my shadow.

It had become confused
in the darkness.

Utiwwwwww . . .
a coyote.

I walked on.

Tu tu tukuuuuuuurrr . . .
an owl.

I continued walking.

Sotz', sotz', sotz' . . .
a bat chewing the ear
of a little pig.

Until the break of dawn.

My shadow was so long
that it hid the road.

LEARNING

In these "spurts"
the urge to write comes upon me,
not because I know something, but
because doing and undoing
is how I learn this craft,
and in the end
something stays with me.

The knolls,
the hills,
the canyons,
the old villages
have bewitching secrets
and I wish to extract these

to transfer them
to sheets of paper.

I must treat this beautiful craft
like an avocation although it pains me,
because I cannot give it as much time as I would like.
(I must work at something else in order to survive.)
My verses are as wet as rain,
or the tears of the evening dew,
and it could not be otherwise,
because they have been taken from the mountain.

Humberto Ak'abal, *Tejedor de Palabras (Word Weaver)*(Guatemala: Fundación Carlos F. Novella, 1996). Spanish translation by the author; English version, Sylvia and Earl Shorris.

At the Side of the Road
by Humberto Ak'abal

It was a brilliant, sunny afternoon. I was coming from a great distance when I arrived at the edge of a canyon, where you could smell the fresh perfume of the grass. The ambience gave the impression of an afternoon after the rain. To cross to the other side I had to make a bridge out of two logs. I crossed the bridge. I felt thirsty. I began to dig a hole with my hands; while I was removing the earth I felt dampness, each time more dampness; then my hands brought up mud, and finally I gave the water its birth. The flow looked like a worm moving in the earth that had been removed. I let it alone. The turbid water began to clear; the mud was left in the bottom of the little well. I dipped my hands into the water, took it up, and drank.

This was a dream that I had when I was a child. Every time that I recall it, I feel the freshness of the water.

What is being told here?

Simply because I believe that this dream marked my life with poetry, or better said, it awoke the poetry in me.

To walk, to dig out, to hope, is the way I go about the writing of a poem. To look for the necessary word, to find the desired word. And these necessary words, desired words, to which I refer, are those used in daily life, common words. So when I need them I do not turn to dictionaries, but to the markets, the plazas, the streets.

This was the cause of my lameness: One day I stumbled over a stone; it spoke; at that moment I forgot my pain and moved closer to listen to it, but the stone said nothing more. As I left there I realized that everything has speech: the wrinkles in the face of my grandmother, the laughter of the sprinkling rain, the pallor of my dead father, the silence of my mother.

I began to record the teachings of my grandfather, the Maya K'iche priest. He taught me to read the storms, to gauge the wind with my fingertips, to interpret the song of the birds, to know the voice of fire and the behavior of animals.

I understood that poetry is the lightning that shatters the night of the poet; it does not last long but it is enough to advance a little on the road.

I do not pretend this to be a pattern or form, much less to represent anyone. I simply write at one side of the road; independently. I tell things as I feel them, as I live them, as I see them; freely. I carry poetry in my pockets, in my head or within my heart.

This is the case; when it wearies my heart because I sweeten it too much, it comes out and hammers my head, or it remains in my pockets annoying me. If I need a penny, in place of the money a poem comes out and a poem does not buy bread.

When I least expect it, it blocks my path on the road. I allow myself to be trapped and to let it choose the theme. And I discover that the themes do not come from outside but from inside. Seizing them produces this thing that is surely a combination of pain and happiness.

I am helped by reading, my environment, and the philosophy of my mother tongue, Maya K'iche'. Speaking this language taken from nature is like chewing cypress leaves: rough, sweet and simple.

And so, without a scheduled time, without a place or established space, I write. I do it on pages of paper, on pieces picked up off the streets, on bus tickets, or on any blank corner of a newspaper. These things add up; at times they make a book.

Once the text is written, I let it rest. When I return to find myself with it, I see that I have too many words, then I begin to undress it, until I leave it with the nakedness of a newborn. At other times the opposite happens to me; I make the idea come out and I must dress it, which is why I go on trying one and another, until finally I think that this is how it should be dressed. I do not always end up satisfied, I feel that something is lacking, and this dissatisfaction torments me.

In producing my poems, I make use of three resources. One is direct language; I lay out a picture. Another is metaphors and images. And when I feel that the words are not capable of giving form to what I want, I resort to onomatopoeia, the language that spewed out of my grandfathers; because this is a language that does not go to the senses but to the spirit, in its intention to translate natural sound to a piece of paper.

Walking this road has opened my eyes wider. My tongue notices more flavors, my sense of smell distinguishes more odors, my hearing has sharpened, and I can discern the beat of the butterfly's wings as it flies to the other side of the river; my touch has become so sensitive that when I say fire, I feel that I am burning. It is a flirtation with madness and at the same time the fear of believing that I am really mad.

Sadness pleases me; at times I wish that it could be eaten. Loneliness pleases me, because it is there that poetry is undressed, and I laugh. I do not seek pain, but those difficult moments give me strength.

I have also suffered crises and I have come to the point of hating this work; in one rabid seizure I wanted to say to hell with it all. And when I have wanted to flee from poetry she has caressed my heart. Then I realize that she is a necessity, like the air, like the water, like a tortilla made of corn.

All that is said is nothing new except for me, because in this insistent writing the person I want to find is myself. Poetry will always be in its proper place, disposed to speak in a dream or in sleeplessness. Poetry is the echo of the shadow of a bird that flies by at the edge of the afternoon. Finally, I write for myself. I laugh and cry and sometimes sing.

> I would like to be
> as simple as a tree.
> Or even something less,
> like a plank.

Humberto Ak'abal, *Tejedor de Palabras (Word-Weaver)* (Guatemala: Fundación Carlos F. Novella, 1996). Spanish translation by the author; English version, Sylvia and Earl Shorris.

BUZZARD
by Humberto Ak'abal

> Buzzard:
> box for the dead,
> grave on the wing,
> but you're not burdened
> with the names of the dead.

Unpublished poem translated from the Quiche by Dennis Tedlock. Tedlock said this poem refers to the U.S. helicopters that were used by the Guatemalan government against the Maya of Guatemala.

Two Poems by Briceida Cuevas Cob

THE PITCHER

The sun beats down.
It brings out the sweat on my brow.
The welcome freshness of the deep well caresses me.
The pitcher is with me,
it is my companion in fortune,
it smiles up at me.

It always laughs, even though it is thirsty.
It feels good to the touch.
I swing the rope, serpent-toy,
that wraps around my feet.
With her the pail of water comes up.
I give the pitcher a drink.
It sings a cheerful song as it drinks.
Its song is the flight of a black and white bird k'au.
The pitcher is no longer thirsty.
With pleasure I put my arm around its neck,
I embrace it,
although it is very forward of me.

Its ear tickles my belly,
and my ribs, too.
Gratefully it spits in my hand.
It refreshes the earth where I walk.
Its mischief never ends.
Nor does the tickling of my belly and my ribs
with its ears.
Perhaps it did not see
that I carried the pail in my left hand,
that I have a rope on my shoulder?
Perhaps it does not think
that just as it makes me laugh,
it could also cause me to let go of it
and that it would break?
It does not see anything,
nor does it think;

it is dedicated only to making me laugh.
I do not see anything,
nor do I think,
I only enjoy belly laughs with it.

THE DOG LAMENTS HIS EXISTENCE

PART VI

Who offers the hard tortilla with his left hand and then raises his right
hand to deliver a blow?

Dog that does not abandon his owner,
dog that bites his master,
dog that loves his love:
lend your tongue to the man
so that he also drools,
wets the earth,
and like you, cultivates the understanding of existence.
Lend your eyes to the man
so that he can see with your sadness.
Lend your tail to the man
so that he can wag it with your joy
when they call KS, KS, KS;
so that he can keep it between his legs with your shame
when they say B'J, B'J, B'J;
lend him your nose
so that he can sniff the goodness that exists only in the hands of the
    child.
Finally,
lend him your fangs
so that he can take a bite of consciousness.

Briceida Cuevas Cob, *Cuadernos de la Casa Internacional del Escritor,* no. 17, el Instituto
Quintannarroense de la Cultura, Quintana Roo. Spanish translation by the author; English
version, Sylvia and Earl Shorris.

The Little Bee (a fable)

Once upon a time, a little bee fell into a puddle of water and began to sink.
At that moment a little bird flew over, and upon seeing that the bee was sink-

ing, the bird went in search of a leaf, which he took in his beak and brought to the bee.

Seeing the leaf at his side, the little bee climbed up on it. And so his wings dried, he was able to fly, and off he went.

Another day, the little bee was flying among the flowers, looking for honey to suck, when he saw a boy with a slingshot who was about to shoot the very bird that had saved the little bee. But the little bee flew at the boy, and stung him on the hand. The boy dropped the slingshot, and ran off crying.

Said the little bee: One good turn deserves another, even if it means one must die.

Barbara Pfeiler, Yucatecan Maya fable; English translation, Sylvia and Earl Shorris.

Book III

Other Mesoamerican Literatures

Nahuatl, a lingua franca through which Mesoamericans could communicate between language groups, as happens today with Spanish, was a language of great contrasts. Beside its several dialectic variants, there was the extremely polite form, proper to nobles, with its subtle system of honorifics, and the other, simpler form, used by ordinary people.

There were (and remain) thirty different Maya languages still spoken in the Mexican states of Yucatan, Quintana Roo, Campeche, Tabasco, and Chiapas, as well as in Guatemala, Belize, Honduras, and parts of El Salvador. Mayan languages—not dialects—are as different one from the other as Spanish, Portuguese, Catalonian, Italian, and French.

But the Mesoamerican linguistic mosaic is considerably larger than these two groups. In the state of Oaxaca, sixteen different languages are spoken today, and in central Mexico, besides Nahuatl, one can hear people speaking in Otomi, Mazatec, Mazahua, Matlatzinca; a few hundred miles to the west, Tlapanec, Tarascan; and to the east, Totonac, Tepehua, and Huaxtec.

How, when, and why did such a proliferation of languages develop?

A branch of linguistics, glotochronology, has sought the answer, going back as far as possible in time (perhaps 300,000 years) to when languages belonging to one family began to differentiate.

It is a fact that Mesoamerica was, and continues to be, a linguistic paradise, or if you prefer, a Babel, for there are so many languages and consequently so many expressions of these languages. No matter what language they speak, people compose songs and poems, tell stories, deliver discourses, utter proverbs, and say their prayers.

This third part of the anthology has to do with Mesoamerican literary production in languages other than Nahuatl or the branches of the Mayan linguistic family. From among the many languages we have chosen a few that give testimony to the creativity of six well-known indigenous groups: Mixtec, Mazatec, Zapotec, Otomi, Purepecha, and Tlapanec. We begin with Otomi literature, the work of a people who have lived for thousands of years side by side with the Nahuas without being absorbed by them.

The Otomis actually witnessed the collapse of the Teotihuacans, as well as that of the Toltecs and the Mexicas. They also saw how Spanish rule came to an end. Their own endurance and sense of humor led some Otomis to ask of modern Mexicans: Who is next?

At the moment there are some 300,000 Otomis. Although many of them live in extreme poverty, they still know how to smile and to celebrate their feasts in an atmosphere of great happiness. In section IV, a short story, three erotic songs, and a poem of a philosophical nature give testimony to their wit, wisdom, and creativity.

The Purepechas—or Tarascans, as they are also known—live in the state of Michoacan and enjoy a reputation as skilled artists and courageous people. They were never conquered by the bellicose Mexica. Today, they remain proud of their own cultural identity and the fact that some 100,000 of them continue to speak their language. Strangely enough, linguists have not been able to relate Tarascan, as with Basque in Europe, to any other language in the world.

Why the Tarascans did not come to the aid of the Mexica, who asked for their help during the Spanish invasion, is told in a narrative included here (p. 641) taken from the *Relación de Michoacán,* redacted in Roman letters around 1540. Contemporary oral tradition provides a text in a different mood (p. 644), one dealing with flowers as part of the cult of the dead.

Oaxca, where (as we have said) a kind of linguistic paradise exists, has been the site of the development of sophisticated cultures by the Zapotec, Mixtec, and Mazatec, among others. The earliest known testimony to Mesoamerican writing come from the Zapotecs. In what is now the archeological center of Monte Alban, many stelae have been discovered bearing inscriptions dated around 600 B.C. From there, these great artists influenced much of the culture of Mesoamerica. Their contemporary descendants, numbering some 400,00, keep alive their tradition as well as their language, which is spoken in several variants. Literary creativity has been a constant throughout their history, manifested first in the early inscriptions, in works produced during the colonial epoch, and today in both oral and written form. The three in section III encompass as many literary genres: a short story, a discourse recalling the *huehuetlahtolli* of the Nahuas, and a modern poem in defense of the Zapotec language; and three poems by the teacher, author of short stories and essays as well as poems, Mario Molina Cruz of Yalalag, Villa Hidalgo, in the northern sierra of Oaxaca.

The Mazatecs of northeastern Oaxaca, although less numerous than the Zapotecs, have also managed to maintain faith in their destiny as a people. They are famous for their ceremonies related to hallucinogenic mushrooms, which have attracted the attention of many foreigners as well as Mexicans.

We include five poems from a contemporary Mazatec poet who enjoys a great reputation, Juan Gregorio Regino. One of his poems is about the famous María Sabina and her mushroom chants; a portion of one of the chants is also given here.

As to the Mixtecs, they now live not only in their original Oaxacan homeland but also in suburbs of Mexico City, Los Angeles, and other parts of the United States and Mexico. Besides their contemporary literary compositions— songs, poems, and various forms of narrative, as well as work from the colonial period—a good many ancient codices, genealogical and historical, have been preserved. Five of them, housed in libraries in Mexico and Europe, are of pre-Hispanic origin; several others, scattered among various repositories, including some in the United States, were produced shortly after the Spanish invasion.

The final poem is by Abad Carrasco Zúñiga from the state of Guerrero on the west coast of Mexico. The Tlapanecos, who live largely in the mountainous areas of the state, speak a language that linguists now say belongs to the Mayan group. When Carrasco says, "The word shall always bloom," meaning the indigenous languages will survive, he has evidence to support his contention. There are now almost 100,000 speakers of Tlapaneco, and their number has been growing steadily since the 1970s.

◎ 1 ◎

Mixtec

*T*he Mixtec Creation Myth opens this part of the anthology. It is a
modern account, which sounds like a "reading" (provided independently by two illiterate Mixtecs from the towns of San Juan and
Santa Crux Mixtepec, Oaxaca, in 1976) of material presented pictorially and with glyphs in the pages of two ancient codices. One is known
as the Vindobonensis, *because it is housed at the National Library in Vienna. The other is the* Selden, *after Bishop John Selden, who donated
it to the Bodleian Library at Oxford University. Such accounts, closely
related to the content of two codices obviously unknown to those Mixtec "readers," demonstrates among other things the vitality of Mesoamerican culture. In this case, a tradition kept alive in both the codices and
the modern oral testimony across the centuries brings to light the story
of the birth of the Mixtec nation.*

The Mixtec Creation Myth

In the beginning, before there were days and years, when the world was dark
and everything in it was in chaos and confusion, the land was covered with
water, and the face of the earth was covered with only mud and slime. At that
time there appeared a god named One Deer, who was also known as Lion
Serpent, and a very beautiful goddess named One Deer, who was also known
as Jaguar Serpent.

As soon as these two gods appeared in human form, omnipotent and
wise, they made a huge mass of rock on which they skillfully built a very
sumptuous palace for their seat and dwelling on earth. At the highest point
of their house was a copper axe, the blade turned upward under the sky.

The rock and the palace were on a high hill, near the village of Apoala in the province of Mixteca Alta. This rock was called Place Where the Heavens Were. It was a paradise for the gods and they spent many centuries in repose and contentment there, while the rest of the world was in darkness.

These two gods, father and mother of all the gods, had two very handsome sons who were prudent and wise in all the arts. The first was named Nine Serpent Wind, after the name of the day on which he was born. The second was named Nine Caverns Wind, after the day of his birth. These two children were raised in great luxury. The older, when he wanted to amuse himself, would turn into an eagle, and soar to the heights. The other turned himself into a small animal, in the form of a winged serpent, and flew through the air with such agility and craft that he could enter into boulders and walls and make himself invisible. The noise they made was heard by those below. They took these forms to show that they had the power to transform themselves.

While enjoying the tranquility of living in their parents' house, these two brothers agreed to make an offering and a sacrifice to their parents the gods, so they took a clay incense burner with some live coals in it and threw some ground tobacco on it. This was the first offering made in the world.

Then the two brothers a made a garden for their enjoyment, in which they planted many flowering trees, fruit-bearing trees, roses, and many fragrant herbs and spices. They amused themselves in the garden almost every day, and next to it they made a very beautiful field with everything they needed for all the offerings and sacrifices they would make for their parents. After the brothers left their parents' house, they lived in the garden, taking care to water the trees and plants and making offerings of ground tobacco. They also made prayers, vows, and promises to their parents, and asked if by virtue of the sacrifices and offerings they had made their parents might create the earth, form the waters and the sky, and bring light into the world, since they had no place to rest but in their small garden. And in order to oblige their parents more to do what they asked, they pierced their ears with stone lancets and let a few drops of blood. They did the same with their tongues, and the blood was scattered in the branches of the trees and plants with a willow wand. Busying themselves this way, they waited for those things they had asked for, all the while showing their submission to their parents the gods and attributing to them far greater power and divinity than they had themselves.

Later, there was a great flood, in which many gods were drowned. After the flood, the god called Creator of All Things began the creation of the heavens and earth. The human race was restored, and this is how the Mixtec kingdom was populated.

Roberta H. and Peter T. Markman, *The Flayed God* (San Francisco: HarperCollins, 1992), pp. 149–51. Translation from the Spanish version by Scott Mahler.

↺ 2 ↻

Mazatec

*T*he sierra of northern Oaxaca is home to more than 150,000 Mazatecs, and in recent years it has attracted many visitors, some of
whom came because of María Sabina (1898–1985), who lived in the village of Huauhtla de Jimenez. She knew better than anyone the traditions, rituals, and forms of consuming the hallucinogenic mushroom,
teonanacatl—"flesh of the gods" (Psylocibe mexicana).

However, many Mazatecs as well as others who are not native to the
region realize that their land is noted for its literature as well as its hallucinogenic mushrooms.

The literature is brilliantly represented here by the Mazatec Juan
Gregorio Regino, who was born in 1962 in Chichicazapan Soyaltepec,
Oaxaca. Although he is still a young man, he has written extensively in
both Mazateco and Spanish, producing several books of poetry and many
articles, in addition to serving as president of the Casa de los Escritores
en Lenguas Indigenas. He is best known for his book of poems, No es
eterna la muerte (Death Is Not Forever). Three gems from that book are
included here. One is deeply ironic; a second carries the title of the
book; and the third is a poem to María Sabina.

She is described by Juan Gregorio as a flower, incantation and wisdom, the soul of the sierra. Here, she herself manages to answer him, and
us. One of her chants, recorded years ago by R. Gordon Wasson, conveys
the words of wisdom and wonder that accompany her multicolored visions.

In this chant, María Sabina uses hallucinogenic mushrooms and
aguardiente to cure a boy of a malady that may be dropsy. There are several sustained chants during the ceremony. In the one given below, the
reader should be aware that the Jesus Christ of whom she speaks is a syncretic deity, part Jesus, part Quetzalcoatl. Wasson speculates on the word
"clown" as used by María Sabina: ". . . the mushrooms are equated with

*Jesus Christ only in post-Columbian times [but] the clowns must go
back far indeed. Some of the 'mushroom stones' may represent clowns on
the stipe. Clowns play a role in most Indian fiestas and in the palo
volador performance. What was that role precisely? Does the clown
mean the same thing to the Mesoamerican Indian and to a European?"*

Chant by María Sabina

Clock woman am I, yes, yes, Jesus Christ says,
Woman who was born thus am I and quick woman am I
Woman above am I, yes, Jesus Christ says,
Woman general am I, yes, Jesus Christ says,
Saint woman am I,
Woman of clean spirit am I,
Woman of good spirit am I, [he] says,
I merely throw here and there, I merely scatter, [the mushroom] says,
I merely throw here and there, I merely scatter all that is dirty, all that
   is useless,
[the mushroom] says,
I give account to him who is my chief, [the mushroom] says,
Woman who was born thus am I, [the mushroom] says,
And woman who came into the world thus am I, [the mushroom] says,
Yes, Jesus Christ says, woman, Jesus Christ says,
Yes, Jesus Christ says, [so]
Woman drummer am I, he says,
Woman musician am I, he says,
Yes, Jesus Christ says,
Woman who thunders am I, he says,
Woman who uproots am I, he says,
Woman doctor am I, he says,
Yes, Jesus Christ says,
Woman of the principal star am I, he says,
Woman of the Star of the [Southern] Cross am I, he says,
No one will frighten us, he says,
No one will be two-faced to us, he says, yes, Jesus Christ says,
I throw about and scatter, he says, yes, Jesus Christ says,
Woman of the clock am I, he says, eagle woman am I, he says,
Yes, Jesus Christ says. . . . [four times]
I merely throw about, I merely scatter, he says, yes, Jesus Christ says,
Woman general am I, he says, yes, Jesus Christ says,
Woman musician am I, he says,
Woman drummer am I, he says, yes, Jesus Christ says,

Woman [male] saint am I, he says, woman [female] saint am I, he says,
Spirit woman am I, he says, illuminated woman am I, he says,
Woman of the day am I, he says, yes, Jesus Christ says,
I am going to the sky, he says,
And I am going even into your presence, even into your glory,
No one will frighten me, he says,
Woman who is *than more* human am I, he says,[1]
Lawyer woman am I, he says,
Woman of affairs am I, he says, yes, Jesus Christ says,
Yes, Jesus says, I only throw about, I only scatter, he says,
Woman of Puebla am I, he says,
Woman with "balls" am I, he says,
Important eagle woman am I, he says,
Clock woman am I, he says,
I am going to show my valor, he says, I am going to show my valor, he
    says,
Even before your eyesight, your glory, he says, (woman who waits am I,
    he says,)
When I shall show my valor, he says,
I am a woman who is *than more* human, he says,
Yes Jesus Christ says, yes Jesus says,
No one frightens me, he says,
No one is two-faced to me, he says,
Yes Jesus says, yes Jesus says,
Music woman am I, he says,
And drummer woman am I, he says,
Woman violinist am I, he says,
Yes, Jesus Christ says,
Woman of the principal star am I, he says,
Woman of the star of God am I, he says,
Woman of the star of the [Southern] Cross, he says,
Launch [canoe] woman am I, he says, yes, Jesus Christ says,
Woman chief of the "clowns" am I, he says, yes Jesus Christ says,
No one frightens me, he says, no one is two-faced to me, he says,
Woman who is *than more* human am I, he says,
Lawyer woman am I, he says,
And I am going to the sky, he says, yes Jesus Christ says,

[1]The urge here is to repair the text to read "more than human." However, Wasson has hewed to the Mazatec language, deliberately avoiding the idea that the chanter is claiming to be "super" human. A Harvard-educated acquaintance of the editors who entered into the mushroom experience with María Sabina described it as a religious experience, not strange or frightening.

Woman [male] saint am I, he says,
I am going to burn the world, he says, yes Jesus Christ says,
I am going to burn the world, he says, yes Jesus Christ says,
Woman of shooting stars am I, he says,
And Saint Peter woman am I, he says,
Whirling woman of the whirlwind am I, he says,
Woman of a sacred, enchanted lace am I, he says, yes Jesus Christ says,
Woman [male] saint am I, he says, spirit woman am I, he says,
Illuminated woman am I, he says, yes Jesus says,
I am going to burn the world, he says, yes Jesus Christ says,
Woman of "balls" am I, he says,
No one frightens me, he says,
No one is two-faced to me, he says,
I'm not surprised, he says, I'm not frightened, he says,
I give account to the judge, he says, I give account to the government,
  he says,
And I give account to my bishop, he says,
The good, clean bishop, he says, the good, clean nun, he says,
Yes Jesus Christ says, yes Jesus says,
Yes Jesus says, yes Jesus Christ says,
I throw about, I scatter, he says,
Yes Jesus Christ says, yes I am going to spread out in the main trail
  [Royal Road], he says
Only ounces, only pounds, he says, yes Jesus Christ says,
Woman who thus was born no less am I, he says, woman who thus
  came into the world no less am I, he says,
Woman of "balls" am I, he says, clock woman am I, he says,
Yes Jesus says, I am going to burn the world, he says,
Saint Peter woman am I, he says, whirling woman of the whirlwind am
  I, he says,
Woman of a sacred enchanted lace am I, he says, yes Jesus Christ says,
Woman of the hunting dog am I, he says,
Wolf woman am I, he says,
Woman who thunders am I, he says, yes Jesus Christ says,
No one frightens me, he says,
No one is two-faced to me, he says,
Yes, Jesus Christ says,
Yes, I am going to throw [it] away there, he says,
Yes, I am going to put it out to dry there, he says,
Only ounces, only pounds, he says, yes, Jesus Christ says,
Woman [male] saint am I, he says, woman who came to the world thus
  am I, he says,

Woman who thunders am I, he says, yes Jesus Christ says, yes Jesus
    Christ says,
Woman [male] saint am I, he says, spirit woman am I, he says,
Yes, Jesus says, there is still God, he says,
There are still saints, he says, there is still God, he says,
Yes Jesus Christ says, I am going to burn the world, he says,
Yes Jesus Christ says, I am a woman who waits, he says,
Yes, Jesus Christ says, Saint Peter says,
I am going to accuse everything he says, yes Jesus says,
Yes Jesus Christ says,
Isn't that so now?

R. Gordon Wasson, George and Florence Cowan, and Willard Rhodes, *María Sabina and Her Mazatec Mushroom Velada* (New York: Harcourt Brace Jovanovich, 1975), pp. 113–21 (1/2 of each odd-numbered page).

Five Poems by Juan Gregorio Regino

DON JUAN'S WOMEN

Don Juan has three women,
three good women.

One is the oldest,
and she is the head woman.
She starts the day,
ending the night,
sending sleep away.
She is the tempo,
and the guide.
She is the wise counsellor.
She is the loyal ambassador
of the loves of don Juan.

The second is the middle one;
her bosom is an inexhaustible fount of love.
She suckles a child of the others
as lovingly as her own.
She is the tortilla woman.
She is the pozol woman.
She is the metate woman.

The third is the youngest,
the one who speaks and sings like a girl.
She is the woman of brilliant ribbons.
She is the woman of party dresses.
She is the woman of jewelled necklaces.
She is the woman chosen
to keep vigil over the body of don Juan.

DEATH IS NOT FOREVER

Dear souls descended from heaven,
death is not forever.
I feel your presence here
in the imperfect world,
where we who have life
are dead
and those who are dead
have life.

We live one day of celebration,
in a momentary escape from death,
in a momentary engagement with life.

Living souls.
Dead souls.
They share our table,
they eat and drink our fruits;
later, we dance with death
hidden behind every mask.

This is our celebration,
our worlds appear together
for an instant.
We have heart,
and so do you.
In this life that is not forever.
In this death that is not forever.

TO MARÍA SABINA

María Sabina:
Soul of the mountain range.
Goddess of the five guardians.
Your spirit soars
in the impenetrable mountains,
in the mountains you soothed
with your wise woman's chants.
Principal woman.
Power of thunder woman.
Guiding woman.
Woman of the muleteer's path.
I speak to you in the language of the wind,
because it is necessary for you to know,
because you must know
that the hill has fallen mute,
the orphan has forsaken the seed,
and the flower withers.
Yes, that flower,
heritage of your ancestors,
muse, poetry,
wisdom, song.
That flower, lucid as your soul,
pure as your spirit,
wise as your talents,
proud as your people.
The one that goes now
in the naked sky.
In the wild current
of distant seas.
That one invokes your spirit,
your speech, your word,
your song, and your name.
Savant María Sabina!

THE SONG OF THE SNAILS

As if they were amused by the brilliance of the sky,
the snails daily sing;
they are the voices of the roots of antiquity.
They are the senses of twilight,

of the sea breeze, the murmuring air,
the dew that comes with the dawn.
They are living languages,
memories of the morrow,
evocations of spirit,
solo guitars, solo violins.
In the colors of our language
there is blood and rootedness.
The sun gives it warmth, the earth makes it fertile,
the wind caresses it, oppression gives it strength.
In the peace and silence of the universe
our language rules.

TWENTY DAYS

We held back our love for twenty days.
Twenty days of peace to begin the purification.
We held back our sex on the petate
to console ourselves and so to delay our life
for the journey to the future.
We held back our restlessness of the dawn,
in the night we made speeches that sent it away
so that nothing might enter or leave the house,
not even the breath of smoke
or the breeze that slaps the wind.
We kill our sensuality with incense,
deterring the passion that consumes us,
because sensuality is a fire that burns.
In this way we reprove our weak flesh
so that our soul may soar and come to a place
without limits or endless depths.
We alone know the door there,
as if it were our house.
Only those who are part of the world
may enter there,
only those who are careful,
who fill the universe with light;
those who can sustain a vigil for twenty days,
during the menstruation of the moon.

Juan Gregorio Regino, *No es eterna la muerte* (Mexico City: Consejo Nacional para la Cultura y las Artes, 1992), pp. 11, 17, 19. Spanish translation by the author; English version, Sylvia and Earl Shorris.

⑥ 3 ⑥

Zapotec

*A*long with the Maya and Nahuatl cultures, the one created by the
Zapotecs stands out in Mesoamerica for its great achievements.
They created the first Mesoamerican written testimonies, including cal-
endric records. Anyone who looks at the great archeological sites scat-
tered across the sierras, valleys, and Pacific Coast of Oaxaca cannot help
but be impressed by the past grandeur of the Zapotecs.

Their literature is represented here by a legendary story about a Za-
potec princess who married a Mexica huey tlahtoani; *a traditional wed-*
ding blessing; and a poem by a contemporary Zapotec author, Gabriel
López Chiñas. The poem can be taken as both the expression of desire
and a prophecy. Answering those who pessimistically anticipate the death
of the Zapotec language, López Chiñas says that yes, their language will
die—"on the day of the death of the Sun."

1. A Historical Legend

First Part

K–sixwɛsa had his palace in the pueblo of Zaachila in a cave. There was a
road by which to reach [this] place where the magician lived. Indeed the older
people said that K–sixwɛsa used to go to Mexico in a cloud. He used to go
thus to get to that place and [once] when he had almost reached there he saw
a beautiful woman bathing in a lagoon.

Then he descended from the cloud and made obeisance to the woman.
K–sixwɛsa did not know what to do that time, for those of the pueblo of Zaachila had begun[?]. He was inflamed in his heart with ardent love. Then

K–sixwɛsa said to the young woman, "What are you doing here, young woman?" then the young woman said that she went there every morning to bathe because she had dreamt seven months before that at this place she was going to meet the one who was going to be her husband. Nothing else would the animal tell [except] that here a king of the Zapotecs would come. This was what this young woman said to K–sixwɛsa.

Then K–sixwɛsa began to speak to the young woman. She said to K–sixwɛsa that her father was the ruler of Mexico. That was what the young woman said to K–sixwɛsa. That man [K–sixwɛsa] said to the daughter of the king that he was the king of the people of Zaachila. K–sixwɛsa told the young woman that he loved her. Then the young woman said to him that if he wished marriage with the young woman [i.e., with her] he should go to see her father. Then they conversed about two hours. Then the young woman said to K–sixwɛsa, "Bathe me!" Then K–sixwɛsa said to the young woman, "But if your father should come I should not wish him to punish you." And the young woman said to him, "Don't be afraid, for if my father should come I would tell him that I love you."

Then K–sixwɛsa took courage to stay in that lagoon and the two of them at that hour pledged their love for each other. Then the young woman put some scented soap on a piece of cloth and put this soaped cloth in a red receptacle. Then K–sixwɛsa bathed the beautiful young woman. When K–sixwɛsa finished the bath, she bathed K–sixwɛsa. Then they embraced, they embraced, the lovers, kissed each other, and swore ardent love.

Second Part

Then the queen told K–sixwɛsa that her father wanted to make himself king of Zaachila or king of the Zapotecs. This is what the queen said to her husband. Then they got ready the four hundred families or so who were in Tehuantepec, which was the limit [of the kingdom]. When the father of the queen heard about this, and that the troops of the people of Zaachila were in Tehuantepec, then he ordered out his troops and soon an army was brought together in order to wage war against the people of Zaachila at Tehuantepec. It took about three days for the troops [those of Mexico] to get together. Then they started out in the direction of Tehuantepec. Then the king of Mexico said to the one who was at the head of his troops, "You know, you are to take K–sixwɛsa a prisoner, if he is in Tehuantepec." That is what he said to the person who commanded his soldiers.

When this man [Awis–1] arrived at Tehuantepec the king of the Zapotecs was ready to carry on the war. The soldiers of Mexico had just about come to the place where their enemy was. Then [suddenly] fear began to attack them. They were not able to march to the place where their enemy was.

They did not even engage in a single battle. Then they turned their backs to the enemy, and many poor fellows perished on the road because they had taken with them very little to eat. They had to cross high mountains full of nothing but lions and tigers. These animals ate many of them. As a result those who finally reached the king were few in number. He who commanded the troops did not reach Mexico, for he stumbled over a stone on the road and broke his foot. His king began to get sad and angry because he had not won the war. He was sad because many of his people had perished. K–sixwɛsa, on his part, was joyful because his people had won.

Paul Radin, *An Historical Legend of the Zapotecs* (Stanford, CA: University of California Press, 1935), pp. 1–26, 123–38.

2. Blessing of the Wedding Couple

In the dark of night, the breezes whisper: This is life's most intense moment for the young. Our beloved divine Mother celebrates this occasion, anointing this couple. She arrived with her face uplifted, saying: Ah! Then search now for the shining face! Ah! Then search for clarity, guided by reason and longing for heaven. Thus you come to the house of God. . . .

Then the sacred face appeared there, the clear, distinct face from the heart of the time. Then the different, but also clear eyes of the other road (bachelor to married man) also appeared.

Approaching the heart of the bosom of the family with my patriarchal character seems to create anticipation of another moment; may it be transported across a wider land; may it hide the night, although that is only one responsibility of the soul. Because it now sounds the choral music of our ancestors and fills us with the holiness of successfully embarking upon this new and clear road. Because the moment has come when, during the uniting of this pair, the Religion of the Holy Mother truly enters the hearts of the relatives gathered here.

Having come to this state of matrimony, they find the extraordinary face of the holy truth, because she comes from God and from Most Holy Mary, for they alone permit life, breath, hope and tenderness in the bosom of the family. Therefore, I implore God whom I adore, that this place, in which the linking petate has been spread out for this pure young virgin, should be considered holy.

Ah! then I arrived at the appointed hour, I came as chief of the land, representing the ancient saint, for whom you and she, united forever, will produce flowers, until old age sends to you heaven.

Listen to my words, storehouse of flowers, sweet storehouse with which I have asked for happiness for you. . . .

Ah! this joining that I carry out is sacrosanct; it is the knot glorified by the Archangel Saint Gabriel and it is finally here, where it comes to be truly recognized by the godfather, the godmother, the family, the parents, the forbears imbued with the divine words. Accordingly, in this very moment, I bless you (the bride and groom) and all of you (those in attendance), as well.

Gilberto Orozco, "Tradiciones y Leyendas del Istmo de Tehuantepec Zapotec," *Revista Musical Mexicana* (1946), pp. 98–99; English version by Sylvia and Earl Shorris.

3. Zapoteco

by Gabriel López Chiñas

They say that Zapoteco is on its way out,
No one will speak it;
It has died, they say,

The language of the Zapotecans.
The language of the Zapotecans
Will go to the devil,
Now that the cultured Zapotecans
Speak only Spanish.

Ay! Zapoteco, Zapoteco,
Those who despise you
Do not know how much
Your mothers loved you.

Ay! Zapoteco, Zapoteco,
Language that gives me life,
You shall die, I know,
On the day of the death of the sun.

Victor de la Cruz, ed., *La Flor de la Palabra* (Mexico City: UNAM and CIESAS, 1999), p. 69; English version, Sylvia and Earl Shorris.

4. Three Poems by Mario Molina Cruz

THE EARTH

You opened your womb,
and I came out of the darkness.
I experienced the light, the air;
I saw the grandeur of the sky,
its lullaby to the earth.
When I crawled, you stayed with me,
and so. . . .
little by little I learned to step on you.
Tirelessly, after every clumsy fall
you picked me up,
to every demand of my being
you changed your season;
in your hands, over time,
I found the rules of life.

Now, grown up. . . .
I do nothing but defile you,
bury you under concrete
or look at you from my terrace.

Every day I damage you,
putting off my own end;
but everyone knows:
that when the goodness of the mother is over,
you open your womb again,
and we are given back to the void.

THE GRINDER

You awaken
and I find you washing the metate,
while the blue smoke tickles the tiles,
revealing the red heart of the oak.
At the same time,
your naked knees rest upon
the husks of sugar cane.

The back and forth of the pestle
is heard
and now and then the cornmeal applauds.
The smell of the hot tortilla
calls,
the coffeepot
perfumes the new day,
the fire whistles . . . crackles,
a song that gives life to the stove.
Meanwhile . . . in silent satisfaction
I contemplate you.
I return to my house
before dawn
and again I find you
on your knees,
your noble strength upon the stone
rhythm driven
then. . . .
my eyes bathe you in affection.
Later,
when darkness takes over the village
and the fire is dying,
when only broken silhouettes are painted,
I come near you,
I lift up your metate,
and when I touch your dark knees
as rough as my hands
I feel that the embers have entered me.

LA NIÑA LIBERTAD
                         —to Chiapas

The volcanoes of the south roared
and the jungles understood the pain,
the overflowing silence;
the pitiful hour was announced,
irrepressible as any birth.

Chiapas the manger,
cradle of the little girl Liberty.
At her side hope revives,

while an old century
hurries toward death.

The inheritors of the great rock,
for centuries marginalized,
tired of eating roots,
of clamoring to a deaf god,
spewed out their righteous anger.

Little girl Liberty,
whom the huts adore,
was born;
men, women, and children
began the ritual,
the pilgrimage was put down
and the jungle burned.

The girl lives,
she will be a woman,
she speaks the only language
that the continents understand.

Mario Molina Cruz, *Volcán de Pétalos* (*Eruption of Petals*) (Mexico City: Dirección General de Culturas Populares, 1996). Spanish translation by the author; English version, Sylvia and Earl Shorris.

☙ 4 ❧

Otomi

*T*he Mexican Revolution of 1910–17, which so profoundly affected
the country, has been told in many forms. Historians and novelists,
both Mexican and foreign, have written about it. Painters as famous as
Diego Rivera and David Alfaro Siqueiros have covered the walls of
palaces, schools, and a great many other public buildings with murals
portraying some of its most dramatic episodes as well as some of its fail-
ures. But few people imagined that there were indigenous people who
left their own records of that social and military convulsion, which also
altered their lives. The first excerpt gives the words of the Otomi Ernesto
Pérez Francisco, from the town of San Antonio el Grande Huehuetla in
the state of Hidalgo, telling the stories his father used to repeat about
what happened in his home town during those years. His brief, dramatic
account is a fine example of what is now known as "oral history."

Poets abound among the Otomis, and they often sing their own compositions. Several examples follow. They combine humor with a marvelous mental acuity. One might say of some that they are erotic, while
others are concerned with philosophical questions.

In the Revolution of 1910

The war was thirty-two years ago. The people suffered greatly. All the poor,
men or women, suffered greatly. In those days many people died, many were
lost.

There was one man who was the chief of one group and another man who
was chief of the other. Everyone followed a different leader. Neither of them
knew when the hour would come to attack his enemy.

One day, during the war, there was a festival. The priest came to say mass.
And that night there was a great disgrace. Seven men died during the fiesta.

At dawn the priest told them: You have done something very bad. In truth, you are very evil. You treated these poor persons that were shot here as if they were not people.

The chief answered: You do not know what happened here in the village. But I do know what we brought. If in truth you came to make a feast day, say the mass and have done with it.

The bodies of the dead, the ones who were shot, were there. They did not want anyone to bury them. They said that the dogs and the vultures (the birds of prey) should eat them. But the priest decided that the poor dead ones must be buried. Although they did not have anything to bury them in, they did not have a box to put them in, they wrapped them up in a petate.

One of the men who did not die was locked up in the jail. He had nothing more than a bullet wound in his ribs. He told the priest of those who had killed the others: Do not finish him off, he has already suffered enough. You can see all the way to his liver. Do not kill him.

This was the answer: No, this man is very bad, he killed many people. For this he will suffer a little first. When they have finished burying his companions, he is going to die, too.

Days passed and the enemies of the chief who had killed the seven men came back and then they killed him. Before dying he said: Ay! little father, they have finished me off now.

The one who killed him spoke to him earlier in this way: Your father is not here. Yesterday and the day before you were a bully. You thought a lot of yourself, but now, here is what you wish. He spoke this way: Do not say that *you* are suffering, because this is the way you did it to the others.

Do you believe that what you did to the others did not pain them? Speak! answer!

Then he killed the leader of the rebels.

A. Echegoyen and C. Voigtlander (from an Otomi informant), "The Wars," *Tlalocan*, vol. ix (1986), pp. 214–17; English version, Sylvia and Earl Shorris.

Seven Erotic Otomi Songs and One Farewell

I

Turn your eyes,
we are going over there.
Turn your eyes,
we are climbing up there.

By the time they find out,
your mom and dad,
we'll be back
from doing what we planned.

II

What are you afraid of?
What are you afraid of?
That you'll stain your petticoat?
La, la, la, la.

III

When you need it, you need it.
When you don't, why not?
When I tell you to come here,
Don't come out with a No.

IV

Tell my pal,
to see if she wants it,
because her guy
is dying of the cold.

V

"Don't do it that way,
sister-in-law."
"How will I do it
standing on the floor?"

VI

—trembling breasts,
apple, little woman, caray!
Open your beautiful thighs,
I have a great urge, caray!

Put the shaft in the earth,
my darling little pigeon.
"Are my petticoats pretty?"
"They are the color of roses."

VI

Touch a piece
with the maguey spike, Celestino.
Touch one very prettily
so that all my cats will jump.

VII

In the sky, a moon;
in your face, a mouth.
In the sky, many stars;
in your face, two eyes alone.

"Los Otomies del Valle del Mezquital, Modas de Vida," *Ethnografia (Folklore)* (1954), pp. 365, 366, 369; English version, Sylvia and Earl Shorris.

FAREWELL

Tomorrow your dark one goes,
your student is on his way,
give him a little kiss if you like,
God knows if he will return someday.

Vicente T. Mendoza, *Musica Indigena Otomi* (Cuyo, Argentina: Universidad Nacional de Cuyo, ca. 1955), p. 205; English version, Sylvia and Earl Shorris.

The River Passes

The river passes, passes,
never stops.
The wind passes, passes,
never stops.
Life passes,
never returns.

Angel María Garibay K., *Historia de la Literatura Náhuatl*, vol. I (1953–54), pp. 238–39; English version, Sylvia and Earl Shorris.

⑤ 5 ⑥

Purepecha

*T*he Tarascans, or Purepechas, have lived for a long time close to the
beautiful lakes and mountains of Michoacan. Speaking a language
unrelated to any other in the world, they have maintained a deep sense
of identity. The Purepechas not only resisted several Mexica attempts at
invasion, but succeeded in defeating them in a war.

The sonority of the Purepecha language—with words like Pátzcuaro,
Tzintzuntzan, and Chupícuaro—adds to the beauty of their compositions. The Chronicle of Michoacan is a historical account given to a
Franciscan friar around 1540 by a Purepecha governor known among
the Spaniards as don Pedro. In dramatic language, he tells of the answer
the Purepechas gave to the Mexica ambassadors when they asked for help
in their fight against the invading Spaniards.

"The Lazy One" is a fable, with a very clear moral, suggesting that the
Purepechas, like all rural peoples, live between the lure of dreams and
the demands of practicality, and that indulgence in dreaming may have
impractical consequences.

Tenderness as well as irony are shown in an anonymous contemporary composition, the song entitled "The Flower of the Dead."

The *Chronicle of Michoacan*

OF THE COMING OF THE SPANIARDS TO THIS
PROVINCE, AS IT WAS TOLD TO ME BY DON PEDRO,
WHO IS NOW RULER, AND WAS THERE, AND HOW
MONTEZUMA, LORD OF MEXICO, SENT TO ASK FOR
HELP FROM THE CAZONCI ZUANGUA

Moctezuma sent ten messengers from Mexico, who arrived at Taximaroa, along with a message to the Cazonci called Zuangua, whose father, the old one, is now dead. And the Lord of Taximaroa asked them what they wanted.

They said that they came with a message sent by Moctezuma to the Cazonci, that they had to appear before him, and that they were to speak only to him.

And the Lord of Taximaroa sent word to inform the Cazonci, who commanded that they not be harmed, the more so because they had just come from afar.

The messengers arrived here at the city of Mechuacan, and went before Lord Zuangua, and they gave him a gift of turquoises, and green feathers, ten bucklers with golden circles, rich mantles and loincloths, and great mirrors. And all the lords and sons of the Cazonci disguised themselves and put on old cloaks, so that they would not be recognized, because they had heard it said that the Mexicans had come for them.

The Mexicans sat down and the Cazonci summoned an interpreter of the Mexican language, one Nuritan who was his Nahuatl interpreter. Then the Cazonci said to him: "Listen, what are the Mexicans saying? Let us see what they want, why they have come here."

And the Cazonci was calm; he had an arrow in his hand that he was tapping on the ground, and the Mexicans said: "The Lord of Mexico called Moctezuma sent us, and other lords, and he told us, 'Go to our brother the Cazonci, who does not know this tribe which has come here and suddenly seized upon us. We have been in battle with them, and they are killing us, those who come on deer, two hundred riders, and those that do not bring deer, another two hundred; and these deer carry men wearing iron armor, and they bring along a thing that sounds like the clouds and gives a great thunderclap, and kills all it finds, so that none remain. They destroy us and leave many of us dead.

" 'The Tlaxcalans come with them, since there were days when there was rancor between us and the Texcocans. We would already have killed them, if it were not that the Tlaxcalans and the Texcocans helped them. They had us encircled, isolated in this city.

" 'How could your sons not come to help—the one who is called Tiri-marasco, and the other Cuini and the other Azinche—and bring your people to defend us? We will provide food for everyone. Those people who have already arrived are in Tlaxcala, where we might all die.' "

Hearing the message, Zuangua responded: "It is good, good that you have come, and made your message clear to our gods Curicaueri and Xaratanga. I cannot now send people, because I have need of those you named; they are not here, they are staying with people in four conquered areas. Rest here a few days, and my interpreters, Nuritan and Piyo, will go with you. They will go to see these people that you want; in the meanwhile all the people come from the conquered places."

And the messengers went out and were put into a chamber and given food and breechcloths and mantles and suits of leather and garlands of clover. The Cazonci called his counselors and told them: "What shall we do? This is a great trouble that the ambassador has brought me. What shall we do? What has happened to us, to which sun that these two kings were accustomed to see, the one from Mexico or this one? We have not heard the other side of the story; here we shall be serving two gods.

"Here it is proposed that I must send people to Mexico, because we keep going to war, and we are close to each other, we and the Mexicans have rancor between us. See how astute the Mexicans are in speaking, how cunning they are! I have no need, as I said to them, look how incautious I am!

"As they have not been able to conquer certain villages, they want to avenge themselves on us and kill us through betrayal; they want to destroy us. Go to these Nahuatl speakers and interpret to them that I have told them to go, that they are not boys to act like boys, and they will know what that is."

His counselors responded: "Lord, you who are king and lord, you command. How could we contradict you? What you say goes."

First he commanded us to bring the many rich mantles and suits of leather, and from the sorcerers the mantles of their bloodstained gods, like those they had brought from Mexico for their gods, and everything else that there was in Mechuacan. They gave it to the messengers to give to Moctezuma, and they went with these Nahuatl speakers to see if what they said was true.

And the Cazonci sent warriors by another road and they took three Otomis and they asked them: "Do you have any news from Mexico?"

And the Otomis said: "The Mexicans are conquered, we do not know who conquered them. All Mexico is breached, with the bodies of the dead, and because of this they are looking for help to free them and defend them; we know this as they have sent to the villages for help."

The Michoacanos said: "So it is true, that they have gone; we know this."

The Otomis said: "Let's go, let's go to Michoacan; take us there, because they will give us mantles, for we are dying of the cold: we wish to be subjects of the Cazonci."

And they came to make known to the Cazonci how they had captured these three Otomis, and what they said and told: "Lord, this is the truth, that the Mexicans are destroyed and the entire city is breached, with dead bodies, and for this they go to the villages seeking succor. This is what they said in Taximaroa, the cacique Capacapecho asked about it there."

Said the Cazonci: "You should be welcome; we do not know how it will go with the poor ones that we send to Mexico. We should wait for them to come, if we are to know the truth."

Fray Jerónimo de Alcalá, among others (Morelia: Fimax Publicistas Editores, 1980); English version, Sylvia and Earl Shorris.

The Lazy One

There once was a person who was very lazy and besides that, very poor. He engaged in the struggle for survival by cutting firewood in the countryside and selling it so he could solve the family's economic problems. At least, this is what he used to say, because the truth is that every day he went to the countryside, but came back to his house with empty hands.

One day he went as always to the hills, and when he arrived at the usual place he saw a deer, and he stopped, motionless, thinking:

If I kill this deer and sell it, I will have money to buy a hen. Every day the hen will lay eggs and so I'll be able to buy a hog; then it will have many little hogs, and when they are big I will sell them, and then I will have a lot of money. After that, I will be able to buy a lamb that will multiply quickly and in a short time I will be able to buy an automobile and some cows that I have really yearned for, and I am going to have many other things, and I will no longer be poor.

If I succeed in buying the cows, many calves will come out of them that they are going to raise until they become bulls, and later I will be able to pick the biggest and handsomest ones to make a team and then I will be able to work the land. . . . No, no, I am not going to work, since I am going to be rich; better to send the peons to work and I will be an important gentleman and I will merely supervise my workers to avoid dirtying my shoes, and moreover, from afar, I will shout at them:

"Hurry up, you slackers!"

At these words, shouted with great determination, the deer leaped and went bounding toward the forest, leaving the gentleman with nothing but his illusions.

Lázaro Márquez Joaquín, *Cuentos Purépechas* (Mexico City: Diana, 1996), pp. 79–80; English version, Sylvia and Earl Shorris.

The Flower of the Dead

There will be no doubt, young lady,
that we are poor little indians;
but we really are the great Purepechas!
We really are, young lady!
We never tire
of planting
the flower of the dead.
Cheer up! Cheer up! young lady,
we have come to the time
when the rains begin.
For we really are the great Purepechas!
we really are, young lady!
We never tire
of planting
the flower of the dead.

Rudolf van Zantwijk, "The Flower of the Dead: A Tarascan Song," *Tlalocan*, vol. V (1965), pp. 122–23; English version, Sylvia and Earl Shorris.

Tlapanec

The Word Shall Always Bloom

by Abad Carrasco Zúñiga

The word shall always bloom.
As long as the cicada sings,
as long as the hummingbird darts,
and if the ant stays on course.
The word shall always bloom.
As long as one child smiles,
as long as your voice is heard,
and if you are with me.
The word shall always bloom.
As long as a flower opens its petals,
as long as the clamor of the river continues,
and if the dawn can be discerned.
Do not disturb the cicada,
do not disturb the ant,
do not disturb the river,
so that the word shall always bloom.

Abad Carrasco Zúñiga, "La Palabra Florida," *Revista de Escritores en Lenguas Indigenas,* I, 1 (1997). Spanish translation by the author; English version, Sylvia and Earl Shorris.

Glossary of Names, Terms, and Concepts

Acolhua—followers of Xolotl, of Chichimeca origin, who arrived in the Valley of Mexico in the thirteenth century. They ruled in Texcoco, then came under the rule of Azcapotzalco until the defeat of that state by Nezahualcoyotl and the Mexica, after which the Acolhuas came to power again

Acolmiztli—"the cat of Acolhuacan," another name for Nezahualcoyotl

Aguamiel—juice of the maguey cactus, from which pulque, a fermented alcoholic beverage, is made

Ahau—Lord

Ahpop Achih—messengers of *Xibalba*

Ah Puch—Maya god of death

Ahuelitoctzin—a warrior during the Conquest

Ahuitzotl—eighth *huey tlahtoani* of Tenochtitlan (1486–1502), among the most bellicose of the Mexica rulers

Ajolote/Axolotl—amphibian once common in the lakes of the Valley of Mexico; mythically connected to Xolotl, who was able to change shapes and become a clown

Akbal—see *Calendar*

Ake—a pre-Classic site east of Merida; also an architectural style known for its "wavy walls" and round corners

Almud—dry measure equivalent to 4.625 liters

Altepetl—literally, "water/mountain"; the Nahua ethnic unit, described by James Lockhart in his work, *The Nahuas After the Conquest* (Stanford, CA: Stanford University Press, 1992)

Altiplano—high plain of central Mexico

Alvarado, Pedro de (Tonatiuh)—one of Cortés's captains, whose blond hair and ruddy complexion earned him the name Tonatiuh, the Sun God, Alvarado was known for his ferocity in battle. After journeying through much of what is now Mexico, Guatemala, and Peru, he was killed in 1541 while trying to put down a Nahua uprising led by Tenamaztle (see León-Portilla, *La*

Flecha en el Blanco, for a full description of the uprising and the later connection of Tenamaztle to fray las Casas)

Amac—Quiche word meaning "tribe," as in *Amac-Tan,* tribe of Tan

Anahuac—"near the waters," denoted the Valley of Mexico, later the entire country

Aquiauhtzin of Ayapanco/Chalco (1430?–1500?)—author of "The Song of the Women of Chalco," probably served in the battle of 1464 in which Chalco was defeated by the Mexica and 16,000 common people fled

Atlatl—a device made of cane used to increase the velocity of a spear; used in war and hunting in the Valley of Mexico prior to the introduction of the bow and arrow

Atlixco—a small *altepetl* under the domination at various times of Cholula, Tenochtitlan, and Tlaxcala

Atole—a corn-based beverage, may be flavored with cacao

Audiencia—in Spain, the courts which heard both civil and criminal cases. In Nueva España, they also had legislative, judicial, and administrative duties. The first audiencia in Mexico was established in 1527 and presided over the worst graft, corruption, and general lack of fairness in economic, social, and political dealings of the colonial period. Other audiencias were established later in Guadalajara with jurisdiction over northern Mexico; and in Guatemala with jurisdiction over the Yucatan, Tabasco, and Chiapas. The audiencias were in competition for power with the viceregal and church authorities

Auilix (Avilix)—"mountain" deity of the Greathouse line, founded by Jaguar Night

Axayacatl—*sixth huey tlahtoani* of Tenochtitlan, reigned 1469–81

Ayacachtli—rattle

Ayapancatl—see Aquiauhtzin of Ayapanco/Chalco; a place near Amecameca

Ayocuan—"White Eagle Coyote," poet, king of Tecamachalco, reigned 1420–41, son of Cuetzpaltzin

Ayocuan of Tecamachalco—early sixteenth-century poet and philosopher, known as Ilhuicamina, "he who launches arrows at the sky"

Azcapotzalco—settled by people of Teotihuacan when the Tepanecs arrived in 1230; ruled by the Acolhuas, who controlled much of the Valley of Mexico—Tenayuca, Culhuacan, Xochimilco, Coyoacan, and Cuauhnahuac—until 1363 when his son Tezozomoc came to power; declined at the end of the first quarter of the fifteenth century

Aztec—those who ruled in *Aztlan,* whence the Mexica escaped. The word did not come into common use until the establishment of the Republic of Mexico, which would have led to some confusion between "Mexica" and "Mexican"

Aztlan—"place of the herons," a real or mythical place of origin for the

Nahuas (Aztecs), variously located in areas as diverse as Lake Chapala in Mexico or the Colorado River in the United States. The name suggests a body of water, but the linguistic evidence points to what is now the Southwest United States. The concept of Aztlan holds great importance for many Mexican Americans as a validation of both their culture and place of residence

Bacab—in Maya mythology the world is supported by four *Bacabs,* or more correctly *Bacabob,* "fathers of the land"—white to the north, black to the west, yellow to the south, and red to the east; these are also the *year-bearers.* Among humans, the *bacabob* are priests or shamans, hence the *Rituals of the Bacabs*

Bacalar—site of the Maya cycle in A.D. 692, on the opposite shore of Lake Bacalar from Chetumal, in the present-day Mexican state of Quintana Roo

Baktun—see *Tun*

Balam (also *Chilam Balam de Tizimin, Chumayel, Mani,* etc.)—"Jaguar"; see *Chilam Balam*

Balche—an intoxicating beverage made of fermented honey

Bolontiku—the Nine Gods of the Maya underworld

Bundle—a collection of objects (bones, feathers, stones, and relics) relating to accomplishments and spiritual activities and beings; a repository of psychological and/or magical power

Caban—see *Calendar*

Cabildo—municipal council, also *ayuntamiento;* composed of councilors or regidores and alcaldes who had greater powers, often including judicial duties

Cabracan—"Earthquake"

Cacama—poet, king of Tezcoco, reigned 1515–20, son of Nezahualpilli and nephew of Motecuhoma; rebelled against Cortés and Motecuhzoma in 1519, was kidnapped by the Spaniards, imprisoned, later tortured with hot irons by Pedro de Alvarado in an attempt to extract more treasure, and in some accounts burned at the stake

Cacamatl—probably Lord of Amecameca, killed in the battle of Chalco, 1417

Cacique—Taino/Arawak word used in Cuba and Santo Domingo, meaning "chief"; the post-Conquest replacement for the *tlahtoani* of the Nahuas, caciques were almost always of noble lineage. In the government under the Spanish viceroys, the caciques were responsible for the welfare of the Indians and for collecting tributes. The cacique could petition the Spanish governors for redress of wrongs against the Indians, but the *macehuales* had nowhere to turn for redress of wrongs done to them by the caciques

Cakchiquel—a Maya linguistic group in present-day Guatemala; in the pre-Hispanic period, frequently at war with the Quiches. Both groups trace their origins to a mythical Tula, from whence they journeyed south, eventually adopting the language of the area

Calendar—

Maya Days:

Imix (alligator/ceiba tree)
Ik (wind)
Akbal (night)
Kan (yellow)
Chicchan (great snake)
Cimi (death)
Manik (deer)
Lamat (flood/lightning)
Muluc (storm/thunder)
Oc (foot)
Chuen (monkey)
Eb (step/frog)
Ben (corn)
Ix (jaguar)
Men (bird)
Cib (wax)
Caban (earth/earthquake)
Edznab (obsidian blade)
Cauac (rain)
Ahau (ruler/lord)

Maya Months of 20 Days:

Pop (mat)
Uo (frog)
Zip (deer)
Zotz (bat)
Zec (skeleton)
Xul (end)
Yaxkin (new sun)
Mol (track)
Che'en (well)
Yax (new)
Zac (white)
Ceh (deer)
Mac (cover)
Kankin (yellow sun)
Muan (macaw)
Pax (drum or break)
Kayab (songs)
Cumku (dark god)

Uayeb (specters)—Mesoamerican calendars were adjusted to the solar
year by the use of five nameless days, which the Maya called Uayeb

There were two Nahua calendars, a solar and a divinatory (*tonalpohualli*)
version, the latter composed of 13 numbers and 20 signs:

Earth Monster (cipactli)
Wind (ehecatl)
House (calli)
Lizard (cuetzpalin)
Serpent (coatl)
Death (mizquiztli)
Deer (mazatl)
Rabbit (tochtli)
Water (atl)
Dog (itzcuintli)
Monkey (ozomatli)
Grass (malinalli)
Reed (acatl)
Jaguar (ocelotl)
Eagle (quauhtli)
Vulture (cozcaquauhtli)
Movement (ollin)
Flint (tecpatl)
Rain (quiahuitl)
Flower (xochitl)

Solar Months:

Izcalli (Resurrection)
Atlcahualco (The waters are leaving)
Tlacaxipehualiztli (Flaying of men)
Tozoztontli (Short watch)
Hueytozoztli (Long watch)
Toxcatl (Dry thing)
Etzalcualiztli (Meal of maize)
Techuilhuitontli (Small feast of the lords)
Hueytecuilhuitl (Great feast of the lords)
Tlaxochimaco (Flowers are given)
Hueymiccailhuitl (Great feast of the dead)
Ochopaniztli (Sweeping)
Teotlelco (Arrival of the gods)
Tepeilhuitl (Feast of the mountains)

Quecholli (Flamingo)
Panquetzaliztli (Raising flags)
Atemoztli (Waters fall)
Tititl (Wrinkled)
Nemontemi—five-day period used to adjust the solar calendar

The Mesoamerican nature of the calendar is illustrated by the Maya month Imix and the Nahua Cipactli. *Imix* is the ancient name for the ceiba or world tree, which symbolizes the duality of earth and water, the origin of life. *Cipactli*—sometimes called a crocodile or alligator—symbolizes earth, from which all vegetation, including the precious maize, the source of nourishment and life, grows. One can see this as well, of course, in the Mixtec man who is born of a tree.

Calmecac—school for the highborn, offering a complete education in Nahua culture at the highest levels

Calpulli—literally, a group of houses; smallest social-political unit, having its own patron deity, economic resources, scribes, schools, communal property, and persons responsible for maintaining order

Camazotz—"Great Bat"

Came—"death"; Lords of Xibalba: *Hun-Came*—One Death; *Vucub-Came*—Seven Death

Cantares Mexicanos—poems and songs redacted in Nahuatl in the sixteenth century, the source of much of the most beautiful and hermetic work by the Nahuas, most of it of pre-Hispanic character, but with Christian concepts inserted (often awkwardly or even incorrectly). Translation of the *Cantares* has proved extremely difficult, leading to widely varied readings of the work

Carranza, Venustiano (1859–1920)—revolutionary leader, named first chief, and in 1917 president of the Republic of Mexico; supported by Villistas and Zapatistas early on, then at odds with them; helped plan the betrayal and murder of Zapata and the devastating defeat of the Villistas at Agua Prieta. As president, Carranza did little to bring about social reforms. He was forced to flee the capital in 1920, and was assassinated perhaps by one of his own guards acting under orders from Alvaro Obregon

Caste War—in 1847, the Maya in the eastern part of Yucatan rebelled against the whites of Spanish descent who had taken their land and water; in the bloodiest uprising of indigenous people in the history of Latin America, more than 10,000 whites and mestizos and at least a quarter of a million Maya, over a third of the entire population, were killed. The war did not end until the early twentieth century

Cauac—see *Calendar*

Ce Acatl Topiltzin—"One Reed, Our Prince," name of Quetzalcoatl

Ceiba—a common tree south of the altiplano, the lower branches often giving it a cruciform appearance; the Maya World Tree takes its form from the ceiba (see *Calendar: Nemontemi*)

Cempoalxochitl—marigold, the flower of the dead

Cenote—a deep, natural well caused by the collapse of the limestone crust above it, both a source of water and a place of ritual importance as in Chichen Itza, because it is thought to be an entrance to *Xibalba*

Centeotl—var. spelling of *Cinteotl*

Chac (Chaak)—Maya rain god—see *Tlaloc, Tohil*

Chalco—a city/nation or *altepetl* of the Valley of Mexico in the pre-Hispanic and colonial periods, built around a now dry lake. Currently a distant and very poor suburb of the capital

Chamula—see *Tzotzil*

Chan Balum (II)—born A.D. 635, ruled 683–702. Son of Pacal the Great of Palenque, his name translates as "Snake Jaguar"

Chicchan—see *Calendar*

Chicha—alcoholic beverage made of fermented maize

Chichen Itza—a great Maya city, now an archeological site, in Yucatan; structures are of pre- and post-Toltec influence. The city-state figures prominently in the history of the pre-Hispanic era; it appears to have been in power for long periods during the Classic era, defeated through trickery by Hunac Ceel of Mayapan at the beginning of the thirteenth century, then coming to power and destroying Mayapan in the fifteenth century. Recent reinterpretation of the famous bas-relief on the wall of the great ball court suggests that the beheaded ballplayer depicted there may have been the winner rather than the loser of the game

Chichimecs—"People of Dog Lineage," a nomadic group from the north of Mexico or the U.S. Southwest that invaded the Valley of Mexico. The term may refer to more than one ethnic group, linked linguistically to either Otomi or Nahautl and assimilated in the Valley of Mexico with more culturally advanced peoples there. The title of Lord of the Chichimecs held great significance in Texcoco; Chichimec also connotes barbarism, especially in the area north of the Valley where the Spaniards fought frequent battles against the Chichimecs during the early colonial period

Chilam Balam—literally, "Jaguar Priest" or "Jaguar Spokesman, "because he was dressed in jaguar skin; also a series of prophetic works named for the cities in which they were found. Fourteen books bear this title, although only five—*Chumayel, Tizimin, Mani, Chan Cah,* and *Kaua*—contain prophecies. The *Chilam Balam of Tusik* contains the Zuyua riddles. The book of *Ixil* is about medicine and *Tekax* and *Nah* are mainly calendrical. Five other books—*Hocaba, Nabula, Telchac, Tihosuco,* and *Tixkokob*—are lost

Chimalmat—the mother of Zipacana and Earthquake (Cabran or Cabracan) and the wife of Seven Macaw; her name is derived from the Nahuatl *chimalli*, "shield"

Chimalpopoca—"Smoking Shield" or "Resplendent," third king of Mexico, reigned 1416–28, assassinated by Maxtla, son of Tezozomoc, king of Azcapotzalco

Chinampas—the floating gardens of the Valley of Mexico, constructed of logs, cane, and rich soil, on which the Mexica grew vegetables, corn, and flowers; canals between the chinampas permitted passage of boats on the lakes

Cholula—present-day name of pre-Hispanic city-state of *Chollolan,* which flowered during the fourth century A.D., occupied by the people of Teotihuacan until they were displaced by later Olmecs in the eighth century. After the fall of Tula, many Toltecs were enslaved by the Olmecs in Chollolan; later domination by Huexotzinco lasted until the beginning of the sixteenth century

Chontal—a word of Nahuatl origin meaning stranger. The Chontales were a powerful group located in various parts of southern Mesoamerica; their leader's name, Talezcoob, was corrupted by the Spaniards into Tabasco, a state in which many Chontales lived; fewer than 100,000 persons now speak Chontal

Chuen—see *Calendar*

Chumayel—see *Chilam Balam*

Cib—see *Calendar*

Cihuacoatl—"Serpent Woman," the feminine aspect of the great dual god of the Mexica, worshipped in her dual aspects, Xochiquetzal, and Coatlicue (who is represented by the single most imposing work of Nahua sculpture), the mother of Huitzilopochtli. Also a term of political organization for a deputy ruler: when the *huey tlahtoani* was absent, the *cihuacoatl* was left in command of the Mexica

Cimi—see *Calendar*

Cincalco—"House of Maize," a cave near Chapultepec, filled with flowers, thought to be an entrance to the paradise of Huemac, Lord of Tula. Motecuhzoma tried to hide in this cave when he heard the Spaniards had arrived

Cinteotl—god of the ear of corn, born in *Tamoanchan,* child of Tlazolteotl and sometime companion of the Sun

Citlalinicue—"Skirt of Stars," feminine aspect of the dual god

Citlatona—her name refers to the Milky Way

Citlallatonac—variant spelling of *Citlatona*

Coacueye—wife of Mixcoatl, founder of Colhuacan; fled following the assassination of her husband, and died while giving birth to Ce Acatl Topiltzin, "One Reed Prince," who later founded Tula and became Quetzalcoatl

Coanacoch—son of Nezahualpilli, reigned over Texcoco, 1520–21

Coatepec/Coatepetl—the Mountain of The Serpent; birthplace of Huitzilopochtli

Coatlicue—"Skirt of Serpents"; see *Cihuacoatl*

Cocom—Maya dynasty of Toltec origin, in power A.D. 968–1441, with many descendants in present-day Yucatan

Codex—an indigenous folded book, painted on deerskin or amate paper (bark of the fig tree)

Colhuacan—founded by Toltecs in A.D. 1064, following the fall of Tula; in one version, Quetzalcoatl was born in Colhuacan. The Colhuaques participated in many alliances, including one that attempted to keep the Chichimecs from settling in the Valley of Mexico. Colhuacan fell under the domination of Azcapotzalco during the rule of Tezozomoc, and did not free itself until Tezozomoc's kingdom declined during his old age. The rulers of Colhuacan in the early fourteenth century were Coxcox, Acamapichtli, and Achitometl II; an internal revolt in 1358 led to a period of instability until Xilomantzin took the throne in 1440, followed by the 64-day reign of Maxihuitzin, then Tlatolcatzin, and Tezozomoctli, 1482–1519. The last ruler, Tizaotzin, was baptized by the Spaniards

Cohuatzin—Tecpanec lord, sovereign of Tepetlixpa

Copal—resin burned as incense

Copil—evil sorcerer whose heart was torn from his chest and buried; from it grew the cactus (*tenochtli*) that gave its name to Tenochtitlan

Cortés, Hernán (1485–1547)—led the Spanish expedition to Mexico; also known as Fernando Cortés, the given name he preferred

Coyoacan—a town conquered by Azcapotzalco; the site of the residence of Hernán Cortés, first *ayuntamiento* (1524); first capital of Nueva España

Coyohuehuetzin—Jaguar Warrior from Tlatelolco

Coyolchiuhqui—see *Tochihuitzin Coyolchiuhqui*

Coyolxauhqui—"Face Painted with Tiny Bells," sister of Huitzilopochtli; moon goddess

Cuacuauhtzin—fifteenth-century poet sent to his death by Nezahualcoyotl

Cuahuitlicac—one of the four hundred gods of the south, uncle of Huitzilopochtli, whom he warned of the plot to kill him

Cuauhatlapal—Lord of Chimalhuacan, killed in 1459

Cuauhtecoatl and Cahualtzin—Mexica soldiers who distinguished themselves in the war against Chalco

Cuauhtemoc or Quauhtemoc—son of Ahuitzotl, ironically named "Descending Eagle," a metaphorical phrase for the setting sun. He was the last significant *tlahtoani* of the Mexica, born 1502, died 1525. His heroic struggle against the Spaniards and tragic end are chronicled in many of the finest works of the colonial period

Cuauhtepetl—"Eagle Mountain"

Cuauhtlatohua—one of the women of Chalco who was conquered by forces of the *huey tlahtoani* Axayacatl

Cuauhtlehuanitl—"Rising Eagle," another name for the sun

Cuauhtliztac—"White Eagle," Lord of Xaltocan

Cuauhxilotl—*cihuacoatl* of Iztapalapa, which was allied with Texcoco during the reign of Ixtlilxochitl; died in the war against the Tepanecs

Cuecuechcuicatl—tickling songs, often accompanied by provocative music and dance

Cuetlaxtlan—a small Totonac city between the Valley of Mexico and the Atlantic Coast, with a Mexica colony

Cuetzpaltzin—father of Ayocuan, "White Eagle"

Cuicatl—a composition in poetic form

Cux—weasel

Difrasismo—the Mesoamerican kenning, sometimes said to be a metaphor; defined by Angel Maria Garibay as two concrete terms used together as a convention to express a single idea. There are numerous examples, including *flower and song*—poetry; *one lip, two lip*—translation; *night and wind*—invisible, as in *Ometeotl; the skirt, the blouse*—the sexuality of a woman; *jade and quetzal plumes*—beauty; *black ink and red ink*—writing/wisdom; *in the box, in the coffer*—secret

Eb—see *Calendar*

Ek—see *Calendar*

Eloquechol—one of the long-necked birds of Mesoamerica

Etz'nab/Eetznab/Edznab—see *Calendar*

Fanega—measure equal to 1.58 bushels

Feast of Toxcatl—great feast, including sacrifice to Tezcatlipoca; during this feast Pedro de Alvarado and his troops entered the temple, sealed the doors, and massacred the participants

Flower—one of the key metaphors in classical Nahuatl composition. In its simplest form, it describes the beautiful sound of a drum; at the next level, it stands for beauty both as noun and adjective; as part of Flowers of the Dawn, it refers to dead warriors; when used with war, it refers to the form of warfare fostered by Tlacaelel for the sole purpose of taking captives for sacrifice; flowers may also mean the warriors themselves; in the *difrasismo* "flower and song," it forms part of the concept of poetry. "Flower," "flowered," "flowers," "flowery," "floral," and "florid" are among the more difficult aspects of translation from Nahuatl, for the word in one of its forms is sometimes used more than once within a single sentence or even a single phrase, e.g., "the flowery house of flowers." The words "quetzal and quetzal plumes" present similar problems in both denotation and connotation

Gucumatz—"Plumed Serpent" in Quiche—see *Kukulcan/Kukulkan, Quetzalcoatl*

Haab—solar year (see *Xihuitl*)

Hacauitz—patron deity of the Quiche

Ho' or T ho'—Maya town now known by the Spanish name Merida

Holom-ocox—the head of a mushroom

Huehuehtlahtolli—"ancient word"

Huemac—"Great Hands," a legendary *huey tlahtoani* of Tula, perhaps its last ruler

Huexotzinco—city-state occupied by late classic Olmecs, then Chichimecs; dominated Cholula, attacked Tlaxcala, then allied with them to conquer Chalco and other city-states; attacked by Motecuzoma I; permitted Nezahualcoyotl to take refuge there. In 1506, Huexotzinco defeated the Mexica in a great war, taking thousands of captives. Soon thereafter Tlaxcala defeated Huexotzinco in a war, leading Huexotzinco to ally itself with the Mexica. Huexotzinco and the Mexica fought Tlaxcala to a standoff. The Mexica, however, insulted the Huexotzincans by placing their tutelary god, Camaxtli, among those of the conquered. When the Spaniards arrived, Huexotzinco allied itself with them against the Mexica

Huey tlahtoani—literally, "great speaker," the high ruler elected by judges and other nobles; see *tlahtoani*

Huipil/Iipiil—probably derived from the Nahuatl, *huipilli* (blouse), an overblouse worn by Maya women, often elaborately embroidered

Huitzilihuitl—a noble of Tlatelolco

Huitzilopochtli—"Blue Hummingbird of the South," tutelary god of the Mexica, born of Coatlicue, who was impregnated by a white feather; war god, associated with the Sun; other names may have been *Mexi* or *Mexitli*, from which Mexico is derived; it was to Huitzilopochtli that the Mexica made sacrifice, including offerings of human hearts

Huitznahuatl/Huitznahuac yaotl—"Warrior of the South"

Hunab Ku—Maya "One God," possibly a Christianization of the Mesoamerican abstract concept of a supreme deity, the Mother/Father, creator of *Itzam Na,* maker of the man of corn, analagous to the Nahua *Ometeotl*

Hunac Ceel—Xiu governor of Mayapan; using deceit, overthrew Xib Chac, the Itza rain priest of Chichen Itza; then captured and destroyed Mayapan in 1451

Hun—One (Quiche)—see *Vucub*

Hunahpu—"One Blowgun," a Hero Twin of the *Popol Vuh;* his head, lost in Xibalba, becomes the Evening Star; also associated with the Sun. Venus and the Sun are referred to in some Maya literature as the Older Twin and the Younger Twin, respectively, since they are seen in the morning sky in that order as they rise out of the darkness (underworld)

Huracan (Hurricane)—a word of Taino or Quiche origin meaning "One Large Raindrop," according to Dennis Tedlock; other names include Heart of Sky and Heart of Earth. Huracan was the one-legged god who caused the flood that destroyed the men of wood; also known as *Tahil,* "Obsidian Mirror," suggesting a connection to the Nahua Tezcatlipoca, again connected to hurricanes. Three forms of lightning are linked with Huracan:

caculha—regular lightning

chipi caculha—small flash of lightning

raxa caculha—green lightning

Iboy—armadillo dance

Icelteotl—"One God or Unified God," as in Maya, *Hunab Ku,* a Christianized concept

Ik—see *Calendar*

Ikim Soots (Zotz)—"Great Bat," a Maya death god

Ilhuicamina—"He Who Launches Arrows at the Sky," one of the names of Motecuhzoma I

Imix—see *Calendar*

Ipalnemoani—Giver of Life

Itzam Na—"Iguana House," offspring of *Hunab Ku,* functioned as a kind of demiurge, associated with the Sun, creator of writing, the first priest; benevolent, shown in glyphs as bearded and toothless. Itzam Na is quadripartite—red for the east, white for the north, black for the west, and yellow for the south; analagous in many respects to the Nahua god Tezcatlipoca

Itza—"Water Witches," elite lineages of eastern Yucatan, in ascendance during the post-Classic and colonial periods; established their major city of Chichen Itza at the end of the seventh century, antedated the Xiu (of Toltec origin) by a full century. In the twelfth century the Itza destroyed their city of Champoton and spent forty years in the wilderness before arriving again at Chichen. In the middle of the thirteenth century in a compromise over calendrical differences, the Itza and the Xiu, constant antagonists, agreed to seat the new cycle at Mayapan. But the alliance lasted only until 1451, when Mayapan was destroyed

Itzcoatl—"Obsidian Serpent," fourth *huey tlahtoani* of the Mexica, ruler of Tenochtitlan, liberator of his people from Azcapotzalco. Reigned 1428–40, and sought to destroy all documents written before his reign in an effort to rewrite the history of the Mexica, casting events in a more favorable light. Uncle of Tlacaelel

Itzpapalotl—"Obsidian Butterfly," a Chichimec goddess, companion of Tezcatlipoca in his aspect as god of the night; she is connected to the paradise of *Tamoanchan,* where she is the leader of women who died in childbirth

Ix—see *Calendar*

Ixchel—"Stretched-out Woman," the moon goddess, companion of the Sun, capable of both good and evil acts toward humans, depicted in the codices as a warrior, with spear and shield; myths about her and the Sun are homologous to that of Huitzilopochtli and Coyolxauhqui

Izcahuitli—a reddish-colored aquatic insect

Kan—"Yellow," see *Calendar;* also "Serpent," as in Kukul*kan*

Katun—see *Calendar, Cycle, Tun*

Kaxlan/Kaslan/Caslan—Castellan as adapted by many Maya language groups

K'iche—see *Quiche*

K'in/Kin—may be translated as "Sun," "day," or "time"

Kinich Ahau—"Sun Eye Lord," the Maya Sun god, one of the aspects of the mother/father dual god

Kukulcan/Kukulkan—"Plumed Serpent," the Maya version of Quetzal-coatl, probably introduced by Toltecs in the tenth century A.D.

Ladino—Spanish speaker in southern Mesoamerica, white or mestizo, genetically or culturally

Lahun Chan—"Ten Molar," name of the Great Star, Chak-ech'; also a place name

Lamat—see *Calendar*

Landa, Diego de—Fransciscan bishop, arrived in the Yucatan 1549, instituted the auto-da-fé, burned the Maya codices; nonetheless, his *Relación de las Cosas de Yucatan* contains much unique and useful information

Languages—170 languages were spoken in Mexico when the Spaniards arrived; at the end of the twentieth century, there were still 62, with approximately 10 million speakers of these languages, although many speakers were beyond childbearing years, which means the languages were in danger of becoming lost. The largest language groups were Nahuatl and Maya

Macehuales/Macehualtin—"the deserving ones," in the sense of deserving the sacrifice of the gods by which life came about, including the restoration of the (Fifth) Sun; the common people; nobles were known as *pipiltin*

Macuilxochitl—"Five Flower," the goddess of art and poetry; also the name of a daughter of Tlacaelel, elegantly educated during the mid-fifteenth-century peak of Tenochtitlan, following its defeat of Azcapotzalco. Her work attests to the fact that women as well as men practiced the arts; however, it is one of the few extant works composed by a woman

Mahucutah—one of the first men; the meaning of his name is unclear

Mani—established after the destruction of Mayapan. It was here that the terrible auto-da-fé was conducted by Diego de Landa in 1562; see also *Chilam Balam*

Manik—see *Calendar*

May—"cycle," from which *Maya* or "those of the cycle" is probably derived; the cycle comprised 13 *katuns*, which Munro Edmonson counts as "260 tuns minus 1300 days, 160 days short of 265 years"

Mayapan—built at the close of the ninth century A.D. as a way to end the wars between Maya city-states by forming the League of Mayapan, which lasted for nearly three hundred years. In the thirteenth century, Hunac Ceel tricked the rain priest of Chichen Itza and gained power over it and Izamal; from then until the middle of the fifteenth century, when it was sacked and burned, Mayapan held political sway over a great area. The period of ascendance of Mayapan marked a serious decline in the culture of Yucatan

Mecatl—"rope," "cord," a Nahua measure equaling 20 units, each of approximately 2.5 meters

Mexica—from *Mexi* or *Mexitli,* one of the names of Huitzilopochtli; the people who gained the post-Conquest name "Aztec" following Mexican independence and the use of "Mexican" to designate all citizens. Originally a nomadic group from the north who settled in the place now known as the Valley of Mexico and founded Tenochtitlan

Miccacalcatl—"He of the House of the Dead"; the effect in this part of the plain song is to indicate that one will grow as clusters of flowers, blossom, and then become yellow, which means to die

Mictlan—Region of the Dead

Mictlantecuhtli/Mictlancihuatl—Lord/Lady of the Region of the Dead; shown in astonishing representation in the Museo del Templo Mayor in Mexico City

Milpa—a Nahuatl word used across Mesoamerica for land on which corn, beans, squash, and other vegetables are grown; the milpa culture is the material basis for much of Mesoamerican culture

Mixcoatl—"Cloud Serpent," the Milky Way, an important Chichimec god; also a historic person, father of Ce Acatl, Quetzalcoatl of Tula

Mixitl, tlapatl—hallucinogenic herbs

Mixtec—Literally, "people of the clouds," a major pre-Hispanic civilization in western Oaxaca, Guerrero, and Puebla. Culturally an outgrowth of early Toltec influence, the Mixtecs developed along unique lines beginning in the eleventh century. They warred frequently against the Zapotecs, eventually occupying Mitla and Monte Alban, which they expanded and decorated in their own fashion. The Mixtec codices are among the most beautiful and important documents to survive the Spanish invasion. Nearly 500,000 people still speak the Mixtec language

Monencauhtzin—fifteenth-century sage/poet; little more is known of him

Motecuzoma/Motecuhzoma/Montezuma/Moctezuma—name of two Mexica rulers:

Motecuhzoma I, Ilhuicamina, fifth *huey tlahtoani,* reigned 1440–69, nephew of Itzcoatl, celebrated warrior and military leader, expanded the empire, held it together during a severe drought, defeated Totonacs, increased public order in the polity and institutionalized social stratification

Motecuhzoma II (*Xocoyotzin,* meaning something close to "Junior") followed the bellicose Ahuitzotl, who had left him a kingdom the size of Italy; reigned from 1502 until the Conquest; last *huey tlahtoani* to enjoy the formal installation proceedings. He mandated changes in the character of government, moving away from the warrior mentality back toward Toltec notions associated with the gentle Quetzalcoatl; scholarly, ruminative as much as intellectual, ascetic yet the master of many concubines, Motecuhzoma II is sometimes described as neurotic; he was the *huey tlahtoani* least prepared to meet the Spanish invasion

Motenehuatzin—fifteenth-century poet/sage of Tlaxcala

Moyocoyatzin—"He Who Invents Himself," another name for the supreme god of the Nahuas

Muluc—see *Calendar*

Muzen Cab—"Dug Up Honey," the Maya bee god

Nacom—"Captain," military or sacrificial

Nagual (nahual)—literally, spirit *(genio)* or wizard; an alternate person or animal who acts as protector and adviser. The newborn infant is often accompanied by a *nagual* in the old literature. In more recent times, it is a wizard who transforms himself into an animal *nagual*

Nahua—A diverse group spread across much of central Mexico and as far south as Nicaragua (Nicaros) and El Salvador. In Mexico alone, there are more than 1.5 million Nahuas who speak Nahuatl in its various forms. The civilization developed in the ninth century in Culhuacan and later in Tula, with roots probably in the Teotihucan culture and as far back as the Olmecs of the Gulf Coast. The Nahuas themselves appear to have come to Mexico from the north, bringing their Uto-Aztecan language with them.

The great Nahua city of Tula, home to Quetzalcoatl, was destroyed in the eleventh century by Chichimec invaders from the north. The second flowering of the Nahua world took place in the high central plain of Mexico, where the legendary seven tribes established themselves. The last of the seven tribes, those we know now as the Aztecs, founded their city of Mexico-Tenochtitlan in 1325. Under a series of expansionist leaders—Tlacaelel, Motecuhzoma Ilhuicamina, Axayacatl, Ahuitzotl, and Motecuhzoma Xocoyotzin—who formed an alliance with Texcoco and Tacuba, the (Mexica) Aztecs extended their political and cultural hegemony across virtually all of central Mexico and south into Central America.

With the Spanish Conquest in the sixteenth century, the Aztec state fell into decline as many of its works were destroyed, its people killed, and its religious and cultural practices outlawed

Nahuatl—a Uto-Aztecan language that served as a lingua franca for much of pre-Hispanic Mesoamerica. The word refers to "speaking clearly," in contrast to people like the Populucas, a Nahuatl word meaning "unable to speak." This focus on language rather than mere being, as in *Dine* (the people), is not common among peoples of the world

Names, translation of—the English translation of Mesoamerican names, and especially people's names, presents a difficult problem. Some translators insist that names like Descending Eagle for Cuauhtemoc, the last king of the Mexica, must be rendered in English for a full comprehension and appreciation of the text. Others argue that the names should be left in the original language and that they should be understood as mere combinations of sounds, just as we understand that the English Brown, Steel, or Towne no longer connotes color, metal, or urban settlement. In the two translations of the *Popul Vuh* given here both methods have been used, providing an opportunity for the reader to make a comparison

Nation—among the Nahuas, a ruling entity, often comprising more than one *altepetl*, sometimes multilingual and pluriethnic, with the lingua franca of the ruling entity; among the Maya these were city-states, often in alliance, sharing the seating of the new cycle

Nezahualcoyotl—"Fasting Coyote," born 1402, died 1472, reigned as *huey tlahtoani* of Texcoco from 1431 until his death. The son of Ixtlilxochitl I, he was famed as a lawgiver, philosopher, and poet

Nezahualpilli—son of Nezahualcoyotl, whom he succeeded to the throne. Born 1460, died 1515; known as a philosopher and poet, his name translates as "Son of the Fasting One"

Nicte—"flower" in Yucatecan Maya

Ometeotl—"Dual God," the supreme deity, creator god, a concept described only through metaphor

Ometecuhtli/Omecihuatl—Lord of Duality/Lady of Duality, the male/female aspects of the supreme deity, as in *Tonantzin/Totahtzin,* Our Revered Mother/Our Revered Father

Otomi (people)—an important group in the Valley of Mexico that did not speak a Uto-Aztecan language; the objects of their culture were less sophisticated than those of other tribes in the area and the circumstances of their arrival in the Valley have been disputed

Otomi (rank)—designation of a high level of accomplishment by a Mexica warrior

Oyal Mut—"Island Pheasant," a *Bacab,* or Maya priest of the south

Pacal the Great—eleventh ruler in the dynasty of Palenque, born 603, died 683, ascended to the throne in 615. During the rule of Pacal many of the most extraordinary buildings of Palenque were constructed, including the Temple of Inscriptions, which served as his tomb. Although the details of his rule have not yet been verified, Pacal (Shield) the Great has been compared to the great kings and conquerors of history

Palenque—Maya city-state located in the Chiapas highlands, flourished 600–900, the Maya Classic period. The art and architecture of Palenque are among the finest in Mesoamerica

Paquime—cliff dwellers of the present Mexican state of Chihuahua; the culture flourished from the eleventh until the mid-thirteenth century, when drought and overpopulation led to its decline; an important trading center where Mesoamerican and southwestern U.S. culture existed contemporaneously

Peten—an area in the north of Guatemala, site of Classic period Maya city-states, declined in the early post-Classic period

Piltzintecuhtli—"Young Lord"

Pipiltin—nobles

Pochteca—merchants, especially those of Tenochtitlan, who traveled all over Mesoamerica, sometimes in great caravans, trading for goods and always spying for the Mexica; they lived in their own quarter of the city, had their own deities, and although often rich, did not engage in displays of wealth. There was an unwritten rule in Mesoamerica allowing the merchants to travel freely wherever they chose to do business, but the custom was not always followed

Posole/Pozole—beverage of ground corn and water

Poyon—hallucinogenic plant, said to cause visions of dancing flowers

Pucbal-Chah—"Place of Sacrifices"

Puhuy—owl

Purepecha—a unique language, unconnected to any other. The Purepechas, sometimes known as Tarascans, live largely in the state of Michoacan; more than 100,000 people still speak the language

Quaquauhtzin—see *Cuacuauhtzin*

Quauhcoatl—"Eagle Serpent"

Quauhtlequetzqui—Aztec high priest who, together with Tenochtli, prophesied the glory of Mexico-Tenochtitlan

Quauhtli—see *Calendar*

Quechol—a bird of brilliant red plumage, flaming or roseate spoonbill; *quechol* describes the shape of the bird's neck rather than its color

Quecholxochitl—a flower

Quenonamican—"Where One Exists in Some Way," the Region of the Dead, the beyond; a place neither of the suffering associated with the Christian Hell nor the glory of Heaven, but a mysterious form of existence. Nahua writers often spoke of a longing for the return of the dead, but no resurrection is described in the literature

Quetzal—trogon, a bird of brilliant plumage, including long green tail feathers; in its adjectival sense, the word means "precious"

Quetzalcoa—high priests, the plural form of Quetzalcoatl, referring to the two highest Aztec priests

Quetzalcoatl—"Plumed Serpent," the mythical culture bearer, of whom the *Codex Chimalpopoca* says, "In truth, it began with him/it flowed out from him;/all art and knowledge/came from Quetzalcoatl." The ascetic who was seduced by Tezcatlipoca into drunkenness and incest; also a person in the ninth century, known for his gentle and highly cultured ways

Quetzalizquixochitl—"Precious Tree of Fragrant Flowers"

Quetzalmamatzin—son-in-law of Nezahualcoyotl, governor of the region of Teotihuacan

Quiche/K'iche'—"Many Trees," the Maya of highland Guatemala (from the Nahuatl also meaning "Many Trees"); Dennis Tedlock describes three quiche lineages: Quiche, Tams, and Ilocs. The Quiche trace their origin to Tula. Under King Quikab (Qikab) of Utatalan (the Nahuatl name for Rotten Cane, the Quiche capital destroyed by Pedro de Alvarado in 1524), the Quiche state expanded until Quikab was defeated by the Cakchiquels

Quilaztli—"The One Who Causes the Vegetable to Sprout," the mother goddess identified with Itzpapalotl and Coatlicue

Quitze—perhaps a form of Quiche, hence Jaguar Quitze or Quiche Priest

Raramuri—language of the people of the Sierra Madre Occidental of Chihuahua State, also known as Tarahumara; spoken by perhaps 75,000 persons

Regidor—member of the municipal council (*cabildo*, now *ayuntamiento*)

Sacbe—"White Road," a road generally of worked stone, raised above the surrounding ground; there were *sacbe'ob* connecting parts of many of the Maya cities, and even from city to city, as in the case of Labna and Kabah

Sahagún, Bernardino de (1499–1590)—Franciscan friar, born in Spain, arrived in Nueva España (1529), where he lived and taught in the College of Tlatelolco until his death. Although fray Sahagún said the purpose of his work with native students was to learn the Nahua religion and customs in order to destroy them, he became the first ethnographer of the hemisphere, more responsible than any other person for preserving the religion and customs of the people in his many works, including the *Florentine Codex* and the *Cantares Mexicanos*. Although the basic elements of his work can be confirmed in pre-Hispanic stone carvings and codices, the degree to which Christian concepts affected the written material remains in dispute

Tamoanchan—a place name of Maya-Huastec origin, interpreted as if it were a Nahuatl word possibly meaning "we are looking for our home." The mythical place of origin of the culture eventually inherited by the Nahuas; there Quetzalcoatl sprinkled his blood upon ground-up bones and brought human beings to life again. A paradise where all is joy and material goods abound

Tarascan—see *Purepecha*

Tecayehuatzin—ruler of Huexotzinco who, along with Ayocuan Cuetzpaltzin, attempted to influence Motecuhzoma II to abandon the militaristic policies of his predecessors; held the meeting of philosophical nobles at his palace in 1490 at which a Nahua aesthetic and moral philosophy were discussed. Tecayehuatzin lived in difficult times, caught in the tensions among Tlaxcala, Tenochtitlan, Cholula, and Huexotzinco. His hold on the throne was not entirely secure and his method for keeping it was largely the use of deceit; at the end of the fifteenth century, Tlaxcala defeated Huexotzinco, burning its crops and destroying Tecayehuatzin's palace

Tecolliquenqui—"Garbed in Charcoal"

Telpochcalli—school for young people, where the duties and responsibilities of the warrior as well as the ways of war were taught

Telpochtli—"young man"

Temilotzin (late fifteenth century–1525)—attended the *calmecac*, where he developed a taste for poetry. Known for his work on friendship, fought valiantly during the siege of Tenochtitlan, friend in peace and companion in battle to Cuauhtemoc

Temoayan—"Place of Descent," another name for the Region of the Dead

Tenochca—residents of Tenochtitlan, "Place of Nopal Cactus"

Tenochtitlan—Mexica capital in the Valley of Mexico, probably settled by Mexica in 1325; at its peak exacted tribute from much of Mesoamerica. The tribute included foodstuffs: grains, vegetables, fruits, cacao, vanilla, chiles, honey, maguey sap, and salt; animals and insects: fowl, deer, dogs, monkeys, amphibians, ants, grasshoppers; clothing: deer and jaguar skins, cotton and maguey fiber cloaks and clothing; as well as arms, metalwork, feathers, paper, pottery, tobacco, hallucinogenics, precious stones, gold, silver, incense, and seashells.

The marketplaces in which most goods and foodstuffs were traded were carefully policed to maintain order and eliminate dishonest practices. That in the suburb of Tlatelolco was the largest in the hemisphere. Order extended beyond the public world; breaches of private as well as public morality were subject to draconian measures: adultery, for example, was a capital crime punishable by stoning.

At the time of the Spanish invasion, the population (approx. 250,000) made it larger as well as far cleaner than any city in Spain. The tutelary god was Huitzilopochtli. Tenochtitlan was allied with the nearby cities of Tacuba and Texcoco and for brief periods with other cities.

Daily life was rich in ceremony: great feasts which required human sacrifice and small moments of speechmaking and prayer played a significant role in a city filled with immigrants as well as nobles, warriors, and common people. Even daily encounters were formalized; well brought up children spoke in the prescribed manner to adults, careful never to raise their eyes, speak out of turn, or use informal language. Every noble, warrior, priest, and functionary displayed status according to a clear dress code.

In 1518, just before the Spanish invasion, the Nahua poets asked, "Who can disturb the city of Tenochtitlan? Who can shake the foundations of heaven?"

Teomicqueh—"deified dead," persons who had been sacrificed

Teoquecholtin—great flamingos

Teotihuacan—flourished from the third to seventh century A.D., after which its collapse was complete. The most important cultural, political center in the *altiplano*, Teotihuacan influenced virtually every Mesoamerican culture that followed; it was devoted to the worship of Quetzalcoatl and perhaps to Tlaloc. The language of the city is unknown, although it appears that sections were occupied by people from other parts of Mesoamerica, suggesting that Huastec, Totonac, Otomi, Zapotec, and Nahuatl were spoken, although there may also have been some sort of lingua franca. Sculpture, architecture, pottery, and the decorative arts were highly sophisticated. The ruins are only 50 kilometers northeast of present-day Mexico City

Teotlahtolli—"divine words"

Tepaneca—one of the original tribes from Aztlan or Chicomoztoc (Seven Caves) that arrived in the Valley of Mexico in the twelfth century and settled in Azcapotzalco; achieved its height during the fabled 78-year reign of Tezozomoc

Tepeyacac—in the current state of Puebla, where it is known now as Tepeaca. Tepeyacac was founded in 1182 by a combined group of Toltecs and Chichimecs. It flowered under Cuetzpaltzin during the first half of the fifteenth century; was conquered in 1459, after which many of the inhabitants migrated to Toluca. They returend in 1464, only to be conquered by Axayacatl, then invaded by Cholula and Tlaxcala in 1491; site of the second Spanish city in Mexico

Teponaztli—a large, horizontal percussion instrument similar to a drum, but with a greater range of tones, played with a rubber-tipped mallet

Tetlepanquetzaltzin—last *huey tlahtoani* of Tacuba, which was destroyed by Tlaxcalans in league with the Spaniards; along with Cuauhtemoc, he was captured and tortured by the conquistadors

Tetzcoco/Texcoco/Tezcoco—said to be the Athens of Anahuac, founded by Quinatzin, a great-grandson of Xolotl, in 1328; attacked by Tezozomoc, who defeated the forces of King Ixtlixochitl and killed him in the presence of his son Nezahualcoyotl. It was divided into zones according to the occupation of the head of the household, by order of Nezahualcoyotl, and may have had as many as 200,000 residents. Came increasingly under the influence of Tenochtitlan from the late fifteenth century until the Spanish invasion

Tezcacoacatl—"Mirror Serpent"

Tezcatlipoca—"Smoking Mirror," known as Night and Wind, in four manifestations as the four sons of Ometeotl; see the General Introduction and p. 17 as well as many of the texts for more information

Tezozomoc—ascended to the throne of Azcapotzalco in 1363; a perfect example of the cliché of a warlike central Mexican *huey tlahtoani,* this bloody conqueror died in 1426 in extreme old age (see also Azcapotzalco, Chimalpopoca, Colhuacan, Tepaneca, and Texcoco)

Tezozomoctli—king of Colhuacan, reigned 1482–1519

Ticociahuacatl—one of the principal Aztec judges, also an elector of the *huey tlahtoani*

Time—a Mesoamerican concept, especially among the Maya, that differed from our present-day understanding of time. Although the concept is not entirely clear, time among the Maya can be understood as discrete units occurring during time itself; i.e., there is time within time. Events happened during days, which took place within great cycles, which occurred in time. The concept developed from observation of the celestial world and its clockwork interplay: the rising and setting of the Sun, the regularity of the Morning and Evening Star, the solar year, and so on. The rhythms of the universe were an obvious homology—the setting and rising of the sun, the cycle of corn, the cycle of the *May*. For a Western parallel, one might think of Socrates speaking of day following night and night following day as dying follows living and living follows. Hence the Maya preoccupation with time and their brilliant mathematics and astronomy as well as the complex astrological interpretations

Titlacauan—"The One We Serve," one of the names of Tezcatlipoca

Tizimin—see *Chilam Balam*

Tizoc—"Bloodstained Leg," seventh *huey tlahtoani* of Mexico, brother of Axayacatl, reigned 1481–86, said to have been a coward and rumored to have been killed by witches; turned his military activities over to the generalship of Tlacaelel

Tlacaelel—"Virile Heart." In 1430–80, served as *cihuacoatl* to four *huey tlatoque*: his uncle Itzcoatl, Axayacatl, Tizoc, and Ahuitzotl. The classic devious and sinister gray eminence, Tlacaelel was also a brilliant military strategist and commander. He promoted the worship of Huitzilopochtli, urged Itzcoatl to burn the codices in which the Mexica appeared as an insignificant people, and may have been the inventor of the War of the Flowers, which he is said to have considered "a marketplace for sacrificial victims"; the number of human sacrifices increased greatly while his views held sway among the Mexica

Tlacahuepan—"Strong Man," a great warrior, cousin of Motecuhzoma II, who lost his life in the war against Huexotzinco

Tlacateccatl—"Leader of Men," military rank, a Mexica captain

Tlacateuhtzin—"Courageous Lord," second *huey tlahtoani* of Tlatelolco, reigned 1408–27, assassinated by order of Maxtla of Azcapotzalco

Tlacochcalcatl—"Lord of the House of Spears," commander of the army

Tlacopan—"Above the Jarilla," known today as Tacuba, the weak partner in the *Triple Alliance* with Tenochtitlan and Texcoco, founded in 1430 after the fall of the Tepanecs of Azcapotzalco

Tlacotzin—*cihuacoatl*, advised the Mexica during the last days and hours of the battle against the Spaniards, then became liaison between the Mexica and Spaniards, eventually aiding in the construction of new buildings in place of those destroyed in Tenochtitlan

Tlahtoani (pl. *Tlatoque*)—"Speaker," the supreme commander of the Nahua state, all-powerful, representing divine power and wisdom, but not himself divine, as Alfredo Lopez Austin explains in *The Human Body and Ideology: Concepts of the Ancient Nahuas* (Salt Lake City, 1988). The *huey tlahtoani* himself was known as the "great spokesman"

Tlailotlaqui—"The One Who Came Back," applied to Quiyeuhtzin, a lord of Culhuacan who took refuge in Chalco

Tlallamanac—"Sustainer of the World," a title of the dual god

Tlallichcatl—"Cotton of the Earth," a title of the dual god

Tlaloc—literally, "The One upon the Earth," the god of rain, one of the oldest and most revered gods of Mesoamerica

Tlalocan—the dominion of Tlaloc; a mythical place of abundance and happiness reserved for those whose death is connected to water, as in drowning

Tlaltecutli—"Lord of the Earth," a dual god, with both male and female aspects, related to Tlaloc, symbolized by *cipactli* (alligator), the first day of the *Tonalamatl*

Tlamaceyhua—verb: to deserve, do pennance, offer sacrifice

Tlamatini—"Those who know something"; wise men

Tlapallan—"Red Place," often associated with Tlillan, "Black Place," in a *difrasismo* meaning "abode of wisdom"

Tlapatl—hallucinogenic herb (Datura Stramonium)

Tlapalteuccitzin—a prince of Huexotzinco

Tlatelolco—"The Hill," occupied since the tenth century A.D., according to recently discovered evidence; later occupied, in 1337, by a separatist group from Tenochtitlan. Home to the *pochtecas* and the largest market in the hemisphere. One of the last places defended by the Mexica against the Spanish invaders; ruling succession: Teutlehuac, 1375; Cuacuahpitzahuac, 1380–1418; Tlacateotl, 1418–28; Cuauhtlatoa, 1428–60; Moquihuix, 1460–73; and the military governors after their defeat by Tenochtitlan: Tlahueloctzin, 1473–88; Tzihuacpopocatzin, 1488–1506; Yollocuanitzin, 1506–20. The inhabitants went to war with Tenochtitlan in 1475, were defeated, their temple closed, but the great market originally established under Cuauhtlatoa remained open and thriving. In the fight against the Spaniards, the people of Tlatelolco were perhaps the most valiant, at one time even accusing Tenochtitlan of cowardice

Tlatlauhquecholtin—Red Flamingos

Tlaxcala—influenced by Teotihuacan during its florescence, then by late Olmec culture, until invaded by Toltec-Chichimec groups and in the tenth-century by Otomis. In its various parts, Tepecticac was the fort, Ocotelulco the market, Tizatlan the center of government, and Quiahuiztlan the craft center. The people lived in an almost constant state of war with the Mexica. Tlaxcala was known for its warriors, and for its three poets, Monencauhtzin, and Xayacamatl and Xicontecatl (father and son). It was the decision of Tlaxcala to ally with the invading Spaniards that no doubt brought down the Mexica

Tloque Nahuaque—"Lord of the Close and the Near," the supreme deity expressed in its most divine form, omnipresent and above all

Tochihuitzin Coyolchiuhqui—fifteenth-century Mexica poet and ruler of a small province near Huexotzinco, son of Itzcoatl and nephew of Tlacaelel, whose daughter he married; helped to rescue Nezahualcoyotl when the Tepanecs assasinated his father and attempted to kill him as well

Tohil—Quiche god of storm, thunder, and rain (see Tlaloc, Chac)

Tollan—"Place of Reeds"—see *Toltec*

Toltec—resident of Tula or Tollan, generally understood to mean "craftsman," the most revered group in the *altiplano*, for theirs was the height of cultural life, inventing mining and metalwork, developing the practice of medicine, producing the most beautiful art, architecture, and craftswork. Acampichtli, the first Mexica *huey tlahtoani*, was said to have Toltec blood and took twenty-two wives to extend the bloodline; the culture refiend from the barbarism of Mixcoatl, father of Quetzalcoatl, and eventually spread to much of Mesoamerica, leaving religious, linguistic, artistic, and other cultural evidence reaching south into the world of the Maya at the end of the tenth century

Toltecayotl—the essence of Toltec culture

Tomine—one eighth of a peso or *real*, one of the first Spanish loan words in Nahuatl, according to James Lockhart, *The Nahuas After the Conquest*

Tonacacihuatl—"Our Lady of Sustenance," a version of *Tonantzin*, the feminine aspect of Ometeotl

Tonacateuctli—"Our Lord of Sustenance" (see above)

Tonalli—day, also destiny

Tonalpohualli—"The Book of Destinies," the astrological calendar

Tonantzin/Totahtzin—see *Ometeotl*

Tonatiuh/Tunadiu—"He Who Gives Light," the name of the sun in Nahuatl, also applied to Pedro de Alvarado, the conquistador

Topantemoctzin—Motecuzoma's storekeeper in Tlatelolco

Topiltzin—"Our Prince," last Toltec *huey tlahtoani*, reigned 1111–16. There is a legend that Huemac said Tula would fall when a child was born with a crown of curly hair. Such a child was born to Topiltzin in 1115, and so it was that the Chichimecs attacked and defeated the Toltecs only a few months later

Toteociteuhtli—supreme ruler of Chalco in the days of Motecuzoma I

Totonicapan—"Over the Hot Water," the Nahuatl name for the Quiche town of Chuvia-Miquina

Totoquihuatzli—"Entrance of Birds," two *huey tlatoque* of Tlacopan; the first reigned 1430–50 and helped to form the *Triple Alliance* with Tenochtitlan and Tezcoco; the second, a poet, reigned 1490–1519

Tototecti—"Bird Lords"

Tozan—a priest of Chalco condemned to death by Motecuzoma Ilhuicamina; but he escaped and found refuge in Huitzilac, where he died in 1411

Tozmaquetzin/Tozmacuechtzin—chief of Chalco

Triple Alliance—of Tenochtitlan, Tezcoco, and Tlacopan, which developed after the decline of Tezozomoc and later ruled central Mexico

Tula—see *Toltec*

Tun—the Maya year of 360 days plus the 5 nameless days, divided into 18 months of 20 days each (see *Calendar*); 20 *tuns* equal 1 *katun*; 20 *katuns* equal 1 *baktun*

Tutul Xiu—ruled Uxmal (Windfall), claimed descent from the Toltecs. The name is half Nahuatl, half Maya: *Tutul* from *Tula* ("Place of Reeds") and *Xiu*, "grasses" in Maya *tzeltzal*; or a Nahuatl loan from *xihuitl*, "grass"

-tzin—Nahuatl honorific suffix, translated as "honored," "honorable," or "revered"

Tzitze—coral seed, used in divining by the Quiche Maya

Tzolkin—Maya astrological calendar of 260 days

Tzompantli—rack where skulls of sacrificed humans were displayed

Tzotzil—a branch of the Maya linguistic family; also the people sometimes known as Chamula. Frequent rebels against colonial authority, they were involved at the end of the twentieth century in the extremely complicated conflict in Chiapas, one of the richest states in Mexico in natural resources but among the poorest in standard of living for indigenous people. Although many members of the Zapatista movement are Tzotziles, not all Tzotziles support the *Zapatistas*. There is a long history of rebellion by the Tzotzil people

Uinal—the 20-day cycle sacred to the Maya; according to Munro Edmonson, "the birth of the uinal is the birth of time itself"

Uinic or Winik—Maya for the number 20; also the word for "person" (one who has 20 digits)

Uxmal—see *Tutul Xiu*

Vucub—"Seven"

—*Came* "Seven Death," Lord of Xibalba

—*Caquix* "Seven Macaw," father of Zipacna and Cabracan, husband of Chimalmat

Xayacamach—ruled Tizatlan (a part of Tlaxcala) during the first half of the fifteenth century; sided with Huaxteca in its war with the Mexica and was killed

Xayacamach Tlapalteuctli—poet, son of Aztahua, ruler of Tizatlan, born in the middle of the fifteenth century, said to have ruled fairly and well. There are two versions of his death: one (perhaps apocryphal) has him living in Tenochtitlan, attempting to flee, and being killed by order of Motecuhzoma II in 1518; in the other, he died quietly before the end of the century

Xbalanque—younger brother of Hunahpu, son of Blood Woman and Hunahpu. Dennis Tedlock suggests the translation of the name as "Little Jaguar Sun," meaning the moon

Xib Chac—"Male Rain," rain priest of Chichen Itza

Xib Yuy—"Male Matasano (Casimiroa) Tree"

Xibalba—"(?) Frightening Place," the underworld, comprising nine distinct levels; possibly accessible through caves or by climbing down sheer cliffs, but more likely only through death. Those who entered Xibalba embarked upon a journey exemplified by that of the Hero Twins, in which they endured many tests. Those who survived the tests could emerge again on earth, which is analogous to the life cycle of maize and the setting and rising of the sun. Physical resurrection of historical persons in Mesoamerica is unknown

Xihuitl—the solar year of 365 days (18 groups of 20 days, plus ominous days at the end of the year)

Xiloxochitl—a silk cotton tree with red flowers like silk corn tassels, beautiful but not fragrant

Ximoayan—"The Place of the Fleshless," resting place of dead souls

Xipe Totec—the Flayed God, a masculine fertility god of the Mexica. People sacrificed to him were flayed and their skins worn by priests

Xiu—residents of Yucatan of Toltec origin—see *Itza*

Xiuhamatl—"Books of the Years"; annals

Xiuhcoatl—read as "Fire Serpent," one of the emblems of Huitzilopochtli, a sun ray; interpreted as "Precious Serpent," it becomes a name of Quetzalcoatl. Also connected with the great serpent that was set afire and paraded by those who were to be sacrificed to the sun

Xiuhquechol—"Fire Flamingo"

Xiuhtecuhtli—Nahua god of fire, akin to Huehueteotl (Old God), also god of the year, perhaps of time itself; persons sacrificed to Xiuhtecuhtli were burned before their hearts were torn out

Xmucane and Xpiyacoc—"Grandmother and Grandfather," the first begetters, the oldest dual gods, creators of man from yellow and white maize, parents of One Hunaphu and Seven Hunaphu

Xochimilco—"Flower Garden," at the south end of the Valley of Mexico, where the mountains leading to Milpa Alta begin; *chinampas* developed in Xochimilco were extremely fecund. Xochimilco was conquered by Azcapotzalco in 1427, liberated by Nezahualcoyotl in 1430, and then fell under the domination of Tenochtitlan. Participated in the betrayal of the Tenochas during the Spanish invasion

Xochiquetzal—"Precious Flower," goddess of happiness and love, patron of embroiderers and "gladdeners," wife of Tlaloc

Xochitl—Nahuatl word for flower; *in xochitl in cuicatl*, "flower and song" (metaphor for poetry: cin some codices the speech scroll is accompanied by flowers); see also *Flower*

Xolotl—"boy/servant," according to Frances Karttunen, *An Analytical Dictionary of Nahuatl* (Norman, OK, 1992), but often interpreted as "monster";

god of monstrous things: clowns, spies, misshapen creatures, and sexual aberrations. The historical Xolotl arrived in the Valley of Mexico in the thirteenth century at the head of the invading Chichimecs, whom he set on the path of acculturation, adopting all that they could of Toltec ways—and successfully, given that the great-great-grandson of Xolotl was Nezahualcoyotl

Xpiyacoc—"Grandfather"—see *Xmucane*

Xquic—daughter of one of the Lords of Xibalba and mother of Hunahpu and Xbalanque

Yaocihuatl—"Warrior Woman," grandmother of Huitzilopochtli. Early in the fourteenth century, the Mexica, supposedly guided by Huitzilopochtli, asked Achitometl of Culhuacan to give his treasured virgin daughter to them so that she could be transformed into Yaocihuatl. Instead, they sacrificed and flayed her, dressed a priest in her skin, and invited Achitometl and the Culhuacans to venerate the goddess. When the Culhuacans realized what had happened, they turned on the Mexica and drove them out, sending them on the last part of their journey to Tenochtitlan

Yancuic Tlahtolli—"New Word"; applied to contemporary literature written in Nahuatl

Yaotl—"Enemy," an aspect of Tezcatlipoca

Yearbearers—the four sacred days that can begin the Mesoamerican year; also associated with the four directions

Yoaltecatl/Yoaltecuhtli—"Lord of the Night"

Yoloxochitl—flower of the heart, a herb used to treat heart disease

Zacatimaltzin—see *Tochihuitzin Coyolchiuhqui*

Zacuan—a bird with black and gold plumage

Zapata, Emiliano (1879–1919)—led the Revolution of 1910 in the south. Born in Anenecuilco, Morelos, he delivered manifestos in Nahuatl, the language of many of his followers. His interest in distributing land to the peasants inspired his army. He was betrayed and killed in ambush at Chinameca

Zapatistas—followers of Emiliano Zapata; also a radical movment, begun in Chiapas, that changed into armed rebellion in 1994 to coincide with the implementation of NAFTA (the North American Free Trade Agreement) and spread throughout Mexico as part of a desire for social and political reform generally, with emphasis on indigenous rights

Zapotec—culturally of Olmec origin, later under the influence of Teotihuacan; builders of Monte Alban, which they abandoned at the end of the ninth century; known for their magic, funerary rites, artisanry, and use of hallucinogens. Later built Mitla, which was overrun by the Mixtecs in the thirteenth century

Zipacna—shown in the form of a crocodile, maker of mountains. Killer of the Four Hundred Youths, he was himself finally killed. Turned to stone (the mountains, the earth) by Hunahpu and Xbalanque, he is similar to the Nahua *cipactli*

Zuyua—a legendary town west northwest of Merida (Ho'), near Motul; Munro Edmonson says it is another name for Tula, which the Maya used to connect their priestly examinations to the Toltecs. The Zuyua riddles were taught only to the highborn, and thus served to eliminate the possibility of common people ascending to the priesthood.

Bibliographical Essay

by Ascensión H. de León-Portilla

The Conquest of Mesoamerica in the sixteenth century brought with it the loss of much of the valuable culture of the Mesoamerican peoples. Not only were their temples, palaces, and the effigies of their gods destroyed, but also their books or codices containing glyphs and signs, the majority of which were reduced to ashes. Many of their priests and wise men perished; and with them their worldview, the memories of their history, their narratives, songs, and poems, were on the point of being obliterated forever.

Nevertheless, in that same century, some humanist friars, informed by the humanism revived in their time, came to appreciate the value of the works we now call the literary creations of the men and women of Mesoamerica. There were also some surviving indigenous wise men who proposed to salvage from oblivion the work they considered their precious heritage. Despite all that was lost, they embarked upon the important tasks of rescue. Among those who undertook this work, two figures stand out: the friars Andrés del Olmos (c. 1490–1571) and Bernardino de Sahagún (1499–1590).

Aided by their Nahuatl-speaking students, both Franciscans transcribed the contents of numerous indigenous codices and other documents of the culture in alphabetic letters. Thanks to Olmos, a set of texts were preserved in Nahuatl: see *Huehuetlahtolli (Testimonies of the Ancient Word)* (Mexico City: Fondo de Cultura Economica, 1991, 1998); and *Of the Manners of Speaking That the Old Ones Had*—Judith M. Maxwell, ed. (Salt Lake City: University of Utah Press, 1992). The fruit of the research by Sahagún taken from the oral tradition and the ancient pictoglyphic books includes many texts in Nahuatl about diverse aspects of the culture—Sahagún, *Florentine Codex, General History of the Things of New Spain*, edited by Arthur J. O. Anderson and Charles E. Dibble, 12 vols. (Santa Fe, NM: School of American Research and the University of Utah Press, 1950–82).

Other friars working in different regions of Mesoamerica did the same thing. Diego de Landa (1524–1579), the very person who had burned many of the codices in the town of Mani, wrote a *Relación de las cosas de Yucatan* with important information about Maya traditions—edited with notes by Alfred M. Tozzer (Cambridge, MA: Harvard University Press, 1941). Among other things, he included a record of syllabic glyphs that has been the Rosetta Stone for deciphering Maya writing. We should give separate mention to Francisco Ximénez (1666–1723), thanks to whom the Maya Quiche text of the *Popol Vuh*, Book of Counsel, was preserved. Ximénez also translated the Quiche text into Spanish (see editions by M. Edmonson [New Orleans: Tulane University Press, 1971], and Dennis Tedlock [New York: Simon & Schuster, 1985]).

In addition to the work by these and other friars, some zealous indigenous people conserved, copied, and in certain cases translated many other testimonies of Mesoamerican culture. We are indebted to Hernando Alvarado Tezozómoc (c. 1525–c. 1615) for an important genealogy in Nahuatl, included in his *Cronica Mexicayotl* (Mexico City: National University Press, 1975), and also for a history of the Mexica, from their early wanderings up to the time of the Conquest, in his *Cronica Mexicana* (Mexico City: Editorial Porrua, 1985).

Other writers in Nahuatl were Cristóbal del Castillo (1525–1606), who left various texts about the history of the Mexica, the life of Nezahualcoyotl, and the pre-Hispanic calendric computations (edited by F. Navarrete, Instituto Nacional de Antropologia, Mexico City, 1991). We should also mention Domingo Francisco Chimalpain (1579–1660), who wrote down in Nahuatl eight historical *Relaciones,* based on the testimony he gathered from various places in central Mexico—Susan Schroeder, ed., *Codex Chimalpain,* 4 vols. (Norman, OK: University of Oklahoma Press, 1997–99). To these names must be added those of Sahagún's students: Antonio Valeriano, Martin Jacobita, Alonso Bejerano, and Andrés Leonardo, who compiled collections of ancient songs, historical annals, and other works.

Indigenous people also were preoccupied with rescuing ancient texts and some pictographic manuscripts in the form of codices. In Yucatan, one of the best known was Gaspar Antonio Chi (c. 1520–1590), who worked on geographic studies commissioned by Felipe II in 1576. Chi drafted a text about Mayan antiquities and collaborated on the works of several friars. Indigenous people also played an important role by uncovering a number of the works of Maya priests and soothsayers (*Chilam Balams)* in Yucatan; availing themselves of codices and oral presentations, they rescued numerous works dealing with astrology, history, and literature: see Munro Edmonson, ed. (Austin, TX: University of Texas Press, 1982, 1986). It was an indigenous Quiche named Diego Reynoso who probably made the first alphabetical version of the contents of the *Popol Vuh,* one of the best-known Amerindian literary works.

During the centuries of the colonial period, scholars once again undertook the task of rescuing the ancient culture. One of these, Fernando de Alva Ixtlilxóchitl (c. 1578–1650), a child of Tezcocan nobility, in addition to writing various annals about the Chichimeca nation and the rule of Aculhuacan-Tezcoco, gathered an important collection of codices and manuscripts: *Obras Históricas,* 2 vols. (Mexico City: UNAM, 1975). After his death, his work was passed on to Carlos de Sigüenza y Góngora (1645–1700). This distinguished humanist, historian, and cosmographer, besides writing works about indigenous culture, enriched his inherited collection of Nahua codices and manuscripts. The Jesuits were later to benefit from this collection. One of them, Francisco Javier Clavigero (1731–1787), having consulted these writings while in Mexico, later wrote his *Historia Antigua de Mexico* (Editorial Mexico City: Porrúa, 1990) during his exile in Bologna.

The Milanese Lorenzo Boturini Benaducci (1702–c. 1751) was a contemporary of Clavigero. He came to Mexico attracted by the cult of Our Lady of Guadalupe and everything about the native culture, and put together another very valuable collection of Nahuatl codices and writings. He copied those worked on by Sigüenza y Góngora and was able to locate others in various locales—see M. León-Portilla, ed., *Museo Indiano* (Mexico City: Editorial Porrúa, 1990). This vast gathering of source materials was to be enjoyed much later by scholars who, especially in the second half of the nineteenth century, set their sights on a wealth of Mesoamerican literature.

The Rediscovery of Mesoamerican Literature

The interest shown by Alexander von Humboldt (1769–1859) actually preceded the rediscovery of Mesoamerican literature. He came to the New World at the end of the eighteenth century, arrived in Mexico in 1803, and soon felt the attraction of the ancient culture. In his *Vistas de las cordilleras y monumento antiguos de los pueblos indigenas,* which appeared in Paris in 1813, he devoted considerable attention to indigenous codices (preserved in various museums and libraries in Europe), aside from those gathered by Lorenzo Boturini and previously mentioned scholars.

One incident of great importance was the publication between 1831 and 1848 of the scholarly work, in nine volumes, entitled *Antiquities of Mexico,* by Edward King, Lord Kingsborough, who gathered up reproductions of numerous Mesoamerican codices, such as the text in Spanish of Bernardino de Sahagún's *Historia General de las Cosas de Nueva España.* Thanks to Kingsborough, there was a worldwide increase in the study of these valuable primary sources from ancient Mexico.

By the last third of the nineteenth century, several researchers of other nationalities were turning their energies to rediscovering the sources of Mesoamerican literature. The American Daniel G. Brinton (1837–1899), a professor at the University of Philadelphia, edited such important texts as *The Comedy of the Güegüenche* (Philadelphia, 1883), the *Annals of the Cackchiquels* (Philadelphia, 1885), and the *Twenty Sacred Hymns* (Philadelphia, 1890) from the collection preserved in the Biblioteca Nacional de Mexico and other manuscripts. This was the start of an awareness of the literary legacy of Mesoamerica in the United States.

Interest was also awakened in France. There, three scholars made important contributions: one was Léon de Rosny (1837–1914), who edited works about Maya writing and their codices, among them the *Peresiano* (Paris, 1872) and the *Trocortesiano* (Paris, 1869, 1883). Joseph Marius Alexis Aubin (c. 1810–1880), who lived for some time in Mexico, collected many manuscripts, some of them pertaining to the ancient collection of Boturini. He later sold these works to Eugenio Goupil, who ultimately donated his collection to the Bibliothèque National. The third was Rémi Siméon (1827–1890), who also contributed greatly to the study of Mesoamerican documents. Among other texts he edited two of the *Relaciones* of Chimalpain (Paris, 1889), and he published a *Diccionario de la lengua nahuatl o mexicana* (Paris, 1885; Mexico City: Siglo XXI Editores, 1990), with corresponding entries in French.

The tradition in Germany initiated by Alexander von Humboldt was continued brilliantly by Eduard Seler (1849–1922). In addition to linguistic, philological, ethnological, historical, and archeological research in many parts of the region, he published numerous studies. He also edited texts in Nahuatl, including some of the work that had been collected by fray Bernardino de Sahagún. Seler produced codices with extensive commentaries, among them the *Tonalamatl de Aubin* (Paris, 1900), the *Cospi* (Paris, 1900), the *Féjerváry-Mayer* (Paris, 1901), the *Vatican B* (Paris, 1902), and the *Borgia* (Paris, 1904–06).

In Mexico itself, during the last third of the nineteenth century, a rebirth of Mexicanism centered on the study of native antiquities. The pioneer in these studies was Manuel Orozco y Berra (1811–1881). We owe to him, besides his great *Historia antigua y de la conquista de Mexico,* editions of various manuscripts, among them the *Tonalamatl de Aubin* and the *Codice Mendocino.* Alfredo Chavero (1842–1916) wrote a *Historia antigua de Mexico,* and for the fourth centenary of the "discovery" of America in 1892, he edited a group of indigenous codices, with commentaries, under the title *Antigüedades mexicanas.* Antonio Peñafiel (1839–1922) edited codices and texts in Nahuatl, and left a body of work, including the *Coleccion de documentos para la historia mexicana* in six volumes that appeared in 1887–1903.

Francisco del Paso y Troncoso (1842–1916) merits special mention. He was probably the most notable compiler of documents touching on the an-

cient and colonial history of Mexico that had been scattered across Europe.
Among many other things, he succeeded in printing a facsimile of the *Codices
matritenses,* 3 vols. (Madrid, 1906–08) with testimonies in Nahuatl gathered by fray Bernardino de Sahagún. He himself was also the editor of such
codices as the *Borbonicus* (1898) and many other manuscripts. Just as Carlos de Sigüenza y Góngora in the seventeenth century and Lorenzo Boturini
in the eighteenth had put together large collections, del Paso y Troncoso
brought later researchers invaluable examples of the enormous wealth of
documents from the Mesoamerican culture.

The Rescue of the Oral Tradition

Only at the end of the nineteenth and the beginning of the twentieth centuries was there a final, concerted commitment to saving the traditional culture preserved by indigenous peoples. Franz Boas (1858–1942), distinguished
professor at Columbia University, conceived and coordinated various projects
to gather the traditions of numerous peoples of the United States and Mexico in their own languages. Thanks to Boas's own personal involvement and
the work of his students, stories, songs, and poems are preserved in more
than a few Mesoamerican languages. Boas demanded that all his disciples
learn the language of the indigenous group with which they worked.

One distinguished disciple was Manuel Gamio (1883–1960). It can be
said that Gamio was the person who brought modern anthropology to Mexico. In his great research into the entire character of the *Poblacion indigena
del valle de Teotihuacan,* 3 vols. (Mexico, 1922), he organized a collaboration
between ethnologists and linguists. One of these, Pablo González Casanova
(1889–1936), working in the region of Teotihuacan as well as other parts of
Mexico, transcribed many oral testimonies (in Gamio, Mexico, 1922). Besides obtaining some in Nahuatl, he also made transcriptions in other
Mesoamerican languages.

The German Konrad Preuss (1869–1938) was also drawn to the indigenous peoples' ancient songs, prayers, poems, and stories. Preuss labored for
some years among Nahuas known as Mexicaneros in the southwestern part
of the state of Durango, and obtained from them—as well as from the Coras,
Huicholes, and Tepehuanes—a considerable body of work.

The tradition begun by Boas, Gamio, González Casanova, and Preuss
was carried on by both Mexican and foreign researchers. We must mention
at least two of them. One, the American Robert Barlow (1918–1951), historian and sponsor of many studies, during his brief life gathered many texts
in Nahuatl, a number of which were published in a magazine entitled *Mexica Itonalamatl.* The second was a Mexican, Fernando Horcasitas Pimentel

(1924–1980), who undertook actual productions of the Nahuatl missionary theater, tracing indigenous creativity in comedies and other forms of representation from the period of Mexican independence right up to the present. Horcasitas also transcribed many tales, in particular, the valuable ones told by Señora Luz Jiménez, a native of Milpa Alta in the Federal District. Her recollections of the period of the Mexican Revolution and her narrations are actually considered classics of the modern literature in Nahuatl.

The Humanistic Appreciation of Mesoamerican Literature

By the middle of the twentieth century the knowledge and spread of this rich literature, especially in Nahuatl and various Mayan languages, had increased considerably, due to the increase in the number of researchers in countries like Germany, France, and the United States. In Guatemala, Adrián Recinos (c. 1895–1968) offered a new translation of the *Popul Vuh* in Spanish, and from that there was soon a new version in English, as well as others produced in the original Quiche. In Mexico, Angel Maria Garibay K. (1892–1967) concentrated, with a humanistic focus, in the field of Nahuatl literature. His translations of many poems, and the later appearance of his *Historia de la literatura nahuatl* in two volumes (Editorial Mexico City: Porrúa, 1953–54), were a further revelation. From then on, work in classical Nahuatl finally came to be seen as no longer merely a curiosity, folklore, or of purely ethnological interest, but as a genuine literary legacy.

At present, many researchers in different countries are studying and disseminating the literature of the ancient pre-Hispanic tradition, as well as works acquired more recently from the oral tradition. Here we can mention only a few of the major contributions.

Arthur J. O. Anderson and Charles E. Dibble, besides editing numerous Nahua texts and some pictographic manuscripts, have translated the great collection of Bernardino de Sahagún into English for the first time, including the *Florentine Codex,* 12 vols. (Santa Fe, NM, 1950–82). Donald Robertson worked with the codices done during the colonial period in his *Mexican Manuscript Painting of the Early Colonial Period* (New Haven: Yale University Press, 1959). Charles Gibson and John B. Glass have described hundreds of codices and indigenous texts converted to the alphabet in vols. XIV and XV of the *Handbook of Middle American Indians* (Austin, TX: University of Texas Press, 1975). José Alcina Franch brought examples of indigenous literature to Spain in his *Floresta literaria de America* (Madrid, 1956). And Munro S. Edmonson has shed new light on the *Popol Vuh* and several of the books of the Chilam Balam in English translation (1971–82).

More recently, Frances Karttunen and James Lockhart have made valuable contributions. Among them, an *Analytical Dictionary of Nahuatl* (Austin, TX: University of Texas Press, 1983), and Lockhart's *The Nahuas After the Conquest*, which elaborated the concept of the *altepetl* (Stanford, CA: Stanford University Press, 1992).

In France, Georges Baudot in his *Lettres Precolombiennes* (Toulouse, 1972) brought a unified vision of the riches of the literature. We conclude this list with the works of Miguel León-Portilla. We are indebted to him, among other contributions, for *La filosofia nahuatl estudiada en sus fuentes (Aztec Thought and Culture)* (Norman, OK: Oklahoma University Press, 1956, 1961); *Vision de los vencidos (Broken Spears)* (Boston: Beacon Press, 1959, 1963); and *Literaturas indigenas de Mexico (Pre-Columbian Literatures of Mexico)* (Norman, OK: Oklahoma University Press, 1963, 1992); as well as for many works that shed important light on the Nahua peoples, as in the case of the *Libro de los colloquios* (Mexico City: UNAM, 1985), in which dialogues of great power between the first missionaries and the surviving indigenous wise men are transcribed. Many of León-Portilla's books have been translated into major European languages, as well as Japanese and Hebrew. Finally, from Ascensión H. de León-Portilla comes *Tepuztlacuilolli, impresos Nahuas, historia y bibliografia*, 2 vols., (Mexico City: UNAM, 1988), in which about 3,000 pieces of printed matter in Nahuatl are listed.

The New Word

During the 1970s, a new literature sprang up in Mesoamerica. Indigenous authors, working independently or with others, have taken up the pen—and more recently the computer—to set down their poetry, essays, and other forms of narrative. A number of examples of their creativity have been included in this anthology. Among the Nahuas, several names stand out: Librado Silva Galeana, Francisco Morales Baranda, Natalio Hernández Xocoyotzin, Delfino Hernández, Alfredo Ramirez, José Antonio Xochime.

Other distinguished writers include Gariel López Chiñas, Andrés Henestrosa, and Victor de la Cruz, all of whom write in Zapoteco. From the Mayan world comes work by Briceida Cuevas Cob, Humberto Ak'abal, Miguel May May, Gerardo Can Pat, and Jorge Cocom Chen that has attracted a good deal of attention. The list of modern Mesoamerican writers could be enlarged. But we must mention María Sabina and Juan Gregorio Regino, both Mazatecos from the state of Guerrero. The former is known worldwide for her songs connected to hallucinatory mushrooms. The latter, currently president of the Association of Writers in Indigenous Languages of Mexico, is widely noted among other works for his book of poems, *No es eterna la muerte* (*Death Is Not Forever*).

The vitality of the new writing is such that in recent years collections have been published in diverse Mexican languages. Four of them can serve as examples here: *Letras indigenas contemporáneas,* 11 vols. (Editorial Diana, 1994); *Relatos: Lenguas de Mexico,* 10 vols. (Direccion General de Culturas Populares, 1994–95); *Letras mayas contemporáneas,* more than 40 vols. (Instituto Nacional Indigenista, 1993–94); and *Letras mayas contemporáneas: Chiapas,* 15 vols. (Instituto Nacional Indigenista, 1996).

Anthologies, too, deserve our attention. The first of these, published in *Estudios de Cultura Nahuatl,* vols. XVIII, XIX, and XX (1986–90) is edited by Miguel León-Portilla and gives abundant examples of Nahua literature of this century, including works in Nahua Pipil from El Salvador. A feature of the collection is the publication of complete works.

There are also outstanding collections by authors of indigenous stock, who in recent years have been interested in gathering texts in their respective languages. *Narrativa Nahuatl contemporánea* (Culturas Populares, 1992) was compiled by Natalio Hernández. In 1990, Librado Silva Galeana and Natalio Hernández published *Flor y canto de los antiguous mexicanos* (Gobierno del Estado de Nayarit), in which they reflect on the interpretation of the literary thinking of their ancestors in light of their own time.

Two more titles must complete this brief discussion of anthologies. The first is *Kotz'ib: Nuestra literatura maya* (Guatemala: Fundación Yaxté, 1997). The Q'anjob'al Pedro Gonazález has succeeded in bringing together a selection of texts from various Maya languages, starting with the diachronic notion that arose with the inscriptions on stone during the Classic period and ending with contemporary poetry. The second title is by Víctor de la Cruz, *Binnizá,* which is to say Zapoteco from Juchitan, Oaxaca. In his book *Guie'sti' diidxazé, La flor de la palabra* (Mexico City: UNAM, 1999; first published 1983), de la Cruz gathers examples of the literary creations of his people, whose poetic inspirations, as much from the oral tradition of the ancient Zapotecos as from the writers of this century, spring to life on the printed page.

The words of Mesoamerica do indeed have life. Today more than ever, the ancient and the new word are read and heard all over the world. The works in this book demonstrate the will of many Mesoamericans who persist, generation after generation, in transmitting their culture, giving it continuity and uniting it in a chain in which every link enriches and revivifies. Thanks to them, the ancient and the new words of the people of Mesoamerican form a profound human legacy, part of the truly universal literature.

Index

PERMISSIONS